Global Sociology

Introducing Five Contemporary Societies

Global Sociology

Introducing Five Contemporary Societies

FOURTH EDITION

Linda Schneider

Arnold Silverman

Boston   Burr Ridge, IL   Dubuque, IA   Madison, WI   New York
San Francisco   St. Louis   Bangkok   Bogotá   Caracas   Kuala Lumpur
Lisbon   London   Madrid   Mexico City   Milan   Montreal   New Delhi
Santiago   Seoul   Singapore   Sydney   Taipei   Toronto

Higher Education

GLOBAL SOCIOLOGY: INTRODUCING FIVE CONTEMPORARY SOCIETIES
Published by McGraw-Hill, a business unit of The McGraw-Hill Companies, Inc., 1221 Avenue
of the Americas, New York, NY, 10020. Copyright © 2006, 2003, 2000, 1997 by The McGraw-Hill
Companies, Inc. All rights reserved. No part of this publication may be reproduced or distributed
in any form or by any means, or stored in a database or retrieval system, without the prior written
consent of The McGraw-Hill Companies, Inc., including, but not limited to, in any network or other
electronic storage or transmission, or broadcast for distance learning.
Some ancillaries, including electronic and print components, may not be available to customers
outside the United States.

This book is printed on acid-free paper.

1 2 3 4 5 6 7 8 9 0 DOC/DOC 0 9 8 7 6 5

ISBN 0-07-299752-4

Editor in Chief: *Emily Barrosse*
Publisher: *Phillip A. Butcher*
Sponsoring Editor: *Sherith H. Pankratz*
Developmental Editor: *Katherine Blake*
Senior Marketing Manager: *Daniel M. Loch*
Managing Editor: *Jean Dal Porto*
Project Manager: *Ruth Smith*
Associate Designer: *Marianna Kinigakis*
Cover Image: *© Bob Krist/CORBIS*
Art Editor: *Katherine McNab*
Photo Research Coordinator: *Brian Pecko*
Senior Media Project Manager: *Nancy Garcia*
Senior Production Supervisor: *Carol A. Bielski*
Composition: *10.5/12 Times Roman by Carlisle Communications, Ltd.*
Printing: *Black, 45 # New Era Matte Plus, R.R. Donnelley/Crawfordsville, IN.*

Credits: The credits section for this book begins on page viii and is considered an extension of the
copyright page.

Library of Congress Cataloging-in-Publication Data
Schneider, Linda.
    Global sociology: introducing five contemporary societies / Linda Schneider, Arnold
Silverman.—4th ed.
        p. cm
    Includes bibliographical references and index.
    ISBN 0-07-299752-4 (softcover: alk. paper)
    1. Sociology. 2. Sociology—Cross-cultural studies. I. Silverman, Arnold R., 1940–II.
Title.
HM585.S36 2006
301—dc   2005043764

The Internet addresses listed in the text were accurate at the time of publication. The inclusion of a
Web site does not indicate an endorsement by the authors of McGraw-Hill, and McGraw-Hill does
not guarantee the accuracy of the information presented at these sites.

www.mhhe.com

About the Authors

LINDA SCHNEIDER is Professor of Sociology at SUNY—Nassau Community College. She received her Ph.D. in Sociology from Columbia University. Professor Schneider has for many years enjoyed teaching introductory sociology and has long been involved in activities related to undergraduate instruction. She has published in the American Sociological Association's journal *Teaching Sociology,* contributed to panels about teaching at conferences of the Eastern Sociological Society, the Community College Humanities Association, the Community College General Education Association, and the American Association of Community Colleges. Professor Schneider has directed several grants from the National Endowment for the Humanities, the Fund for the Improvement of Postsecondary Education, and the National Science Foundation for multidisciplinary and global curriculum development.

ARNOLD SILVERMAN is Professor of Sociology at SUNY—Nassau Community College. He received his Ph.D. in Sociology from the University of Wisconsin, Madison. Professor Silverman has published widely, and his articles have appeared in the *American Sociological Review, Built Environment, Contemporary Sociology, Social Service Review,* and elsewhere. He is the co-author of *Chosen Children,* a longitudinal study of American adopting families. Professor Silverman has also been active in efforts to improve the quality of undergraduate instruction. He co-directed a faculty development effort financed by the Fund for the Improvement of Postsecondary Education to encourage active learning in undergraduate teaching. He has been chair of the Eastern Sociological Society's Committee on Community Colleges, and coordinator of Nassau Community College's Freshman Learning Communities program.

Photo Credits

Contents

List of Tables

Introduction: To the Student

Global Sociology

Today, no one can afford to ignore the variety of the world's societies. If you go to work in the business world, it is very likely that in selling your products, or buying supplies, or managing your company's factories, you will need to deal with people from other societies. So will you, too, if you join your country's military forces. The better you understand cultures that differ from your own, the more likely it is that you will be successful. When you go on vacation or listen to music, you may come into contact with unfamiliar cultures. You will enjoy yourself more if you are comfortable with diversity. *Global Sociology* is a sociological introduction to the diversity of the world's societies.

Sociology has an important message for you: There are many ways to arrange human lives—many different kinds of families, economies, and governments, and endlessly varied values, beliefs, attitudes, and customs. Until very recently in human history, most people lived quite isolated lives, seldom meeting people from other societies. People readily believed that their own way of life was the only way, or the best way, and that other societies were strange or evil. In today's global world, condemning other societies leads to misunderstanding and violence. The world's peoples need to learn about one another. We believe that the more you know about different ways of life, the more profoundly you will appreciate how much all humans have in common.

We chose five societies to include in this book:

Japan: The Importance of Belonging

Mexico: Nation of Networks

The Bushmen of Namibia: Ancient Culture in a New Nation

Egypt: Faith, Gender, and Class

Germany: Social Institutions and Social Change in a Modern Western Society

It was hard to choose just five societies from all the hundreds in the world today. First of all, we chose societies from different parts of the world and different cultural traditions. One society in this book is in Asia, one in Latin America, one in

Europe, and two in Africa (although one of these, Egypt, is culturally part of the Middle East). Japan and Germany are rich, industrialized nations. Mexico, Namibia, and Egypt are "developing" nations that are struggling with poverty.

We looked for societies very different from your own in order to illustrate the range of the world's social diversity. Egypt is an Islamic society, where five times a day the call to prayer penetrates every street and house. Many people pray at every call and strive to follow the laws of Islam. In Japan, people enjoy celebrating the holidays of many religions. At Christmas, Japanese people give each other presents and eat takeout fried chicken. Afterwards, they attend a ceremony in a Buddhist temple. But only 10 percent of Japanese people consider themselves religious.

The Germans and the Bushmen could not be more different peoples, but they have in common the experience of rapid social change. The Bushmen are one of the last peoples on earth who have lived by gathering wild food. They are now losing their land and their way of life, marking the end of a major chapter in the story of humanity. Since reunification, Germans have struggled to merge two very different societies, one capitalist and one socialist.

In Egypt and Mexico there are tremendous disparities between the rich and the poor. Rich Egyptians have made their country one of the world's largest importers of German luxury cars, but poor Egyptians, desperate for housing, have taken to living in cemeteries. A decade ago, impoverished Indian peasants in Chiapas, Mexico, took up arms against local landowners and the government. Today, farmers, Indians, and poor Mexicans still protest government policies.

Learning Sociology from Diversity

Learning about many different societies will help you deepen your understanding of sociological concepts. Sociology textbooks teach concepts like values, norms, roles, socialization, deviance, social stratification, modernization, and so forth. The five societies in this book were chosen to illustrate these and other important sociological concepts. When you understand how sociological concepts can be applied to differing societies, you will understand the concepts much better.

Let's take an example: the concept of social inequality. For this book, we have chosen societies with highly varied forms of social inequality. In Namibia the Bushmen lived for centuries with almost complete equality. No one had any more possessions or any more power than anyone else. Learning about the Bushmen will sharpen your ability to see inequalities in other societies, including your own. In Egypt, there are very sharp inequalities between men and women. In Japan, people pay close attention to status differences in age, gender, education, and occupation, but income inequalities are quite minimal. In Mexico, millions of people earn the minimum wage of under four dollars a day, while the richest Mexicans have imported cars and air-conditioned houses and send their children to colleges and universities abroad. When you learn about many different systems of social stratification, you will understand the concept better.

In order to help you understand what life is like in different societies, we have included in each chapter a number of *vignettes:* short, fictional sketches of individuals, their life situations, and their feelings. None of the characters in the vignettes are real people. We made them up, inspired by people we read about and people we met.

Learning through Comparison

Comparison and contrast are very important means of learning. The Bushmen spent all their lives in groups of 15 to 40 people, related by kinship. Imagine how hard it would be to teach them the concept of "bureaucracy." They have never waited in a line at the Department of Motor Vehicles or filled out forms for registration at college. When you study the Bushmen, you will learn how new and unusual bureaucracies are in the human experience.

Comparison has always been the essence of sociology. Sociologists know that when you are immersed in your own society, you take for granted and assume that its ways are part of human nature, universal and unchanging. We most easily discover what our own society is like when we learn about a different society. As sociologists say, "The fish is the last to discover the water."

Comparison is a wonderful means by which to apply concepts and theories and deepen your understanding of their meanings. Comparison is also a challenge to intolerance. Studying world societies shows us that there is no one *right* way to live, and that the most fundamental characteristic of "human nature" is our tremendous flexibility in creating diverse cultures.

Active Learning

Suppose you wanted to learn to play basketball and someone told you to listen to another person talk about the game, and then watch other people play it. You would be disgusted with this advice because you know that in order to learn basketball, you must play the game yourself and then practice, practice, practice. If you have a coach or someone else to watch you and give you pointers, you will learn even faster.

Will you be surprised to hear that learning sociology (or any other college subject) works the same way? Just reading or hearing someone else present sociological ideas isn't enough. You must practice your own sociological reasoning, aloud and in writing, and have others coach you in your work in order to learn the subject.

Global Sociology is designed so that you can practice applying sociological concepts to a descriptive "database" of information about five different societies. As you read this book, ask yourself: "Can I talk about these societies using the language of sociology?" Try to describe the values of each society, or the roles they expect men and women to play. Think about how family life is organized in each society, or what social groups are most important in peoples' lives. Questions at the end of each chapter will help you put your knowledge of sociology to active use.

One of the best ways to practice sociological thinking is to make comparisons. We invite you to compare each of these societies to your own society: What similarities and what differences can you see? You can also compare the societies in this book with one another. In writing this book, we have been greatly tempted to make comparisons ourselves, but we have tried to discipline ourselves and stick to description. We want to leave the work and play of comparison to the students and instructors who use *Global Sociology*.

Preface: To the Instructor

We wrote this book to give students a broader context for understanding both sociology and their own societies. For several years both authors had assigned William Kephart's *Extraordinary Groups* when teaching introductory sociology. We liked Kephart's case-study approach. Reading his descriptions of a variety of American religious groups, students were exposed to diverse cultures and social structures. Despite these advantages, we were unhappy confining our comparisons to religious sects. Linda's student Mike Godino put it nicely when he told us, "You know, introductory sociology is great. I'm learning about ways of life I never imagined, and it makes me see my own society so much more clearly by contrast. But I'm not sure I want to know this much about these little religious groups. Isn't there a book that does the same thing for countries, important countries that we should understand?"

Mike's comment crystallized our desire to extend the range of comparisons, and we searched around, but there wasn't such a book. There were plenty of ethnographies, but these were anthropological rather than sociological. Then there were "global" textbooks. We liked these texts, but we were looking for a supplement with in-depth case studies.

Finally, we decided to write the book ourselves: *Global Sociology* is a soft-cover supplement to any standard sociology text, providing broad and comprehensive sociological description of five diverse contemporary societies. We aimed for wide geographic distribution: We chose one Asian society—Japan; one Latin American society—Mexico; one European society—Germany; and two African societies—Egypt and Namibia. Two of the societies are wealthy and industrial, and two are poor "developing" nations. For greater contrast we include a special focus on the hunting-and-gathering Bushmen of Namibia.

One of our concerns in writing *Global Sociology* has been to create a text that instructors can use without being specialists in the study of Japan, Mexico, Egypt, Germany, or Namibia. General knowledge and a sociologist's understanding of how societies work provide ample background for using *Global Sociology*. We are confident that you will see how easily *Global Sociology* can be introduced into your courses. Although it is interesting to read some of the more specialized studies we have recommended, it is by no means a requirement for the effective use of *Global Sociology.*

A Comparative Framework

The five societies described here vary in many ways: in their definitions of male and female roles, in their degree of inequality, in the salience of religious values and norms in their cultures, and in their population dynamics. *Global Sociology* includes two different socialist societies, the former East Germany and Egypt, and it examines the post-socialist transformations of East Germany. The book also examines two different wealthy capitalist societies—Germany and Japan—whose styles of capitalism contrast with that of the United States.

Global Sociology is structured to parallel the major sections of a standard sociology text. Each chapter is organized around basic sociological topics: culture, social structure and group life, socialization, deviance, social institutions, social stratification, and social change. Earlier chapters place more emphasis on topics usually introduced first in introductory sociology. Chapters on Japan, Mexico, and the Bushmen of Namibia provide much discussion of culture, social structure, socialization, and deviance, although they include other topics as well. Later chapters on Egypt and Germany touch more briefly on beginning concepts and emphasize social stratification, social institutions, and social change.

Global Sociology will help bring to life abstract textbook presentations of concepts with a wealth of vivid illustrations. Reading about Japanese greeting norms, or Mexican patronage politics, or the effects of population growth in Egypt, or East Germans' first encounters with capitalism, or how the Bushmen avoid conflict, students will see the universal relevance of sociological ideas. Questions posed at the end of each chapter lead students to make sociological comparisons and to apply sociological concepts to descriptive knowledge.

Comparison is one of the great strengths of sociology. By comparing other societies with their own, students learn about the range of social variation, and they learn what makes their own society distinctive. Reading *Global Sociology,* students will spontaneously make comparisons with their own society, and they can be encouraged to compare the diverse societies described in the book. To aid in this effort, the text provides a variety of tables that summarize important comparative data for Japan, Mexico, Egypt, Germany, Namibia, and the United States.

Although most of our students were born and raised in the United States, an increasing number are from countries as diverse as El Salvador, Haiti, Jamaica, Iran, China, Greece, and the former Soviet Union. It is exciting to see that these students can use *Global Sociology* to make meaningful comparisons with the societies and cultures they have been born and raised in. *Global Sociology* doesn't require that students carry the assumptions, insights, and values of an American childhood and schooling.

Learning about other societies helps all students become aware of their ethnocentrism and reach beyond it. Students develop a sense of attachment to the societies they study, even when some of what they read disturbs them. To help students use their imaginations in picturing unfamiliar societies, we have included fictional vignettes of individuals in each society. Vignettes help students make human connections across cultural divides.

We have found that reading *Global Sociology* heightens student interest in other societies. News from abroad becomes absorbing when students have a framework in which to place it. *Global Sociology* presents societies that are often in the news, and our own students have become alert to news coverage about the societies they study. After September 11, 2001, with the United States fighting wars in Afghanistan and Iraq, our students became very interested in news coverage of Islamic societies. As they compared Egypt with Afghanistan, Iran, and Pakistan, they learned that while Muslim societies are linked by a common religion and face similar problems of wrenching economic and political transformation, they respond very differently because of their diverse histories and cultures.

The Fourth Edition

World events move quickly. The fourth edition has been revised to keep students up to date. First of all, the statistical tables have been updated with the latest information available. We have searched out the best sources of world statistics on the Internet, and Web references are noted with the tables and in the bibliography. You and your students can continue to update data by using these sources. In many cases, Web sources will allow you to generate your own tables by selecting variables.

Global Sociology has been carefully revised to reflect current events. The chapter on **Egypt** now offers in-depth analysis of the role of Islam in Egyptian life, carefully distinguishing between the revival of religious piety and the growth of both jihadi and political Islam. We discuss the development of democratic institutions in **Mexico** and the obstacles to establishing the rule of law. The fourth edition tracks rapid social change in **Japan** in the past few years, tracing the disruptive effects of a decade-long recession on male and female roles, marriage, children and schooling, career paths, and politics. The chapter on **Namibia** reports on a peaceful transition of power from the founding president of the nation to a democratically elected successor, and follows the vexed issue of land redistribution. We have updated material in the chapter on **Germany** about educational and economic institutions and political change.

As we follow events in *Global Sociology*'s five societies and the world, we see two overarching themes of change, which we have tried to illustrate and incorporate in the fourth edition. First of all, we see everywhere the effects of **globalization.** Global media and the global economy touch every society, making their material cultures more similar, and widening the secularizing impact of capitalist economic institutions and democratic politics. We ask ourselves, Will *Global Sociology* become outdated as all the world's societies become alike? Our answer is, No, because the secularizing and homogenizing effects of globalization have been greeted in every society by efforts to assert particularistic identities, be they national, cultural, or religious. So the world's societies—including those in *Global Sociology*—are becoming both more similar and more different all the time. *Global Sociology* describes this two-way flow of social change.

Below, we highlight specific material that is new to the fourth edition:

- Fuller discussion of the impact of religious revival on popular culture and daily life (Islam in Egypt and evangelical Christianity in Mexico).
- A much broadened analysis of deviance and social control, applying important sociological theories to understanding phenomena such as crime, suicide, and youth rebellion (Japan, Mexico, Egypt).
- Expanded discussion of changing male and female roles (Japan, Egypt).
- New analyses of the challenges of creating and maintaining democratic governmental institutions (Egypt, Mexico).
- Fuller coverage of Islamism in Egypt, clarifying the differences among cultural Islam, political Islam, and jihadi Islam.
- Additional exploration of the importance of global shifts in the demand for low-wage labor in Mexico. Also, updated discussion of the importance of migration to Mexico's economy, and the effects of migration on family and community life.
- More analysis of the impact of global economic competition on Germany, and the resulting social strains in educational institutions, labor-management relations, and politics.

Events, no doubt, will continue their rapid pace. We have tried to give you access to current news about the societies in this book so that it will be easy for you to keep up. Please use the Web Guide in the Instructor's Manual that accompanies *Global Sociology*. It includes English-language newspaper websites for all five societies. We have carefully selected websites that are reputable and reliable, easy to access, and constantly updated. They should be a good source for news for you and your students.

We have enjoyed using *Global Sociology* with our own students. We appreciate their sense of wonder as they confront diverse societies, and we are continually impressed with how much they learn about their own society when they study other societies. We hope you and your students will enjoy the book too.

Supplementary Material

Accompanying *Global Sociology* is a combined Instructor's Manual and Test Bank. It opens with an Introduction with hints on "Using Global Sociology." For each chapter, it includes a chapter overview highlighting the important themes; an annotated list of suggested readings; a film/video guide; an annotated list of websites; exercises and assignments; discussion/study questions; essay questions; and multiple-choice and true/false test questions.

Acknowledgments

We would like to acknowledge the help that so many people gave us throughout the writing of this book. First, we need to thank our students, whose responses first led us to this effort and who "field tested" earlier editions of *Global Sociology*. We owe a tremendous debt to our Developmental Editor at McGraw-Hill, Kathy Blake, who has been our constant support through four editions of *Global Sociology*. We could never have kept up with the whole project without the continuity she provided and her steady encouragement. Her sound judgment was invaluable. McGraw-Hill's Sociology Editor, Sherith Pankratz, and Marketing Manager, Dan Loch, were continuously encouraging and insightful.

Brian Pecko, our photo editor at McGraw-Hill, was resourceful in locating images we needed for the fourth edition of *Global Sociology*.

A panel of reviewers gave us useful comments and suggestions and generously shared their knowledge of the societies described in *Global Sociology*. For the fourth edition, we want to give special thanks to Jan AbuShakrah of Portland Community College and Gary Brock of Southwest Missouri State University. Thanks also go to Cynthia Cook, Creighton University; Susan Cox, Bellevue Community College; L. M. Hynson, Oklahoma State University, Stillwater; Robert Ingoglia, Felician College; Emily LaBeff, Midwestern State University; and James Wolfe, Butler University. Our reviewers' insights into the teaching arts have helped to make this book a more useful classroom document.

Alicia Sanchez of Nassau Community College's Library was indispensable to our efforts to read and review the wide range of contemporary scholarship on our subject matter. Tsubasa Kamei's understanding of the dynamics of Japanese popular culture made it possible to discern trends that had not yet made it into the scholarly literature. Shiva Balaghi of New York University's Hagop Kevorkian Center for near Eastern Studies was continually helpful in bringing to our attention scholarship on gender and popular culture in the Islamic cultures of North Africa and Asia. Our colleague Yih-Jin Young was an invaluable resource to us as we threaded our way through census materials. Our Departmental Secretary, Mavis Loschin, went out of her way to make our lives easier as we pursued both teaching and writing.

Howard Becker's remarks on careers delivered at the Eastern Sociological Society in 2004 helped us place the human consequences of a changing Japanese economy in sociological perspective. Juergen Paffhausen of the *Statistisches Landesamt Berlin* was especially kind in helping us interpret changes in the reporting of German demographic data. Gonca Okur, of the Developmental Data Group of the World Bank, responded graciously to our requests.

For their help with earlier editions, we are also indebted to our colleague Eric Wood; to Louise Forsyth of Brooklyn Poly Prep; to Janet Abu-Lughod of the New School University; and to Lila Abu-Lughod of Columbia University.

Finally, we recognize our debts to our respective spouses and children, who encouraged us and endured our preoccupation with researching and writing *Global Sociology.*

Linda Schneider
Arnold Silverman

Global Sociology

Introducing Five Contemporary Societies

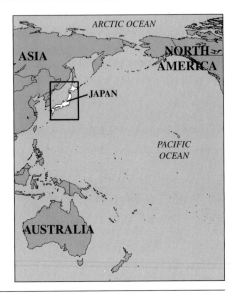

To reach Japan from the United States or Canada you would fly across the North Pacific almost to the mainland of Asia. Narita airport outside Tokyo is one of the busiest airports in the world. Rising from defeat in World War II, Japan has become the world's second largest economy.

LOCATION: Japan is located on the eastern edge of Asia, 200 miles from Korea and across the Sea of Japan from China and Russia. East of Japan lies the Pacific Ocean.

AREA: Japan consists of four large islands of Hokkaido, Honshu, Shikoku, and Kyushu (145,000 square miles or 420,000 square kilometers). Together they are the size of California or Germany. Honshu is the largest island and the site of Tokyo, the capital, and other large cities.

LAND: Japan is mountainous and rugged. Mt. Fuji, a dormant volcano, is 12,000 feet high. Less than 1 acre in 6 is flat; most of this is along the coasts where cities compete with farms for space. Almost half the population lives in three major metropolitan areas.

CLIMATE: Similar to the east coast of the United States. It is colder on Hokkaido and nearly subtropical in southern Kyushu. Japan receives 50 inches of rain a year, much of it falling as snow.

POPULATION: In 2000 there were 127 million people; by 2050 the population will likely fall to 101 million. Japan's population is aging; 18 percent are over age 65.

INCOME: U.S. $34,510 per capita GDP in 2003.

EDUCATION: Japan has one of the highest average educational levels and the highest literacy rate in the world.

RELIGION: 75% combine Buddhism and Shinto, a unique Japanese religion; less than 2% are Christian.

MINORITIES: Korean Japanese, Ainu, Burakumin.

CHAPTER ONE

Japan: The Importance of Belonging

INTRODUCTION

If you visit downtown Tokyo today, you might think you are in New York, or London, or Beirut for that matter. Young people sit in coffee bars and talk on their cell phones. The women carry Vuitton bags and wear Prada and Burberry clothes. You can eat lunch at McDonalds or KFC, shop at the The Gap and see the latest Hollywood action movie. In some ways, all our societies are becoming more similar, as a global consumer culture spreads around the world. Perhaps in your society, people eat both hamburgers and sushi, watch both *Friends* and Japanese anime. Does it still make sense to read a book like this one, devoted to describing what makes five societies different from each other?

This is an old question in Japan, a really old question, going back at least a thousand years. Japan's history has a very clear story line. It is the story of a society that repeatedly adopted elements of culture from other societies, but nevertheless remained distinctly "Japanese."

JAPAN'S HISTORY

Japanese history is interesting and contradictory. It shows us long conservative periods when the Japanese guarded and preserved their traditions and shut out foreign influences. It also displays repeated crises in which Japanese society transformed itself, rapidly adapting foreign cultures and creating new Japanese "traditions."

The Great Opening to China

The first great turning point in Japanese history happened more than a thousand years ago, in the seventh century. Japan was at that time a tribal society in which people lived by gardening and fishing, without cities, with only a weak national government and a ruling family whose importance was largely symbolic. But early in the seventh century, a prince of the ruling family, Prince Shōtoku, began to import cultural practices from China, at that time the world's most advanced nation. Prince

Shōtoku began by importing Chinese Buddhism and Buddhist art. Typically, for Japan, planned change and the adoption of foreign ideas was orchestrated from the top, by the elite of Japanese society. For the next three centuries, Japan's rulers continued to study China and adopt Chinese institutions, arts, and technology, deliberately "improving" Japanese society. Japan adopted China's courtly manners and arts, its Confucian philosophy, its centralized government and elaborate bureaucracy, its tax system and system of writing. The Japanese even built elaborate Chinese-style capital cities, remarkable in a society that previously had lacked even towns! But it is important to understand that this was a self-transformation. Japan was not conquered or colonized by China. All of its borrowings were voluntary. In fact, after the ninth century, Japan retreated into isolation and slowly digested all its borrowed Chinese culture, blending it with native ways, and finally producing a new, distinctly Japanese culture (Reischauer, pp. 41–51; Bellah, pp. 9–15).

The Tokugawa Era: Contact with the West Refused

By the sixteenth century Japan was enjoying a period of commercial growth and artistic expression. It was a relatively open time when individual self-expression flourished. When Portuguese missionaries and traders reached Japan, they were greeted with curiosity and interest. In the next 100 years, more than 300,000 Japanese were converted to Christianity. But then Japan's rulers decided things had gone too far and forced thousands of Japanese Christians to renounce their religion or face execution. By 1638, they had completely sealed off Japan from the outside world. Laws banned firearms, forbade the Japanese from building ocean-going ships or trading with foreigners, and only a few foreign traders—Koreans, Chinese, and Dutch—were allowed to enter Japan. During two centuries of isolation, from 1638 to 1853 (known as the Tokugawa Era, after the leading family of *shoguns,* or rulers, of the period) Japan was peaceful and stable. Important changes took place, though, including the development of a class of entrepreneurs, the rise of a centralized government, and the forging of a strong sense of national identity. A few Japanese scholars read Dutch books and kept up with news of the scientific and political revolutions taking place in the West (Christopher, pp. 47–48; Bellah, p. 22).

The Meiji Restoration: The First Opening to the West

Japan's second contact with the West had a very different outcome. It resulted in another great self-transformation. By mid-nineteenth century, western powers had colonized Africa, India, and much of Southeast Asia, forcing trade concessions upon China as well. Finally, in 1853, the American navy forced Japan to open its ports to American ships and sign a series of trade treaties. Fear of subjection to foreign powers brought on a national crisis in Japan. In 1868, rebel provincial rulers, backed by reform-minded middle and low-ranking *samurai* (members of Japan's hereditary warrior caste) seized power from the shoguns. Their rule was called the *Meiji Restoration,* because they claimed to restore power to the emperor, the heredity monarch. In fact, however, they ruled in his stead. Japan's new rulers decided to take radical defensive action against European colonization. They successfully argued that the only way Japan could enjoy equality with western powers was to modernize and adopt western technology. Under Meiji leadership Japan was able to deliberately bring about its own modernization and fend off European colonization.

The new government soon abolished feudal domains and began dismantling the caste system. It instituted universal primary education and universal conscription. Then, the top leaders of the new regime went off on a long voyage during which they visited the United States and many European countries. In effect, the Meiji government went shopping for new institutions, finding a model for its navy in Britain, its army in France, its universities in America, and its constitution in Germany (Tasker, p. 21; Bellah, pp. 30–31). Meiji rulers created a new government bureaucracy, based on European models and staffed by a new university-educated civil service. They adopted a modern court system and public school system. Meiji Japan promoted economic modernization, making peasants owners of the land they farmed, and encouraging modern agriculture, based on American models. The government created western-style banks, railroads, and ports, and developed mining, steel and weapons production, and silk manufacture. They sent students abroad to learn western skills and hired western experts to come to Japan. And all of this was done by the end of the nineteenth century!

Japan also emulated the imperial ambitions of western countries, both to demonstrate its military strength to the West, and also to build an empire of its own. In 1894–1895, Japan defeated China in a war for control of Korea, and in 1904–1905, it fought again for Korea, this time against Russia, gaining Korea and several other possessions in its victory. By World War I, Japan was a major colonial power, the equal of western powers. Militarism intensified in Japan during the difficult years of the 1920s and 1930s. Imperial ambitions once again led Japan into war with China, a war that dragged on and finally escalated into the Pacific theater of World War II. Japan's defeat opened a new chapter in its westernization and economic development.

The Occupation Reforms: The Second Opening to the West

Japan was utterly devastated by the war, and its people demoralized and disillusioned with militarism. They were open to change and new ideas. And the American occupying forces, in their self-confident, well-meaning American way, were eager to make over Japanese society. General Douglas MacArthur, acting as Supreme Commander for the Allied Powers, dismantled Japan's military, reformed its government and constitution, broke up its industrial monopolies, and redistributed land ownership. MacArthur's reforms were radical, giving individuals rights beyond what is guaranteed in the U.S. Constitution, including equal rights for women, the right of labor to bargain collectively, and the right of all individuals to an equal education. As we will see, in the years since the occupation, Japan has strengthened the reforms that were compatible with its culture and ignored the rest. A new combination of western institutions and Japanese centralized government, created with Japanese-style drive, brought about Japan's postwar "economic miracle."

Japan rapidly rebuilt from wartime ruin and then went on to industrialize and develop cutting-edge export-oriented industries, producing cars, radios, televisions, computers, and other consumer electronics. Japan is a small country, essentially lacking in raw materials and energy resources. In forty years, the nation grew to become the world's second largest economy. Japanese workers were content to dedicate themselves to the nation's goal of economic advance because they benefited. Wages doubled and redoubled. Companies promised job security and rising wages in exchange for worker loyalty, and once-radical unions were declawed. The Japanese "embraced the drama of business growth," making business their national identity (Chapman, pp. 120–121). People looked up to big companies and business life became glamorous. The company man going to work became a kind of warrior, headed into battle, with the nation cheering him on.

JAPANESE CULTURE

In its long history, Japan has repeatedly adopted foreign institutions and practices. And they haven't just nibbled a little around the edges. Japan has swallowed entire foreign institutional systems, technologies, and forms of government. Nevertheless, when they borrowed foreign ways, the Japanese didn't feel humiliated or dominated. Even in the case of the American Occupation, when the United States did indeed force changes on Japan, the Japanese remained confident that their society could digest all its foreign borrowings, while remaining true to itself in essential ways. In Japan, you can still hear an old slogan from the Meiji Era, "*wakon yosai*" (Japanese spirit and western knowledge), and Japanese people will tell you that the foreign models they adopt are transformed by the addition of a "Japanese heart" (Tasker, p. 21; Feiler, pp. 36–37). What is this "Japanese heart"? It is the critical core of Japanese culture, consisting of elements of nonmaterial culture: values, beliefs, language, symbols, and norms and sanctions. **Values** are a central element in all cultures. They are ideals, abstract expressions of what people consider important. Even if people don't explicitly articulate their values, values infuse the decisions they make, the way they see the world, and how they relate to each other.

The Value of Belonging

In Japan, belonging is the most fundamental value. Let us take some time to thoroughly explore what belonging means in Japan. After all, in every society people want to belong. If you ever went to junior high school or high school, you have had intense, personal experience of the human need to belong. And belonging is the basic subject matter of sociology, which studies the groups people construct and how these groups shape their lives.

A Sense of "Peoplehood"

Belonging in Japan begins in a sense of national solidarity. People in Japan are told constantly that their society is special, like no other, because the Japanese people are, literally, one family. Tradition holds that Japan is a sacred land, created by the gods, and that all Japanese are biologically a single family, descended from a common ancestress, the sun goddess, Amaterasu. The emperor, said to be a direct descendant of Amaterasu, symbolizes the government, the people, and divinity, fused together (Bellah, pp. 35–38). The Japanese see themselves as a unique people, physically and

Belonging is a constant in Japanese society, but what group you belong to and how you show your group identity can change rapidly. These young Japanese women have dyed their hair pink and orange and dressed in similar "cute" outfits to tell the world they belong.

racially different from all the rest of the world's peoples. Many Japanese people believe that their society's economic success, low crime rate, and high level of education are the result of its people's distinct racial stock.

But Japanese racial identity is in reality a social belief, not a physical fact. Anthropologists tell us that the Japanese people are part of the Mongoloid group of peoples, which includes the Koreans and the Han Chinese. There is some variety too in the appearance of the Japanese people—different shades of skin color, and hair and eyes ranging from black to brown reflect a heritage of Polynesian, Chinese, and East Asian ancestry. And while they believe that Koreans are physically distinctive, the Japanese are unable to identify Japanese-born Koreans by their appearance (Tasker, pp. 15–16, 34; Feiler, p. 135).

Although it is not a physical fact, the Japanese sense of "peoplehood" has a firm social foundation. Japan, like most other societies, is inhabited by people whose ancestors came from many places. Japan is a chain of islands, about two hundred miles off the coast of Korea. The most ancient people to arrive in Japan were the Ainu, a distinctive race which dates back thousands of years into prehistory. After the Ainu, other peoples came to Japan from southern and northern Asia. But it is important to know that there has been no significant immigration into Japan for more than a thousand years. For all that time, the peoples of Japan mingled, until they developed the world's most racially and culturally unified society. There are in fact some minority groups in Japan (which we will examine later), but they are few and small in size. The Japanese sense of distinctiveness is reinforced by language: Unlike the rest of the world's major languages, Japanese is spoken by only one ethnic group, and by relatively few foreigners (Tasker, p. 26).

While the Japanese people are not the separate race they believe themselves to be, they are indeed an unusually homogeneous people, much more so than the people of other societies. Their sense of peoplehood has given them unique advantages that other societies don't have. They are able to merge the concepts of racial and national identity, and their acute sense of distinctiveness, carefully cultivated by Japan's leaders, helps to foster an unusually strong feeling of group solidarity and national purpose in Japanese society.

"An Island Nation"

"Japan is an island nation," schoolchildren are repeatedly told, "surrounded by seas and enemies, so we must depend on each other." Though their country is perceived by others as a giant power in the global economy, the Japanese people share a sense of national vulnerability. Many Japanese think of their country as small, even weak, unprotected from assault by outside forces. They are acutely aware that Japan, though self-sufficient up to the twentieth century, is now highly dependent on the world economy, more so than any other major power. Japan has no oil, almost no raw materials, and must import much of its meat and grain. Since the land is very mountainous, only a small portion is suitable for agriculture, and almost the entire population is squeezed into only one-fifth of the total area. The Japanese play down their early twentieth-century history as an aggressive imperial power, which invaded China and other Asian nations and provoked the United States to war (Tasker, pp. 8–10; Feiler, pp. 88, 141).

Group Membership

The importance of belonging in Japan starts on the level of the nation, or people, but this group membership is then expressed in all the social groups that make up Japanese society. Japanese groups are like little "family states, tightly cohesive and all-consuming in their demands," American sociologist Robert Bellah explains. Individuals owe their groups intense loyalty and devoted service (Bellah, pp. 39, 188). In Japanese society, the group comes first. Being alone, outside the web of group life, is unthinkable. In the Japanese view, it is only in groups that people develop as individuals, experience the pleasures of human feeling, and enjoy a sense of secure interdependence with others.

Do you remember the recent craze for Pokémon cartoon superheros? It is interesting that Pokémon was such an international success, because it teaches quintessential Japanese values, including the value of group membership. Unlike American superheros, who generally work alone, the Pokémon characters work as a team, taking risks to save each other from danger. The older, more experienced Pokémon characters befriend the younger ones and guide them, and in return the younger ones give them loyalty (Strom, Nov. 7, 1999, p. WK4).

Of course there are individualists in Japan: brilliant entrepreneurs who start billion-dollar companies alone, and iconoclastic artists and writers. But they are not celebrated in Japanese society. They are not cultural idols and children don't look up to them and imitate them. Popular legends attach instead to the loyal company man, the "salaryman," who puts his company first, despite his personal wishes and problems. Novels, television series, and movies portray him.[1]

Group Life and Adaptability

Now that you know something about the importance of belonging in Japan, you can begin to understand why Japan has so readily incorporated practices and institutions borrowed from other societies. Bellah explains that group life is the heart of Japanese culture. It is, in his words, like a "container," uncommitted to any particular set of beliefs or institutions, which persists even when the "contents"—all those foreign borrowings—change (Bellah, pp. 189–190). In fact, group life, or belonging, is the "Japanese heart," which can encapsulate and transform foreign culture by implanting it firmly within the structure of Japanese group life. So Japan was devoted to war and conquest in the 1930s and 1940s, and then when Japan was defeated and occupied by the Americans, the society turned around and devoted itself to economic growth and peace. The transition was smooth, because the whole culture of group life continued; only the "content" changed.

Value Clusters

Sociologist James Henslin offers us a concept very useful in understanding Japan. He suggests that we can often discern one or several values that are of supreme importance in a culture, and then we can see subsidiary values, or satellite values so to speak, connected to those central values (Henslin, pp. 46–49). In Japan, we can see a number of values connected to the value of belonging.

The Value of Harmony

People in Japan will tell you that because their island is crowded it is important to maintain public harmony and avoid conflict. But, as sociologists, we can see that restricting conflict helps people keep up important relationships in groups. Public life really is harmonious: There is little crime, so you needn't lock your car nor fear being mugged, and couples can safely walk in the park at midnight. It would be very rare to see people arguing in public or come upon a fight outside a bar. Japanese norms require people to be willing to apologize and humble themselves. So after a car accident the drivers will jump out and apologize and bow to each other. In the Japanese version of the fairy tale Little Red Riding Hood, the wolf apologizes, the grandmother is saved and forgives him, and they all sit down together to tea. As you can imagine, lawsuits are uncommon in Japan; people are more likely to avoid confrontation and reach informal compromises. But lest you get the idea that the Japanese are inhumanly perfect, you should understand that people must work very hard

---

[1]*Sarariman* translates in English to "salaryman." It is used to describe managers who are, almost without exception, men. Women work in business as "office ladies"—secretaries. There is no gender-neutral language in Japan (like "businessperson") to describe employees, because men and women play sharply different workplace roles.

to maintain public harmony and order. Japanese people get insulted or angry just like anyone else, but in their society values and norms forcefully promote self-control and the avoidance of direct personal confrontation.

The idea of two people openly expressing disagreement fills Japanese people with horror. In business or personal life, people avoid committing themselves to hard and fast positions; they try not to acknowledge or clarify their disagreements. Instead, Japanese people proceed by cautiously feeling each other out, making ambiguous statements, and using nonverbal clues to figure out what others prefer, aiming for compromise without revelation of conflict.

Decisions in Japanese corporations are usually made after a long process of consultations, often through the circulation of memos, typically written by middle-ranking associates and usually vaguely phrased. Each reader puts his seal on the document and may add comments to it. The memo is gradually revised as the members of the staff edge toward agreement. By the end, everyone is familiar with the problem under discussion, but no one stakes out a clear position from which they might have to retreat, and there are no clear winners and losers. There is one tremendous advantage to this procedure: Once a decision is reached there is no losing minority, licking its wounds and grudging support. On the other hand, decision making is slow and cumbersome, and in a crisis, like an earthquake or a financial panic, Japanese institutions are infuriatingly slow to respond (Smith, pp. 54–55).

Another way the Japanese avoid conflict is by use of a *go-between,* a neutral person who literally goes between two parties when there is some matter to be worked out. Go-betweens are frequently used in Japan in negotiating marriages. With a go-between, one need not turn down a potential bride or groom to her or his face, avoiding open disagreement and embarrassment.

The Value of Maintaining Relationships

In Japanese society, people value being part of a group, and they work at getting along. But life in Japanese groups takes a great deal of time and work, because of the emphasis placed on avoidance of conflict. Self-assertion, overtly disagreeing with others, making demands, or even clearly stating one's wishes all look like threats to group harmony and are out of the question. Such behavior is downright frightening to the Japanese. In relating to others, it is far preferable to express your feelings and wishes indirectly.

In Japan people try not to call attention to themselves. This *enryo* or "reserve" restrains people from giving opinions, expressing desires, or even making choices if they are offered. But how can a group function if no one can express their wishes? Because of *enryo,* it is of fundamental importance that people are highly sensitive to the unspoken wishes of others. The Japanese value *ninjo,* which means compassion, sympathy, rapport, or "fellow feeling." A good person strives to empathize—to understand the feelings of others and the situational difficulties others may be experiencing. In Japan, if something bad happens to you—if someone close to you dies, or your mate leaves you, or you fail your exams—your friends will rally around. They will keep you company and bring you food and try to distract you from your troubles. But they will never say "you must feel terrible about . . ." or even "do you want to talk about . . ." That would seem terribly crude. In Japan, your friends support you by showing you they understand, but people don't believe that expressing feelings directly is especially useful or healing.

In ordinary Japanese life a good host knows a guest well enough to anticipate what food will be pleasing and sets it before the guest, so no choices are required. Good guests eat what they are given so as not to cause embarrassment by implying that the host has misunderstood their desires. If you make your wishes known, it is an insult to others: It implies that you believe the other person is too insensitive to perceive them. For example, the worst thing a husband can say about his wife is "I have to ask for what I want." Members of Japanese groups also expect other group members to anticipate their unexpressed desires (Smith, pp. 57–58).

How do the Japanese manage to do this? For one thing, spending a lot of time together helps. People who are in constant contact, in informal as well as formal situations, come to understand each other intuitively. Also, the Japanese place great emphasis on nonverbal communication. Because of *enryo,* people's words are not a good guide to their feelings. From childhood, people practice observing others' behavior for tiny hints in body language, tone of voice, the timing of silences. Just as children in many cultures can read their parents' disapproval in a glance or body posture, so members of Japanese groups come to read each other. In fact, a person who insists on explicit rational explanation is called a "reason freak" and is considered immature (Smith, p. 58).

The Value of Conformity

Conformity helps people fit into groups. It is related to reserve, a Japanese reluctance to stand out, an unwillingness to separate oneself from the group. (Just think about those groups in your high school and how carefully everyone followed the unspoken dress code of their group.) If you observe the way people dress in Japan you will see conformity in action. Businessmen dress very conservatively; the salaryman outfit of dark blue suit and white shirt is legendary. A gray suit or a blue shirt stands out. Salesclerks in department stores wear uniforms and so do all the workers and supervisors in factories. Adult women usually dress quite conservatively too; they wear skirts and avoid bright colors. When they shed their school uniforms, rebellious adolescents conform to the styles of their "tribes," like the subculture of young people who tint their skin dark and wear braids or Rastafarian hair.

People also conform to the norms of public life. Subway riders wait in two neat rows for the train doors to open. Women carefully separate their household trash for recycling and wait on the correct day to trade their old newspapers for rolls of toilet paper. Every family devotedly sweeps their sidewalk and entryway. A person who finds a lost object in the subway or on the street turns it over to the police, who carefully catalog it and place it in the local lost and found center. In 2002, people brought $23 million in lost cash to the Tokyo center (of which 72 percent was returned to its owners) and 330,000 umbrellas, among many other items. Unclaimed money or objects are eventually offered to the finder (Onishi, Jan. 8, 2004, p. A1).

The Values of Loyalty, Duty, and Self-Sacrifice

Chushingura is a classic Japanese tale, based on a true story from the early eighteenth century, often performed as theater. (You may know it as the film *Forty-Seven Ronin,* with Toshiro Mifune.) The story goes like this: When Lord Ako, the hero, is baited by Kira, the villain, into drawing his sword in the shogun's castle, he commits a deadly breach of etiquette and is ordered by the shogun to commit suicide. Ako's men, his samurai, become *ronin,* masterless men. Their loyalty to their lord Ako is so strong, however, that they plot revenge against Kira and succeed in killing him a year later. They do this knowing that they, in turn, will be obliged to commit suicide.

Many Japanese say the story remains so popular because people still admire the samurai code, which emphasized loyalty and a dedication so great that its followers were willing to sacrifice themselves (Web-Japan, Feb. 7, 2003). Though the time of the samurai is long past, ties of loyalty still matter greatly in Japanese groups. It is obvious that during World War II, the government leaned heavily on the values of loyalty and self-sacrifice. We remember the kamikaze pilots, but all Japanese were asked to make terrible sacrifices to show their loyalty to the emperor and Japan. Today, in a peaceful Japan, the bonds of loyalty and duty still tug on people.

During the economic recession of the 1990s, small businessmen struggled to keep their enterprises from going under, because they felt obliged, by ties of loyalty, to continue to employ their workers. Some ran up enormous debts borrowing money to pay wages. One man used his entire personal savings to pay his workers "sorry money" when the company finally went under (Belson, Dec. 28, 2002, p. BU1).

Chushingura also illustrates the classic Japanese conflict between *giri* (duty) and *ninjo* (human feeling). Everyone knows the folk saying, "you can't be there when your father dies," which reminds Japanese people that public duty to nation, company, community, or school often takes priority over private feeling. Today, a Japanese employee will think twice before taking off time from work to bring his child to the high school entrance exams, or his mother to the hospital. As Robert Bellah puts it, Japan is a society "where social obligations act like steel cables pulling and controlling one's acts regardless of what one's own feelings are" (Bellah, p. 205).

Before World War II, during the whole Meiji Era, the bonds of duty were very strong. Bellah says that at the time "any pursuit of purely private happiness was considered almost criminal" (p. 205). And social obligation was often set in hierarchical situations where someone in a position over you made demands that you demonstrate your loyalty and do your duty. Nowadays, more people feel resistant towards the coercive power of companies and schools. They care more about private life and personal happiness. Survey data revealed in 1993 that only 4 percent of Japanese respondents said that they would like best "to live a life devoted entirely to society without thought of self." In 1940, 30 percent had chosen that option. The option most frequently chosen in 1993—40 percent—was "to do what you find interesting, regardless of money or honor" (Sugimoto, p. 70). Now the meaning of group loyalty is shifting, from a context of threatened punishment, to a softer dependence on reward. People remain loyal because of the rewards of group membership, because they find acceptance in groups and feel dependent on other group members, or because bosses and teachers and others with authority demonstrate caring (Bellah, pp. 194–205).

The recent Japanese film *Shall We Dance,* which is widely available outside Japan, illustrates this shift well. The hero of the film, who is a diligent but unenthusiastic worker at his company, becomes involved in learning ballroom dancing. The film tells the story of how he gets to know the other students at the dance studio, who are all fairly odd characters. In true Japanese fashion, however, this group of dance students bonds. They come to sympathize with each other; loyalty and obligation become willing, not forced.

Another Value Cluster: The Value of Achievement

Japan is an achievement-oriented society. People believe that what you accomplish in life should be more important than who you are when you are born. They are proud that in Japan, there are opportunities for hardworking people of even the most modest background to rise to positions of prestige and power.

Today, more than ever, the kind of achievement that matters is educational achievement. By the time they reach junior high school, children must understand that excelling in school is the unavoidable gateway to good jobs and high status. Education is becoming more and more important all over the world, but in Japan, it has been the supreme arena of achievement for a long time, since entrepreneurship garners little prestige. If you do well on the high school entrance exams, you can go to a prestigious academic high school. Do well on the college entrance exams and you can get a high-status job with a major corporation or the government bureaucracy. Flunk the exams, and you will find yourself restricted to part-time, temporary manual labor.

This pattern of advancement through exams has been generalized throughout Japanese society. The arts are organized in "schools" of painting, flower arranging, acting, calligraphy, etc. To advance in your art you take classes and exams.

The value of achievement is linked to several other Japanese values, including perseverance, discipline, dedication, competition, and perfectionism. In the film, *Shall We Dance,* the characters enrolled in the school of dance practice constantly, for one character, to the point of exhaustion, with the goal of winning a ballroom dancing competition.

The Value of Perseverance

Japanese contains many words, used constantly, that tell people to endure, or persevere, bear, accept, or accommodate. Children must endure after-school cram classes and long nights of study to pass their high school and college entrance exams. Principals tell their students that school is "life's first big battle," and they must put their all into it. Businessmen must endure after-hours parties with clients, even if they would rather be home sleeping or spending time with their families. Even a person lugging a heavy suitcase up a street in Japan can count on others to call out encouragingly, "go on, *gambatte* (keep going), you can do it" (Feiler, pp. 60–61).

Perseverance is linked to another Japanese value, dedication, or *seishin.* People judge others by how hard they try, how hard they work at whatever task or role is their lot. They are willing to make excuses for poor work, as long as great effort went into it, while good work produced without effort does not impress them. *Seishin* literally means "spirit"; it means the spiritual development that results from effort, discipline, and self-control. It doesn't matter what the task is: It can be studying for exams, paving a road, or learning the tea ceremony; if you persevere in working at it and try to do it perfectly, you will become a better person and people will respect you (Bayley, pp. 118–119).

Japanese Norms

Every society has values that tell its members what the society considers in general to be important, desirable, ideal. Also, all societies have **norms** that tell people, in detail, how they are expected to behave in specific situations. You have already read about many Japanese **norms** or **social expectations** in this chapter. Can you go back through the chapter and find all the norms? One is obviously that if you find lost

These Japanese businessmen conform to their culture's norms of greeting. You bow higher or lower depending on whether your status has more or less prestige than the person you are greeting. Where you stand is not always clear. If you are the president of a small company greeting a Toyota executive, do you bow lower or does he? Japanese must be able to make these decisions rapidly. Does your culture have norm for greeting others? Do you greet superiors in the same way you greet equals?

property in Japan, you should turn it over to the police. What are some other Japanese norms?

Being Japanese requires self-control. Not only must you restrain the expression of your feelings, you must devote enormous effort to behaving properly in all situations. "Good form," compliance with very strict and specific norms of good conduct matters greatly. Good intentions, or "having one's heart in the right place," don't count. And there are very few all-purpose norms to rely on: Japanese norms tend to be **particularistic** (pertaining to a specific situation), rather than **universalistic** (good in all situations). You must bow lower or higher to people of different statuses. When you drink with others, you must lift the bottle to fill their glasses, never your own. You must switch from shoes to slippers when you enter someone's home and switch your slippers for special bathroom slippers when you go to the bathroom. It is acceptable to tell the boss dirty jokes in a bar, but not in the office.

Norms are so particularistic that Japanese people learn to be very tuned in to the behavior, dress, and language of others, so as to understand how they should behave. They find strange groups and new social situations anxiety-provoking, because the norms are unknown and one might unwittingly fail to conform. For example, Japanese don't like to drink in bars where they don't know people. Westerners sometimes regard Japanese people as insincere, or even dishonest, because they see them behaving very differently in different social situations (for example, deferential and reserved in one situation, aggressive or joking in another). To a Japanese person, the western expectation of consistent individual behavior seems immature and foolish: The wise person matches his or her behavior to the requirements of the situation.

Situational Norms

In every society, norms are **situational:** They prescribe expected behavior in a particular situation. The Japanese are unusually conscious of how norms vary depending on the social situation. They place special emphasis on the difference between two fundamentally different kinds of situations: *omote* and *ura. Omote* is the surface, or front of an object, the official, public face of a person, event, or social institution; *ura* is its back, its reverse or private side. In Japan, it is outward compliance to social norms that counts. People accept your conventionalized *omote* behavior at face value; they know your private feelings may not match it, and you can expect them to intuit your real feelings and have unspoken compassion for you. While standards for *omote* behavior are rigorous, and appearances are highly valued, they are not expected to correspond to realities (Tasker, pp. 67–71). Private feelings and behavior are never condemned as "bad," inappropriate, neurotic, etc., as long as they remain in their place. Private feelings are accepted as only human, and outward behavior alone is judged.

Ura is the private side of life, the situations in which people are with close friends or family and can be relaxed, informal, and spontaneous and express their emotions. They will sit in the informal family room and loosen their clothing, drink from the old teapot and cups, and joke and gossip. Women friends or male co-workers spending the weekend together at an inn will put on *yukata,* the cotton robes the hotel supplies and drink and eat in a private room, after relaxing together in the hotel's hot tub.

Children are controlled and orderly in the classroom, but are given frequent play-ground breaks when they are left to their own devices and play wildly and noisily. People are not "free" of norms in the world of *ura,* but the norms are different: They allow more spontaneous self-expression (Bachnik, p. 166).

Religion and Japanese Culture

In some societies (like Egypt) religion is of major importance and norms and values are closely linked to religious belief. Some people think that it is only when people are religious that values and norms are taken seriously. This is not the case in Japan. Though most people carefully conform to the society's norms, very few Japanese people consider themselves religious believers and few are observant of religious practices. But although formal religion has little influence, Japan has an interesting religious heritage which in a very general sense infuses its culture.

There are many religious traditions in Japan: Shinto, Buddhism, Confucianism, Taoism, and Christianity, as well as a number of more modern religious sects usually referred to as the New Religions. Except for a very small number of people (less than 2 percent) who are practicing Christians, most Japanese don't feel they must choose a single religious identity from this heritage. Instead, they practice a kind of folk religion, observing Shinto, Buddhist, and Christian holidays, having Buddhist funerals, and weddings that combine elements of Shinto and Christian rituals, and choosing lucky days by the Taoist calendar.

Shintoism is the most ancient Japanese religion; its tradition extends back to Japan's prehistoric past. Shinto reveres nature in the form of *kami,* deities that embody natural objects, like trees, mountains, the sun, and animals, and represent the life force. *Kami* are everywhere and they are worshipped at Shinto shrines where people ask for their blessings (Earhart, pp. 16–17). No one really takes the Shinto *kami* literally today, but Shinto is a lively part of Japanese folklore, and shrines and shrine festivals figure in folk religion. According to Bellah, Shinto has had a very important influence on Japanese society in that it is a religion of rituals, not principles. This explains why norms in Japan are situational, or **particularistic,** not **universalistic,** and why the forms of group life are more important in Japan than the cultural contents of the groups (Bellah, pp. 1–15).

The Meiji rulers who militarized Japan in the twentieth century revived Shinto and separated it from Buddhism, identifying the emperor as a living *kami* to heighten group identification and create nationalism (Bellah, pp. 35–39). Today, militarized state Shinto is rejected, but Shinto influence survives in a love of nature which is a deep current in Japanese culture, expressed in poetry, landscape painting, and traditions of pottery, landscaping, and architecture that stress subtle, natural materials.

Buddhism, a religion that began in India, came to Japan via China in the sixth century A.D. In Japan it is both a monastic tradition and a family religion that honors family ancestors and offers the possibility of salvation and an afterlife in a Buddhist paradise. For almost a thousand years, Buddhism was a very important part of Japanese culture and society, until, in the sixteenth century Japan's Tokugawa revolution attacked Buddhism as the religion of the old political system and substituted a new emphasis on Confucianism (Reischauer, 1988, pp. 206–207). Today

Buddhism permeates Japanese values in a very subtle way: The Japanese belief in perfectionism, the idea of improving one's spirituality through dedication to any task, no matter how humble, is deeply Buddhist. It is notable that in Buddhism (and Shinto), it is the family, not the individual, that is the basic unit of religious participation. People participate in religious rites as family members and maintain family altars and objects of ancestor worship in the home. Traditional religions helped shape Japan's dominant group consciousness (Earhart, pp. 69–71).

Confucianism is not a religion in the same sense that Buddhism, Shinto, or Christianity are religions. It is a philosophical tradition, named for Confucius, its originator in China in the fifth century B.C. Confucianism became prominent in China in the twelfth century A.D., as a rational, ethical system with strict norms, stressing loyalty to the ruler, obedience towards one's father, and proper behavior. Confucianism has no priests, no temples, no religious rituals. From the sixteenth century to the late nineteenth century, Confucianism was very important in Japan, shaping values in a lasting way. Its influence is felt today in the Japanese stress on loyalty and obedience, and in the importance of education, hard work, and doing one's duty to family, employers, and the nation (Reischauer, 1988, pp. 203–204).

Christianity came to Japan in the sixteenth century and it spread rapidly before being suppressed by the Tokugawa rulers. When Christianity was permitted again in the late nineteenth century, Protestant and Catholic missionaries entered Japan but found only small numbers of converts. Today, however, Christian culture has come to Japan as part of a larger western influence, and most Japanese people celebrate Christmas, know bible stories, and respect Christian values, although they are not themselves Christians (Reischauer, pp. 212–213).

Japanese people today who feel a strong need for religious faith generally turn to the New Religions, popular religious movements, the best-known of which are *Soka Gakkai* and *Tenrikyo,* which combine ideas and rituals from Shinto, Buddhism, Taoism, and sometimes Christianity. The new religions offer their members help in solving personal problems through faith and religious observance, and perhaps even more important, they offer close-knit communities, with festivities, rallies, study groups, and leadership hierarchies (Inoue, pp. 220–228).

SOCIAL STRUCTURE AND GROUP LIFE

In Japan, group life comes first. People think of themselves primarily as members of groups, and only secondarily as individuals. Japanese sociologists consider this **group consciousness** or **group identification** a traditional part of Japanese culture.[2] Over the course of the twentieth century, different groups have risen to preeminence in Japanese life, but group identification remains the basic pattern.

Up to the start of World War II, people in Japan lived out their lives "embedded" in *extended,* multigenerational families and in their village or neighborhood (Fukutake, p. 214). Villages were small, consisting of not more than one hundred households, and

[2]See, for example, Nakane, pp. 1–22; or for a recent discussion, Kuwayama, pp. 121–151.

they were closed, self-sufficient communities, within which most people spent their entire lives. Villages were self-governing units, responsible as a whole for collecting taxes imposed on the village, not its households. The households of a village worked together in the fields, or in maintaining the village irrigation system. They helped each other build and repair houses and hold weddings and funerals. Ties between superiors and subordinates were emphasized in the village as well as in the family since wealthier, landowning families, and their tenants and laborers were in constant interaction (Fukutake, pp. 33–39).

Group Life in Modern Japan

The old-fashioned family and village community have all but disappeared in Japan today. Since World War II, the size of Japanese households has gotten smaller and smaller. In the 1990s, Japan had the world's third lowest birthrate, with Japanese women bearing an average of only 1.46 children each. As a result, the size of the average household numbered only about three people. Twenty-eight percent of households are single-person households. This figure has risen since 1980, when it was 20 percent, now that Japanese men and women postpone marriage into their late twenties and venture to live independently. At the same time, however, 9.5 percent of households are three-generation households. There are still many elderly people who live with their married children, though not as many as in the past (Sugimoto, pp. 73, 163; *United Nations Demographic Yearbook,* 1995, pp. 650, 950, 952; *Japan Statistical Yearbook 2004,* Chapter 2, Tables 16, 18). (See Table 1.1.)

TABLE 1.1 Persons Per Household (1992–2003)

Egyptians and Mexicans are more likely to live in large households than are Japanese or Germans.

	Percent of Population in One-Person Households	Percent of Population in Households of 2–4 Persons	Percent of Population in Households of 5 or More Persons	Percent of Population in Households of 8 or More Persons
Egypt 2000	1	21	75	27
Namibia 1992	2	15	79	46
Mexico 2000	6	53	41	7
Japan 2000	10	65	24	1
United States 2003	10	68	21	Data Not Available
Germany 2002	17	73	10	Data Not Available

Sources: Demographic and Health Surveys, STAT compiler. http://www.measuredhs.com (Egypt, Namibia)

2000 Population Census of Japan, http://www.stat.go.jp/english/data/kokusei/2000/kihon1/00/hyodai.htm

National Institute of Statistics, Geography, and Informatics http://www.inegi.gob.mx/inegi/default.asp (Mexico)

U.S. Census Bureau, Annual Social and Economic Supplement: 2003 Current Population Survey, Current Population Reports, Series P20-553, "Americas Families and Living Arrangements: 2003" http://www.census.gov/population/socdemo/hh-fam/tabHH-4.pdf

The modern nuclear family is a much less dominating group than the traditional extended family. Typically, the husband has less authority than the old head of household and he almost always works outside the home, often quite far away. Long commutes and many hours of work result in fathers spending little time with their children. Salarymen, whose long hours are legendary, must return home after their children are asleep and leave home before the children awaken in the morning. Mothers and children are close, but children typically spend long hours at school and after-school activities. Husbands and wives usually have different friends and don't socialize as a couple. Their leisure activities and even their vacations are spent separately (Fukutake, pp. 123–126).

Postwar industrialization has also broken up the village community. After the war, massive migration from the countryside to cities emptied the villages, as young Japanese searched for industrial jobs. Today, most Japanese, even those in rural areas, commute long distances to work, so few people both live and work in the same community. People are less involved in local community life, and less concerned about what their neighbors think of them, especially in big cities (Fukutake, pp. 134–36).

Many western sociologists expected Japan to follow a pattern observed in Europe and North America: When societies industrialize, people spend less time in **primary groups** (small, personal, face-to-face groups), like families and villages, and more time in **secondary groups** (large, relatively impersonal, goal-oriented organizations), like cities and corporations. Then, group membership becomes less important in people's lives and they begin to think of themselves as individuals and to value their liberty to make individual choices. Away from the close supervision of family and neighbors, people feel freer to defy social norms. In western societies industrialization has meant more individual freedom, but less social order. This is an important observation, worth pondering. Ask yourself—is there too little freedom in your society? Is there too much? Is there too little order, or too much?

Japan is fascinating to sociologists because there the social consequences of industrialization have been different than in the West. When Japan became a modern, industrialized nation, the family and the community became much less important. But individualism didn't take their place. Instead, Japan has been remarkably successful in creating new primary groups within the secondary groups of school and company, so much so that these new groups have become the focus of Japanese life.

Group Life in School

School dominates the lives of Japanese children. They have long school days and short summer vacations. In junior high school, children attend club meetings after school and sports practices and games in the early morning and late afternoon, and on weekends. Teachers, not parents, are in charge of these events. Children are often away from home from seven in the morning until seven in the evening (Fukuzawa and LeTendre, pp. 98–100). The authority of the school extends outward into the community and the home. Teachers make home visits, and each elementary school child has a little notebook in which the teacher writes notes to the child's

The children at Mikala Middle School have changed out of their regular uniforms and moved the chairs and desks into informal groups for lunch. The whole *kumi* eats together in the classroom, relaxing and joking around. At the end of the school day, children usually walk home from school in groups, along routes that are chosen by the school. After kindergarten, children are not picked up by parents.

mother and the mother replies. When police see children behaving improperly, they call their principal as well as their parents.

In elementary and junior high school, Japanese children are taught to see themselves first and foremost as members of their homeroom class, or *kumi*. (The word *kumi* is old: Originally it meant a band of samurai warriors.) Starting in first grade, children spend nine years together in the same *kumi*. In elementary school, they stay with each teacher for two years. Each *kumi* of about 40–45 children is encouraged to think of its classroom as the children's own collective home. They arrange and re-arrange its furniture, bring in plants and flowers from home, and each day the *kumi* and teacher completely clean the room—scrubbing the desks and floors, washing windows, cleaning blackboards and erasers. Each *kumi* also takes a turn cleaning the school halls and toilets, the teachers' room, and the street outside the school. The *kumi* eats lunch in its own room, and even in junior high school, teachers for differ-ent subjects move from classroom to classroom, while the students stay in their own room. On the playground, members of a *kumi* play on the same team, competing with other *kumi* in their grade.

Teachers divide *kumi* into smaller groups called *han,* which are like study or work groups. Han stay together for several months before they are reshuffled. Each *han* elects a leader or *han-cho,* whose job it is to lead the group into harmonious decision making by patiently eliciting a consensus. *Hans* are expected to resolve conflicts and solve problems themselves, without appealing to adult authorities (Duke, pp. 25–29). Japanese schools do not practice ability grouping, and typically children from both rich and poor families attend the same school. The emphasis is on keeping the whole class moving through the work at the same pace, with the more able students helping their slower *han*-mates. *Hans* compete against each other in the classroom.

Keiko's Story: The Han

Keiko is nervous as she arrives in her seventh grade classroom. Today her han must present its report on the Tokugawa Era. They've been working on it in school and for the past two days they have met after school at Yukichi's house to practice making the oral presentation. Keiko is afraid she will make a mistake and let down her han. She hardly hears the music over the loudspeaker that signals the official start of the school day, and she follows the kumi through the prescribed exercises without even noticing. But her teacher, walking up and down the rows, does notice. "Keiko seems distracted; not concentrating," she writes in her little notebook.

After the presentation, Keiko is giddy with relief. They did well! The teacher gives Keiko's han gold stars for preparation and presentation. They are the only han with no demerits! Today Keiko's han has its turn to serve lunch and she gaily wraps herself in the white apron and puts on the surgical mask. She and her han-mates haul the heavy pots and bins of rice, stew, and salad up to the classroom from the school kitchen and dish them out. The whole kumi chants grace together, then breaks out in laughter and conversation while they eat. Keiko is particularly animated. She has done her part in supporting her han.

Working and playing so closely together, members of a *kumi* come to know each other intimately and think of themselves as a group. Children work hard, not to please the teacher, but to avoid letting down their *han*-mates. Habits of group loyalty, a preference for uniformity, and the learned skill of building group consensus through patient negotiation prepare children for the all-important work groups of Japanese adult life (Feiler, pp. 99–102; Leestma, p. 3).

But as much as group life in school illustrates the strength and importance of group life in Japan, it also illustrates its dark underside. It was American sociologist William Graham Sumner (1840–1910) who long ago articulated the principle that the more closely people identify as a group and the stronger their **in-group** feelings, the more hostility they direct toward **out-groups** or people outside the group. We see this in Japanese schools in the practice of *ijime,* or bullying, usually after school or during free play, or even through e-mail, when children single out one child who is different in some way (perhaps Korean, or foreign-born, or poorer or richer than the others) and subject him (it is usually a boy) to ceaseless torment. They tease him, make fun of him, kick and punch, sometimes extort money, or pressure him to commit petty theft. The Japanese are ashamed of *ijime,* but even though they are disturbed about it, they seem unable to prevent it. Sometimes teachers ignore bullying or even abet it. Every year there are several reports of suicides of 12- or 13-year-old children who are victims of *ijime*. Bullying shows us that as much as the Japanese value harmony, it is harmony within the group that matters; hostility towards outsiders, towards those who are different, is tolerated. Is it possible that bullying those who are different is essential to maintaining the tight cohesion of Japanese school groups (Yoneyama, pp. 161–185; Sugimoto, pp. 127–128)?

The Work Group

Following World War II, as Japanese industry expanded, and drew in an ever larger workforce from the farms and villages, Japanese companies encouraged their workers to see the company as their family. They invented a new focus for group identity in modern Japanese life. Large corporations hired their employees right out of high school or college. Promised lifetime employment and guaranteed promotion, employees spent their whole working lives in one company, advancing in step with all those hired in their year. Company housing, company sports teams and recreation complexes, cafeterias, health clinics, and company discount stores re-created the all-absorbing village within the company. Today, although no more than a third of Japan's labor force is employed by large corporations, their organization has set the tone for Japanese work life. Government employees, as well as employees in smaller companies, look to work for a sense of community. They find it in the work group, or "section," of the office or factory.

Hiroshi's Story: The "Section"

When the bullet train suddenly slowed, Hiroshi glanced out the window and saw beside the track the village where he had been born. Staring, Hiroshi thought about how different his life was now from his village childhood. He spotted his family's old house—a large wooden structure with its own courtyard and small garden, where he had lived with his parents, brother and sisters, and grandparents. Hiroshi looked down into the quiet streets of the town where he had spent his days at play, even as a two-year-old, watched by his brother.

Now Hiroshi lives in an apartment house outside of Tokyo. He is home so little that he doesn't even know his neighbors and his children never play outside. They hurry from school to lessons to homework. Really, his office is now the focus of his life. Hiroshi knows his family wants him at home, but he feels he has to give his all to his job. He doesn't do it to get a raise, or even a promotion; he just wants to do a good job.

Every morning the nine men of his section assemble, greet each other, and drink their first cups of tea together. Takeshi has become a close friend: He really knows what is in Hiroshi's heart. But all the men are important to him. That year when Hiroshi's mother was dying so painfully, they knew how he felt without his having to explain. They took over most of his duties at work and took him out after work, making sure he ate and gently distracting him with stories and songs. Kenji-san had introduced Hiroshi's son to his niece, and they were soon to be married. Mr. Fuji, the department chief, looked after them all, and was now arranging a marriage for Masao, the only unmarried man in the section. After work, and before the long commute home, the section and its chief usually go out together to a local bar, to drink and chat more informally. Hiroshi enjoys the monthly evening parties paid for by the company, and the twice-yearly weekend retreats when the whole section goes away together to a country inn. His real home, he thinks, is at the office with his office "family."

SOCIALIZATION

Japan is a demanding society: It asks of individuals a high level of conformity with very detailed norms, and it demands self-discipline in subordinating individual needs to the requirements of the group. Most people conform. The Japanese pride themselves on how orderly their society is, and they find it very threatening if order seems to break down. Most people embrace Japanese values, identify with their roles, and do what is expected of them. Foreigners often wonder: How does Japanese society achieve such a high level of conformity?

One good answer is that conformity is carefully taught in Japan. Japanese people learn the beliefs and role expectations of their culture and learn to play their roles properly through the process sociologists call **socialization.** While all societies and social groups socialize their members, in some cases the process is haphazard and disorganized and people may be largely unaware that socialization is taking place. In Japan, socialization is highly consistent, explicit, and carefully planned. Studying Japan provides a wonderful opportunity to understand the process of socialization, how socialization actually takes place, because the Japanese carry out socialization so thoughtfully.

The Process of Socialization: Explicit Instruction

In school, at work, and in many other situations, Japanese people are used to receiving a great deal of **explicit instruction** about what is expected of them, followed by opportunities to **practice** proper behavior. Elementary schools in particular are designed to socialize children into Japanese values and norms. Teachers consider this "moral education" even more important than teaching reading and writing and math (Lewis, pp. 44–61).

In school, posters on classroom walls and in hallways exhort, "Let us not run in the corridors," "Let us keep our school toilets clean," "Let us greet people with a smile," etc. Students actually make up these goals themselves, and then later hold self-criticism sessions in which they decide whether they have met the goal, and if not, what should be done next. So the exercise also teaches children to take responsibility, since no one in authority tells them, "You are still running in the corridors." They are expected to recognize this themselves and devise a remedy.

Schoolchildren through junior high school are drilled in proper bowing, formal greeting, sitting and standing (all together), answering their teachers (immediately and loudly), and arranging their desktops for study (in a set format). A teacher, preparing eighth graders for a class trip, arranges chairs on the floor of the gym in the shape of a bus, and for hours students practice getting in and out of the seats in orderly fashion (Hendry, p. 102; Feiler, p. 264; Leestma, p. 27).

Several western analysts of Japanese society have called Japan a "nanny state" because of the active role the government takes in giving its citizens corrective advice. Loudspeakers tell bus and train passengers to be careful getting off and even warn bus riders to hold on because "the bus is turning a corner." A passenger running for a train and gratefully slipping in just before the doors close, can expect to be reprimanded by the loudspeaker: "never run for a train." Bruce Feiler reported that highway signs approaching his town proclaimed "patience and humility prevent accidents." On the ski lift too, messages blare out: "remember to lift your ski tips" (McGregor, pp. 113–114; Feiler, p. 16).

Role Models Aid Socialization

The Japanese believe in providing **role models** to help people learn expected behavior. Mothers and teachers consciously "model" correct behavior for children. Nursery school teachers wash their hands and brush their teeth alongside their charges, and elementary school teachers eat lunch with their students and work alongside the students during the regular daily cleaning period. At home and at school older children are urged to set a good example for younger ones, and take pride in their roles as "elder brother" or "elder sister" (Hendry, p. 149).

Ceremonies Support Socialization

Initiation ceremonies, marking the transition to new roles, are an effective part of Japanese socialization. Ceremonies help people learn to recognize that they are in a new stage of life, with new roles and norms. Carefully staged ceremonies are an important part of children's progress through school. Interestingly, the Japanese place more emphasis on ceremonies that mark the beginning of different stages of education than on graduation ceremonies. Children begin their elementary schooling with a special welcome ceremony. Their mothers attend, dressed in their best clothes, and the children dress up too. Usually there is a formal photo taken of the whole class and their mothers. It is customary in Japan for parents to give each child a special study desk at the beginning of elementary school. The desk is expensive. It has a special built-in light, shelves, and drawers. The message is clear: "You are embarking on a new stage in life that really matters a lot. We're investing a lot of time and effort in you."

Defining the Situation

Sociologist Peter Berger used the term **"the definition of the situation"** to explain that the way people respond to situations is conditioned by how they "define" or interpret and evaluate those situations (Berger, p. 94). If you get together with your friends, it is up to you to define the situation as a party or a study session. Depending on which you choose, you will behave differently, in fact adopt different roles. But we find ourselves in many situations which others have defined. Think of a courtroom. When you enter the court, it is not up to you to define the situation and decide how to behave. Those who designed the court have already decided that your role is to be humble and respectful, to literally look up to the judge, seated on his platform. We find ourselves in many situations that have been defined, or socially structured, to induce us to view reality in particular ways and adopt certain roles and ways of relating to others. This is an indirect form of socialization. If you are Japanese, from infancy through adulthood you find yourself in situations defined in such ways to emphasize group consciousness and dependence on the group.

Socialization to dependence on the group begins at birth, according to Takeo Doi, a famous Japanese psychiatrist, because of the way mothers define the situation for their babies. Care of infants is based on the assumption that babies should experience as little anxiety as possible. Caregivers try to anticipate the baby's needs, and satisfy them before crying and fretfulness signal a problem. Cribs are placed beside adult beds, and children are never put in their cribs to fall asleep alone; they are sung to sleep before being laid down. The Japanese also avoid playpens, preferring instead that the child be protected by the constant close attention of an adult. They almost never employ baby-sitters. Doi argues that mothers' all-embracing, unconditional love and support fosters in children a taste for dependency that is later expressed in adult group life. Children learn implicitly that if you conform, and do what others expect of you, then people will be kind and considerate, and they will gratify your wishes without your having to ask (Hendry, pp. 116, 97, 18–25; Christopher, pp. 68–70; Doi, 1977).

Defining the Situation in School

Elementary schools carry out a tremendous amount of **anticipatory socialization,** socialization that prepares children for adult roles by teaching them to be part of Japan's all-important groups. Schools stress the similarity of all children, and the importance of the group. In the typical elementary school, teachers put a lot of thought into forming *hans.* For example, the teacher will pair an immature, needy child with a child who enjoys taking care of others (Lewis, p. 82). The purpose is to bring children to enjoy belonging to the *han,* to find pleasure in their dependence on others. Teachers seldom address children individually, or overtly recognize differences in individual ability, and they minimize situations in which children compete individually with each other. Instead, each *han* is held responsible collectively for the progress of all its members.

Also, teachers do not discipline individual students in Japanese schools. Rather, if a class or an individual is unruly, the teacher will turn to that day's assigned monitor and request him or her to restore order. The classroom situation is structured to emphasize group participation, group loyalty, and the responsibility of the individual to the class. In this situation, students experience no conflict between loyalty to their friends and conformity with school norms (Feiler, pp. 30, 100–102; Leestma, pp. 3, 27). You may be amazed to learn that there are no substitute teachers in Japanese elementary schools. When a teacher is absent, other teachers, the principal, or assistant principal stop in occasionally and assign work which the children do on their own. This is possible because the children are so well socialized to taking responsibility for each other and controlling each other's behavior (Lewis, p. 114).

Teachers are well aware of the importance of defining the situation for socialization. For example, Bruce Feiler describes a seventh-grade class trip to Tokyo's Disneyland defined in such a way as to encourage students' dependency on their *han.* Students were required to stay with their *han* during the visit. In each *han* one member was assigned to carry the money, one to wear the watch, one to take the photos, and one to take notes. "The management of this trip," Feiler explained, "revealed the skill with which Japanese schools transfer abstract goals into concrete educational practices" (Feiler, p. 266).

Japanese offices are crowded; desks are lined up side by side. Office workers have to be very conscious of each other in close quarters. You have to consider others when you do your work; you must speak softly when others are on the phone. The arrangement of desks defines the situation in a way that reinforces the Japanese values of harmony and teamwork. Have you ever worked in an office? Was its arrangement different? What values did it convey to you and other office workers?

Many preschools provide wooden blocks for play, but these blocks are different from the ones you may be familiar with: They are 3 to 5 feet long and very heavy. Just think about how these blocks define the situation. The children must work together in order to lift them. In fact, they organize themselves to carry the blocks all over the school—from gym to classroom to yard—and build enormous structures with them, two-story buildings sometimes, in which they play, even eat their lunches (Lewis, pp. 20, 114, 115).

Socialization in the Workplace

Socialization doesn't end with childhood. We all continue to be socialized and **resocialized** throughout our lives. When people in Japan leave school and enter the world of work, they find familiar patterns of socialization. Companies use explicit instruction and drill. Large companies maintain an in-house staff of trainers, who create company slogans and chants, inspirational comic books and poems, and conduct training sessions. Corporations often provide elaborate welcome ceremonies for new recruits (described by one observer as "a cross between a coming-of-age ceremony and initiation into an American fraternity"). Starting in the 1950s, companies devised rituals in which cohorts of new employees, and in some cases their parents too, were first greeted and lectured by company officials in welcome ceremonies at the factory, then escorted on several days of touring and partying (Chapman, pp. 131–134). When Mazda opened its first U.S. auto plant in 1985, employees were given a training program lasting ten to twelve weeks, time the company considered necessary to communicate to American workers the values and expectations of a Japanese company. Training included a week of work on "interpersonal relations," using group discussions with a trainer, videotapes of "correct" and "incorrect" ways to interact, workbooks, and role-playing exercises. For example, in one workshop trainees practiced the proper way to tell a co-worker that his body odor was offensive. (Incidentally, some of the Americans hated the training and dropped out, but many loved it. They said that the new techniques for relating to others transformed their home lives.) (See Fucini, pp. 71–74.)

Corporations also rely on role models to socialize employees. Building on the familiar pattern of the elder child as role model, companies appoint "elder brothers" to instruct new recruits in proper behavior. In business, government, and even organized crime, young men seek out "mentors" to guide their progress.

Companies take care to **define the situation** in the workplace to maximize group identification. The employees of offices and factories are organized in "sections," groups of eight or nine workers who share responsibility and are expected to make suggestions for improving efficiency and to monitor their own progress in implementation. The arrangement of the furniture actually helps to define the situation. Offices are huge undivided areas, but each section's desks are arranged in two facing rows, all touching, so as to form one huge tabletop, with the section chief's desk perpendicular across the end. Among the eight or nine section members, every conversation is a group affair, every memo can be read by all. Even telephones are shared. The director's desk stands alone, but nearby, not in a separate room (Feiler, pp. 19–20, 28).

DEVIANCE IN A DEMANDING SOCIETY

Japan is a demanding society; there is strong pressure to conform to very detailed, explicit norms. Socialization is extensive. Families, schools, and businesses work hard to make sure their members learn their roles and play them properly. Under these circumstances, would you expect there to be very little, or a great deal of **deviant behavior** in Japan? Deviance is universal: Every society establishes norms and in every society people defy socialization and group pressure; they violate norms, incurring disapproval and some sort of punishment. But in some societies there is a great deal more deviance than in others. In some societies crime rates are high, teenagers drink and take drugs, and many people engage in sexual behavior that scandalizes others. This is not the case in Japan. Although it doesn't take much to violate social norms in Japan, there is, in fact, very little deviance.

Low Levels of Deviance

Crime rates are unusually low in Japan. With a population one-half the size of the United States, Japan has fewer robberies in a year than take place in two days in the United States; fewer rapes than in one week. In 2001, there were 1,340 homicides in all of Japan, compared to 16,307 in the United States. Twenty-two of the homicides in Japan were committed with handguns, while more than 12,000 killings were done with handguns in the United States. (Thirteen of the twenty-two victims of shooting in Japan were members of organized crime syndicates.) Handguns are outlawed in Japan, except for sports use. There are only forty-nine legal handguns in the whole country and they are registered with the police and must be kept at the shooting range. There are about 425,000 rifles and air guns in Japan, held by people who have passed exams and rigorous licensing procedures, repeated every three years. (Compare this to the estimated 200 million guns owned by individuals in the United States.) More minor crimes are also uncommon. There is little drug use in Japan, and no graffiti or litter on the streets (Tasker, pp. 71, 73; Kristof, May 14, 1995, p. 8; U.S. Bureau of Justice Statistics; *Japan Statistical Yearbook,* 2004, Chapter 25, Table 1). (See Table 1.2.)

However, it is important to recognize that rates for certain kinds of crimes and other deviant behaviors are rising in Japan. Homicide has not increased significantly, but robbery rates, though still low, have more than tripled since 1990. There are twice as many cases of extortion (*Japan Statistical Yearbook,* 2004, Chapter 25, Table 1).

So we have two interesting questions to answer: Why are rates of deviance in Japan relatively low, and why is deviance increasing? We might even ask why some kinds of deviance (like robbery) and are increasing at rates much faster than other kinds (like homicide). Luckily, sociology offers three powerful theories to help us answer these questions: **control theory, labeling theory,** and **strain theory.**

Effective Social Controls: Control Theory

Control theory, as developed by Walter Reckless (1973) explains that when social controls work effectively, people are more likely to conform to society's norms. One reason why rates of deviance are relatively low in Japan is that social controls operate very well. Thorough socialization to strict standards is followed by constant supervision and effective **social sanctions.** In every society sanctions are the muscle behind social control. Social sanctions reward those who conform and play their

TABLE 1.2 Murder and Suicide (2000–2002)

The rate of murder is far higher in the United States and Mexico than in Germany and Japan. But though Japan has a low murder rate it has a high suicide rate.

	Total Number of Suicides	Number of Suicides among Every Million People	Total Number of Murders	Number of Murders among Every Million People
Germany 2001	11,156	135	564	7
Japan 2002	29,949	238	730	6
Mexico 2001	3,784	38	10,148	101
USA 2000	23,319	104	16,590	59

Source: WHO Mortality Database

Number of Registered Deaths

http://www3.who.int/whosis/menu.cfm?path=whosis,inds,mort&language=english

roles well, and punish those who fail to shape up. In Japanese society there are a variety of **positive sanctions** that are real incentives, coupled with **negative sanctions** that people very much wish to avoid. You could say that in Japanese society people are managed very effectively. The Japanese themselves say, "The nail that sticks up, gets pounded down."

With great consistency and regularity, the reward for role conformity in Japanese society is inclusion in the warm and pleasant life of the group. Those who fail to play their roles correctly face exclusion: Misbehaving children are excluded from family activities or left standing alone outside the classroom or playground, ignored by teachers. A mother may say, "If you keep doing that, the garbage collectors will come and take you away," or she may punish extremely serious offenses by locking the child out of the house (Lebra, p. 149).

Ridicule is also a common sanction, and children are actually encouraged to make fun of a child who fails to conform. Mothers commonly censure misbehavior by telling children, "If you do that, people will laugh at you." Children come to fear ridicule, and this fear continues into adult life as an important social pressure to conform (Hendry, pp. 106–108, 114–115).

In Japanese corporations social sanctions back up all the slogans and chants and exhortations to work hard and be loyal to the company. Those who work for big companies are looked up to by others; their sons are sought out in marriage. They find it easier to get a home mortgage. Company expense accounts fund visits to bars and nightclubs and golf club memberships. Once past his twenties, a man who leaves his company pays a heavy price. Not only does he lose company benefits, but he loses his friends at work. If he finds a new job (and most companies won't hire a man they label as disloyal for leaving his company), he finds it hard to make new friends among men who have worked together for years. Positive and negative sanctions ensure that it pays for a corporate employee to act loyal, even if he doesn't feel loyal (Chapman, pp. 137–139).

Criminal sanctions in Japan are a serious matter. Japan's prison population has grown in the last decade, but it is still comparatively small—only 48 people out of every 100,000 people are in prison, compared to 638 per 100,000 in the United States and 97 per 100,000 in Germany (The United Nations Office on Crime and Drugs, 1990–2000). Jail sentences are relatively short, but harsh. Prisoners are often kept in isolation and not even allowed to talk to each other. There are no gangs in Japanese prisons, nor any prison rapes or assaults. White collar offenders are treated the same as ordinary criminals. Also, Japanese people are ashamed to have relatives in jail. They seldom visit them and often refuse to accept them back home once they are released (Kristof, May 14, 1995, pp. 1, 8; McGregor, p. 94). (See Table 1.3.)

"Friendly Authoritarianism"

Japanese society is unusual in the sureness with which negative sanctions follow deviance. You can be certain that if you violate norms in Japan, someone will notice, and they will definitely take action, and you will surely pay a price. Yoshio Sugimoto calls the Japanese system of sanctions "friendly authoritarianism," because authority figures in Japan are usually warm and caring. They help people and give them rewards and people come to trust them. But people also know that if they

TABLE 1.3 Prison Population
Mexico imprisons a far higher percent of its population than does Japan.
Incarceration rates are highest in the United States.

		Prisoners	Prisoners Per 100,000 Population
Egypt	1994	32,257	56
Germany	2000	79,507	97
Japan	2000	61,242	48
Mexico	2000	154,765	158
United States	2000	1,799,582	638

Source: The United Nations Office on Crime and Drugs

United Nations Surveys of Crime Trends and Operations of Criminal Justice Systems covering the period 1990–2000

http://www.unodc.org/unodc/crime_cicp_survey_seventh.html#responses

don't conform, these same authorities can be very harsh. Police, for example, are very polite and helpful. They lend people umbrellas when it rains and they lend money to people who have lost their wallets or are short on trainfare (and people almost always return the umbrellas and pay back the money) (Sugimoto, pp. 245–258; Kristof, June 4, 1995). Police often decide not to prosecute for minor offenses, but only if the suspect writes out a sincere apology. The same police, however, are given great leeway in searching and questioning people. They can hold suspects without a formal hearing for up to twenty-one days, and often subject them to long interrogations and pressure to confess. Evidence obtained illegally is admissible in court (Kristof, May 14, 1995, p. 8).

Surveillance

In Japan, strict norms are enforced through constant surveillance. People come to feel that the eyes of others are always upon them. People have a word for this in Japan; it is called the *seiken* (the watchful community). Let's say that a 100-yen note has been dropped and is blowing along the street. No one stoops to pick it up! Each person fears being seen by others and condemned as dishonest, or greedy, or petty. Bruce Feiler, an American who taught in Japan, has written of his surprise at the tightness of Japanese social controls. Feiler used a bicycle to travel around his town, and late at night, when there was no other traffic, he saw no need to stop for red lights. But someone observed him, and called the Board of Education, which called his principal, and Feiler found himself rebuked by his supervisor (White, 2002, p. 9; Feiler, p. 25).

Schools organize regular after-school patrols of the neighborhood by parents and teachers (to watch students, not to protect them from others, since all neighborhoods are quite safe). Police take an active approach to surveillance, visiting each household in their district yearly and discreetly keeping track of the private lives of all district residents (Tasker, p. 73). Police will actually take a teenager into custody for smoking, an act considered seriously delinquent, then call both parents and the school guidance counselor to the police station (Leestma, p. 46).

Social Controls in School

Japanese schools are a good place to study social sanctions. In the lower grades, school is a warm and pleasant place. The children are lively and noisy and cheerful and teachers react tolerantly to mischief. The most important lesson of elementary school is that conformity will result in a warm, happy feeling of belonging.

But when children reach junior high school age, their lives change drastically. Junior high and high school are designed to socialize children into the norms of obedience and hard work and accustom them to dealing with hierarchy. As much as children are indulged in elementary school, they are toughened by struggle in junior high and high school. In junior high school, children must wear uniforms and conform to a dress code. Academic classes are much more regimented than in elementary school. Group work and class discussion is replaced by lecture and note taking. Students take multiple-choice exams, and their grades are based almost entirely on these tests. After-school clubs are an important part of junior high school life, but clubs are dominated by upperclassmen. Younger students must learn to adapt to the sometimes harsh demands of their older classmates (Fukuzawa and LeTendre, pp. 56–57).

Social controls are very powerful in Japanese schools because how well a person does, even in junior high school, has serious effects that can last a lifetime. Junior high schools are neighborhood schools, but high schools are not. At the end of junior high school, students must all take high school admissions tests. High schools are ranked in a hierarchy, the higher-status schools serving as feeders for the most prestigious universities. Almost everyone goes to some high school, but only students with good school records are even permitted to take the tests for the highest-ranked high schools.

At the end of high school, students must again take very competitive exams for admission to college. Those who excel can gain admission to prestigious "national" universities. As many as three-quarters of the people hired for upper-level civil service jobs and almost half the company presidents in Japan are graduates of prestigious Tokyo University. Many companies don't even bother to recruit employees outside a few select universities. For students who attend technical high schools, any chance of getting a full-time job, with good pay and some security, depends on school performance. Schools place only their best students in such jobs.

Japan's Social Compact

What is your reaction to reading about social controls in Japan? Are you saying to yourself, "I would never go along with a system like that"? Studying social control lets you see just how demanding and exacting Japanese society is. Why do most Japanese go along? The answer is that for most people the rewards of being part of Japanese society are sufficiently satisfying to compensate for the difficulties. Sociologist Travis Hirschi (1969) explained that the **outer controls** of social sanctions are complemented by **inner controls.** The more strongly connected we are to our social groups, the more we want to conform. We want the approval of our fellow group members. We want the group to accept us. The more we care about belonging to the group, the more we **internalize** group values and norms and make them our own. We are moved by inner controls. In Japan, most people feel like they belong, like they are part of a team—a *han,* a section, the nation itself. Also, as part of the group, people find they share in the national prosperity and participate psychologically in its prestige. And in Japan it is important that people share pretty equally in prosperity, so no one feels that they have sacrificed and someone else has benefited. You can also see that if order, belonging, and social equality were ever undermined, Japanese society might well be in trouble.

Defining Deviance: Labeling Theory

Sociologists have long understood that deviance is a matter of social definition. **Symbolic interactionists,** who use **labeling theory,** point out that actions are deviant only if people see them that way. Behavior labeled as deviant in one society might not be considered a problem at all in another society. One reason why there is so little deviance in Japan is that a lot of behavior condemned as deviant in other societies is acceptable in Japan, as long as it remains private. The paired concepts of *omote* and *ura* are fundamental to Japanese life. Japanese society required outward conformity in a person's *omote* or public life, but behind the scenes, on the *ura* side, Japan is very accepting. It is characteristic of Japanese culture that no human behavior, and no person, is considered intrinsically bad, or sick, or evil: What matters is that you keep your behavior appropriate to the social situation. The world of *ura* may be seen as a safety valve for Japanese society. In *ura* social settings people can express individualism and rebellion and let off steam that builds up in the pressure cooker of Japan's conformist public life.

Drinking is one such release. Alcohol plays an important role in Japanese life. Most drinking takes place in groups, in bars or restaurants. Levels of habitual alcohol consumption that would be labeled alcoholism in other societies are not seen as deviant in Japan. Drinking together, business associates or co-workers are able to ease the tensions of formal, *omote* relations. Often groups in bars engage in *karaoke* singing, taking turns singing into a microphone to a taped accompaniment. A TV screen shows the words of the song, with accompanying pictures. Laughing and singing together, participants are relieved of the need to make conversation (Sugimoto, p. 227).

It is common for the whole staff of a work section, including the boss (and sometimes the female workers), to go out drinking together after work. Drunk, the boss may make a fool of himself, singing and crying, but the next day in the office, when he is once again his proper, formal self, no one's respect for him will be in the least diminished. Employees, under cover of "drunkenness" may complain to the boss openly about their treatment, but the next day no one will "remember" that it happened.

Hostesses in bars offer their male guests flirtation and flattery. Nearby, men can visit Japan's "soaplands," baths where massages and other sexual attentions are available for purchase. Sexually explicit stripper shows even feature (illegal) "open stage" events, in which a member of the audience joins the stripper in public sexual acts. Until they were closed down, "no-panties waitress" coffee shops, with glass or mirrored floors, offered the option of looking without touching (Condon, pp. 76, 82, 247; Bornoff, pp. 263–272, 295–296, 312–322). The women who work in such establishments may preserve an *omote* public life in distant apartments where they raise their children with propriety. Pornography is also ubiquitous. Pornographic comic books, often filled with violence, are sold in vending machines and porn videos are shown in bars. Popular animated films have many scenes of sex and violence (often cut from the exported versions of the films) (Tasker, pp. 111, 113–114).

Japanese society is matter-of-fact about sex—in its proper *ura* place. While a husband would never kiss his wife goodbye in public at the train station, nevertheless Japan is dotted with conspicuous "love hotels"—fantastically decorated as castles, or pirate ships, or chalets—which rent rooms by the hour, and these hotels are much used by young people, adulterous couples, and even married pairs looking for privacy. In the past, the world of bars and sex was just for men, but increasingly, women and girls participate too. Teenaged girls look cute and innocent in their school uniforms, going about in giggling groups, but behind the scenes two-thirds of the girls engage in sex by age 15. Some teenaged girls go further, working on telephone sex lines or even as prostitutes. The schoolgirl look is considered the last frontier in illicit sexual appeal, so girls are much in demand (White, pp. 170–189).

Sexual Harassment

You can see how much deviance is a matter of social definition if you consider the topic of sexual harassment. Until very recently, sexual harassment didn't exist in Japan. Of course there was and is sexual molestation, quite a lot of it in fact. Men

Private fantasies play themselves out privately in the "Space Odyssey" room of this Tokyo love hotel. Love hotels help the Japanese maintain the distinction between the polite and proper realm of *omote* and the backstage world of *ura,* where feelings and fantasies can be more freely expressed.

grope young women on trains, and in offices men take advantage of women's subordinate position to touch them, make unwanted sexual advances, and spread sexual rumors about them. Recently, 70 percent of female government workers told interviewers they had been sexually harassed. But all of this was just taken for granted. Police ignored sexual molestation, and women were warned not to complain, since complaining would bring them shameful attention and people would assume they had dressed or acted provocatively. It was not until 1999 that the government established regulations banning sexual harassment in the workplace. But the rules lack clear penalties and very few women have dared to sue. In the most famous recent case, the complainant used a false name and testified in court sitting behind a screen. So even though the government is conducting a campaign against sexual harassment, with posters in the Tokyo subway, most people don't yet see harassment as deviant. Really, it is complaining about sexual abuse that is labeled the deviant act (French, July 15, 2001, pp. 1, 10).

Domestic Violence

In Japan, as in other societies, there are groups of people that try to redefine certain behaviors, or certain people, as deviant. Sociologists call such activists **moral entrepreneurs.** In the past few years, several organizations in Japan have worked to change the way the Japanese view domestic violence—specifically assaults by men on their wives. In a nationwide government survey in 2000, 27.5 percent of Japanese wives said their husbands had beaten them, but most Japanese don't see such violence against women as a crime. Nevertheless, activists, lawyers, and some outspoken victims of wife battery actually succeeded in 2001 in getting the Japanese legislature to pass a law permitting courts to issue restraining orders against wife beaters. It is one step in relabeling spousal abuse as an act of deviance, rather than a domestic dispute that should be hushed up (Kumbayashi, Feb. 4, 2004, p. 11).

Deviance and Stigma

You may be surprised to learn that in Japan it is sometimes seen as more deviant to adopt a deviant identity than to engage in deviant behavior. **Primary deviance,** that is, deviant acts, is much more readily forgiven than is **secondary deviance,** or the adoption of deviant statuses. When Japanese people adopt a deviant identity— one that proclaims their difference from other Japanese—they are strongly **stigmatized** or publicly labeled as different and deviant. For example, homosexual sex acts are not seen as perverted or sinful in Japan, but people who announce that they are gay scandalize others and they bring shame on their family members who will experience difficulty getting jobs and finding spouses. Having AIDS is a matter of the deepest shame, and many AIDS sufferers move to Hawaii before their symptoms show so as to spare their families from ostracism. Even people with disabilities occupy a deviant status in Japan. People in wheelchairs are almost never seen in public and indeed, there are no wheelchair ramps or other accommodations for them (Sesser, 1994). We can say that in a very real way being different is deviant in Japan.

How Strain Theory Accounts for Deviance

Why is it that in Japan (or in any other society for that matter) some people decide to risk negative social sanctions and stigmatization and commit acts of deviance? You might look at this as a matter of individual choice, but sociologists see patterns in who engages in deviance, and they locate the causes for deviance in society.

Robert Merton's (1956, 1968) **strain theory of deviance** offers a powerful analysis of social patterns of deviance. Every society, Merton said, has both generally approved goals (its values) and widely approved means for achieving those goals (its norms). If people who follow the norms regularly achieve the values they treasure, then conformity pays off and people will generally conform. Deviance arises when some people find obstacles in their path to achieving the approved goals by following the approved means. The more obstacles people encounter, the more they will experience strain or frustration and the more likely they are to resort to deviant behavior (Henslin, pp. 148–149).

Merton saw four possible kinds of deviant responses to strain. **Innovators** continue to strive for the accepted goals of society, but resort to disapproved means for achieving them. **Ritualists** give up on the accepted goals, but continue to cling to following the norms. **Retreatists** give up entirely, rejecting both the accepted goals and the normative means for achieving them. And finally, **Rebels** reject both the goals and the norms, but try to substitute new goals and new norms they consider superior.

Sources of Strain in Japanese Society

Merton's **strain theory** is enormously helpful in understanding Japanese society. It explains both why there has been so much conformity in Japan and why deviance has recently increased. In the forty years that followed World War II, the Japanese created a remarkably successful society. People devoted themselves to work, sacrificing their personal time and family lives. Children studied intensively for exams, denying themselves time for hobbies and social life. But nevertheless, people found life good. They conformed by working hard, but they were rewarded. Children who excelled in school got good jobs and men who loyally worked for their companies enjoyed constantly rising pay, economic security, and eventual promotions. They were sought after as husbands and found fulfillment as valued members of their companies. They took pride in helping to create Japan's economic miracle. Wives were told they made it all possible by taking over all the household responsibilities. Everyone belonged.

Today, however, the postwar social order is breaking down. There are many signs of strain and rising levels of deviance. The fundamental source of strain in Japan today is an economic recession that began with the bursting of the "bubble economy" in 1991 and only began to end in 2003. Economic growth and prosperity were the basis of the late twentieth century Japanese social order. Now the most disruptive force in Japan is unemployment. Official unemployment is still relatively low—about 5 percent. But even 5 percent unemployment is unprecedented for Japan, where a 2 percent rate was taken for granted throughout the 1980s. Also unprecedented is the youth unemployment rate: 14 percent in 2001 for young men aged 15–24 who are not in school (The Japan Institute for Labor Policy and Training, 2002/2003).

Now Japanese men who once assumed that their loyalty to their company would be rewarded with lifetime job security must worry about being cast out of the company. Young people, who had always known that a high school or college degree guaranteed a job and inclusion in a corporate "family," now worry that they will find no job or only temporary freelance work. Women wonder why they should marry men who seem to lack a secure future (Brooke, Oct. 16, 2001, p. A3; *The Economist,* July 1, 2000, pp. 26–28).

Innovative Deviance in Japan

There is certainly innovative deviance to be found in Japan, but in a way it is the most acceptable form of deviance. Deviant innovators still embrace the supreme Japanese value of belonging; they just find ways of belonging that are deviant.

The *Yakuza*.   Japan's organized crime syndicates, called the *Yakuza,* are a form of innovative deviance with a long history. Approximately 90,000 *Yakuza* members are organized into three main syndicates and 3,000 groups, running prostitution, pornography, gambling, drugs, extortion, and labor rackets, and taking in billions of dollars a year. The *Yakuza* also engage in violence on behalf of legitimate authorities who wish to avoid the use of violence themselves. They have broken strikes, silenced dissenters, and evicted tenants from valuable real estate. The *Yakuza* have worked for corporations, the ruling Liberal Democratic Party, the American CIA, and the police. The *Yakuza* also police the ranks of criminals, making sure that all who engage in crime belong to one of their organizations.

The *Yakuza* occupy a somewhat contradictory position in Japanese society. Obviously they are seen as engaging in deviant activity. But as an organization, the *Yakuza* enjoy a legitimacy and acceptance in Japanese society very different from their American counterparts. The *Yakuza* is accepted as a public presence in Japan; their offices publicly display gang insignia on the door, like an insurance office or loan company. Members wear gang badges, like the company pins Japanese salarymen wear. People who join the *Yakuza* become part of a social group like others in Japan—one that stresses group identity and conformity to group norms (Wildeman, unpublished material; Tasker, p. 78; Sterngold, Oct. 21, 1992, pp. A1, A6).

The *Yakuza* have long attracted those Japanese who have the hardest time being accepted by Japan's mainstream groups: outsiders, mostly people of Korean and *burakumin* ancestry. (Koreans in Japan are mostly descendants of people brought to Japan in the early twentieth century when Korea was conquered by Japan. *Burakumin* are descendants of Japan's ancient hereditary **outcaste** group. See pages 54–56 for more on both these **minority** groups.) Nowadays, *Yakuza* advertisements for new members are drawing responses from high school dropouts and disgraced former employees (*Mainichi Daily News,* Nov. 16, 2003, p. 1).

Yakuza members are genuinely innovative. They constantly come up with new rackets to adapt to changing times. Since environmental activism has increased in Japan, the *Yakuza* have started creating fake environmentalist groups that make demands that are very inconvenient for companies. Then, in exchange for bribes, they cease their campaigns. Another new *Yakuza* business is contract killing of suicidal unemployed men who want to die without depriving their families of their life insurance (Shih, May 15, 2004; Pearson, Jan. 23, 2004, p. 44).

Cult Groups.   There are about 18,000 groups classed as "new religions" in Japan, groups neither Shinto nor Buddhist (McGregor, p. 29). Japanese society is ordinarily very tolerant of religious cults. They too fit the pattern of innovative deviance: they offer a way to belong to people who feel alienated from mainstream society. Most cult groups follow the familiar pattern of a secretive group, led by a mystical guru, who demands members' loyalty and total involvement. For example, Pana Wave is a doomsday cult whose members dress all in white and do not bathe. They travel Japan in caravans searching for places to avoid electromagnetic waves (French, May 14, 2003, p. A10). The most famous Japanese cult is *Aum Shinrikyo,* which killed twelve people in a sarin gas attack in the Tokyo subway in 1995. At the time of the attack, *Aum* had as many as 10,000 members in Japan and 30,000 to 40,000 in Russia. Until the attack, the organization was not seen as a threat. Its leader ran for parliament in 1990 and appeared on television. Even now that the cult leader has been sentenced to death, the organization has been allowed to keep operating, though it now has only 1,650 remaining members (Onishi, Feb. 28, 2004, p. A3).

Ritualist Deviance in Japan

There are a few examples of ritualist deviance in Japan, but these cases don't excite much outrage. They are seen rather as pathetic. One example is the sad ex-salarymen who have been forced by their companies to retire prematurely. Some of them continue to leave the house every morning in suit and tie and take the train into Tokyo. Then they while away the hours in the public library, public buildings, or movie theaters before returning home. They are ashamed of being fired and don't want their neighbors to know. Some have not even told their wives.

Retreatist Deviance in Japan

Many of the forms of deviance that upset the Japanese the most could be classified as retreatist. That's not surprising when you remember the importance of belonging, of group membership, in Japanese culture. Retreatists reject belonging in a way that is the ultimate threat to Japanese society.

Suicide.   Suicide is clearly the most radical possible retreat from society, and the Japanese are very concerned about their rising suicide rate. Japan began the 1990s with a relatively moderate rate of suicide, comparable to that of most European countries. But with the economic recession, the suicide rate shot up, rising 50 percent between 1990 and 1999 (though it has since leveled off a bit). The suicide rate has been highest for men between the ages of fifty-five and sixty-four, precisely the group that devoted their lives to the company and then abruptly faced new company demands, layoffs, and forced retirements. This is the same age cohort that is also experiencing an increased divorce rate. These men continued to follow the norms as usual, but nevertheless felt rejected both at work and at home (*Japan*

Statistical Yearbook, Chapter 25, Table 15; World Health Organization Statistical Information System, 1999, Table 1; Nathan, pp. 74–75).

Japanese newspapers carry many reports of suicides on the rail lines, particularly the express lines which lead from Tokyo to the surrounding suburbs. One company has installed mirrors across the tracks from passenger platforms in the hope
that if jumpers see themselves, they may hesitate. All the rail lines now charge the
families of suicide victims for the expenses caused by the suicides. It is widely ru-
mored that the most suicides take place on the rail line that charges the least (French,
June 6, 2000, p. A4). Recently there have been many news articles about young people using the Internet to enter into group suicide pacts with strangers. How ironic
that people who feel so alienated from society that they would take their lives still
want company as they do so! (Brooke, Oct. 18, 2004, p. A11).

School Refusal.   Another form of deviant behavior that is of serious concern
in Japan is the growing number of children, usually of junior high school age, who
refuse to go to school. Often they won't even leave their houses, and sometimes they
imprison themselves in their rooms. There are many news articles about school refusal. Teachers and parents worry about it, and the government conducted a special
study in 1999. It found that by 1997 over 20,000 elementary school students and
over 80,000 junior high school students were identified as school refusers (an eight-
fold increase over 1978). According to Fukuzawa and LeTendre, some people suggest that the real figure may be as high as 350,000, or 5 percent of all students.
School refusal worries the Japanese way out of proportion to its rate of incidence,
because it challenges their belief in school as a "family society," an all-inclusive
group to which children should enjoy belonging (Fukuzawa and LeTendre,
pp. 81–87; Nathan, p. 39).

Youth Violence.   School refusal is often associated in public discussion with
youth violence, also a much publicized problem. There are constant stories in the
media about students armed with knives, horrible murders committed by middle
schoolers, and attacks on drunken salarymen by gangs of youths. Rates of juvenile
crime have risen since 1990, but are actually much lower than they were back in the
1960s and 1970s (*The Economist,* Oct. 25, 2003, pp. 39–40; Fukuzawa and
LeTendre, p. 87; Nathan, pp. 31–37; *The New York Times,* June 2, 2004, p. A12).

Japanese experts understand child violence and disobedience very much in
Merton's terms. Parents' expectations for their children are rising; they have smaller
families and demand that their one or two children excel in school, attend prestigious
colleges, and get high-status jobs. But children see the means to achievement col-
lapsing. They see young people with excellent records in school who still fail to get
secure jobs with good companies. They lose their trust in society, their belief that
following the approved norms will lead to achieving desired goals (French, Sept. 23,
2002, p. A6, quoting Noaki Ogi, an education expert).

Responses to Deviance

Characteristically, Japanese society responds to deviance by assuming there has
been a failure of human relations in groups. The focus is less on the deviant

individual and his or her problems and more on devising a way to reintegrate that individual into a close-knit group. So, for example, when a child persistently misbehaves in elementary school, the teacher invites the child to spend Saturday with her, in order to deepen the emotional bond between them. When LeTendre interviewed teachers in Japan, they kept telling him that school refusal and school violence came about when teachers had been unsuccessful in creating emotional connections with students, in building a sense of community (*kazoku-teki shakai,* or "family-society") in the class. They saw violence in school resulting when teachers didn't work together, when divorce disrupted families, and when employment kept mothers from participating in the PTA, breaking connections between parents and school (Fukuzawa and LeTendre, pp. 86–87).

Some schools and communities have set up programs for students who avoid school and seem at risk of dropping out. Often school nurses set up a special room for these children, where they can be coaxed out of their shells. "They need to be closer to teachers. They need to feel the teacher's warmth," one nurse said. New alternative schools offer school-refusing children a chance to start over in a rural town, boarding with local families and forming an acccepting group of their own in school (Fukuzawa and LeTendre, p. 85; Nathan, pp. 40–43; Onishi, June 6, 2004, p. 3).

Recently, the *Yomiuiri Shimbun,* Japan's major conservative newspaper, detailed the decade-long rise in crime rates and fall in arrest rates. The cause, the newspaper explained, was selfishness by police officers, who were neglecting routine police work in order to concentrate on cases that might help them win promotion. To control crime, the newspaper recommended that the focus of policing return to the *koban,* the local "police box," from which officers make themselves a part of the community (Masui, Jan. 18, 2003).

GENDER ROLES: A FOCUS FOR REBELLION

Most rebellious deviance in Japan today centers on rejection of traditional gender roles. Young men and women spurn the goals their society assigns them and the approved means for achieving those goals, and instead, they adopt new, alternative goals and new norms. To understand the rebellion of young people, you must first know what are the dominant role expectations and then recognize what forces have created stress around these expectations. So far, young Japanese women are far more rebellious than young men, but there are signs of rebellion among men too.

Traditional Gender Roles for Women

Everyone in Japan is familiar with traditional expectations for women. The subordination of women is built into Japanese institutions, shaping family life, education, and the economy. Women are seen as fundamentally different from men and inferior to men. Almost everyone assumes that the purpose of a woman's life is to serve others: her children, her husband, perhaps her in-laws, the men at work. Women are expected to be patient and "endure" and put their own needs last. Women are expected to defer to men: they giggle behind their hands, act shy, cute, and submissive, and lower their eyes. They are taught to listen and quietly observe men to interpret men's feelings and anticipate their needs. When women do speak, they are expected to have small, high voices and to use forms of speech that express hesitation.

But while women are certainly subordinate in the public realm of life, "off-stage" at home they exercise considerable power. Japanese wives are in charge of family budgets and with their husbands away at work so much, they are the emotional center of family life. Many psychologists and anthropologists claim that Japanese women manipulate their husbands and children by playing the role of the martyr. Feeling guilt for inflicting suffering on their wives and mothers, Japanese men and children spontaneously strive to please them. Other analysts depict Japanese men as dependent on their wives, both physically and psychologically. Anthropologist Takie Sugiyama Lebra describes the traditional wife as offering her husband so much "around the body care" that he cannot even find his socks without her. Women speak of their husbands as like another son, only older (Kato, pp. 184–185; Lebra, 1984, p. 133).

Shoko's Story: A Conformist Marriage

Shoko Sato was born in 1965 in a small city near Kyoto. She graduated high school and began working in the office of a local construction company. She enjoyed working very much. Her department chief was very kind to her and he allowed her an unusual amount of responsibility for organizing the paperwork on contracts. When she was 24 Shoko married Taichi. The match was semi-arranged. She knew Taichi from high school and from neighborhood temple festivals. When Taichi's boss, who knew her father, suggested the marriage, they found themselves very drawn to each other. Shoko wanted to continue working after she married, so she felt terribly flustered and confused when her boss immediately began to talk about a party for her "retirement" when he learned of the engagement. It was too embarrassing to try to explain that she had imagined she could keep working, and she didn't want to suggest that he hadn't understood her. So Shoko went along. Anyway, her first child was born just a year after the marriage, and Shoko firmly believed that she should fully devote herself to her children.

While Shoko plunged into the world of babies and mothers, she was still in some ways disappointed in her marriage. The companionship she and her husband Taichi had enjoyed in the beginning of their marriage seemed to vanish in the face of his obligation to work long hours and travel frequently for his company. Shoko made his breakfast every morning, and waited up for him at night until he returned at 10 or 11, since he didn't carry a key to the apartment. At any rate, she wanted to give him dinner and run his bath for him and lay out his clothes for the morning. Taichi turned his paycheck over to her and she arranged the family finances. They moved several times and each time Shoko searched for the new apartment and made the decision to buy it, since her husband was too busy at work to join her. Raising her children was a great joy to Shoko. At every milestone, like starting first grade, or graduating junior high school, she relived her own happy childhood and strove to make her children's as secure and loving as her own. Shoko became active in the PTA and kept up her friendships with several women she had known ever since junior high school. Now, helping her son and daughter with their homework and driving them to lessons take a lot of her time. She works on the yearly festival of their local shrine and studies flower arranging in the town cultural center. Last year she began working part-time for a nearby bank. Shoko feels her life is full, but she doesn't really know her husband very well any more.

Gender Segregation

One thing is clear about Japanese adult men and women: Their roles are highly segregated. They lead separate lives. The word wife in Japanese literally means "inside person" (Condon, p. 1). It is the wife's role to be in charge of the home and children. The husband is the "outside man," who goes out into the world, relieved of all worries at home. He is sometimes referred to as a "boarder," so uninvolved is he in household matters. In a real way, the primary ties in the family are those between mothers and children. Women are expected to live through their children, taking pride in their successes and blaming themselves for failures. Childcare and housework are demanding jobs in Japan. Mothers are expected to teach their children to read at home before they enter kindergarten and to spend hours a day helping their children with homework. Apartments are very small and few women have cars, so they must shop for groceries every day. A very significant obligation for women is care of the elderly. They are expected to care for their husband's parents, and often their own as well.

Women and Work

In Japanese society, everyone is expected to marry, and almost everyone does. Adulthood doesn't really start until marriage, so single people in their late 20s or early 30s are considered peculiar. By then one should definitely have found a mate. Between high school or university graduation and marriage, women are expected to work outside the home. But when their first child is born, usually within a year of marriage, three-quarters of women leave work. They begin working again, on a part-time basis, once their last child has begun school. (See Table 1.4.)

Young Women and Work.   Young women find they have few job alternatives. The jobs available to them keep them dependent, separated from and subordinated to men, usually without prospect of promotion. Unmarried women work in offices,

TABLE 1.4 Working Women (1970–2002)

Increasing numbers of Japanese women work, but their income is less than half of men's income.

	Percentage of Women in the Adult Labor Force		Women's Income as a Percent of Men's Income
	1970	2002	2002
Egypt	*	36	38
Mexico	19	40	38
Japan	39	51	46
Namibia	39	54	51
Germany	39	48	52
United States	37	59	62

Source: United Nations Human Development Report 2004

http://hdr.undp.org/statistics/data/advanced.cfm

*Data Not Available.

Note: Adult labor force is defined as those 15 years old and older.

in factories, and in retail stores. A job considered highly desirable for young women is "office lady" (called OL), especially with a prestigious company. OLs are selected for looks, since their duties are minimal: They do photocopying and filing, make tea, and tidy up. They are really a corporate status symbol, employed to be decorative and act as hostesses for business guests. Newly hired OLs are trained in bowing, greeting phone callers correctly, and offering tea. They are expected to live with their parents, and most companies will not hire girls who don't live at home, unless they live in the company dormitories provided for some female factory workers (Tasker, pp. 102–103; Condon, p. 194). (See Table 4.3, p. 241.)

Within the last decade it has become possible for women to get "career track" managerial or professional promotion track jobs, but, in fact, very few women do so. A woman in a "career track" job must work overtime, be willing to transfer to distant offices, and work through their childbearing years, just like men. Only university graduates are eligible and only 21 percent of female high school graduates go to a university.[3] Sometimes women can find promotion-track jobs with foreign companies or in the very few female-owned companies. But overall, very few women in Japan hold high-ranking jobs. Of the 27,000 companies listed on the Tokyo stock exchange, only twelve are headed by women and ten of these are family businesses. There are only fifty-eight women in the top four levels of the Japanese bureaucracy (out of 5,573 such employees) (Condon, p. 276; Sugimoto, p. 147).

Working Mothers.   The typical Japanese woman today re-enters the workforce once she is in her 40s and her children are school age or grown, both to occupy her time and to help pay rising family expenses. Since 1977, more employed women have been married than single, and 40 percent of the workforce is female (Condon, pp. 219, 263; Sugimoto, p. 142). But married women work on terms even more disadvantageous than do single women. Accommodating the needs of their families, most married women find unskilled work with flexible hours, near home in supermarkets, fast-food shops, department stores, and small factories (Condon, p. 194; Tasker, p. 103). Under the pressure of economic competition, more and more Japanese companies now hire a small core of men for full-time, lifetime security jobs, and then adjust their workforce to the ups and downs of the business cycle with part-timers, often women.

Young Women Challenge Traditional Roles

Japanese women are still seen primarily as wives and mothers, and it is as wives and mothers that they are registering their strongest rebellion against their roles. Women are postponing marriage, prolonging that pleasurable time after leaving school and before marrying when they are relatively independent and have jobs and money of their own. While 90 percent of all Japanese marry by the age of 40, young women are postponing marriage more and more. More than half of all Japanese women are still single at age 30, compared with 37 percent in the United States (Orenstein, p. 31). Japanese men complain about their difficulty in finding wives. Farmers and

[3]Of that 21 percent, only 1 percent take career track jobs (Sugimoto, pp. 145–147).

fishermen find it particularly hard to persuade women to live in rural areas and in the same house with their in-laws. Marriage bureaus do a big business in arranging marriages for Japanese men with Chinese, Taiwanese, and Filipino women (Jolivet, pp. 40, 146–147).

What do Japan's young women want? They are not demanding job equity. Most women say they don't envy men their long hours, grim devotion to work, and lack of time for any other activity. What women do want is even more subversive. Over and over again, unmarried women in their 20s in Tokyo told journalist Peggy Orenstein, "I just want to live for myself and enjoy my life" (Orenstein, p. 34). This statement might sound completely ordinary to you, but it is revolutionary in Japan where self-sacrificing devotion to family and duty has been the unquestioned norm for women. The popular name for unmarried women in Japan is now "parasite singles." They live with their parents, pay no rent, do no housework, and do as they please. Though their wages are not high, they have disposable income for cell phones, designer clothes, restaurant meals, and travel. These women are *wagamama*, people say, meaning selfish and willful. And the parasite singles have defiantly adopted *wagamama* as their own self-characterization, moving its meaning towards "self-determining" (Orenstein, pp. 32, 33).

Makiko's Story: "Parasite Single"

Makiko Yokimura is 29 years old and still unmarried. She lives with her parents in Tokyo and works as an OL for a big pharmaceutical company. Her work, she says, isn't unpleasant, but it's unchallenging. Mostly she answers the telephone and acts as receptionist for visiting businessmen. She earns the equivalent of $28,000 per year. But her life, she says, is good. She wears Comme des Garçons clothes and carries Gucci handbags. She lightens her hair in the trendiest salon and spends a fortune on makeup. Her cell phone seems to ring constantly. After work at 5 o'clock she meets her friends in fashionable cafes. She takes lessons in conversational French and classical shoko playing. Last summer she and a friend took a trip to Paris.

"Sure I'll get married," Makiko says, ". . . some day. "But I don't want to think about it now. If I were married I'd be stuck at home all the time, worrying about what my husband wants. I'd have to do all the housework and be a servant to my in-laws. My mother tells me I should get married, but she also complains all the time about how her in-laws exploit her and how my father is a stranger to her." But doesn't she miss having a man in her life, we asked Makiko? "You have to understand," she replied, "Japan is not a 'couples culture.' Even if I were married, or had a regular boyfriend, I'd still be spending most of my time with my girlfriends. Men and women just aren't companions for each other."

Older Women Rebel

Increasingly, the mothers of today's twenty-somethings are also rebelling against their roles as wives, often encouraged by their daughters. In the past decade, the divorce rate for middle-aged couples has shot up, perhaps tripling, as wives decide to leave abusive or empty marriages. Howard French quotes Tomoko Masunaga, a woman who divorced her executive husband against his wishes: "He had promised he would support me if I decided to work some day and then he betrayed me. What's worse he got old very quickly. For the first ten years at least he made an effort at conversation. But the company was everything for him, and after a while, he would just come home tired and sit silently watching TV, drinking his beer" (French, March 25, 2003, p. A3).

Middle-aged divorcees must be determined and brave because although the legal requirements for divorce are simple, there are tremendous social barriers for older, divorced women. They face the disapproval of family and neighbors, who expect a wife to *gaman,* to deny herself for the sake of her family. Then, middle-aged divorced women find it hard to get jobs, loans, mortgages, or even credit cards (French, March 25, 2003, p. A3).

Unhappy wives who are afraid to divorce have initiated an unusual new trend: They arrange to be buried separately from their husbands, leaving them in death, if not in life. Cemeteries that accommodate such women have only appeared since 1990, but there are close to 400 of them now (French, May 9, 2002, p. A4).

Women and the Population Crisis

The rebellion of women is reshaping Japan in many ways. It has consequences for consumer culture, business, men, and the care of old people. But no consequence has attracted more attention than the impact of women's decisions on birthrates.

We have heard so much in the past few decades about the problems of rapid population growth that you may be surprised to hear that Japan has the opposite problem: its population is shrinking! How can a country's population grow smaller? It is easy to understand. Demographers tell us that for population size to remain stable in Japan, the number of births per woman (**the total fertility rate**) would have to average 2.1 children. At this rate, taking childhood mortality into account, each couple would just about replace themselves with their children. If each woman has more than 2.1 children, total population grows, and if each woman has fewer than 2.1 children, population falls. By 2000, Japanese women were averaging only 1.4 children each. According to sociologist Merry Isaacs White, we can see the problem more clearly if we look separately at married and unmarried women. Birthrate data for all women aged 15–49 shows 1.30 children born per woman. But married women in that age bracket have an average of just over two children each. So postponement of marriage is the real culprit in Japan's birthrate problem (White, 2002, pp. 209–210).

But, whatever the reason, at this current low birthrate, not only will Japan's population shrink in the twenty-first century, it will age. There will be fewer children in the population and more old people, especially since old people are living longer and longer. In 2000, the number of Japanese over 65 topped the number of those below age 15 (Sims, June 20, 2001). Who will support these old people? Twenty years ago, there were four working-age people for every retired elderly person in Japan. Taxes on the working people provided retirement benefits for the old people. But in 20 years there will be only 2.2 people of working age for every old person (*The Economist,* July 1, 2000, p. 28). People in Japan know that today's unemployment problems will soon disappear. There will be a shortage of workers.

Japan is not alone in facing this problem of a declining birthrate. Many rich countries are in the same boat. Spain's total fertility rate is only 1.1. In Germany, the rate is only 1.3 and in Italy it is 1.2. The United States would have a falling population were it not for the large families of immigrants (*UN Population Division,* pp. 37, 43). (See Table 2.5, p. 119.)

In Japan there has been a great deal of discussion about the problem of falling birthrates. It is clear that there are several possible solutions for the problem. One solution is to follow the example of the United States and open Japan to immigration. People in poor countries all over Asia: China, Thailand, the Philippines, Indonesia, and others, would like to immigrate to Japan. But the number of immigrants would have to be quite large. The UN estimates that Japan would need to admit about 380,000 immigrants a year to stabilize its population at the 2005 projected level. This is a solution that is profoundly distasteful to Japanese policymakers. They attribute Japan's economic success and social harmony to its racial "purity." Sentiments like those of Tokyo mayor Ishihara, who said that foreigners in Japan commit "atrocious" crimes, are widespread in Japan (*United Nations Population Division,* p. 49; Sims, April 11, 2000, p. A6).

What else could Japan do about its falling birthrate and shrinking working age population? Another possible solution is to allow women a more active role in the labor force. If more women worked and worked full-time in real careers, this would add to the labor force and help support the old. This is another solution that produces very little enthusiasm in Japan. As we have seen, there is tremendous resistance to admitting women to career track jobs. In many ways, Japanese society depends on women remaining in the home, at least while they have children at home. Men work such long hours that they can't help much with child rearing, and there are few babysitters, after-school centers, or summer camps.

Are there any other possible solutions? Well, people could work many years longer before they retire, although that would only partially solve the problem. If the economy suddenly became much, much more productive, then maybe the smaller number of working adults could support the larger number of retired elders, but nobody knows how to bring that about. The simplest solution would be to raise birthrates again! That is probably the solution Japan's leaders would like best. Already, several large companies have offered bonuses to employees who have a second child. One company pays as much as $10,000 for each child after the first (Sims, May 30, 2000; Kristof, August 1, 1999, pp. 1, 4). We can imagine a concerted campaign, orchestrated by the bureaucracies, to convince women that it is their duty to Japan to have more children. Do you think the campaign would work?

Japanese Men: Trouble with Roles

You must pity the poor Japanese male! Even the most willingly conformist man is likely to have trouble with his roles, at work and at home. Japanese men know they are expected to devote themselves to their jobs, out of loyalty to their company, and to help Japan compete and advance. But the economic crisis in Japan has produced a collapse of careers. Men can no longer count on what used to be stable patterns of hiring, promotion, and compensation. Middle-aged salarymen who have been dedicated team players all their lives may suddenly experience harassment designed to drive them into retirement. David Slater, an anthropologist who studies bullying in Japanese companies says it often takes the form of ignoring the targeted individual, acting as if he doesn't exist, not responding when he speaks. You can imagine how humiliating this is. It suggests that the person isn't really there in the group; that he is nobody (Jessica Smith, *Marketplace,* Sept. 17, 2003). And the executives who do the bullying also feel ashamed, because they can no longer reward their subordinates for loyal efforts. Those who keep their jobs may be overwhelmed by the increased workload (Strom, July 15, 1999, p. A8).

A smooth transition from school to work is no longer possible for many young Japanese. In the recent past, companies actively recruited high school and college graduates. In 1992, Japanese companies offered 1.67 million permanent full-time jobs to high school graduates. By 2003, only 220,000 such jobs were offered. The decline for college graduates has been less striking, but severe nonetheless. The number of college graduates recruited for permanent full-time work dropped by a third in the same ten-year period (Kosugi, pp. 52–53).

At the same time, men experience a kind of loss of meaning. It wasn't so long ago that Japanese men saw themselves as players in a grand national drama. They were like a band of samurai warriors, fighting to bring Japan back from its defeat in World War II and make it a world economic power. That fight was won—and then, in a way, lost—in the economic recession of the 1990s. Japan is no longer the envy of the world. Americans no longer fear that Japan will take over the U.S. economy, and Japanese men no longer understand what it is that they are to sacrifice for. John Nathan quotes a 48-year-old bank manager who told him:

> We had big dreams until the early nineties. . . . We wanted things and we worked desperately hard to bring our material life up to the American standard. The family cooperated; it was a team effort. No matter how late we had to stay at the office working, Saturdays and Sundays and no vacations, they understood and supported us. And we created unbelievable wealth. . . . But since the bubble burst it feels as though our hard work is unavailing. And people my age and older have to ask ourselves why are we working so hard. What's the point. . . . We've lost our dreams and now we must rethink our way of life. (Nathan, p. 67; also see Roberson and Suzuki, pp. 6–7, 9.)

Marriage and Family Life

Today, Japanese men's battered self-esteem has come under further attack, an assault by women. Being a salaryman is suddenly *dasai* (uncool). Younger women call the ubiquitous dark-suited company warriors *nakakenai* (clueless) and their wives call them the *nure-ochiba zuku* (the "wet leaf tribe," "clingy, musty, and emotionally spent," according to Howard French). Young women publicly make fun of middle-aged men for having "old man smell." Cosmetic companies are experiencing record sales of special deodorants for older men (French, Nov. 27, 2002, p. A4; Sims, March 17, 2000, p. A8).

When it comes to marriage, men find themselves caught between contradictory demands. If they are lucky enough to find full-time, salaryman-style jobs, their employers demand that they marry. Salarymen need wives. They work such long hours that they really can't take care of themselves at home and they certainly can't take care of children. But young women don't want the lifestyle of the salaryman's wife. At the same time, young women are also reluctant to marry men without secure incomes.

Men also face conflicting demands from wives. A recent large Japanese government survey of family relations found that 68 percent of Japanese wives believed that husbands should give first priority to their work. Remarkably, at the same time, 77 percent believed husbands should share equal responsibility for child rearing! Another 48.3 percent said they were unsatisfied with their husband's participation in household work and child rearing (National Institution of Population and Social Security Research, *The Second Survey of Japanese Family Households Report,* 2000). Young women talk about the "3 C's" they seek in a prospective husband: He should earn a "comfortable" income, be "communicative," and be "cooperative" with housework and children. Gordon Mathews reports an interview with one salaryman in his late thirties who reported that his wife almost left him because he stayed late at work, wasn't affectionate, and didn't take her anywhere on weekends. So he promised to have breakfast with the family every morning and spend Sundays with them. But he still feels stressed and exhausted: He is under great pressure at work, and now home, rather than a retreat, is one more source of stress (Mathews, pp. 115–116).

Men Respond: Ritualism, Retreatism, and Rebellion

As discussed earlier, we can see many examples of men engaging in retreatist deviance in Japan: from suicide to school refusal to dropping out. There is a small, but growing number of homeless middle-aged men who have lost their jobs and left their families because of shame. You can see them in orderly squatter settlements in public parks and under bridges, or in spotless shelters put up by city authorities (French, Feb. 2, 2001, pp. A1, A8). Some men go on working and supporting their families, playing the expected male roles, but they find no meaning or fulfillment in any of it. It does not look like deviance, but Merton would call it ritualistic deviance.

The varied forms of rebellion among Japanese men deserve fuller description. Some men are rejecting the traditional role of company man and instead, like the "*wagamama* girls," are seeking a more personal self-fulfillment. Masayoshi Toyoda is widely known in Japan as the man who built a network of men's liberation groups devoted to helping men get in touch with their feelings, communicate their thoughts, and find pleasure in the ordinary moments of family life (French, Nov. 27, 2002, p. A4).

Many young men have rejected conventional jobs, choosing to work only for the money they need to enjoy life. They are called "freeters" (from a combination of the English word "free" and the German word "arbeiter," or worker). The government estimated in 2000 that there were 4.17 million freeters, aged between 15 and 34, up from 1.5 million in 1997 (*Japan Today,* Feb. 6, 2004). Freeters take part-time jobs or temporary jobs; they are unmarried and live with their parents. They travel, pursue personal hobbies, and enjoy free time. (There are women freeters too, but since women aren't expected to have career jobs, the meaning of their lifestyle is different.) When a recent survey asked freeters why they chose their way of life, the most frequent response was "to give priority to the things I myself want to do" (40 percent). But many worked as freeters because they couldn't get career jobs.

The freeter rebellion against traditional male roles can be summed up in the number-one pop song of 2003, "Only One Flower in the World," which asked, "Why do we want to be No. 1 when each of us is different? Small flowers, big flowers, none of them alike. So its OK not be No. 1. Every one of them is the only one" (*Web-Japan,* Feb. 4, 2002; Onishi, Feb. 2, 2004, p. A4).

Not all men who rebel do so by dropping out in search of personal fulfillment. Shuji Nakamura rebelled by insisting on personal recognition and personal compensation for his inventions. He sued his company for a share of royalties on patents for his device: a blue-light emitting diode. Nakamura's actions push Japan towards a more U.S.-style society, where employees are free agents, money is important, and individuals who innovate are admired (Markoff, Sept. 18, 2001, pp. C1, C4).

A very different group of young rebels created a huge scandal in Japan in 2003. They were members of an elite Waseda University social club. The club arranged parties, to which members sold tickets, and at the parties women were gang raped while drunk. The club's leader, Shinichiro Wada, was reported to have made $100,000 from ticket sales. Before the scandal broke, Wada had been admired by other students for making so much money while still a student. It was truly an act of rebellious deviance to risk his status at a prestigious university in order to make money, and by such universally disapproved means as well (*Mainichi Interactive,* Sept. 17, 2003, Dec. 27, 2003; Bender, Oct. 3, 2003).

Interlocking Changes

The 1990s were a period of rapid change in Japan. Against a background of economic recession, crime rates rose, suicide rates spiked up, and women and men began to challenge traditional roles. Now we need to examine patterns of inequality in Japan and how these too have been changing.

SOCIAL INEQUALITY IN JAPAN: CLASS, STATUS, AND POWER

Inequality is universal; it can be found in every society, but that doesn't make all societies similar. Actually, societies differ quite a lot, both in how much inequality they contain and what forms these inequalities take. Max Weber's classic discussion of social stratification is useful for understanding the varieties of social inequality in Japan. Weber said that there are three basic aspects of inequality: class, status, and power. **Class** has to do with the wealth and income people enjoy as the result of their property or job. **Status** refers to prestige. It is the cultural dimension of inequality, because it results from the way a culture views different groups of people—men and women, ethnic or racial groups, people in different occupations, people from particular families. Weber defined **power** as the ability to make people do what you want, even against their will. In every society, some individuals and groups have more power than others.

In Japan class inequalities make people uncomfortable. The Japanese don't want to have great inequalities of wealth or income or opportunity in their society, and they have made great efforts to minimize them. But the economic recession and the economic restructuring that resulted from it have strained class equality in Japan, creating new tensions in the society. There are interesting changes in status inequality as well. Women, as we have seen, are challenging their subservience to men. But other status inequalities are growing, as Japan's minority populations expand. Inequalities of power in Japan have seen little change. Power is still closely held in the hands of a small elite of government bureaucrats, politicians, and business leaders. Significant challengers have appeared on the scene, but it is not yet clear how successful they will be in dislodging the elites. You should be aware, however, that changes in the structure of inequality are not without precedent in Japan. Japan's history is full of such transformations.

A History of Change

For most of its history (up until the Meiji Restoration), Japan was a society of hereditary status rankings: it was a **caste society.** Everyone was born into their parents' **caste,** as aristocrat, samurai, commoner, or (those in the most menial occupations) outcaste. Caste was destiny: Everyone had to live and marry within the caste, no matter what his or her talents might be, and there were rules regulating what members of different castes and subcastes were permitted to do and wear (Reischauer, p. 158).

Meiji Inequality

Then, in one of Japan's most remarkable self-transformations, the Meiji government declared that "the four orders are equal" and legal distinctions between the castes were officially discarded (Fukutake, pp. 27–28). Remarkably, most caste distinctions faded from people's awareness after they were legally abolished. The emperor and his family are the only nobility recognized in Japan today, and while descendants of samurai are proud of their ancestors, people don't try to marry within the samurai caste. The only exception is the descendants of the outcastes, the *burakumin:* Those still identifiable face a persistent, though unacknowledged prejudice (Reischauer, pp. 159–160).

But inequality by no means disappeared from Meiji Japan; rather, it changed its character. In the early twentieth century, class inequalities grew, as Japan industrialized. Rural land was concentrated in the hands of a wealthy landlord class, while the growing industrial economy quickly came to be dominated by a small number of vastly powerful, family-owned business conglomerates with close ties to government and the military (Chapman, p. 198).

Postwar Equality

But the story is far from over, for remarkably, World War II ushered in yet another era of Japanese social stratification. Defeat destroyed Japan's industry and left nearly everyone poor. Many inequalities were leveled by the American Occupation reforms, which broke up the landlords' estates and distributed the land to the peasants, dismantled the great industrial empires, and purged their executives as war collaborators. Occupation authorities instituted progressive income taxes and (briefly) supported labor unions. Building on occupation reforms, Japan's leaders reconstructed the society on egalitarian foundations (Chapman, p. 198).

Contracts between labor and management followed the principle of equal pay for equal work, regardless of the education, skill, or status of the employees. Unions aimed for a "livelihood wage" for all, and there was little difference in the pay received by blue and white collar employees. New schools, shaped by the Occupation authorities, and by teachers' socialist unions, tried to create equal opportunity through education. Teachers told their students that everyone had equal ability; hard work and perseverance were what counted for success. Schools did no IQ testing or ability grouping, so each class was a cross-section of the community. Individuals in high positions took their cue from the government and tended to disguise their wealth. Executives avoided conspicuous luxury in dress or housing and took buses and trains like their employees (Chapman, p. 199). The government even worked to even out regional and rural-urban inequalities by channeling large subsidies to poorer areas. It paid for much of the local budgets in poor areas and kept people employed on public works projects. By doing this, the government redistributed tax revenues from wealthy industrial areas like Tokyo and Osaka to poorer rural areas (Strom, July 27, 2001, p. A3). In the postwar years the Japanese came to believe that class inequalities of wealth, income, and opportunity were unfair and should be minimized, and this belief persists today.

Class Inequality in Japan Today

Much of the postwar egalitarianism has survived into the present. Class differences are weaker in Japan than in most advanced capitalist societies. Traveling in Japan, you will look in vain for rundown, crime-ridden neighborhoods with abandoned buildings, decaying schools, and corner drug dealers. Nor will you find gated suburbs filled with huge homes, with private pools and gyms. Only 1.2 percent of the Japanese population receives any welfare payments, and the number of people who are homeless alcoholic men, petty criminals, or able-bodied but permanently unemployed dropouts is very small (Fukutake, p. 158). In survey after survey, about 90 percent of Japanese identify themselves as middle class, reflecting their sense of economic equality. It is also true that to an unusual degree people of different classes mix socially. In city neighborhoods, modern luxury towers have been built in the midst of shabby old houses, and since almost all residents send their children to neighborhood public schools, children from different class backgrounds become friends. Also, school uniforms mask class differences.

In addition, cultural differences among Japanese people of different social classes are minimal: There are no class accents, and styles of dress, leisure pursuits, even the newspapers and magazines people read vary very little along class lines. Japanese people spend a lot of time in association with those higher or lower in class position than themselves in the close group associations of school and office. They spend little time in groups which bring together those of one class or status. Even Japanese unions are distinctive in this respect, joining both blue- and white-collar workers of a particular enterprise. Class equality in Japan has supported people's belief that they are all in it together; that there is a place for everyone, working together to achieve their nation's goals.

Income, Occupation, and Social Class

People in Japan don't like to acknowledge the existence of class inequalities in their society. People value equality, and they try to maintain an *omote* depiction of Japan as a very egalitarian society. For example, official government statistics on income distribution include the earnings of full-time workers, but omit part-time workers. Let us try to puzzle out just how much class inequality there really is in Japan.

According to Yoshio Sugimoto, about 10 percent of Japanese are part of an upper-middle class of university-educated managers and professionals. They have income more than twice the national average and they have some wealth—fancy cars, stocks and bonds, costly memberships in sports clubs. They can afford expensive sports like golf and sailing, and attend theater and concerts. At the other end of the income spectrum is a much larger working class—as much as 30 percent of Japanese who have completed only junior high or high school. They are manual workers and farmers and their incomes are only about half the national average.

Most Japanese fall somewhere between the richest 10 percent and the poorest 30 percent, and for this large population class differences are blurred. Many "salarymen" and professionals have university degrees and prestigious jobs, but their incomes are only in the middle range. Blue-collar employees of big corporations earn less, but not a great deal less. Many self-employed workers—owners of small businesses and skilled tradesmen like plumbers and electricians—earn more on average than the salarymen, though they enjoy less prestige (Sugimoto, pp. 37–39).

The best-paid Japanese earn less than the best-paid Americans. And they accumulate less wealth too. According to a 2001 survey by an American management consulting firm, the average income of chief executive officers of U.S. manufacturers with annual sales of at least $500 million was $1.93 million. Equivalent Japanese CEOs averaged only $500,000. Without high incomes, Japanese executives are unable to accumulate great wealth. High inheritance taxes and heavy taxes on high incomes also make it difficult to pass on any wealth amassed. As a result, while the U.S. economy is twice the size of Japan's, America's billionaires outnumber Japan's ten to one: 277 to 22 (*The Asahi Shimbun,* July 19, 2003; *Forbes,* "The World's Richest People"; Chapman, p. 200).

Table 1.5 displays differences in income distribution in five societies. In the United States, those in the poorest 20 percent of the population receive 5.4 percent of the total income earned by all individuals. In Japan, the poorest 20 percent

TABLE 1.5 Distribution of Income in Six Societies
Income is shared more equally in Japan and Germany than in the United States, Mexico or Namibia

	Percent of Income Received by Poorest 20% of the Population	Percent of Income Received by Richest 20% of the Population	Ratio of the Income Share of Richest 20% to the Income Share of the Poorest 20%
Egypt 1999	8.6	43.6	5.07
Germany 2000	8.5	36.9	4.34
Japan 1993	10.6	35.7	3.37
Mexico 2000	3.1	59.1	19.06
Namibia 1993	1.4	78.7	56.21
United States 2000	5.4	45.8	8.48

Source: United Nations Human Development Report 2004
http://hdr.undp.org/statistics/data/advanced.cfm

receives almost twice as much—10.6 percent of all the income earned. The richest 20 percent in the United States gets 45.8 percent of total national income, while in Japan the corresponding figure is only 35.7 percent. You can see that inequalities between the richest fifth of the population and the poorest fifth are greater in the United States than in Japan, more than twice as big.

The Bubble Economy.   During the 1980s, Japan enjoyed a period of unprecedented economic boom. The stock market was pushed higher and higher by speculation, and real estate values rose at a tremendous rate. Company profits went up fast. But inequalities also increased during the 1980s. Those who happened to own land or stock found themselves suddenly rich and speculators amassed fortunes. Old values of frugality and restraint gave way to a burst of conspicuous consumption. Expensive western goods—designer-label clothes, foreign cars, and artwork—became fashionable, and credit cards were introduced. Corporate executives lived lavishly at company expense, enjoying headquarters in palatial office towers and sometimes even company apartments. The luxurious corporate lifestyle was emulated by the newly rich and by young women and middle-aged couples who spent their earnings on consumer goods, rejecting traditional habits of saving (Chapman, pp. 174, 190–194).

The Crash and Recession.   Most Japanese disapproved of these new economic disparities. Perhaps that is why the public at first registered little concern over the crash and recession of the 1990s, when real estate prices fell as much as 80 percent, the stock market crashed, and expense account living was cut back drastically. Executives' bonuses shrunk and in many working-class families wives entered the labor force to supplement family income. Businesses replaced full-time workers with part-timers or temps, often women. As a result, the population became more **stratified,** with a layer of remaining privileged career workers and new layers of less secure and more poorly paid workers. Many of these latter are women, many are young people, and some are immigrants.

Equality of Opportunity and Economic Change

Japanese society actually prizes equality in two different ways. First, people think it right that incomes and wealth should be relatively equal throughout the population. (We call this **equality of reward.**) Then, they also think everyone should have an equal chance to compete for the more prestigious, somewhat better-paying jobs. (This latter kind of equality is called **equality of opportunity.**) Think about it: Some societies value equality of opportunity, but they are untroubled by vast inequalities of reward. Is your society like this? Or is it more like Japan, in valuing both kinds of economic equality?

Because the Japanese value equal opportunity, they support an educational system that puts tremendous effort into making sure that children from all classes start out equal in a competition to achieve success through education. All public schools in Japan are centrally controlled by the Ministry of Education, and it is ministry policy to make sure that all elementary and junior high schools are of uniform quality. There are no budget disparities between schools in rich and poor communities in

Japan. All have the same facilities, and teachers get the same high salaries in every school. (Teaching is a prestigious career in Japan and a very competitive field to enter.) Teachers are even rotated from school to school every five years to ensure that all children have the same quality of instruction. This system works to provide greater upward mobility for poor children than exists in most other industrialized nations. One in three children from the poorest 20 percent of Japanese families ends up attending a university, an unusually large percentage.

To a remarkable degree, Japanese society is a **meritocracy,** a social system in which one's place in the social stratification system is based solely on merit, or achievement, not on inherited advantage (or disadvantage). Education is the heart of Japan's meritocracy, which makes sense in a modern, technological society where education is the gateway to jobs. In Japan, academic excellence and high scores on achievement tests are the ticket to high status jobs. Other good qualities like creativity, or entrepreneurial flair, which aren't measured by tests, are not rewarded. But take careful note: An educational meritocracy may be fair, but it doesn't make life easy for children. A child's school performance, at an early age, has a lifelong impact, and there are very few second chances. As a result, competition is fierce and childhood is a serious time. From junior high school on, children are occupied with preparation for exams. They put in long hours of study and attend cram schools, called *juku,* for many hours after school and on Saturdays. The purpose of cram schools is just to prepare students for the exams. It's like attending school twice every day.

The Japanese were content with their meritocracy as long as there was room in it for everyone. In the 1970s and 1980s, children who worked hard and finished high school could count on getting jobs, full-time jobs, with benefits and some economic security. In a labor-short economy, high school graduates were so prized by employers that they were known as "golden eggs" and were well rewarded. Young men who finished college could expect prestigious jobs in large companies or with the government. Only the high school dropouts got stuck with dirty, unskilled, temporary work. But in the 1990s and 2000s, economic changes resulted in less hiring, more intense competition for education and jobs, a greater number of losers in the competition, and more anxiety all around. Now young people could finish high school and still find no job. They could even finish college and end up unemployed. People began to perceive the system as "unfair."

Polarization

In order to recover from the recession, Japanese businesses began to restructure. Manufacturing companies began to move their factories to China, where wages were a fraction of Japanese wages. Companies hired fewer career workers with lifetime security, and more contract workers. Japanese men and women are now more likely to be part-time workers than their counterparts in the United States or Germany. In 2000 11.8 percent of Japanese men held part-time jobs, compared to 7.9 percent in the United States and 4.8 percent in Germany. Twice as many women worked part-time in Japan as in the United States. The growth of part-time work in Japan has created what sociologists call a **polarized** economy. A minority (less than a quarter of full-time workers) are still in the old lifetime security system. They tend to be middle aged. At the same time, an increasing number of workers, especially young workers, are much less well off. They work part-time, often for smaller companies and at lower wages. Sometimes their "part-time" jobs require 35 or 40 hours a week, but include no benefits or security, and they don't belong to unions (The Japan Institute for Labour Policy and Training, Japan Working Life Profile, 2003, p. 40).

Young people can no longer depend on being rewarded for excellence. They have become anxious and disillusioned and angry. They resent the relentless emphasis on tests that no longer guarantee success in adult life. More and more working-class children feel "thrown away." If they don't plan to go to college, they don't see how working hard in high school will benefit them. For middle class children, the pressure to compete and excel has increased. Cram school enrollment is rising. Parents feel desperate to ensure their children prosperous futures.

Even in the early 1990s, parents who could afford it began to send their children to private junior high and high schools, schools with special relationships with the most prestigious colleges. In 1992 a Japanese television special revealed that at Tokyo University, the top university, half of the students were graduates of the twenty top high schools in Japan and eighteen of those high schools were private schools. Many expensive private high schools started their own junior highs so their students wouldn't have to take the grueling high school entrance exams (Sugimoto, pp. 117–119; Sanger, 1991, p. 4). Education became more expensive too. *Jukus* are expensive and while fees for public high schools and universities remained moderate, tuition at private schools rose.

Some wealthy parents were able to give their advantages to their children in other ways. Doctors passed their practices to their doctor offspring and the children of politicians took over their fathers' seats in parliament and their carefully nurtured political support groups (Chapman, p. 203). People in Japan don't fully appreciate that their society still has less class inequality than most other industrialized societies. They see increasing inequality, and they find it very offensive.

Is this story of polarization and competition familiar to you? In many ways, the changes in social stratification we have been describing have become a worldwide pattern, experienced in all the rich nations. Do you notice polarization in the job market, increasing competition for good jobs, and increasing pressure to go to college in your society too?

Status Inequality in Japan: Minority Groups

Japan is a very homogeneous society; it has few groups that differ racially or ethnically or socially from the rest of the population, and those it does have are very small. At most, 4–5 million people out of the total population of 120 million could be classified as members of **minority groups,** groups which are seen as inferior and are treated unequally by the **majority** population. Japan's minority population is growing, but rather slowly, as low birthrates and a changing economy have created a niche for immigrant workers. Most Japanese minorities look little different from other Japanese. Though they can't be recognized by their physical appearance, minorities are nonetheless treated with distaste and face considerable discrimination (Reischauer, pp. 32–33; Tasker, pp. 23–24).

Sociologists note that there is a variety of ways that societies treat their minority groups, ranging from **pluralism** to **genocide**. A **pluralistic** society takes a positive view of group diversity and minorities are permitted, or even encouraged, to keep their separate identities, languages, and customs. Pluralistic societies believe that people can be different without being unequal. Many societies reject pluralism and aim for **assimilation** of minorities, requiring that they adopt the values, language, and customs of the majority. If assimilation works, minorities join majority culture and they are accepted and become equal. Japanese society officially promotes assimilation of minorities; but actually minorities, who may not be very different from majority Japanese, are often excluded from mainstream society. They face **discrimination** in employment and marriage, and **segregation** in their place of residence. But in modern times Japan has never gone to the extreme of **genocide,** the physical extermination of minorities, which has happened in many other societies.

The Ainu

The oldest Japanese minority is the descendants of the Ainu, the ancient race that inhabited Japan before Asian settlers arrived more than a thousand years ago. The Asians pushed the Ainu north into the less desirable, wintry islands at the top of Japan. They also intermarried with the Ainu, so that today many of the Ainu have been absorbed into the majority population. About 20,000 Ainu still live as a distinct group. They are poorer than other Japanese and are looked down upon. Today, the Ainu are becoming more conscious of themselves as a minority group. They are writing down their aboriginal language before it disappears and have come to identify themselves with the aboriginal peoples of Alaska and northern Canada with whom they believe they are racially linked, and whose experience with settlers they see as similar to their own (Reischauer, pp. 32–33; Tasker, pp. 23–24).

Ethnic Japanese

Only about 1,800,000 foreigners live in Japan—about 1 percent of the total population—and most of these are Koreans and Chinese whose families migrated or were brought to Japan during the period when Japan annexed Korea in the aggression which led up to World War II. Even those Koreans who were born in Japan and speak only Japanese are not automatically granted citizenship. They cannot vote and face discrimination by employers (Ministry of Justice, Statistics on Foreign Residents, 2003; French, Nov. 20, 2000, p. A4; Reischauer, pp. 32–35; Tasker, pp. 23–24).

A new minority in Japan is the growing community of approximately 300,000 people of Japanese descent who were born in Brazil and Peru. Faced with a shortage of unskilled workers, and fearful of illegal immigration from other Asian countries, the Japanese government decided to welcome Japanese of foreign descent whose ancestors had emigrated in the past. These new immigrants are racially identical to the Japanese, but culturally they are different. They speak and laugh loudly and embrace in public, and hold street festivals with salsa and samba music. The Latin Americans face discrimination in Japan: They are treated fearfully in restaurants and stores and often exploited by labor contractors. "The Japanese treat us like some kind of inferior race," said one Brazilian immigrant (Ministry of Justice, Statistics on Foreign Residents, 2003; Weisman, p. 1).

Immigrants

Japan's population of recent Asian immigrants, mostly from China, the Philippines, and Vietnam is growing, but still small. Demographers say that Japan needs immigrants. If the nation wants to keep Japan's population of 120 million from falling to 60 million by the end of the twenty-first century, immigration will be necessary. Even business spokesmen are now openly calling for Japan to allow in more immigrants. But foreigners, even other Asians, and even immigrants who have adopted Japanese names and speak fluent Japanese, are not well accepted in Japan. "Living in Japan," said one student from China, "is like staying in a hotel forever, never in a home. I'm always waiting to go home." Though the government has agreed to encourage migration of immigrants with specialized skills or knowledge, in fact most immigrants fill the most undesirable jobs, providing cheap labor to a polarizing economy. They work in what the Japanese call 3-K jobs, translated in English: as dirty, dangerous, and difficult. Many Thai and Filipino immigrants work in construction, and factory owners employ Africans and others indoors, where they are less likely to be seen. Many Asian women immigrants work in bars and in the sex trades.

There are more than 100,000 foreign students in Japan, 65 percent of them Chinese. Many foreign students overstay their visas or work illegally to support themselves in expensive Japan. It is widely believed that foreign students are responsible for rising crime rates in Japan and criminal acts by foreigners get headlines in the press. Recently, in reaction, the government tightened visa requirements for foreign students (Onishi, March 28, 2004, p. 3; French, July 24, 2003, p. A1).

The *Burakumin*

Not all Japanese minority groups are racial or ethnic minorities. The *burakumin* are Japanese, but they are rejected nonetheless. They are the descendants of Japan's ancient "outcastes," those who did dirty jobs (like butchering or leatherwork) considered offensive by others. In Tokugawa times the *burakumin* were required to live in separate villages and were forbidden to enter temples, shrines, and festivals. Though the *burakumin* became legally equal to other Japanese during the Meiji period, discrimination continued. The *burakumin* today are physically and culturally indistinguishable from other Japanese. Only their family names and sometimes the neighborhoods where they live mark them out for discrimination and distaste. Estimates of the number of *burakumin* today range from 1.2 million to 3 million, no more than 2 percent of the population (Pharr, pp. 76–77).

Today, *burakumin* face discrimination in employment and marriage. It is common practice in Japan for families to hire a "marriage detective" to research the background of a prospective spouse whose family is not known to them. Marriages are canceled when the family is traced to a *burakumin* village. The same thing happens when employers research the family background of new hires. "Buraku place-name registers" are (illegally) sold in Japan. As a result of this discrimination, *burakumin* have lower incomes and less education than majority Japanese; they follow more insecure occupations, and have higher crime rates than other Japanese, and this feeds the contempt in which they are held, perpetuating their disadvantage (Pharr, pp. 77–79).

Inequalities of Power in Japan Today

Everyone in Japan knows that political and economic power is very unequally distributed. Power is concentrated in the hands of a small elite—a three-way partnership among government bureaucrats, legislators, and industrialists. But the truth is that as long as Japan enjoyed its long post–World War II prosperity, no one cared. People were willing to entrust their nation's rule to an elite that was wisely managing the society for the good of the entire nation. But once the long economic boom ground miserably to a halt and Japan's economy got stuck in recession, people became cynical about the power elite of their society. Politicians had never been much respected in Japan. Now people began to question the honesty of bureaucrats too, and their respect for business leaders faltered as the economy failed. So far, discontent has not led to any real change, but the nature of inequalities of power in Japan has become clearer.

Government and Business: Western Structures, Japanese Spirit

Formally and officially, Japan is a western-style parliamentary democracy. After Japan's defeat in World War II, democracy was imposed by the American occupying forces. Occupation authorities created a legislature (the Diet) with an upper and a lower house, political parties, a prime minister, and a liberal constitution guaranteeing free speech, universal suffrage, labor's right to organize, and the rule of law. In theory, the people govern by electing representatives who make laws implemented by the bureaucracy. Japan's economy was also remade to resemble western ideals. The Occupation destroyed Japan's powerful family-owned conglomerates hoping to encourage a free-enterprise economy in which economic power also would be widely and equally distributed among a great many small companies.

Japanese society did not turn out the way Occupation forces intended. After the Occupation, the Japanese retained the American preference for a weak executive who cannot make decisions alone and a weak military excluded from political power. To the American formula they added a very Japanese preference for centralized power, for cooperative over confrontation, and for behind-the-scenes compromise over public debate. Though Japan today has a legislature, political parties, labor unions, and stockholders, these western institutions function in a distinctly Japanese fashion. As they say, it is a case of *wakon yosai,* western structures transformed by Japanese spirit. Most power-holders are not elected, and power is exercised almost entirely behind the scenes.

The Bureaucracy

In Japan's tripartite power structure, commonly called the "iron triangle," the central government bureaucracy in Tokyo stands at the top, coordinating its power with that of business leaders and elected officials. Bureaucrats today, who work in the various government ministries, like the famous MITI (the Ministry of International Trade and Industry) and the Ministry of Finance, actually draft the legislation that is brought to the floor of the Diet. According to Atsushi Ueda, "we might go so far as to say that a Diet session is a kind of ceremonial performance, to give people inside and outside Japan the impression that decisions are being made democratically" (Ueda, p. 129). Then after passage, the bureaucracy implements laws and policies it has developed and sent to the legislature. But bureaucratic power extends further, because the bureaucracy doesn't simply mechanically apply the law; it exercises what is known as "administrative guidance," flexibility in enforcing regulations.

The bureaucracy was the guiding hand behind Japan's fabulously successful post–World War II economic growth. In each important industry, MITI selected a few strong companies and encouraged them to compete with each other for market shares and profits, while sheltering them from foreign competition. The bureaucracy supplied capital to companies they supported and denied it to others. Bureaucrats rather than individual companies decided which types of foreign technology would be imported and manufactured in Japan. They decided where to send Japanese products for export and taught companies how to produce for export. So both political and economic power in Japan were centralized (Chapman, pp. 103–107; van Wolferen, p. 33).

Who are Japan's powerful bureaucrats? They are an educated elite. Young people who have excelled in school and graduated from Japan's top universities are hired as bureaucrats, and it is considered very prestigious work. Traditionally, people have seen the bureaucrats as society's best and brightest. They have seen them as apolitical: Bureaucrats are not allied to any political parties (Ueda, pp. 130, 134–137). Until recently the Japanese accepted bureaucratic power because it was traditional in their society and because they agreed with the goals of the ministries: economic growth, increased market share abroad, the protection of Japanese businesses, and restraint on the growth of inequality. However, by the late 1990s there was a crisis of public confidence in the bureaucracy. Faced with the stubborn economic recession, the ministries stumbled. They couldn't seem to get the Japanese economy moving again; they couldn't deliver on the goals people had trusted them to accomplish. As a result, distrust in the bureaucracy grew. Japanese bureaucrats had never been viewed as corrupt or incompetent, but now scandals involving bureaucrats began to surface.

Business and Bureaucrats

Businesses cultivate their relationships with bureaucrats. In a way it is difficult to decide whether bureaucrats are the masters or the servants of business, since all their efforts are aimed at maximizing the long-run expansion of industry. For example, until the scandals of 1998, every bank designated a number of young employees to spend all their time developing relationships with bureaucrats at the Ministry of Finance. They "dropped in" at ministry offices and they entertained ministry officials at bars and restaurants, getting tips about new policies, scheduled bank inspections, anything that might help their bank. Sometimes they sent birthday gifts to the bureaucrats' wives. When these young *MOF-tans* (ministry handlers) moved on to other assignments in the bank, they took their connections with them. In the 90s, as it became clear that the Ministry of Finance had protected banks from the consequences of their bad loans, the Japanese public became much more cynical about relationships between businessmen and bureaucrats, and business entertainment spending, formerly accepted as a normal part of business, came to be seen as a form of bribery. Banks abolished their *MOF-tans* and some ministry officials were even arrested for taking bribes (WuDunn, Oct. 29, 1995, p. E14; March 17, 1998; Jan. 27, 1998, pp. D1, D12; May 19, 1998, p. A4).

Business Organization

Today industry in Japan is far different from the thousands of competing small firms Occupation authorities envisioned. Japanese business is big business and it is highly organized to coordinate economic activity. Industries are organized by sector: auto manufacturers in one association, iron and steel companies in another, their industrywide organizations setting unwritten rules for business operations and successfully pressuring members to comply.

But this is only the beginning of business organization. Most large corporations also belong to conglomerates: There are six giant ones that date to the early postwar years and a number of newer, smaller ones. Conglomerates organize companies from many industries around a bank, also bringing in real estate, insurance, and trading firms. It is customary for 60–70 percent of all shares in Japanese companies to be held by other companies in their conglomerate. These shares are never traded: Held off the market, they link the companies of a conglomerate together and make outsider takeovers of companies impossible. Organization goes further: Each member of a conglomerate heads a *keiretsu,* a hierarchy of subsidiaries, suppliers, distributors, and subcontractors. Small enterprises produce for firms higher up in their *keiretsu,* both protected from the market and dependent on the larger companies (van Wolferen, 1989, pp. 34, 46–47).

In Japan this is called "the convoy system": Strong companies (the big ships) protect and help weak companies (the little ships) with which they sail, often at the bidding of the ministries, so all survive. In the financial crisis of the 90s, strong banks held up the weak ones, and that meant that banks which had made too many bad loans were not permitted to fail and the whole economy was burdened by an unresolved banking crisis. Of course, it also meant that bank employees' jobs were protected, and the businesses that couldn't keep up payments on their loans were protected too. Even within a company, protecting managers and workers, customers, and vendors takes precedence over maximizing profits for shareholders (Safire, p. 16; Kristof, July 15, 1997, pp. A1, A6).

The Elected Government

The official institutions of Japanese power, that is, the legislature, the political parties, the prime minister, the cabinet, and the electorate, are probably the weakest partner in Japan's ruling triumvirate. This was especially true after 1993 when the long domination of the Liberal Democratic Party (the LDP) began to weaken, without other strong parties emerging.

For forty years, the LDP held power and dominated Japanese politics, running what was essentially a single-party system. The LDP was a vote-getting machine: Politicians treated politics as the business of getting elected. The legislature seldom legislated. The prime minister was often a relative unknown installed by behind-the-scenes kingmakers and had very limited power; and the cabinet served a merely ceremonial function, automatically approving policies developed by the bureaucrats (van Wolferen, pp. 45, 110).

So what do Japanese politicians really do? What power do they have? Politicians are mostly engaged in what Americans call "pork barrel politics"—securing government funding for their constituents in exchange for political support (Kristof, July 5, 1998, p. A4; Ogawa, p. 4). Politicians play the role of go-between linking citizens with business and bureaucrats and helping all three groups informally trade favors and influence each other. The politics of the construction industry illustrates this relationship. The Ministry of Construction controls licenses for the entire industry, and it has a huge budget to spend on government construction. It has spent over $6 trillion in the last nine years alone, building bridges, railroads, airports, museums, dams, and roads. Politicians, especially those from rural areas, use their contacts in the ministry to get construction projects approved for their home districts. Then the communities that elected them benefit from jobs and local spending. These contracts are really important. Ten percent of the Japanese labor force is employed in construction, and these workers have loyally voted for the LDP. Local construction companies are big contributors to political campaign funds, and they are rewarded with contracts. Then politicians reward retired construction ministry bureaucrats by helping them gain election to the Diet (the legislature), reinforcing the connections between politicians and the ministry (van Wolferen, pp. 114–120; Strom, July 8, 2001, p. 16).

SOCIAL CHANGE AND THE FUTURE

What will happen to Japan in the future? Will the economy recover fully? Will crime rates continue to rise? Will birthrates keep falling? Will young women remain selfish "*wagamama* girls"? Will young "freeters" continue to scorn traditional careers? Westerners, particularly Americans, tend to assume that Japan has embarked on a sort of inevitable process of becoming more and more like the United States. They expect its economy to become more of a free enterprise system, its government more voter oriented, its men and women more individualistic. If you are familiar with the American context, Japan today will remind you of the 1960s in the United States, with its rapid social change, disillusionment with government and business, challenges to gender roles, rebellious youth, dropouts, and hippies. But let the comparison be your guide: In the United States, the revolutionary days of the 1960s were followed by decades of reaction, in which the society became more religious, more conservative and business oriented, and traditional gender roles and "family values" were reinvigorated. Which way will Japan go: towards continued liberalization? Or towards a conservative reaction?

John Nathan argues that Japan is actually going in both directions at the same time: in one direction, towards a greater emphasis on individualism and personal fulfillment, and in the opposite direction, towards a revival of nationalism, militarism, and self-sacrifice. Popular new politicians who threaten to shake up Japan's established power structures head up each of these tendencies.

The Individualists

The best-known symbol of the new individualism is Yasuo Tanaka, first elected governor of Nagano Prefecture in 2000. Tanaka is an eccentric figure, a playboy novelist, known for his tight leather suits, who decided to run for governor just six weeks prior to the election. In the campaign Tanaka declared that he stood for "a call for individualism and a triumph for the citizens' movement." He told John Nathan, "I want people to think for themselves and to take responsibility for transforming their society into the place they want it to be" (Nathan, p. 214). Now Tanaka travels through his rural district holding novel town meetings. He has built a new symbolically "transparent" glass-walled office on the ground floor of the government building. Visitors can stand in a waiting room next door and watch him work at his desk, meet with his staff, or eat his lunch (Nathan, pp. 214–215; Strom, Jan. 10, 2001, p. A4; Sims, April 18, 2000, p. A10; *The Economist,* June 16, 2001, pp. 41–42).

After taking office Tanaka fired off a frontal attack on Japan's pork-barrel politics by canceling a $240 million dam project. Preserving the environment, he said, was more important than collecting government subsidies (Nathan, p. 217). Inspired, in part, by Tanaka, citizens groups are springing up all over Japan to oppose government construction projects: dams, nuclear power plants, high speed trains, bridges, etc. They say these projects are a waste of taxpayer money and a boondoggle, in which the construction companies that get the contracts make political donations to the politicians. The opposition is environmentalist. People see huge construction projects despoiling the countryside of Japan (French, Jan. 20, 2000, p. A4, Sept. 24, 2000, p. 22). In Teshima, locals succeeded in getting rid of a toxic waste dump after a 25-year battle. In Fukushima and Nigata, organized residents insisted on enhanced safety procedures for nuclear power plants (French, July 2, 2003, p. A9; *The Economist,* June 16, 2001, pp. 37–38; April 19, 2003, p. 41). More maverick governors have been elected, several of them women, most allied with local activist movements. This is a pretty dramatic break with the past. Up to now, Japan's 47 prefectural governors had generally been in the pocket of the Home Affairs Ministry, which controls their budgets. In fact, half of the governors are still ex-bureaucrats. Local activism is quite radical in Japanese society. It challenges the traditional Japanese trust in central authority and obedience to authority that is taught from childhood. Perhaps more profoundly, local activists must overcome their reluctance to make a fuss, to criticize, to create conflict, rupturing the social harmony (French, July 18, 2000, p. 6).

Protest and Change

The individualist perspective is heard on many issues in Japan today. In 2002 the government instituted a new computerized national registry that assigned each citizen an 11-digit number. It was met by widespread protest and complaints that the system would violate individual privacy. Yokohama and half a dozen smaller cities refused to participate (Brooke, Aug. 6, 2002, p. A3). Some young radical politicians have pressed for "free market" deregulation of Japan's economy to cut the whole web of interlocking relationships between government and business. The Ministry of Education itself decided that Japanese schools are too regimented, stifling individualism and producing people who are good at getting along in organizations, or following orders, but lack creativity and enterprise. In 2002 the ministry cut out one-third of the required elementary and junior high school curriculum and ended Saturday morning classes. This "sunshine approach," they said would give children more time to think for themselves (French, Feb. 25, 2001, p. 6; *The Economist,* Dec. 16, 2000, p. 48).

The Neonationalists

Shintaro Ishihara, the provocative governor of Tokyo is Japan's leading nationalist, or as he would say, "patriot." Governor of Tokyo is an important position in Japan, with more power than an ordinary city mayor and great influence over all of Japan. In national polls in 1999 and 2000, respondents called Ishihara Japan's most effective leader (Nathan, p. 184). In Ishihara's view, the problem with Japan is that the nation has become weak and the people have lost their confidence. Japan needs to rediscover its proud national heritage, Ishihara says, and restore the traditional values that put the nation, the emperor, loyalty, and duty before individual needs.

Ishihara traces Japan's problems to the nation's humiliating subservience to the United States. Japan is still apologizing, he says, for its supposed misdeeds in World War II, while no one mentions the cruelty of the U.S. firebombing of Tokyo and the atomic bombing of Hiroshima and Nagasaki. Alone among the world's important nations, Japan has a constitutional provision that forbids the use of military force except in self-defense and forbids the development of nuclear weapons. The neonationalists propose changing the constitution to allow Japan to use military force at will, and about 60 percent of the population supports the idea. The neonationalists supported sending Japanese troops to Iraq. They want Japan to be more assertive with North Korea and China. Ishihara and his allies are also quite anti-immigrant. In 2000, Ishihara asked troops stationed in Tokyo to be ready to intervene in case immigrants from China, Taiwan, and Korea rioted following an earthquake (Nathan, p. 192; French, July 22, 2003, p. A1; Onishi, Nov. 19, 2003, p. A1; French, June 8, 2002, pp. 1, 4).

For many Japanese, especially older people, this kind of talk evokes the militarism of the World War II era. They find it frightening and repellent; pacifism has been engrained in Japan since the Occupation. But many people are sympathetic to the neonationalist nostalgia for a time of greater national confidence and glory. They are tired of being ashamed of their past. They like Ishihara's plan to take Yokata Air Base back from the United States and his plan to tighten discipline for Japan's newly unruly students (Nathan, p. 185). Prime Minister Koizumi has adopted some of the neonationalist approach, approving new history textbooks that praise Japan's pre-1945 military past and leave out atrocities committed in Korea and China. Koizumi also set off a storm of controversy and protests from China by visiting Yasukuni Shrine, a Shinto shrine honoring Japan's war dead, including some convicted war criminals (French, July 26, 2001, p. A8). The neonationalists seem to suggest that if a more assertive Japan could rally its people behind some grand national enterprise, devotion to duty and a sense of belonging would return.

Japan and Asia

One thing seems certain: However the conflict between conservative neonationalists and liberal individualists plays out, Japanese society, economy, and culture are experiencing an important reorientation, away from the United States and towards Asia. Japan spent the whole second half of the twentieth century working out its relationship to the United States—first as an occupied nation, then as a host for U.S. bases, junior ally, and economic competitor. The United States was Japan's best market and its cultural ideal. Every Japanese schoolchild learned English, and hundreds of English "loan-words" worked their way into Japanese, along with McDonalds, Kentucky Fried Chicken, Hollywood movies, and country and western bands. But now, the Japanese are losing interest in the United States. Attention is shifting to Asia, both culturally and economically.

A Cultural Shift

John Nathan notices a process of disillusionment with the United States in Japan. The neonationalists' constant criticism of Japanese dependence on the United States has had an effect. There are now TV shows and comedians that make fun of Americans. And many Japanese have been offended by comparisons of the 9/11 attack with the Japanese assault on Pearl Harbor, and by American insistence on the enormity of its losses. Japanese movies and films from China, Korea, and other Asian countries have been gaining audiences in Japan, while Hollywood blockbusters attract fewer viewers. Vietnamese restaurants and Chinese teahouses have replaced American chain cafes as the "in" places for young people. More people are studying Chinese and Russian, and tours to China are now more popular than travel to the United States (Nathan, pp. 240–243).

An Economic Shift

Now that China is growing in importance in the global economy, it is no surprise that China's economic importance to Japan is also growing. Some people say that China is the engine of Japan's present economic recovery (and that if growth in China slackens, Japan will fall back into recession). China (and to a lesser extent Russia and southeast Asia) plays a dual role for Japan, both as a location for cheap manufacture of Japanese products and as a market for Japanese goods (Onishi, Jan. 19, 2005, p. A4).

Wages in Japan are 20 to 30 times higher than wages in China, where a very good factory job pays $95 a month. So Japanese companies have swallowed their scruples about lifetime security for Japanese workers and moved manufacturing, particularly low-cost mass production of simple products, overseas to China. Since 1991, Japan has lost 2.5 million manufacturing jobs—a 25 percent decline—some to overseas production and some to automation. It has done wonders for company profits. Some jobs, like chip assembly, which are done in Japan by robots, can be done more cheaply in China by female workers. Honda and Toyota are rapidly expanding production in China and the electronics industry is quickly doing the same. Japanese companies now do about one-sixth of their manufacturing abroad (compared to more than a quarter of American manufacturing). Japanese businesses have tried, however to keep the most sophisticated and precise high-tech production at home, both to preserve the best jobs for their own people and to guard against theft of trade secrets in China (Belson, Feb. 17, 2004, pp. W1, W4; Brooke, July 11, 2002, pp. W1, W7; Belson, Oct. 21, 2003, pp. C1, C4; *The Economist,* April 10, 2004, pp. 57–59).

At the same time, China is growing in importance as a market for Japanese goods. With its population of two billion, China is a huge market, and its people are just beginning to buy consumer goods. Imagine two billion people buying their first refrigerators, cell phones, cars, and computers! China and the rest of Asia now account for 48 percent of Japan's exports. The U.S. share is down to 24 percent. Also, many Japanese factories in China are producing for the Chinese market. Other Japanese companies are selling capital goods—machinery used to produce other goods—to Chinese entrepreneurs (*The Economist,* Nov. 29, 2003, p. 38; Brooke, Nov. 21, 2003, pp. W1, W7).

Japan Looks East

Overall, Japan's reorientation to Asia is clear. Japanese companies need to know more about China in order to adapt their products to the Chinese market. Some companies are beginning to hire Chinese communications technology specialists to work in Japan on designing export products (Asahi Shimbum, June 7, 2004). Other Japanese companies are planning to move some of their research and development operations to China, for the same reason. There are even Japanese managers and engineers, many of them middle-aged people forced into early retirement, who now work in China for lower pay. (Brooke, April 21, 2002, pp. BU1, BU11; Nathan, p. 246). Eastern Russia is even closer to Japan geographically than is China. Japanese used cars are increasingly finding their way to Russia, and Japanese companies are rapidly investing in Russia's far east, especially in oil and gas production, and in a pipeline that will bring oil from the interior to a port in Sakhalin near Japan (Brooke, Nov. 21, 2003, pp. W1, W7; June 30, 2004, pp. W1, W7; Feb. 12, 2003, pp. C1, C6).

Japan's new relationship to Asia is stimulating anticipation and fear in about equal measure. Kenichi Ohmae, author of *China Impact,* published in Japan in 2002, argues that "for most of its history Japan has been a peripheral country to China. . . . In the future, Japan will be to China what Canada is to the United States, what Austria is to Germany, what Ireland is to Britain" (Brooke, Nov. 21, 2002, pp. BU1, BU11). For the neonationalists, China looms as an economic competitor, a possible military threat, and the ally of an unpredictable (and probably nuclear-armed) enemy—North Korea. A series of recent incidents have heightened tensions between Japan and China. In 2004, a Chinese navy nuclear submarine was discovered in Japanese waters and chased out by the Japanese navy. Later, Prime Minister Koizumi called for cuts in Japan's foreign aid to China and a 2005 government military document described China as a potential threat (Onishi, Jan. 19, 2005, p. A4). The government's increasingly assertive posture towards China has delighted the neonationalists by offering a vision of a new national mission, a crusade to assert Japan's interests, one that might have the potential of unifying the society again.

Thinking Sociologically

1. When you read Chapter 1, were you ethnocentric in your reaction to the Japanese?
2. Using a highlighter pen, go through pages 6 to 22 of Chapter 1. Highlight descriptions of Japanese values in blue and descriptions of norms in yellow. Are you confident you understand the difference between values and norms?
3. When some large American luxury cars were recently put on display in Tokyo, many Japanese shoppers said they wouldn't want to purchase them. "I would get a lot of attention if I drove that car," one woman said. Using what you now know about Japanese society, decide what kinds of cars you would choose to export to Japan if you were making this decision for an American auto company.
4. What are some Japanese values that contrast sharply with values in your own society?
5. What social groups are most important in the lives of the Japanese? What groups are most important in your life, in your society?
6. How are offices in your society physically arranged? (Are the desks separated, or all touching, as in Japan? Are there cubicles? Separate offices with doors?) Are offices in your society similar to Japanese offices or different? What kinds of interaction and attitudes does office arrangement in your society encourage?
7. Turn to Table 1.2 (p. 28) and compare homicide rates in Japan to those in the United States. Thinking sociologically, can you explain what causes the tremendous difference in these rates?
8. Are there any similarities in the roles of women in Japanese society and in your society? What differences are there?
9. Compare the educational system in your society with the educational system in Japan. Which system is more of a meritocracy?

For Further Reading

BELLAH, ROBERT, *Imagining Japan.* Berkeley: University of California Press, 2003.

BUMILLER, ELIZABETH, *The Secrets of Mariko: A Year in the Life of a Japanese Woman and Her Family.* New York: Times Books, Random House, 1995.

DOWER, JOHN W., *Embracing Defeat: Japan in the Wake of World War II.* New York: W. W. Norton and Co., 1999.

FEILER, BRUCE S., *Learning to Bow: An American Teacher in a Japanese School.* New York: Ticknor & Fields, 1991.

FOWLER, EDWARD, *San'ya Blues: Laboring Life in Contemporary Tokyo.* Ithaca: Cornell University Press, 1996.

FUKUZAWA, REBECCA ERWIN, AND GERALD K. LETENDRE, *Intense Years: How Japanese Adolescents Balance School, Family and Friends.* New York and London: Routledge Falmer, 2001.

LEWIS, CATHERINE C., *Educating Hearts and Minds: Reflections on Japanese Preschool and Elementary Education.* Cambridge: Cambridge University Press, 1995.

NATHAN, JOHN, *Japan Unbound: A Volatile Nation's Quest for Pride and Purpose.* Boston: Houghton Mifflin Company, 2004.

OSASAWARA, YUKO, *Office Ladies and Salaried Men: Power, Gender and Work in Japanese Companies.* Berkeley: University of California Press, 1998.

ROBERSON, JAMES E., AND NOBUE SUZUKI, eds., *Men and Masculinities in Contemporary Japan.* London and New York: RoutledgeCurzon, 2003.

SUGIMOTO, YOSHIO, *An Introduction to Japanese Society.* Cambridge: Cambridge University Press, 1997.

WHITE, MERRY ISAACS, *Perfectly Japanese: Making Families in an Era of Upheaval.* Berkeley: University of California Press, 2002.
YONEYAMA, SHOKO, *The Japanese High School: Silence and Resistance.* London and New York: Routledge, 1999.

Bibliography

Asahi Shimbun, "More Firms Put Directors' Retirement Bonus Out to Pasture," July 19, 2003.
———, "Chinese Recruits to Rise," June 7, 2004, Lexus Nexis Document, pp. 6–7 (last accessed Nov. 1, 2004).
BACHNIK, JANE, "Kejime, Defining a Shifting Self in Multiple Organizational Modes," in Nancy R. Rosenberger, ed., *Japanese Sense of Self.* Cambridge: Cambridge University Press, 1994.
BAYLEY, DAVID H., "The Forces of Order in Japan and in the United States," in Gregg Lee Carter, ed., *Empirical Approaches to Sociology.* New York: Macmillan, 1994, pp. 101–119.
BELLAH, ROBERT, *Imagining Japan.* Berkeley: University of California Press, 2003.
BELSON, KEN, "Japanese Capital and Jobs Flowing to China," *The New York Times,* Feb. 17, 2004, pp. C1, C7.
BERGER, PETER L., *Invitation to Sociology: A Humanistic Perspective.* New York: Doubleday Anchor, 1993.
BORNOFF, NICHOLAS, *Pink Samurai: Love, Marriage and Sex in Contemporary Japan.* New York: Simon & Schuster Pocket Books, 1991.
BRENDER, ALAN, "Six Members of Elite Student Club Plead Guilty to Rape in Tokyo," *Chronicle of Higher Education,* Oct. 3, 2003, p. A36.
BROOKE, JAMES, "Young Japanese Breaking Old Salaryman's Bonds," *The New York Times,* Oct. 16, 2001, p. A3.
———, "Japan Braces for a 'Designed in China' World," *The New York Times,* April 21, 2002, pp. BU1, BU11.
———, "Japan Carves Out Major Role in China's Auto Future," *The New York Times,* July 11, 2002, pp. W1, W7.
———, "Japan's Used Cars Find New Lives on Russian Roads," *The New York Times,* Feb. 12, 2003, pp. C1, C6.
———, "Japan in an Uproar as 'Big Brother' Computer File Kicks In," *The New York Times,* Aug. 6, 2003, p. A3.
———, "Japan's Recovering Economy Is Relying Heavily on China," *The New York Times,* Nov. 21, 2003, pp. W1, W7.
———, "Gas and Oil Bring Japanese Money to Russia's Far East," *The New York Times,* June 30, 2004, pp. W1, W7.
———, "Strangers in Life Join Hands in Death as the Web Becomes a Tool for Suicide in Japan," *The New York Times,* Oct. 18, 2004, p. A11.
BURUMA, IAN, *The Wages of Guilt: Memories of War in Germany and Japan.* New York: Farrar, Straus & Giroux, 1994.
CHAPMAN, WILLIAM, *Inventing Japan: The Making of a Postwar Civilization.* Englewood Cliffs, NJ: Prentice-Hall, 1991.
CHRISTOPHER, ROBERT C., *The Japanese Mind: The Goliath Explained.* New York: Simon & Schuster, 1983.
CONDON, JANE, *A Half Step Behind: Japanese Women of the Eighties.* New York: Dodd, Mead, 1985.
DOI, TAKEO, *The Anatomy of Dependence.* Tokyo: Kodansha, 1977.

DUKE, BENJAMIN, *The Japanese School.* New York: Praeger, 1986.

EARHART, H. BYRON, *Religions of Japan.* San Francisco: Harper & Row, 1984.

The Economist, "After Japan's Election: Sunset for the Men in Suits," July 1, 2000, pp. 26–28.

———, "Japan: Less Rote, More Variety," Dec. 16, 2000, p. 48.

———, "The Day of the Governors," June 16, 2001, pp. 41–42.

———, "Small Victories, Big Lessons," April 19, 2003, pp. 37–38.

———, "Crime in Japan, Insecure," Oct. 25, 2003, pp. 39–40.

———, "Learning to Love a Growing China," Nov. 29, 2003, pp. 38, 39.

———, "(Still) Made in Japan," April 10, 2004, pp. 57–59.

FEILER, BRUCE S., *Learning to Bow: An American Teacher in a Japanese School.* New York: Ticknor & Fields, 1991.

FORBES MAGAZINE, *The World's Richest People,* http://www.forbes.com/billionaires (last accessed Nov. 2, 2004).

FOWLER, EDWARD, *San'ya Blues: Laboring Life in Contemporary Tokyo.* Ithaca: Cornell University Press, 1996.

FRENCH, HOWARD W., "U.S. Copters? No, No, No. Not in Their Backyard," *The New York Times,* Jan. 20, 2000, p. A4.

———, "Japanese Trains Try to Shed a Gruesome Appeal," *The New York Times,* June 6, 2000, p. A4.

———, "Lone Voice No Longer, a Japanese Gadfly Catches On," *The New York Times,* June 18, 2000, p. 6.

———, "Japan's New Bullet Train Draws Fire," *The New York Times,* Sept. 24, 2000, p. 22.

———, "Brooding Over Its Homeless, Japan Sees a Broken System," *The New York Times,* Feb. 2, 2001, pp. A1, A8.

———, "More Sunshine for Japan's Overworked Students," *The New York Times,* Feb. 25, 2001, p. 6.

———, "Fighting Sex Harassment, and Stigma, in Japan," *The New York Times,* July 15, 2001, pp. 1, 10.

———, "Koizumi Plan to Visit Shrine Raises Warning from China," *The New York Times,* July 26, 2001, pp. A1, A8.

———, "Death Does Them Part (Wives Make Sure of That)," *The New York Times,* May 9, 2002, p. A4.

———, "Taboo against Nuclear Arms Is Being Challenged in Japan," *The New York Times,* June 9, 2002, pp. 1, 4.

———, "Educators Try to Tame Japan's Blackboard Jungles," *The New York Times,* Sept. 23, 2002, p. A6.

———, "Teaching Japan's Salarymen to Be Their Own Men," *The New York Times,* Nov. 27, 2002, p. A4.

———, "As Japan's Women Move Up, Many Are Moving Out," *The New York Times,* March 25, 2003, p. A3.

———, "Japanese Cult Vows to Save a Seal and the World," *The New York Times,* May 14, 2003, p. A10.

———, "Japanese Winning Cleanup Battles," *The New York Times,* July 2, 2003, p. A9.

———, "Japan Faces Burden: Its Own Defense," *The New York Times,* July 22, 2003, pp. A1, A7.

———, "Insular Japan Needs, but Resists, Immigration," *The New York Times,* July 24, 2003, pp. A1, A3.

FUCINI, JOSEPH J., AND SUZY FUCINI, *Working for the Japanese: Inside Mazda's American Auto Plant.* New York: Macmillan, Free Press, 1990.

FUKUTAKE, TADASHI, *Japanese Society Today,* 2d ed. Tokyo: University of Tokyo Press, 1981.

FUKUZAWA, REBECCA ERWIN, AND GERALD K. LETENDRE, *Intense Years: How Japanese Adolescents Balance School, Family and Friends.* New York and London: Routledge Falmer, 2001.

GARON, SHELDON, *Molding Japanese Minds: The State in Everyday Life.* Princeton: Princeton University Press, 1997.

HENDRY, JOY, *Marriage in a Changing Japan: Community and Society.* New York: St. Martin's Press, 1981.

HENSLIN, JAMES, *Essentials of Sociology,* 5th ed. Boston: Pearson, 2004.

HIROMI, MORI, *Immigration Policy and Foreign Workers in Japan.* New York: St. Martin's Press, 1997.

HIRSCHI, TRAVIS, *Causes of Delinquency.* Berkeley: University of California Press, 1969.

HOLLOWAY, SUSAN D., *Contested Childhood: Diversity and Change in Japanese Preschools.* London and New York: Routledge, 2000.

INOUE, SHOICHI, "Religions Old and New," in Atsushi Ueda, ed., *The Electric Geisha: Exploring Japan's Popular Culture.* Tokyo: Kodansha International, 1994, pp. 220–228.

ISHIDA, HIROSHI, *Social Mobility in Contemporary Japan.* Stanford, CA: Stanford University Press, 1993.

ISHIDA, TAKESHI, *Japanese Political Culture: Change and Continuity.* New Brunswick, NJ: Transaction Books, 1983.

IWAO, SUMIKO, *The Japanese Woman: Traditional Image and Changing Reality.* New York: Free Press, 1993.

THE JAPAN INSTITUTE FOR LABOUR POLICY AND TRAINING, *The Labour Situation in Japan, 2002/2003,* http://www.jil.go.jp/english/laborinfo/library/situation2003.htm (last accessed Nov. 8, 2004).

———, *Japan Working Life Profile, 2003,* http://www.jil.go.jp.english/laborinfo/library/index.htm (last accessed Nov. 2, 2004).

JAPAN MINISTRY OF JUSTICE, "Number of Non-Japanese Residents in Japan by Country," *Statistics on Foreign Residents,* 2002.

———, *Statistics on Foreign Residents, 2003.*

Japan Statistical Yearbook, 2002, http://www.stat.go.jp/english/data/nenkan/1431-25.htm (last accessed Nov. 8, 2004).

Japan Today, "Living in an Era of 'Freeters'," Feb. 6, 2004, http://www.japantoday.com/e/?content=kuchikomi&id=284.

JOLIVET, MURIEL, *Japan: The Childless Society? The Crisis of Motherhood.* London and New York: Routledge, 1997.

KAMBAYASHI, TAKEHIKO, "A Defender for Japan's Battered Women," *Christian Science Monitor,* Feb. 4, 2004, p. 11.

KATO, RYOKO, "Japanese Women: Subordination or Domination," in James Curtis and Lorne Tepperman, eds., *Haves and Have-Nots: An International Reader on Social Inequality.* Englewood Cliffs, NJ: Prentice-Hall, 1994.

KOSUGI, REIKO, "The Transition from School to Work: Understanding the Increase in Freeter and Jobless Youth, *Japan Labor Review,* Vol. 1, no. 1 (Winter 2004), pp. 52–67.

KRISTOF, NICHOLAS D., "Japanese Say No to Crime: Tough Methods, at a Price," *The New York Times,* May 14, 1995, pp. 1, 8.

KRISTOF, NICHOLAS D., "Empty Isles Are Signs Japan's Sun Might Dim," *The New York Times,* Aug. 1, 1999, pp. 1, 4.

———, "A Neighborly Style of Police State," *The New York Times,* June 4, 1995, p. E5.

———, "Real Capitalism Breaks Japan's Old Rules," *The New York Times,* July 15, 1997, pp. A1, A8.

————, "Japan Voters Send Message: No Change," *The New York Times,* July 5, 1998, p. A4.

KUWAYAMA, TAKAMI, "The Reference Other Orientation," in Nancy L. Rosenberger, ed., *Japanese Sense of Self.* Cambridge: Cambridge University Press, 1994, pp. 121–151.

LEBLANC, ROBIN M., *Bicycle Citizens: The Political World of the Japanese Housewife.* Berkeley: University of California Press, 1999.

LEBRA, TAKIE SUGIYAMA, *Japanese Women: Constraint and Fulfillment.* Honolulu: University of Hawaii Press, 1984.

————, ed., *Japanese Social Organization.* Honolulu: University of Hawaii Press, 1992.

LEESTMA, ROBERT, *Japanese Education Today.* U.S. Department of Education, Washington, DC: Government Printing Office, 1987.

LEWIS, CATHERINE C., *Educating Hearts and Minds: Reflections on Japanese Preschool and Elementary Education.* Cambridge: Cambridge University Press, 1995.

LO, JEANNIE, *Office Ladies, Factory Women: Life and Work at a Japanese Company.* Armonk, NY: M. E. Sharpe, 1990.

MAINICHI DAILY NEWS, "Yakuza Place Want Ads to Find New Blood," Nov. 16, 2003, p. 1 http://mdn.mainichi.co.jp/ (last accessed Nov. 4, 2004).

Mainichi Interactive, "Ex-Elite Students Admit to Gang Rape," Sept. 17, 2003, http://www12.mainichi.co.jp/news/mdn/search-news/902078/rape20trial-0-5.html (last accessed April 20, 2004).

————, "Best and Brightest on Rape Rampage," Dec. 27, 2003 file://E:NEWFOL~1\ Global03\Japan\JAPANE~1\BESTAN~1.HTM (last accessed June 4, 2004).

MARKOFF, JOHN, "Rebel Wants Japan's Inventors to Get Some U.S.-Style Rewards," *The New York Times,* Sept. 18, 2001, pp. C1, C4.

MARTINEZ, D. P., ed., *The Worlds of Japanese Popular Culture: Gender, Shifting Boundaries and Global Cultures.* Cambridge: Cambridge University Press, 1998.

MASUI, SHIGEO, "Back to Basics to Beat Crime," *Daily Yomiuri,* Jan. 18, 2003, http://www.yomiuri.co.jp/index-e.htm (last accessed Nov. 2, 2004).

MATHEWS, GORDON, "Can a Real Man Live for His Family?" in ROBERSON and SUZUKI, EDS., *Men and Masculinities in Contemporary Japan.* London and New York: RoutledgeCurzon, 2003, pp. 109–125.

MCGREGOR, RICHARD, *Japan Swings: Politics, Culture and Sex in the New Japan.* Tokyo: Yenbooks, 1996.

MERTON, ROBERT K., *Social Theory and Social Structure,* enlarged edition. New York: Free Press, 1968.

NAKANE, CHIE, *Japanese Society.* Berkeley: University of California Press, 1970.

NATHAN, JOHN, *Japan Unbound: A Volatile Nation's Quest for Pride and Purpose.* Boston: Houghton Mifflin Company, 2004.

NATIONAL INSTITUTE OF POPULATION AND SOCIAL SECURITY RESEARCH, JAPAN, *The Second National Survey on Family in Japan Report,* March 2000, http://www.ipss.go.jp/English/ nsf (last accessed Nov. 2, 2004).

OGASAWARA, YUKO, *Office Ladies and Salaried Men: Power, Gender and Work in Japanese Companies.* Berkeley: University of California Press, 1998.

OGAWA, AKIO, "Public Works Opposed, But System Hard to Break," *Asahi Evening News,* July 19, 1998.

OKANO, KAORI, AND MOTONORI TSUCHIYA, *Education in Contemporary Japan: Inequality and Diversity.* Cambridge: Cambridge University Press, 1999.

ONISHI, NORIMITSU, "Japan Heads to Iraq, Haunted by Taboo Bred in Another War," *The New York Times,* Nov. 19, 2003, pp. A1, A4.

————, "Never Lost, but Found Daily: Japanese Honesty," *The New York Times,* Jan. 8, 2004, pp. A1, A4.

———, "This 21st-Century Japan, More Contented Than Driven," *The New York Times,* Feb. 4, 2004, p. A4.

———, "The Japan-China Stew: Sweet and Sour," *The New York Times,* Jan. 19, 2005, p. A4.

———, "Mood Sours for Japan's Other Asian Students," *The New York Times,* March 28, 2004, p. 3.

———, "An Aging Island Embraces Japan's Young Dropouts," *The New York Times,* June 6, 2004, p. 3.

ORENSTEIN, PEGGY, "Parasites in Pret-a-Porter," *The New York Times Magazine,* July 1, 2001, pp. 31–35.

PEARSON, BRENDAN, "Japan Despairs of Dying Trends," *Australian Financial Review,* Jan. 23, 2004, p. 44.

PHARR, SUSAN J., *Losing Face: Status Politics in Japan.* Berkeley: University of California Press, 1990.

RECKLESS, WALTER, *The Crime Problem,* 5th ed. New York: Appleton, 1973.

REISCHAUER, EDWIN O., *The Japanese.* Cambridge, MA: Harvard University Press, 1977.

———, *The Japanese Today: Change and Continuity.* Cambridge, MA: Harvard University Press, 1988.

ROBERSON, JAMES E., AND NOBUE SUZUKI, eds., *Men and Masculinities in Contemporary Japan.* London and New York: RoutledgeCurzon, 2003.

ROBERTSON, JENNIFER, *Takarazuka: Sexual Politics and Popular Culture in Modern Japan.* Berkeley: University of California Press, 1998.

ROHLEN, THOMAS P., *Japan's High Schools.* Berkeley: University of California Press, 1983.

ROHLEN, THOMAS P., AND GERALD K. LETENDRE, eds., *Teaching and Learning in Japan.* New York: Cambridge University Press, 1998.

ROSENBERGER, NANCY R., ed., *Japanese Sense of Self.* Cambridge: Cambridge University Press, 1994.

SAFIRE, WILLIAM, "Ratcheting Up the Periscope," *The New York Times Magazine,* July 21, 1998, p. 16.

SANGER, DAVID E., "Best College Money Can Buy (Can It Be Bought?)," *The New York Times,* June 24, 1991, p. 4.

SESSER, STAN, "Hidden Death," *The New Yorker,* Nov. 14, 1994, pp. 62–89.

SHIH, BRIAN, "Yakuza, The Japanese Mob," *National Public Radio,* weekend edition, May 15, 2004.

SIMS, CALVIN, "Behold, the Fragrant Japanese Man!" *The New York Times,* March 17, 2000, p. A8.

———, "Japan's Employers Are Giving Bonuses for Having Babies," *The New York Times,* May 30, 2000, pp. A1, A8.

SMITH, JESSICA, "Bullying within the Japanese Workplace," *Minnesota Public Radio, Marketplace,* Sept. 17, 2003.

SMITH, ROBERT J., *Japanese Society: Tradition, Self and the Social Order.* Cambridge: Cambridge University Press, 1983.

STERNGOLD, JAMES, "Mob and Politics Intersect, Fueling Cynicism in Japan," *The New York Times,* Oct. 21, 1992, pp. A1, A6.

STROM, STEPHANIE, "Japanese Family Values: I Choose You, Pikachu!" *The New York Times,* Nov. 7, 1999, p. WK4.

———, "Governors Taking a New Broom to Japan's Politics," *The New York Times,* Jan. 10, 2001, p. A3.

———, "The Twist of Koizumi's Reforms: Supporters Could Suffer," *The New York Times,* July 27, 2001, p. A3.

SUGIMOTO, YOSHIO, *An Introduction to Japanese Society.* Cambridge: Cambridge University Press, 1997.

TASKER, PETER, *The Japanese: Portrait of a Nation.* New York: Penguin Books, New American Library, 1987.

TOBIN, JOSEPH, "Japanese Preschools and the Pedagogy of Selfhood," in Nancy R. Rosenberger, ed., *Japanese Sense of Self.* Cambridge: Cambridge University Press, 1994.

UEDA, ATSUSHI, "How Bureaucrats Manage Society," in Atsushi Ueda, ed., *The Electric Geisha: Exploring Japan's Popular Culture.* Tokyo: Kodansha International, 1994, pp. 127–138.

UNITED NATIONS, *Human Development Report, 2001,* http://www.undp.ord/hydro/highlights/statistics.html.

THE UNITED NATIONS OFFICE ON CRIME AND DRUGS, *United Nations Surveys of Crime Trends, 1990–2000,* http://www.unodc.org/unodc/crime_cicp_survey_seventh.html (last accessed Nov. 7, 2004).

UNITED NATIONS POPULATION DIVISION, DEPARTMENT OF ECONOMIC AND SOCIAL AFFAIRS, *Replacement Migration: Is It a Solution to Declining and Ageing Populations?,* March 21, 2000.

U.S. BUREAU OF JUSTICE STATISTICS, *Homicide Trends in the U.S., 2002,* http://www.ojp.usdoj.gov/bjs/homicide/tables/totalstab.htm (last accessed Nov. 3, 2004).

VAN WOLFEREN, KAREL, *The Enigma of Japanese Power: People and Politics in a Stateless Nation.* New York: Knopf, 1989.

WASWO, ANN, *Modern Japanese Society, 1868–1994.* Oxford: Oxford University Press, 1996.

Web-Japan, "What Do You Think of 'Freeters'?", Feb. 4, 2002, http://web-japan.org/trends01/article/020204fear.html.

———, "Chushingura: Loyalty That Never Goes Out of Style," Feb. 2, 2003, http://web-japan.org/trends01/index.html.

WEINER, MYRON AND TADASHI HANAMI, eds., *Temporary Workers or Future Citizens: Japanese and U.S. Migration Policies.* New York: New York University Press, 1998.

WEISMAN, STEVEN R., "In Japan, Bias Is an Obstacle Even for the Ethnic Japanese," *The New York Times,* Nov. 13, 1991, pp. A1, A10.

WHITE, MERRY, *The Material Child: Coming of Age in Japan and America.* New York: Free Press, 1993.

WHITE, MERRY ISAACS, *Perfectly Japanese: Making Families in an Era of Upheaval.* Berkeley: University of California Press, 2002.

WILDEMAN, JOHN, "Crime and Crime Control in Modern Japan," unpublished material.

WORLD BANK, *World Development Indicators, 2004,* http://www.worldbank.org/data/wdi2004/cdrom/loi.html (last accessed Nov. 5, 2004).

WORLD HEALTH ORGANIZATION, *Statistical Information System,* http://www3.who.int/whosis.

WRAY, HARRY, *Japanese and American Education: Attitudes and Practices.* Westport, CT: Bergin and Garvey, 1999.

WUDUNN, SHERYL, "The Japan Bank Alarm," *The New York Times,* Oct. 29, 1995, p. E14.

———, "Two Top Japanese Bank Inspectors Arrested and Accused in Bribery," *The New York Times,* Jan. 27, 1998, pp. D1, D7.

———, "A No Pan Shabu Shabu Scandal in the Ministry of Finance," *The New York Times,* March 17, 1998.

———, "Like the Geisha, the Good-Time Bar Is Endangered," *The New York Times,* May 19, 1998, p. A4.

YONEYAMA, SHOKO, *The Japanese High School: Silence and Resistance.* London and New York: Routledge, 1999.

You can fly to Mexico from New York in five hours, from London in ten, or you can walk across a border bridge from Texas in five minutes. You will find yourself in a society created from two clashing cultures: the Native American culture of Mexico and the Spanish culture of the European conquerors.

LOCATION: Mexico is a North American country, just south of the American states of Texas, New Mexico, Arizona, and California. Mexico is bordered on the east by the Gulf of Mexico and on the west by the Pacific. To the south Mexico borders Guatemala and Belize.

AREA: One-fifth the size of the United States or Canada, Mexico (756,000 square miles or 2,128,600 square kilometers) is four times the size of Germany.

LAND: A rugged, mountainous country. Mexico City, the country's capital, is several thousand feet above sea level.

CLIMATE: Hot, humid, and tropical in the south; arid and desertlike in the north. Temperatures cool as one climbs higher. The year alternates between rainy and dry seasons.

POPULATION: 2000: 102 million people. 21.6 million people live in the capital. The population is relatively young. One-third of the population is under the age of 15.

INCOME: U.S. $6,320 GDP per person per year in 2002. 23 percent live in absolute poverty.

EDUCATION: 89 percent of adult women and 93 percent of adult men are literate.

RELIGION: 93 percent are Roman Catholic; 3 percent are Protestant.

MINORITIES: 7 million people (8 percent of the population) belong to indigenous Indian groups, including the Nahua, the Zapotec, the Maya, the Totonac, the Mixtec, and many smaller populations.

CHAPTER TWO

Mexico: Nation of Networks

INTRODUCTION

Visitors to Teotihuacán, the ancient Indo-American ruins 25 miles northeast of Mexico City, come upon richly carved walls, crammed with intricate patterns, picked out in sharp relief by the bright sunlight of the mountains. These stone carvings might well symbolize Mexico itself, a diverse society marked by strong social and cultural contrasts. There are many Mexicos: urban and rural, rich and poor, European and Indo-American.

Mexico City is a twenty-first century megacity (Kandell, p. 8): It points the way to the problems of urbanization increasingly visible all over the world. Twenty million people live crowded into Mexico City's high, mountain-ringed valley: in apartment towers, leafy middle-class suburbs, and squatter shantytowns. They jam its highways, buses, subways, and markets, their cars spewing out a toxic haze of air pollution, their accumulating sewage and garbage a constant hazard. But when city people go home to visit their relatives in the countryside, they find a very different way of life. Most villages now have electricity and roads, but the modern world is distant. People grow the food they eat, often without machinery, and build their own houses; some wear traditional Indian dress. In the most remote villages, paths, not streets, link the houses; there are seldom any newspapers, and perhaps not even a telephone.

Even in Mexico City, the rich and the poor live so differently they might inhabit different societies. A rich teenager may drive an imported car, live in his family's air-conditioned house, wear European designer clothes, and dance at a club built to look as much as possible like one in New York or Los Angeles. The family's maid will probably travel four hours a day on packed buses and trains, returning at night to a one-room shanty with a bare light bulb (wired illegally to a city streetlight), a single mattress, and no refrigerator or running water.

Understanding Mexico: The Conflict Perspective

Mexican society seems to call for analysis with the **conflict perspective.** When we examine Mexico, we see all sorts of divisions and disagreements within the society. Diverse groups struggle for control of scarce resources and justify their claims with conflicting worldviews. Those who hold power use it to dominate others and to protect their own privileges. Disagreement about values is common. A conflict theorist, looking at Mexico's long history, would contend that conflict and value **dissensus** (disagreement, the opposite of consensus) are the normal condition of society, and any period of order is really a period of domination by one or another ruling group.

MEXICAN HISTORY

In order to better understand both the conflict perspective and Mexican society, you must first know something about Mexico's dramatic history. Mexicans themselves believe that their history holds the key to their character, and they relish its romance and extravagance. In every period in Mexican history, different groups struggled to control society so as to benefit themselves. Mexico's history is divided by dramatic events into three clearly marked periods: the pre-Columbian, the colonial, and the modern.

The Pre-Columbian Period (c. 300 B.C.–A.D. 1519)

The earliest period of Mexican history was the longest: This was the pre-Columbian period (c. 300 B.C.–A.D. 1519) when the great Maya and Aztec and other Indo-American empires ruled Central America. By the first century B.C., there were great civilizations in Mexico, the equal of anything in Europe. The Indo-Americans built large cities, developed sophisticated systems of writing and mathematics, kept astronomy records, and built monumental works of architecture. These empires also fought frequent wars to subjugate neighboring peoples and make them pay **tribute** (goods that conquered people had to pay to their conquerors) and also to take captives who were made into slaves or sacrificed to the gods (Rudolph, pp. 5–8; Ruiz, pp. 18–20).

The Aztecs

The last Indo-American empire was that of the Aztecs, who rose to power in the fourteenth century. Dedicated to conquest, the Aztecs glorified fighting and bravery. Nobles ruled and merchants enjoyed a relatively high status, but commoners, conquered people, and slaves labored hard to build the gleaming pyramids, roads, and aqueducts of their capital, Tenochtitlán (site of today's Mexico City). The Aztecs exacted more and more tribute from subject peoples to make their gorgeous feathered cloaks and jewelry, and the resentment and hatred of the conquered peoples grew (Ruiz, p. 24; Rudolph, p. 14; Kandell, pp. 49–54).

The Conquest

The pre-Columbian period in Mexico ended in a new episode of struggle and domination in 1519, the year of the Spanish Conquest. Aztec religion predicted periodic destruction and renewal of the world, with the next destruction predicted for the year 1519. Legend held that at that time the white-skinned Quetzalcoátl (god of the earlier Toltec people) would return from the sea and take back his empire from the Aztecs and their god, Huitzilopochtli. The prophecy proved uncannily accurate, since in 1519 Aztec society was indeed destroyed—but at the hands of the Spanish *conquistadors,* led by Hernán Cortés.

The Spaniards. At the time of the Conquest, Spanish society had much in common with Aztec society: Both were shaped by war and religion. The most important force in Spain was the *Reconquista,* the politico-military "crusade" to recapture all of Spain from the Muslims or "Moors" who had ruled it for seven centuries. Under the leadership of Ferdinand and Isabella, Granada, the last bastion of the Moors, was reconquered in 1492. The crusader mentality glorified war and looked down upon agriculture and manufacture, which it associated with the Moors, and also looked down on finance, associated with the despised Jews (expelled from Spain in 1492). Spanish warriors found it proper to live off the labor of those they conquered, the crown rewarding them with land grants and "infidel" serfs.

Cortés and Moctezuma. Hernán Cortés was the very model of a conquistador, thirsting for adventure, greedy for gold, aggressive, brave, and ruthless. He was a brilliant strategist, able to switch gears instantly and turn misfortune to advantage. In 1519, at the age of 33, Cortés assembled 11 ships, 500 soldiers, 100 sailors, 200 Cuban Indians, weapons, and 16 horses and sailed from Cuba for the Yucatán (the southeastern coast of Mexico).

Cortés' invading force was tiny, compared to the military might of the Aztecs. Three special weaknesses made the Conquest possible. First was the power of ideas: Belief in the coming end of their world undercut Aztec resistance. Second, the Aztecs had made many, many enemies among neighboring peoples, who gladly joined Cortés, swelling his army from 500 to 10,000. It was not really Cortés who conquered the Aztecs, but the Aztecs' Indian enemies. Finally, if any European force really mattered, it was an army of European germs: smallpox—absent in the Americas—which arrived with the Spanish and ravaged Tenochtitlán.

The Colonial Period (1519–1810)

The Conquest ushered in 300 years of colonial rule in Mexico, now christened New Spain. Mexico's native peoples were inclined at first to see the Spanish as just the next in a long series of conquerors, but in many ways the Spanish empire was harsher and more destructive than any previous Indo-American rule.

The Spaniards wanted wealth from Mexico, gold or silver, ideally, but also sugar, indigo (a valuable dye), cattle, or wheat for export. They were not much interested in settling Mexico. The Spaniards in Mexico wanted to become rich and they wanted to do so by using Indian labor to extract the wealth of the land. The Spanish monarchy had similar ambitions: The king and queen hoped to tax Mexico's exports. The colonizers in Mexico had another goal too: They wanted to save souls and to convert the Indians to Catholicism and stamp out the worship of pagan gods.

A Genocidal Beginning

Spanish rule turned out to be much more disastrous for the native Mexicans than Cortés' Indian allies could ever have imagined. First of all, Spanish rule began with a tragedy—a "biological catastrophe"—a terrible plague of Old World diseases to which the Indo-Americans had no immunities. Measles and influenza, minor diseases in Europe, became killers in Mexico (as everywhere in the New World). Smallpox became epidemic. Demographers estimate a population of 25 million in central Mexico at the time of the Conquest; by 1650, only 1 million native Mexicans survived there (Kandell, p. 149; Wolf, p. 195). Disease wiped out families, villages, ruling classes, and whole cultures.

The *Hacienda* System

Without an abundant Indian labor force, Spanish colonizers' plans for wealth were frustrated. It took them until the seventeenth century to work out a sustainable system for colonizing Mexico: the *hacienda system*. The *hacienda* was an estate or plantation on which Indians were forced into a kind of slavery. Spanish colonizers helped themselves to the best land, and then offered to employ the now-landless Indians. They tricked the Indians into debt by giving them advances on their wages until they owed so much money they could never finish working off the debt. *Haciendas* were land-hungry: the more Indian land they could take, the more Indians they could force into dependence. They also imported some black slaves (Wolf, pp. 203–208; Ruiz, pp. 81, 102–103; Rudolph, p. 23).

The society the Spanish created in Mexico was highly race-conscious and racially stratified. Every person had an official racial classification: white, followed by *casta* (mixed white and Indian), with Indian and black at the bottom. People had different rights based on their race.

The Modern Period (1810–Present)

The modern period in Mexico began with the War of Independence, which freed Mexico from Spanish rule. Much of the modern period has been characterized by a high level of conflict between different groups. From 1810 until the early twentieth century, Mexico was in an almost constant state of upheaval as the different strata of Mexican society fought for justice, recognition, equality, or power. Every group had grievances: The wealthy colonists wanted more political independence, the middle class wanted greater economic opportunities, and the poor and the Indians wanted land, food, jobs, and an end to slavery and to tribute payments.

After declaring independence from Spain in 1824, rural guerrilla bands, royalists, and republicans fell to fighting each other. The next fifty years were marked by government instability and corruption and a succession of coups by generals. There were forty-two different governments between 1821 and 1855 (Kandell, p. 319). During this period of disintegration, Mexico lost Texas to the United States, lost the Mexican-American War, and suffered a French invasion and occupation. Finally, a new middle class emerged as the ruling elite. They looked toward Europe and sought to remake Mexico according to the ideals of the French and American Revolutions, as a capitalist republic. Mexico abolished slavery, established constitutional government on the American model, and guaranteed freedom of religion, but these paper reforms had little practical effect.

Order and Revolution

Order was finally imposed by a brilliant politician, Porfirio Díaz, whose eight terms of office as president, between 1876 and 1911 are known as the Porfiriate. Díaz advocated order and progress and threw all his tremendous power into modernizing the economy, securing international recognition, and attracting foreign investment. He built railroads and ports, extended electric and telephone service, modernized Mexico City, strengthened mining and agriculture, began oil exploration, and balanced the national budget. Díaz was ruthless in his exercise of power. He executed rival generals, massacred rebellious Indians, held fraudulent elections, and censored the press. The wealthy enjoyed a golden age during the Porfiriate, but the misery of the poor intensified, paving the way for Mexico's next great upheaval.

Mexico's revolution, begun in 1910, was one of the great early twentieth-century revolutions, like the Russian Revolution. The Mexican Revolution spoke for workers and peasants whose living and working conditions had steadily worsened in the late nineteenth century. The revolution rejected Europe as a model, asserted an Indian identity for Mexico, and committed the government to providing security for peasants and workers by redistributing land and income.

Middle-class liberals who wanted democracy started the revolution, but it blazed into violent struggle as it attracted those who had suffered most under the Porfiriate. Peasants and Indians, led by the famous Emiliano Zapata and by Pancho Villa, waged guerrilla struggles to take back land from the *haciendas.* Fighting continued for almost two decades, with every region convulsed by conflict between rival armies. A radical constitution promulgated in 1917 stipulated restoration of all Indian lands and national ownership of all natural resources, guaranteed free public education, an eight-hour workday, equal pay for equal work, and the right to organize and strike. Amid the prevailing disorder, most of these provisions were not put into practice for years, if ever (Fuentes, *The Buried Mirror,* pp. 299–306).

Revolutionary Change

It was not until the 1930s, and the presidency of Lázaro Cárdenas that the government finally made good on its promises to retrieve for the Indians lands stolen by the *haciendas.* Cárdenas redistributed 46 million acres of land. Two-thirds of Mexican farmers received land, mostly through the creation of *ejidos*—landholdings given to villages to be held in common and assigned by the village for individual use—on the traditional Indian model. (Later, in the 1950s and 1960s, the government redistributed more land through *ejidos.*) Cárdenas also nationalized the whole oil industry (mostly foreign-owned), another enormously popular action.

Finally, poor rural Mexicans saw some improvements in their lives. Schools, roads, electricity, and hospitals began to reach the countryside. The number of people dependent on *haciendas* decreased. Now it became possible for the government to move from revolutionary change to the consolidation of power. Those who had benefited from reform were readily rallied as supporters of the government: *Ejidos,* trade unions, and government workers were all organized into subsidiary units of the

Institutional Revolutionary Party, the PRI. The party dominated Mexico for the next seven decades, making politics orderly, channeling benefits to organized peasants and workers, but also substituting one-party rule for democracy.

Mexico Today

In Mexico today we can see both continuity with the past and dramatic change. Mexico continues to be a Catholic culture with persistent Indian subcultures. Mexicans still focus their lives and their loyalties on their families. Rural poverty remains a major problem and source of tension in the society. Politically, contention continues between middle-class modernizers like Porfirio Díaz and their opponents who focus on issues of land and income distribution. In the last decades of the twentieth century, Mexico's government chose the economic strategy of free trade and foreign investment. President Carlos Salinas signed the North American Free Trade Agreement (NAFTA), making Mexico, the United States, and Canada free trade partners. As you will see in the pages ahead, in the midst of rapid economic change, Mexicans have also seen major changes in family life, migration, crime, and political life.

More and more Mexicans now spend at least some period of time in the United States, and more and more rural communities depend on the money migrants send home. Actually, the whole **border region,** along both sides of the Mexico–U.S. border, is being reshaped by migration. As movement of people and goods has increased along the border, narcotics trafficking has become a really big problem. The drug trade has brought a huge crime wave to Mexico, and drug money has corrupted the government and criminal justice system. Mexico is now experiencing rapid political change. The PRI's claim to be the party of order and stability has been undermined by revelations of government corruption. A revolutionary movement in rural Chiapas state has challenged the PRI, as have two major opposition parties. In 2000 the PRI lost control of the presidency for the first time in 71 years, with the election of Vicente Fox. A new era in Mexican political life has begun.

MEXICAN CULTURE

Every era of Mexican history has left its own ambiguous cultural legacy. A distinctive society developed, in which Indo-American, Spanish, western European, American, socialist, and Catholic influences were adapted and combined. Mexicans debate the effects of Spanish colonialism on their society. In one view, Spanish and Indo-American cultures blended in Mexico. The Spanish colonizers tried their best to destroy Aztec civilization—its religion, cities, government, army, and system of social stratification—and to substitute their own church, Spanish law, and the *hacienda* system. They succeeded in eliminating Aztec institutions, but were less successful in destroying Indo-American culture. Instead, similarities between the two cultures facilitated blending: Both cultures were warlike, hierarchical, and religious. Their family structures and norms were similar. Celia Falicov argues that "today the Spanish and Indian heritages are so fused that it is difficult to separate them" (Falicov, p. 135).

Some analysts (like Mexican writer Octavio Paz) have seen the colonial legacy as much more destructive. Paz argued that the experience of conquest and colonial domination caused lasting damage to the Mexican psyche. Mexicans, he contended, saw their origins in a historical act of violation and wished to deny both their Spanish and their Indian origins. Some contemporary socialists argue that today Mexico continues to be enmeshed in economic colonialism, distorting its development to serve the needs of multinational corporations, while unemployment, poverty, and undernourishment increase. In this view, relations of economic dependency are deeply embedded in Mexican society, shaping its political system as well as its economy (Paz, pp. 86–87; Barkin, pp. 11–22, 93–95).

Other Mexicans identify with their country's revolutionary tradition. Mexicans still see the revolutionary murals of Diego Rivera, and they faithfully remember President Lázaro Cárdenas. "Subcommandante Marcos," leader of the Zapatista rebels, aligns himself with Mexico's historic revolutionaries. All these figures have stressed Mexico's heritage of resistance rather than dependence—resistance to Spanish colonialism, to the *hacienda* system, to undemocratic government. The legacies of cultural blending, colonial domination, and resistance can all be seen in Mexico's religious heritage.

Catholicism in Mexican Culture

The most enduring legacy of the Conquest was Catholicism. Mexico became, and remains, a Catholic country. Colonial churches and images of Catholic saints are seen everywhere. Catholicism is so much a part of Mexico that it is as multisided and contradictory as Mexican culture itself.

Catholicism arrived with the Conquest. Spanish friars immediately set about converting the conquered Indians. In Mexico City, one friar, Pedro de Gante, baptized Indians at the rate of 14,000 per day. Many writers have wondered why the work of conversion was so successful. In some measure, force was responsible: The Catholic Church drove out the old priests, destroyed the idols and temples, ended human sacrifice, and burned sacred books. Indians who refused to accept the new religion were sometimes tortured or whipped. But the Catholic clergy also offered genuine concern and care for the Indians and sometimes defended them against abusive colonial practices. Probably most important, the Church declared Indians to have immortal souls, to be human. In a dehumanizing colonialism, the Church offered Indians hope for justice.

In some ways too, Catholicism offered the Indians a way to continue their religious traditions after their own gods had failed. Colonial Mexico, like Aztec Mexico, was a society permeated by religious faith and ritual. There were similarities between Catholicism and Indo-American religions, so it was not difficult to join them. The Indians looked on the Catholic saints as an array of gods, similar to their own. They were familiar with rituals of baptism, confession, and communion, enacted in their own religion too. The cross was even familiar to the Maya, though their cross emerged from a base of carved snakes and represented the god of fertility.

In fact, the Indians adapted Catholicism to meet their own needs for religious grace and human respect. Nowhere is this clearer than in the legend of the Virgin of Guadalupe, still today the patron saint of Mexicans. The story tells that in 1531, the Virgin Mary appeared before a humble Indian man at Tepeyac, just north of Mexico

City, at the site of a temple to Tonantzin, the Aztec mother of gods. Miraculously her image appeared on his cloak, and lo! she was a dark-skinned Mary. Worship of the Virgin of Guadalupe spread rapidly in Mexico, and after initial opposition the friars accepted her, implicitly conceding the full humanity of the Indians (Wolf, pp. 165–175; Ruiz, pp. 66–70).

Catholicism in Mexico (as elsewhere in Latin America) absorbed and became joined to deep Indo-American religious feeling. Shrines and altars, incense and flowers, religious ceremonies and processions make Catholicism in Mexico "a sensuous, tactile religion" (Fuentes, March 30, 1992, p. 410).

Popular Religion

Everywhere that it has gone in the world, the Catholic Church has adapted to local practices of folk religion, and Mexico is no exception. Mexican Catholicism has absorbed local *fiestas* (festivals) and local Indo-American saints. All over Mexico, villages celebrate the saint's days of their patron saints with brass bands and processions, bright costumes, special masses, colorful decorations of the church and town, fireworks, bullfights, sports contests, food, drink, and dancing, and street sales of fruits, candy, and toys. Some *fiestas,* like Holy Week, Christmas, and the Festival of Our Lady of Guadalupe are national holidays.

El Día de Los Muertos. Probably the most famous of Mexico's *fiestas* is El Día de Los Muertos (The Day of the Dead). By an odd coincidence, both the Spanish and the Aztecs commemorated the dead on November 2, and this holiday fuses the two celebrations (as well as the Christian All Saints Day, November 1).

Weeks before November 2, candy vendors begin selling skulls of white sugar, decorated with sequins, ribbons, and foil, with first names on their foreheads. People buy skulls with the names of their dead relatives and set them on homemade altars, along with statues of saints, ears of corn, fruit, candy, foods the dead especially liked, soda, liquor and cigarettes, incense, and candles. People give each other gifts of cookies shaped like skeletons, or chocolate skulls, or sugar coffins (Braganti and Devine, p. 156; Nolen, pp. 48–49).

Before midnight on November 1, Mexicans spread a path of flower petals from their doors to the altar, and settle down to await a visit from the dead. The next day, they jam the roads to the cemeteries, to bring flowers and candles and perhaps a toy for a dead child, and to clean up gravesites. There is a party atmosphere, as people picnic and chat with graveside neighbors. Afterward, at home, they feast on the food which the dead have enjoyed in spirit (Reavis, pp. 194–198).

The Saints. Every village in Mexico adopts a patron saint who watches over villagers. If you visit a village church, you will see a statue or doll representing the saint at a special altar. People pray to their patron saint and ask for miracles, often cures for illness, or good harvests. The saint of San Juan Jaltepac, for example, is a 3-foot-tall plaster statue of the Virgin of Candelaria. In Zapopan, the tiny doll-like Our Lady of Zapopan, covered in jewels, is said to protect against floods (Oster, p. 200; Reavis, pp. 200–203). People often devote part of the main room of their house, or a special separate room to a home altar where they light candles, hang religious pictures, and spend time in prayer.

Doña Ana's Story: The Believer

Doña Ana is a woman in her fifties who works as a maid for a middle-class family. Every night she takes the subway and two buses and returns to her family in Colonia Caultepac at the northern edge of Mexico City, where she lives with her husband, daughter, and granddaughter. When her granddaughter fell ill with hepatitis, the doctors at the clinic said they weren't sure they could save her. Doña Ana prayed to the Virgin of Candelaria. A special room in her house contains an altar: a shelf covered with a lace tablecloth, decorated with marigolds and a picture of the saint. Doña Ana burned candles to the Virgin and prayed every night. When her granddaughter recovered, Doña Ana cried with joy. She felt bad that she couldn't go to the Virgin's own church in San Juan Jaltepac to thank the saint. So Doña Ana saved her money and the next year, on the Virgin's own saint's day, she made the long trip to her village, bringing the saint flowers and candles. Doña Ana's foolish son José laughed at her, but she felt she did the right thing and that there could be no better use for her precious savings.

In Mexico, even criminals have patron saints. In the dangerous neighborhood of Tepito in Mexico City, Santa Muerte ("Saint Death") has become the local patron saint. Despite the opposition of church officials, people come to her skeletal statue to ask for her help. Fernando Sanchez has tattooed his chest with images of Santa Muerte, Jesus, and the devil.

Some saints are of more recent origin. In Sinaloa, pilgrims come to the shrine of Jesús Malverde, "the Angel of the Poor," in Culiacán. Malverde was a legendary late-nineteenth-century bandit said to have stolen from the rich to give to the poor. He is also known as "the Narcosaint," the patron saint of Sinaloa drug smugglers. The shrine is hung with thank-you letters, plaques from grateful pilgrims—"thank you for saving me from drugs"—and pleas from other visitors—"please let them leave my family alone"—as well as plastic flowers, faded baby pictures, and the odd artificial limb (Quinones, pp. 225–232).

In Jalisco, Toribio Romo, sainted by Pope John Paul II in 2000, is known as "the Patron of Immigrants." He is known to appear to desperate immigrants as a miraculous *coyote,* bringing them safe passage across the border. Thousands come for special masses, or to kiss the saint's coffin or buy medallions of his portrait. Vendors sell a small "Migrants' Prayer Book" which includes "the Prayer for Crossing Without Documents: I feel I am a citizen of the world and of a church without borders" (Thompson, Aug. 14, 2002, p. A4).

Popular Religion and the Church

Religion permeates Mexican culture, but there is always a tension between folk religion, religion created by ordinary people, often poor Indian farmers or slum dwellers, and religion as laid down by the Catholic Church. Mexicans have long felt suspicious of the political role of the church in their society. In the beginning, the Church worked hand in hand with the conquistadors, although some clerics, like Fray Bartolomé de las Casas criticized the treatment of the Indians and spoke movingly on their behalf. Many leaders of the fight for independence were clerics like Miguel Hidalgo, but the Church, itself a huge and wealthy landowner, was seen as part of Spanish colonialism by the independence fighters. The revolution was anti-Church, and the Constitution of 1917 institutionalized a strict separation of church and state, making the Catholic Church subject to civil authority and forbidding clerics from teaching in primary schools or even from wearing their religious robes in public. Today, religious organizations are still forbidden to own media outlets in Mexico (Thompson, Aug. 2, 2002, p. A6).

When the Pope visited Mexico in 2002, President Vicente Fox was the first Mexican president ever to attend a papal mass or kiss the Pope's ring. Mexicans gave the Pope an enthusiastic welcome, and the churches are always full for Sunday Mass, but Mexicans are quite comfortable ignoring church doctrine. Surveys show majorities of Mexicans favor birth control, wish to permit abortion, and oppose religious education (Bruni and Thompson, Aug. 1, 2002, p. A6; Thompson, July 30, 2002, p. A3).

Catholic Deacons. In rural Mexico, especially in the State of Chiapas, the poorest, most Indian state, local bishops have appointed several hundred deacons, or lay preachers. They are married men who perform baptisms and weddings and conduct services. However, they don't serve communion or hear confessions. Almost all the deacons are Indians, who preach in their native languages. In many places, deacons' wives are considered deacons too and help with services, baptisms, and teaching. The Vatican has now ordered Mexican bishops to stop appointing deacons. This controversy is linked to an ideological dispute within the Catholic Church (Thompson, March 12, 2002, p. A8).

In the 1960s and 1970s many Mexican clergy were attracted to **liberation theology.** Religious leaders like Bishop Samuel Ruiz, former head of the Roman Catholic diocese in Chiapas, argued that the Church must take an active role in seeking justice and a better life for the poor. But other priests and members of the Church hierarchy appointed by Pope John Paul II are much more conservative. President Fox's party, the PAN, has long been seen to speak for conservative Catholics. Under Fox's leadership, the government reversed its historic bans on religious schools and clerical garb (Preston, May 28, 1997; Thompson, Aug. 29, 2000, p. A3).

Evangelical Protestants. In Chiapas, it has been clear that the appointment of deacons was a defensive measure, taken by the Church to try to counter the growth of evangelical Protestantism in Mexico during the past twenty years. Evangelical missions first came to Mexico from the United States and Europe, but Mexico and Guatemala now have organizations of their own. The evangelical movement has been particularly successful in Chiapas, where almost 14 percent of the population is now Protestant (overall for Mexico, 7.3 percent of the population is Protestant, mostly evangelical).

Two explanations stand out in accounting for the recent success of evangelicals in Mexico, particularly among the indigenous population. First of all, these groups are less hierarchical than the Catholic Church. Native people are able to take a more active role in evangelical churches, preaching and using native language, songs, and symbols. Secondly, evangelical opposition to the use of alcohol has proved very popular. In poor Mexican communities, male alcoholism is a scourge of family life. Wives are attracted to the evangelical church, and then coax their husbands to join. It gives them a church-based social life that is alcohol free, in contrast to the culture of Catholic folk religion, in which many traditional festivals involve heavy consumption of alcohol (Brandes, p. 33; *The Economist,* July 27, 2002, pp. 34–35; Thompson, March 12, 2002, p. A8).

A Culture of Opposites

Mexicans tend to see the world divided into two opposite realms: the "City of God"—the world of the sacred, of religion, home, and loyal friends—and its opposite, the "City of Man"—the public world of power struggle, appearances, and dishonesty. It could certainly be argued that Mexicans' colonial experience contributed to their dualistic view of the world. In colonial times, the public world was indeed a hostile, exploitative place for Indo-Americans. Developing a strong, protective family life was a healthy response.

Family and home represent loyalty, trust, and warmth to Mexicans. The family is "a fortress against the misery of the outside world" (Goodwin, pp. 3, 6). It is "the hearth, the sustaining warmth" (Fuentes, March 30, 1992, p. 410). Today, Mexicans who can afford it build high, solid walls around their homes, sometimes topped with broken glass. The mother is seen as the caring heart of the family, taking pleasure in serving her children and treasuring the loyalty they return. While respect for the father may keep him a somewhat remote figure, siblings are often very close, even in adulthood. For men, a small group of old friends may form another inner world of trust in which they freely let down their defenses and express their feelings, especially in the forgiving setting of a drinking party. In the popular mystery novels of Paco Taibo, for example, the hero is always rescued in a crisis by his drinking buddies or his sister and brother.

Idealization of the Mother

In Mexican culture, women and men are often depicted as deeply and tragically different from each other. Women, as mothers, belong to the City of God, set apart in the protected and protecting home. Motherhood is a sacred value in Mexico, and through motherhood, women become spiritual creatures, long-suffering, and patient, offering unconditional love and care to their families. The treasured national symbol of the mother is the Virgin of Guadalupe, the miraculous Mexican Virgin Mary, the virtuous, humble mother who looks after her suffering Mexican children.

The *Macho*

Corresponding to the sacred ideal of the mother in Mexican culture is an equally stereotyped image of the *macho* (more or less, "the real man"). Men are depicted as belonging to the City of Man. They live in the dangerous public world where they must guard their honor, protect their families, and battle for respect. Every man's life is an adventure story, a quest for recognition in a corrupt society. The *macho* is courageous and capable of violence, and it is understood that he is sexually active. Mexico's famous essayist, Octavio Paz described these gender dualities so forcefully in his 1950 book *The Labyrinth of Solitude* that his work helped to confirm the ideals, even though he wrote about them critically (Paz, pp. 29–31, 38–39).

We must investigate what connection there may be between the cultural ideals of the mother and the *macho* and the roles people actually play in real life. You will find that discussion on pages 92–95. But for now, let's look further into the cultural implications of Mexican's dualistic view of the world. Important traditional norms help Mexicans, especially men, negotiate the dangers of the City of Man.

Negotiating the Public Realm. In contrast to the inner world of family and friends, the outer world is perceived as a dangerous, treacherous, corrupt place. Business, government, the police, unions, schools, towns, and neighbors are not to be trusted. Social relations in the public world require watchfulness. Outside the family, Mexicans hide their feelings and fears behind "masks of formality" (Riding, p. 10). Like actors, they practice what symbolic interactionist Erving Goffman called **role distance,** self-consciously playing a role fit for a situation, but not identifying with the role. Formal language, empty phrases, false promises, and even lies allow Mexicans to meet role expectations without risking their real selves. Goffman would say that for Mexicans the world outside the family is a **frontstage** where people play their roles carefully and engage in **impression management** to try to control how others see them, while at home in the **backstage** they relax their guard.

Respect and Dignity. In the public world Mexicans try to attain and keep respect and dignity. *Respeto* in Spanish has a different meaning than does the corresponding word respect in English. In English, when one person respects another, it has a connotation of individuals acknowledging their essential equality. In Mexico, *respeto* is more like deference: It means that one person acknowledges the high status of another. Mexicans agree that people ought to be respected by others of lower status, by younger people and children, and that men ought to be respected by women. Respect allows people to preserve their *dignidad*. Mexicans attach greater importance to honesty and the preservation of their dignity than they do to individual achievement. People will proudly depict themselves and their families as "poor but honest" (Falicov, p. 138).

Norms of Public Formality. Interaction in the dangerous outer world is smoothed by norms of public conduct that help people show respect to one another and avoid unwanted provocation. Mexicans make heavy use of honorific titles to show respect. New acquaintances met at a party are addressed as *señor, señora,* and *señorita.* In business, people address managers with titles like director, doctor, *ingeniero* (engineer), or *licienciado* (someone who has a higher education degree). Many Mexican folkways involve showing respect to others and allowing them to protect their dignity. Men reassure each other with rituals of physical contact. The *abrazo,* an embrace demonstrating friendship, always follows the same pattern: a handshake, a hug, two backslaps, another handshake, and a shoulder slap. Recoiling from the *abrazo* would be highly insulting, as would failing to say a formal goodbye when departing, or evidencing dislike for the food someone has served you. Showing respect is important in little gestures too. It is insulting to place money on the counter, rather than in the cashier's hand, and you would never toss a key to someone. If you bribe a policeman, or tip a maid, you tuck the money into their pocket or apron, so they needn't humble themselves by acknowledging it (Riding, p. 10; Braganti and Devine, pp. 139–155).

In the formal public world, appearances matter a great deal. Men try to impress each other with their importance. Being late to an appointment makes you appear a busy man; buying drinks a prosperous one. Poor neighborhoods bristle with TV antennas, although there may be no TVs inside the houses (Goodwin, p. 4).

Individualism and Familism

The cultural ideal of the Mexican man bravely and aggressively making his way in a hostile world can certainly be described as "individualistic." In part, individualism in Mexico derives from a frontier mentality, what Sam Quinones calls "ranchero culture." *Ranchos* are the tiny settlements made by landless people who moved out to the arid frontier in central and northern Mexico, away from the *haciendas* and cities. Quinones quotes Esteban Barragán, a leading rural historian, who says, "people who live on the frontier have to take care of problems on their own. There's no police to solve conflicts, no judges to resolve problems with others, no ambulances. It's him alone against everything else. And an attitude develops around this. People who grew up in this don't feel tamed." "Ranchero culture values daring and individual initiative," says Quinones, as typified in the figure of the *valiente,* celebrated in Mexican *corridos* (ballads) and classic films. You could call the *valiente* a bandit, or a lone avenger (Quinones, pp. 252–253).

The romantic individualism of ranchero culture is reflected in the way Mexicans admire the matador or the boxer more than the team player in soccer or basketball.

Mexicans personalize their history, telling it as a story about heroes and villains like Cortés, Zapata, Porfirio Díaz, and Lázaro Cárdenas. Successful politicians are never simply party functionaries; they build their own faction or following within the party, and the most successful, like Cárdenas, attract supporters through charismatic appeal (Wolf, pp. 238–239; Riding, p. 5).

But while their culture idealizes the *valiente,* in real life Mexicans are **familistic:** They are intensely loyal to their families and pride themselves on their willingness to put their families first. It is not uncommon for Mexicans to sacrifice opportunities for individual advancement or enrichment in order to remain near their parents, or support their widowed sisters or other relatives. Individuals who work in the United States send a lot of what they earn home to their families. Mexicans see their status in society as an attribute of their families, not an individual quality.

Cynicism and Fatalism

Another aspect of the culture of the City of Man, of the *macho* individualist, is cynicism. Mexicans don't trust the government to make rational decisions and they are skeptical of government promises to solve social problems through legislation and government action. Mexicans believe it would be foolish to make business decisions or career plans based on government forecasts and foolish to plan too far ahead. If you save now for retirement, the banks could fail, inflation could skyrocket; it makes more sense to spend your money now on a house that will last or a business that will generate income.

Also, Mexicans are cynical about the idea of "progress," about the value of modern science and technology. When things go wrong—when corrupt governments disregard the Constitution; when modern technology pollutes the countryside—Mexicans are cynically unsurprised. If the bus fails to arrive, if the store is out of what you need, people shrug and cynically say *"ni modo"* (literally "no way," but with the connotation, "that's life"). They are likely to tell you that people always make mistakes; that something inevitably goes wrong, even with the best intentions. They cite the old proverb "There is no evil that does not come from good."

Anticipating your cynicism, Mexicans minimize their own accomplishments. A Mexican who is ambitious says, *"tengo ilusiónes"* ("I have illusions"). He calls his ambition a weakness, and if you call him ambitious, it is a criticism. It is more acceptable to praise a person for their good qualities—their strength, bravery, intelligence, or skill, than their accomplishments. People usually attribute a person's success to luck (Reavis, pp. 289–293).

SOCIAL STRUCTURE AND GROUP LIFE

Sociologists often find it useful to distinguish between **culture** and **social structure.** So far, we have been discussing Mexican culture: Mexicans' distinctive norms and customs, their particular beliefs, attitudes, and values. When we are introduced to an unfamiliar society, we notice culture first. Sometimes it seems exotic: Other peoples' religion, their holidays, food, art, and music may be noticeably different from our own. It takes longer to notice social structure, but it is equally important. Put most broadly, culture always involves meaning, while social structure describes how people organize their social lives. In Mexico, people may idealize the brave loner, but in fact they create a rich fabric of social groups: the family, the village, the political party, the evangelical church, the union, and others, to help them deal with life's difficulties. All of these groups are built out of **status positions,** like "student," "woman," or "employee," linked together in a **status system,** together with **roles** and **norms.** Don't confuse **status positions** with status in the sense of prestige. Sometimes status positions are ranked in a hierarchy, with different levels of prestige. But now we want to focus on status in its meaning of position, or social location. The social structures built out of status positions may be small—like a nuclear family built of three statuses: mother, father, child—or they may be large and complex, like a corporation or university. Three distinctive types of social structures are found in all societies: **social networks, groups,** and **social institutions.**

Social Networks in Mexican Society

People in every society are members of networks. Networks are webs of relationships that connect each person to other people, and through them to yet others. People have family networks, and networks of friends, neighbors, co-workers, and so forth, and sometimes these networks interlock. You may find a job, or an apartment, or meet your spouse-to-be through your networks.

Networks are of enormous importance in Mexican society. Mexicans place great value on family loyalty, and as we have seen, they are distrustful of public institutions and nonrelatives. There is nothing in Mexican life equivalent, for example, to the importance of the company and the school in the lives of the Japanese. This leaves Mexicans with a problem: Everyone needs relationships beyond the family, particularly in modern cities where one cannot count on being surrounded by relatives.

Compadrazgo and Personal Networks

Mexicans create relations of trust beyond the family by developing personal networks. One way they do this is by adapting the traditional Latin American practice of *compadrazgo,* or godparenthood. It is customary for important occasions in a child's life, like baptism, confirmation, marriage, or even nonreligious events like graduation, or a first haircut, to be marked by the appointment of godparents, or "sponsors." A child then has many sets of godparents and the relationship between parents and their children's godparents is a special one. *Compadres,* as they are called, might be equals like neighbors, friends, or co-workers. Often people seek as *compadres* and *commadres* those of greater wealth or power, like bosses or local politicians. *Compadres* have a special relationship: They treat each other with formality and respect. They don't drink together or discuss personal matters. Because of this mutual respect, *compadres* can turn to each other for favors, like a loan of money. *Compadrazgo* creates personal networks, but not necessarily social groups, because each person's *compadres* are different, and one individual's *compadres* may not all know each other (Goodwin, pp. 8–9; Falicov, pp. 142–143).

Patronage

Mexicans also may construct networks by seeking out **patron-client relation-ships. Patronage** is a special kind of relationship between unequals; between a **patron,** a person with power of some kind, and a **client,** a person who gives the patron loyalty and perhaps something else of value in exchange for the patron's protection and help. Traditionally, in rural villages, people sought out the local elite as *compadres,* to establish a kind of protected relationship with them. Nowadays, ordinary people are likely to become clients (or dependents) of patrons (or bosses) in other ways: by joining a political party, or community organization, or by becoming a follower of a local boss who controls access to stalls in a market or unionized jobs. Clients owe patrons loyalty, sometimes votes, and often payments of one kind or another. Patrons will often lend money in time of need, attend the client's saints' day celebrations, or even find ways to register a favored client in the national social security system (Selby, Murphy, and Lorenzen, p. 121; Cross, pp. 123–127, 151–153).

Reciprocity Networks

Through kinship, friendship, *compadrazgo,* and patronage, ordinary Mexicans create what they call *redes de seguridad* (literally, "security networks"), or, as anthropologist Larissa Lomnitz terms them, **reciprocity networks.** Members of such networks are linked by exchange: They help each other find work; they lend each other food, money, pots, and pans, even clothing. They visit back and forth and watch each other's children. They care for each other when ill, and in a crisis, they take in each other's children, for a day, or even for years. Economists used to talk of reciprocity as a mode of exchange found only in traditional societies (like the Bushmen) and absent in modern industrial societies, except for minor practices like Christmas gift giving. Lomnitz argues that reciprocity remains an important pattern in complex, modern societies, existing alongside exchange of goods for money: "The enduring importance of social connections and influence peddling in societies as different as Mexico, the United States, and the Soviet Union attests to the fact that reciprocity as an economic force is today very much alive" (Lomnitz, p. 4).

A good example of a Mexican reciprocity network is a *tanda,* an informal, rotating credit arrangement. The members of a *tanda* are usually close relatives, neighbors, or co-workers who join together to help each other save and who must trust each other to continue contributing (Lomnitz, pp. 88–89).

> ### Rosa's Story: The Tanda
>
> *Rosa, Carmen's daughter, is desperate to get married and leave home, but there is no money. She has only a slim hope. Next month is Rosa's turn for the* tanda. *She and Carmen and their two neighbors and two cousins each contribute 10 pesos weekly to the* tanda, *and then every month a different person gets to take the whole 240 pesos. When they began the* tanda *they drew lots to establish the order and now it is Rosa's turn. Her great plan is to use the money as a down payment on a sewing machine. With the machine, she figures that she and Héctor, her fiancé, will be able to afford to marry. They can live with Héctor's family, and she can sew piecework at home.*

Social Groups in Mexican Society: The Household

Groups are more highly structured than networks. Group members occupy statuses and play roles that are special to the group, and have some kind of group culture: shared values and norms, perhaps group folkways, and even some special way of talking. Finally, group members interact regularly and they see themselves as a group, drawing a boundary between those who are members and those who are outsiders. Most people belong to many social groups: families, friendship groups, work groups, teams, clubs, and other organizations.

The social group of greatest importance to most Mexicans is the household, the group of people with whom they live. For poor urban Mexicans, it is household sharing and reciprocity that enables them to get along, to feed and clothe their families. In the majority of cases, the members of a household form one **nuclear family** (a family composed of two parents and their children), but it is considered desirable for households to shelter an **extended family** (several nuclear units linked by kinship), and, in fact, extended family households tend to be better off economically. Households may also include more distant relatives, godchildren, or even friends or neighbors.

Most urban Mexicans live in a detached house on a small plot of land (a *solar*). Ideally, they want a brick house with a wall to close the household off from the street. In this small domain, the household sets about *defendiendose*, or "looking after themselves" (Selby, Murphy, and Lorenzen, pp. 70, 89). Many households are productive units, a functioning part of the economy. Households often raise animals for their own consumption or for sale; they sometimes open tiny workshops that produce textiles, carpentry, upholstery, or custom ironwork; or sidewalk businesses that do auto and truck repair or customize trucks. Sometimes household members take in washing or run sidewalk stands or rudimentary stores, selling fruit or milk, beer, crackers, and candy (Selby, Murphy, and Lorenzen, p. 71).

The Gómez' Story: The Household

The Gómez household, consisting of fourteen people, lives in Ciudad Nezahuacóyotl, the huge working-class neighborhood east of Mexico City. Their solar *contains a series of rooms grouped in a U-shape around a central patio. Here live three related nuclear families and two individuals, linked to the household by kinship. There is Don Ramón, the head of the household, his wife Consuela, their two teenage children, and a 5-year-old godchild, who all share the main room. Don Ramón's older son and his family live in another room, and a younger son and his family live in a third room. Both daughters-in-law have orphaned younger siblings living with them too. When each son married, the whole family worked together to build a new room. The children of all three families are raised by everybody in the household, and the women go out together to shop and visit church. They borrow food, money, and other items from each other.*

Many facilities in the solar *are shared by the whole household. There is a small pen for pigs, rabbits, and chickens, and a privy. Also, there is a woodstove, a barrel for water, which all share in refilling, and laundry tubs used by all. Consuela and her two daughters-in-law help support the household by taking in laundry. The two teenagers carry the laundry for Consuela when she collects and delivers it, and the two young mothers wash the clothes at home. The married sons work in the same factory and the older helped the younger get a job. Sometimes, when the factory is busy, they are able to get Don Ramón*

*hired too. Each nuclear family keeps its separate finances, but the two married sons give
their father a weekly allowance in exchange for the use of his solar. Don Ramón says that
they all "stick up for themselves and keep going." (See Selby, Murphy, and Lorenzen,
p. 70, and Lomnitz, pp. 112–114, for descriptions of similar households.)*

SOCIAL INSTITUTIONS

The Gómez household is a social group, but it also illustrates a third aspect of social
structure. It shows us some of the characteristics of the Mexican family, a major
Mexican **social institution.** While social groups are concrete units of real people,
social institutions are patterns of behavior. Sociologists use the term **social institution** when they need to discuss how clusters of social groups and organizations, statuses and roles, and associated norms and values operate to serve some important
need in social life. In modern societies there are five major social institutions: the
family, political institutions, the economy, educational institutions, and religious institutions, each performing functions that are vital to the continued existence of the
society. Each of these institutions can be organized in a variety of ways, as you have
seen in this book; but in each society, social institutions are long-lasting and widely
accepted. Often, people don't even imagine different ways of organizing their society's institutions, and when institutions do change (see Chapter 5, Germany), they
find it difficult to adjust.

Mexican Social Institutions: The Family

Families in all societies do similar things for society (that is, they perform basic
functions), though they do them in different ways. Families regulate sexual activity,
supervising their members to be sure they conform to sexual norms. Families are in
charge of reproduction to keep the society going, and they socialize the children they
produce. Also families provide physical care and protection for their members. They
provide emotional support and caring as well. When sociologists discuss "the family," they are talking about a cultural ideal: how families are supposed to work in a
given society. The ideal may or may not coincide with what things are actually like
in any given family group.

The Mexican family fulfills these universal functions in a distinctive way. The
structures and the values, norms, beliefs, and attitudes that permeate family life are
characteristically Mexican or Latin American. According to Selby, Murphy, and
Lorenzen, "it is difficult to overemphasize the importance of the nuclear family in
Mexico, for it truly is the emotional center of the psychological and social life of all
Mexicans" (p. 98). Ordinary Mexicans don't go downtown to shop, or eat out in
restaurants, or go to clubs or concerts or sports events. Their lives revolve around
home and work; family TV watching, family celebrations, visits among relatives and
neighbors, and for men, going out drinking with close friends. Although Mexican
families are typically large, only the well-to-do in Mexico live in houses with many
bedrooms. Ordinary Mexicans will even rebuild the interiors of houses to make
fewer bedrooms and more shared common space for family work and socializing
(Selby, Murphy, and Lorenzen, pp. 22, 26, 98).

TABLE 2.1 Divorce

Divorce rates more than doubled in Japan between 1971 and 2002. At the same time, divorce rates in Egypt fell by half. Mexico's divorce rate rose but remained low. Divorce rates in the United States rose and remained at a very high level.

	Divorces per 100,000 Persons per Year	
	1971	1999–2002
Japan	99	227
Germany	131	240
Mexico	41	52
United States	372	419
Egypt	209	117

Source: 1990 Demographic Yearbook, United Nations, 1992

2001 and 2002 Demographic Yearbooks, United Nations Statistics Division, Demographic Yearbook System

http://unstats.un.org/unsd/demographic/products/dyb/dyb2.htm

Practically everyone in Mexico lives in a family-based household, and most of these are headed by a man who is the principal wage earner. In 2000, 20.6 percent of households were female headed (compared to 36 percent in the United States). Mexicans tend to marry young (only 37 percent of Mexican women aged 20 to 29 have not been married) and stay married. In Mexico there are only 5.2 divorces per year per hundred marriages.[1] Almost no one lives alone (only 6 percent of Mexicans lived in one-person households in 2000), and indeed it is almost unthinkable to do so, and very inconvenient too, since Mexican society assumes the presence of children or servants in every household to run errands, stand in line to pay bills (since the mails are so unreliable), or to carry messages (since so many people lack telephones). The average household size in Mexico is still rather large: 4.3 persons (compared to 2.6 in the United States), because most adults have children living in the house with them, and often grandchildren as well. Forty-one percent of Mexicans live in households of five or more (Mexican National Institute of Statistics, Geography and Informatics, http://www.inegi.gob.mx/inegi/default.asp., United States Census, American Fact Finder, Households and Families 2000, http://census.gov.). (See Table 2.1, above and Table 1.1, p. 18.)

Family Structure

In Mexico the ideal nuclear family is part of an extended family network, and the household willingly expands to include grandparents, uncles, aunts or cousins, related children who are orphans or children of divorced parents, or relatives who are single, widowed, or divorced. People feel close to their third and fourth cousins. Extended family members rely on each other to take care of children, help with money,

---

[1] Mexico's extremely low divorce rate is puzzling. It results in part from the large number of couples who live together in common-law marriages without a legal marriage. If they part, there is no divorce to register. Also, because Mexico is a Catholic country, people are reluctant to divorce. They are more likely to separate but remain legally wed. There is tremendous social pressure on wives to stay with their husbands, even in the face of physical or psychological abuse. If a woman considers divorce, her parents will likely tell her she must endure the marriage so the family won't be ashamed of her. "He is my cross to bear," said one woman of her abusive husband (Vargas, 1998, p. A1).

or provide friendship and support. People live in families at every stage of their lives and families demand loyalty. "What you have to do," an informant told Selby, "is care for your family, so your family will care for you" (Falicov, p. 138; Selby, Murphy, and Lorenzen, p. 5).

Families are also hierarchical: The old have authority over the young, and men have authority over women at every stage of the life cycle. People are expected to remain loyal to their family of origin throughout their lives. Indeed, ideally, married sons and their families will share households with their parents, and married daughters often do so as well. Married sons and daughters who live separately will try to live nearby and visit often, and sons will contribute money to their parents' household. According to Falicov, family values stress proximity, cohesiveness, respect for parental authority, and cooperation. Confrontation and competition are discouraged, and individual autonomy and individual achievement are not emphasized (Falicov, p. 138).

Roles in the Mexican Family

Earlier in this chapter we described a pair of gender stereotypes deeply ingrained in Mexican culture: the self-sacrificing mother and the *macho*. At the beginning of the twenty-first century, do these stereotypes still have power in Mexican culture? Do people accept these role ideals and try to portray them in their own lives? Did they ever? Mexico's gender dualities are contested terrain: Everyone knows them but not everyone accepts them, and not everyone who accepts them actually plays them in real life. Mexican women fought alongside men in the revolution, worked in factories, and participated in Mexican public life. Though they did not gain the right to vote in national elections until 1953, women have since become deputies and senators, have occupied seats on the Supreme Court, and have held high positions in political parties. In 2003, 116 out of 500 members of the federal congress were women. In the assembly of Mexico City, 33 percent of the seats are held by women. The leader of the PRI in the lower house of congress is a woman, Elba Ester Gordillo. Rosario Robles, another influential woman politician, was first mayor of Mexico City and then the leader of the PRD, the major left-wing opposition party. Women have also taken the lead in neighborhood organizations and have been influential union organizers (Ruiz, pp. 425, 449; Preston, Feb. 28, 2000, p. A4; Thompson, Nov. 1, 2001, p. A3; *The Economist,* Sept. 20, 2003, p. 36).

On the other hand, most women do not work outside their homes (40 percent were in the labor force in 2002), and women are paid less than men. On average, working women earn only 38 percent of what working men earn (see Table 1.4, p. 41). In the government, women find themselves appointed to "soft-issue" ministries like tourism and culture, not the powerful departments of economy and justice. School hours run from 9 A.M. until 1 or 2 P.M., so children have to be picked up in the middle of the day, and there is very little formal day care available (*The Economist,* Sept. 20, 2003, p. 36). Probably for most families, traditional role ideals still hold sway.

Role expectations for husbands and wives stress complementarity. Ideally, the husband is hard working and continuously employed. He disciplines and controls the family. The husband hands over his wages to his wife, who manages the household. It is her task to maintain the home, physically and emotionally. She creates an emotional shelter, a refuge for her family, where they can recover from the stresses of life in the public world outside. Taking care of everyone is the mother's task: She sustains and nurtures and serves her family.

Traditionally, the roles parents play in relation to their children are considered much more important than the roles they play toward each other as spouses. They don't expect much romantic intimacy or friendly companionship, but rather respect, consideration, and control of anger. As Falicov explains, "it is thought that *el amor de madre* (motherly love) is a much greater force than wifely love" and "a Mexican woman feels more challenged to perform as a mother than as a wife, companion, or sexual partner" (Falicov, pp. 140, 149). In fact, since Mexican families are large, and adult children remain close, husbands and wives rarely live without children and are able to transfer their early involvement in raising their children to a lasting relationship with their grandchildren.

Children are expected to respect and obey their parents, but they wouldn't think of being friends with them. Ideally, children put the family's needs before their own. When they see their parents working so hard to maintain the family, they feel tremendous gratitude and a sense of protectiveness toward their mother. They are eager to help by working with their parents, or if they obtain paid work, by contributing their wages. Selby, Murphy, and Lorenzen estimate that by the time working children are 20, they will have paid back their parents all the expenses entailed in raising them. When adult children live with their parents, or regularly give them money, parents soon realize a net gain in the financial calculus of child rearing (Selby, Murphy, and Lorenzen, p. 55).

Siblings are expected to have very close ties throughout their lives. Brothers and sisters and cousins are encouraged to play together, and it is not unusual for Mexican children to have few friends who are not relatives. Older siblings are usually given some authority over younger ones and these age hierarchies may continue into adult life. Adult brothers and sisters may quarrel and carry grudges, but they seldom break off relations with each other, because family celebrations or crises reunite them.

Changing Families and Changing Roles

The institution of the family is changing in Mexico today, and gender roles are changing along with it. Two changes are leading the trend: People are having fewer children and more women are working outside their homes. Obviously these two big changes are related in complex ways. Both changes may be a response to Mexico's economic problems, as families try to make ends meet. But it is also true that when women have fewer children they are freer to work, and conversely, when women work, they are likely to have fewer children. In 1967, Mexican women bore an average of 6.8 children in their lifetimes. By 1980, it had fallen to 4.6, and by 2004, this **total fertility rate** was down to 2.5. Falling fertility rates are reflected in smaller household sizes (U.S. Bureau of the Census, International Data Base, http://www.census.gov/cgi-bin/ipc/idbsprd; United Nations Human Development Report, 2004). (See Table 1.1, p. 18.)

More Mexican women are working for wages outside their homes—as maids, in factories, in small shops and markets, in agriculture and in family enterprises. The *maquiladoras* (foreign-owned assembly plants) concentrated along the border, but found elsewhere in Mexico as well, employ workers who are mostly female and young—aged 16–24. In 2004, 40 percent of Mexican women were in the labor force, a tremendous change from 1950, when the corresponding figure was only 8 percent. (See Table 1.4, p. 41.)

Migration and Changing Roles.   Men and women are migrating out of rural Mexico today, both to the United States and to the border region to work in *maquiladoras,* the foreign-owned factories there. When men migrate alone, the women left behind assume new responsibilities and freedoms. They must make decisions for their families, and usually, they must work. Many put on jeans and farm the family plot or even work as farmhands. They get used to more independence. But this is a story without a happy ending. In many cases, the men fail to return home again. Gradually, they stop sending money. They get involved with women in the United States and start new families there. Then their wives in Mexico are abandoned, impoverished, and alone. When husbands do return, it may mean a wrenching return to old roles for their wives. "Once their husbands return, women have to slip quietly back into their traditional role," explains sociologist Monica Gendreau Maurer, of the Latin American University in Puebla, Mexico (Tayler, Oct. 21, 2001, p. A12).

Maquiladora Workers.   When the first factories were built in the border region, people expected that they would employ men, but in fact, almost the only people hired were women, especially young women between the ages of 16 and 24. Young women come to Juárez, or other border cities, and suddenly find themselves freed from family control. *Maquila* cities have huge numbers of bars and dance halls, filled on weekend nights with groups of girls who arrive together and pay their own way. The clubs even feature male strippers. There are also many more female-headed families in the border cities, and more women who must fend for themselves without family or the other networks of village life to watch over them and back them up (Quinones, pp. 139–149).

Gains and Losses for Women.   At this point you may be asking yourself, have women in Mexico become more "liberated"? That's a hard question to answer because it involves how people act and how they feel, not just whether or not they work or how many children they have. Many Mexican women would prefer not to work. After all, if you had to leave your children and your house to work at cleaning someone else's house and caring for their children, wouldn't you prefer not to work? Many Mexican women work out of necessity, to feed their families, at jobs that are menial and badly paid. They work a "double day," working for wages all day outside their homes, then grocery shopping, cooking, cleaning, and caring for their own children. The poorest women, who have no refrigerators, must shop for food every day and also must fill and carry containers of water from the nearest public tap. Many commute two hours each way besides! In contrast, being a housewife in Mexico is a desirable and honorable job. It is still seen by many as a woman's highest calling and it carries another sort of prestige as well. A woman who can afford to be a housewife tells the world that her husband (and/or sons) makes enough money to support the family without her working (Isaac, pp. 125–130).

At the same time, when women work and leave their homes for the public world, there is something liberating about it, especially when they work in factories or other situations where there are many female employees. Women talk together, they give each other advice, and they develop a broader social perspective on their lives. Some move on to union or political activism. Women who run their own businesses, even as laundresses or market stall proprietors, feel a sense of pride in their business skills and in what they have built up. Also, when women bring home some of their family's income, it does have an effect on roles within the family: "Breadwinners" have a say in making decisions. If they are unhappy in their marriages, a wage-earning job may make it possible for them to divorce or separate from their husbands.

Changing Roles for Men. If women can work, support themselves, or leave their husbands, then men's roles must also change. Matthew Gutmann documents the positive side of this change and Sam Quinones, the negative side. In his 1996 book, *The Meaning of Macho: Being a Man in Mexico City,* Matthew C. Gutmann found Mexican men playing more companionate roles in their marriages, spending more time at home with their wives, and even discussing child care. He could find no case among ordinary working Mexicans of the legendary philandering *macho,* supporting a mistress on the side. Robert Fox and Pedro Solis Camacho found Mexican men as involved in child care as their American counterparts (Fox and Camacho, pp. 489–495).

Though it is becoming more acceptable for the husbands of working women to "help out" at home, both men and women speak of it as "helping out." The belief that the home is primarily the woman's responsibility is unchanged in Mexico. But when men "help," especially with child care, they learn how much work it is, and it makes them think differently about how many children they want and whether use of contraceptives is acceptable to them.

Quinones describes husbands in Juárez who have become newly dependent on their wives and are angry and resentful about it. "*Maquiladoras* . . . created a new Mexican woman," Quinones says, "But this same process did not create a new man." Community activists in Juárez talk about men from rural areas who are used to controlling women. But when their wives get work in the *maquiladoras,* those women become more independent, talk back to their husbands, and socialize with coworkers, including men. Some men respond with violence, beating or even killing their wives (Quinones, pp. 144–145; see also Shorris, pp. 535–536).

Mexican Political Institutions: The Patronage System and Democracy

Every society develops some means to maintain order, protect the members of the society from outside threats, control crime, and resolve conflicts among different groups. All modern societies have separate political institutions that exist to serve these functions: governments, political parties, the military, and legal institutions.

Mexico's political institutions are in transition. For years, Mexico was ruled by a one-party **patronage system.** Although this system is under attack today, it still exists in many states, cities, and towns governed by the PRI, within labor unions and other organizations, within Mexico's criminal justice system, and within political parties. Increasingly though, Mexicans are demanding a **representative democracy,** with competing parties, free elections, and the rule of law. Let's first examine Mexico's traditional patronage system and then see how Mexico's political institutions are changing.

Patronage Politics and the PRI

Until very recently, Mexico was really a **single-party system.** The PRI was a "big tent" party that worked to include everyone: Farmers, factory workers, small businessmen, white-collar workers, and so on, all found their place within the PRI. The PRI organized them all in confederations under its wings. These groups made the PRI a powerful machine for getting votes and channeling benefits (Riding, pp. 53–55). The party became the **patron** of all its subsidiary groups, and in exchange, all the **clients** acknowledged the supremacy of the party and accepted its choice of president. The PRI's success was based on its ability to deliver real benefits to Mexicans in exchange for their political loyalties.

One reason why the PRI was so successful is that it was firmly based in Mexican culture and social structure. The party was a hierarchical network of patron–client relationships, based on personal favors, gratitude, and personal loyalty. Sociologists and political scientists call this way of running a government **patronage politics.** Patronage politics is highly developed in Mexico, but it is found in many, many other societies too.

The system took shape under President Lázaro Cárdenas, who is remembered with gratitude to this day. Cárdenas began by organizing Mexican peasants into their own federations under the PRI. Between 1934 and 1940 Cárdenas redistributed 46 million acres of land, formerly held in large estates, creating more than 180,000 *ejidos* (tracts of land held communally by villages, which could be inherited but not sold), farmed by 750,000 families. Peasants received land and vital loans from state banks to buy seeds and equipment. The government invested in rural development—road construction, power lines, wells, health clinics, and schools—that benefited peasants and also created jobs for construction workers, teachers, health care workers, and government bureaucrats. The PRI organized these workers into party-affiliated unions and professional organizations. Then these groups received wage increases, benefits, and also access to jobs in industries newly taken over by the state, like the railroads, the oil industry, and as time went by, thousands of smaller state companies as well. But people who didn't join and support the PRI were cut off from benefits.

Don Miguel's Story: The Patron

Don Miguel is a PRI jefe (or boss). He is the president of the Citizens Action Committee of Colonia "Lázaro Cárdenas," a newly settled colonia populare *(or squatter neighborhood) on the outskirts of Oaxaca. Five years ago, Don Miguel got involved with his neighbors in order to build a much-needed school. To his own astonishment, he found he had a talent for organizing and leading people. With Don Miguel as president, the Citizens Action Committee collected signatures on petitions, visited the mayor's office, and searched for every possible personal connection to officials of the city government. Demonstrations in front of city hall finally culminated in a memorable visit by the mayor to the* colonia, *when he promised to provide sewer service.*

> *By the time the bulldozers arrived, Don Miguel found he had a new profession. Residents of the* colonia *came to him with all sorts of problems: This one's brother needed a job; that one's son was brilliant, but needed a scholarship; that one's mother was senile and kept wandering off and getting lost. As he got to know the officials at city hall better, Don Miguel found he could get help for some of his neighbors. They looked up to him as a kind of protector, a patron, and they willingly gave 5 pesos a month per family to finance the Citizens Action Committee. In turn, Don Miguel felt grateful and loyal to the mayor and the other PRI officials for their help. When they asked him to bring his people to a campaign rally in Oaxaca to cheer the mayor and the PRI, he was glad to do it, and his neighbors were happy to come to show their gratitude and loyalty to him. The PRI even served them all a free lunch when they arrived.*

Although the citizens of Lázaro Cárdenas know, in an abstract way, that the city is obliged to provide sewer service, they haven't demanded it with a feeling of entitlement. Rather, they believe that it is their personal relationship with a patron, Don Miguel, and his relationship with his patron, the mayor, which made the sewers possible.

Social Mobility and the PRI. Ambitious Mexicans often thanked the PRI for providing them with opportunities for **upward social mobility** (that is, movement to a higher social rank or position). Like a good patron, the PRI "sponsored" the rise of politically talented individuals up the ladder of power. It was possible to become active in your local union or *ejido* or student group and then, supported by the power of the organization you controlled, to be tapped by the party for higher positions. Sociologists call this pattern of improving your social position **sponsored mobility.** In this way, some people who came from quite poor origins ended up in congress or in high government positions (Riding, p. 75). At the same time, the PRI created networks that linked together potentially opposed groups, granting benefits to each and absorbing into itself the natural leadership of each group.

What Price Stability?

If you are thinking that this political system sounds too good to be true, you are right. There is a substantial downside to a one-party patronage machine, a downside that worries more and more Mexicans. Because, for so long the PRI was really identical with the Mexican government, certain kinds of abuses of power readily occurred.

Co-optation and Repression. Faced with any new organization, like a newly settled community, or a new union, the PRI/Mexican government followed a consistent policy. When local authorities judged the new group and its leaders willing to play the game, the organization was **co-opted**—that is, it was given some benefits, allowed to achieve some of its goals in return for becoming a loyal part of the PRI. Leaders could be co-opted personally with recognition and paid positions. But organizations with interests and goals that conflicted with those of the PRI, or organizations bent on achieving power independent of the PRI, were ruthlessly repressed. Because the PRI and the government were identical, it was an easy matter for the party to call out soldiers to bulldoze the too-independent shantytown, or police to crush the too-radical union.

Lack of Democracy. In theory, the PRI gave representation to all groups through its subsidiary organizations. But in fact, this system was a far cry from representative democracy. Power was held by a hierarchy of bosses: union chiefs, or local leaders who were appointed by those above. Election was a mere formality. Even the president was essentially appointed (by his outgoing predecessor); the election just legitimated his selection. Basically, Mexican elected officials were accountable to the patrons who appointed them, not the people they represented (Cornelius and Craig, p. 25).

The PRI, as the governing party, organized all the elections held between 1929 and 2000. No PRI nominee for president ever received less than 50 percent of the votes, and one president, José Lopez Portillo, was elected in 1976 with 100 percent of the ballots. In fact, no other name was listed on the ballot. Mexican historians suggest that in the presidential elections of 1929, 1940, 1952, and 1980, as well as in many local elections, the PRI won through fraud, stuffing ballot boxes, destroying ballots, buying votes, and intimidating voters (Dillon, March 12, 2000, pp. 1, 18; June 28, 2000, p. A3).

Also, the PRI siphoned money from the public treasury to finance its party operations. It used government resources for party business, for example assigning public officials to run party election campaigns and using government cars and trucks to carry supporters to rallies. When the state of Nuevo Leon elected a mayor from the PAN in 1997, he began an investigation which found that $8 million had been transferred from the state treasury to the PRI. The former PRI party leader admitted that he had received $130,000 a month in public funds that he used to pay the party payroll (Dillon, March 27, 2000, p. A6). The PRI's subsidiary organizations also misused funds. In 2002 allegations surfaced that officials of the state-owned oil company, PEMEX, and the leaders of the oil-workers union had jointly siphoned $100 million out of union funds. The money was given to the PRI and used in the 2000 presidential campaign (Thompson, Jan. 21, 2002, p. A6).

Corruption. The practice of patronage, combined with the *sexenio,* the single six-year presidential term of office for the president and legislators, fostered corruption in Mexico. Every high-level PRI politician had his following of loyal clients, who helped him rise. When a politician was elected, his patronage network struck it rich. Every client could expect a government job, or perhaps a government contract, an import license, sewers and streetlights for the community, or other government funds, a portion of which found their way into the private wealth of the client. But the largesse lasted only six years, after which another politician and other clients took over. The temptation to line one's pockets as fast as possible usually proved irresistible. Corruption filtered down to lower civil servants, police, judges, businesspeople, and the media.

Newspaper reporters, paid low wages, made a living by accepting bribes of money (a sum of perhaps triple a monthly wage is typical) or even food, liquor, cars, prostitutes, or airline tickets from the government agency, industry, or criminal operation they were assigned to cover. Editors printed *gacetillas,* propaganda pieces that pretended to be news, in exchange for bribes (Weiner, Oct. 29, 2000, p. 10; Riding, pp. 123–124, 126). In business it was difficult to accomplish anything without kickbacks and payoffs to suppliers, government bureaucrats, or union officials.

Many union leaders used their power primarily to obtain the largest possible payoff in return for not striking. And union bosses often filled jobs by selling them to the highest bidder.

Police corruption was probably most notorious, and though President Fox has worked hard to clean up the criminal justice system, you can still see police corruption at work today. It starts with hiring. To become a police officer in Mexico City, you don't take an exam or train at a police academy. You must know someone in city hall and then you will have to buy your job with a payment to the bureaucrat in charge of hiring, or to someone to whom he owes a favor. The job itself is hardly worth having, since the pay is absurdly low. It is valuable only as an opportunity for corruption, for *la mordida* ("the little bite"), as police payoffs are called. In Mexico you can expect to be stopped for tiny, or imaginary infractions of the traffic laws, but the police officer will be happy to "pay your ticket for you" if you give him the fine. Peddlers must bribe police to stay on their corners, and men learn to keep loose bills in their pockets for the police to find when they search them randomly for drugs or weapons. Police are also paid off by drug dealers and prostitution operators. They must be "tipped" before they will investigate a crime, and small criminals can buy their way out of charges. Like police officers, judges are poorly paid. Some simply give the decision to the party that makes the biggest payoff. In prisons, guards sell drugs, sex, and liquor, protection and even escape, if the price is right (Riding, p. 117; Weiner, Jan. 29, 2001, p. A7; Thompson, Nov. 24, 2000, p. A32).

Institutional Change: A Crisis of Legitimacy

Social institutions are crucially important building blocks of every society. It is not easy to change institutions, and when they do change, disruption and reorganization spread widely through the society. The PRI's hold on Mexican political institutions was so firm and lasted so long that no one really believed the party could be dislodged. But the PRI was dislodged from domination in 2000. It lost the presidency, a major blow, and it lost its majority in congress (though it still controls the largest block of votes). It lost 12 of 31 governorships and a third of the local legislatures. Tellingly, the PRI now gets fewer and fewer votes from the young, from people with education and skills, and from urban Mexicans.

By 2000, many Mexicans had lost faith in the PRI as a governing party. Now the question is, has their faith in government been renewed under the presidency of Vicente Fox and his PAN party, or has cynicism about government become broader and more profound? Mexico is experiencing what Max Weber called a crisis of **legitimacy.** Weber drew a distinction between **power** and **authority.** Power, he said, is just the ability to make people do what you want, even without their consent. If you force them against their will, that is called **coercion.** But when people believe in the right of those who have power to make decisions for others, that is called **legitimacy.** Both local governments and the federal government in Mexico are suffering a crisis of legitimacy as people question government honesty and effectiveness.

The Zapatista Rebels. Mexico's crisis of legitimacy was most dramatically expressed by the Zapatista National Liberation Army. In 1994, just months before presidential elections, this unknown peasant revolutionary movement in the state of

Chiapas took Mexico by surprise. They seized the state's major city, San Cristóbal de las Casas, and several other villages and towns, installing their own governments, courts, and jails. In the weeks that followed the initial armed attack, peasants in at least a dozen other towns seized their town halls and demanded the removal of local (PRI-selected) authorities. By 1998 Zapatistas ran parallel governments in 33 different villages. Sympathetic protesters held rallies in Mexico City and other cities to support the Zapatistas' demands for honest elections, redistribution of land, better treatment of Indians, and government development aid (Golden, Feb. 9, 1994, pp. A1, A9).

The Indian Zapatistas reminded Mexicans of their revolutionary heritage and their national hero, Emiliano Zapata, peasant leader of the 1910 revolution. The Zapatista's masked leader "Subcommandante Marcos" captured Mexicans' affections with his clever manifestos and good humor. He was treated as a celebrity, and "Marcos" dolls became the latest hot toy. To avoid alienating voters, Mexico's government agreed to "negotiate" with the Zapatistas, instead of moving against them militarily. But when peace talks collapsed in 1996, the federal government and state governments used troops and paramilitary forces to attack Zapatista villages. The

Mayan Indian women clear fields for planting corn on confiscated property near Ososingo, in Mexico's poorest state—Chiapas—in 1998. The property was seized when the rebel Zapatista National Liberation Army rose up in early 1994. The local landowners' association says that Indian peasants sympathetic to the rebels occupied nearly 90,000 acres of private land. Although corn has been the staple crop of Mexican farmers and the essential food for most Mexicans, most corn consumed by Mexicans is now imported from the United States. Cheaper corn from the United States has driven many Mexican farm families from the land.

governor of Chiapas declared the Zapatista towns illegal and promised to "eradicate" them. But Zapatista leaders replied that "the federal and state governments aren't legitimate because they weren't chosen by the people." When forty-five Zapatista supporters were massacred in the village of Chenalhó in December 1997 by a paramilitary force allied with the government, the PRI fell further in public opinion (Wager and Schulz, p. 11; *The New York Times,* Aug. 3, 1998, p. A22; Preston, May 17, 1998, p. 14; Fisher, Dec. 25, 1997, p. A8).

When Vicente Fox was elected president in 2000, he tried hard to solve the conflict in Chiapas through negotiations, and he scaled back government military forces. Pablo Salazar, who became governor of Chiapas by defeating the PRI candidate, also tried to end the rebellion. He stopped funding anti-Zapatista paramilitaries, and he jailed all twenty-five regional police commanders. The governor made it possible for some people displaced by the conflict to return to their villages, but almost 14,000 remain expelled. At best, the conflict in Chiapas has reached a stalemate, with rebels entrenched in their villages and on disputed land, and opposing armed forces reined in (*The Economist,* Jan. 12, 2002, p. 35).

Deviance and Legitimacy

Every society experiences deviance, though the amount of deviance, the forms it takes, and its causes vary greatly. Mexico is distinctive because not only is there a great deal of deviance that is criminal in nature, but also deviance is very much a political issue. People see government officials involved in crime and unable to stop crime. The legitimacy of the government, and the future of the PAN, hinges on its ability to get crime under control.

Murder and the Breakdown of Social Organization

At least 300 women have been murdered in the industrial border city of Juárez in the past decade, many of them raped, some mutilated, their bodies dumped in ditches or in the desert. Most of the victims have been young, between 15 and 25 years old. They were poor and relatively dark skinned: students, store clerks, and many, many *maquiladora* workers. Officials say that at least 100 of them were victims of serial killers, but that more than one killer is involved. Very few of the killings have been solved. The police have arrested several suspects, each time declaring the crime wave at an end, only to see the murders resume while the suspect was in jail. In fact, only half the bodies have been identified, and there are no missing persons reports or descriptions to match up with the unidentified women.

What is going on? We probably need to investigate many factors to understand the unsolved murders, including police incompetence and male rage over the displacement of male workers by women. But one factor that stands out is the changes in the city of Juárez. Women have come to Juárez from all over Mexico, many without their families. The population of the city has grown rapidly, from 407,000 inhabitants in 1970, to probably 1.5 million today. Thousands of people arrive and depart every day, on their way to the United States, on their way back home to their villages. But the social organization of the city has failed to keep up with its rapid growth. Shantytowns spread out into the desert, without water or sewers, lighting or paved streets. There are no street addresses. Five different gangs battle for control of the streets.

¡JUSTICIA!

Silvia Elena Rivera Morales
7/junio/95 (muerta)

Ramona Morales wears a photo of her 16-year-old
daughter, murdered in Ciudad Juárez. Morales was
photographed speaking at a press conference with other
relatives of the more than 340 girls and women murdered in
Ciudad Juárez and Chihuahua City, Mexico in the past few
years. The murders reflect the disintegration of Juárez's
social fabric as thousands of young women pour in from the
countryside to work in the city's *maquiladoras.*

Juárez has the kind of anonymity that goes with a new city. Not only is there a
lack of formal government, family networks have not yet developed and neighborhood organization is just beginning. Many of the murdered women were unknown
to their neighbors, and their families back home had lost touch with them or assumed
they were in the United States. Lack of social organization means there are fewer informal controls on crime (Quinones, pp. 139–148; Guillermoprieto, Sept. 29, 2003;
Thompson, Dec. 10, 2002, p. A20; Navarro, Aug. 19, 2002, p. B3).

Kidnapping and Social Strain

There were 732 kidnappings for ransom officially reported in Mexico in 2001, but
since so many others went unreported the real total was probably five times as large.
Kroll, a major security company, says there were 3,000 kidnappings in 2000 and the

number is rising. Celebrities like Laura Zapata, a well-known actress, and especially wealthy businessmen, are targeted for huge, multimillion dollar ransoms. Recently, more middle-class people have been kidnapped for ransoms of "only" around $100,000. And then there are the "express kidnappings" in which people are grabbed and forced, over a period of hours or days, to use their ATM cards to empty their bank accounts. The number of kidnappings and other violent crimes rose between 1990 and 1995, and then began to rise even more rapidly after the serious economic recession of 1995. In 2005 there was an outbreak of kidnapping of Mexicans and visiting Americans in the cities along the border with Texas. Often the kidnappings are done by city police officers who are working for local drug gangs that have gone into the business of kidnapping for ransom.

It makes sense to look at a great deal of the crime and corruption in Mexico in the context of Merton's **social strain theory of deviance** (see pp. 35). When Mexicans cannot achieve a widely accepted goal like making money, in a legal, conformist way, some people (but by no means all) engage in **innovative deviance.** They find deviant means of achieving conformist ends. Police officers, who make as little as $250 a month, find ways to supplement their salaries. These range from the familiar small bribes to major and disruptive acts of deviance. Some police rent out their uniforms and badges to con men, called godmothers. Other Mexicans turn to car theft, picking pockets, and petty theft: such crimes all abound. Recently, many kidnappings have turned more violent, with female victims raped and male victims beaten and mutilated, ears cut off and sent to relatives. Some speculate that this reveals an edge of class hatred, born of economic hard times (*The Economist,* June 19, 2004; June 15, 2002; Weiner, Jan. 16, 2003, p. A4; June 7, 2002, p. A5; Oct. 12, 2002, p. A6; Thompson, Jan. 23, 2005, p. 3).

Drug Trafficking and Ineffective Social Controls

Have you ever lived in a neighborhood or town where there was a lot of illegal drug dealing? If so, you will understand how much drug trafficking increases crime. Dealers fight over turf and commit assaults and murders. Drug addicts feed their habits with holdups and thefts. And the gangs that transport the drugs corrupt police and courts and border agents with bribes. All this and more has taken place in Mexico, starting in the 1990s, as Mexico became a major route for the transport of cocaine from Columbia to the United States, and more recently a center for the manufacture of heroin and methamphetamines. U.S. officials estimate that the Arellano Félix cartel, one of the major drug rings, paid $1 million per week in bribes to local, state, and federal officials. The local wisecrack in Tijuana was that out of every ten police officers, eleven were on the drug cartel's payroll. The cartel moved the drugs into the United States using trucks, airplanes, ships, and even a 1,200 foot long underground railroad tunnel. Then it moved the money back across the border in several ways. There were couriers, usually part of the Los Angeles and San Diego gangs that sold the drugs. Then, some of the money was wired to cooperative Mexican banks that were paid 1 or 2 percent for their help in exchanging drug profits for bank drafts in dollars. Some of the money was laundered through what appeared to be ordinary currency exchange businesses (Weiner, April 19, 2002, p. A8; April 12, 2002, p. A5; March 11, 2002, p. A3; April 26, 2002, p. A3). Drugs that fail to make it across the border are sold in Mexico, so drug use is rising, especially crack co-caine use by young people in the poorest communities (Thompson, Jan. 11, 1999, p. A4).

In 1998 the United States charged three major Mexican banks and 26 bankers with laundering drug money (Van Natte, May 19, 1998, p. A6; Preston, May 20, 1998, p. A6). Later that year, the jailed former head of Mexico's national police tes-tified that he collected $1,500 for every kilo of cocaine that he permitted to move through the country (Golden, July 15, 1998, pp. A1, A6).

Mexicans believe that when it comes to crime and punishment, the whole sys-tem is a mess. Crime rates are rising, but many police seem to be implicated in the crime, not controlling it. In 2005, Mexico's government was forced to send troops to take over control of three major high security prisons from wealthy drug dealer inmates who had bribed wardens and guards to let them bring guns into the prisons and run their gangs from jail. One drug lord had an enemy assassinated in the visit-ing room of the prison. At the same time, the government announced it had discov-ered one of the president's aides was selling information about President Fox's movements to a drug cartel. Even aside from police corruption, the criminal justice system is almost ludicrously disorganized and ineffective. The central part of Mex-ico City has about 8 million people, about the same number as metropolitan New York City, but it has only one-third as many police, divided into three poorly coor-dinated forces. The SSP (the Ministry for Public Security) can only patrol to prevent crime; they cannot investigate or prosecute it. That function belongs to the PGR (the Prosecutor-General's Office). Then there is the federal police force and several spe-cial police forces devoted to the drug trade. Police are poorly paid and poorly trained. Lacking investigative expertise, they rely on torture to extract confessions. The court system is slanted in favor of the prosecution, with few jury trials and few competent lawyers (*The Economist,* June 28, 2003, p. 33; Oct. 19, 2002, p. 34; McKinley, Jan. 15, 2005, p. A3; Feb. 7, 2005, p. A3).

As a result, Mexicans have so little confidence in the criminal justice system that only about one-fifth of crime victims even report the crime. And only 7 percent of reported crimes lead to convictions. It is clear to criminals that if you commit a crime you have a very good chance of getting away with it. Ineffective sanctions re-sult in increased deviance (*The Economist,* June 28, 2003, p. 33; Weiner, Oct. 17, 2002, p. A4).

Building the Institutions of Democracy

Mexico is now at a crossroads in its political life. The election of President Vicente Fox in 2000 was a potent symbol of the end of the era of PRI domination. But it is far from clear where Mexico is heading. In many states and localities the PRI polit-ical machine is still working. The PRI still dominates the unions, a powerful source of patronage. And the party has used its control of the largest block of votes in con-gress to stymie Fox's agenda and leave him with few accomplishments to show the Mexican people. It is perfectly possible that the PRI will regain the presidency in 2006 and restore its old system of government. In a 2004 opinion poll, over 80 per-cent of Mexicans expressed dissatisfaction "with the way democracy works in your country." Seventy-five percent said that "only a democratic system can bring development," but at the very same time 67 percent reported they "wouldn't mind a non-democratic government if it solved economic problems" (*The Economist,* Aug. 14, 2004, p. 36). If Mexico is to become a democratic society, it needs democratic institutions to put in place of the PRI's patronage system. What progress has been made in building democracy?

Free Elections

In a democracy, the legitimacy of the governments rests on elections. It rests on public belief that elections are free and fair and that an official or party that loses an election will follow the law by leaving office and making way for the victor. In the PRI years, the legitimacy of Mexico's government was undercut by the widespread belief that the PRI manipulated and falsified elections. Mexicans remain convinced that Cuahtemoc Cárdenas really won the election of 1988 and the PRI dishonestly installed Carlos Salinas as president in his place. Indeed the outcry was so great that the PRI decided it had to clean up its act and risk losing elections in order to preserve its legitimacy. And, in fact, with PRI cooperation, Mexico has made considerable progress towards free and fair elections.

For the first time, in 2000, presidential elections were supervised by an autonomous agency, The Federal Elections Institute, with a budget of $918 million to prevent fraud and ensure an honest vote count. There were new voting booths, with curtains to ensure privacy, citizens selected at random to be pollwatchers, and a computerized vote-reporting system to ensure that results were posted on the Internet before tampering could occur. The government issued costly new photo-ID voter registration cards and compiled more accurate voting lists. Foreign observers monitored the vote (Dillon and Preston, May 9, 2000, pp. A1, A4; Dillon, June 28, 2000, p. A3).

Did the reforms succeed? Was the 2000 election free and fair? The answer has to be both yes and no. The actual process of voting was remarkably clean and the PRI must be given credit for establishing democratic procedures, risking, and in fact forfeiting, the party's power. But at the same time that federal officials were building new democratic institutions, the PRI political machine was engaging in old-fashioned dirty tricks—buying votes, coercing voters, and exchanging favors for votes. In 2004, in state and local elections, the PRI continued some of its old practices. In Oaxaca, a stronghold of the PRI, the party's patronage system is still in place, co-opting people who might be effective opponents with offers of jobs and contracts. The opposition candidate for governor in Oaxaca charged that the PRI's narrow victory in 2004 was achieved by tampering with paper ballots and computer tallies. PRI supporters clubbed a man to death in front of photographers during the campaign (*The Economist,* Aug. 7, 2004, p. 29).

A Free Press

In its heyday, the PRI manipulated elections by controlling the media. The party made sure that opposition candidates got no coverage, or negative coverage, in newspapers and on television, and made sure that PRI candidates were lavishly praised. Nowadays, Mexico's newspapers and TV are much freer. In Mexico City, dozens of small daily newspapers, which had been covertly financed by the PRI, have collapsed.

There are now new newspapers—*El Norte,* in Monterrey, *Reforma* and *El Financero* in Mexico City, which are financed through advertising and can be completely independent of the government. In television there have been big changes. Televisa, which for decades was given virtual monopoly over TV broadcasting (in exchange for loyalty to the PRI) now has a new major competitor, TV Azteca; and at Televisa, a family business, the old guard has given way to a new, younger owner who says he is trying to "re-create our credibility" through freer coverage. Televisa now runs Mexico's most popular show, *El Mañanero* ("The Morning Quickie"), with foul-mouthed, smutty Brozo the Clown, who mocks both Mexican prudishness and Mexican politicians (Preston, June 7, 2000, p. A3; *The Economist,* March 11, 2000, p. 44; Weiner, Oct. 29, 2000, p. 10; Thompson, Jan. 14, 2002, p. A4; Guillermoprieto, Aug. 12, 2004, pp. 40–43).

The Rule of Law

Mexicans are most outraged today by politicians, police, and military officers who continue to defy the law. Mexicans call it "impunity"; they say that people with power in Mexico break the law with impunity, that is, without risk of being held accountable. The powerful take bribes, use torture and murder, and distort the law for political advantage.

President Fox took office with admirable plans to restore the rule of law, but there have been many obstacles. Soon after the election he announced plans to create a new national police force. He also promised to end the use of torture by the police and to put a halt to police violating the law with impunity. He said he would strengthen and modernize the federal courts. Finally, the new president promised to create a "transparency commission" that would investigate all the hidden abuses of power of the PRI era (Weiner, June 17, 2001, p. 17; July 10, 2001, p. A4; Dillon, July 6, 2000, p. A6; Thompson, July 5, 2000, pp. A1, A8).

What has Mr. Fox actually been able to accomplish? Congress has passed a freedom of information act, opening government records to the public. It is considering legislation to reform the antiquated criminal justice system and the federal police forces (Thompson, May 2, 2002, p. A6; Weiner, March 30, 2004, p. A12). Mexico has also created a new elite antidrug unit, which the United States so far sees as free of corruption. Its most stellar accomplishment has been defeating the Arellano Félix drug gang through a long campaign capped by the arrest of Benjamín Arellano Félix, after the death of his brother, Ramón. Top leaders of several other gangs have been arrested too (Weiner, April 26, 2002, p. A3; March 11, 2002, p. A3). Unfortunately, when the Arellano Félix gang was knocked out, it resulted in a turf war between other drug cartels, with a wave of some seventy killings. Some of the victims were executed by local police on orders from one of the gangs (*The Economist,* March 11, 2004, p. 34). There seems to be an endless supply of corrupt police and government officials to be linked to drug cartels, arrested and fired. Most discouragingly, in Baja California, where the PAN has been in power for a decade, drug-related crime has not lessened. Although the government has repeatedly fired corrupt police officers, new ones are readily corrupted. In 2002, María de los Ángeles Tames, an elected PAN official of a town outside Mexico City, was assassinated while investigating corrupt PAN officials. The local mayor was charged on suspicion of ordering her killing. This evidence that corruption and impunity are not restricted to the PRI, but have readily spread to the PAN, has been profoundly discouraging to Mexicans. Voters are losing faith in the ability of the PAN to fight crime and establish democracy, and voter participation rates, high at the start of the PAN era, have fallen to new lows (Weiner, March 18, 2001, p. 10; Golden, Jan. 9, 2000, pp. 1, 8; Thompson, Sept. 5, 2002, p. A10).

The Story of Digna Ochoa: A True Story

Digna Ochoa, 37, was shot to death at close range in her Mexico City law office on October 19, 2001. Born in the state of Veracruz, Ochoa was a former nun, the daughter of a bricklayer, and the fifth of thirteen children in the family. Ochoa was best known for her defense of Rodolfo Montiel and Teodoro Cabrera, two peasant farmers who protested logging by political bosses in their community. The two men had been imprisoned since 1999 on dubious drug and gun charges, despite official evidence that they were arbitrarily arrested and then tortured. Ms. Ochoa had received death threats for years, and in 1999 was kidnapped and beaten, then later tortured while tied up and blindfolded in her own home. No arrests were ever made for these attacks. This time, the assassins left behind a note warning other human rights lawyers that they would be next.

The attack on Digna Ochoa was widely reported in Mexico and in other countries. It was an embarrassment for President Fox. The attorney general he appointed, Rafael Macedo de la Concha, an army general, was the chief military prosecutor against Monteil and Cabrera. It was Macedo who ended the investigation into the earlier attacks on Ochoa. This time, Fox ordered the creation of a civilian commission to monitor the official investigation into Ochoa's death. Later, he ordered the release of Montiel and Cabrera. In 2004, the human rights commission of Mexico City released a report saying that government prosecutors did not properly investigate Ms. Ochoa's death, and even concealed vital pieces of evidence. And in 2005, the government opened yet another investigation. Rumors are still circulating in Mexico linking the murder to the military and suggesting that the military and the police still operate with impunity outside the law (Thompson, Oct. 22, 2001, p. A6; Oct. 28, 2001, p. A10; Nov. 9, 2001, p. A12; Nov. 18, 2001, p. A10; July 21, 2004, p. A3; McKinley, Feb. 27, 2005, p. 8).

Competition between Political Parties

In a democracy, voters have a choice between real alternatives. This seems to work only when there is competition between at least two political parties, identifiably different in their beliefs and policies. For the seventy years of PRI domination, there was no real political alternative in Mexico.

Now there are three major parties in Mexico, and also a number of minor ones. The PAN and the PRD represent clearly opposed political philosophies. The PAN is a socially conservative party that speaks for business, and it is popular in the north. It favors limited government, free trade, and foreign investment, and it opposes unionization, increased environmental regulation, and abortion. The PRD, the weakest of the three parties, is an old-fashioned party of the left. It speaks for peasants and poor city residents, primarily in the south. The PRD opposed NAFTA and opposes free trade and calls for redistributing more land to peasants. The PRD is in favor of increased government help for the poor, broader recognition of the rights of

Indians, and tariff protection to help small farmers. It supports labor organizing in *maquiladoras* and wants to put more taxes on *maquiladoras* to pay for water and sewage and schools in surrounding towns.

The PRI offers a contradictory mix of all these policies. Its support is greatest among rural voters. It favors free trade and NAFTA, but it also advocates government spending to help the poor, largely through the sort of patronage programs that have supported its power in the past. The PRI is divided between two factions. The "technocrats" are the younger, mostly U.S.-educated leaders, like past president Ernesto Zedillo, who engineered NAFTA and opened the way to free elections. They are opposed by the "dinosaurs," the old-style operators of the political machine who blame the technocrats for losing the 2000 election. The PRI's national president, Roberto Madrazo, who will probably be the party's candidate for president in 2006, is a "dinosaur" machine politician.

The PAN achieved great victories in the 2000 election, at the national, state, and local levels. But this was not an endorsement of the PAN platform. Mexicans were voting for "the change," as they called it, voting for clean government and democratic politics. They were voting against the PRI. Since 2000, there have been many reasons to celebrate the change. The old system of "presidentialism," in which the president had almost unlimited personal powers and was immune to justice, has ended. The president no longer dominates his party or congress. He no longer can use government funds as personal assets, nor can he order electoral fraud (Dominguez and McCann, pp. 14–15; Krause, Aug. 10, 2004, p. A23). At the same time, however, Mexicans are disappointed in their new democracy. They now have competition between political parties, but they do not have effective government.

Fox was a wonderful candidate, but he was a weak president. In part, that resulted from the constitutional requirement that it takes the votes of two-thirds of the members of congress to pass a bill. Neither the PAN nor the PRI controlled that many representatives. It necessarily required negotiation, compromise, and coalition building to enact legislation. But Fox was not very skilled or interested in these activities, and as a result, little of his legislative agenda was enacted. Economic problems added to Fox's difficulty in delivering the economic growth and new jobs he promised. Probably Fox will be remembered for his most successful program, a government housing initiative that has already helped 1.3 million families move out of slum neighborhoods and buy modest homes in low income housing developments all over Mexico (Malkin, Dec. 17, 2004, pp. W1, W7).

But as the three major parties, the PRI, the PAN and the PRD position themselves for the 2006 election, it appears that the recent change to democratic politics might be under threat. The front-running candidate for president is Andrés Manuel López Obrador, the PRD mayor of Mexico City. But several recent events have seemed designed to remove López Obrador from the race. First, in 2004, viewers of Brozo the Clown saw a secretly filmed videotape of López Obrador's closest political aide stuffing his pockets with cash from the suitcase of a rich businessman. He had either been caught out, set up, or both. Next, congress, where the PRD is a minority party, threatened to impeach López Obrador and strip him of official immunity to prosecution over contempt charges in an obscure lawsuit about a government construction project. In that case, he would be barred from running for office. Many people in Mexico see these charges as a naked power play by a coalition between the PRI and the PAN in an effort to remove their most formidable rival for the presidency in 2006. That would be a major setback for free and fair elections in Mexico. It would probably result in the election of the PRI candidate for president. If the effort to disqualify López Obrador succeeds, it will feed voters' cynicism about the possibility of democracy in Mexico. "All the parties are the same," said one voter. "They say they will bring change and things stay the same. Better the old man you know than the bad one you don't" (Weiner, Nov. 3, 2003, p. A5; *The Economist,* Nov. 15, 2003, p. 35; Guillermoprieto, Aug. 12, 2004, p. 40; Thompson, Aug. 30, 2004, p. A3; Feb. 17, 2005, p. A6; July 9, 2003, p. A4).

SOCIAL INEQUALITY

What do sociologists mean when they say that a given society has deep inequalities, or that another is relatively egalitarian? How do we judge the extent of inequality in a society or compare the amount of inequality in different societies? In every society there are scarce resources that are distributed unequally: Some people receive more and others less. Sociologists usually point to three categories of scarce goods: **power, prestige,** and **wealth.** Then, in examining any society, they ask who, which groups or categories of people, have more or less power, prestige, or wealth.

In every society there is some degree of inequality between men and women. (We call this **gender inequality.**) We have seen how in Mexican society women are often economically dependent on men and defer to their husbands and fathers. In Mexican society (and in many other societies) there are also **racial inequalities** in which some races (or ethnic groups) enjoy higher status than others, more wealth, and more power over other races. Finally, in Mexico, as in many other societies, we can distinguish distinct groups or **strata** (layers) of the population whose access to power, prestige, and wealth differs because they start out with different economic resources. We call these groups **social classes** and this kind of inequality **class inequality.**

Racial Inequality in Mexican Society

Mexico is a racially diverse society, and it began as a **caste** society: one in which everyone was racially classified at birth and race determined people's rights and obligations. Modern Mexico has explicitly rejected caste structures. Race consciousness has been greatly reduced, but there are still racial inequalities.

Race and Class in Colonial Mexico

Colonial Mexico was a society of vast inequalities, in which a person's status was set mostly by race, but also by wealth. Most basically, there was a three-level pyramid, with whites at the top, followed by *castas* (mixed bloods) in the middle, and Indians at the bottom, with blacks (originally brought to Mexico as slaves) even below them.

Whites, while they dominated colonial society, were never more than a tiny minority of the Mexican population. In 1570 there were approximately 7,000 Spaniards and three and a half million Indians. In fact, during the whole three centuries of colonial rule, no more than about 300,000 Spaniards ever came to Mexico. The *conquistadores* took Indian mistresses as soon as they arrived, fathering the growing *casta* population. By 1810 Indians were approximately 60 percent of the population and people of mixed race nearly 40 percent (Ruiz, p. 85; Kandell, p. 213).

The colonial administration, highly race-conscious, tried to classify and regulate Mexico's varied people. Whites born in Spain were *peninsulares* and they had the most privileges. Whites born in Mexico were *criollos.* A person born of Indian and white parents was a *mestizo;* someone of mixed black and white ancestry, a *mulato.* A person classified as Indian was entitled to a share in village communal lands, but couldn't own land as an individual. A person of African and Indian parents could not be enslaved, but had no rights to communal lands. Every racial category had a different legal standing.

But as time went on, *criollos* mixed with *mestizos,* with Indians who had left their communities, and with the descendants of African slaves. People came to call all poor urban dwellers *mestizos,* so the word became social, rather than racial in meaning. Today, a person stops being an Indian and becomes a *mestizo* through a social change of identity, by adopting the Spanish language and western dress.

The Revolution and Mexican Identity

After the 1910 revolution, Mexican intellectuals embarked on a period of intense soul-searching about their national identity. They rejected the idea that Mexico should try to be like a European country, and began to find value in their Indian past. A very influential essay by José Vasconcelos (1882–1959), *La Raza Cósmica (The Cosmic Race)* praised Mexico's mixed-race character as a crowning achievement in world history, forging from the world's four races (whites, blacks, Asians, and Indians) a new "fifth race" (Russell, p. 172). The revolutionary murals of Diego Rivera depict Mexicans as proud brown-skinned people, and a plaque at Tlatelolco Plaza proclaims: "On August 13, 1521, heroically defended by Cuauhtémoc, Tlatelolco fell into the hands of Hernán Cortés. It was neither a triumph nor a defeat: it was the powerful birth of the mestizo nation that is Mexico today" (quoted in Riding, p. 3).

Race in Mexico Today

In Mexico today school textbooks and politicians proudly depict the *mestizo* as the ideal Mexican. The PRI reminds Mexicans that it is the party of the revolution, still carrying the banner of a multiracial Mexico. Mexican society doesn't force people to choose between polar racial identities: Anyone can adopt a *mestizo* identity. In its official census, the Mexican government does not ask people to classify themselves by race, a practice it says is racist. No data is collected on the percentages of Mexicans of different races and their residences, occupations, incomes, education, and so forth. Indians are recognized as a culturally distinctive group, but blacks, who are viewed as culturally identical to other Mexicans, are not recognized as a minority group (Russell, p. 95).[2] In general, in Mexico, as in other Latin American societies, skin color

---

[2]Sociologists have had to estimate the percentage of Mexicans of different races. Russell suggests that Mexico's population is now 79 percent *mestizo,* 15 percent Indian, 5 percent white, and less than 1 percent black and Asian (p. 95).

is viewed as an individual rather than a group attribute. Individuals may be lighter or darker skinned. Even within a family, one sister may be described as "white" and another as "black" without their feeling they belong to different racial groups.

But while government policies have minimized race consciousness in Mexico, racial inequalities persist. The government's refusal to collect data about race makes it hard to document racial inequalities that obviously exist. There is a strong association between skin color and status, and skin color and wealth. Whiteness is admired: *la güera* ("the blonde") is the ideal of feminine beauty, seen in advertisements, on television, and in the movies. Light skin and European features are associated with wealth and success; government officials and corporate executives look European. Dark skin is associated with Indians, with poverty, ignorance, and dirt. To call a person an *Indio* (Indian) is an insult. Cuauhtémoc Cárdenas, opposition candidate in the 1988 and 1994 presidential elections, was the first candidate to be seen in decades with dark skin and Indian features. His son, Lázaro Cárdenas, elected governor of Michoacan State in 2001, has a black wife who is from Cuba, and his wife's race was the subject of attacks during the campaign (Thompson, Nov. 11, 2001, p. A10).

Indian Minority Groups. While Mexico collects no statistics about people who are racially Indian, data is available about people who speak Indian languages. In 1990 the Mexican census recorded about seven million people (or 8 percent of the population) who spoke fifty-five different Indian languages and dialects. The largest language groups were the Zapotec (512,000 speakers) living in Oaxaca and neighboring Guerrero and Puebla, the Maya of the Yucatán (with 740,000 speakers), the Totonac of Puebla and Veracruz (with 256,000 speakers), the Mixtec, living chiefly in the State of Oaxaca (with 230,000 speakers), and the Nahua, Mexico's largest indigenous group, of 1,687,000 members, speaking the language of the ancient Aztecs (Grimes, http://www.sil.org/ethnologue/countries/Mexi.html). Indians are much more likely than non-Indians to live in rural areas, and they are more likely than other Mexicans to be self-employed peasant farmers. They are also much poorer than other Mexicans. Of Indians living in Indian counties 77 percent earn less than the minimum wage (compared to 27 percent of all Mexicans). Their median monthly income is only $30. Half live in houses without electricity, 90 percent have no indoor plumbing, and 45 percent are illiterate (Russell, pp. 125–128).

Class Inequality in Mexican Society

Is there a great deal of class inequality in Mexican society? Is there more or less than in other societies? In trying to answer these questions, we can start with two relatively simple comparisons. First, we can ask, do most people in this society make pretty much the same amount of money? Are there just a handful of rich people and a sprinkling of poor people, with everyone else clustered in the middle? Or are people spread out over the whole range of incomes? Second, we can ask, how big is that range from the richest to the poorest? Do the richest people receive double the share of total income that the poorest receive? Ten times as much? One hundred times as much? These are questions about **income distribution.**

According to these measures, Mexico is quite an unequal society: There are many poor people and they are very poor indeed, both **relatively,** compared to others, and **absolutely,** in terms of the absolute minimum necessary for human survival. Real wages today in Mexico have fallen below their 1981 level and 53.7 percent of Mexicans live in poverty, with average earnings of $4 a day. Relative poverty is an interesting phenomenon in Mexico. In years past, poor Mexicans compared themselves to the local middle class, or perhaps the *hacienda* owners. Today, the United States is the standard of comparison, since most Mexicans see the United States on television, or they have been there themselves or heard about *el norte* from relatives (Thompson, Sept. 25, 2002, p. A4; Sept. 4, 2002, p. A3).

Even within Mexico, great disparities are easily seen. In Monterrey, for example, there is a huge contrast between rich and poor. Monterrey, an industrial city only two hours from the Texas border, has wealthy suburban enclaves, with air-conditioned malls, that rival any in the United States. There are millionaires living in Monterrey. Ten miles away are shantytowns like Fernando Amilpa, where 18,000 people live without indoor plumbing and with little running water. Some of the people in the shantytowns work in the hotels and restaurants that serve Monterrey's rich (Weiner, March 21, 2002, p. A8).

Income Distribution

Sociologist James W. Russell calculates that Mexico's upper class is tiny—making up less than 1 percent of the population. The middle class, including well-off small business owners, privileged bureaucrats, managers, and well-paid professionals, is very small, encompassing only 16.5 percent of the workforce and their families. All other Mexicans, a group that includes farmers and farm workers, blue-collar workers, and most self-employed people, make up a huge 83 percent of the labor force and their families. Approximately half of this majority lives in poverty (Russell, p. 69).

We can learn a lot about the extent of inequality in a society by looking at income distribution by "income fifths," or **quintiles.** This calculation adds up all the income everyone receives, then divides up all the households into five equal size groups: the 20 percent who are the top income earners, the 20 percent who are the bottom income earners, and the three-fifths in the middle.

In Mexico in 2000 the richest income fifth received 59.1 percent of total income earned, and the poorest fifth received only 3.1 percent. That means the richest fifth received 19 times as much income as the poorest fifth. Compare this to Egypt (in 1999) where the richest fifth received only 5 times as much of total income as the poorest fifth; or Germany where the richest fifth received 4.34 times as much; and the United States, where the richest fifth received 8.48 times as much (see Table 1.5, p. 51).

Social Classes and Standards of Living

Income distribution figures will make more sense if you know how much money rich people and poor people earn, or at least what their money will buy them. The official minimum wage in Mexico is $3.42 per day, or approximately $100 per month (and $1,200 per year), a wage typical for unskilled workers in the city or countryside, but one that leaves them very, very poor. Earnings of approximately $1,000 a

TABLE 2.2　Inequalities in Pay (1997–1998)

Average income is much lower in Mexico than Japan, but executive pay is similar.

	Average Executive Pay and Benefits for CEOs of Major Companies*	Average Income**	For Every $100 the Average Person Takes Home, CEO Takes Home
Japan	$ 420,855.00	$32,350.00	$ 1,300.94
Germany	$ 398,430.00	$26,570.00	$ 1,499.55
United States	$1,072,400.00	$29,240.00	$ 3,667.58
Mexico	$ 456,902.00	$ 3,840.00	$11,898.49

Sources: *Bryant, Adam, "American Pay Rattles Foreign Partners," *The New York Times,* Sunday, January 17, 1999, page 2 WK;

**World Bank. World Development Indicators 2000 CD-ROM.

month (or $12,000 a year) put you squarely in the middle class. Rich Mexicans receive a great deal more income: Russell estimates that $60,000 a year puts you in the Mexican upper class, a level that fewer than 1 percent of Mexicans can attain. A very tiny minority of Mexicans, many of them top executives of companies that do an international business, have extremely high incomes, similar to those of their counterparts in the United States (Russell, pp. 78–79; Thompson, Sept. 4, 2002, p. A3). (See Table 2.2, above.)

People with similar incomes and about the same amount of wealth often resemble each other in many aspects of their lives. Their income enables them to buy one or another standard of living, and they also develop shared values, norms, and customs. They live in the same neighborhoods, send their children to the same schools, and usually marry each other as well. We call these groups **social classes.** In Mexico the various social classes live apart from each other and follow very different ways of life.

The Upper-Class Way of Life

Upper-class Mexicans have sufficient money to live like the wealthy of rich western societies, with cars, vacations abroad, designer clothes, and investments in foreign real estate. They think of themselves as an elite group, setting standards for their society (Rudolph, pp. 115–116).

María Asunción Aramburozabala's Story: The Heiress

This is a true story. María Asunción Aramburozabala, 39, a divorced mother of two is on Forbes magazine's list of the richest people in the world. Her father was one of the owners of Grupo Modelo, the brewer of Corona beer. When he died suddenly, with no male heirs, business associates scrambled to control the company, assuming that Ms A, her mother and her sister, who had never been involved in the family's economic interests, could be pushed aside. Instead, María did something rare for a wealthy woman in Mexico. She abandoned her life of shopping, lunching and supervising her staff of servants. She studied the company, held onto her father's seats on the board of directors and his shares of stock. Today, she makes deals for the company. Her last—selling a non-controlling interest in Grupo Modelo to Anheuser-Busch—netted her family about $500 million. She also acquired a 20 percent stake in Televisa, Mexico's giant media company.

Ms A looks impeccably rich and feminine, with high heels, tight clothing, gold jewelry and perfect makeup. Her office is on the twenty-fifth floor of a building in the fashionable northwest edge of Mexico City. She finds time to travel in Europe with her girlfriends and on her last trip to the United States she gave a speech at the Harvard Business School. In 2005 she became engaged to the American ambassador to Mexico, Antonio O. Garza Jr., a friend of President George W. Bush (Thompson, July 20, 2002, p. A4, Feb. 1, 2005, p. A6).

Traditionally, there are three somewhat overlapping sectors of the Mexican upper class, which are distinct, but linked through kinship and social interaction.

The Industrial Elite. Business fortunes in Mexico are often held by extended families, like the Garza Sada family fortune begun in the 1890s when the family founded Cervecería Cuauntémoc, today Mexico's largest brewery. Descendants have invested in chemicals, oil, steel, banking, insurance, and finance. Families like the Garza Sadas intermarry with each other. They give relatives jobs in various family-controlled businesses and form alliances with other family business groups (Rudolph, pp. 116–117).

The Landowning Elite. Another group of wealthy people in Mexico are rural large landowners. They are the owners of the (mostly northwestern) large estates of good, irrigated land used to grow winter vegetables for export to the United States. Large landowners make enough money to invest in the most modern farm technology: irrigation systems, farm machinery, fertilizers, herbicides, and pesticides. Many have also invested in commerce, industry, and banking, forming alliances with Mexico's industrial elite (Rudolph, pp. 117, 124–125).

The Political Elite. Politics is the most conspicuous route to wealth in Mexico. It is almost expected that elected officials and the networks of clients they bring with them into office will spend their six-year terms skimming government budgets and accumulating payoffs. Today, with drug money, the sums elected officials accumulate are staggering. Raúl Salinas' $132 million is one example, and he was only the president's brother! A former mayor of Mexico City, Oscar Espinosa, was charged with stealing $45 million between 1995 and 1997 (Althaus, Nov. 26, 2000, p. J8).

The Middle-Class Way of Life

Middle class in Mexico is an elusive term. Some people, like teachers, have professions usually considered middle-class, but in Mexico they are paid so little that in terms of their income they are poor. Other Mexicans own businesses, but their businesses are so small that they have no employees and their earnings don't keep them out of poverty. More than half the Mexican middle class earn less than $10,000 a year. At these wages it is hard to afford goods produced for the world market, like cars and TVs, which cost as much in Mexico as they do in the United States. But lower-middle-class families may still employ cheap household help. Often they are better off than their income indicates: Many civil servants (and some unionized workers) enjoy government benefits like subsidized housing, pensions, free medical care, even coupons to exchange for food. Such families are part of the richest fifth: better off than the other 80 percent of all Mexicans.

Prosperous business owners, the top managers of Mexico's small number of big businesses, top bureaucrats, and well-off professionals make up the Mexican upper middle class. Though they earn less than $60,000 a year, they can afford a suburban middle-class life similar to that of their counterparts in the United States. Their children go to private schools and universities and are taught to be conscious of proper language and manners (Rudolph, p. 113).

Bernardo and Francesca's Story: The Struggling Middle Class

Francesca drives down the hill towards downtown Mérida busy doing arithmetic in her head. She owes the wholesaler 5,000 pesos on last month's shipment. Her daughter needs a new school uniform and her tooth—Díos míos, her tooth hurts, but can they afford another dentist bill? Between her dress shop and her husband's two jobs—the day job as a math teacher and the night job as an accountant—they are barely making it. At least the car is still running. It's an embarrassing old VW Beetle, but it keeps her off the smelly, crowded buses. They were doing much better before the 2001 recession. Now, with interest rates so high, their mortgage payments take half their income. And the new Wal-Mart scheduled to be built out on the highway—Francesca fears it will drive her out of business.

Bernardo complains, but Francesca thinks they are lucky that his mother has come to live with them. She cooks for the family and is always there to pick María and Salvadór up from school. And Bernardo's younger brother Juan pays them rent for his room. They are trying to save that money to send María and Salvadór to university. But who knows—another economic crisis and they could fall right out of the middle class.

The Lower-Class Way of Life

You have to admire the resourcefulness, tenacity, and hard work with which **lower-class** families struggle to put together sufficient income to survive. There is no safety net to fall back upon: no welfare, no unemployment insurance, no social security pensions. People can rely only upon their families and their networks of patrons and friends.

If a family has more than one adult wage earner, a favored strategy is for one person to find a job for wages—in a factory, as a bus driver, or even as a teacher. Such jobs often pay no more than minimum wage, but they are desirable if they carry health benefits, pension, and access to other government subsidies. Other family members look for work in the **informal sector,** where there is a chance of earning more, but no benefits. (See Hellman, especially pp. 220–221, for discussion of "survival strategies.")

The Informal Sector. One important difference between Mexico (and other "developing" nations) and the "developed" industrial nations is that many Mexicans lack "formal" paying jobs in business or government. Many are "informally" self-employed in tiny businesses that usually have no employees or employ other family members working without wages. These businesses have no official licenses and pay no fees or taxes. Russell estimates that more than a quarter of the Mexican labor force is self-employed in this way. Often people work for wages when they can, but if they are laid off they hustle work until they can find employment again. Many peddle goods or services from place to place (Russell, p. 59; Castells and Portes, pp. 11–37).

There are few chain stores or chain restaurants in Mexico, but lots of "Mom and Pop" groceries and cafés. Outdoor markets are crowded with stalls selling fruit and candy, cooked food, appliances, new and used clothing, and anything else you might want. In sidewalk workshops people make and sell shoes; they print stationery and business cards; they sew dresses. On a busy street or square you can buy a song from a mariachi band, have your shoes shined, hire a child to watch your car, or watch a sword swallower or fire-eater who hopes for your tip. In Mexico City, 2,500 people work as garbage pickers, sorting through the city's huge garbage dump for recyclable materials to sell. (Incidentally, most of these "informal sector" occupations can't be adopted casually. The market or the street corner or the dump has its boss, and you must pay him or her for your spot. You will become his client and he will try to provide you some protection from shakedowns by police and competition from other peddlers.) Struggling for a livelihood, poor Mexicans find every possible niche in the economy.

Absolute Poverty. The bottom line for Mexican families is that, if they cannot somehow earn enough for necessities, they will simply have to do without. If they cannot afford rent, they will live in a shack in a squatter settlement, without electricity, running water, or sewage pipes. In 2004, a quarter of Mexicans had no toilet, not even a latrine. It is usual for the families of an apartment building or a squatter

A woman and her child walk through a squatter community where they live in Tijuana, Mexico. Most of the people in this community work in nearby *maquiladoras* and lack basic services such as running water, sewage, electricity and adequate roads. Many advocates for Mexico's poor have argued that economic changes resulting from NAFTA—the North American Free Trade Agreement—widened the gap in Mexico between rich and poor.

neighborhood to share a single water tap that runs continually. Often there is a rotating schedule for filling each family's containers at the tap: today your turn may come at 3 A.M. Less money frequently means less food: 20 percent of Mexicans eat no eggs or meat; 40 percent never have milk. In the poorest Mexican states 80 to 90 percent of the population don't eat eggs, meat, or milk (United Nations, *Human Development Report,* 2004; Hellman, p. 15). When you learn about the poorest Mexicans, the term **life chances** really becomes vivid. Lack of food results in malnutrition for children and mothers, weakening their health. The poorest Mexicans also lack access to good medical care, which results in high infant mortality rates. (See Table 2.3, below.)

The Way of Life of the Rural Poor

So far, we have been describing the lives of poor people in urban areas, but actually more than half of Mexico's poor families live in the countryside. A quarter of Mexicans depend on agriculture for a living (compared to less than 3 percent in the United States). The southern agricultural states of Chiapas, Oaxaca, Campeche, Yucatan, and Quintana Roo are the poorest in the nation. (See Table 2.4, p. 118.)

A third of the people living in poverty in rural areas work their own farms or *ejido* plots. They produce most of the food they consume: corn tortillas and beans and possibly eggs, chicken, and pork. Any surplus they sell for cash. A small percentage of households (3.2 percent) are really living outside the modern money economy: The value of what they grow for their own use exceeds their money income. Two-thirds of the rural poor have no land. They work for the large landowners, increasingly as seasonally employed migrants, moving around the country from harvest to harvest, living in shacks in the fields, and often paid less than the minimum wage (Russell, pp. 71, 79; Rudolph, pp. 125–126).

TABLE 2.3 Death and Disease

The relative poverty of Mexico, Egypt, and Namibia is reflected in shorter lives and the deaths of mothers in childbirth (2000–2005).

	Number of Person with HIV/AIDS	Mothers Dying in Childbirth for Each 100,000 Births	Percentage of Women Not Expected to Survive to Age 65	Percentage of Men Not Expected to Survive to Age 65	Tuberculosis Cases per 100,000 Persons
Namibia	230,000	300	69.2	75.3	478
Egypt	8,000	84	22	32.1	38
Mexico	150,000	83	17.9	28.5	44
United States	900,000	11	13.6	21.9	4
Japan	41,000	10	7	15	44
Germany	12,000	8	9.8	18.3	8

Source:. United Nations Statistics Division, Demographic and Social Statistics, Statistics and Indicators on Women and Men, Table 3.8 , http://unstats.un.org/unsd/demographic/products/indwm/table6C.htm; United Nations Human Development Report 2004 , http://hdr.undp.org/statistics/data/advanced.cfm

TABLE 2.4   Men and Women Working in Agriculture and Their Families

In Mexico and Egypt, the number of people working the land has increased, but at the same time, farmers and their families are a smaller percent of the total population.

	Men and Women Working in Agriculture and Their Families, 1950	Agricultural Families as a Percent of the Total Population, 1950	Men and Women Working in Agriculture and Their Families, 2000	Agricultural Families as a Percent of the Total Population, 2000
Egypt	15,400,000	71	24,900,000	37
Germany	15,800,000	23	2,100,000	3
Japan	39,400,000	47	5,100,000	4
Mexico	17,500,000	63	23,500,000	24
Namibia	413,000	81	862,000	49
United States	21,700,000	14	6,200,000	2

Source: Food and Agriculture Organization, On-Line FAOSTAT Database, 2001, http://apps.fao.org.

Historically, rural Mexicans have tried to improve their lives through political action, supporting the Mexican Revolution and then petitioning the government to create or expand *ejidos*. Though the government was obligated under Article 27 of the Constitution to redistribute land to any Mexican who would work it, after Lázaro Cárdenas, government enthusiasm for this commitment weakened greatly. *Ejidos* were created on the poorest land: steep, rocky, and dry. Although it was forbidden to sell *ejido* land, many peasants found their only alternative was to enter into arrangements with landowners in which they lost control of their land and had to work it as employees. Many found that as the fertility of their land decreased, and their families grew, they could no longer make a living off the land.

Population Growth and Rural Poverty

The problems of poor, rural Mexicans have been exacerbated by rapid population growth. Stagnant for centuries, Mexican population growth took off after World War II. There were approximately 28 million Mexicans in 1950, 35 million in 1960, and 70 million in 1980. Population growth is slowing now; there were 100 million Mexicans in 2000.

As population grew, rural Mexicans found themselves with limited alternatives. Poor families didn't have enough land to divide among all their children. As a result, the number of landless peasants who had to work for wages also grew. Large-scale commercial farming created some jobs, but it also damaged the land by pouring unregulated pesticides and other chemicals over it and by draining rivers and groundwater for irrigation. When peasants tried to remain on their own land, they often caused environmental damage too, by clearing more and more of the infertile common lands, formerly considered unsuitable for farming. In poverty-stricken Chiapas, so much of the rainforest has been cleared that the border with forested Guatemala

TABLE 2.5 Total Population Growth (1950–2050)

Mexico and Egypt have tripled their populations since 1950. Japanese and German populations are expected to decline by 2050.

	Total Population, 1950	Total Population, 2000	Total Population, 2050 (estimated)
Egypt	21,197,691	68,359,979	113,002,084
Germany	68,374,572	82,797,408	79,702,511
Japan	83,805,000	126,549,976	101,228,471
Mexico	28,485,180	100,349,766	153,162,145
Namibia	463,729	1,771,327	2,464,890
United States	152,271,000	275,562,673	403,943,147

Source: U.S. Bureau of the Census, International Database 2000, http://www.census.gov/ipc/www/idbsprd.html.

TABLE 2.6 Urban Population Growth (1950–2000)

Mexico and Japan are significantly more urban today than they were 50 years ago.

	Urban Population, 1950	Urban Population as a Percent of the Total, 1950	Urban Population, 2000	Urban Population as a Percent of the Total, 2000
Egypt	6,800,000	31	31,300,000	46
Germany	49,200,000	72	72,400,000	88
Japan	42,100,000	50	99,700,000	79
Mexico	11,800,000	43	73,600,000	74
Namibia	48,000	9	542,000	31
United States	101,200,000	64	214,500,000	77

Source: Food and Agriculture Organization, On-Line FAOSTAT Database 2001, http://apps.fao.org.

is visible from space. Overall, rural population in Mexico has increased about 30 percent since 1940. The percentage would be higher, were it not for the fact that so many rural Mexicans have left the countryside and moved to the cities or across the border to the United States. (See Table 2.5, above.)

Since the 1940s, rural Mexicans have been flocking to the cities in search of work. And the youthful population of cities continued to grow through natural increase. Fifty years ago, 57 percent of Mexicans lived in rural areas and 43 percent lived in towns and cities. Today, only 26 percent live in the countryside and 74 percent live in urban areas. As they grew, cities engulfed rural areas at their edges. Mexico City's population is now twenty times greater than it was in 1950; approximately 20 million people are living today in and around the capital. (See Table 2.6, above and also see Table 4.2, p. 235.)

Mexican women are having much smaller families now than they did in the past (see p. 93) and as a result, Mexico's rate of population growth is gradually slowing. By 2045, the population will virtually stop growing. That will give Mexico what experts call a "demographic bonus," a period when the working age population is large, but the number of old people and children to be supported is small. This "demographic window of opportunity," as demographer Rodolfo Tuiran puts it, will be the perfect time for Mexico to increase investment and economic growth (Dillon, June 8, 1999, pp. A1, A12).

SOCIAL CHANGE AND MEXICO'S POOR

Mexico today is in the midst of major economic change. Increasingly it is part of a global economy, with especially tight links to the United States. Economic globalization has had a major impact on poor Mexicans in rural areas and cities. We hear about globalization all the time these days, but you may not be quite sure just what globalization means. Often, when we think of globalization we think of products. We think that all over the world people are wearing Nike sneakers or eating McDonald's hamburgers or buying Hello Kitty accessories. But it is important to realize that it is not just consumption that has been globalized. Social institutions have been globalized too. In Mexico, globalization has had profound effects on where people live, what work they do, and how their families and communities are organized. We can see the impact of globalization in Mexico by contrasting the present "global" era with earlier times.

Protectionist Mexico

For forty years, Mexico's economy was protectionist—the very opposite of a globalized economy. The government set high tariffs (import taxes) to protect Mexican companies from foreign competition. The goal was to develop Mexican industries that would employ Mexicans and sell their goods to the Mexican market. The government also helped Mexican businesses by giving them loans and sometimes subsidies. The government itself became a major industrialist and employer, operating railroads, the oil industry, telephone service, and thousands of smaller companies. The government protected peasants too, by granting them land in *ejidos*. Protectionism worked well for many years; the economy grew and Mexicans' standard of living rose.

But by the 1970s, the protectionist system had begun to break down. Protected against foreign competition, Mexican industries became less efficient and lacked incentives to improve production. Mexicans wanted to buy foreign products, but they couldn't sell what they made in return. The Mexican economy stagnated. Only the money earned abroad by the state-owned oil industry provided some foreign exchange. Mexico had to borrow money abroad to pay for its imports. When oil prices fell, in 1982, Mexico no longer had enough to pay even the interest on its loans.

The International Monetary Fund agreed to help Mexico pay off its debts, but as a condition of its help, it required the Mexican government to cut tariffs, eliminate subsidies to Mexican companies, and reduce spending on social services. Some

800,000 Mexicans lost their jobs and many Mexican businesses failed. The cost of food and other essentials increased to ordinary Mexicans as businesses lost their subsidies. The standard of living dropped for most Mexicans (Hellman, pp. 8–9).

The New "Free-Market" Mexico

The PRI's leadership understood that they needed a new strategy for Mexico's economy. The United States, the World Bank, and many others told Mexico that it needed to increase its involvement in the world economy. This **free market** philosophy fell on the receptive ears of a new generation of Mexican presidents educated in the United States—Carlos Salinas and Ernesto Zedillo. Salinas and Zedillo opened Mexico to foreign trade and investment as never before. Foreign, mostly U.S., companies located in Mexico and invested in the Mexican economy. Foreign investors made loans that enabled Mexico to buy abroad. In some ways, the free trade policy worked very well; the economy grew rapidly. But depending on foreign investment left Mexico very vulnerable to crises in the world economy. The Mexican economy now echoes and amplifies the pattern of U.S. recessions. In 1995, 1998, 2000, and 2001, Mexico suffered financial crises, bankrupt businesses, falling wages, and higher unemployment (Otero, 1995, pp. 320–321; *The Economist,* July 7, 2001).

NAFTA

NAFTA is probably the best-known part of Mexico's new free-market economy. NAFTA (the North American Free Trade Agreement) is a trade treaty that links Mexico with its two wealthy northern neighbors, the United States and Canada. NAFTA removed trade barriers so that goods and money could move more freely across borders. NAFTA's advocates argued that freer trade would help all three nations. Mexico would benefit from increased foreign investment, both in Mexican companies and in factories built by foreign companies. That would create more jobs and improve Mexico's trade balance by increasing the amount of Mexican goods imported into the United States and Canada (Burgoon, p. 2).

Ten years after the passage of NAFTA we can see that the agreement fostered the expansion of manufacturing, but had deadly consequences for small farmers. Mexico gained 500,000 jobs in manufacturing, but it lost 1.3 million jobs in agriculture. Economic growth has been slow over the decade, with GNP increasing a mere 1 percent per capita on a yearly average. At the same time, real wages have fallen an average of 0.2 percent per year and income inequality has grown more than 10 percent for the decade. Not all of these outcomes are due to NAFTA, but they show that NAFTA has not been the miraculous economic tonic that was promised (Audley et al., p. 6; Stiglitz, Jan. 6, 2004, p. A23).

Maquiladoras

The *macquiladora* sector is the part of the Mexican economy most closely tied to the global economy. Foreign assembly plants are known in Mexico as *maquiladoras.* Most are owned by U.S.-based multinational firms that send partly finished materials to Mexico for assembly into finished goods. Almost all *maquiladoras* are clustered near the United States–Mexico border so that the materials for clothes or

Many *maquiladoras* employing unskilled workers have moved to China and other Asian countries where wages are even lower than in Mexico. The factories that are left produce more complex products that require more skilled labor. These women are assembling televisions for export to the United States.

electronics can be sent to Mexico one day and returned to the United States as finished goods on the next. *Maquiladoras* come to Mexico for cheap wages. Big companies like GE, Alcoa, RCA, and General Motors, as well as many smaller businesses, have set up *maquiladoras* in Mexico. While the *maquiladora* program was first begun in the 1960s, its greatest growth was in the 1980s and 1990s (Russell, pp. 189, 195). By the end of 2000, Mexico had 3,700 *maquiladoras* employing 1.3 million people. These factories paid $4 to $5 a day for entry-level unskilled workers, and an average for all employees of about $65 a week.

Maquiladoras exist because Mexicans are so desperate for jobs that they are willing to move to often-desolate border areas, accept low wages, long hours, and frequently unsafe working conditions, just to have a job. *Maquiladora* workers usually live in shantytowns, with unpaved streets, and without running water or sewage systems, because they can't afford to pay rent. Prices on the Mexican side of the border aren't much lower than in the United States, so $12.00 a day won't go far. Most workers in the assembly plants are women in their teens and twenties, some as young as 13 or 14 (Clark, p. 2; *The Economist*, Feb. 16, 2002, p. 36; Thompson, Dec. 26, 2001, p. C1; Forero, Sept. 3, 2003, p. A3).

The Ortegas' Story: Maquiladora Workers

Pedro and Maria Ortega count themselves lucky. Because they both have maquiladora *jobs, they are able to earn as much as $120 a week. Back home in their village there was no work for Maria, and Pedro only managed to find work during the planting and harvest seasons. Now that they both work and earn equal wages, Maria says their marriage feels more like a partnership. But it isn't completely equal, she says. The way Pedro budgets their money, his wages pay for food and rent and water, the essentials, and her wages pay* *for "extras"—school uniforms, money sent home, etc. Maria is still "in charge" of the cooking and housekeeping, even though she works full time, just like Pedro.*

They live in San Isidro, a settlement on the east side of Juárez, a huge border city with 1.3 million inhabitants and almost 300 maquiladoras. But although San Isidro is 15 years old, it still doesn't have running water or a sewage system, so Pedro and Maria spend $12 per week for bottled water, delivered by truck. The Ortegas and their son Juan take showers twice a week, by standing on their back step and pouring water over themselves with a dipper. Maria gives Juan as much drinking water as he wants, but she restricts herself to one glass a day.

Pedro has dug a pit for an outhouse out in back of the one-room tin-roofed shack they rent for $15 a week. San Isidro smells of human waste and of the garbage that piles up, since there is no city garbage collection. The Ortegas are saving up money to buy concrete blocks to build their own house, and they also send money home to their elderly parents in the village. When Juan started school this year, he needed sneakers, a book bag, the school uniform, notebooks and pencils. Maria figured out that it took her 44 hours of work to pay for it all (Dillon, Feb. 15, 2001, p. A6; Thompson, Feb. 11, 2001; Young, p. 66).

The year 2000 proved to be the peak of the *maquiladora* boom. When the United States economy went into recession, the border region went with it. In 2001, more than 500 *maquiladoras* closed and 280,000 jobs were lost. By 2004, the industry was reviving, but it had changed profoundly. Much of the light manufacturing of textiles and electronics moved to China. These products were easy to ship, and total costs for unskilled labor are much lower in China: 25¢ an hour, as compared to $1.50 to $2.00 in Mexico. Companies that remained in Mexico employed fewer workers and more machinery, and they hired more temporary workers without rights or benefits. Nowadays it is heavy industry that is moving to Mexico: cars, auto parts, televisions, and refrigerators that are expensive to ship from Asia. These industries pay more and hire more men, but they are more heavily automated. Rapid change like this is typical of the global economy, but it is hard for Mexican workers to keep up with the pace of change (Jordan; Malkin, Aug. 26, 2004, pp. W1, W7; Thompson, June 29, 2002, p. A3).

Free-Market Agriculture

During the 1980s, President Carlos Salinas set in motion the most fundamental changes in Mexican agriculture since the revolution. His purpose was modernization: to replace the inefficient subsistence farmer with modern "agribusiness"—big farm companies, often multinationals—to grow food for export to the world market.

The most radical of Salinas' reforms was the revocation of Article 27 of the Constitution, the article that had promised land to any Mexican who would work it himself and had protected small farmers by prohibiting the sale of *ejidos*. (If *ejidos* were salable, the old reasoning went, then bad harvests or debt would force peasants to sell them.) The *ejido* was a "sacred" symbol of Mexico's commitment to its Indian heritage and to peasants. Many Mexicans who would never benefit from its provisions felt attached to the revolutionary hopes embodied in Article 27.

Since the 1980s, there has been far-reaching change in Mexican agriculture. More food is being produced, much of it on large, modern farms, many owned by foreign companies. Mexican agriculture now produces more food for export and more grain to feed animals, but production of food for domestic consumption has fallen. Mexico is in the seemingly contradictory situation of no longer being self-sufficient in food, even while foodstuffs are a major export. Rural Mexicans especially (like many people in other third-world countries that export food) are eating less and eating worse and experiencing more unemployment (Barkin, pp. 11, 16–22, 28–32; Klein-Robbenhaar, pp. 1–14).

Farmers and NAFTA

Millions of farmers in Mexico grow crops on tiny plots of land, no more than four or five acres, and sell their crops through wholesalers. For example, there are 3.5 million corn growers in Mexico. They are in a state of shock as the agricultural provisions of NAFTA are put into effect. With tariffs and subsidies scaled back, cheap subsidized corn from the United States has flooded into Mexico. The price of corn has dropped 45 percent in three years, to a level below the costs of production for Mexican farmers. Corn, rice, sugar, and coffee farmers have been protesting all over Mexico, demanding new subsidies and protesting free trade. In January 2003, small farmers from all over Mexico marched into Mexico City to protest. They wanted the government to renegotiate NAFTA, impose protective tariffs, and provide credit to small farmers so they can switch to more profitable crops. In Campeche rice farmers took over two cereal processing plants. Five thousand sugar cane farmers marched through Mexico City and blocked access to government offices. The sugar industry is Mexico's second largest employer (with approximately 3.5 million workers), so these protests made legislators take notice. Congress decided to impose a tariff on imports of fructose from the United States so that Mexican soft drink manufacturers would buy Mexican sugar. The government also nationalized almost half of the nation's sugar mills to keep them from closing down (Thompson, July 22, 2001, p. 1; Jan. 21, 2002, p. A6; Malkin, June 9, 2004, pp. W1, W7; Rosenberg, March 3, 2003, p. A22; Rendon, p. 24).

Economists estimate that free trade in agricultural products will force 1.4 million Mexicans off the land (Andreas, in Wise, p. 212). But few of them will be needed on the huge commercial farms. Modern agribusiness uses machines and chemicals; it needs far fewer workers than peasant agriculture. Where will displaced peasants go? Most peasants live in the impoverished south. There are fewer jobs for unskilled workers now in the northern *maquiladoras,* and it is also harder to cross the border into the United States.

This is where globalization is having its most rapid and far-reaching effect in Mexico today. Peasant farmers, many of them Indians, who until recently lived cut off from the larger Mexican society, are suddenly being drawn out of their isolation into not just the Mexican economy but the world economy. Often their new roles are marginal, insecure, and exploited. Vegetable growers in Sinaloa send buses south every year to recruit 200,000 poor Mexicans to pick fruits and vegetables, mostly for export to the United States. Whole families come north, to live in workcamp shantytowns, one room per family, and bathe in pesticide-soaked irrigation canals. In one of the first scandals of Vicente Fox's administration, Mexican reporters revealed that packing plants owned by the president's family were employing child workers (Thompson, May 6, 2001, p. 10).

The Story of San Jeronimo

San Jeronimo Progreso is a remote mountain village in Oaxaca. It is so remote that there wasn't even any road linking the village to the nearest large town, until the villagers built one themselves fifteen years ago. There are about 2,000 inhabitants in 250 households. All land is owned communally and all the land that could possibly be cultivated has already been cleared. There is no more land for growing families to farm. Nowadays, the people of this apparently isolated "traditional" Mixtec Indian village survive through their connections with the global economy.

Luis Ortiz, his wife Ana, and their three children can raise only enough corn and beans to feed themselves for two and a half months of the year. They must find some source of cash to buy food the rest of the year. Twenty years ago, when Luis was a boy, his whole family wove palm hats in the wintertime. They got ten cents a hat from the merchant who bought them and each of the six family members could weave two hats a day. Last winter, Luis and his oldest son spent four months in El Campo de Las Pulgas (Flea Camp), a labor camp in Baja California, where they picked tomatoes for export to the United States. The money they earned bought food for the family, fertilizer for their plot of corn and beans, and last winter, bags of cement to pour a floor for their house.

Luis and Ana are considering moving the whole family to Tijuana next winter. San Jeronimo has a "daughter enclave" in a squatter settlement there, where they can live near relatives and neighbors from their town who will help them get jobs and find a place to live. Luis may even decide to risk a trip to the United States to live in another "daughter enclave" in Oregon and work the apple harvest there. Luis says that if he is to go, it must be soon. By age 35 he will be too old and worn out for migrating. He will "retire" to San Jeronimo and work the family land, with the help of cash that his migrating sons and daughters will send. (This vignette is derived from research presented by Nagengast and Kearney, pp. 453–469.)

Globalization and Migration

Today, the Mexican government estimates that there are 10–12 million Mexicans living in the United States, as much as 12 percent of the country's population of 100 million. Perhaps three and a half million of the migrants are "undocumented," that is, they have no immigration documents and would be arrested and deported if found by the INS. Three-quarters of all Mexicans in the United States live in seven states: the border states of California, Texas, and Arizona, nearby Colorado, and also Illinois, Georgia, and New York (Thompson, Oct. 28, 2003, p. A14; *The New York Times,* March 20, 2003, p. A31; Gori, July 6, 2002, p. B3; *The Economist,* Jan. 25, 2003, p. 37).

At least half a million people from the dry, impoverished state of Zacatecas work in the United States. The isolated town of El Porvenir ("The Future"), population 1,200, is silent and empty; half the working-age men are in the United States. Population is shrinking in 35 of Zacatecas' 57 counties. There are 80 people living in the ghostly village of Jomolquillo, but 300 others live in Los Angeles. It is surprising that many of these empty towns look fairly prosperous. Their unoccupied houses are built of concrete with American-style facades. The streets are paved, and there is a new bridge or a school yard playground. These improvements have been paid for by **remittances,** money sent home by migrants working in the United

States. The total of remittance money is now up to an estimated $14 billion per year, second only to oil as Mexico's most important source of income. One bank study found that one Mexican in five regularly receives money from relatives north of the border. The money goes, first of all, to pay for food and clothing and housing, but an increasing percentage is invested in small businesses or higher education. Mexicans are also organizing home town clubs that put together money to finance village development. The Mexican government now matches these funds with state and federal money on a two-for-one basis, to build roads, schools, and health clinics (Lizarzaburu; O'Murchu; Thompson, March 25, 2002, p. A3).

Mexicans in the United States work as migrant farm workers, as laborers on lawn-care crews, in restaurants, and on construction. Some work in factories or as maids. They are beginning to open businesses or move up to skilled industrial jobs. Even at minimum wages, migrants can make many times more than Mexican wages. It's no surprise then that Mexicans are increasingly living binational lives. They make repeated trips to the United States often joining relatives or neighbors there. Teenage boys, and more and more, teenage girls too, see the trip across the border as a "rite of passage," a risky, but inevitable part of life, since there are no opportunities at home. They expect to send money home and then retire some day to Mexico, when they are too old for the hard life of the migrant, to be supported in their remodeled home by their children in the United States. Recognizing this binational life, the Zacatecas state legislature voted to allow migrants living in the United States to run for political office in Mexico and reserved two seats in the legislature for migrants only. In 2004, Andres Bermudez, "the tomato king," who grew rich-growing tomatoes in California, was elected mayor of the town of Jerez, Zacatecas. In addition, many Mexicans in the United States made trips home to vote (Thompson, July 5, 2004, p. A4).

Migration and Mexican Politics

Early in his presidency, Vicente Fox took the unprecedented step of openly acknowledging the importance of migrants to Mexican society. When he called Mexicans who migrate to the United States "heroes," he made news and deeply moved many Mexicans. Previous presidents had treated migration as an embarrassment, a subject to be avoided (Weiner, Dec. 14, 2000, p. A12). In 2000 two of the three presidential candidates campaigned in Mexican communities in the United States, and there were even attempts to set up polling places in U.S. cities where Mexicans could vote in Mexican elections. President Fox created a new cabinet post for migration issues, and the migration minister immediately set to work creating new financial networks for migrants to use in sending remittances home, cutting the fees they pay from 25 percent to 2.3 percent (Weiner, March 3, 2001, pp. A1, A4). He also pressured the United States to accept a Mexican "consular identification card" for Mexicans lacking other documents. Though the United States government has refused to accept the card, several cities and counties do accept it (Gori, July 6, 2002, p. B3). Finally, Fox announced early in his campaign that he believed the border should be as open to the movement of labor as it is to the movement of capital. One of his first actions as president was to meet with U.S. President George W. Bush to negotiate a new migration policy. But after September 2001, any progress towards regularizing the status of Mexicans illegally in the United States came to a halt, a casualty of the terrorist attacks and the economic recession (Schmitt, Aug. 10, 2001, pp. A1, A4).

Globalization and the Environment

Just as it has brought a contradictory mix of benefits and costs to Mexico's poor, when it comes to Mexico's environment, globalization has been a two-edged sword. The economic development of the border zone has brought uncontrolled pollution to a fragile desert environment. Border cities like Tijuana, Nogales, Agua Prieta, and Ciudad Juárez have seen their populations increase by more than 50 percent in the last ten years. Ciudad Acuna, where Alcoa and GE and Allied Signal, among other companies, run *maquiladoras,* has seen its population double. All along the border, the air and water are polluted with industrial and human waste. On average, cities can treat properly less than 35 percent of the sewage generated (*The Economist,* July 17, 2001). Resort development along the coast of Guerrero has polluted the beautiful bay the tourists come to enjoy. In Chiapas, timber companies and peasants have cut down most of Mexico's last rainforest. If President Fox's plan to bring dams, railroads, highways, and industries to Chiapas becomes a reality, the destruction will increase. And in Mexicali, two new power plants will generate power for California, a very small number of jobs for Mexico, and abundant pollution for both sides of the border. The plants are built in Mexico because costs and environmental regulations are less there (Weiner, Feb. 13, 2003, p. A4; Dec. 8, 2002, p. 16; Sept. 17, 2002, p. A3).

At the same time, globalization has brought Mexico's small environmentalist movement powerful international allies. Efforts to save Mexico's splendid natural landscapes—its deserts, rainforests, coasts, and offshore waters—and its stunning biological diversity have been embraced by powerful NGOs. The Mexican government has learned that if it seeks international investment, then it must also take into account international public opinion. For example, in 2000 the government canceled a joint project with the Mitsubishi Corporation of Japan to build an enormous salt plant on the shore of a lagoon in Baja California where gray whales give birth. The Natural Resources Defense Council, an American group, led the campaign against the plant, with ads throughout Mexico and the rest of North America, an international Internet and press campaign, and a planned campaign to boycott Mitsubishi stock and products (Preston, March 5, 2000, p. 13). Another international campaign helped villagers in Tepoztlán, a village outside Mexico City, to block the building of a golf course. Similarly, building was halted for a nuclear waste processing facility in Sierra Blanca on the Texas border (*The Amicus Journal,* summer 2000, p. 15). In Chiapas, though, where the rainforest is being destroyed, the Zapatista rebel movement criticizes the environmentalists for caring more about preserving the rainforest for rich, foreign tourists than about the livelihood of poor, land-hungry peasants (Weiner, Dec. 8, 2002, p. 16).

The Future

Who can predict what the future will bring? It is particularly risky to speculate about Mexico's future because the society is now so closely tied to the fate of the global economy. In the past, PRI domination of the government provided stability, though at a price. Now, as Mexican political life has opened up, unpredictability has increased.

Here are three possible scenarios for Mexico's future. In the most optimistic scenario, democracy will grow and stabilize. Elections will be free and fair, and various political parties will contend. The government will be able to bring drug trafficking under control, bring down crime rates, and cleanse corruption from the police and government bureaucracy. Stable government will make Mexico attractive to foreign investment, and free of corruption, the government will be able to devote tax revenues to improving education, building infrastructure, preserving the environment, and helping the poor. This is a very attractive scenario, but many dangers stand in the way of its achievement.

What if the world economy continues to sour, Mexican wages fall again, and farm prices fall, putting small farmers of corn, rice, and coffee into greater and greater crisis? What if the government is unable to control drug trafficking and corruption? Then we might see a scenario of growing disorder: rising crime, greater political influence by drug cartels, and spreading rebellion and violence by peasants in the south. In this scenario we might also look for increasing conflict in the north, as population grows along the border, *maquiladora* workers battle for union recognition, and the drug traffic grows.

In a time of crisis, Mexicans might lose faith in the PAN and call back the PRI to restore order. They might decide that corruption with order and stability is better than democracy and crisis. This scenario might involve growing power for the military and perhaps more nationalistic hostility to free trade and the United States. Both the wealthy industrial nations of the world and the "developing" third world are watching to see if Mexico's bold experiment with democracy and free trade will work.[3]

Thinking Sociologically

1. Describe some norms that are important in Mexican culture.
2. Are there any similarities in the roles men are expected to play in Mexican society and in Japanese society? What differences are there?
3. Explain what is meant by the term *reciprocity network*, using examples from Chapter 2. Do people in your society form reciprocity networks? Can you give an example of a reciprocity network from your own experience?
4. Compare the Gómez family household in Mexico (pp. 89–90) with the Sato family household in Japan (p. 40). Which of these does your own household resemble more?
5. Can you explain what political patronage is and how it works? Can you find an example of political patronage in your own society?

---

[3]Michael Mazarr proposes a series of scenarios similar to these in his book *Mexico 2005: The Challenges of the New Millennium* (The CSIS Press, 1998) and "What's Next for Mexico: Potential Surprises from a U.S. Neighbor" (*The Futurist*, October 1999).

6. Look up the most recent data you can find on income distribution by quintiles in your society. Is your society more like Mexico or more like Japan in its degree of inequality?
7. Does the social category of "mixed race" exist in your society, as it does in Mexico, or does everyone have to be classified as belonging to one race or another? Which way of thinking about race would you prefer?
8. Refer to Table 2.1 (p. 91) and compare the rates of divorce in Mexico and in the United States. Use Chapter 2 and your introductory sociology textbook to help you explain why the divorce rate is so much higher in the United States than in Mexico.
9. What are some of the problems that have caused a "legitimacy crisis" for the Mexican government? Do people in your own society question the legitimacy of the government?

For Further Reading

GUILLERMOPRIETO, ALMA, *The Heart That Bleeds: Latin America Now.* New York: Knopf, 1994.

HELLMAN, JUDITH ADLER, *Mexican Lives: Conversations on the Future of Mexico.* New York: New Press, 1994.

KATZENBERGER, ELAINE, *First World, Ha Ha Ha! The Zapatista Challenge.* San Francisco: City Lights Books, 1995.

KRAUSE, ENRIQUE, *Mexico: Biography of Power.* New York: HarperCollins Pubs., 1997.

MARNHAM, PATRICK, *Dreaming with His Eyes Open: A Life of Diego Rivera.* New York: Knopf, 1998.

MARTÍNEZ, RUBÉN, *Crossing Over: A Mexican Family on the Migrant Trail.* Metropolitan Books, 2001.

PRESTON, JULIA, AND SAM DILLON, *Opening Mexico: The Making of a Democracy.* New York: Farrar, Straus and Giroux, 2004.

QUINONES, SAM, *True Tales from Another Mexico.* Albuquerque: University of New Mexico Press, 2001.

SELBY, HENRY A., ARTHUR D. MURPHY, AND STEPHEN A. LORENZEN, *The Mexican Urban Household: Organized for Self-Defense.* Austin: University of Texas Press, 1990.

SHORRIS, EARL, *The Life and Times of Mexico.* New York: W.W. Norton & Co., 2004.

STEPHEN, LYNN, *Zapata Lives! Histories and Cultural Politics in Southern Mexico.* Berkeley: University of California Press, 2002.

WOMACK, JOHN JR., *Rebellion in Chiapas: An Historical Reader.* New York: The New Press, 1999.

Bibliography

ALTHAUS, DUDLEY, "Corruption Eats at the Heart of Mexico's Society," *The Houston Chronicle,* Nov. 26, 2000, p. J8.

AUDLEY, JOHN J., et al., *NAFTA's Promise and Reality.* Washington DC: The Carnegie Endowment, 2003.

BACON, DAVID, *The Children of NAFTA: Labor Wars on the U.S./Mexico Border.* Berkeley: University of California Press, 2004.

BARKIN, DAVID, *Distorted Development: Mexico and the World Economy.* Boulder, CO: Westview Press, 1990.

BENNETT, VIVIENNE, *The Politics of Water: Urban Protest, Gender and Politics in Monterrey, Mexico.* Pittsburgh: University of Pittsburgh Press, 1995.

BRAGANTI, NANCY, AND ELIZABETH DEVINE, *The Travelers' Guide to Latin American Customs and Manners.* New York: St. Martin's Press, 1989.

BRANDES, STANLEY, *Staying Sober in Mexico City.* Austin, TX: The University of Texas Press, 2002.

BRUNI, FRANK, AND GINGER THOMPSON, "Bolstering Faith of Indians, Pope Gives Mexico a Saint," *The New York Times,* Aug. 1, 2002, p. A6.

BURGOON, BRIAN, "The Job-Eating Villain: Is It NAFTA or Mexico's Currency Crisis?" *Dollars and Sense* (July–August, 1996), pp. 12–20.

CAMP, RODERIC AI, *Mexico's Mandarins: Crafting a Power Elite for the Twenty-First Century.* Berkeley: University of California Press, 2002.

CASIQUE, IRENE, *Power, Autonomy and Division of Labor in Mexican Dual-Earner Families.* New York: University Press of America, 2001.

CASTAÑEDA, JORGE G., *Perpetuating Power: How Mexican Presidents Were Chosen.* New York: The New Press, 2000.

CASTELLS, MANUEL, AND ALEJANDRO PORTES, "World Underneath: The Origins, Dynamics, and Effects of the Informal Economy," in Alejandro Portes, Manual Castells, and Lauren A. Benton, eds., *The Informal Economy.* Baltimore: Johns Hopkins University Press, 1989, pp. 11–37.

CLARK, CAROL, "NAFTA's Effects on Mexico Are Grim," *Greensboro News and Record,* May 31, 1998.

CORNELIUS, WAYNE A., AND ANN L. CRAIG, *The Mexican Political System in Transition.* La Jolla, CA: Center for U.S.–Mexican Studies, University of California, San Diego, 1991.

CROSS, JOHN C., *Informal Politics: Street Vendors and the State in Mexico City.* Stanford: Stanford University Press, 1998.

DAVIS, DIANE E., *Urban Leviathan, Mexico City in the Twentieth Century.* Philadelphia: Temple University Press, 1994.

DILLON, SAM, "Smaller Families to Bring Big Change in Mexico," *The New York Times,* June 8, 1999, pp. A1, A12.

———, "In Mexico's Election, the Race Is Real," *The New York Times,* March 12, 2000, pp. 1, 18.

———, "Mexico's Ruling Party Accused of Diverting Public Money," *The New York Times,* March 27, 2000, p. A6.

———, "Clean Vote Vowed in Mexico, but Fraud Dies Hard," *The New York Times,* June 28, 2000, p. A3.

———, "Familiar Foe for Mexico's New Leader: Corruption," *The New York Times,* July 16, 2000, p. A6.

———, "Profits Raise Pressures on U.S.-Owned Factories in Mexican Border Zone," *The New York Times,* Feb. 15, 2001, p. A16.

DILLON, SAM, AND JULIA PRESTON, "Old Ways Die Hard in Mexican Election despite the Pledges," *The New York Times,* May 9, 2000, pp. A1, A4.

DOMINGUEZ, JORGE L., AND JAMES A. MCCANN, *Democratizing Mexico: Public Opinion and Electoral Choices.* Baltimore: Johns Hopkins University Press, 1996.

———, *Democratizing Mexico.* Baltimore: Johns Hopkins University Press, 1996.

The Economist, "Mexico: Free to Be Bad," March 11, 2000, p. 44.

———, "Special Report: The U.S.–Mexican Border," July 17, 2001, pp. 28–30.

———, "Politics in Mexico: Post-Rebellion Pains," Jan. 12, 2002, p. 35.

———, "Crime in Mexico: Critical Threat," June 15, 2002, p. 36.

———, "Religion in Mexico Staying Alive," July 27, 2002, p. 34.

———, "Mexico and the United States: Half an Enchilada," Jan. 25, 2003, pp. 37–38.

———, "Crime in Mexico: Wakey Wakey!" June 28, 2003, p. 33.

———, "A Rising Star in Mexico: The Man Who Would Be President," Nov. 15, 2003, p. 35.

————, "Drugs in Mexico: War without End," March 6, 2004, p. 34.

————, "Crime in Mexico: Fear of Captivity," June 19, 2004, p. 37.

————, "Dinosaurs on the Prowl Again," Aug. 7, 2004, p. 29.

————, "Attitudes and Ambiguities," Aug. 14, 2004, p. 36.

————, "Politics in Mexico: A Close-Run Thing," Sept. 11, 2004, p. 34.

FALICOV, CELIA JAES, "Mexican Families," in Marian McGoldrick, John K. Pearce, and Joseph Giordano, eds., *Ethnicity and Family Therapy.* New York: Guildford Press, 1982, pp. 134–163.

FAOSTAT Database, http://apps.fao.org.

FISHER, IAN, "In Mexican Village, Signs of Death Hang Heavy," *The New York Times,* Dec. 25, 1997, p. A8.

FORERO, JUAN, "As China Gallops, Mexico Sees Factory Jobs Slip Away," *The New York Times,* Sept. 3, 2003, p. A3.

FOX, ROBERT A., AND PEDRO SOLIS CAMARA, "Parenting of Young Children by Fathers in Mexico and the United States," *Journal of Social Psychology,* Vol. 137, no. 4 (August 1997), pp. 489–495.

FUENTES, CARLOS, *The Buried Mirror.* Boston: Houghton Mifflin, 1992.

————, "The Mirror of the Other," *The Nation,* March 30, 1992, pp. 408–411.

GOLDEN, TIM, " 'Awakened' Peasant Farmers Overrunning Mexican Towns," *The New York Times,* Feb. 9, 1994, pp. A1, A9.

————, "In Breakthrough, Mexican Official Testifies in Texas," *The New York Times,* July 15, 1998, pp. A1, A6.

————, "Mexican Tale of Absolute Drug Corruption," *The New York Times,* Jan. 9, 2000, pp. 1, 8.

GOODWIN, PAUL, ED., *Global Studies: Latin America.* Guilford, CT: Dushkin Publishing Group, 1991.

GORI, GRAHAM, "U.S. and Mexico Battle over Sweetening Drinks," *The New York Times,* Jan. 17, 2002, p. W1.

————, "A Card Allows U.S. Banks to Aid Mexican Immigrants," *The New York Times,* July 6, 2002, p. B3.

GRIMES, BARBARA, ed., Ethnologue. Dallas, Texas: Summer Institute of Linguistics, Inc., 1996, http://www.sil.org/ethnologue/countries/Mexi.html.

GUILLERMOPRIETO, ALMA, *The Heart That Bleeds: Latin America Now.* New York: Knopf, 1994.

————, "A Hundred Women," *The New Yorker,* Sept. 29, 2003, pp. 82–93.

————, "The Morning Quickie," *The New York Review of Books,* Aug. 12, 2004, pp. 40–43.

GUTMANN, MATTHEW C., *The Meaning of Macho: Being a Man in Mexico City.* Berkeley: University of California Press, 1996.

HELLMAN, JUDITH ADLER, *Mexican Lives: Conversations on the Future of Mexico.* New York: New Press, 1994.

ISAAC, CLAUDIA B., "Class Stratification and Cooperative Production among Rural Women in Central Mexico," *Latin American Research Review,* Vol. 30, no. 2 (1995), pp. 123–150.

JORDAN, MARY, "Mexican Border Factories Move to Asia," *The Monterey Herald,* June 21, 2002, http://www.montereyherald.com/mld/mcherald/2002/06/21/business/356040.htm (last accessed Dec. 24, 2003).

KANDELL, JONATHAN, *La Capital: The Biography of Mexico City.* New York: Random House, 1988.

KLEIN-ROBBENHAAR, JOHN F., "Agro-Industry and the Environment: The Case of Mexico in the 1990s," *Agricultural History,* Vol. 69, no. 3 (Summer 1995), pp. 395–419.

KRAUSE, ENRIQUE, *Mexico: Biography of Power.* New York: HarperCollins Publishers, 1997.
———, "Past Wrongs, Future Rights," *The New York Times,* Aug. 10, 2004, p. A23.
LEWIS, OSCAR, *Five Families: Mexican Case Studies in the Culture of Poverty.* New York: Wiley, 1959.
———, *Tepoztlán, Village in Mexico.* New York: Holt, Rinehart & Winston, 1960.
LIZARZABURU, JAVIER, "Mexican Migrants Growing Influence," *BBC News,* May 18, 2004, http://news.bbc.co.uk/go/pr/fr/-/1/hi/world/americas/3582881.stm.
LOMNITZ, LARISSA, *Networks and Marginality: Life in a Mexican Shantytown.* New York: Academic Press, 1977.
McKINLEY, JAMES C., JR, "Prosecutors in Mexico Reopen Inquiry in Rights Lawyer's Death," *The New York Times,* Feb. 27, 2005, p. 8.
———, "Mexico Says Drug Cartel Had Spy in President's Office," *The New York Times,* Feb. 7, 2005, p. A3.
———, "Mexican Troops Seize Prison after Drug Lord Violence," *The New York Times,* Jan. 15, 2005, p. A3.
MALKIN, ELISABETH, "In Mexico, Sugar vs. U.S. Corn Syrup," *The New York Times,* June 9, 2004, pp. W1, W7.
———, "Mexico's Working Poor Become Homeowners," *The New York Times,* Dec. 17, 2004, pp. W1, W7.
———, "A Boom along the Border," *The New York Times,* Aug. 26, 2004, pp. W1, W7.
MAZARR, MICHAEL, *Mexico 2005: The Challenges of the New Millennium. Significant Issues,* Vol. 20, no. 4, Washington DC: The Center for Strategic and International Studies, 1998.
———, "What's Next for Mexico: Potential Surprises from a U.S. Neighbor," *The Futurist,* Oct. 1999.
Mexican National Institute of Statistics, Geography and Informatics, http://www.inegi.gob.mx/inegi/default.asp
MIDDLEBROOK, KEVIN, *The Paradox of Revolution: Labor, the State, and Authoritarianism in Mexico.* Baltimore: Johns Hopkins University Press, 1995.
———, *The Paradox of Revolution: Labor, the State and Authoritarianism in Mexico.* Baltimore: Johns Hopkins University Press, 1995.
MORRIS, STEPHEN D., *Corruption and Politics in Contemporary Mexico.* Tuscaloosa: University of Alabama Press, 1991.
MURPHY, ARTHUR D., AND ALEX STEPNICK, *Social Inequality in Oaxaca.* Philadelphia: Temple University Press, 1991.
NAGENGAST, CAROLE, AND MICHAEL KEARNEY, "Mixtec Ethnicity: Social Identity, Political Consciousness and Political Activism," in Michael B. Whiteford and Scott Whiteford, eds., *Crossing Currents, Continuity and Change in Latin America.* Upper Saddle River, NJ: Prentice Hall, 1998.
NAPOLITANO, VALENTINA, *Migration, Mujercitas, and Medicine Men: Living in Urban Mexico.* Berkeley: University of California Press, 2002.
NAVARRO, MIREYA, "Who Is Killing the Young Women of Juárez? A Filmmaker Seeks Answers," *The New York Times,* Aug. 19, 2002, p. B3.
———, *The New York Times,* "U.S. Mexicans Gain Dual Citizenship," March 20, 2003, p. A31.
———, "Traffickers Reportedly Donated to Mexicans," Aug. 3, 1998, p. A22.
NOLEN, BARBARA, ed., *Mexico Is People: Land of Three Cultures.* New York: Scribner's, 1973.

O'MURCHU, SEAN, "In Zacatecas, America's the Future," *MSNBC News,* Feb. 15, 2001, http://msnbc.msn.com/id/3071713/ (last accessed Feb. 2, 2004).

OPPENHEIMER, ANDRES, *Bordering on Chaos: Guerillas, Stockbrokers, Politicians and Mexico's Road to Prosperity.* New York: Little Brown, 1996.

OSTER, PATRICK, *The Mexicans: A Personal Portrait of a People.* New York: Morrow, 1989.

OTERO, GERALDO, "Mexico's Political Future(s) in a Globalizing World Economy," *The Canadian Review of Sociology and Anthropology,* Vol. 32, no. 3 (August 1995), pp. 315–338.

———, *Farewell to the Peasantry: Political Class Formation in Rural Mexico.* Westview Press, 1999.

PAZ, OCTAVIO, *The Labyrinth of Solitude: Life and Thought in Mexico.* New York: Grove Press, 1961.

PRESTON, JULIA, "1 Blunt Bishop. Pope Steps In. Now There Are Two," *The New York Times,* May 28, 1997, p. A4.

———, "Mexico Sees Both Carrot and Stick Fail in Chiapas," *The New York Times,* May 17, 1998, p. 14.

———, "Mexicans Belittle Drug-Money Sting," *The New York Times,* May 20, 1998, p. A6.

———, "In Mexico, Nature Lovers Merit a Kiss from a Whale," *The New York Times,* March 5, 2000, p. 13.

———, "Mexican TV, Unshackled by Reform, Fights for Viewers," *The New York Times,* June 7, 2000, p. A3.

PRESTON, JULIA, AND SAM DILLON, *Opening Mexico: The Making of a Democracy.* New York: Farrar, Straus and Giroux, 2004.

QUINONES, SAM, *True Tales from Another Mexico.* Albuquerque: University of New Mexico Press, 2001.

RAMOS, SAMUEL, *Profile of Man and Culture in Mexico,* trans. Peter G. Earle. 1934. Reprint. Austin: University of Texas Press, 1972.

RANDALL, LAURA, ED., *Changing Structure of Mexico: Political, Social and Economic Prospects.* Armonk, NY: M. E. Sharp, 1996.

———, *Reforming Mexico's Agrarian Reform.* Armonk, NY: M. E. Sharp, 1996.

REAVIS, DICK J., *Conversations with Moctezuma: The Soul of Modern Mexico.* New York: Quill, Morrow, 1990.

RENDON, JOEL ESTUDILLO, "A Time for Politics," *Business Mexico,* Vol. 11, no. 10 (October 2001), p. 24.

RIDING, ALAN, *Distant Neighbors: A Portrait of the Mexicans.* New York: Knopf, 1985.

RODRIGUEZ, VICTORIA, AND PETER M. WARD, *Opposition Government in Mexico.* Albuquerque: University of New Mexico Press, 1995.

ROSENBERG, TINA, "Why Mexico's Small Corn Farmers Go Hungry," *The New York Times,* March 3, 2003, p. A22.

RUDOLPH, JAMES A., ed., *Mexico: A Country Study* (Area Handbook Series). Washington, DC: U.S. Government Printing Office, 1985.

RUIZ, RAMON EDUARDO, *Triumphs and Tragedy: A History of the Mexican People.* New York: Norton, 1992.

———, *On the Rim of Mexico: Encounters of the Rich and Poor.* Westview Press, Boulder, CO. 1998.

RUSSELL, JAMES W., *After the Fifth Sun: Class and Race in North America.* Englewood Cliffs, NJ: Prentice-Hall, 1994.

SELBY, HENRY A., ARTHUR D. MURPHY, AND STEPHEN A. LORENZEN, *The Mexican Urban Household: Organized for Self-Defense.* Austin: University of Texas Press, 1990.

SHORRIS, EARL, *The Life and Times of Mexico.* NY: W.W. Norton, 2004.

SIMON, JOEL, "Moment of Truth," *The Amicus Journal* (Summer 2000), pp. 12–15.

STAUDT, KATHLEEN, *Free Trade? Informal Economies at the U.S.–Mexico Border.* Philadelphia: Temple University Press, 1998.

STEPHEN, LYNN, *Zapata Lives! Histories and Cultural Politics in Southern Mexico.* Berkeley: University of California Press, 2002.

STIGLITZ, JOSEPH E., "The Broken Promise of Nafta," *The New York Times,* Jan. 6, 2004, p. A23.

TAYLER, LETTA, "Changes in Mexican Families," *Newsday,* Oct. 21, 2001, p. A12.

THOMPSON, GINGER, "Cocaine Doesn't Just 'Transit': Some of It Seeps," *The New York Times,* Jan. 11, 1999, p. A4.

———, "Victor in Mexico Plans to Overhaul Law Enforcement," *The New York Times,* July 5, 2000, pp. A1, A8.

———, "A Victory of Sorts for Abortion Rights in a Mexican State," *The New York Times,* Aug. 29, 2000, p. A3.

———, "In Mexico, a Man with a Badge Isn't the Good Guy," *The New York Times,* Nov. 24, 2000, p. A32.

———, "Chasing Mexico's Dream into Squalor," *The New York Times,* Feb. 11, 2001, pp. 1, 6.

———, "At Home, Mexico Mistreats Its Migrant Farmhands," *The New York Times,* May 6, 2001, pp. 1, 10.

———, "Farm Unrest Is Roiling Mexico, Posing Challenge for New Chief," *The New York Times,* July 22, 2001, p. 1.

———, "Mexican Human Rights Lawyer Is Killed," *The New York Times,* Oct. 22, 2001, p. A6.

———, "A Death in Mexico Symbolizes the Slow Pace of the Police Reforms That Fox Promised," *The New York Times,* Oct. 28, 2001, p. A10.

———, "Fighters for the Forest Are Released from Mexican Jail," *The New York Times,* Nov. 9, 2001, p. A12.

———, "Race Strains a Mexican Campaign," *The New York Times,* Nov. 11, 2001, p. A10.

———, "Tough Road for Mexico's Top Lawman," *The New York Times,* Nov. 18, 2001, p. A10.

———, "Fallout of U.S. Recession Drifts South into Mexico," *The New York Times,* Dec. 26, 2001, p. C1.

———, "Now the Morning News Is Earthy and Unsparing," *The New York Times,* Jan. 14, 2002, p. A4.

———, "Congress Shifts Mexico's Balance of Power," *The New York Times,* Jan. 21, 2002, p. A6.

———, "Vatican Curbing Deacons in Mexico," *The New York Times,* March 12, 2002, p. A8.

———, "Big Mexican Breadwinner: The Migrant Worker," *The New York Times,* March 25, 2002, p. A3.

———, "Mexico: Freedom of Information," *The New York Times,* May 2, 2002, p. A6.

———, "Mexico Is Attracting a Better Class of Factory in Its South," *The New York Times,* June 29, 2002, p. A3.

———, "Daddy's Girl Turns Beer-and-TV Billionaire," *The New York Times,* July 20, 2002, p. A4.

———, "Pope to Visit a Mexico Warmer toward the Church," *The New York Times,* July 30, 2002, p. A3.

———, "The 'Pilgrim Pope' Fondly Bids the Mexicans Farewell," *The New York Times*, Aug. 2, 2002, p. A6.

———, "A Saint Who Guides Migrants to a Promised Land," *The New York Times*, Aug. 14, 2002, p. A4.

———, "Sleepy Mexican Border Towns Awake to Drug Violence," *The New York Times*, Jan. 23, 2005, p. 3.

———, "Free-Market Upheaval Grinds Mexico's Middle Class," *The New York Times*, Sept. 4, 2002, p. A3.

———, "A Mexican Reformer Who Looked Too Close to Home," *The New York Times*, Sept. 5, 2002, p. A10.

———, "The Rich, Famous and Aghast: A Peep-Show Book," *The New York Times*, Sept. 25, 2002, p. A4.

———, "Wave of Women's Killings Confounds Juárez," *The New York Times*, Dec. 10, 2002, pp. A1, A20.

———, "A Surge in Money Sent Home by Mexicans," *The New York Times*, Oct. 28, 2003, p. A14.

———, "Why Mexico's Political Machine Keeps Chugging," *The New York Times*, July 9, 2003, p. A4.

———, "Mexico: U.S. Ambassador to Wed Beer Billionaire," *The New York Times*, Feb. 1, 2005, p. A6.

———, "Mexico City's Mayor, Facing Arrest, Is Taking His Case to Streets," *The New York Times*, Feb. 17, 2005, p. A6.

United States Census, American Fact Finder, Households and Families 2000, http://census .gov.

———, "On Mexico's Mean Streets, The Sinners Have a Saint," *The New York Times*, March 26, 2004, p. A4.

———, "Hundreds of Thousands in Mexico March against Crime," *The New York Times*, June 28, 2004, p. A6.

———, "Mexico's 'Tomato King' Seeks a New Title," *The New York Times*, July 5, 2004, p. A4.

———, "Mexican Panel Challenges Ruling on Rights Lawyer's Death," *The New York Times*, July 21, 2004, p. A3.

———, "Thousands Protest Effort to Oust Mayor of Mexico City," *The New York Times*, Aug. 30, 2004, p. A3.

TIANO, SUSAN, *Patriarchy on the Line: Labor, Gender and Ideology in the Mexican Maquila Industry.* Philadelphia: Temple University Press, 1994.

UNITED NATIONS, *Human Development Reports, 2004*, http://hdr.undp.org/statistics/data/ index_indicators.cfm.

———, *Human Development Reports, 2001*, http://hdr.undp.org/reports/global/ 2001/en/.

———, Statistics and Indicators on the World's Women, http://www.un.org/Depts/ unsd/gender/1-3dev.htm.

UNITED NATIONS STATISTICAL DIVISION, *2001, 2002 Demographic Yearbook*, http://unstats .un.org/unsd/demographic/products/dyb/dyb2.htm.

UNITED NATIONS STATISTICAL DIVISION, *Demographic and Social Statistics, Statistics and Indicators on Women and Men*, http://unstats.un.org/unsd/demographic/products/indwm/ table6c.htm.

U.S. BUREAU OF THE CENSUS, U.S. Current Population Survey Report—The Foreign Born Population: 1996, http://www/census.gov/population/www/socdemo/foreign96.html.

———, International Data Base 2000, http://www.census.gov/ipc/www/idbsprd.html.

VAN NATTE, DON, JR., "U.S. Indicts 26 Mexican Bankers in Laundering of Drug Funds," *The New York Times,* May 19, 1998, p. A6.

VARGAS, ALEXIA, "For Many Immigrants, Marriage Is Too Much of an Endurance Test," *The Wall Street Journal,* Nov. 18, 1998, p. A1.

WAGNER, STEPHEN J., AND DONALD E. SCHULZ, "Civil-Military Relations in Mexico: the Zapatista Revolt and Its Implications," *Journal of Interamerican Studies and World Affairs,* Vol. 37, no. 1 (Spring 1995), pp. 1–42.

WEINER, TIM, "Mexico Ending Coziness for Press and Powerful," *The New York Times,* Oct. 29, 2000, p. 10.

———, "Mexico Chief Pushes New Border Policy: Free and Easy Does It," *The New York Times,* Dec. 14, 2000, p. A12.

———, "Mexican Jail Easy to Flee: Just Pay Up," *The New York Times,* Jan. 29, 2001, p. A7.

———, "Mexico Seeks Lower Fees on Funds Sent from U.S.," *The New York Times,* March 3, 2001, pp. A1, A4.

———, "Mexico's New Leader Vows to End Longstanding Impunity for Torture in Justice System," *The New York Times,* March 18, 2001, p. 10.

———, "Power Fight in Mexico on Peering into the Past," *The New York Times,* June 17, 2001, p. 17.

———, "Fox Urged to Uphold Pledge on Justice Reforms," *The New York Times,* July 10, 2001, p. A4.

———, "Mexican Drug Lord's Arrest Helps Fox as He Awaits Bush," *The New York Times,* March 11, 2002, p. A3.

———, "Mexico Holds 41, Including Tijuana Police Chief, in Crackdown," *The New York Times,* April 12, 2002, p. A5.

———, "New Web of Trust Topples a Mighty Mexican Cartel," *The New York Times,* April 26, 2002, p. A3.

———, "Notorious Kidnapper Arrested in Mexico, but Problem Rages On," *The New York Times,* June 7, 2002, p. A5.

———, "U.S. Will Get Power, and Pollution, from Mexico," *The New York Times,* Sept. 17, 2002, p. A3.

———, "Mexico: Kidnapped Actress Freed," *The New York Times,* Oct. 12, 2002, p. A6.

———, "A Town on the Wild Side Awaits Sheriff Giuliani," *The New York Times,* Oct. 17, 2002, p. A4.

———, "Growing Poverty Is Shrinking Mexico's Rain Forest," *The New York Times,* Dec. 8, 2002, p. 16.

———, "Enter Consultant Giuliani, His Fee Preceding Him," *The New York Times,* Jan. 16, 2003, p. A4.

———, "For All to Read: A Mexican Resort's Dirty Secret," *The New York Times,* Feb. 13, 2003, p. A4.

———, "Monterrey's Poor Sinking in Rising Economic Tides," *The New York Times,* March 21, 2003, p. A8.

———, "A Fresh Mexican Standard-Bearer Emerges," *The New York Times,* Nov. 3, 2003, p. A5.

———, "Mexico: Fox Sends Congress Justice Reforms," *The New York Times,* March 30, 2004, p. A12.

WISE, CAROL, ED., *The Post-Nafta Political Economy: Mexico and the Western Hemisphere.* University Park, PA: The Penn State University Press, 1998.

WOLF, ERIC, *Sons of the Shaking Earth.* Chicago: University of Chicago Press, 1959.

WOMACK, JOHN JR., *Rebellion in Chiapas: An Historical Reader.* New York: The New Press, 1999.

WORLD BANK, HEALTH, NUTRITION AND POVERTY STATISTICS 2001, http://devdata.worldbank.org/hnpstats.

———, *World Bank Development Indicators, 2004,* http://www.worldbank.org/data/wdi2004/cdrom/loi.html.

———, *World Development Report 1997.* New York: Oxford University Press, 1997.

YOUNG, GAY, *Women, Work and Households in Ciudad Juárez.* Washington DC: Institute for Women's Policy Research, 1992.

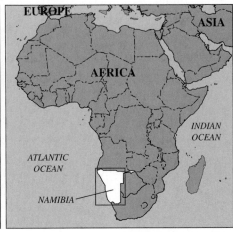

To get to Namibia you will have to fly to the southern tip of Africa. You may get a direct flight to Windhoek, the capital of Namibia, or you may have to fly to Johannesburg, South Africa, and change planes there. It will be a very long day's flight from Toronto or Los Angeles. In Windhoek you will need to hire a jeep and a guide if you want to visit the Bushmen described in this chapter.

LOCATION: Namibia is on the west coast of southern Africa. South Africa is to its south; Botswana to the east and Angola to the north.

AREA: Namibia covers 318,261 square miles (or 824,292 square kilometers). It is about twice the size of California or Japan.

LAND: The Namib Desert extends along the entire Atlantic coastline. The rest of the country is a high, grassy plain, dryer towards the south and east and wetter in the north. In the Kalahari Desert along the eastern edge of Namibia there is dry grassland that gets less than 10 inches of rainfall yearly.

CLIMATE: In the desert areas, temperatures reach seasonal extremes—as high as 120 degrees F in the summer and as low as 10 degrees F in the winter.

POPULATION: Total population was just about 2 million in 2005. Namibia is a young country: 43 percent of its people are under age 15.

INCOME: Namibia is a developing nation. Its per capita income (GNP) is $1,463 in dollar equivalents.

EDUCATION: 83 percent of Namibians are literate. Nearly all adult Namibians have at least some high school education.

MINORITIES: Namibia has many ethnic groups. The Ovambo number over 600,000 and are the largest ethnic group. There are 80,000 whites and 36,000 Bushmen. The Kavango, Damara, and Herero groups number about 100,000 each. There are also many other, smaller groups.

CHAPTER THREE

The Bushmen of Namibia: Ancient Culture in a New Nation

INTRODUCTION

Of all the societies described in this book, Namibia may be the most unfamiliar to you. Perhaps you know little about any of the countries of sub-Saharan Africa. Many westerners avoid thinking about Africa altogether. It seems to them to be a continent of disasters, plagued by drought, famine, war, and disease. You may know that most of the poorest nations of the world are in Africa. But we think you will find many surprises in this chapter. First of all, you will learn about African diversity. Do you think of Africa as a "black continent"? Did you know that there are people of several different races in Africa and that there are many ethnic groups and many languages?

If you were born in the last decades of the twentieth century, you may think it has been a long time since African countries were European colonies, and you may know little about the wars Africans fought for independence. We think you will be surprised to learn that Africa's colonial past is actually very recent and that it casts a long shadow over Africa today.

Namibia was the last colony in Africa to become an independent black nation—in 1990! Today it is a stable democracy with a free press and the most democratic constitution of any African nation. Namibia is rich in resources—it mines diamonds, uranium, lead, and zinc and has a thriving fishing industry. Cattle and sheep ranching predominate on the dry central plain and Namibia exports beef and sheepskins. In the north, bordering Angola, where there is more rainfall, family farmers herd cattle and goats and raise crops for their own subsistence. Namibia is a "middle income" African country. Yearly per capita GNP is about $1,990 in dollar equivalents and the economy is growing by about 25 percent per year (The World Bank, *World Development Indicators*). But Namibia's income is very unequally distributed. Two minority racial groups stand out: In a country with a total population of 1.9 million, there are 80,000 whites whose incomes are way above average. They own most of the good land and live in modern European-style houses, with cars and servants, TVs, computers, and cell phones. Their children attend private schools and universities (*Statistical Survey,* p. 764).[1]

---

[1]This pattern of a small white minority dominating land ownership is typical of southern African countries like Namibia, South Africa, Zimbabwe, and Mozambique.

At the other end of the economic spectrum are the 36,000 Bushmen who are the focus of this chapter. Looked down upon by blacks and whites alike, most Bushmen live in the Kalahari Desert, the driest, most undesirable part of Namibia. Most own no land and no cattle, and they are dependent on white ranchers and black farmers for work, or on the government for life-saving food supplies. Yet the Bushmen are the original people of Namibia; they were here long before whites or blacks arrived. Their story is interwoven with the whole history of Namibia. When you understand the Bushmen you will know a lot about the importance of Africa in human history, about the tragedy of colonialism, and about the challenges facing African nations today.

Who Are the Bushmen?

The Bushmen of southern Africa are a people sharply different from all the other groups in this book. For centuries, and probably for thousands of years, they were a **hunting and gathering** (or **foraging**) people who lived in small bands of ten to fifty people and gathered wild plant foods and hunted game. Systematically moving among food and water sources, the Bushmen were **nomadic:** they made no permanent homes and carried with them their few possessions. They had no rulers, no schools, no money, no written language, no police, no hospitals, and no inequalities of wealth or privilege. Bushmen lived in southwestern Africa long before black people from southeastern Africa or whites from Europe arrived. Archaeologists have found evidence of people like the Bushmen living in this region as long ago as 11,000 years before the present and occupying the area without interruption ever since (Tobias, pp. 4, 30–31).

> Bumping along sand tracks in the Kalahari Desert in dry season, you do not see the Bushman camp until your jeep is almost upon it: a circle of shelters roughly built of sticks and grasses, facing inward toward a cleared area, and almost invisible in the surrounding landscape of dry brush. The full band of perhaps twenty individuals gathers around their campfires. You see small people with yellowish-brown skins, partially clothed in animal hides, blending readily into their environment.
>
> It is dusk and they are blowing their fires into flames to cook the evening meal. Women are sorting through their day's collection of wild foods: mangetti nuts, tsama melons, water-bearing roots, perhaps birds' eggs or a snake, or in a wetter season, wild onions, leafy greens, tsin beans, or baobab fruit. The men have killed a small antelope and they are distributing the meat among their relatives. You hear many voices: Men tell the story of their hunt; women report on the tracks they have seen while out gathering; people gossip, tease, and joke. You hear the children's games, played to a rhythm of clapping and singing. The Bushmen come forward to meet you, carefully leaving their weapons—their small bows with the lethal poison-coated arrows—behind. They will doubtless invite you to share their food and water, but they will expect you to return their hospitality.
>
> The year is 1957.

When anthropologists and others talk about "Bushmen," they are generally thinking of people with three important traits. First of all, Bushmen are hunters and gatherers; they feed themselves by foraging. They don't herd animals or farm. Second, Bushmen are associated with a distinctive physical appearance. They are quite small in stature (the men under 5 feet 3 inches; the women considerably under 5 feet), and they have light brown or "yellow" skin, small heart-shaped faces with wide-apart eyes, eyefolds, and flat-bridged noses. Physically they are very different from the black Bantu-speaking people of Africa, who are tall and dark.

Also, Bushmen are known for speaking "click languages," which will probably sound quite unusual to you. There are three related click languages which include a dozen or so click sounds, made by clicking the tongue against the teeth, the roof of the mouth, the cheek, etc., as if you were going "tsk tsk" or signaling to a horse. The clicks usually function as consonants in forming words. Bushmen themselves had no written language, so only anthropologists have attempted to write down these click sounds and they have developed a system of denoting the different clicks with symbols like these: !, /, //.

As you might expect, all Bushman peoples are not exactly alike. The Ju/'hoansi or !Kung Bushmen, described in this chapter, fit the above description best. Elsewhere in southern Africa, some Bushman peoples (like the !Xu) live near rivers or in more fertile country, and do some fishing, herding, and gardening, in addition to foraging. Other Bushman peoples, like the Hai//om, speak languages related to those of the Nama and Damara, dark-skinned herding people. These Bushmen are also often taller and darker than the Ju/'hoansi (Barnard, 1992, pp. 6–13, 16–28).

Problems with Names

People who study the Bushmen have had a lot of trouble deciding what to call them. The problem is that, since Bushmen have long been looked down upon in southern Africa, all the names for them have taken on derogatory meanings. The name "Bushman" seems to be derived from the Dutch *bossiesman,* which means "bandit." Some anthropologists have preferred to use the term *San,* the word in the Khoekhoe language for Bushmen or foragers. But *San* is also a negative term, meaning "tramps" or "rascals." Recently, in Botswana, the Bushmen have been called *Basarwa,* a name meant to be respectful, but which has picked up the insulting connotation of "those without cattle." We have chosen to use the term "Bushmen" in this chapter (despite its racist and sexist overtones) because the Ju/'hoansi and other foraging peoples are now calling themselves Bushmen to emphasize the links between hunting and gathering peoples all over southern Africa (Gordon, pp. 4–8; Kelso, p. 51; Barnard, pp. 8–9; Wood, personal communication).

Where Do the Bushmen Live?

Once Bushmen lived all over southern Africa, but today they are concentrated in the nations of Namibia and Botswana, mostly in the huge dry expanse of the Kalahari Desert. The Kalahari Desert is a vast basin of sand, occupying almost a third of the African subcontinent. Much of the Kalahari is too dry to sustain human habitation, but in the more northerly parts, around places like Nyae Nyae in Namibia and Dobe in Botswana, where the Ju/'hoansi live, and in the central Kalahari in Botswana, where the G/wi and the G/ana live, there is enough rain to support drought-resistant plants, grasses, scattered trees, and the animals that feed upon them. There are many kinds of antelope, like eland, kudu, and gemsbok; there are warthogs, hares, and tortoises, and also giraffe. (There are predators too, like lions and hyena, but the Bushmen don't hunt these for food.) The rainy season leaves temporary pools of surface water, and greens up the landscape, so plants bear fruit, nuts, berries, and seeds. But rains are localized and unpredictable; while some areas receive abundant rainfall, others nearby may suffer drought. The whole region experiences drought approximately two years out of every five, with severe drought one year in four. There are dry riverbeds in the Kalahari, but they are rarely filled by runoff, perhaps only once in a decade. The Namibian Bushmen are sustained during the dry season by a small number of permanent waterholes, where underground water comes to the surface.

The Kalahari is "big sky country," flat and monotonous, with endless vistas of brush out to the horizon. Outsiders easily lose their way in the markerless landscape. To this austere landscape is joined a harsh climate. During the hot, dry season of September and October, temperatures reach 115 degrees Fahrenheit in the shade, 126 degrees in the sun, and the temperature of the sand reaches 140 degrees. The Kalahari winter of May to August is cold and dry, with nighttime temperatures often below freezing (Marshall, pp. 62–71; Lee, 1979, pp. 87–88).

A few Bushmen peoples live outside the Kalahari: the Ovokango River Bushmen and the Hai//om of Namibia, the !Xu of Angola, and the /Xam and the "Mountain Bushmen of Lesotho" in South Africa.

The Bushmen and Prehistory

Using research by anthropologists, archaeologists, and historians, sociologists have concluded that in all of human history there have been just four basic kinds of societies. The first human societies were **hunter/gatherer bands,** like the Bushmen. Humans, and their prehuman ancestors before them, lived like this for hundreds of thousands and perhaps millions of years. They lived in small nomadic bands, following game and harvesting wild foods. It was only about 10,000 years ago that humans learned to raise their own food. They settled down, often along rivers, and made gardens and raised tame animals. These people lived in **horticultural villages.** At about this same time, other peoples began to live as pastoralists, herding animals and often moving about with their herds. Approximately 6,000 years ago what we think of as "civilization" began, with the invention of agriculture. Agriculture applied new technologies (the plow) and new methods (fertilizing and rotating crops) so people could farm the same fields generation after generation. Farming raised more food and made it possible for some people to live on food others grew. They became craftsmen, priests, monks and nuns, kings and queens, professional soldiers, sailors, cathedral builders, artists, scientists and inventors, and all the other inhabitants of cities in **agricultural states.** Finally, the most recent type of society to develop (in the last 250 years) is **industrial nations,** in which farming has become so productive that most people can devote their lives to other work, producing goods in factories, building large cities, inventing new technologies, waging war, etc. All four types of societies still exist today, but there are fewer and fewer hunter/gatherer and horticultural societies.[2]

---

[2]Sociologists owe this commonly used classification scheme to Gerhard and Jean Lenski (Lenski, Lenski and Nolan, 1991).

The Importance of Hunter/Gatherers

Since the first humans were foragers, sociologists and anthropologists have long regarded hunter-gatherer bands as the cradles of human nature and culture. The first families must have been formed in hunter-gatherer bands, the first specialized roles and the first religions. It is easy to speculate (but difficult to prove) that early conditions of foraging bands fundamentally shaped human nature. Those who study hunter-gatherer societies have often asked whether widespread human characteristics—like competitiveness, or aggression—are a heritage from those first societies.

It is hard to learn much about societies that existed 50,000 or 100,000 years ago when all the world's peoples were hunter/gatherers. Archaeologists dig up fossilized human and animal bones and the remains of hearths and sometimes huts, weapons, garbage heaps, and fossilized pollen, but these remains can tell us little about how people interacted in prehistoric times. To learn about humanity's ancient past, anthropologists and sociologists have turned to hunter/gatherer societies that still exist today. They have hoped that study of the Bushmen will open a window on the common ancestors of all humans—the ancient hunter/gatherer peoples.

Hunter/Gatherers and Human Nature

When you study the Bushmen, you must put away stereotyped images of "cavemen" fighting each other in a brutal competition for survival. The Bushmen are peaceful people and in this they are quite typical of hunter/gatherers. They avoid conflict and competition and share what they have so that everyone can survive. They have no formal leaders, no privileged class or deprived lower class. They don't hate or fight their neighbors. Though they live in a harsh environment, their lives are not brutal or debased. They value generosity and graciousness, joking and kidding around, and they find plenty of time for relaxation, playing music and singing, dressing up, and holding ceremonial dances, like parties that go on all night. If this is what our earliest ancestors were like, then we cannot blame our own greed and violence on our evolutionary heritage.

Living with Nature

The Bushmen have exemplified a kind of society we may well call the most successful human way of life of all times. The hunter/gatherer life sustained humanity for millions of years. Variations of foraging cultures allowed people to live in many different environments, gentle or harsh: by the shore, in forests, open grasslands, deserts, rainforests, and arctic tundra. Wherever they live, hunter/gatherers live close to nature: Their food comes directly from nature, and everything they use—houses, tools, clothing, containers, jewelry, and weapons—is made by hand from natural materials. Hunter/gatherers use nature, but they don't use it up. They live in such a way that they don't kill off the animals they depend upon; they don't use up the water or pollute the land. They can go on living on the same land for thousands and thousands of years without harming it. Sociologists call this **sustainability.** In the last 10,000 years, since people learned to cultivate seeds and plants and to domesticate animals, human impact on the environment has constantly increased. Industrial society now pollutes the air and water and land. It pumps carbon dioxide into the atmosphere, creating a "greenhouse effect," and it alters ecosystems, so many animal species become endangered or extinct. Many people are now asking: Is our industrial way of life sustainable? Perhaps we can learn from the Bushmen about creating an environmentally sustainable society.

Anthropologists and the Bushmen

Eager to learn about hunters and gatherers, anthropologists have studied the Bushmen, especially the Ju/'hoansi in Namibia and Botswana, with exceptional thoroughness. Dutch and English scholars in South Africa began publishing studies of the Bushmen as early as the nineteenth century. From the early 1950s through the present, anthropologists, linguists, archaeologists, musicologists, and ecologists have almost continuously lived with and observed one or another group of Bushmen. These social scientists made a very detailed record of Bushman life, in books and films, which we will draw on in this account.

The first major studies of the Ju/'hoansi and the G/wi were done by Lorna and Laurence Marshall in the 1950s. The Marshalls made many trips to the Kalahari, accompanied by their daughter, Elizabeth Marshall Thomas, who wrote a famous book about the Bushman, *The Harmless People,* and their son, John Marshall, who filmed Bushman daily life. In the 1970s, anthropologist Richard B. Lee and his team studied several groups of !Kung, as reported in his books, *The Kung San* and *The Dobe Ju/'hoansi.* Today, a new generation of anthropologists, from South Africa, the United States, Norway, Japan, and other countries, has come to Namibia and Botswana to observe the Bushmen.[3] Their primary focus has been on how Bushman culture is now changing as former foragers settle in villages and adopt cattle-herding.

Some present-day anthropologists (like Robert Gordon and Edwin Wilmsen) (Gordon, 1992; Wilmsen, 1989) have questioned the portrait of the Bushmen painted by earlier anthropologists. These scholars, they suggest, were too eager to discover in the Bushmen an isolated living survival of Stone Age times. Anthropologists portrayed the Bushmen living in a timeless present and often failed even to mention what country they inhabited. Gordon and Wilmsen caution that for a long time— perhaps as long as 2,000 years—Bantu and Khoi herders lived near Bushmen, and well-used routes for trade in iron, glass beads, and shells passed through Bushman territory. Bushmen, they contend, have long herded animals and traded goods when they could.

HISTORY OF THE BUSHMEN

We know very little about the history of the Bushmen for all the thousands of years before their contact with Europeans in the seventeenth century. The modern history of the Bushmen, recorded first by white settlers, then by colonial governments, and now by African governments, began in the seventeenth century. It is a tragic story of genocide and displacement.

---

[3]They include John Yellen, Susan Kent, James Denbow, Edwin Wilmsen, Robert Hitchcock, Robert Gordon, Thomas Widlok, Megan Biesele, and Claire Ritchie.

Settlers and the Bushmen

In the seventeenth century, an estimated 200,000 Bushmen lived all over southern Africa—in the desert, the mountains, on grasslands, and along the coasts. When the Dutch settled the Cape of Good Hope region at the southern tip of Africa in the 1650s, an indigenous (native) group of Bushmen, called the Khoi, were living there, fishing, hunting, gathering, and herding cattle and goats. Seizing their good land, the Dutch slaughtered the Khoi and drove them northward.

Other groups of Bushmen lived in more remote areas, in small bands, and without domesticated animals. The Dutch were especially contemptuous of them and considered them "wild" people, little better than animals. In the eighteenth century, white settlers moved north and almost completely exterminated the Bushmen, killing the men and enslaving the women and children. Some Bushmen fought back, raiding settlers' farms and stealing cattle, and in remote areas they were able to hold off the whites for years. By the end of the nineteenth century, the Bushmen had been virtually wiped out in all of the country of South Africa. White South Africans then began to settle further north, in Namibia, joined by German traders and missionaries. However, few ventured into the harsh lands of the Kalahari Desert.

In the late nineteenth century, the Kalahari Desert Bushmen came into contact with another group of settlers: Bantu-speaking blacks from southeastern Africa. Relationships between the Bushmen and the Bantu peoples were not always harmonious. Both sides tell stories of armed conflict, cattle theft, and disputes over women, and the Bantu have considered the Bushmen an inferior people. However, these forms of conflict have never become as extreme as the European genocide against the Bushmen, and in the twentieth century, trade and intermarriage between Bushmen and Bantu have peacefully developed. As a result of intermarriage, some Bushmen, who live along the eastern edge of the Kalahari have come to resemble their Bantu neighbors physically. Two different Bantu cattle-herding peoples, the Tswana and the Herero, settled the margins of the Kalahari. Bushmen men worked for the Tswana as trackers and porters, and later as cattle-herders, receiving tobacco and cow's milk in exchange for seasonal or temporary work. Many Bushmen, especially in Botswana, became attached to Herero farms, as unpaid dependents (Lee, 1979, pp. 32–33, 77–84; Lee, 1984, pp. 17–18; Lee, "Ecology of a Contemporary San People," in Tobias, ed., pp. 94–96; Silberbauer, p. 181).

The Colonial Era in Namibia

Namibia became a German colony in 1884; it was known as German Southwest Africa. Germany was a powerful industrialized society with advanced weaponry, while Namibia was sparsely populated and vulnerable. At that time the Herero and Nama peoples were the largest ethnic groups in the country and they lived in the central plateau, grasslands well suited to animal-raising. The German colonial powers gradually took over this land, between 1893 and 1903, pushing the Herero and the Nama onto the edges of the plateau, where there was less rainfall and the land quickly became overcrowded and the soil exhausted. When the Herero and the Nama tried to resist this policy of "highland clearance," the Germans responded with purposeful genocide. In two military campaigns, in 1904 and 1908, the German armed forces in Southwest Africa slaughtered three-quarters of the Herrero and half the Nama. The Herero and Nama population in Namibia today is still smaller than it was in 1904. As Leys and Saul point out, this first genocide in a century of carnage prefigured Nazism. It even began with an "extermination order" issued by the German Chief of Staff, Von Trotha (Leys and Saul, pp. 8–9; Slotten, p. 277).

Having killed off the native inhabitants, German settlers found there were not enough people available to work on their ranches and in the mines. So they set up a system of *apartheid* (separation of races), dividing Southwest Africa into two sections. The south was for whites only, except for blacks who had passes showing they worked for whites. North of the official "red line" or "police line" the Germans created reserves for the Ovambo, Kavango, and Makololo peoples who were allowed to live under the authority of their own chiefs, as long as they responded to German recruiting and sent migrant laborers south to the German ranches and mines. There they worked as "contract laborers" for wages amounting to about 5 percent of white wages (Slotten, p. 1; Leys and Saul, pp. 9–10). In this period the first German settlers began to appear at the edges of the Kalahari Desert, taking over Bushman waterholes and pushing them onto drier land. It wasn't unusual for settlers to kill Bushmen or kidnap ("blackbird") them and force them to work on white farms (Gordon, pp. 201–205).

South Africa Takes Over

Germany was defeated in World War I and as a result it lost its African colonies. The League of Nations awarded Southwest Africa to Great Britain, which turned it over to South Africa (a white-run former British colony, by then a member of the British dominion). For the people of Southwest Africa this was no improvement at all. They went from the hands of one brutal master into those of another. South Africa kept the German system of apartheid, as it did in its own territory. It gave the white minority in Southwest Africa some limited self-government and kept the black majority suppressed and exploited. Afrikaner settlers (people of Dutch descent from South Africa) gradually replaced German settlers and they kept pushing out the remaining blacks on the plateau. By 1963, 48.7 percent of the land was controlled by white farms. Black migrant laborers from the north were not allowed to bring their families south with them. They were forced to live in miserable "compounds" and allowed to return home only once every two years. South Africa was as willing as Germany had been to use violence to maintain this system. The police, the army, and a counterinsurgency unit all made expeditions to punish resistance by northern peoples, and political activists were beaten, tortured, and killed (Saunders, p. 755; Slotten, p. 278; Leys and Saul, pp. 9–10; Gordon, p. 201).

Formalizing Apartheid

In 1964 South Africa formalized its system by creating "self-governing homelands" for Namibia's eleven ethnic peoples. In a kind of mockery of "separate but equal," whites ruled Namibia, but blacks were permitted their own local governments on reservations to which they were confined. Of course all the wealth, businesses, mines, diamonds, and minerals were in the south, so the northern reserves or *bantustans* had no tax revenues to work with (Slotten, p. 278; Leys and Saul, pp. 9–10).

Bushmanland

For the Bushmen apartheid meant the loss of most of their last refuge: the Kalahari Desert. South Africa established two "homelands" for the Bushmen, Bushmanland in the Kalahari and West Caprivi in the far north. But Bushmanland comprised only 10 percent of the land around Nyae Nyae, so the Ju/'hoansi lost 90 percent of their land and all but one of their permanent water holes. Most of the land they were left is deep sand, without water holes, with little plant or animal life. The government made southern Nyae Nyae into Hereroland East, a "homeland" for the surviving Herero, and joined northern Nyae Nyae to the Kavango homeland.

The Bushmen suffered further losses. The Southwest African government set up game and nature reserves on their land. In the 1950s the Hai//'om were driven off their lands that were turned into the Etosha Game Reserve. The Kxoe were expelled from their land on the Kavango River for another nature reserve. Finally, in 1968, about 6,000 Ju/'hoan people were evicted from the West Caprivi (Weinberg, p. 8; Biesele and Weinberg, pp. 1–2).

The Fate of Hunter/Gatherers

As recently as 100 years ago, there were dozens of foraging peoples still living in isolation in the most remote corners of the globe—in the deserts of Africa and Australia, the rainforests of the Amazon, Africa, and New Guinea, and the arctic wastes of Canada. Today, the Bushmen number among the last surviving foraging societies (along with some Eskimos and some Australian aborigines). Modern societies have not been kind to indigenous foraging peoples. Industrial societies have penetrated every corner of the earth, exploring, searching for precious metals, or oil, for trees to log or land to clear for farming and ranching. Everywhere, they have dismissed indigenous hunter/gatherer peoples as subhuman savages. Settlers and explorers have not hesitated to kill indigenous people or take away their land, their means of survival. Western diseases spread through indigenous populations in devastating epidemics, and the bewildered survivors were converted by missionaries and enticed or forced into working for the outsiders. Under the assault of modern societies, indigenous cultures all over the world have disappeared. Surviving hunter/gatherers have been forced into the least desirable environments on earth.

Will the Namibian Bushmen survive? Will they be forced to abandon the foraging life? Will their culture adapt and persist in the modern world or will it be changed beyond recognition? This chapter is written in two parts. In the first part we will begin by describing Bushman life as it was lived up until they lost most of their land in the late 1960s. Then, in the second part of the chapter we will continue our history of the Bushmen in Namibia and examine what happened to the Bushmen during Namibia's war for independence and after 1990 in independent Namibia.

Let's return, for now, to the 1950s, a time when the hunting and gathering life was relatively undisturbed. You must keep in mind that even in the 1950s, when there were many more people living by foraging, the Bushmen were not fossils of the past. Prehistoric hunters and gatherers lived in a world of hunters and gatherers. Then, the whole world was wilderness; there were no towns, no governments, no roads, no lands cleared for farming. Small bands of people traveled about following game and harvesting wild plants, and meeting another band was a rare and important event. We can use our knowledge of twentieth-century hunter-gatherers to help us picture the past, but we must remember that even in the 1950s, the Bushman world was shaped by governments, settlers, and world events.

PART I: BUSHMAN CULTURE: A DESIGN FOR LIVING

You can do a brief "thought experiment" to help you understand Bushman culture. Imagine that like characters in a movie, you and your friends are suddenly dropped into the Kalahari Desert, circa 1957. Will you survive? Unlike the animals of the Kalahari, you will not know instinctively how to find water or food or shelter, or how to organize your group life. You will lack special physical adaptations to desert life. Your evolved human capacity to create culture will have to see you through.

Bushman groups, like all human societies, learned how to secure the necessities of life. They divided up their tasks efficiently. They learned to keep order, resolve conflicts, and protect the group from outside threats. Their beliefs about the meaning of life sustained them. Even reproduction was not just left to nature; the Bushmen made sure they had enough children, but not too many, and they taught their children how to live in their society and their difficult environment.

Sociology textbooks often adopt anthropologist Clyde Kluckholm's definition of **culture** as "**a design for living.**" Every human group must solve the basic problems of adapting to their environment: Groups do so through **culture** and **social structure,** and if they are successful, the group survives. But there are many possible "designs for living" (Kluckholn, 1949).

All the various Bushman peoples were similar in the fundamentals of their life, but they differed somewhat in their customs. For example, they had varying religious myths and gods, did different sacred dances, and used different kinship terminologies. To avoid confusion in this part of the chapter, we will focus mostly on one group, the Ju/'hoansi Bushmen who live around Nyae Nyae in northeastern Namibia and directly across the border at Dobe in Botswana. The Ju/'hoansi are the most intensively studied Bushman group, so there is a lot of anthropological information to draw on.

Nyae Nyae: 1957

Let us describe traditional Ju/'hoan society to you in the present tense, so you can imagine yourself there, in the Kalahari, in 1957 or before. Even in their harsh environment the Ju/'hoansi Bushmen have found a way to live that is environmentally sustainable, psychologically rewarding, and physically healthy. Four elements of Bushman culture make possible a more than adequate living in the Kalahari Desert. These are: the Bushmen's comprehensive **knowledge** of their environment and its food sources; the custom of **nomadism,** or movement from one temporary encampment to another; customs of childbearing and child-rearing that result in **population limitation;** and **values** that stress sharing, modesty, and cooperation.

Knowledge

Foremost in importance is the Bushmen's detailed knowledge of their environment, itself a form of control over nature. Knowledge of plants, water sources, and animal habits enables the Bushmen to use the desert as a larder, neither cultivating nor storing food, but rather turning systematically from one resource to another, each in its season. To some degree, knowledge is gender based, since women gather plants and men hunt animals, but both women and men have some basic store of knowledge about animal tracks and plant properties.

Bushman hunters are superb trackers. Not only can they identify animals from their tracks in the sand and their droppings, they are able to deduce detailed information from tracks. They can single out the tracks of a single animal (perhaps the one injured by an arrow) from those of a herd, tell if it is male or female, old or young, whether it is injured and how badly. Examining the freshness of tracks, hunters can deduce how long ago an animal passed, whether it was feeding, how fast it was going, whether it passed during the morning or afternoon (did it seek the shade to the east or west of bushes and trees?) or at night. Both men and women can read human footprints in the sand, identifying the tracks of every individual.

Intimate knowledge of resources makes the foraging life possible. The Bushmen know and name hundreds of plants, insects, animals, and birds. Tiny arrows derive their lethal power from a poison coating made from the larvae and parasites of three different kinds of beetles.[4] In the dry season, when plants wither to near invisibility, women unerringly locate underground water-storing roots from the evidence of a few tiny leaves hidden in the dry grass. They know exactly when each plant resource will be ready to harvest, under various weather conditions. And they know how much water each permanent and temporary waterhold can be expected to provide, so they are never caught short.

Nomadism

The Bushmen adapt themselves to the desert by living in small **nomadic bands.** The Ju/'hoansi have no permanent place of residence, but they cannot be said to wander either. They move about the desert in a planned, rational fashion, making temporary camps to exploit local resources of water and food, then move on when these become scarce. In the dry season, they retreat to permanent water holes. In this way, the Bushmen neither wear out nor pollute the desert; they distribute their impact over a wide area.

But nomadism means traveling light. When the Ju/'hoansi move, they carry on their backs all their possessions, plus their young children. In fact, all of a person's belongings can fit into a leather bag the size of an overnight carrier, and weigh no more than 12–15 pounds. Possessions include a woman's *kaross* (her leather all-purpose garment and blanket), her digging stick, items of personal adornment like beads and headbands, ostrich eggshell water holders, and nowadays, an iron pot. A man carries his hunting kit—arrows, bow, and quiver—and his fire-making kit; other possessions include musical instruments, toys, pipes, ceremonial rattles, tortoise

---

[4]The poison acts on the central nervous system, through the bloodstream, so animals killed by the poison can be safely eaten.

shell bowls, nets, and leather bags. All possessions (except the pot) are handmade and can readily be made anew. Houses are built at each camp out of branches and grasses, and abandoned when the camp is moved. The Bushmen possess little, but until they become involved in the modern cash economy, they desire no more and feel no deprivation.

Population Control

Ultimately, the desert can support the Bushmen because they keep their population proportionate to its resources. In the 1970s, in the central Kalahari, population density was no more than one person per each 4 to 6 square miles! (Silberbauer, p. 184). Significantly, it is a low birthrate, rather than an usually high death rate, that keeps the Ju/'hoan population small. Women reach puberty late and generally don't have their first child until their late teens. Thereafter, children are widely spaced, without modern means of birth control, with an interval of approximately four years between babies. How this spacing is achieved has fascinated anthropologists. Richard B. Lee, who studied the Dobe Ju/'hoansi, concluded that the nomadic foraging life and population control are closely linked. Ju/'hoan women nurse their children for as long as four years, and during that time they carry them everywhere, on daily foraging trips as well as on longer migrations, and they carry them in such a fashion that the child can nurse at will. Nursing is known to inhibit ovulation, but in most societies it is an ineffective means of birth control. Lee argued that Ju/'hoan babies nurse so frequently that ovulation is more effectively inhibited. Ju/'hoan women who settle on cattle ranches or farms carry their babies less and also give birth at more frequent intervals.

The Ju/'hoansi understand the importance of spacing their children: It is very difficult for a mother to carry two children at once, and also, since young children live so entirely on their mother's milk, they believe that if a mother had two babies nursing, her milk would be insufficient and both would probably die. **Infanticide** (the killing of newborn infants) is infrequently practiced, but seen as a possible tragic necessity should a new sibling come too soon after the birth of a baby or in the rare case of twins. Infant and child mortality is high by modern western standards, but not compared to most poor agricultural societies. Close to 20 percent of Ju/'hoan children die before their first birthday, and only half of those born live long enough to marry (Shostak, p. 182).

The Value of Sharing

Critical to Bushman survival is the emphasis they place on sharing. The worst one can say of a person is that he or she is "far-hearted" or stingy. Generosity, graciousness, and modesty are highly valued. Indeed, it would be fair to say that sharing is a subject of constant discussion among the Ju/'hoansi, with the question "who will give me food?" always on people's minds. As the Bushmen see it, sharing is important because it is the way to create and maintain relationships.

A **functionalist** sociologist would explain sharing differently, as a practice that helps the society to survive. A functionalist might say that sharing is the Bushman "social security system." They cannot store food for future use and they cannot buy food with money or any other goods, so when food is scarce, life is threatened. A man could be the best hunter, but if he is injured or falls ill, there is no unemployment insurance or welfare, no savings account or pension plan. He must rely on the people in his family and band to feed him. Everyone needs to help others, so that they can be helped in turn. A person who shares gets something else of value in return also: prestige or social advantage. A hunter who shares shows he is fit to be a husband or qualified to be a hunting partner (Roue, p. 24).

Sharing is not only a prime value in Bushman culture, it is a constant practice integral to their way of life. Sharing takes place on many levels. The plant foods women gather are cooked and shared with their immediate families. Big game is shared on a wider basis. The hunter to whom the meat belongs cuts it into large chunks and distributes these among his immediate relatives: his wife, in-laws, parents, and siblings. These recipients give some of their share to those who eat at their fire, but they also cut much of the meat into smaller pieces and make presents of these to their relatives, who pass it on in turn to theirs. In the end, everyone in a camp shares the meat, not in a wholesale distribution, but as a personal gift from some connection, and the meat is quickly consumed. The idea of a person hoarding meat is horrifying to the Bushmen: It seems savage and uncivilized. "Lions might do that; people could not," they explain. Lorna Marshall noted that in one large dry-season encampment, the meat of a single eland (a large antelope) was ultimately distributed to sixty-three individuals (Marshall, p. 302).

But the Bushmen struggle with sharing; it doesn't always come easily and sometimes hunger or possessiveness win out over generosity. People grumble if someone keeps a particularly desirable ornament or tool, instead of passing it on as a gift. Disputes often arise over the sharing of food. Among the Ju/'hoansi, custom facilitates sharing by blurring the ownership of meat. Meat belongs not to the man who brings it down, but to the owner of the arrow which first penetrates the quarry. And a hunter will usually carry arrows from many individuals—his own, and also those borrowed or received as gifts from others. Even a poor hunter may thus come to be the owner of meat, and people will not be put in the position of constantly receiving gifts of meat from the same superior hunter.

Sharing takes place on a wider basis too: between bands as well as within them. Kalahari resources are unevenly distributed, since localized drought may temporarily render one area barren while another is productive. At times like these, whole bands or individual families visit relatives in more fertile or better-watered areas. At another time, when conditions are different, they will reciprocate as hosts. Sharing evens out inequalities—between youthful and aging families, between talented and inept hunters, women and men, and people in different areas. Sharing constantly reinstates equality, ensuring that differences in individual ability or luck will not accumulate into institutionalized economic or status stratification.

A Flexible Culture

Knowledge, nomadism, low population growth, and sharing are critical elements of Bushman culture. Together they make possible the distinctive flexibility of forager societies. People shift readily from one food source to another. Tsin beans, mangetti nuts, meat, government-supplied cornmeal; Bushmen turn readily from one to another. Without jobs or permanent houses, they are available to pull up stakes and go where food and water can be found. Small families are flexible too. There aren't too many babies to carry, and as we will see, families easily break away from one band to join another, allowing band size to adapt to resources. Wherever they go, Bushmen can rely on their friends and relatives to share with them. There is no bureaucracy to slow down decision making, nor do possessions tie them down. It is customary to think of hunting and gathering societies as fragile, since we have seen so many destroyed by loss of their land; but actually, the fluidity and flexibility of Bushman society is a great strength when they are forced to adapt to other peoples and societies. As Mathais Guenther points out, the Bushmen are as willing to forage for ideas as for food, making their culture relatively resilient in the face of outside influence (Kent, *Cultural Diversity,* pp. 6–7, 12–14; Guenther in Kent, pp. 73–74).

How Hard Is the Foraging Life?

Until recently, life in hunter-gatherer societies was believed to be harsh and difficult, with constant labor the only shield against starvation, and population kept from outrunning resources only by famine, disease, and infanticide. In the late twentieth century, studies of the Ju/'hoansi Bushmen and other foraging societies have resulted in a much rosier view of foraging societies, and, by implication, of early human history. One of the most significant new insights is that foragers don't work very hard. In fact, they spend fewer hours working and enjoy more hours of leisure than people in agricultural and modern industrial societies. In a typical band observed by Lee, women went out gathering on an average of nine out of twenty-eight days. Counting all foraging, tool-making and fixing, and housework, women put in an average workweek of 40 hours. Ju/'hoan men spent more days in hunting, an average of twelve out of every twenty-eight days, and counting all hunting, gathering, tool-making and fixing, and housework, their average workweek was 44.5 hours. Even at this low level of work, the Ju/'hoansi are generally adequately nourished, and they have infant mortality rates and adult life expectancies somewhat better than those of most agricultural societies.[5]

Work and Affluence

The Bushmen work little, but from our modern western point of view, they are poor and deprived. It is important to understand that Bushmen living traditionally don't feel deprived. They don't crave permanent houses, running water, refrigerators, jeeps, or diapers. They accept occasional hunger, secure in the knowledge that there will be food soon enough. In effect, they have made a tradeoff—living at a low level of material affluence, they needn't work much, and can enjoy a great deal of leisure. And, in reality, since they live in a sparse environment, greater work would not necessarily produce greater abundance over the long run; it might instead disturb the ecological balance. For example, more intensive hunting might temporarily provide

[5]Richard B. Lee collected this data in 1964. See Lee, 1979, pp. 254–280. Lee notes that work in child care was not included in the calculations, but if it had been, the work totals for women would have been considerably higher, since they do 60–80 percent of all care of young children.

abundant meat, but it might also threaten the welfare of the wild herds, and therefore ultimately, the survival of the Bushmen.

Leisure

The Bushmen devote their leisure to nurturing group life, cultivating relationships between individuals, and elaborating their culture. Perhaps it was the abundant leisure of foragers that allowed our ancestors to create human culture, incrementally freeing humanity from the bonds of instinct and biological necessity.

Those who study the Bushmen all note that they are great talkers. They spend an enormous amount of time sitting around their campfires talking, joking, arguing, exchanging news, telling stories, repeating the events of a hunt, planning tomorrow's hunting or gathering. There is a constant buzz of conversation in a camp, and uproarious laughter breaks out often. Women and girls sit close together at the campfire, their shoulders and knees touching, as do the men and boys. Members of a band truly seem to enjoy each other's company.

Playing Games. Unlike the children of farming and herding societies, Ju/'hoan children do not have to work. This is, in its way, a sign of affluence: You could say that the Ju/'hoansi enjoy such abundance that they don't need the labor of their children (or of old people) to support the band. Since children don't go to school either, they are free to play all day long, until, in their teen years, girls and

Surrounded by miles of open land, this band of Ju/'hoansi adults and children, men and women, cluster close together, talking, telling stories, joking, and arguing in typical Bushman fashion.

boys begin to accompany their elders in gathering and hunting. Adults also like to play games when they are at leisure in camp or in the evenings.

The games the Ju/'hoansi play reveal much about their culture. There are no games in which people keep score or care greatly about winning or losing. Games are all played in groups, and in many, the players are bound together in rhythmic chorus and close physical contact. Typical is the ball game played by girls who stand in a line, singing and clapping. Each girl takes the ball in turn, at the right point in the music, dances with it, then tosses it to the next in line (Marshall, pp. 313, 322, 332–336).

A Musical Culture. Music is not only a part of Bushman games, but a constant accompaniment to camp life. The Ju/'hoansi have a rich musical culture in which everyone participates in some way. Their homemade instruments make subtle, vibrant sounds, and their compositions are always complex. The traditional *guashi* is a stringed instrument made from a hollowed-out log strung with animal sinew or hair. There is also a traditional one-string violin, and the more recently introduced drums (adapted from their Bantu neighbors), and the thumb piano, a handheld instrument made of wood and strips of tin. Women as well as men play the *guashi* and thumb piano. Talented men even produce music by plucking their upended bows. People carry instruments with them on trips, and, traveling or in camp, they often sit listening to a musician, sometimes softly improvising a sung harmony interwoven with the intricate rhythm (Biesele, "Religion and Folklore," in Tobias, ed., pp. 165–166; Thomas, pp. 223–225; Shostak, pp. 14, 310; Marshall, pp. 363–375).

Music is a means of individual self-expression for the Bushmen. People who are troubled or sad or bothered by some trying incident may sit alone and compose "mood music"—songs with titles, but without words, that touchingly express emotions, often wistful or ironic. One song Elizabeth Marshall heard, called "Bitter Melons," expressed the musician's feelings when he returned to a remembered field of melons but found them too bitter to eat. Another song expressed the composer's guilt and sorrow about an incident when his brother-in-law, lost in the bush near camp, had shouted to the band, and no one had bothered to answer him (Thomas, pp. 122–123). Some songs are mocking and sung under cover of darkness, with words that reproach an individual for misbehavior.

There are also sacred songs, like the Eland Song, the Gemsbok Song, the Giraffe Song, and the Sun Song, which are part of the religious and ceremonial life of the group. These songs are sung at sacred *trance dances,* and some are also sung at important ceremonies, like the Eland Song sung by women at the ceremony for an adolescent's first menstruation.

Sacred Dances. Trance dances are a regular feature of Bushman life, held on an average every ten days, with dances more frequent during dry season, when the nearness of several bands at a water hole makes social life more intense and exciting. Dances involve everyone in the band or bands, and last entire nights, with the women seated in a line or circle, shoulder to shoulder, singing the sacred songs and clapping complex rhythmic accompaniments. The men, their steps emphasized by the shaking of cocoon rattles tied around their legs, dance themselves into a trance in which they can converse with the spirits and heal the sick. Children excitedly dance and clap along, then, as the night wears on, fall asleep in their mothers' laps.

Trance dances may begin spontaneously, as fun, often initiated by children, or they may be arranged in response to serious illness or misfortune. Trance medicine, *n/um*, is a kind of power, "owned" by the people who have learned how to achieve a trance state and use it to cure others. About half the adult men and a third of the women have achieved trance at some time. Smaller numbers are accomplished healers, the greatest of whom may travel from camp to camp when needed.

In trance, the healer is able to draw illness out of the bodies of the sick and throw it away. The Ju/'hoansi believe sickness (and misfortune and death) are caused by tiny invisible arrows shot into the sick person by the spirits of the dead. These spirits are not malevolent, but lonely, and wish the living to be with them. The spirits are especially likely to take away a person who is ill-treated by others. In trance, healers lay their hands on the afflicted persons and draw the arrows into their own bodies. Then, at a moment of crisis, healers violently shudder and shriek, hurling the arrows away again. It is believed that in deep trance healers' spirits can leave their bodies to meet and talk with the spirits of the dead, to find out why they want to take the sick person, and try to persuade them to reconsider (Megan Biesele, "Religion and Folklore," in Tobias, ed., pp. 167–168; Shostak, pp. 291–299; Lee, 1984, pp. 109–113).

Megan Biesele emphasizes that the dancer's *n/um* cannot be activated without the support of singers (or drummers for the women's drum dance). Singing actually protects the dancers as their spirits leave their bodies. The trance dance is thus "a concerted effort by the entire community to banish misfortune" and a central unifying force in Bushman life. As **Emile Durkheim** pointed out a century ago (in *The Elementary Forms of the Religious Life*), dances like these are important shared experiences. Joining together in a sacred and risky ceremony intensifies group feeling, strengthening the bonds of group solidarity. While the Bushmen may think of their dances as serving a practical-spiritual purpose—curing the sick—dances also fulfill a **latent function,** a secondary purpose of which the Bushmen themselves are unaware, that of drawing the group more closely together (Durkheim, 1962, p. 432).

As a student of sociology, you will recognize that trance dances are both religious and medical. There are no Bushman hospitals or doctors, though the role of "healer" is one of the few specialized roles in Bushman society. There are no priests or churches: Everyone participates in sacred dances and many people learn to enter trance. But sacred dances are nevertheless part of religious life, as Durkheim recognized. Through the dances the Bushmen enter the realm of the sacred and communicate with spirits. They seek otherworldly help for their misfortunes and affirm their beliefs.

Gift-giving and Visiting. A great deal of the Bushmen's abundant leisure is devoted to cultivating relationships—in talk and games, music-making and ceremony—that reinforce group solidarity. Leisure activities also link individuals with individuals in ties of friendship and reciprocal obligation. Marshall found that Ju/'hoansi all over northern Namibia are connected in face-to-face acquaintance through visiting. In rainy season, individuals, couples, and small family groups break off from their bands to visit relatives, especially people they like (Marshall, pp. 180–181; Lee, 1979, p. 72).

Visits are often occasions for gift-giving, though gifts are also bestowed within the band and exchanged by spouses. Gift-giving is a constant preoccupation and a subject of talk second in prominence only to food. Interaction about gifts expresses feelings and carries weight in relationships. People talk about whom they plan to give gifts to; sometimes they complain about gifts they have received, or about people who take too long to reciprocate gifts. A person may ask someone for the gift of a particular object, as a way of inviting a closer relationship, or to cause discomfort because of jealousy or anger. It would be very rude to refuse a gift, and one must reciprocate, but not too soon, for owing a return gift links people together in friendship and is really the whole point of the exercise.

The objects given as gifts are really of secondary importance to the relationships created and sustained. Anyone can make any of the objects in daily use, or readily borrow them, and people tend to keep the gifts they receive for just a short while, before passing them on as gifts to someone else. People give objects in common use: ostrich shell bead headbands and necklaces, musical instruments, wooden bowls, arrows, pipes, dance rattles, or valued materials like eland fat (Marshall, pp. 303–305, 309–310).

SOCIAL STRUCTURE AND GROUP LIFE

One important lesson you can learn from studying the Bushmen is that people create social structure themselves, through interaction. When you live in a large, complex society, statuses and roles and institutions often seem like "givens." You are confronted with politicians or bosses, teachers or nurses, schools or courts, and you may feel you have had nothing to do with creating them. In Bushman society, it is clear that statuses and roles emerge as the result of repeated interaction between individuals. We can see the building of social structure very clearly, because Bushman society is limited to the family and the band. The Ju/'hoansi are distinctive (though typical of hunting and gathering societies) in that they have an extremely limited selection of statuses, roles, groups, and institutions. There are no chiefs or officials, priests, managers, employees, doctors, or servants, or any of a long list of specialized statuses and roles that may be found in your society. There are no committees, gangs, classes, clans, teams, parliaments, or clubs. Neither are there churches, courts, prisons, hospitals, schools, armies, governments, markets, or businesses.

Bushman society is a social system based on kinship: The band, the family, and kin statuses comprise all social structure and must serve all needs. It is most helpful to think of Bushman society not as socially impoverished by its lack of varied social structure, but as focused with extraordinary intensity on family relationships. Since social structure is created and maintained through interaction, it is easy to understand that the Bushmen are constantly involved in forming and elaborating family relations.

Authority and Anarchy

Here's another important point to think about: There are no authorities in Bushman society. No one person has any more power than another. There are no police officers, no bosses, no teachers, no generals, no presidents, nor kings. No one can tell you what to do—not even your parents! Kalahari Bushmen have a tremendous amount of individual freedom. They are not in the habit of taking orders from anyone, and if a person doesn't like what others are doing, their most usual response is to pick up and leave—go off visiting, or join another band. And there are no institutionalized rules—no legal code, no tax laws, no school policies, no traffic regulations, nor gun laws. Some modern societies pride themselves on individuality and freedom of choice, but compared to hunters and gatherers, people in modern societies are totally hedged about with bosses. Of all the ways humans have arranged their social lives, the bands of hunter-gatherers come closest to the life of mutual aid envisioned by anarchists. You should realize, though, that Bushman survival requires constant interaction, as autonomous individuals must continually discuss, persuade, negotiate, and plead to organize daily life.

The Family: Putting Flexibility First

The small **nuclear family** (the reproductive unit of parents and children) is the basic unit of Bushman society. Families are "modular" and flexible. Nuclear family modules may link together to form larger **extended families,** and extended families may also break up into their constituent nuclear units. A series of nuclear and extended families links together to form a **band,** but bands are not necessarily permanent arrangements: Some families may leave and others join, and sometime a band will break up entirely. At certain seasons, bands come together in larger encampments forming more or less defined **band clusters** (Guenther, pp. 79–80). The modular structure of Ju/'hoan families and bands may readily be seen as a form of **cultural adaptation,** permitting flexible adjustment of group size to available resources.

Creating Nuclear Families

While a couple and their children form a long-lasting, firmly bonded group in Bushman society, nuclear families never live independently. (However, they may temporarily go off visiting on their own.) Nuclear families are small. In the 1950s, 60s, and 70s, anthropologists found that the average Ju/'hoan woman gave birth to only four to five children altogether, and the average family comprised only two to three living children. Marriage creates nuclear families, and also links them in larger extended families and in an even broader kinship network.

When a couple marries, the Ju/'hoansi expect the husband to move in with his new wife's family. Typically, they explain this custom in terms of food. The boy must feed his wife's parents, who are getting old, and he must feed his bride, they say, and prove he is capable and responsible (Marshall, p. 169). Members of the same band are not forbidden to marry, but such marriages are unusual. Consequently, marriages usually involve some reshuffling of band membership. This is especially so since the new husband may bring others with him to his wife's band. He remains responsible for his parents and dependents, and they may come with him. Ju/'hoan men are allowed to have more than one wife (**polygyny**), though this practice is rare, and in such a case, a man will bring his first wife, their children, and perhaps her relatives with him (in addition to his own) when he joins his new wife's family.

There is no set duration for this **bride service** with the wife's family (people say it should last long enough for three children to be born), but afterwards a man has the right to return to his own people, taking his wife and dependents. He may or may not do this, depending on how well he gets along with his wife's band and what kinds of resources are available to each band. The couple and their dependents may in fact move back and forth between his relatives and hers (Marshall, p. 170). One way of understanding this is to say that Ju/'hoan society is **ambilocal:** People live with either the husband's or the wife's relatives. It is also **bilateral:** They reckon kinship on both their mother's and their father's sides.

The Band: Linking Families

There is no rigid pattern for band formation. Band members are always related to each other in some fashion (through ties of blood or marriage), but the actual linkages vary. The band grows like a chain, as in-marrying spouses bring their parents, siblings, and spouses, who in turn bring theirs. But band members are not mandated by kinship ties to remain together. People choose to stay in a band because they get along well living and working together. If they don't get along, families are free to leave the band, affiliating themselves with relatives in some other band. This is a real option, frequently exercised. Often families break off from their band to visit others—to exchange gifts, or news, or arrange a marriage, or attend a ceremony. Because bands are flexible, people can adjust the size of their group to environmental conditions and resources. Most people, Lorna Marshall found, have relatives who are parents, offspring, or siblings in five to thirteen other bands (Marshall, pp. 180–181, 195, 200). But everyone belongs to a family and a band; there are no unattached people in Bushman society.

> ### Dabe's Story: The Visitors
> *Dabe saw the straggling line first. A dozen people approached slowly through the bush. Dabe broke into a smile as he recognized his mother's favorite brother /Gao at the head of the line. /Gao had once lived for two years with Dabe's band and had taught Dabe to track and hunt. Dabe rushed to meet his uncle and shouted to attract his attention. /Gao embraced Dabe and croaked out a sad and weary tale. /Gao's band's water hole had run dry and they had walked north for six days, searching the area for Dabe's band. /Gao's infant daughter had died three days ago when her mother's milk dried up. As /Gao spoke, Dabe's mother Karu rushed forward and embraced her brother.*
>
> *Then /Gao's wife limped up, and her mother and brother and his family, and his wife's widowed sister and her sons. Karu brought water that had been stored in ostrich eggshells; soon the travelers had their first deep drink of good water in days. An hour later, Dabe's father Kwi and several other men of the band appeared, returning from a hunt. Kwi greeted his relatives warmly and invited them to make their camp next to his. Later, he gave them a share of the eland he had killed, but his heart was full of anxiety. There was not enough water here for even two small bands. How would they all survive?*

The next day it was decided: /Gao and his band would stay with Dabe and Karu and Kwi. They were too worn to go farther. But the other people in Dabe's band decided to go to stay with their relatives at Nyae-Nyae, where there was a permanent water hole and the rains usually began first.

Kinship: Elaborating Connections

Kinship systems vary from one Bushman people to another. The Ju/'hoan system has been carefully described. You will no doubt find it surprising and interesting. Ju/'hoan kinship is rudimentary in some ways; extraordinarily complex in others. The Ju/'hoansi are not much interested in keeping track of relatives more than two generations back in time, or beyond second cousins. But they have developed several interesting devices for creating extra kinship bonds, weaving additional threads into the net of family that unites all Ju/'hoansi.

The *K'ausi* and the *N'ore*

An important part of Ju/'hoan kinship has to do with the relationship of bands to their territories. Every band is attached to a territory—a water hole and the land and resources surrounding it, called a *n'ore*. It would be impossible for a band to exist without a *n'ore* (and since the number of water holes is limited, this serves to limit the number of bands). Each band is identified with a group of related older people, who have lived in the band a long time—usually siblings or cousins, who are considered to be the "owners" or *k'ausi* of the *n'ore*. Visitors traveling through a territory would ask the *k'ausi* for permission to gather plant foods and use the water hole.

The *k'ausi* are not formal leaders. They "own" the resources, but can't give them away or sell them; neither can they decide who joins the band or tell people what to do. They may not necessarily be the informal leaders of the band either; they may be too old or lacking in the personal qualities needed for leadership. Leadership is then likely to be exercised by someone else who has a strong personality (but is not arrogant or selfish) and who has qualities of wisdom and judgment (Lee, 1979, pp. 61–67; 1984, p. 88).

Generations and the Joking Relationship

Another kinship principle profoundly shapes life in Ju/'hoan society: the principle of alternating generations (Lee, 1984, pp. 63–66). Ju/'hoan kinship terms pair up alternating generations. You, your grandparents, and your grandchildren share a special kin relationship; so do your parents and your children. Special reciprocal kin terms are used by the alternating pairs.

Just to make all this more complicated, there is another principle related to alternating generations: the joking relationship. All of a Ju/'hoansi's kin are either people they joke with or people they avoid. The "joking relationship" is relaxed, affectionate, and familiar; the "avoidance relationship" is respectful and formal. Generally speaking, you joke with relatives in your generation, your grandparents' generation, and your grandchildren's generation, and you avoid relatives in your parents' and your children's generations. An important rule is that you may never marry someone in the avoidance relationship.

Xama's Story: The Joking Relationship

At the end of the long dry season, when everyone was waiting impatiently for the rains to begin, five bands gathered at the large permanent water hole at Nyae Nyae. They had to— it was practically the only water left—but it was also a wonderful distraction from worries about the rain. Xama thought this was the best time of the year. She saw her married older brother and her best friend who had gone to live with her husband's band. Almost every night there was a trance dance at one camp or another. Xama was sixteen and knew she was ready now to get married.

At the water hole, Xama met her mother's uncle /'Ase, who had long ago left Xama's band to do his bride service in his wife's band. "Come walk with me," he laughed, "I am so old that I need help from my grandchildren." Xama laughed also. In his mid-30s, /'Ase was muscular and smooth-faced. He stood half a head taller than Xama; he was known as "Tall /'Ase." "Here is someone who makes me feel small,"/'Ase said, as a hazel-eyed young man walked into view. As tall as /'Ase, Tu was in his early twenties, and, in Xama's eyes, very handsome.

"This is Tu," /'Ase introduced the young man, "he is your cousin's cousin." This made Tu a marriageable partner for Xama, and after a few comments, /'Ase left the couple alone. In a few days Xama had decided that the future would offer few better opportunities than the tall young man with the hazel eyes. But there were problems. Xama's aunt confronted her and said, "You must not joke with Tu; people are talking. Tu is the brother of your uncle's second wife. You cannot marry him; he is of your parents' generation."

Xama was stunned and frightened, but Tu reassured her. "I am your cousin's cousin; that's what's most important. People will see that." Tu's father and brother argued openly with Xama's mother. Tu and Xama, they said, could marry. No one could agree and Tu and Xama were miserable. Tu's father said he would take them to his cousin's band. They wouldn't see any problem with the marriage. The young couple waited anxiously for the rains to come and make travel possible.

Fictive Kin: Making Kinship Really Complicated

Here is the tricky part: The Ju/'hoansi take the whole kinship structure—relationships by blood and marriage, alternating generations, joking and avoidance relationships—and apply it to fictive (imaginary) kin. The system is based on names. Anyone who has your name addresses your kin as his—he calls your wife "wife," your father "father," etc. And you can do the same: Anyone with your mother's name you can address as "mother," anyone with your son's name you may call "son," and so on. Anyone with your sibling's name or your grandparent's name, etc., stands in a joking relationship to you. Those with your father's name or your child's, you treat with avoidance. Also, and very importantly, you may not marry anyone who shares the name of a relative you are forbidden to marry (your sibling, or parent, or child, or sibling's child).

Fictive kinship extends the benefits of kinship to everyone who bears a Ju/'hoan name. With it, no one among the whole people need be a stranger or an outsider. In the very few cases in which people have no blood relatives, they live in a band with fictive kin. It also makes kinship a complex intellectual challenge, since there are very few Ju/'hoan names (only about 35 first names for each sex, and no last names) (Lee, 1984, pp. 68–71).

Why do the Ju/'hoansi bother to maintain such an elaborate kinship system? You may find the **functionalist perspective** very helpful in understanding Ju/'hoan kinship. In a society without specialized roles kinship finds places for all people. It helps the society function smoothly by ensuring that any two members of Ju/'hoan society will always know where they stand in relation to each other and what roles they should play. Depending on their actual kinship, their ages, and their names, individuals will quickly establish kinship status and determine whether they have a joking or an avoidance relationship.

Roles: Focusing on Gender

In addition to kinship and age, the other fundamental basis of Bushman status and role is gender. More than anything else, who you are and what you do in life is determined by your gender. Male and female are the basic "specialties"; there are no other specialized occupations. One way of putting this is to say that the Bushmen, like other hunting and gathering societies, have only the most basic **division of labor,** for there are only two jobs, two economic roles. And since these roles are gender roles, they are part of family life. In effect, there is no economy separate from the family and the band.

Is There a "Breadwinner" Role?

Bushman women and men both "commute" to work (Fisher, p. 103). The work roles of men and women are different, but there is no sense in which women do "housework" and men "go to work."

N!uhka's Story: The Gatherers

N!uhka is hungry, but happy. Her brother found a field of tsin beans while hunting and she is off to harvest them. Tsin beans have been scarce, so many women are eager to come along. Even N!uhka's mother, who is less active than she once was, comes along. Gathering tsin beans is work, but it's also a social occasion, a break in routine. Twikwe, N!uhka's best friend, plays a tune on her thumb piano as they walk along, and the women join in, singing a rhythmic chorus. Even though N!uhka is burdened with her heavy toddler, whom she carries in her leather kaross, her step is light and her face is smiling.

Everyone seems lifted by the prospect of the beans. Even Dasina, whose running fight with her husband has made her sullen for weeks, is smiling and singing. Suddenly, as the women enter the bean field, a duiker, a tiny antelope, breaks from its hiding place and dashes away. The women take up the chase with enthusiastic shouts. Although the duiker can race faster than any Ju/'hoansi, it is young and confused and runs in circles. N!uhka and Twikwe pelt it with stones, knocking it over, but the duiker recovers and bounds off. All the women are disappointed. On other harvesting trips they have run down small game and feasted on the meat.

Soon the women turn to the work of harvesting beans and by afternoon have collected a huge pile, which they roll in their karosses. With her kaross tied around her waist, each woman will carry 15–30 pounds of beans, the babies perched on top. Weary and joking, the women return home, knowing they can rest in camp for three or four days without further gathering.

These young women have walked out from camp for the day, to a place where they know grewia berries are ripe. Behind them stretches the Kalahari Desert; rolling grasslands, punctuated with clusters of trees and bushes.

Women's Work

Anthropologists calculate that the food women collect constitutes about 75 percent of the Ju/'hoan diet. Gathering is not random; the women have a plan and a clear objective. They know where fruits are ripe or roots and tubers may be found. When the band moves camp, women carry all their belongings and their young children. Lee estimates that each year the average Ju/'hoan woman carries her child 1,500 miles. Women also gather wood, and tend fires and cook vegetable foods. They build shelters and repair them and keep the family's living area clear of ash and grasses. They make household objects like ostrich eggshell water holders, tortoise shell bowls, and personal ornaments. Women don't use bows and arrows or spears to hunt, but they do kill snakes and tortoises and birds and occasionally even small animals (Marshall, pp. 92, 97, 102; Lee, 1979, pp. 310–312).

Men's Work

Hunting is the focus of male activity and talk. Men hunt small game with spears, clubs, or snares, and they hunt big game with bow and poisoned arrow. They hunt on an irregular basis, sometimes alone, but by preference in groups of two to four.

They may stay around camp for weeks at a time, then hunt for several days in a row, but averaged out, they hunt around two or three days a week.

Debe's Story: The Hunters

Debe and N!eisi were very tired. They had followed kudu tracks all day, without sighting the animals. "Let's go back to camp," sighed Debe; "I'm tired; my back hurts. Sa//gai will rub my back." "Your wife will rub her belly in hunger if we return without meat," N!eisi protested. "Let's go on just a little longer." Debe and N!eisi were lucky. They suddenly came upon the kudu in the slanting light of late afternoon, grazing as they settled for the night. Crawling to a clump of bushes only a few feet from the kudu, Debe used his bow. The poisoned arrow hit a young male kudu in the flank and it fled. By morning, the poison would weaken and then paralyze the three hundred pound animal. Debe and N!eisi hurried back to the camp. They would need help to carry the meat.

The next morning they returned to the hunt with four more men from their band. They soon found the wounded kudu, but it was closely watched by a pair of lions. N!eisi tried to chase the lions: "Go lions; this is our meat, not yours!" he commanded, tossing a clod of earth in the big cats' direction. The lions would not move and growled alarmingly as N!eisi tossed another clod.

Debe raised his bow, but only in frustration. The lions would devour the foolish hunters long before the weak Ju/'hoan poison could do its work. Debe turned toward camp and shouted at N!eisi: "Now we can all rub our bellies!" "There are other kudu to hunt," N!eisi called out, but Debe kept walking toward camp.

Game is used for many purposes besides food; almost nothing is wasted. Men make animal hides into clothing and bags, bone and horn are used for tools, sinews for bowstrings and nets. Men craft all their hunting gear—bows, arrows, quivers, spears, clubs, and implements for trapping. They collect the beetle larvae from which arrow poison is distilled and carefully prepare and spread the poison. Men also butcher and cook meat, especially the meat of large animals. They light fires, by twirling sticks, or in recent decades, by use of a flint and tinder. At a Ju/'hoan campground, both men and women are engaged in domestic tasks. Men know how to gather and sometimes do so—when they return empty-handed from a hunt, or when they go with women on overnight gathering trips (Lee, 1979, pp. 216–226; Marshall, pp. 124, 132–137).

SOCIAL INEQUALITY

Everyone who has studied Bushman societies has been struck by their lack of inequality. As we have seen, there are no economic or **class** inequalities: sharing and gift-giving ensure that food and material objects are distributed equally in families and bands. Visiting evens out resources between bands and *n'ore*. There are not inequalities of **power** either. There are no official chiefs. Informal leaders do develop in bands, but they don't have the power to give orders or make people do things against their wills. They lead by example and by their interpersonal skills. The only kind of inequality discernable in Bushman societies is **status** inequality. Some people enjoy more prestige and respect than others, perhaps because of their skill as hunters or musicians or healers, or perhaps because of their pleasant personalities. But their prestige doesn't result in increased wealth or power. Admired individuals don't eat better or have more possessions than others; they aren't given special titles or privileges. They may be sought out in marriages or as band members. But take note: these status inequalities are personal, not social; they result from individuals' personal traits, not from their membership in social groups, like classes or races. The only status inequality in Bushman societies that is social in nature is inequality between men and women. Gender inequality does exist, but it is minimal.

Gender Inequality

Women and men are not perfectly equal in Ju/'hoansi society, but they come pretty close. Women work longer hours than men, in gathering, child care, and household work, but their enormous contribution to subsistence is recognized, and the food they gather is considered theirs. Men don't scorn womens' work, and they do sometimes go gathering. Women have a great deal of autonomy and power. They are not expected to obey men; they don't wait on men, and they don't eat less or inferior food than men. Women are seldom physically assaulted or coerced by men, and in fact, women hit men about as frequently as they are struck by them. Women have a voice in group discussions and a say in making arrangements. There are no formal statuses or laws that give power to men (Marshall, p. 177).

In marriage too, women are not disadvantaged. Mothers and fathers share authority over children, and divorces are as likely to be initiated by women as by men. Because of bride service, young women don't end up as powerless newcomers in their husbands' families. And finally, though there is polygyny (multiple wives) and not polyandry (multiple husbands), its rarity seems to be the result of women's firm opposition.

Gender and Personality

In societies where men and women are very unequal, they are often socialized to develop personality traits that reinforce their inequality. In such societies, boys are taught to be aggressive and domineering and girls to be passive and dependent. Personality differences between Ju/'hoan men and women are minimal. The Ju/'hoansi find conflict and violence abhorrent (as we will soon see) and they disapprove of men who are aggressive, boastful, or dominating. It is no compliment to say that a man is a fighter, and in Ju/'hoan culture boys are never urged or taught to fight. Men who are easygoing and skillful and who help ease tensions in the group are preferred. Self-assertion, demandingness, and boldness are also discouraged in women, but perhaps slightly more so than in men. Women are expected to be gentle, modest, and gracious, and to comply with the wishes of others (Marshall, p. 176).

Gender Segregation

In many societies, women's lower status is reflected in their extensive segregation from men and from public life in general. Among the Ju/'hoansi, women and men are segregated in some of their roles, but overall, the degree of segregation is not great. Most of the time, women and men work separately, each going into the bush with friends and relatives of their own gender. But this separation is not rigid. Parties of men and women do go gathering together, especially in major expeditions to the mangetti groves, or the tsin bean fields, and these are usually rather festive occasions. Women are sometimes part of the party that returns to track down and carry home big game fatally wounded in a hunt. Within the camp, men and women sit on opposite sides of the fire, but beyond this, there is a great deal of mixing of men and women, and boys and girls. Children of both sexes play together, and spouses are commonly real companions, sitting and talking by their fire and even arranging "getaways" to visit relatives or go gathering together in the bush.

The "Masters of Meat"

Anthropologists disagree about just how equal Bushman men and women are. Lorna Marshall argued that Ju/'hoan men did enjoy an advantage over women, an advantage in influence and prestige, which stemmed from the glamour of hunting. As she explained it, "There is no splendid excitement in returning home with vegetables." People crave meat and they call men the "masters of meat" and "the owners of hunting" (Marshall, p. 178). News of success in a hunt, particularly of big game, spreads rapidly even beyond the camp. Visitors arrive and everyone feasts and parties. Hunting confers not only prestige, however, but also concrete influence. Women distribute their plant food within their own families, but men distribute the enticing meat widely, and their gifts are a kind of investment, which gathers in honor and obligations, and grows into influence (Fisher, p. 215).

But more recently, Susan Kent has replied, "Only foreign anthropologists consider hunting as somehow better than collecting (gathering), or as an activity in which everyone should want to participate" (Kent, 1995, p. 520).

DEVIANCE AND SOCIAL CONTROL

Do you think that there is more deviance in your society or in Bushman societies? If you think about this you will see that it is puzzling. The Bushmen have no laws or police or courts, no authority figures to make rules or mete out punishments. There are no **formal sanctions**—positive or negative—to make people conform: no diplomas to work for, no scholarships for merit, no promotions, no jobs to win or lose, no jail sentences, parole, or court-martials. The Bushmen rely entirely on the **informal sanctions** of small group life. Negative sanctions include the mocking song heard in the darkness, gossip and ridicule, teasing and avoidance. The Bushmen fear having others laugh at them. Positive sanctions include group approval, loving attention, and companionship. Inclusion in group life is emotionally so essential that these informal sanctions are highly effective.

While there certainly is deviance in Bushman society, there are no **deviant roles** or **deviant careers.** There are no gang members, or burglars, no confidence men, no punk rockers, no cross-dressers who inhabit subcultures condemned as deviant by the rest of their society. Most of the time, members of Bushman societies accept group norms and act and talk and think in ways that are expected of them. But they sometimes commit deviant acts, like failing to share food, or fighting, or boasting, or engaging in adultery, or even killing another person.

Deviance and Social Interaction

In the Bushmen's small bands, many norms concern how people are expected to interact with each other, and much of Bushman deviance involves disapproved modes of interaction. Sociologists distinguish four types of interaction, found in all societies: **social exchange, cooperation, competition,** and **conflict.** In every society, people value some of these forms of interaction and they disapprove of others. For the Bushmen, exchange and cooperation are desired, competition and conflict feared and avoided.

Social Exchange and Cooperation

Many sociologists see exchange as a universally important interaction process, and the Bushmen would agree. They tend to see the world in terms of exchanges (you give me a gift and then I'll give you one; you give me meat when you are successful hunting, and then I return the favor; you extend hospitality to my family or band when we are in your territory, and later we will do the same for you). In exchange, each person gives something in order to get something else—gifts, assistance, love, food, attention, companionship, etc. Like people in other societies, the Bushmen are careful to reciprocate appropriately. Their society, like others, has many norms that sociologists call **norms of reciprocity.** These norms tell people what to exchange, how, with whom, and when. The Bushmen worry about whether this relative or that deserves a shoulder of the antelope, or whether it would be better to give the hindquarter as well, and they think carefully about the timing of gifts as well as their nature—to reciprocate too quickly, or to wait too long could both be insulting.

People usually can find some way to reciprocate. Those who are too old or handicapped to hunt or gather can stay in camp with the children, or shell nuts or make music. People who fail to reciprocate are teased or reproached or avoided. Some people work harder than others at reciprocal gift-giving, spending many hours making ostrich-shell beads and jewelry, for example. They are rewarded with an extensive network of social connections from whom they can expect gifts, perhaps help in matchmaking, or a place they will be welcome to visit.

For the Bushmen, exchange often takes the form of cooperation, when people pitch in together and pool their resources to achieve a common goal. We see this in the dry-season sharing of permanent water holes, in the help people give each other in carrying home large kills or heavy mangetti nuts. Most games illustrate and teach cooperation, as the whole group works together to keep the ball aloft, or the rhythm going. In one popular game, girls make a circle, each girl crooking one leg around her neighbor's, then hop in unison. When one falls, the circle collapses and the game is over.

Competition

Like cooperation, competition requires agreed-upon social rules, but competition is repugnant to the Bushmen, and they work constantly to squelch competitive tendencies in individuals and suppress arrogance in those more talented or successful. Acting competitive is a form of deviance.

Ju/'hoan norms call for extreme modesty in presenting one's accomplishments. A man whose arrow badly wounds an antelope will return to his hearth silent and dejected. Asked about the hunt, he will doubtfully admit that he just might have grazed his quarry. Then the camp will celebrate, for they know this means the hunter has scored a certain hit and there will probably be meat tomorrow. As one Xai/Xai man, /Gaugo, explained to Richard Lee, when the carrying party finds the kill, they will loudly disparage the meat:

> You mean you have dragged us all the way out here to make us cart home your pile of bones? Oh, if I had known it was this thin, I wouldn't have come.

The Ju/'hoansi call this "insulting the meat." Anyone who shows open pride is relentlessly teased, and the object of their pride disparaged. Tomazho, a famous healer explained:

> When a young man kills much meat, he comes to think of himself as a chief or a big man, and he thinks of the rest of us as his servants or inferiors. We can't accept this. We refuse one who boasts, for someday his pride will make him kill somebody. So we always speak of his meat as worthless. In this way we cool his heart and make him gentle. (Lee, 1984, pp. 151–57)

Conflict

Conflict occurs when normative consensus breaks down, but actually, in most cases, the events of a conflict follow an accepted script, escalating through stages recognizable to all. In conflict, people try to meet their goals by destroying an opponent. The Ju/'hoansi are horrified, and very much frightened by conflict, especially violent conflict, and make every effort to prevent disagreements from escalating into physical fighting. Much as they oppose conflict, the Ju/'hoansi are only moderately successful in preventing it. In the worst case, arguments progress to insults and then into wrestling and hitting, followed by a general melee in which many people may be wounded or killed (Lee, 1984, pp. 93–95; 1979, pp. 396–399).

> ### Kushe's Story: The Fight
>
> *It seems like it has gone on all day. As Kushe sits shelling mangetti nuts, she carries on an endless shrill monologue, complaining about her husband. "He is so stingy; too stingy," goes the refrain. "He doesn't give me presents. He doesn't bring home enough meat." The whole band ignores her, and her husband's parents, who are visiting, tactfully disappear into the bush. By the time Ukwane and his brother-in-law return from hunting, the tension is so high you can practically see it. Ukwane begins to butcher the kudu and hands the first share to his mother. Kushe jumps between them, furious: "You're not going to give me any, are you?" she demands. Taken aback, Ukwane tries to deflect her with kidding: "No, of course not; I never give you anything." Kushe is beside herself. "That's right," she screams, "you don't; no food and no babies," as she hits and claws at him. Amazed by the suddenness of this emotional storm, Ukwane grabs Kushe and literally throws her out of his way. Kushe runs back and assaults him again. Ukwane's mother and Kushe's mother are now pushing and shouting at each other. Momentarily shocked, the rest of the group finds its feet and leaps into action, separating and holding the combatants. Everyone is talking and shouting and milling about.*
>
> *Tempers have cooled by the following morning, but Ukwane wants no part of Kushe or her family. "They are like warthogs, not people!" Ukwane's mother spits out. "They all look*

*like warthogs," grunts his father. Ukwane rises, declaring, "I want to go to hunt kudu, not
to live among beasts!" Having said this in a voice loud enough to carry across the camp,
Ukwane leads his parents off on the long trek to his brother's camp near the Herero village.*

Managing Conflict. How do the Ju/'hoansi ensure that most conflicts do not
escalate to the point of violence? After all, they cannot call the police or campus security. While there are no separate political or legal institutions, the Ju/'hoansi do
have norms and procedures for handling conflict—within the band and the family.

One way the Ju/'hoansi manage conflict is by providing plentiful opportunity
for harmless venting of complaints. The Ju/'hoansi are an exceptionally verbal people, and feelings like grief, envy, resentment, anger, or alarm are readily expressed
in conversation. A great deal of the constant interchange in groups takes the form of
semiserious argument, called "a talk," in which real discontents are jokingly aired.
In such sessions, people complain about others' laziness or stinginess, about people
who don't distribute meat properly or don't reciprocate gifts generously. (Though
complaints like these are common, the underlying problem in uncontrolled, fatal
fights is usually adultery, or anger over a previous homicide.) "Talks" are potentially
dangerous, but most of the time, the danger is defused by laughter.

A "Fight." If "talking" fails, then people lose their good nature and begin angry argument. When they begin to make sexual insults (*za*) against each other, then
you know that anger will mount and actual physical violence is likely. Women are
as likely as men to be involved in hand-to-hand violence, with men or with other
women. In most cases, once people separate the combatants, they are usually able
to use joking to calm everyone down.

Conflict Control. Separation in fact is one of the most effective means of limiting conflict available to the Bushmen. It is relatively easy for one party or the other
in a dispute to pick up and leave the group temporarily, and people often do so. Conflict avoidance and flexible group composition are closely intertwined, with
conflict-induced separations keeping groups small, and flexible group composition
making conflict-avoidance possible.

The most extreme form of conflict-management practiced by the Ju/'hoansi
(and the one that comes closest to the exercise of political authority) is group execution. It is a last resort to even the score when people hold a grudge for a previous
murder, or to put an end to fighting caused by a single, dangerously violent individual. Richard B. Lee has recorded several such cases, in one of which a whole community joined in shooting and stabbing a probably psychotic killer (Lee, 1984, p. 6;
1979, pp. 393–395).

Since the Tswana and the Herero have settled in the Kalahari, the Bushmen have
been glad to make use of their legal institutions to manage conflict. As early as 1948,
the Tswana appointed a !Kung-speaking Tswana, Isak Utigile, as "headman" (really
a kind of justice of the peace, or magistrate) of the Ju/'hoansi, and his "court" became very popular as a place for mediation of disputes by a trusted authority (Lee.
1979, p. 396; 1984, pp. 96–97). Nowadays, as the Bushmen settle down in villages,
people are less able to avoid conflict by leaving the group, so they are turning more

and more frequently to Herero or Tswana headmen or to government officials to mediate disputes. Susan Kent describes a Bushman village in Botswana where villagers turned repeatedly to the Game Scout (the nearest government official) in cases of conflict (Kent, 1989).

SOCIALIZATION

One reason why there is relatively little deviance in Ju/'hoan society is that socialization is quite successful. Bushmen learn to play new roles all through life, as they move from childhood through adulthood to old age. These age-specific roles are in fact the major roles in Ju/'hoan society since, besides the basic gender division, there are no other specialized roles. Like the rest of life, socialization takes place in the family and the band and people are socialized by their friends and relatives. There is no formal socialization, since there are no schools or other formal institutions. However, there are formal ceremonies that mark important life transitions.

Ju/'hoan socialization has a special quality because children can rely on their adult roles being just like their parents. Adults have valuable knowledge and skills to transmit to children, and old people's long experience with the conditions of bush life makes them respected advisors. Life is filled with difficulties, but has a reliable consistency from generation to generation. No Ju/'hoan child needs to worry about what they will be when they grow up; but they don't have very many choices either. Everyone has to accommodate their talents to the small number of gender and kinship roles that exist.

Childhood Socialization

The Ju/'hoansi begin their lives with an immensely secure early childhood. Babies sleep beside their mothers at night and are carried all day in slings that permit constant skin-to-skin contact. They have free access to the breast, and nurse on demand, several times an hour. The Ju/'hoansi believe babies need no training or discipline. Young children are carried and nursed up to the age of 3 or even 4, but once out of infancy, they spend more time out of their mothers' arms—in affectionate play with their fathers, held by the various aunts and uncles, grandparents and cousins who surround them in the band, and often carried, like dolls, by the older siblings.

But then, when a child is 3 or 4 years old, they are suddenly required to stop breast-feeding, relinquish the role of an infant, and adopt the much more independent role of a child. Ju/'hoansi mothers bear children with an average birth interval of four years. Ideally, a new pregnancy occurs because the still-nursing toddler is self-weaning to solid food. Much of the time, however, the toddler is still emotionally wedded to nursing, and with the new pregnancy, mother and child enter a stressful period of angry conflict. The child feels rage and rejection, sometimes still unresolved by the time of the new birth. But the weaning crisis gradually abates as the 4-year-old tires of hanging around mother and infant and is drawn off into the more exciting life of the children's play group (Shostak, pp. 57–58).

Children Socialize Each Other

Children from about ages 7 to 12 spend almost all their time in each others' company, playing in mixed-age and often mixed-sex groups. They play in the cleared central "plaza" of the camp, or, even more often, in a nearby "children's village," out of sight, but not out of hearing of the adults. Children play traditional games, give their smaller siblings rides on an old *kaross,* or on their backs, and endlessly "play house." Girls build rough shelters and pair off with boys or with each other as "mommies and daddies." Children gather berries or roots in the nearby bush, snare small birds or collect caterpillars, or pretend to kill and butcher an animal. Girls and boys hold their own "pretend" trance dances. Away from disapproving parents, children also experiment with sex, imitating parents glimpsed in the dark, looking and touching, but not initiating actual intercourse (Lee, 1979, p. 236; Shostak, p. 83; Marshall, pp. 318–319). A great deal of childrens' play is obviously **anticipatory socialization,** in which they learn by observing and imitating the roles they will play as adults.

Gai's Story: Learning to Be a Man

"We are masters of the meat," shouts 9-year-old Gai, as he leads two younger boys in a mock hunt through the tall grass. Gai and //Oma use their toy bows to shoot at the grasshoppers they disturb as they run. Suddenly a shout from the youngest boy, Gwe, reveals a 3-foot-long grass snake. The three boys chase the snake, shooting at it, tossing rocks, and finally killing it with a branch used as a club. "We must cook our meat!" exclaims Gai, as they build a fire and roast the unfortunate snake.

Gai enjoys his new role as "hunter" and distributes meat to the younger boys. Four girls, including Karu, an 8-year-old who often plays "house" with Gai, look on hungrily, but no food comes their way. Finally Karu shouts, "Where is my food? I am your wife; you have to give me some!"

Gai's pals are beside themselves with laughter. Karu, nearly a head shorter than Gai, chases him around the clearing. What starts as a game soon becomes a tug of war, as Karu grabs the charred snake and Gai pulls back on the other end. The snake splits and the pair are dumped on the ground. Karu and Gai scream at each other until Karu's older sister arrives and shouts at both of them, "You're acting like a bunch of babies! Grown-ups share their food, especially husbands and wives!"

Actually, children learn a great deal from each other. Older children are patient with younger ones who try to join their games and instruct them in the proper way to play. Older children act as peacemakers and mediators in the frequent minor conflicts of the informal playgroup. They often intervene when one child teases another, grabs someone's melon or toy, or when disagreements turn to physical fighting. They punish aggression—generally with ridicule—and give comfort to the victims. Also, they sometimes make fun of children who don't participate in games, or who play badly (Eibl-Eibesfeldt, p. 135). As children grow up, they gradually move from freely expressing aggression to controlling aggression in others, then to an adulthood in which suppressing their own aggressive, competitive impulses will be expected.

Adults Socialize Children

Children spend a great deal of time with adults of all ages and learn from them by imitation and informal instruction. They learn to control their tempers and avoid offending others. When young children fight, mothers' most common response is to separate or distract them. Mothers may scold and compel the return of a grabbed object. Though threats of beatings are common, actual physical punishment is rare (Eibesfeldt, pp. 132–33, 135).

Children also learn the many norms of daily life. They learn to receive food in outstretched hands, not to grab, to wait until asked to share food; to take a modest serving from a passed bowl, and to eat with restraint, not revealing eagerness. They are scolded for greed or stealing. Girls and boys also learn the norms of sexual modesty. They learn that adults do not hug or kiss each other in public. Girls learn to sit modestly, so their genitals are not visible. Both girls and boys learn that it is dangerous to sit where a person of the opposite sex has sat. The Ju/'hoansi believe that if a man sits in a place touched by a woman's genitals, his ability to hunt will be impaired, and if a woman sits in a man's place, she will get an infection (Marshall, pp. 244, 249, 293–294, 311).

In adolescence children begin to go gathering or hunting with adults, in order to learn these vital skills. Girls begin to gather in earnest as soon as they marry, which could be as young as 10 or 12, but is more probably about age 16. But even then, the young wife gathers in the company of her mother, or perhaps her aunt or sisters. The transition to adult responsibilities is gradual. At about the age of 12, boys' fathers give them their first small bows and arrows and quivers, and they begin to hunt birds and rabbits. This is a time when they may also accompany an older man, perhaps a grandfather, in setting snares and tending a trapline. Finally comes the big step of going with their fathers, uncles, and older brothers on a hunt (Shostak, pp. 83–84).

Rites of Passage to Adulthood

In traditional Ju/'hoan society, major events mark the passage to adulthood: for boys, the first kill of a large animal, and *choma,* initiation into manhood, and for girls, first menstruation and marriage. All four of these events are marked by public ceremonies; they are the **rites of passage** that mark and celebrate a person's change in status before the whole community.

The First Buck Ceremony

A boy becomes a fully adult hunter when he kills his first big antelope with a poisoned arrow. Killing the first big animal is the result of hard work on hunting, and this is recognized with two important ceremonies—for the first male and first female animals killed. These ceremonies are male business, performed while the women are out of camp. The young man is given small cuts and tattoos on his chest, back, and arms; these mark him as a hunter in the eyes of the world. Further cuts are rituals to strengthen his vision, stamina, aim, and determination. Then the men gather to cook and eat some of the young hunter's meat. The ritual ends with the dramatic tale of a hunt (Lee, 1979, pp. 236–240). After killing his first buck, a young man is considered eligible for marriage.

Choma

Sometime between the ages of 15 and 20, boys participate in *choma*, a sacred six-weeks-long initiation rite. *Choma* is an elaborate rite, in which sacred male knowledge is passed on to a new generation. It is usually held every few years during the winter dry season when several bands gather at a permanent water hole, bringing together a large enough group of boys. *Choma* is a challenging experience of hunger, cold, and thirst. The boys sing the men's songs and dance to exhaustion. Like the first buck ceremony, *choma* is performed away from women (Lee, 1979, p. 365; Shostak, p. 239).

Marriage

Marriage and first menstruation are two important transitions in the life of a Ju/'hoansi girl that are marked by formal ceremony. It will probably seem quite strange to you that of the two events, a traditional Ju/'hoan girl would be likely to experience marriage first. Neither event signals an abrupt transition to adulthood, and marriage especially should be thought of more as a process—beginning with marriage negotiations and ending with the birth of a child—than as a sudden change of status.

Marriage is a stormy period in a girl's socialization. First marriages are usually arranged by parents or other close relatives (who will also arrange subsequent marriages if the spouses are still young). Arranging a marriage involves a lot of visiting, discussions, and gift-giving, and it may actually be difficult to find a suitable mate within the restrictions of actual and fictive kinship. The marriage ceremony itself is an almost casual, hearthside occasion, attended mostly by children.

But learning to play the role of a wife is a very difficult, and often long transition. Girls typically resist marriage. They are usually preadolescent, and they are in no hurry to grow up. The disparity in ages and sexual maturity of the bride and groom is a source of real difficulties. The groom is sexually mature, but he is expected to marry a child and wait, often as long as five years, before he has sex with her. During that time he must sleep by her side, live with and help her family, and probably put up with her rejection, fear, and anger. Young men find this situation very frustrating, but they usually accept it, because marriageable girls are scarce. **Polygyny,** though uncommon, unbalances sex ratios, and young men know that if they reject a marriage, they may have to wait for another potential bride to grow up. Newly married girls are often frightened. Frequently an adult woman, usually a close relative, sleeps next to the bride on her wedding night, and longer, to reassure her, but nevertheless, a girl's introduction to adult sex is likely to be traumatic. Sexual relations may be postponed for years, but will be unavoidable as soon as she begins menstruation (at about 16) (Shostak, pp. 129–130, 148, 150).

Khoana's Story: The Bride

When she wakes up, Kai doesn't see her daughter in her usual place, sleeping next to her fire. Could it be, she wonders happily, that Khoana has relented and agreed to sleep beside her new husband in their hut? But Khoana isn't in the hut and Kai's pleasure turns to panic. That girl has surely run away again! Hours later, they find her sleeping beneath a mangetti tree, hidden by sand dunes. "Are you crazy, girl," shouts Kai, "a lion could have eaten you!" Khoana bursts into tears and begins ripping the bracelets off her arms. "I won't go back to him. I'm afraid. I'm still a child; I'm not old enough yet for marriage."

Ju/'hoan society tolerates a girl's free expression of her objection to marriage. She may rage and storm and may even threaten or attempt suicide. Basically, if she insists, a girl can force an end to her marriage, either by driving her husband away with unpleasantness or by enrolling family members on her side. Divorce is very common in the early years of marriage, before children are born, and it is usually initiated by the wife. It is common for a girl to enter several such "trial marriages" before finally having children and settling down to a stable marriage (Shostak, pp. 130–131, 148).

First Menstruation

The onset of menstruation is celebrated in a more public, ceremonial manner than is marriage. The girl, elaborately ornamented, stays in a special hut, while the women of the band dance and sing in a sometimes suggestive fashion. Men must not see the girl, but they watch the dancing women from a distance, making bawdy comments. The rite marks sexual maturity, but not full adulthood. Girls are unlikely to conceive a baby for about two years after menstruation begins, and in this period, their relatives still help them with gathering, cooking and other household tasks, while they continue to play with their friends (Shostak, p. 149).

After her first menstruation, a girl usually begins to settle down, with her original or a new husband. She may come to love her husband and enjoy a period of romance before the first child is born. The married couple grow into an easy, relatively equal relationship, in which they go about together, exchange opinions, and make decisions jointly. Fear of her husband usually eases into acceptance and even enjoyment of sex. Also, the girl may come to enjoy the status of married woman, the presents given her by her husband and his family, and the meat he brings to her fire (Shostak, p. 150).

With the birth of a first child, a woman becomes fully adult. She and her husband are now referred to as the parents of their children ("/Toma's father" or "Nisa's mother") rather than by their childhood names, and they settle down to their major life roles in rearing children and provisioning their household. The Ju/'hoansi love and enjoy children and wish to have many, though not too closely spaced.

New Roles in Maturity

Growing into mature adulthood and then old age, Ju/'hoan adults must adjust to new roles. Both men and women in maturity find opportunities to express their talents, as hunters, storytellers, craftsmen, musicians, healers, and informal leaders. A few men will be able to enjoy the advantages of polygynous marriage. But because of relatively high death rates, almost every adult has experienced the death of at least one child, and many the death of a spouse. Family roles change as the result of deaths.

The Ju/'hoansi are adequately nourished, in good physical condition, and suffer little from stress or diet-related diseases. But lacking modern antibiotics and other medicines, infectious and parasitic diseases like influenza, pneumonia, gastroenteritis, tuberculosis, and malaria take a high toll of children and adults. Close-knit nuclear and extended households are repeated disrupted by death. The Ju/'hoansi support each other in deeply felt mourning. People travel to attend funerals; women publicly cry and wail and men sometimes also cry. Family members struggle to understand the death of a child or sibling, asking why God would take a person so prematurely. But after a relatively short time, relatives and friends encourage the bereaved to stop mourning.

Death often causes the reorganization of families. After the death of the head of an extended family, the group may split up, with some of its constituent nuclear families leaving the band. There are many more widows than widowers, and they almost always marry again. Some remarriages also take place after divorce, which is relatively infrequent among adults, but readily accomplished by mutual consent, or as the result of one spouse leaving the other. No formal grounds of divorce are necessary, and there is no property to divide. Children remain with their mother, except for teenage boys who may choose to stay with their father or visit with both parents.

Polygyny

Adulthood is also the time when some Ju/'hoansi men (approximately 5 percent at any time) are able to achieve their fantasy of having more than one wife. **Polygyny** has real advantages: a new sexual partner, more children, another person to gather food, and the forging of a whole new set of relationships with in-laws in another band, another *n'ore*. A second marriage may increase a man's status or political influence (Shostak, p. 169). But there are serious disadvantages too. A man must be a very good hunter to attempt polygyny, and he may even then regret his disruptive second marriage. The first wife will probably object, feel jealous and rejected; the two wives may fight so bitterly that the second one leaves. Polygynous marriages have the greatest chance of success when the second wife is the widowed sister, or the unmarried younger sister of the first (Shostak, pp. 170–171).

The Roles of the Old

Few of the Ju/'hoansi live to old age: Barely 20 percent of those born reach age 60, but those who do will, on the average, live another ten years. The old are relatively free of high blood pressure, heart disease, and deafness, and many are still vigorous. Old widows (over 40 percent of the women over 60) may marry again, or live with children or grandchildren. Old people are treated with respect and often have an influential voice in the group. The older they are, the more likely they are to be the *k'ausi* of their band. Old people are consulted because their experience is valuable. They know how people are related, who married whom, and who is comparatively older or younger. They have seen so many seasons go by that they know where to find food under unusual conditions. They know the recent history of the people and the region and the folktales, songs, and legends. As long as the group continues to live the traditional hunting and gathering life, old people play an important role in the band.

Healthy old people continue to forage, but on a reduced scale. Old women may gather closer to home; old men may set snares and gather along with their wives. But most old people contribute little food; they are supported by sharing with their relatives. Old age may be a time of intense religious exploration, especially for women, who often wait until their children are grown before learning trance dancing and curing. For some people, spiritual powers strengthen with age; they achieve great control over their ability to enter trance and become valued healers and teach apprentices how to enter trance and cure.

For some people, old age is a satisfying time. If they are surrounded by children willing to provide for them, and grandchildren to be loved and cared for, they may enjoy inclusion in the life of the band: sharing the feasts and dances, telling and hearing the stories, sharing gossip, debating the merits of marriages. But for those who outlive their children and spouses (20 percent of all women, but relatively few men) and become a burden on those with less affection for them, old age may be far less pleasant (Shostak, pp. 324–325).

PART II: SOCIAL CHANGE AND THE FUTURE: THE POSTCOLONIAL ERA

As we look into the future of the Bushmen, we must tell more than one story. For most of the Bushmen, life in modern Namibia has been tragic. They have been pushed off their land, caught in a brutal war, and treated with racist contempt by other Namibian peoples. So wise in the ways of the desert, Bushmen have been unprepared to succeed in a modern society. They are illiterate and uneducated, stranded in the most remote, unpromising areas. And there have been terrible losses to alcoholism, depression, violence, and disease. But the Bushmen have responded to their misfortunes with their usual resiliency and ingenuity. They have found a variety of different ways to survive. To tell their story properly, we must go back to the Ju/'hoansi and we must also introduce you to other Bushman peoples, following different paths.

Nyae Nyae, 2001

As your jeep speeds along the Transkalahari Highway west into Bushmanland, Namibia, you watch eagerly for the turnoff for the village of /Aotcha. Aside from the road, the Kalahari seems unchanged. Dry grass and scattered trees stretch as far as the eye can see in every direction. But when you reach /Aotcha the changed life of the Ju/'hoansi is readily apparent. First you see a cattle kraal, made of poles cut in the bush. Then there are plots planted with pumpkins, millet, and corn (maize). There are a few old-style Bushman grass huts, but many more Bantu-style round, more permanent houses, made of poles with grass roofs. Nearby is the borehole (the water pump). As the villagers run up to your jeep, you see that they are wearing western-style clothes—shorts and T-shirts, hats and sweaters, though these garments are dusty and worn. The children circling your jeep have just run over from school—a spot of deep shade under a big baobab tree. Their parents are in animated discussion on the shady side of the largest building. It is a meeting of the Nyae Nyae Farmers' Cooperative, being taped by a visiting anthropologist.

/Gomais, 2001

The roads are poor going north from Bushmanland to /Gomais, and you arrive dusty and tired. At first glance, the Hai//om settlement at the edge of /Gomais looks like nothing has

> *changed in twenty years. There are three circles of grass huts (and a few pole houses), but no cattle kraals, no gardens, no permanent buildings. But by evening you can see that much has changed. Old Naberos happily climbs down from her ride on a government ranch truck with three sacks of mangetti fruits she has picked at a distant grove. She bustles off to sell the fruits to a couple in the nearby Ovambo settlement who brew alcohol from mangetti. She returns pleased with the bottle of liquor and sack of millet they have given her in exchange. Naberos is a lucky woman; her son is one of the few who have jobs at the government ranch. He is often away checking fences. !Gamekhas and her two daughters have spent the day cultivating corn at an Ovambo garden. The girls are not in school. Her brother and three other men are gathered under a tree working at a portable forge. They are using a pile of scrap metal to repair pots, forge and sharpen knives, and make arrowheads. When another man comes by with a sack of cornmeal from the church mission, several of the ironworkers break away from their work to try their luck at the mission. The Hai//om live on the margins, but they resourcefully look to the government ranch, the mission, the Ovambo farms, and the bush as they piece together a living.*

The days are long gone when the Bushmen lived in the Kalahari Desert and moved freely over borders, careless of national boundaries and uninterested in colonial powers. Now the Bushmen are keenly aware that they live in Namibia or Botswana, Angola or South Africa. To survive, they must deal with government officials, foreign aid organizations, other ethnic groups, and commercial organizations. They have learned from their experience in the liberation struggle and in the new nations of postcolonial Africa.

The Liberation Struggle

We left off our history in the first part of this chapter with South Africa in control of Namibia, having just formalized a system of ethnic "homelands," an apartheid system. Under South African rule in the second half of the twentieth century, it became harder and harder for the Bushmen to maintain the traditional culture you have just read about.

Namibia's other ethnic groups also suffered under South Africa's repression, and they began to resist. As early as 1946, Namibian tribal chiefs had petitioned the United Nations to stop South Africa from absorbing Namibia. Later the chiefs asked the UN to declare South Africa's occupation illegal and to start the process of achieving independence (Leys and Saul, p. 10). The formation of SWAPO, the Southwest African People's Organization, in 1960, was a big step forward to seeking independence. Although SWAPO first developed in the Ovambo farming region of the north, SWAPO's leadership soon passed to an educated black elite, drawn from the capital and many other regions of Namibia. SWAPO always saw itself as a national, multiethnic organization. In 1966, after repeated petitions, the UN finally declared South Africa's mandate to govern Namibia at an end. That sounds like a triumph, but in fact South Africa continued to rule illegally and the struggle for independence went on for twenty-three years more!

The Thirty Years War

It is important to understand Namibia's fight for independence in its proper context. First of all, it was part of what Leys and Saul call "The Thirty Years War in Southern Africa" (1960–1990), the anticolonial struggles and wars of liberation that at long last resulted in the replacement of white regimes by black self-rule in South Africa, Namibia, Zimbabwe, Angola, and Mozambique (Leys and Saul, pp. 2–3). In Africa and elsewhere, this was the era of **decolonization,** the end of European and American colonies abroad and the birth of many new nations.

Namibia's fight for independence was never a simple struggle between Namibians and their South African rulers. It was always part of a broader, global conflict. We need to see Namibia's struggle in the context of the Cold War, that ideological and sometimes armed struggle between the Soviet Communist Bloc and the American-led pro-capitalist alliance. The Cold War lasted from the end of World War II in 1945 until the break-up of the Soviet Union in 1989. During the Cold War both superpowers were interested in poor, distant countries (countries like Namibia, Korea, Vietnam, and Afghanistan) because each side feared the other side would get a foothold there.

From the beginning SWAPO was a very sophisticated movement that operated in the arena of world politics. SWAPO kept up a presence at the UN, looked in Europe for political support against South Africa, and got military support from Soviet Bloc nations. After 1972 SWAPO had its military headquarters in neighboring socialist Angola and worked militarily with Cuban troops sent there to help fight South Africa.

The Bushmen and the War for Namibia

It wasn't long before the Bushmen were drawn into the protracted warfare between the South African army SWAPO guerillas and Angolan troops. Bushmen were recruited by the South African army as scouts and infantrymen, because they were such skilled trackers. South Africa located its "Bushman battalion" headquarters in the desert of western Bushmanland. Barakwengo, Hai//'om, and Vasekela Bushmen who had been dispossessed of their land were particularly attracted to the army, perhaps because they had nowhere else to go, perhaps because the wages were good, perhaps because the Ovambo and other black Namibian peoples had been their historic enemies. By the end of the war, 9,000 Bushmen (a quarter of the Bushman population in Namibia) were dependent on army pay and services. They were also out of work, without land, and on the losing side (Slotten, p. 228; Biesele, pp. 1–2).

Independent Namibia

There were many milestones on the road to Namibian independence. While the UN General Assembly had voted in 1966 to end South Africa's mandate to govern Namibia, it was not until 1978 that the UN Security Council passed Resolution 435, a plan for UN supervised elections in Namibia, the withdrawal of South African troops, and the release of political prisoners. It took another two decades of UN-led negotiations and of warfare between South Africa and SWAPO and Angolan forces before South Africa agreed to implement Resolution 435.

Finally, in November 1989 elections for an independent government were held, with more than 95 percent of the people voting. Competing with nine other parties, SWAPO won 57 percent of all the votes and emerged with a majority in the constituent assembly. In February 1990 the assembly elected Sam Nujoma, SWAPO's leader, to be president, and in March 1990 Namibia finally became independent (Saunders, pp. 755–757). Now SWAPO and Nujoma have led an independent Namibia for more than a decade. How has the new nation fared?

Democracy Endangered

Inevitably, Namibia's progress is measured against the condition of other new nations in Africa. A certain kind of threat to democracy is common in Africa. In many African countries power has become personalized. Government is identified with the president and the party becomes the president's personal instrument. There is no longer any real mechanism for handing over power to other parties or other candidates. The government becomes a kind of shell; there may be ministers, courts, officials, and governors, but actually all power lies in the hands of the chief of state and his networks, and all the wealth of the state flows into their hands. They really rob their people and usually send their wealth abroad for safekeeping. Mobuto Sese Seko of Zaire typified this kind of autocrat, until he was thrown out in 1997 and Zaire was renamed Congo (*The Economist,* May 13, 2000, pp. 22–24). Societies like Zaire are sometimes referred to as "kleptocracies."

Another real threat to democracy in Africa is ethnic breakdown, in which competing politicians arouse ethnic tensions in order to further their political careers. In its worst form, as in Rwanda, or Yugoslavia, states dissolve in ethnic warfare, hundreds of thousands or even millions are killed, and it is difficult or impossible to recreate any kind of functioning political authority again. The fate of democracy in Namibia matters intensely for the Bushmen. They are a tiny minority, likely to survive and prosper only in a democracy that grants rights to all ethnic groups.

Democracy in Namibia. Are any of these political disasters likely to befall Namibia? A recent United Nations report ranked Namibia as the most democratic of seven nations in southern Africa. The nation has a thoroughly democratic constitution and system of government. Citizens are guaranteed free speech, freedom of the press, and the right to join organizations, including political parties and trade unions. The right to strike and the right to a living wage are guaranteed in the constitution too. There are mechanisms for removal of cabinet members and even the president by the Assembly (Good, pp. 67–71). (See Table 3.1, p. 179.)

Since independence there have been three elections, in 1994, 1999, and 2004, and all clearly were free and fair elections. That's a very real democratic accomplishment, a standard many countries with "democratic" constitutions fail to reach, on all continents. There are active, vociferous opposition parties and a genuine free press, which is ever critical of the government and of SWAPO. Radio call-in shows feature lively, sometimes offensive political critique as well (Good, pp. 73–74).

On the other hand, Sam Nujoma, the leader of SWAPO, was twice elected president, in 1989 and 1994, and then, in 1999 his party's large majority in congress authorized a change in the constitution to allow him a third term in office. In the lead-up to the 2004 election, there was some fear that Nujoma and his party would engineer a fourth term. That has not happened. Rather heroically following in Mandela's footsteps, Nujoma has given up the presidency voluntarily, something almost

TABLE 3.1 Corruption 2004

In the Corruption Perceptions Index, a high score means that a country is seen as honest and lacking in corruption by businesspeople, academics, and risk analysts. Namibia scores higher than half of the 146 nations ranked, and above Mexico and Egypt.

Country	Rank 2004	CPI Score
United States	17	7.5
Germany	15	8.2
Japan	24	6.8
Namibia	54	4.1
Mexico	64	3.6
Egypt	77	3.2

CPI scores range between 10 (highly clean) and 0 (highly corrupt).

Source: Transparoxy International Corruption Perceptions Index 2004,
http://www.transparency.org/cpi/2004/cpi2004.en.html.

unheard of in Africa. Nujoma's protegé, Hifikepuye Pohamba, has been elected in his stead, so that while there has been a handover of power to a new president, SWAPO continues as the ruling majority party. And Nujoma will continue as the party president, at least until 2007, with considerable patronage power. It remains to be seen whether Pohamba will function independently or as a puppet of Nujoma. And SWAPO's majority, now up to about 75 percent, is so large that the boundaries between party and state are starting to blur (*The Economist,* Dec. 4, 1999, p. 44; Nov. 20, 2004, p. 50; *The Namibian,* Dec. 6, 1999; *Business Day* (South Africa), May 31, 2004, p. 7).

We must realize though that Namibians really want SWAPO to remain in power. They identify the party with national liberation, democracy, and stability. And in African perspective, Namibia's democracy is a huge success. Namibia is a relatively law-abiding country with regular elections and a functioning parliament. Nujoma was not an autocrat and he did not divert the wealth of the state to his own bank accounts. Probably most important, SWAPO remains committed to national unity. Nujoma did not build his power on the deadly game of ethnic politics.

Problems with Poverty and Land

For the Bushmen, and for Namibia's other peoples, the need for land was the country's most serious problem at independence. Most people made their living from the land and many were without land. This was so despite the fact that Namibia is rather sparsely populated. Land is plentiful; good land, land that can be farmed, is scarce. Rapidly growing population makes the problem worse (Saul and Leys, pp. 196–197).

Today, about 4,000 white farmers still own just about half the land that can be farmed. The other half is shared by roughly 800,000 black farmers. At first the government tried to increase black farm ownership by making available low cost loans so black farmers could buy land offered for sale by whites. Only about 700 black farmers were able to take up that offer. Then the government tried to buy white-owned farms directly and lease them to black farmers, but since 1995 it has settled only about 1,000 black farmers by this method. There are still 243,000 people on the waiting list. In the meantime, black farm workers are getting impatient. They have organized the Namibian Farm Workers Union, which threatens land invasions. In an effort to calm things, the government has promised to compel about 2,000 white farmers to sell their land, amounting to 23 million acres, or about a third of all the commercial farmland owned by whites. But since only about $8 million is available to the government each year to buy land, it will take twelve to twenty years to buy it all (LaFraniere, Dec. 25, 2004, p. A3).

Perhaps you are thinking now that there would be a certain justice in it if the government simply confiscated land without compensation. After all, that's how the white settlers got the land themselves. There are two reasons why the Namibian government does not do so. First, in order to get western support for Namibian independence, SWAPO promised that white farmers would not be forced off their land without compensation. This was written into the constitution and the Namibian government obeys the constitution. The second reason has to do with neighboring Zimbabwe, where the government permitted land invasions and expropriations of white-owned farms by landless black farm workers. The new black farmers lacked the capital to produce commercially and grew little more than enough to feed themselves. That resulted in food shortages in the cities and an economic collapse. Namibia's government wants to redistribute land to black farmers, but it knows the nation needs large commercial farms (Saul and Leys, p. 197; *The New York Times,* Aug. 9, 2000, p. A8).

The Landless. What do landless people do to support themselves in Namibia? The government estimates unemployment at 30–40 percent (*The New York Times,* Aug. 9, 2000, p. A8). There is little manufacturing, and an active mining industry is substantially mechanized and employs few people. At present, most people who work for wages are employed in agriculture as very poorly paid farmhands on commercial ranches. Other unemployed people in the countryside depend on employed relatives or on government food aid (Saul and Leys, pp. 196–197; Sparks, pp. 760–763).

Namibia's employment problem is growing as population grows and people leave the countryside for the cities. War in the 1970s and 80s and drought in the 90s led to a huge urban migration, with shantytowns rapidly growing around all the cities. People there survive in the "informal economy." They live off the wages of employed relatives; they peddle goods, collect saleable scrap metal and glass, do laundry, work as servants or as prostitutes. Unemployment and migration are associated with homelessness and crime. Namibia's newspapers lament rising crime rates and call on the government to combat crime. In Namibia, as elsewhere, it scares the government to have thousands of marginally employed or unemployed people, many of them young men, living around the capital. SWAPO would dearly love to solve Namibia's problems with land and jobs (Saul and Leys, p. 197; *Africa News,* June 18, 2004).

The Bushmen in Modern Namibia

For the Bushmen, as for other Namibians, land is the key to their fate. Those who have land struggle to hold it and to produce enough to feed themselves. Those without land must scrounge a living, working on white-owned farms, or in the north, for Ovambo farmers, or hunting and gathering on other people's land. They may live on government aid, or find a niche in the informal economy, making and selling home brew, working as prostitutes, or collecting scrap.

The Ju/'hoansi of Nyae Nyae (whose life before Namibian independence we detailed in Part I of this chapter) have been extraordinarily lucky in the years since independence, and they have built capably on their luck. The Ju/'hoansi have managed to establish ownership of a small part of their former land and to find ways to live independently on it. We will tell their story next. But other Bushman peoples in Namibia have not been so lucky. They have not been able to establish claims to their land and so they have had to patch together ways of surviving as landless people. We will tell the story of one landless Bushman people, the Hai//om, who live in the northern part of Namibia.

The Lucky Ones: The Ju/'hoansi of Bushmanland

They weren't lucky in the beginning. You'll recall that the Bushmen of Nyae Nyae lost 90 percent of their land in 1970 when the South African government established Bushmanland. Only one permanent water hole was located in the land they were allotted. Then the South African authorities made the town of Tjum'kui into an administrative center and collected the Ju/'hoansi to live permanently there. Tjum'kui sounded promising, but it was a disaster. There was a school, a health clinic, a church, a prison, and a store, but there was no work for the Bushmen. Government promises to help with gardening and animal-raising came to nothing. The government gave people "welfare"—free cornmeal—and, most disastrously, subsidized the "bottle store" that sold liquor. If you had visited Tjum'kui in the 1970s or 80s you would have seen a slum, with all the chaos and pathology that word implies. On paydays, Bushman soldiers crowded the town, pushing to be served in the bottle store, lying drunk by the side of the road, or fighting behind the store. Transistor radios blared South African pop music and trash piled up behind buildings. Prostitutes patrolled the street in front of the store. The Ju/'hoansi called Tjum'kui "the place of death" (Weinberg, pp. 8, 10–11; Biesele and Weinberg, p. 7).

Return to the Bush

Remarkably, the Ju/'hoansi did not succumb to despair and alcoholism. Group by group they organized themselves to leave Tjum'kui and return to the bush. And this is where luck comes in. The Ju/'hoansi had three important things going for them: leadership, land, and outside help.

=Oma N!oa was one of the first to lead his people back to the bush. If you have seen either of John Marshall's famous films, *The Hunters* or *Bushmen of the Kalahari,* you will know =Oma, or remember him as "Toma." =Oma was a Bushman-style informal leader. He had no inherited or appointed position. He was simply influential. People respected and trusted him because of his wisdom, his skill in hunting, and his ability to persuade and organize people. In the late 1970s, =Oma took his people back to /Aotcha, which was his *n!ore,* and by great good fortune, the location of the only remaining permanent water hole within what was left of Bushmanland (Biesele, p. 7). Biesele quotes =Oma as saying:

> So I asked the man, what do you mean that we should go where there's only a borehole surrounded by rocks and no natural water? If that borehole dies we'll have to leave. I have cattle, the cattle will die; and I will die. I won't move to a well where you can't count on the water. The thing to do is to move back to /Gautscha (!Aotcha). God's water, !Xu's water, is there and I can dip it up and give it to my cattle. That's where I'm going to return and settle. That's what I told him. That's what I told the whites. (Biesele, page unnumbered)

Now at least twenty-five groups have made settlements in their families' old *n!ores,* all depending on wells with pumps. This is where outside help has been so important. The Ju/'hoansi found a savvy and energetic advocate in John Marshall, who had lived at /Aotcha as a boy and felt a deep attachment to =Oma and to all the Ju/'hoansi. When Marshall visited Tjum'kui in the 1970s he was horrified by the squalid settlement and wasted lives. He started the Bushman Development Foundation which facilitated the return to the bush. The foundation gave settlers a few head of cattle, seeds, and tools and help in making gardens. It raised money abroad to pay for drilling the new boreholes. Most important, it effectively opposed a planned government takeover of Eastern Bushmanland for a game reserve (Butler, p. 2; Weinberg, p. 8).

Conflict over Resources

The Ju/'hoansi of Nyae Nyae have been troubled recently by a conflict that may surprise you: conflict between people and animals and the organizations and officials that advocate for each. What do you think: Should Namibia preserve the elephants, giraffe, and eland in their natural environments, even if it means that the Bushmen must be removed from their native soil? Or should humans take precedence? Is there some way of protecting both? For years conservationists accused the Ju/'hoansi of overhunting Nyae Nyae and the Ju/'hoansi blamed the government-built fences, which they said impeded animal migration. Now the conservationists and the Bushmen may have found a way to get along, with the help of several governments and an international nongovernmental organization.

In 1993 the Namibian Ministry of Environment and Tourism established a $14.6 million plan called the Living in a Finite Environment (LIFE) Project, which receives funding from the U.S. Agency for International Development and is funded by the World Wildlife Fund. The plan is to set up seven "conservancies" or areas where local people protect and manage the wildlife themselves and make money from tourism and trophy hunting. One of these areas is Eastern Bushmanland. The idea is that conservancies will enlist the local people in conservation, since the wildlife becomes their livelihood (Butler, p. 4).

You can visit a conservancy enterprise outside Tjum'kui, where a Bushman group runs an ecotourism camp, together with a tour operator from Windhoek. Visitors can stay the night in huts, with showers and toilets, go hunting, buy local crafts, and watch Bushmen dance. Visitors pay the Ju/'hoansi operators directly, $25 Namibian dollars a night, a stunning sum in Bushmanland (Weinberg, p. 16).

Cultural Adaptation at Nyae Nyae

The Ju/'hoansi have survived by giving up some, but not all, of their traditional culture and by adopting some new cultural practices. The biggest change is that they are no longer nomadic. They still gather wild plant foods and pass that knowledge down and they still hunt and trap animals, but hunting yields relatively little. They still sing and dance around the fire at night. They still own their land communally

Meet =Oma N!oa, the elderly Bushman who led his band in leaving Tjum'kui and returning to their traditional *n'ore,* their territory of /Aotcha in Bushmanland. In this photo =Oma is telling a story, revealing some of the wisdom and personal charisma that made Bushmen turn to him for leadership.

and own businesses like the safari camp as a group. But a lot has changed. The wonderful thing is that the Ju/'hoansi have been able to institute changes themselves, changes they are proud of.

New Leadership

One of the clearest accommodations the Ju/'hoansi have made to modern life is the replacement of traditional informal leadership with new formal leadership and formal political organization. The people who returned to their *n!ores* in Bushmanland created a political organization—the Nyae Nyae Farmers' Cooperative. NGOs (nongovernmental organizations) gave them advice and grants to help in the task. Tsamkxae =Oma, the son of =Oma N!oa, became the chairperson of the cooperative. By 1996 his position had turned into a full-time paid job (Weinberg, p. 16). It is clear that in choosing Tsamkxae as their leader the Ju/'hoansi have not simply created an hereditary headmanship. Tsamkxae is a skilled political leader, a strategist, and what is very important for the Bushmen, an inspired speaker.

Early in its existence the Farmers' Coop undertook to write a Ju/'hoan constitution. The document was written by a committee of Ju/'hoansi and then transcribed into both English and !Kung by hired scribes. Representatives from all the villages traveled through Eastern Bushmanland explaining the document. It is an inspiring constitution, formulating the traditional laws of the *n!ore* and explaining the need for formal political organization. Biesele quotes the constitution as follows:

> Our Ju/'hoan land of Nyae Nyae is now small and we are many. We need the strength of unity under law to keep the land that remains to us. We need the strength of thought under written law to use the resources of our land for our individual well-being and our common good. . . .
>
> Today Ju/'hoansi are people dispossessed of land and the right to own land. Without land on which to produce food to eat and without work, too many Ju/'hoansi die of hunger and disease. The Council of the cooperative must become the mothers and the fathers of the dispossessed, and give them *n!ores* on which to live. (Biesele, pp. 8–9)

In 1988 and 89, as Namibia prepared for the end of South African rule and the first free elections, a Farmers' Coop team traveled around the settlements of Eastern Bushmanland, explaining what elections are and why the 1989 election mattered and listening to the issues Ju/'hoansi villagers raised. Alcoholism and education emerged as big issues. At a meeting of the coop, many villagers criticized those who became drunk on home-brewed beer. It is interesting: Here are modern society issues, but speeches drew deeply on traditional values and traditional speech conventions. You'll recognize the themes in what Dabe Dahm said:

> Those who drink are the ones who cause anger and fighting. Those who don't drink just sit quietly. . . . We're not saying don't drink at all, but just drink slowly and wisely. . . . I think we should say to ourselves, I have work to do before I drink. First I'm going to do my work.
>
> When you drink you shouldn't go around thinking like a Boer and telling people that you are a big shot. If you do that, someday people will become angry with you and their

hearts will grow big against you. You don't go saying you're a chief. Instead, you sit together and understand each other. None of us is a chief, we're all alike and have our little farms. So when you drink, just think clearly about it and talk to each other about being careful. (Biesele, p. 11)

The Ju/'hoansi of Eastern Bushmanland agreed about the importance of education—so that people could get modern jobs if they chose; so they could learn veterinary medicine; so they could better deal with government administrators and the press, because they understand that coverage in the media can be a powerful tool in defending Bushman rights. With the help of NGOs, the Ju/'hoan language has been transcribed into written form and children are now taught in their own language (Weinberg, p. 9).

Continuity and Change: Democracy and Egalitarianism

Sometimes when people in rich industrial societies think about what it must be like for indigenous peoples to enter the modern world, they think first of modern products—sneakers and sunglasses, canned soda, TV, cars, and computers. But cultural adaptation is actually much more subtle and interesting. It is a two-way street in many ways. People draw upon their traditional cultures as much as they abandon them. For example, you might think that electing leaders and participating in political organizations is something totally new and strange for the Bushmen. After all, the Ju/'hoansi told Richard Lee in the 1970s that "we have no headman, each one of us is headman over himself." But actually, democracy calls up many themes deeply embedded in traditional Bushman culture. The Ju/'hoansi have long called themselves "the owners of argument," meaning that they believed themselves to be particularly skilled in talk and debate. They also believe it is very important for issues to be openly discussed by everyone together so no one will feel excluded or resentful. South Africa's paternalistic dictatorship angered them. If you think about it, you can see how democracy would make sense to an egalitarian people (Biesele, p. 17). At one meeting Tsamkxao said:

> "I thank the old people who have spoken, but we also need to begin to hear from the young people about their *n!ores*. Everyone must work together. Do you see these sticks in my hand? If you pick up lots of sticks, you can't break them. But one stick alone breaks easily. So we want things from now on to be done on paper, legally, beginning with meetings where everyone comes together to listen. We don't want a Ju/'hoan representative who just stuffs news into his own ears and doesn't speak to us. If you speak for a group of people to a government, and if you speak badly, it doesn't just affect one person. It affects everyone. When you do something, all your people should have a way of learning about it. Political parties are for letting people know things." (Biesele, p. 18)

The Ju/'hoansi of Eastern Bushmanland know themselves to be the lucky ones. They are forging a broader identity, as Namibians, but especially as Bushmen, an identity that links them to the less fortunate Bushmen elsewhere. As Tsamkxao said:

> We want to help everyone we can. Its important that we who are the Ju/'hoansi have our own government and do our own work. We have only a small place, but we want to go

to the Gobabis farms and find our people who were long ago taken away. We want to get them and bring them here. Can we find a way to help everyone? (*Quoted in Biesele,* p. 19)

Let us now search for those other Bushmen and see how they are faring.

Landless Bushmen: The Hai//om

There are about 11,000 Hai//om Bushmen altogether. Many live in northern Namibia between the deserts of Bushmanland and the densely populated farms of Ovamboland. Unlike the Ju/'hoansi, the Hai//om have been little studied by anthropologists. This account will rely primarily on recent work done by Thomas Widlok in the area he calls "Mangetti."

Hai//om Bushmen have lived in the Mangetti area as long as anyone can recall, but they own none of the land there, having been dispossessed during the colonial period (Widlok, pp. 3–4). South Africa gave much of their land to white settlers and later made part of it into Ovamboland, the "homeland" for the Ovambo people under apartheid. Elsewhere the Hai//om were evicted from Etosha, which was made into Etosha Game Park. The Hai//om did not receive any land of their own after Namibia became independent. So how do these Bushmen survive? Have they been forced to give up their hunting and gathering life? Have they lost their traditional culture or been absorbed into the neighboring Ovambo people and their culture?

Living in a Mixed Culture and a Mixed Economy

The Hai//om of Mangetti are illiterate and unschooled. Unlike the Ju/'hoansi of Eastern Bushmanland, they have formed no political organizations and have developed no self-leadership. No international foundation has stepped forward to take them under its wing. Nevertheless, the Hai//om have found ingenious ways to survive and to preserve some aspects of their culture, in a setting where they are geographically displaced and socially despised.

Vilho's Story: Surviving on Mangetti

Vilho (see Widlok, p. 40) is living with his family at Botos in the communal Ovambo area of Mangetti. He lives in a settlement built on Ovambo communal land, just a short distance from an Ovambo homestead. The settlement consists of two circles of Ovambo-style huts, with a fence around it. Vilho's circle includes huts for his wife and children, his widowed mother, and his younger sister and her husband. Another widowed woman also lives in their circle. Vilho, his wife, and his sister and brother-in-law all work on the Ovambo homestead during the growing season, from December through June, planting, cultivating, harvesting, and threshing millet and sorghum. They are paid in food or beer, which they bring home and share with their whole settlement. The Ovambo don't mind if their farmworkers bring their families and friends to live with them and share their food. In fact, during busy times the Ovambo feed all the local Hai//om on their homestead. (Barnard and Widlok, pp. 95–98)

Occasionally Vilho and his brother-in-law go off hunting and sometimes bring back a duiker or a springhare, but larger animals are rarely seen and it is illegal for Hai//om to kill them (Widlok, pp. 67–68). Sometimes the women of the settlement go out and gather mangetti nuts in the nearby groves, often bringing back other wild fruits and roots too. The Ovambo don't mind if the resident Hai//om gather on their land.

So what sort of life is this? It appears that the Hai//om have accommodated themselves to the agricultural economy of the Ovambo, who own the land. They combine work as agricultural laborers with hunting (a little) and gathering (quite a bit). They also combine Hai//om and Ovambo customs. They have built Ovambo-style houses and established separate hearths for men and women, Ovambo-style. "Vilho" is an Ovambo name. At the same time, they continue to share gathered foods and perform trance dances (Widlok, p. 97).

Seasonal Migration. Widlok noted that the Hai//om even preserve some of their old nomadic existence. When the harvest is finished and the dry season begins, they pick up and leave Botos and move to !Gai=nas, an area they consider their original *n!ore* where they stay near another band of close relatives who remain at !Gai=nas year round. This too is on Ovambo land, but there is little work on the homestead at this time of year and the Hai//om depend primarily on hunting and gathering. At !Gai=nas Vilho is known as Xareb, his Hai//om name, and the band builds small grass huts arranged in a circle without a fence, Bushman-style (Widlok, p. 40; Barnard and Widlok, p. 98).

Sometimes the Hai//om make shorter trips into the bush. They may stay for as long as two weeks at distant mangetti groves, building temporary shelters and gathering nuts. Men are sometimes hired by commercial cattle ranches to hunt lost cattle in the bush, with the understanding that if they find the cattle dead, they may keep the meat (Widlok, p. 129).

Other Living Situations. There are yet more ways that the Hai//om manage to make a living. /Gomais is a central town like Tjum/kui in Eastern Bushmanland and many Hai//om live permanently there. During the war, the South African army cleared Hai//om from the combat zones to the north and gathered them at /Gomais. Now there is a large ranch there run by the First National Development Corporation, an enterprise partly controlled by the government. A small number of Hai//om men work on the ranch. There is wild food available and there is also a church that runs a school and sometimes gives out free food. When Vilho/Xareb visits /Gomais he is known as "Samuel," his Christian name. Also, some Hai//om gather mangetti fruits to sell to some local Ovambo who use the fruits to brew liquor. Sometimes they are paid in liquor (Barnard and Widlok, pp. 99–100).

Hai//om also work on white-owned commercial farms, where they have less freedom to practice their traditional culture. Farmers sometimes provide stone houses or provide poles and sheet metal for square houses and each house is fenced separately, so nuclear families are more separated from each other. White farmers don't allow Hai//om to bring their bands with them onto the farm; they allow only immediate relatives. At private farms Hai//om workers are more likely to own things like bicycles or even bank accounts and they may write their initials or signs on their possessions (Barnard and Widlok, pp. 100–101).

Wherever they live, Hai//om men collect scrap iron and do blacksmithing work, making tools like spades, screwdrivers, knives, and arrowheads. They produce these items for themselves and also on order for the Ovambo. That is, they will forge an adze to order, usually in exchange for other useful items, like clothing, but they don't do blacksmith work as a business; they don't produce a stock of goods for sale (Widlok, pp. 120–122).

Change and Continuity: Foraging and Sharing

The Hai//om have no land of their own, so they are always living on land that belongs to someone else: the Ovambo, the white commercial farmers, or the government. Consequently, they are always in dependent relationships with others who have more property and power than they do. But be careful how you think about the changes in their culture. You may assume that change will mean adopting the customs of modern industrial nations. Actually for the Hai//om change has meant adopting some of the customs of their Ovambo neighbors—making separate hearths for men and women, using Ovambo names, making Ovambo-style houses. Only a few Hai//om who work on commercial ranches have done anything so modern as having bank accounts, and their employers really handle these for them.

Widlok points out that in the most fundamental way the Hai//om have not changed; they remain foragers. They are no longer living as traditional hunters and gatherers, but instead they "forage" their new environment, moving about from one resource to another, one day foraging the bush for wild food, another day foraging the church mission for free food, or the dump in /Gomais for iron scrap, old tires to make into shoes, plastic pipes for bracelets, wire for snares, bottle tops for dance rattles, old bottles and used engine oil for lamps (Widlok, p. 127). It turns out that there is a substantial niche for foragers in a commercialized setting. Hai//om work for the Ovambo in exchange for food, and then when the season changes and that resource is at an end, they move on to another setting, the bush, the town, the ranches. This really isn't so different from traditional hunting and gathering.

Foraging lies at the heart of traditional Bushman culture. It is not just a set of practices; it is a basic orientation to life. Foragers don't save; they don't invest; they don't plan for the future. Today they take care of today's subsistence needs, and they assume that something will turn up for tomorrow. Foragers move around and travel light.

Moreover, as Widlok points out, foraging is intimately linked to sharing. Sharing makes the foraging life possible, because you can ask your friends and relatives to give you food if your foraging efforts that day have been fruitless. At the same time, however, as Widlok makes clear, sharing (he calls it "demand sharing") prevents the Hai//om from saving, investing, and planning. Take the distilling business, for example. The Hai//om often gather mangetti fruits and sell them to the Ovambo for use in making liquor for sale. Returns to the Hai//om are meager—a sack of millet, or perhaps a bottle of liquor. Why don't the Hai//om themselves go into distilling? They can make or borrow the simple apparatus and they have already gathered the fruits. Liquor sells for much more than mangetti. Widlok realizes what the problem is as he observes a Hai//om couple distilling. By the end of the day, all their relatives and friends have come by and each has demanded a drink. The mangettis are gone, the liquor is gone, and the enterprising couple are left with nothing (Widlok, pp. 100–105). Similarly, Hai//om who make their own gardens and herd their own cattle find themselves socially excluded. They cannot allow friends and relatives to take food from their gardens and they cannot slaughter a cow whenever people are hungry.

As they settle down to live in towns and villages, Bushmen
find they need cash income. These men have been lucky to
find work as janitors at the local school. Unable to live any
longer by hunting and gathering, Bushmen become part of
the modern world at its lowest levels.

So the practice of sharing both supports the Hai//om in foraging and also restricts
them to foraging. In a way, you could say that the Hai//om have strongly and successfully resisted changing their culture. They have resisted the influence of people
and cultures more powerful than they. Their resistance has taken the form of clinging
to foraging and sharing. But as so often happens, their resistance has had a downside;
it has contributed to keeping the Hai//om dependent and poor in modern Namibia.

The Future of the Bushmen

The Bushmen of Namibia have shown a remarkable ability to adapt to the changed
circumstances of their lives. Their hunting and gathering culture was flexible, and

they have taken flexibility with them into modern Namibia, becoming farm workers, independent farmers, blacksmiths, and craft producers, tourism workers, hunters, and guides, as opportunities permit. It is hard to make generalizations about all Bushmen because, as we have seen, different groups of Bushmen have found themselves in quite different situations and taken varied paths. The Ju/'hoansi of Eastern Bushmanland have been able to rely more on independent gardening and cattle-raising, but the landless Hai//om of Mangetti have had to seek work on farms and cattle ranches. Gathering has remained a part of people's lives in both groups. But even while the Bushmen struggle to adapt and survive, Namibia is changing.

New Ways of Using the Land

Namibia is quite sparsely populated and up until now Namibians have always had a sense that there is unlimited "bush," wild land, out there somewhere. In the north, while the Ovambo are relatively crowded on the arable portions of their land, they have been quite willing to allow the Hai//om to live in the mangetti groves and dry hinterlands of their homeland. Bushmen have also lived on government-administered land and on the remoter edges of commercial ranches. But now the way people use land in Namibia is changing. Land is becoming commercialized. "Unoccupied" communal land in the southeast of Ovamboland where the Hai//om live has been taken over and fenced by wealthy Ovambos and thus effectively turned into private commercial ranches. Widlok counts ninety-seven of these new ranches. The same thing has happened further east on Kavango communal land. Land that is used for subsistence, either by subsistence farmers or by foragers, is coming to be seen as "underused," in contrast to land that produces crops for sale, or profits (Widlok, pp. 33–36). As land is commercialized, there is less space for the landless Bushmen.

Commercialization of land, particularly of the marginal, uninhabited land, poses an environmental threat in Namibia. Especially in periods of drought, cattle overgraze the land, stripping away vegetation. Africans call this process **desertification,** since the denuded land becomes a real desert, in which trees and grasses do not grow back and the wind erodes the soil. When rain falls, the ground doesn't hold it, and the water table gradually drops. Ranchers must then move on to less desirable, drier land, which is all the sooner exhausted. As a growing human population tries to graze more and more cattle, the process of desertification accelerates. Population growth, displacement, and desertification feed each other in a destructive cycle. Desertification is a real problem in many parts of Africa. It may be Namibia's future, but so far, sparse population and incomplete commercialization have shielded the bush.

New Patterns of Work

While the Bushmen have been very creative in piecing together a livelihood, the bottom line is that increasingly they must work for others for wages or make things for sale. They are no longer able to live independently, self-sufficient in the Kalahari Desert. They have become dependent on farmers and ranchers for employment, or even on tourists who buy their crafts or pay to look at them pretending to hunt (McNeil, Nov. 13, 1997, Daley). They are dependent too on foreign relief agencies. Many Bushmen have become dependent on government welfare—mostly handouts of flour—when they move into towns. In many cases, even Bushmen who live independently at Nyae Nyae, still need government food rations in order to survive. While they may have more possessions, better houses, animals to ride instead of walking, Bushmen have lost something valuable: their independence. They have become a very small part of a global economy, dressing up as hunter-gatherers for European and American tourists, raising cattle, and mining gold for export, hoping to buy goods, like flashlights, iron pots, sneakers, or radios that have been imported from other countries.

Changing Roles and Relationships

Wage work and the commercialization of land point the way to changing relationships. Hai//om who work on commercial ranches are not permitted to bring their whole band with them to the ranch. They must live only with their immediate families in separate, private, fenced-in houses, where cooking is done indoors, rather than outdoors, in a communal central space. Widlok tells us that these Bushmen label their possessions with their names or signs and store them indoors.

Gender Inequalities. Several anthropologists have also found that inequalities between men and women have grown among the Bushmen living in villages and towns, leaving women in a more dependent, subordinate position. In their old hunting and gathering days, all life was family life, but modern society draws a line between "public" and "private" life. In most cases, Bushman men are more able than women to get paid work, so their work takes them out more into the public realm. They learn more about dealing with other ethnic groups, with ranchers and farmers and the government. Men control the money or goods they bring home and the possessions they buy with it. Women become more tied to the home by housework, carrying water and wood, repairing houses and cooking food. The work they do is devalued because it is unpaid; it no longer appears to be work. Tied down by babies, no longer the main providers of food, women become more dependent on men (Draper, 1975, p. 85; Draper and Cashdan, 1988, p. 361).

Furthermore, when Bushmen live near the Ovambo, or other Bantu-speaking peoples, they adopt their customs and beliefs along with their technology. Ovambo society is strongly male dominated. Men own the cattle and the fields, male and female roles are sharply differentiated, and men control political decision making. Women lack legal rights and sons are preferred to daughters. These patterns influence Bushmen associated with the Ovambo (Kent, 1995, pp. 528–534).

A Damaged Sense of Self

For the Bushmen, as for other isolated indigenous peoples around the world, contact with modern society often damages individuals' self-esteem. If tourists, dressed in gaily colored sports clothes, pay to look at you, almost naked, as if you were an animal in a zoo, you begin to feel less than fully human. You begin to feel inferior. The tourists seem fabulously rich; they spend more on craft items in a day than the Bushmen earn in a month or even a year. Compared to them, the Bushmen feel poor. Even the neighboring Ovambo are richer than the Bushmen: They have cows and permanent houses with dried mud walls and tin roofs. Many Bushmen admire the Ovambo, respect their chiefs, and wish to adopt their system of farming and herding, their norms for relationships between men and women. But the Bushmen are seen as inferior by the Ovambo neighbors. When you want to be like people who reject you, that is psychologically wounding.

Sociology offers some powerful concepts to help you understand the psychological state of the Bushmen. One is the concept of **marginality,** associated with two famous American sociologists, Louis Wirth and Robert E. Park. The "marginal man," said Park, "lives in two worlds in both of which he is more or less a stranger" (Park, p. 356; Wirth, p. 73). Marginality is an important American concept because it describes so well the situation of many immigrants, who find they are changed by the American experience. They no longer fit into the society they came from, while at the same time, they are not fully accepted in the dominant American society. The Bushmen experience marginality when the hunting and gathering life no longer seems sufficient to them, but they are still rejected by Bantus and whites in modern Namibia.

Anomie. The most famous sociological concept that can help you understand the Bushmen is Emile Durkheim's concept of **anomie.** Anomie means literally a state of normlessness, a social condition in which shared norms no longer effectively regulate individual desires. Durkheim saw anomie occurring in times of rapid social change, when old norms fail to apply to new conditions, and people are no longer sure what they can expect in life (Durkheim, 1951, pp. 248–250). Anomie is a condition of society, not a psychological state, but it is regularly associated with certain individual symptoms like depression, feelings of meaninglessness and aimlessness. When societies suffer from anomie, Durkheim said, rates of suicide rise, and we notice nowadays that rates of alcohol and drug abuse rise too. The concept of anomie can help us understand why the Ju/'hoansi living in Tjum'kui seemed to lose their social moorings. Caught between the values of a lost culture, and those of another, not yet their own, some town-dwelling Bushmen lapsed into unemployment, dependency, drunkenness, and violence.

The Future: Resistance and Adaptation

Commercialization, dependency, breakdown of band solidarity, feelings of inferiority, and anomie: This is a really depressing catalog of what may go wrong for the Bushmen. It's important to emphasize that while some Bushmen have been overwhelmed by their experiences in modern Namibia, others have kept their strength and pride. For the Ju/'hoansi of Nyae Nyae, a little land of their own and a little help from international NGOs have made all the difference. They have resisted dependency and drunkenness and adapted one of the strengths of their culture—egalitarianism—to develop new democratic institutions. The Hai//om of Mangetti have had no help, but nonetheless they have kept their forager ethic, finding niches in the mixed economy of the north and continuing to share.

Namibia: Challenges for the Future

Of course we can't really make any predictions about the future of the Bushmen separate from the future of their nation. So many things may go wrong and harm the Bushmen as well as other Namibians. AIDS is probably the most immediate threat.

The disease is spreading rapidly, overwhelming hospitals, orphaning children, shortening lifespans, contributing to the shortage of teachers and health care workers, and undermining the economy. War is not far behind as a danger to Namibia. Warfare has plagued the nations of southern Africa since independence, helping to spread the AIDS epidemic, leaving famine, poverty, and displaced people in its wake, and preventing African governments from devoting their resources to solving the problems of poverty and development. Namibia is unlikely to sink into internal warfare, but old alliances may drag the country into wars in neighboring countries.

AIDS

People in the developed world have avoided talking about the AIDS epidemic in Africa, for fear that they will stigmatize Africans or be seen as racist. But the truth is that the epidemic is too big to ignore, and Africa needs international help. Almost three-quarters of all the people in the world who are infected with HIV/AIDS live in Africa (French, July 21, 2000, p. A8). And Namibia is one of four countries with the highest AIDS rates in the world (neighboring Botswana, Zimbabwe, and Swaziland are the others). At least 20 percent of all sexually active adults in Namibia are infected with HIV/AIDS, and AIDS is now the leading cause of death. Life expectancy at birth in Namibia was 58.8 years in 1995 but the UN has predicted a fall to 46 years by 2005 (*The Economist,* Jan. 17, 2004, p. 11). (See Table 3.2, below.)

Why has AIDS spread so widely in southern Africa? How can the epidemic be stopped? The UN and several NGOs have conducted quite a lot of research on AIDS in Africa in recent years and there are some answers available. AIDS in Africa is overwhelmingly spread by heterosexual sex. AIDS rates are higher for women than for men, but men are more likely than women to be the carriers of the epidemic. AIDS spreads when people move around. In Africa, that happens when men leave their villages to work in urban areas, in the mines or fisheries, or when they join the army and move around as they fight. Migrant men go to prostitutes and have affairs and then they bring AIDS home to their wives. All the countries with the highest AIDS rates have large migrant labor forces and many have been involved in wars (Joint Report, p. 2; Slotten, p. 278).

In Namibia, as elsewhere, AIDS rates are higher in cities and lower in the countryside. For example, at the clinic for pregnant women in Gobabis, near Bushmanland, 1 percent of the women were infected with HIV/AIDS in 1994 and 9 percent

TABLE 3.2 Birth and Death Rates in Namibia
Namibia's rapidly rising death rates reflect the impact of HIV/AIDS. Birthrates remain high, so Namibia's population continues to increase.

Year	Births per 1,000	Deaths per 1,000	Total Population
1990	38.63	10.69	1,409,069
2000	35.23	19.49	1,771,327
2010*	30.62	28.59	1,908,483
2020*	29.1	26.17	1,956,406

Sources: U.S. Bureau of the Census, International Data Base 2000, http://www.census.gov/ipc/www/idbsprd.html.
Note: *Estimated.

in 1998. In a similar clinic in Windhoek, the capital, 4 percent were infected in 1994 and 23 percent in 1998 (*Joint Report,* p. 2).

When we compare African countries with high and low AIDS rates, two factors stand out. The epidemic is worse where men seldom use condoms and it is worse in areas where other STDs (especially syphilis and genital herpes, both of which cause genital ulcers) are widespread. When people have untreated STDs, ulcers allow the HIV virus easy entrance. In a way these are encouraging facts. Few Africans will ever be able to afford the drugs westerners use to treat AIDS and prolong life, but education and basic public health care are relatively cheap. Senegal, for instance, has kept its AIDS rate below 2 percent by an aggressive program of public education and a system of free health clinics to treat all STDs (Altman, *The New York Times,* July 16, 2000, p. 4). Namibia badly needs a program like this.

War

Since its independence Namibia has tried to maintain a difficult balancing act: The nation has tried to support neighboring governments that helped SWAPO during its liberation struggle, without itself being drawn into war. As a result, Namibia became involved in lengthy conflicts in neighboring Angola and the Democratic Republic of Congo. The civil war in Angola lasted for twenty-five years, with half a million people killed during the 1990s. Congo's civil war began in 1998 and took as many as two million lives. Namibia, Zimbabwe, Angola, Uganda, and Rwanda all became involved in the war in Congo. After a peace accord was signed in 1999, Namibia's troops were pulled back from Congo in 2001. But even after a final peace settlement was signed in 2003, fighting continued to break out sporadically. There have been rumors that Namibia's military will again become involved in Congo, but the government denies such plans (*The Namibian,* July 5, 2001, June 23, 2004; *Facts on File World Digest,* April 2, 2003, p. 381).

Namibia has been skillful and fortunate in pursuing a careful balancing act in its foreign policy. It has been able to help old allies militarily, without being pulled into full-scale war. Nevertheless, military spending leaves less money for land reform and other government action to help the landless and homeless. Any major war would plunge Namibia into the familiar African devastation of displacement, famine, disease, and dictatorship. So Namibia continues its careful balancing act, supporting UN efforts to reach a settlement in the Congo (Itano, Feb. 26, 2002, p. 7; *Houston Chronicle,* Sept. 3, 2001, p. 32; Cauvin, Nov. 26, 1999, p. A12; *The Namibian,* Feb. 27, 2002).

It will take very skilled political leadership for Namibia to deal with its present challenges: to confront the AIDS crisis, help its poor majority, satisfy the demands of western donors and investors or find some way to do without their help, and negotiate the tricky politics of neighboring warring states. If Namibia fails, the suffering of the Bushmen and all of Namibia's peoples will increase.

Thinking Sociologically

1. Explain what the authors mean when they say that in the past the Bushmen "lived close to nature."

2. Can you use the functionalist perspective to explain why the Bushmen, in their lives as hunters and gatherers, emphasized sharing, were nomadic, and had small families?
3. When the Bushmen lived as hunters and gatherers, what were their most important social groups?
4. Compare the status and roles of women in Bushman hunter/gatherer society and in Japanese society. Is the status of women in your society more similar to that of Bushman women or that of Japanese women?
5. Which of the four types of social interaction (social exchange, cooperation, competition, and conflict) predominated in Bushman hunter/gatherer society? How about in your society?
6. What social changes in Namibia changed the lives of the Bushmen?
7. In what ways have foreign anthropologists and aid organizations helped the Bushmen? Have they harmed them?
8. Compare and contrast the ways that the Ju/'hoansi and the Hai//om have managed to adapt to life in modern Namibia.

For Further Reading

GOOD, KENNETH, *Realizing Democracy in Botswana, Namibia and South Africa.* Africa Institute of South Africa, 1997.

LEE, RICHARD B., *The Dobe Ju/'hoansi,* 2nd ed. New York: Harcourt Brace College Publishers, 1993.

LEYS, COLIN AND JOHN S. SAUL, eds., *Namibia's Liberation Struggle: The Two-Edged Sword.* London: James Currey, 1995.

SHOSTAK, MARJORIE, *Nisa.* Cambridge, MA: Harvard University Press, 1981.

THOMAS, ELIZABETH MARSHALL, *The Harmless People.* New York: Knopf, 1959.

WIDLOK, THOMAS, *Living on Mangetti: 'Bushman' Autonomy and Namibian Independence.* Oxford: Oxford University Press, 1999.

Bibliography

Africa News, "Issues That Pohamba Will Have to Face," June 18, 2004.

Africa South of the Sahara, 1999, London: Europa Publications, Ltd., 28th edition.

ALTMAN, LAWRENCE K., "Africa's AIDS Crisis: Finding Common Ground," *The New York Times,* July 16, 2000, p. 4NE.

BARNARD, ALAN, *Hunters and Herders of Southern Africa.* Cambridge: Cambridge University Press, 1992.

BARNARD, ALAN, AND THOMAS WIDLOK, "Nharo and Hai//om Settlement Patterns in Comparative Perspective," in Susan Kent, ed., *Cultural Diversity among Twentieth-Century Foragers: An African Perspective.* Cambridge: Cambridge University Press, 1996, pp. 87–107.

BIESELE, MEGAN, "Religion and Folklore," in Phillip V. Tobias, ed., *The Bushmen: San Hunters and Herders of Southern Africa.* Cape Town: Human & Rousseau, 1978, pp. 162, 165–168.

———, *Shaken Roots.* Marshalltown, South Africa: EDA Publications, 1990.

BUTLER, VICTORIA, "Bushmen at a Crossroads," *International Wildlife,* Vol. 27, no. 4 (July–August, 1997), pp. 20–27.

CAUVIN, HENRI E., "A Flood of War Refugees from Angola Strains Namibia," *The New York Times,* Nov. 26, 1999, p. A12.

The Corruption Perceptions Index, 2001, http://www.transparency.org/documents/cpi/2001/cpi2001.html.

Daley, Suzanne, "Endangered Bushmen Find Refuge in a Game Park," *The New York Times,* Jan. 18, 1996, p. A4.

Draper, Pat, "Kung Women: Contrasts in Sexual Egalitarianism in Foraging and Sedentary Contexts," in Reyna Reiter, ed., *Towards an Anthropology of Women.* New York: Monthly Review Press, 1975.

Draper, Pat, and E. Cashdan, "Technological Change and Child Behavior among the !Kung," *Ethnology,* Vol. 27 (1988), pp. 339–365.

Draper, Pat, and M. Kranichfeld, "Coming In from the Bush: Settled Life by the !Kung and Their Accommodation to Bantu Neighbors," *Human Ecology,* Vol. 18 (1990), pp. 363–384.

Durkheim, Emile, *Suicide.* New York: The Free Press, 1951.

———, *The Elementary Forms of the Religious Life.* New York: Free Press, 1915, 1965.

Eibl-Eibensfeldt, Irenaus, "Early Socialization in the !Xo Bushmen," in Phillip V. Tobias, ed., *The Bushmen: San Hunters and Herders of Southern Africa.* Cape Town: Human & Rousseau, 1978, pp. 132–135.

The Economist, "Half a Cheer for Namibia's Nujoma," Dec. 4, 1999, p. 44.

———, "Africa: The Heart of the Matter," May 13, 2000, pp. 22–24.

———, "Namibian Land Reform: Talking Like Mugabe," Sept. 14, 2002, p. 49.

———, "A Survey of Sub-Saharan Africa: Love and Death," Jan. 17, 2004, p. 11.

———, "Namibia: A New Old Man," Nov. 20, 2004, p. 50.

Facts on File World News Digest, April 2, 2003.

Fisher, Helen E. *The Anatomy of Love.* New York: W. W. Norton, 1992.

French, Howard W., "Africans Fault Rich Nations on Aid to the World's Poor," *The New York Times,* July 21, 2000, p. A8.

Gelles, Richard J., and Ann Levine, *Sociology, An Introduction,* 6th ed. New York: McGraw-Hill, 1999.

Good, Kenneth, *Realizing Democracy in Botswana, Namibia and South Africa.* Captown: Africa Institute of South Africa, 1997.

Gordon, Robert J., *The Bushman Myth: The Making of a Namibian Underclass.* Boulder, CO: Westview Press, 1992.

Guenther, Matthias, "Diversity and Flexibility: The Case of the Bushmen of Southern Africa," in Susan Kent, ed., *Cultural Diversity among Twentieth-Century Foragers: An African Perspective.* Cambridge: Cambridge University Press, 1996, pp. 65–86.

Herbstein, Dennis, "Jobs and Land," *Africa Report,* Vol. 38, no. 4 (July–August 1993), pp. 52–55.

Hitchcock, Robert, "Decentralization and Development among the Ju/wasi in Namibia," *Cultural Survival Quarterly,* Vol. 12, no. 3 (1988), pp. 31–33.

Hopwood, Graham, "Swapo Sweeps It," *The Namibian,* Dec. 6, 1999.

Houston Chronicle, "Namibia Pulls out of Congo as UN Chief Pushes to End War," Sept. 3, 2001, p. 32.

International Partnership Against Aids in Africa, *Joint Country Mission Report—Namibia, 31 May to June 4, 1999,* http://www.unaids.org/africapartnership/files/Namibia_report.doc.

Itano, Nicole, "Dialogue Brings Hope for Peace in Congo, " *Christian Science Monitor,* Feb. 26, 2002, p. 7.

Kelso, Casey, "The Landless Bushmen," *Africa Report,* Vol. 38, no. 2 (March–April 1993), pp. 51–53.

KENT, SUSAN, "And Justice for All: The Development of Political Centralization among Newly Sedentary Foragers," *American Anthropologist,* Vol. 91, no. 3 (Sept. 1989), pp. 703–712.

———, "Does Sendentarization Promote Gender Inequality: A Case Study from the Kalahari," *Journal of the Royal Anthropological Institute,* Vol. 1, no. 3 (Sept. 1995), pp. 513–537.

———, "Cultural Diversity among African Foragers: Causes and Implications," in Susan Kent, ed., *Cultural Diversity among Twentieth-Century African Foragers: An African Perspective.* Cambridge: Cambridge University Press, 1996, pp. 1–18.

———, ed., *Cultural Diversity among Twentieth-Century Foragers: An African Perspective.* Cambridge: Cambridge University Press, 1996.

KLUCKHOLN, CLYDE, *Mirror for Man.* New York: McGraw-Hill, 1949.

LEE, RICHARD B., "Ecology of a Contemporary San People," in Phillip V. Tobias, ed., *The Bushmen: San Hunters and Herders of Southern Africa.* Cape Town: Human & Rousseau, 1978, pp. 94–96.

———, *The !Kung San.* Cambridge: Cambridge University Press, 1979.

———, *The Dobe !Kung.* New York: Holt, 1984.

LAFRANIERE, SHARON, "Tensions Simmer As Namibia Divides Hs Farmlard," *The New York Time,* Dec. 25, 2004, p. A3.

LEE, RICHARD B., AND IRVEN DEVORE, eds., *Kalahari Hunter-Gatherers.* Cambridge, MA: Harvard University Press, 1976.

LENSKI, GERHARD, PATRICK NOLAN, AND JEAN LENSKI, *Human Societies: An Introduction to Macrosociology,* 6th ed. New York: McGraw-Hill, 1991.

LEYS, COLIN, AND JOHN S. SAUL, eds., *Namibia's Liberation Struggle: The Two-Edged Sword.* London: James Currey, 1995.

MALETSKY, CHRISTOF, "Nujoma's Successor Selected," *Business Day (South Africa),* May 31, 2004, p. 7.

MARSHALL, LORNA, *The !Kung of Nyae Nyae.* Cambridge, MA: Harvard University Press, 1976.

MCNEIL, DONALD G., JR., "In Bushmanland, Hunters' Tradition Turns to Dust," *The New York Times,* Nov. 13, 1997, p. A3.

———, "Aids Stalking Africa's Struggling Economies," *The New York Times,* Nov. 15, 1998, pp. 1, 20.

MOYO, TABBY, "Future Generations Will Pay for Military Spending Spree," *The Namibian,* Jan. 28, 2000.

The Namibian, "Government Urged to Speed Up Land Reform," April 15, 1999, http://www.reliefweb.int/IRIN/sa/countrystories/namibia/19990415.html.

———, "Defense Official Says Troop Pull-Back from DRCongo Going 'Smoothly,' " July 5, 2001.

———, "Congolese Talks Suspended Amid Row over Delegates," Feb. 27, 2002, http://www.namibian.com.na/.

———, "Namibia Has No Immediate Plan to Get Involved in DRC Conflict," July 23, 2004.

The New York Times, "Cruelty-Free Diamonds," July 15, 2000, p. A26.

———, "Namibia: Support for Zimbabwean," Aug. 9, 2000, p. A8.

———, "Namibia's Black Communal Farmers Urge Whites to Speed Pace of Land Reform," Aug. 21, 2001, pp. A7, A9.

NTINDA, ASSER, "Biting the Land Reform Bullet," *African Business,* no. 194 (Dec. 1994), p. 26.

PARK, ROBERT E., *Race and Culture.* New York: The Free Press, 1950.

REGIONAL SURVEYS OF THE WORLD, *Africa South of the Sahara, 1999.* Old Woking, Surrey: Europa Publications Ltd., 1999.

ROUE, MARIE, "An Economy of Sharing: There Is No Place for Selfish Individualism in Nomadic Hunter-Gatherer Societies," *UNESCO Courier* (January 1998), pp. 23–25.

SAUL, JOHN S., AND COLIN LEYS, "The Politics of Exile," in Colin Leys and John S. Saul, eds., *Namibia's Liberation Struggle: The Two-Edged Sword.* London: James Currey, 1995, pp. 41–65.

SAUNDERS, CHRISTOPHER, "Recent History," in *Africa South of the Sahara.* Old Woking, Surrey: Europa Publications Ltd., 1999, pp. 755–759.

SHOSTAK, MARJORIE, *Nisa.* Cambridge, MA: Harvard University Press, 1981.

SILBERBAUER, GEORGE B., "The Future of the Bushmen," in Phillip V. Tobias, ed., *The Bushmen: San Hunters and Herders of Southern Africa.* Cape Town: Human & Rousseau, 1978, p. 181.

SLOTTEN, ROSS A., "AIDS in Namibia," *Social Science Medicine,* Vol. 41, no. 2 (1995), pp. 277–284.

SPARKS, DONALD, "Economy of Namibia," in *Africa South of the Sahara.* Old Woking, Surrey: Europa Publications Ltd., 1999, pp. 759–764.

TAPSCOTT, CHRIS, "War, Peace and Social Classes," in Colin Leys and John S. Saul, eds., *Namibia's Liberation Struggle: The Two-Edged Sword.* London: James Currey, 1995, pp. 153–170.

THOMAS, ELIZABETH MARSHALL, *The Harmless People.* New York: Knopf, 1959.

TOBIAS, PHILLIP V., ed., *The Bushmen: San Hunters and Herders of Southern Africa.* Cape Town: Human & Rousseau, 1978.

U.S. BUREAU OF THE CENSUS, *International Data Base 2000,* http://www.census.gov/ipc/www/idbsprd.html.

WEINBERG, PAUL, *In Search of the San.* Johannesburg, South Africa: The Porcupine Press, 1997.

WIDLOK, THOMAS, *Living on Mangetti: "Bushman" Autonomy and Namibian Independence.* Oxford: Oxford University Press, 1999.

WILMSEN, EDWIN N., *Land Filled with Flies: A Political Economy of the Kalahari.* Chicago: University of Chicago Press, 1989.

WINES, MICHAEL, "Namibia: Seizures of White Land Planned," *The New York Times,* March 27, 2004, p. A14.

WIRTH, LOUIS, *The Ghetto.* Chicago: University of Chicago Press, 1928, 1956.

WOOD, ERIC, personal communication, 1995.

WORLD BANK, *Taking Action to Reduce Poverty in Sub-Saharan Africa.* Washington, DC: The World Bank, 1997.

———, *World Development Indicators,* 2000, CD-Rom.

———, *World Development Indicators Data Query,* http://devdata.worldbank.org/data-query/ (last accessed Nov. 12, 2004).

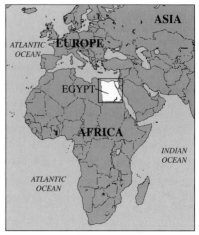

You can reach Cairo, Egypt's capital, in a short flight from anywhere in the Middle East or the Mediterranean. Athens, Rome, Damascus, and Jerusalem are only hours (or minutes) away. You will set down in one of the oldest human civilizations. Thirty centuries before Christ there were cities, scholars, and kings in Egypt.

LOCATION: Egypt rests in Africa's northeast corner bordered by Israel and the Red Sea on the east, the Sudan on the south, Libya to the west, and the Mediterranean Sea to the north.

AREA: 384,000 square miles or 1,113,600 square kilometers. Egypt is as large as Texas and New Mexico combined or about the size of Ontario.

LAND: Egypt is mostly desert. Population is concentrated in the Nile Valley and on the Delta—one of the world's most densely settled areas.

CLIMATE: Hot and dry. The coast gets 8 inches of rain per year, while south of Cairo there is almost none. Egypt is hot from May to October (up to 107° F) and cooler from November to April (55 to 70° F).

POPULATION: In 2005 there were 74 million people; 35 percent were under the age of 15. By 2050 population is projected to reach 113 million.

INCOME: An average of U.S. $1,354 GDP per person in 2004. 44 percent of Egyptians live on less than what $2.00 a day would buy in the United States.

EDUCATION: 44 percent of Egyptian women are literate, as are 67 percent of Egyptian men.

RELIGION: 91 percent of Egyptians are Sunni Muslims; at least 5 percent are Coptic Christians.

MINORITIES: Coptic Christians and Saidis—people from the southern part of Egypt.

CHAPTER FOUR

Egypt: Faith, Gender, and Class

INTRODUCTION

It would be a good idea to start this chapter by thinking about what you already know about Egypt. When you think of Egypt, do pyramids, palm trees, and mummies come to mind? Do you think of veiled women and Muslims kneeling in prayer? Does your mind turn to terrorism and militant Islamic fundamentalists? For many people, Egypt is a faraway place with an exotic past and a frightening present. Why should you learn more about it?

Nowadays, more than ever, studying Egypt will help you understand the world. Egypt will be your key to understanding the Muslim world, the Arab world, and the Middle East. The next time *jihadi* terrorists strike, the next time there is a revolution or an invasion in the Middle East, you will be much better able to make sense of events. You will know something about Islam, the religion, and about the political movements that take Islam as their focus. Also, you will be acquainted with the conditions of life in the Arab world, the dilemmas young people face, and the discontents that seek political expression.

Egypt is at once an Islamic society, an Arab society, and a Middle Eastern society, but the first thing you need to understand is that these terms are not synonymous. Islam is one of the world's great religions, practiced by more than 1.2 billion people worldwide. Followers of Islam are known as Muslims. But Muslims live in many countries and belong to many different ethnic groups. All of the Arab countries have large Muslim populations. Several (like Egypt and Iraq) also have Christian minorities. The Arab countries (including Saudi Arabia, Egypt, Iraq, Yemen, Syria, Lebanon, and Morocco) are inhabited by only 12 percent of the world's Muslims. The three nations with the largest Muslim populations (Indonesia, Pakistan, and Bangladesh) are Asian, not Arab and not Middle Eastern. There are millions of Muslims in Central Asia too (including Iran, Afghanistan, Kazakhstan, Uzbekistan, and western China), and also in Africa (including Nigeria and Sudan). Also, Muslim population is now growing in Europe and the United States as the result of immigration.

If you study only one Muslim society, Egypt would be a good choice. Politically and culturally, Egypt has played a leading role in the Arab and Muslim worlds. From

President Nasser's Pan-Arabism, to early twentieth-century feminism and on to Sayyid Qtub's radical Islamism, Egypt has set the trend. Egypt's sensitive geographic location makes it important too—in the Arab oil-producing region, adjacent to Israel, in North Africa, and not far from Europe. Conflict in Egypt makes the news and reverberates around the world.

Egypt and its African, Middle Eastern, and Asian neighbors have something important in common: they are all former European colonies, struggling to define their place in the modern world and cope with poverty, economic development, and rapid population growth. But in one way, Egypt is very different from some of its neighbors. Egypt has an unambiguous national identity and stable national boundaries. Egypt was a nation long before it was a colony. The kinds of deep divisions which exist in Iraq between Sunni and Shia and Kurdish Muslims, or between Pashtun and Dari tribes in Afghanistan have no real place in Egypt. There are some tribal identities: Bedouin in the northern deserts and Nubians in the south, but people think of themselves as Egyptians first and foremost and there are no separatist movements. Everyone speaks Arabic.

We expect that if you come from a western nation, you will find Egypt very different from your own society. You will learn a lot from contrasting the two. Three aspects of Egyptian society are absolutely central: faith, gender, and class. In Egypt the Islamic faith imbues all aspects of life: People understand the values they cherish and the norms they follow in religious terms. They debate government and law and politics in the light of their religion.

Another aspect of Egyptian society that may make a great impression on you is the contrasting roles played by men and women. Egyptian men and women have different religious obligations, different family responsibilities, and different legal rights. In public and private, Egyptian men and women usually carry on their lives separately from each other.

We would like you to meet Saad and Lima. They lead very different lives, and it is unlikely that they would ever meet. Islam is very important to both of them, but they understand and live it differently.

Two Egyptians: Their Stories

Saad is tired. At 14 he rises very early each morning to study for his high school classes. His father is a small shopkeeper, but Saad badly wants to be a professional with a good salary and a house in a fashionable part of the city. He interrupts his studies only for a cup of tea, a roll, and morning prayers. As busy as he might be, Saad, like his father Ibrahim, prays five times a day. Ibrahim has a "raisin" on his forehead: a small dark bruise raised by touching his forehead to the ground thousands of times in a long lifetime of prayer. Although the future that Saad dreams of may be very different from his father's, Saad cannot imagine a life outside Islam. It is as much a part of him as his family, his friends, and his hopes. Every morning Saad spends the long walk to school listening to the Quran (the holy book of Islam) recited on his Walkman.

Lima is a professor of legal studies. She was raised in a secular family of teachers and doctors and her interest in Islam developed only when Islamic marriage norms became a focus of controversy in Egypt. Lima soon found that the problems of interpreting Islamic law were at least as fascinating as the business law she studied and taught. Some of the Islamic issues were even closer to her life: Could a woman sue for divorce? Could a marriage contract forbid a man to take a second spouse? Lima soon joined a study circle of educated women who met at a mosque on the college grounds to study Islam. "I never learned much about Islam at home," she told a friend. "We considered religion not at all interesting for educated people. We observed the fasts but not much else. My father wasn't happy when he learned I was studying Sharia (Islamic law) and could cite passages and precedents from the Quran." "I never thought I'd live to see the day," he said, "when I had a son who never reads the Quran and a daughter who quotes it." After several years of study, Lima and her circle challenged a ruling by a leading cleric forbidding young couples to take out mortgages to buy apartments. The cleric responded harshly to Lima's group. Writing to a leading Cairo newspaper he argued that the circle's interpretation ignored important points of Sharia. Lima was not dismayed by his response. "When you have the country's leading clerics arguing Sharia with you in the daily papers," she told her fiance, "you've moved women into a role they haven't had in this country for a long time."

Class contrasts are unavoidable in Egypt. There are sophisticated young men and women who live in luxury apartments in Cairo's modern high-rise towers who would not be out of place in New York, Paris, or London. Their clothing comes from Milan and Paris, their luxury cars from Germany, their electronics from Japan, and their income from high-level jobs in Egypt's banking and legal establishments. Not far from the apartments of such wealthy Egyptians, poor people fill the narrow alleys of Cairo's oldest quarters. Many are recent migrants from villages in southern Egypt, where life still revolves around fields and family.

To understand why Islam is fundamental to Egyptian culture, how class inequalities have come to divide Egyptian society so deeply, and why the position of women is the subject of such passionate debate in contemporary Egypt, you need information about Egypt's long and fascinating history.

EGYPT'S HISTORY

In some countries, people look to the future and pay little attention to the past. "That's history," people say dismissively. For Egyptians, however, the past counts for a good deal in the way people look at themselves and their lives. Evidence of a glorious past surrounds Egyptians, a past in which Egypt dominated or led the world. The pyramids are a visible reminder of the advanced civilization that flourished in Egypt before the classical cultures of Greece and Rome emerged. Cairo's mosques and Al Azhar University (established in the tenth century and considered the oldest university in the world) remind Egyptians that they were once in the center of an Islamic civilization that overshadowed Christian Europe.

When Egyptians see that Egypt today is politically and economically dominated by the Christian West, that Egypt is no longer a center of scientific, economic, and artistic innovation, they feel weak and humiliated. But they take courage from the testimony of their history. They know that in the course of its history Egypt suffered conquest after conquest by other societies that successively imposed their cultures and social structures. Egypt embraced some of the invading societies and absorbed their cultures, but resisted others. In its long history Egypt has changed its language and religion three times. After the ancient pharaonic period (c. 3100 B.C.–671 B.C.),

Egypt was conquered and became part of the Greek and Roman empires (333 B.C.–A.D. 641). Next came the Arab-Islamic conquest of Egypt, and the long period of Islamic civilization (641–1798) that followed. In recent centuries, Egypt was conquered once again, this time by Europeans, and subjected to European colonialism (1798–1952). Then, in the midtwentieth century, Egypt entered its present era of postcolonial independence (1952–present). Throughout its history, Egypt has been an intellectual and cultural center. The great library at Alexandria brought together all the knowledge of the ancient world. Later, Cairo became an important focus for Islamic scholarship. And in the nineteenth and twentieth centuries, Cairo was the literary and cultural leader of the Arab world, a magnet for novelists, filmmakers, journalists, and political activists, who argued and inspired each other in the literary coffee houses and shaped cultural life in the whole Arab world.

The Pharaonic Period

One of the world's first great civilizations developed in Egypt. Egyptians began farming as early as 9,000 years ago, and by 4,000 years ago they had built towns, and wealthy people lived in elaborate houses, adorned with gold and glass ornaments, musical instruments, pottery, and cloth. Merchants traveled and traded with other societies in Africa and the Middle East. By 3000 B.C. the reign of the pharaohs began, which lasted nearly 3,000 years. Pharaonic Egypt created some of the first government bureaucracies, complete with record keepers and tax collectors. The power of the pharaohs and the energy and knowledge they commanded is still visible today in their surviving monuments: the pyramids, temples, deserted cities, and tombs of the Egyptian desert.

Greek and Roman Empires

Pharaonic Egypt lasted until 332 B.C., when Alexander the Great conquered Egypt—one step in a stunning series of victories over all of Greece and then over the armies of Asia and Africa. Alexander was the young ruler of Macedonia, a small, poor country in the Balkans, but he put together a historic empire. After Alexander's death, one of his generals, Ptolemy, took over rule of Egypt. Ptolemy and his successors drew Egypt into the Greek world. Greek replaced Coptic, the ancient language of Egypt. Egyptian decorative arts began to follow Greek artistic ideas, and depictions of Egyptian gods began to resemble Greek gods. Ptolemy and his successors built a new capital city, Alexandria, on the shore of the Mediterranean, facing toward Europe.

Greek conquest brought great changes to the lives of Egyptian men and especially Egyptian women. Women had been respected in pharaonic Egypt. There were important female deities and priestesses, and women and men were equal before the law. Women could own property and sue for divorce and they could socialize freely in public with men (Ahmed, pp. 31–33). All this changed with the Greek conquest. In Greek civilization, free women (as opposed to slaves) were **secluded** (that is, they were kept separate from men and out of public view). They could not be seen by any men except close relatives. Men engaged in public life—in the marketplace, the gymnasium, and the political assembly—while women stayed home in special rooms at the back of the house. Greek women were expected to be silent and submissive, and most important, to provide male heirs for a society that was focused on the male line. Women could not own property, and anything they inherited was held in trust for them by male relatives (Ahmed, pp. 28–31).

The Roman Conquest and Christianity

Not long after Alexander's conquests, the city of Rome came to dominate much of Mediterranean Europe. Then, in the first century B.C., Rome defeated the Ptolemies and added Egypt to the expanding Roman Empire, which now ringed the Mediterranean Sea. International trade led to a burst of economic and intellectual productivity in Egypt. Egypt grew the wheat for Rome's bread, and Alexandria became the intellectual center of the entire Roman world.

In the years after Christ's birth, Christianity came to Alexandria and found a receptive audience. For several centuries, Christianity spread throughout Egypt, gradually replacing the worship of the ancient gods of the Nile. Christian ideas about women were similar to Greek ideas. Early Christian women were frequently covered from head to toe in voluminous gowns and veils and they were strictly segregated in order to protect men from temptation (Ahmed, pp. 35–36).

But while Christianity blossomed in Egypt, the Roman Empire declined. The empire had grown so large, stretching from the Atlantic Ocean to the Red Sea, that Rome could not effectively rule it. In the fourth century A.D., Rome divided itself into an Eastern and a Western Empire. The Eastern Empire, which included Egypt, was to be ruled from the ancient city of Byzantium (today Istanbul, in Turkey). Byzantium proved to be a less friendly ruler than Rome. The Byzantine rulers objected to the way Egyptians practiced Christianity and persecuted Coptic (Egyptian) Christians. By the seventh century, Egyptians regarded the Byzantines less as brothers in Christ and more as hated tyrants.

The Arab/Islamic Conquest

When the seventh century began, Egypt was a Christian country; its language was Greek and it identified with the cultural traditions of Greece, Rome, and Jerusalem. All this was to change forever with the explosive growth of a new religion: Islam. Islam originated in the Arabian city of Mecca (now in Saudi Arabia), at that time a crossroads of trade between India and the Byzantine Empire. In the seventh century, Muhammad, a 42-year-old merchant, had a revelation from God and announced a new faith—Islam—that built upon Arab culture, Christianity, and Judaism. By 632 Muhammad's followers dominated Arabia. In 639 the militant followers of the new faith swept across the borders of the Byzantine Empire and rapidly conquered Egypt, Syria, and Palestine. In the centuries that followed, they swept beyond Egypt, west through North Africa, and on to Spain and east to the borders of China.

Although the Arabs came as conquerors, they were not entirely unwelcome in Egypt. The bitterness that Egyptians felt toward the Byzantines led them to stand aside as the Arabs crushed the Byzantine forces. The Arabs, for their part, demanded much less than had the Byzantines: Only obedience and taxes were required.

Although the Arabs devoutly wished for converts to their new faith, they did not forcibly convert Egyptians—whether Christians or Jews or worshipers of the ancient gods.

Islam gradually transformed Egyptian society. Arabic became the common language of Egypt, replacing Coptic, the language of ancient Egypt, and the Greek of the Greco-Roman period. Cairo, a new Islamic city, replaced Alexandria in importance and became a world center of Islamic learning. By the fourteenth century, most Egyptians had embraced Islam, and Islamic beliefs and practices became a fundamental part of Egyptian culture. (However, a minority remained Christians. About 6 percent of Egyptians today are Copts, Coptic Christians.) Arab literature, music, and the arts were absorbed into Egyptian culture.

Islam didn't much change the status of women in Egypt. It shared Christian gender norms and attitudes toward women. Islam did give Egyptian women limited rights to sue for divorce and a limited right to inherit, but it also introduced into Egypt the Arab practice of **polygyny** (which allowed men to marry more than one wife) (Ahmed, p. 33).

Islamic Civilization

People in the Islamic world remember something that westerners forget: For many centuries after the foundation of Islam, the Islamic world was the center of civilization and progress. At the same time that Europe declined into its "Dark Ages," a period when government disintegrated, knowledge was lost, and trade withered, the Islamic world flourished. Old knowledge of science was preserved in Egypt and elsewhere in the Middle East and new scientific and mathematical knowledge was created. The great library at Alexandria preserved all the books and knowledge of the ancient world. Much of the heritage of classical Greece and Rome was preserved and passed on to the modern world by Muslim scholars. In the eleventh and twelfth centuries the Fatamid dynasty ruled North Africa, Sicily, Syria, and Palestine from its center in Cairo (Donner, pp. 44–49). Manufacturing and commerce expanded so that the Islamic world became the hub of the world's economy. The most desired products, like coffee, sugar, and paper, were available only from Muslim merchants. Islamic governments offered unprecedented freedom of thought and tolerance of minorities, so much so that groups like the Jews, persecuted in Europe, fled to Islamic countries for refuge (Lewis, p. 45). Islamic civilization was creative and energetic, spreading through Asia and into Europe and establishing empires like the Turkish caliphate.

European Colonialism

In the fourteenth and fifteenth centuries no one could have imagined that Europe would someday replace the Islamic world in dominance. But in fact Europe began to develop and expand, gradually pushing aside the Islamic world. Europeans forced Arab rulers out of Spain in 1492. They took over trade with India in the sixteenth century, and in 1798, a French army, led by Napoleon, conquered Egypt itself. The French were soon expelled by the British and Turks, with whom they were at war, but European political and economic domination of Egypt continued. England, in particular, believed it had a major interest in Egypt; it wanted Egyptian customers for its products and it wanted to control the Suez Canal, the most direct route to India, Great Britain's largest colony.

Some Egyptians prospered during this colonial period of European domination. An elite of landowners, government officials, and professionals, who cooperated with the Europeans, came under the influence of European culture and ideas. They adopted French (rather than Arabic) as their everyday language and sent their sons to schools where they were taught in French and read European books. They ate European food, drank wine, and read European literature. Many thought and wrote about how a society could be at once modern and Islamic. Egypt's elite also absorbed European ideas about democracy, the right of nations to self-rule, and the need for equality between women and men. During the colonial period, some affluent Egyptian women publicly removed their veils and participated in the political struggle for independence. However, for most Egyptians life became much harder during the colonial period. Many peasants lost their land, weavers, tailors and other skilled workers could not compete against machine-made European goods, and the growing ranks of industrial workers labored long hours for very low wages. Poor Egyptians had little contact with European culture: They spoke Arabic and took consolation in Islam. Both the economic and the cultural distance between rich and poor widened.

The European powers made increasingly restrictive demands on the Egyptian government, and in 1882 a revolt against these restrictions by the Egyptian army led to the occupation of Egypt by the British. From 1882 through 1954, the object of modern Egyptian politics was the end of the British occupation. Although a popular revolt in 1919 led the British to proclaim Egypt independent in 1921, the British army remained in occupation and the newly created king and parliament were dominated by the British ambassador. In 1952, following a humiliating defeat of the Egyptian army by the forces of Israel, the newly independent Jewish state, a group of junior officers deposed King Farouk and took control of the government. In 1954 these officers, led by Gamal Abdul Nasser, expelled the British army and created real independence for Egypt for the first time in 100 years.

An Independent Egypt

It is ironic that western ideas played so large a role in Egypt's revolt against European domination. Nasser, Egypt's greatest twentieth-century figure, transformed Egypt's government and economy and greatly improved the lives of the poorest Egyptians. While he respected Islam, Nasser looked to the West, to the United States, the Soviet Union, and Europe for political values and institutional models. Nasser moved his country in the direction of a **secular** (that is, not religious) authority: a system of business law separate from Islamic family law, a school system separate from religious education, and western-style parliamentary government separate from religious authority. Nasser established a public school system that was open to all but the poorest Egyptians and open to women as well as men. He chose to build a **socialist** economy, in which most enterprises were government owned and the government was the society's largest employer.

Nasser also challenged Egypt's deep economic inequalities, particularly in the countryside. His first target was the great landowning families who owned more than a third of Egypt's land. Nasser seized the land belonging to the royal family and required the other rich families to sell more than half their land. He redistributed this land to hundreds of thousands of poor peasant families. Many poor families received no land, and even those who did acquired only very small plots, but all felt grateful to Nasser; they felt released from oppressive landlords and they hoped to be given more land in the future. Egypt's peasants benefited in a limited way from Nasser's land reform. But Nasser's attack against the great landowners transformed the rural middle class. They bought much of the land the elite was forced to sell and turned themselves into prosperous commercial farmers (Hooglund, pp. 122–123; Mitchell, T., pp. 22–23; Vatikiotis, pp. 396–399).

Politics in Independent Egypt

Nasser won wide support from Egyptians because he helped many people become more prosperous and he succeeded in evicting the British. At the same time, however, he severely restricted democracy. The army crushed strikes and suppressed militant Islamic groups and jailed their leaders.

In 1956 the British, French, and Israeli armies once again invaded Egypt. Britain and France wanted to reassert their control over the region, and Israel wanted to end Nasser's support of the Palestinians who attacked Israel. Although Egypt's armies were defeated in the fighting with Israel, Nasser persuaded the United States and the Soviet Union to force the invaders to withdraw. Nasser emerged as the hero, not only of Egypt, but of the Arab world as a whole. Strengthened by political and economic support from the Soviet Union, Nasser led Egypt into a period of prosperity and international leadership. Other Arab countries recognized Nasser as the leader of "pan-Arabism," a movement for political unity among Arab nations. "Nonaligned" countries—those like India and Yugoslavia, that sought to avoid becoming a part of either the Soviet bloc or the U.S.-led western block—also looked to Nasser for leadership.

But much of Egypt's progress was brought to a halt by the 1967 war with Israel. Israel defeated Egypt's armed forces so completely that it humiliated both the Egyptian leadership and ordinary Egyptians. Many Egyptian soldiers were killed or injured and Egypt's economy was shattered by the closing of the Suez Canal, the capture of the country's developing oil fields in the Sinai Peninsula, and the wave of refugees that poured out of war-torn areas.

After the triumph of independence and the heady early Nasser years, Egyptians found their country's progress disappointing and frustrating. Egypt never recovered its leadership of the Arab world after the 1967 defeat and the 1979 Camp David treaty with Israel. Both Anwar Sadat, Nasser's successor, and Hosni Mubarak, the president after Sadat, sought peace with Israel and alliance with the United States. They were rewarded with huge sums of U.S. foreign aid, but earned the contempt of many Arab nations.

Social tensions within Egypt increased as Egypt's economy failed to keep pace with the growing size and expectations of its population. In 1947 there were 19 million Egyptians; by 2000 there were 68 million. In the 1950s, millions of Egyptians moved from the countryside to the city and found work and housing in an expanding economy. By the 1990s, there was neither work nor housing for poor Egyptians who continued to flock to Cairo, Alexandria, and other cities. For decades millions of Egyptians were forced to find work outside the country, mostly in the oil-rich nations of the Middle East and the Persian Gulf.

When Anwar Sadat became president, he reversed many of Nasser's policies. Sadat tried to move Egypt away from socialism and towards a capitalist economy by encouraging private enterprise. He repressed the socialist political organization that Nasser had supported. Sadat permitted Islamist parties to operate openly, because he saw them as a counterweight to the socialists. But Sadat's economic policy of *infitah* (or "opening the door") failed to bring substantial benefits to most Egyptians. Many people came to believe that Sadat's regime created benefits only for a few rich businessmen. Despite his foreign policy successes, Sadat faced growing hostility in the streets. In October 1981, during a celebration of the 1973 war against Israel, Anwar Sadat was assassinated by one of the Islamist groups he had encouraged that was operating as a secret cell within the military.

Egypt Today

Sadat's successor, Hosni Mubarak, still ruled Egypt in 2005, when this book was written. In 1981 he was an airforce general, unknown to most Egyptians. Mubarak stepped to the controls of a society increasingly torn by economic inequality and political conflict. As time went on, and the government proved unable to deliver benefits to all Egyptians, Mubarak focused more and more single-mindedly on staying in power. He resorted increasingly to police repression, eliminating free speech and political choice and suppressing any possible source of opposition to his government, from socialists, from Islamists, and from those who want Egypt to be a democracy. Growing numbers of Egyptians, alienated from a corrupt and repressive government and distressed by the subordinate position of Muslim countries in the world economy and in world politics, have been looking for answers in religion. Those who joined militant Islamic groups, fighting to overthrow the Mubarak regime and establish an Islamic state, have been harshly repressed by the government. But far more Egyptians have become part of a broad religious revival that has brought religion much more into the foreground of Egyptian culture.

EGYPTIAN CULTURE

Two conflicting forces are gaining strength in Egyptian culture today. A pair of opposing sociological concepts can help us to understand the two sides. Sociologists follow Max Weber in contrasting **secular** and **sacred** societies. In **sacred societies,** religion permeates life. People treasure their religious rituals and ceremonies. They apply religious values and ideas to every aspect of life. Science, law, education, and government are all ruled by religion. When people make decisions, religious considerations trump any other factors. In **secular societies,** religion exists, but it exists in its own separate, sharply delineated space. The rest of life is, as Weber said, "disenchanted," it loses spiritual meaning and people assume that religion has no place there. In secular societies church and state are separated. People accept the idea that some aspects of life are ruled by government and law and other parts of life are ruled by religion. They are used to disagreements between religion and science. When individuals make personal or business decisions, they may think about religious values, but they often think about personal happiness, getting ahead, profit and loss, patriotism, or other nonreligious goals.

We can understand the concepts of sacred and secular societies best as what Weber called **ideal types,** constructed ideals that don't exist anywhere in pure form, but that help us understand some aspects of the real world. What society in the world seems to you to come closest to being a sacred society? Did you say Afghanistan under the rule of the Taliban? That comes pretty close. How about Iran? The Iranian revolution in 1979 was an explicitly religious revolution, aimed at setting up an Islamic state, governed by Islamic law and custom. But Iran still has a parliament separate from its religious authorities. Its business law is adapted to meet the needs of European businesses. How about Egypt? We could say that Egypt has an Islamic culture, but a secular government. Egypt is not ruled by Islamic authorities and most of its law is secular law. Its economy is increasingly under the influence of secular, international corporations. But its culture is in large part Islamic culture. In Egypt even people who are not devout Muslims (and even those who are Christians) live in a world filled with Islamic values and norms. Phrases such as *insha'Allah* (God willing) and *alhamdu lillah* (thanks be to God) fill everyday conversation. Egyptians use these expressions easily and sincerely. People pray and talk about religion every day. When they get dressed, go out, go shopping, or buy a CD, religion is involved. When they need advice they often turn to a local religious authority or an Islamic Web site or advice column.

Now, let's ask: What is the most secular society you can think of? Where would you say religion has less influence, in the United States or in Japan? In the United States, as in Egypt, many people would like to see religion play a more dominant role in all aspects of life. But much of American culture is secular. To a lesser, but still real extent, it is in Egypt too. You can go to the movies and see American action films that have nothing to do with religion. You can watch *Friends* or *Baywatch* on satellite television. People study engineering or medicine or computers and the principles of these disciplines are completely separate from religion. People in Egypt are becoming more religious at the same time that Egyptian society is becoming more westernized and secular. People talk about this dual trend constantly and debate which direction their culture should go in and whether and how both directions can be reconciled (Roy, pp. 3–13).

You have probably experienced a secular culture yourself. But to fully understand Egyptian society, you need to know more about its sacred culture, Islam.

Egypt's Islamic Beliefs, Norms, and Values

Any Muslim will tell you that it is easy to get to know Islam; you need to begin with the five pillars of faith: declaring belief in God, prayer, charity, fasting during the holy month of Ramadan, and pilgrimage. Each of these fundamentals reveals important Islamic beliefs and each has major implications for the conduct of everyday life.

Declaring Belief

Five times a day, in the largest cities and the smallest villages, the voice of the *muezzin* (the prayer caller) cries out from the *minaret* (the highest tower) of the *mosque* (the Islamic house of worship). Nowadays the voice is likely to be recorded and broadcast over a public address system.

> God is great (Allahu Akbar), God is great, God is great. I witness that there is no god but Allah. I witness that there is no God but Allah. I witness that Muhammad is his messenger. I witness that Muhammad is his messenger. Come to prayer, come to prayer. Come to prosperity, come to prosperity. God is great. God is great. There is no God but Allah. (Esposito, 1991*a*, p. 89)

The call is echoed by Muslims indoors and out, who all join in affirming their belief. They thus daily and repeatedly declare their faith: their faith in God and their belief in one single god ("there is no god but God"). You may take **monotheism** (the belief that there is only one god) for granted, but in the history of the world's religions, monotheism is relatively unusual. Most of the world's religions recognize many gods, major and minor. For example, when you read about Japan in Chapter 1, you learned that all the major religions of Asia—Buddhism, Hinduism, Taoism, and Shinto—honor multiple gods. Islam, Christianity, and Judaism all believe in a single god, and he is the same god, the god of Moses and Abraham. Islam recognizes Jesus as one of the four messengers of God—Moses, David, Jesus, and Muhammad—but Jesus is not believed to be the son of God.

All that is necessary to become a Muslim is to make the affirmation of faith: "There is no god but God, and Muhammad is the messenger of God" in the presence of other believers. But professing faith in God commits you to accepting the word of God, as transmitted through his messenger Muhammad and recorded literally in the *Quran,* the holy book. The word *Islam* actually means "submission" in Arabic, meaning submission to the will of God. *Muslim* means "one who submits" (Lippman, 1990, p. 1).

Values and Norms.   Muslims believe in a Judgment Day on which each person will be sent by God either to paradise or to hell. Islam tells people that God is stern, and on Judgment Day terrible agonies await the sinner, while paradise is filled with delights. Pious Muslims fear the wrath of God if they do not live by Islamic values and norms. For example, Islam values honesty, modesty and chastity, charity toward the less fortunate, and religious faith. To be virtuous and win paradise, the good man or woman must strive to submit to God, to make life a spiritual exercise so that in every situation he or she struggles to act virtuously, not for worldly benefit, but to honor God. It is important to follow detailed norms, but they must be obeyed in the spirit of faith.

The good Muslim does not drink alcohol, or profit from lending money, or gamble, gossip, or seek revenge. The good Muslim does not have sex outside marriage, gives to charity, helps orphans, and of course carries out the prescribed religious obligations of prayer, charity, fasting, and pilgrimage. Many of these norms are described in the Quran, which is so important that many Egyptians try to memorize it in its entirety. In Egypt the Quran is chanted continually on the radio and in the traditional schools that boys attend. Over one-third of the millions of cassette tapes sold in Egypt yearly are Quran readings, and the most popular readers are treated with the acclaim of rock stars. One public performance by a Quranic star attracted 600,000 people. Tapes of sermons by popular preachers are also best-sellers. (Jehl, Mar. 6, 1996, p. A4). Other Islamic norms are recorded in the *hadith,* the collection of Muhammad's words as interpreted by religious scholars. *Sharia* is the code of Islamic law derived from the Quran and *hadith.* In Egypt *Sharia* law holds for cases involving family and marriage, but the rest of civil and business law is secular (Rodenbeck, p. 105; Campo, p. 105; Lippman, 1990, pp. 30–32).

Prayer and the Social Construction of Time

Prayer is the second of the five pillars of faith. Muslims are required to pray five times a day: at sunrise, noon, midafternoon, sunset, and night, in response to the call to prayer. Daily prayers may be recited alone or in company, in a mosque or at one's place of work. In rural areas, men may keep clear a small spot in their fields for daily prayer. In busy cities, traffic may be blocked by rows of men kneeling on mats and rugs for the noon prayer. Some people, who are not religious, or not Muslims, do not pray, but these days, more and more people pray. Increasingly, banks, shops, even government offices shut down during the hours of prayer (Jehl, March 6, 1996, p. A4; Abdo, p. 4).

Many norms prescribe the proper way to pray. People take off their shoes before entering a mosque and they ritually wash themselves before prayer. All believers face in the direction of Mecca (the city, today in Saudi Arabia, where Muhammad first heard the word of God) when they pray, so if there are many praying together, you will see them lined up in orderly rows. In daily prayer people recite standard texts; they don't make individual appeals to God. Recitation is accompanied by sequences of bows and prostrations, when people kneel, then lower their foreheads to the ground. Women generally pray separately from men, since the postures of prayer might prove immodest. In the street or the field, people avoid touching the dirty ground by praying on a small rug or even a piece of cardboard (Bassiouni, pp. 30–31). There is tension in Islam between the "official" religion of the mosque and the holy texts and the folk religion practiced by villagers and the urban poor. They often visit shrines and make personal appeals to popular saints. These practices are condemned by Muslim clergy.

Prayer Structures Time. How is time ordinarily divided in your society? Do you think in terms of the week and the weekend? The hours of classes? The time the coffee cart comes around in the office, lunchtime, and the end of the workday? In Muslim countries like Egypt, the hours of prayer divide the day, marking the passage of time as clearly as the clock. Businesses open after the morning prayer and the best bargains may be found before the call to noon prayer (Rodenbeck, p. 105).

In Egypt Friday is the day of special religious observance. The week hurries toward Friday, when schools and government offices are closed. Women who work in private businesses, as typists or engineers, struggle to finish work early so they can go home and clean their houses by Friday afternoon, when the eye of God will be upon them. In towns and villages, the Friday market is the largest, since people flock

On a busy Cairo street, traffic comes to a halt for noonday prayers. Public space in Egyptian cities is "male" space and all those praying in the street are men. Since they face toward Mecca, they easily arrange themselves in neat rows. Not all Egyptians, not even all Muslims, pray regularly. Behind those at prayer you can see other people on errands and at work.

into town for Friday prayers. People gather in the markets to shop for sugar, tea, or cassette tapes (Fakhouri, pp. 51–52; Campo, pp. 126–127).

On Fridays, Islamic tradition requires that Muslim men pray together in the mosque. Women may attend too, to pray in a separate part of the mosque, but it is not required. The prayer leader or *imam* leads Friday prayers and also delivers a sermon. He is not a priest, but rather an ordinary worshiper, normally someone with extra religious training. In a city, the *imam* is probably a person who has done a great deal of special study, but in a village he would likely be an artisan who has studied for a few years at a village religious school (Lippman, 1990, p. 14).

Finally, in Egypt religious holidays punctuate the year. The most important of these is *Ramadan,* which lasts for a whole month. Because the Islamic calendar is a lunar calendar, Ramadan begins on a different date in each year and it is not associated with a particular season. Observance of Ramadan is so demanding that people must structure their year around it.

Ramadan and the Value of Unity

Observance of Ramadan is another of the pillars of Islam. Ramadan is the Arabic name of the month in which God began to reveal the Quran to Muhammad. During Ramadan all Muslim adults must fast from dawn until dark (neither eating nor drinking anything) unless they are pregnant, nursing, traveling, or ill, and refrain from smoking and sex. Fasting teaches self-restraint and it reminds people of how the poor suffer. You can imagine how these obligations disrupt normal life during Ramadan. Especially when the fast occurs during hot weather, life slows to a crawl, with people working shorter hours and resting indoors as much as possible away from the desiccating sun. Families rise before dawn to eat the leftovers from the previous night's dinner and to take their last long drinks of water before the sun rises. Then, after dark, everyone celebrates, with a feast called the *iftar* ("breakfast"). Even the poorest Egyptians, who rarely see meat on their tables, will scrimp and save to eat meat during Ramadan. Egyptians are much more observant of Ramadan now than they were twenty or thirty years ago. Restaurants in Cairo now close during daylight hours in Ramadan, and if there is anyone who smokes or eats before sundown, you will not see them do so in public (Murphy, p. 26).

Like daily prayers, Ramadan vividly demonstrates the cultural and religious unity of Muslims. The rigors of fasting are shared and people feel linked in common endeavor with their community, their nation, and the worldwide community of Islam. In cities and towns all over the country, people who have fasted will sit before tables piled high with food and drink, waiting for the broadcast cannon shot with which Radio Cairo announces sunset prayers and the end of the fast. Radio and television, which often act as instruments of secularization, work in this case to reinforce the culture of a sacred society (Esposito, 1991*a,* pp. 91–92).

Charity and the Value of Equality

Charity (or *zakat*) is a major Islamic value and it is one of the five pillars of Islam. All Muslims are obliged, as an act of worship of God, to support Muslims in need and the Islamic faith. Some Muslims interpret *zakat* as requiring them to give a fixed percentage of their income and wealth to charity every year; or to leave money to charity in their wills. Others donate money to help build mosques. During Ramadan, charity-givers spend hundreds of dollars a day provisioning free *iftar* meals on the streets for the poor, feeding as many as 2,000 people a day. Egyptians also give money to the homeless on the streets or outside mosques (Bassiouni, pp. 30–31; Lippman, 1990, p. 19; Campo, pp. 122–124).

Consideration for the needy is part of Islam's traditional emphasis on equality. In the mosque, all are equal; there are no preferred pews for the rich or influential—all kneel together. Anyone can lead prayers and give the sermon; there is no church hierarchy, no official priests or sacraments, no recognized saints, no monks or nuns. Islam also requires that the rich respect the poor, even though they may be ragged and hungry. Kindness and compassion are the essence of what Egyptians refer to as *saddaqa.* The Quran warns, "A kind word with forgiveness is better than charity followed by insult" (Bassiouni, p. 30). Much of the moral energy and appeal of the current Islamic revival comes from a sense that the rich and powerful have long since ceased to care about the needs of ordinary Muslims. Even when help does come from government agencies, it often comes with a kind of contempt that is especially resented because it violates the sacred norms of Islam. In the absence of government services Islamist groups have organized clinics, built housing, and provided loans for the poor, and this dedication to charity earns them the respect of other Muslims and attracts many followers (Campo, pp. 130–137; Lippman, 1990, pp. 78–90; Hedges, Oct. 4, 1993, p. A8).

Pilgrimage: A Culmination of Faith

The final pillar of faith and the last major obligation of all Muslims is to make the pilgrimage or *hajj* to Mecca at least once in their lifetime. Both personally and socially the pilgrimage sums up the meaning of Islamic faith. To make the journey to Mecca is certainly an affirmation of faith. In the past, when pilgrims journeyed overland, it was a grueling trip. Today, airplanes ease the journey, but it is still challenging, especially in summer. Also, for many Egyptians, the *hajj* represents an enormous expense, the fruit of many years' savings, and perhaps a person's single trip ever away from his or her village. As prayer and holy days structure the Islamic day and year, planning and making the pilgrimage are key events in a lifetime. In many villages you will see "pilgrimage murals," depicting the airplane and Mecca and the crowds, painted on the outside walls of their houses by those who have made the *hajj.*

Finally, the pilgrimage expresses with special emphasis the Islamic values of community and equality. The pilgrimage is a yearly event, taking place only on specified days. During that short time, hundreds of thousands, even millions of pilgrims pour into Mecca from all over the world. In the huge crowds that walk through the required rites of the pilgrimage—trekking to the Sacred Mosque and back and forth to other holy places—you will see people of many races, speaking dozens of languages, visibly united by their Islamic faith. Symbolically, they all put on the special clothing of the pilgrimage, white wraps for the men and loose white dresses, without facial veils, for the women, reminding them that in Islam differences of race and class are surmounted (Lippman, 1990, pp. 22–27).

The Question of *Jihad*

Nowadays we often hear the term *jihad,* and the Islamists who commit terrorist attacks are often called *jihadis.* This is a good place to explain the meaning of *jihad.* The term translates from Arabic as "holy struggle" or "striving," and historically it has been understood in two ways. The "greater jihad" is the struggle inside you, the internal struggle each Muslim should engage in to improve himself or herself, to submit to God and restrain sinful impulses. The "lesser jihad" is the external struggle to defend Islam against its enemies, to protect and perhaps extend the faith. In external jihad violence is sometimes permitted, but only under strict conditions. Most Muslims would say that it is never permissible to kill other Muslims and it is never permissible to kill women and children who are not soldiers. In Egypt, in the

1990s, when Islamist groups staged violent attacks within Egypt, public disapproval was overwhelming. But today an Egyptian who went off to participate in jihad on behalf of the Palestinians, or against the Americans in Iraq, would probably be congratulated.

Do They "Hate Freedom"?

In 2004 George W. Bush said that Islamic terrorists attack the United States because "they hate freedom." Was he right? Do the terrorists hate freedom? Do other Egyptians and other Muslims hate freedom? This is a really helpful question because it allows us to clarify Egyptian political values and understand something about the range of opinion about values in Egypt.

The great majority of Egyptians value freedom and very much want to have it. They want freedom of speech, freedom of the press, fair trial and the rule of law, freedom to join political parties and to freely elect the government of their choice. Is this what you mean by freedom? Egyptians, whatever their political opinions, feel deprived of these freedoms because Egypt has an authoritarian government determined to stay in power by squelching all opposition, Islamist or secular. One of the biggest complaints Egyptians have about the United States is that despite America's devotion to freedom, it has supported the Mubarak government, never criticizing its suppression of opposition parties, detention of political prisoners, and use of torture. The U.S. contribution of $2 billion per year helps keep Mubarak in power. It was unprecedented when, in 2002, U.S. President Bush pressured Mubarak to retry and exonerate Said Eddin Inbrahim, a secular advocate of democracy, who holds dual U.S.-Egyptian citizenship. Egyptians wondered why this one American drew Bush's attention when he never commented on the 20,000 other political prisoners held in Egypt's jails.

Islamist groups, of course, want political freedom as much as any other Egyptians, because if free elections were allowed, they would probably be elected to positions of power. Would they still permit political freedom once elected? The Islamist regime in Iran permits a limited parliamentary system, but forbids many critics of the regime from running for office. In Turkey an Islamist government was elected to power, but it has not changed democratic political processes or secular laws (*The Economist,* Sept. 13, 2003, pp. 10–11).

Personal Freedom. But perhaps to you the word *freedom* has less to do with political freedom and more to do with personal, individual freedom, the freedom to make choices and express yourself. Do Egyptians value personal freedom? The answer would have to be yes, but within a religious context. If you live in Europe or Canada, this answer may seem strange, but if you are American, it will probably be familiar. Like so many Americans, young Egyptians seeking to find themselves very often search through religious experience. So the personal freedom they value is the freedom to explore religious ideas, hear different preachers (not just the official, government-appointed ones), go to Quran study groups, and experiment with just how pious they wish to be. Media coverage of glamorous, newsworthy young actresses in Egypt often focuses on their religious conversions, their decisions to leave acting, stop dressing provocatively and put on the veil (Kamel and Mashour, *Cairo Times*).

Another qualification: In Egypt's religious atmosphere, everyone agrees that personal freedom should stop short of "debauchery." It would be hard to find someone defending alcohol or drug use, homosexuality or promiscuous sex, and no one likes to identify themselves as a feminist. People expect their politicians to believe in God and go to prayers. This too should be familiar from the American context.

Democracy and Justice. We have established that Egyptians very much want political freedom and democracy, but to clarify, we'd really have to say that neither of these is the most important political value in Islamic societies. Justice is the pre-eminent value. A just government impartially applies the rule of law, without favoritism, bribery, or nepotism. A just government is not corrupt. Justice, for Muslims, is closely associated with equality, not only with legal equality, but economic equality. When Egyptians look at their society, they see the children of high government officials enriching themselves through government contracts, while the government does nothing to help the poor. And this state of affairs seems to them to violate the essential spirit of Islam.

The Value of Community in Egyptian Culture

As you can see, much of Egypt's culture is religious culture, derived from the sacred values and norms of Islam. But there are other important values in Egypt, values like community, generosity, and honor, which are traditionally Egyptian but are not specifically religious.

In every situation, Egyptians would rather be with others than alone. It is easy for them to establish a sense of community within a crowd of strangers. Sociologist Andrea Rugh describes how affluent Egyptians pitch their umbrellas close to one another on the beach, rather than seeking privacy. Expensive movie theaters and cheap buses fill up in the same way: People sit next to others already seated, rather than spreading out. Visiting is a major leisure-time activity in Egypt. Friends and relatives spend a great deal of time just sitting around and talking and visits last for hours. Even in illness, Egyptians prefer company. A man who has a headache, or a fever, will be surrounded by a stream of friends and relatives who bring him soda, food, aspirin, and advice. Hospitals are crowded with relatives and friends visiting patients. Egyptians also will make considerable sacrifices to live out their lives in the company of their families. Andrea Rugh describes a young city woman who refused a good job as a live-in companion to a wealthy widow. Despite the fact that her family was so poor they could hardly feed her, she regarded this well-paid job with horror, because she would have to sleep in a room alone, apart from her family (Rugh, 1984, pp. 36–38). A sly joke about the unsophisticated Saidis of southern Egypt reveals not only how Egyptians from the big cities of Cairo and Alexandria feel about Saidis, but also the comfort that all Egyptians take in the presence of their countrymen:

> *An Alexandrian, a Cairene, and a Saidi are stranded in the desert with no transportation and no water. Suddenly a genie appears and offers each of them one wish. The young man from Alexandria wishes that he was back on that city's beautiful beach—and in a flash he is gone. The Cairene wishes to be returned to the Hussein Mosque in Cairo—and in an*

> instant he too vanishes. The genie then approaches the Saidi and asks, "what is your
> wish?" "I'm so lonely," cries the Saidi, "can't you bring my friends back?" (Rodenbeck,
> p. 100)

In the countryside, people live in a village, not spread out in farmsteads in the fields. Houses are tightly clustered, along narrow alleys, filled with children, water buffalo, and the bustle of everyday life. A village teacher asks children to find what's missing in a chalked outline of a peasant home, and their immediate reply is "the neighbors" (Fakhouri, pp. 17–21). According to a familiar Arabic saying, "the most important thing about a house is its neighbors" (Fluehr-Lobban, p. 58).

The Importance of Personal Ties

In Egypt, when people have problems they must solve, they rely on personal contacts. To find an apartment, a job, or a spouse, people turn first to their relatives, then to neighbors and friends. Friendship in Egypt is an active, intense relationship that takes a lot of time and energy. Friends constantly do favors for each other. In fact, you don't really have to even ask for a favor. If you express a wish—"I just feel like getting out of the city today"—a friend will feel obliged to help make it happen for you. A friendship implies a commitment, even if you have long been out of touch. Andrea Rugh describes a middle-aged, middle-class Egyptian woman in difficult economic circumstances who is sure that the president's wife will help her. After all, they went to college together, 30 years before (Wilson, p. 149; Rugh, 1984, p. 40)! A network of favors given and received: a car borrowed, the children watched, money loaned, binds individuals tightly together.

In a similar preference for the personal and informal over the formal and institutional, Egyptians may make great efforts to turn large groups into close-knit units. Men who own businesses, for example, will organize their enterprises around family connections even when this limits their expansion or economic flexibility. Egyptian businessmen like to think of themselves as "fathers" to their employees and often expect their employees to behave like children might: running employers' little personal errands and seeking their boss's advice on personal matters (Rugh, 1984, p. 43).

The Value of Generosity in Egyptian Culture

Linked to Egyptians' broad sense of community is the value they place on generosity and hospitality. Anthropologist Carolyn Fluehr-Lobban traces Egyptian generosity to the influence of Arab culture, now absorbed into Islam. She describes the ancient nomadic desert life of the Arabs, when everyone might someday be a traveler, dependent on strangers for shelter, life-saving water, and food. Today, Fluehr-Lobban says, "generosity . . . is a core value in Arab society the importance of which has not diminished over the centuries or been fundamentally transformed by urban life and empire, by class division and social stratification." A generous person is a moral person, and everyone looks for generosity in friends, marriage partners, and politicians (p. 46). Thus, in Egypt today, shopkeepers offer their customers tea and a pleasant chat, motorists stop to offer help to a driver with a flat tire, bureaucrats offer coffee when you visit their office, and relatives and friends visit each other often, sitting down to tables piled with food and drink, as high as family finances afford. Visitors are urged to stay longer, eat more, and have another cup of tea.

Fluehr-Lobban also explains that in Egypt "sharing is so deeply engrained that to notice its expression is an oddity." It would be very impolite to refuse the offered cup of tea, and impolite as well to thank your host for it. Generosity is **normative:** It is expected and you don't have to thank people for their generosity. People in Egypt don't say thank-you to the store clerk or the taxi driver or the waiter. On the other hand, if someone is generous to you, it would be polite to reciprocate at some later time. You should invite your host to your home, and you may bring fruit or candy to the family of the person who fixed your flat tire (p. 46).

Egyptians prize a quality of lightheartedness they call *dem-khefeef.* Those who have it ease the burdens everyone bears by gently laughing and joking, making light of their troubles, and poking fun at their own feelings. Egyptians love to tell jokes and they treasure their comic movie actors who bring the whole country together in laughing acknowledgment of their absurd problems (Fernea, 1970, p. 279).

The Value of Honor

Egyptians will tell you that their family's honor is utterly precious to them. Individuals are judged by the reputations of their families and when Egyptians think about their own personal honor, they are thinking about how their actions will reflect upon their families. Carolyn Fluehr-Lobban defines honor as "the pride and dignity that a family possesses due to its longstanding good reputation in the community for producing upright men and women who behave themselves well, marry well, raise proper children, and above all adhere to the principles and practices of the religion of Islam" (p. 52). In everyday life, people try to avoid shameful behavior so they won't dishonor themselves and their families. Even future generations of their family would have to live with the dishonor. Use of foul language is shameful, so is losing one's temper, or gossiping in a way that harms others; failing to help a relative or neighbor when one could really do so is shameful, as is failing in one's obligation to support family members (Fluehr-Lobban, p. 53).

We will have to return to a discussion of honor later, when we talk about gender roles, because honor is closely linked to sexual propriety. Right now, though, let's investigate how honor, community reputation, and religion are involved in social control in Egypt.

DEVIANCE AND SOCIAL CONTROL

In the previous section, you learned a lot about Egyptian values and norms. Obviously, in Egypt, as in every other society, it makes sense to ask, do people actually follow the norms of their society? What forces in their society produce conformity or deviance? We are worried that your images of social control in the Muslim world have been shaped by news coverage of the Taliban in Afghanistan. Are you picturing religious police beating women who show a bit of wrist or ankle? Are you picturing beheadings or the stoning of adulterers? The first thing you need to know is that these extreme forms of social control are not common in the Islamic world and they do not exist in Egypt.

Formal and Informal Controls

Egypt is really interesting because it has high rates of social conformity without very repressive social controls, at least in terms of formal mechanisms of social control. Sociologists distinguish between two kinds of social controls: **formal controls** and **informal controls. Formal controls** are used by institutions: governments, the police, the courts, or even schools, churches, and businesses. Typically, formal controls are **institutionalized.** They are codified in rules and procedures, and the penalties or sanctions for deviance are formalized too. For example, the government of the state of Minnesota says that if convicted of vehicular assault, you can be sentenced to a certain number of years in jail, or your college will put you on probation if you accumulate a certain number of Ds, Fs, and Ws. **Informal controls** are different. They take place in different social contexts, and they consist of different sorts of penalties. The members of small groups bring informal sanctions to bear on each other. The sanctions are not codified and they are typically interpersonal in nature, involving the way others see and respond to you. So, for example, if you steal your friend's girlfriend or boyfriend, the other members of your social circle will—well, what? Shun you? Stop including you in the group? Regard you as dishonorable? Gossip about you to others? These are all informal sanctions. Which do you think are more effective in getting people to conform—formal or informal sanctions? Would you be more likely to refuse to drink alcohol because your government says you are too young or because your friends disapprove of drinking?

Egypt's Government and Formal Sanctions

The Hosni Mubarak regime is harshly repressive of certain sorts of deviant behavior, but rather lax about most others. The government is dedicated to rooting out political dissent of any kind, and it is particularly forceful in suppressing any criticism of President Mubarak and his family. This policy goes back about ten years to the early 1990s, when Mubarak abruptly set out to destroy Islamist organizations like al-Gama'a al-Islamiyya and Islamic Jihad, which had grown strong during twenty years of government tolerance. Gama'a and Jihad, and subgroups related to these organizations, developed thriving followings in poor urban squatter neighborhoods and rural towns. They violently enforced their interpretation of *Sharia,* trashing liquor stores, burning churches, attacking Coptic Christians and tourists. The government responded by ruthlessly hunting down members of Gama'a and Jihad and even members of the Muslim Brotherhood, an illegal, but much more moderate Islamist organization. Every terrorist attack was followed by immediate arrests, summary convictions, and executions. The government shut down mosques where radicals preached, arrested preachers, jailed and tortured Islamists, invaded activist neighborhoods, and threatened or arrested Islamists' relatives. Then, for good measure, it did the same to secular organizations that merely worked for democracy. Egypt's prisons are full of political prisoners, many held without trial. Those who are tried and acquitted are released and then often immediately rearrested on another charge. Under emergency laws, militants are tried by military courts where sentences cannot be appealed. Sixty-seven militants have been executed in the decade-long crackdown. The repression continues today. Every few months the government announces arrests of another few dozen militants in what it calls "pre-emptive operations" (Ajami, pp. 202–203; Hasan, pp. 60–63; *The New York Times,* Sept. 25, 2002; Jun. 14, 2002; Dec. 12, 2003; Jan. 3, 2003; Mar. 26, 2004; May 13, 2004).

But when it comes to nonpolitical deviance, the Egyptian government and criminal justice system are relatively lax. You could say that Egypt is an authoritarian state, but not a police state. There is quite a lot of personal freedom. It is easy to buy alcohol. You can see belly dancers. In most cases, the government is uninterested in what people do in their private lives and what they say. There is no official policy on whether women must or must not be veiled. Moreover, while tourist sites and tourist hotels are conspicuously surrounded by armed police, poor Cairo settlements and rural towns have little police presence, except when raids on Islamists take place.

Corruption

Very significantly, Egypt's government does nothing to control corruption, bribery, and favoritism, which Egyptians consider the most troubling form of deviance in their society. They call corruption *kossa* ("zucchini") probably because wealth from corruption grows suspiciously fast. Corruption of those at the top is particularly resented. Egyptians complain about the "Gang of Sons," the children of a number of important officials in the government, including the sons of President Mubarak, who are believed to collect bribes and use their fathers' positions for business advantage (Weaver, 1995, p. 56). They are also angered by bureaucrats who give business licenses, property deeds, or visas to those who can afford to give the biggest bribes, and by officials who give no-bid contracts to their relatives and friends.

> *Egyptians find this joke very funny; it rings true to them. "U.S. President George W. Bush visits Cairo and gets to talking with the waiter who serves him in his hotel there. The waiter pours out his heart and tells Bush about his sick wife and his son who can't afford to marry. President Bush is very moved and tells the waiter he will pray for him. He puts his arm around him and gives him a nickname. When he gets back to Washington, Bush calls President Mubarak and tells him, 'I've sent you $5,000. Please give it to Ibrahim Sayed, who works in the Hilton Hotel in Cairo. Mubarak calls in an aide. 'Here's $2,500 from George W. Bush. Find Ibrahim Sayed at the Hilton and give it to him. The aide calls his assistant. 'Go to the Hilton and find Ibrahim Sayed and give him this $1,000 from President Bush.' The assistant calls his assistant. 'This $500 is from George Bush. Find Ibrahim Sayed and give it to him.' The assistant calls his secretary. 'I want you to find Ibrahim Sayed and tell him George Bush prayed for him and God will provide.' "*

Working your connections to get rich is called *wasta,* and it reminds Egyptians of the old proverb, "How great is the luck of one whose uncle is chairman" (Murphy, pp. 18–19). But corruption is not restricted to the rich. Egyptians also see consumer fraud and scams all around them in everyday life. Construction companies charge for the best materials, buy the worst, and pocket the difference. A parking lot in downtown Cairo parks your car and asks when you will return, then rents your car out as a taxi in the interim.

Homosexuality

Until recently, one sign of permissiveness in Cairo was the existence of a substantial gay scene, underground in a sense, but hidden in plain sight. Men were never openly gay, in fact, most participants in the gay scene were married with children. But it was common knowledge that gay men gathered on certain nightclub boats on the Nile. Online, there were Web sites and chat rooms where gay men talked and arranged meetings.

Then, in 2001, the government began an all-out assault on homosexuals, raiding a nightclub called The Queen Boat (the name is said to refer to the wife of the former king, Farouk) and arresting fifty-two men on charges of "debauchery." (There is no law against homosexuality in Egypt or in *Sharia.*) That began a continuing crackdown on homosexuals in which the police even ran sting operations online, with officers who posed as gay men. Human Rights Watch said that seventeen people died in police custody in 2003 because of torture, used against gays and militants. Egyptians speculate that the government suddenly launched this operation in response to the growth of religiosity in Cairo. Mubarak wanted people to believe he cared about religious norms without, however, letting up in his attacks on Islamists. Homosexuals were simply an easy target (*The New York Times,* March 2, 2004; Kersaw, April 3, 2003, p. A3; Sherif, *Middle East Times,* March 12, 2004; Goldberg, p. 55).

Social Integration and Informal Social Controls

What is most significant, however, is that despite the government's mixed record in applying formal social controls, there is actually relatively little deviance in Egypt, other than corruption. Rates of violent crime are very low. In Cairo, 84 percent of residents say they feel safe walking in their neighborhoods after dark. Less than one percent report having been assaulted in the previous year. Rates of robbery are similarly low. There are few stories about crime in Egypt's newspapers, and those that do appear are funny human interest stories about bumbling thieves (United Nations, Surveys on Crime Trends, 1994; Del Frate, 1998). Why is Egypt such a safe place?

From a sociological point of view, the answer lies in strong informal social controls. Ordinary Egyptians belong to a variety of social groups, including the family, the clan, the neighborhood, and the village, that are very important in their lives. These groups exercise robust informal social controls. Groups discipline their members, and group members also monitor and restrain their own conduct in order to maintain their reputations—their honor—and the reputations of their groups. Let us now examine important social groups in Egyptian society, first examining social groups in rural Egypt and then turning to social groups in urban Egypt.

Social Groups and Social Controls in the Countryside

Today, half of all Egyptians live in rural areas. Roads, buses, radio and television, schools, and health clinics link villages to modern cities, and villagers themselves move to the city or abroad to find work; but villages remain a distinctive social environment. Think for a moment of the geography of Egypt: Life hugs the Nile. Green fields line its banks, interspersed with villages; but not far from the river, the barren sand begins. As a result, the countryside is crowded. People use as much of the good, irrigated land as possible for growing crops; so families never build houses in the midst of their farmland. They all live in houses clustered together in villages, along narrow, winding lanes. Villagers farm tiny plots of land, scattered in different locations. When men and women leave the village to work in their fields, relatives and neighbors are never very far away. Poor families may have just a couple of rooms, built around a courtyard; rich families occupy a walled compound, with offices, storerooms, kitchen, and living quarters. In Egypt's heat, where rain may not fall for years at a time, much of daily life takes place out of doors in the courtyards where women prepare food and bake in outdoor ovens, on the rooftops, in the streets, and in the village center, where the mosque, the market, the coffeehouse, and the school are located (Fakhouri, pp. 119–123; Early, pp. 41–48; Rugh, 1984, pp. 1–4).

Egyptian peasants or *fellahin,* as they are called in Arabic, must cooperate with each other in order to prosper. Without rain, agriculture is entirely dependent on irrigation from the Nile's water. A village's land may be miles from the river and channels must be dug and maintained to sustain the flow of water to each field. *Fellahin* must work together to keep the irrigation system working and share the water. No single farmer and no single family could do it alone.

Male Networks in the Countryside: The Clan. In villages related extended families are linked together in **clans,** theoretically descended from a long-ago common male ancestor. The men of a clan, especially the elders, usually form a tight-knit social group. They are brothers, cousins, brothers-in-law, neighbors, and lifelong friends, who have played and gone to school together as children. They have spent their lives helping each other in the fields, sitting together in the coffeehouse, attending the same weddings and funerals. In practical terms, clans are political alliances of men. Village politics often consists of the maneuverings of rival clans (Fakhouri, pp. 56–57).

Female Networks in the Countryside. Women too live in a world filled with relatives. One of the greatest sources of satisfaction that countrywomen have is the community of women who share an extended household. These women share **primary** ties, bonds that are close, personal, and intimate (Sadat, pp. 181–190). Sisters-in-law and the unmarried daughters of their household work together to prepare food, store crops, make clothing, and do the housekeeping. Village festivals, weddings, and funerals bring together large groups of women. After a funeral, a bereaved woman's home fills with her female relatives and neighbors. Day after day they bring cooked dishes and sit together crying and wailing and praising and telling stories about the deceased individual. Women visit each other on ordinary days too, and sit chatting over coffee and snacks, surrounded by their children. They exchange news of the village, analyze other people's problems and personalities, and give each other advice. The importance of the community of women in Egyptian life is marked by the many jokes men tell about the power of gossiping women.

The Importance of the Family

Families are central to understanding why Egypt is a relatively orderly society. They are also key to understanding the day-to-day life of most Egyptians. In many western societies, whom you spend time with and whom you marry are individual decisions. Contemporary Americans and Europeans hold their families dear, but these families must often adapt to choices individual members make. A person may choose to marry someone of a different religion than their relatives or a different ethnic background. An individual may choose to move far away from his or her family. Individual Egyptians, in contrast, must adapt to the values and needs of their families. Families are demanding and they care deeply about the behavior of family members.

The Extended Family. The basic group of rural life is the **extended family,** an economic unit of production and consumption. Such a family might include an older married couple, their two adult sons and their wives and children, and perhaps, if one of those children is old enough, a grandson and his wife and children. The constituent **nuclear families** may all live in one building or in separate houses. Either way, they operate as a single household. Extended family members carry out household tasks, work in the fields, and take care of the very young and the very old. When a father with married sons dies, the extended household formed by his sons' families dissolves. Each son then creates his own extended family including his sons, their wives and children (Fakhouri, pp. 55–63).

Marriage and Divorce

Marriage and divorce are family matters, not individual concerns, in rural Egypt, and in urban Egypt too for that matter. Everyone is expected to marry and in most cases the choice of a spouse is a family decision. Since a newly married couple becomes part of the husband's family, the bride and her relatives must be acceptable to the groom's whole family, and especially to his mother, who is often the one who actually searches for and selects the bride. The bride's family, if they are wise, must concern themselves not only with the groom, but with the whole extended family with whom their daughter will live. Consequently, village marriages are a matter of careful negotiation between families.

The Marriage Contract. Arranging a marriage is a complex process, culminating in the signing of a marriage contract. Although people have a religious obligation to marry, marriage itself is a contract between two families, almost like a corporate merger. It is not a religious sacrament. The contract is a detailed document that includes an agreement about what the groom and his family will give to the couple's new household—carpeting, furniture, kitchen equipment—and what sum of money they will give the bride. This money becomes the bride's own property. The bride may require that the contract include a promise by her husband never to take any additional wives, or to permit her to work. While **polygyny** (the practice of a man marrying more than one wife) is legal in Egypt, as in most Islamic societies, it is actually quite rare. Definitive data are hard to find, but experts estimate that throughout the Middle East only 3 to 4 percent of women are wives in polygynous marriages (Omran and Roudi, p. 31). Few men can afford polygyny and few would attempt it against a wife's objections, so it is most common when a first marriage has produced no children.

The six months or a year between the signing of the marriage contract and the wedding is the closest Egyptians come to dating. Then the young man may visit his fiancée's house and get to know his future wife—in the company of her relatives— or the young couple may actually be permitted to go out together.

Weddings are joyous events in Egypt. They are one of the few occasions when young men and women can socialize together, perhaps even flirt with each other or see each other dance, albeit under the careful observation of their parents and relatives. Traditionally, weddings lasted for as long as a week of music, dancing, and feasting, culminating in a public procession of the groom and his friends and family to the house of the bride, where they picked up the bride and her entourage and accompanied her to the groom's house, to the music of a hired band (Fluehr-Lobban, pp. 70–71; Fakhouri, pp. 63–70).

Divorce. Divorce is permitted in Egypt, but divorce rates are rather low. For every 100,000 people, there are 117 divorces yearly in Egypt. (Compare this to the United States, where there are 419 divorces yearly for every 100,000 people.) (See Table 2.1, pp. 91.) According to Islamic law, an Egyptian man may divorce his wife easily, just by stating three times "I divorce thee." It is not that easy in reality; he must file legal papers and relatives often try to arrange a reconciliation. Women are now legally permitted to divorce their husbands and they needn't cite any grounds for divorce, although they do lose any claim to their dowry. But men regard being divorced by their wives as so humiliating that they will go to any lengths to avoid it, including suing for divorce themselves, thereby forfeiting the dowry. However, a woman's family may pressure her to stay with her husband because if she is divorced they will be responsible for supporting her. Also, in cases of divorce, the woman may keep her daughters until they are 10 years old and her sons until they are 8, but after that the father may legally take over their custody. These problems of course discourage women from trying to divorce. Another interesting Egyptian custom has helped to hold down divorce rates. The marriage contract specifies the sum of money the groom must give the bride at marriage. The sum has grown to be very large, and it is usually divided into two parts: the "prompt" and the "deferred." The "deferred" part must be paid only at the time of a divorce, so it is kind of an insurance policy against divorce (Fluehr-Lobban, pp. 64, 69, 116–117, 124–130; Wilson, pp. 132–134).

Cousin Marriage. There is one more important custom in Egypt that makes kin relationships even richer and more complex. That custom is cousin marriage. Both rural and urban Egyptians agree that the ideal marriage partner for a man is a paternal first cousin—a daughter of his father's brother. A more distant cousin on his father's side would also be preferable to a nonrelative. Marrying someone who is not kin is called "stranger marriage" (Fluehr-Lobban, pp. 65–67). The ideal cousin marriage is not often attainable in practice; only one marriage in five is actually between first cousins. But as recently as 1995, more than 40 percent of Egyptian women married men who were relatives of some kind (Fakhouri, pp. 63, 64; Kishor, pp. 52–56). Inheritance in Egypt is patrilineal, that is, the family name and most of the land are inherited through the male line. When cousins marry, the dowry paid by the husband also stays in the family, as does any property the wife inherits. Also, since the families know and trust each other, it is also easier to negotiate the marriage, and the bride's family can have confidence she will be well treated by her in-laws, who are her own kin.

In fact, if two brothers marry their children to each other, the young bride may be able to remain in the same household as her mother. This is because rural marriages are **patrilocal,** that is, once married a bride moves to her husband's home and joins the household there, which includes his parents, his brothers, and their wives and children.

Social Controls in the Village

In the countryside, men and women must act in ways that do not dishonor themselves or their families. A young woman is expected first of all to be chaste, to "save herself" for marriage. Chastity means avoiding any interaction with men that might spoil her reputation, or imply that her male relatives are too weak or careless to protect her. A young woman who meets alone with an admirer, or a married woman seen alone with a man not her husband, commits a terrible violation of Egyptian **mores.** She would be suspected of forbidden sexual activity. Her husband or brothers or father might well lock her inside the house, or even beat her. If the family agrees that adultery has taken place, custom allows her husband to kill her, to "wash away the shame with blood" and restore the family's honor. Such murders, considered "crimes of honor," are punished with prison terms of only one to three years, rather than the usual death penalty. In 1995, Egypt last reported relevant statistics, and 52 murders were reported as honor killings out of a total of 819 for the whole country (Fluehr-Loban, p. 55; Daniszewski, p. A9; Jehl, June 20, 1999, p. 8).

While Egyptian men certainly enjoy wider freedoms than women, they too must constantly protect their honor and the honor of their families and clans. To avoid shame, men must protect their female relatives—their mothers, sisters, wives and daughters—accompanying them in public and watching to make sure that no man compromises their reputations. The obligation to protect women extends to supporting them. A husband must feed, clothe, and shelter his wife and children and any other female relative dependent on him—his old aunt, his widowed sister, his deceased father's second wife.

A man's obligations go beyond avoiding shame. Every man must also defend his family against disrespect and insult. A man whose neighbor shouts insults at him in a drunken quarrel would be dishonored. So too would a man whose wife, gossip suggests, flirts with others. If one man steals crops from another man's field, it is an insult to the victim and his whole clan. Even an accidental death might still be seen as an assault on the honor of the victim's family.

In the traditional setting of a rural village, with strong family and clan ties, all these slights to honor must be erased; a man cannot ignore an insult or injury, even though Islam condemns revenge. If he does not respond to insult, a man will be seen as weak and unmanly. His family too will be obliged to back him or revenge him, and they may be drawn into disastrous and criminal violence. You might say that this is one reason why drinking alcohol and gossiping are both so much condemned in Islamic culture: They pave the way to conflict, insult, and destructive revenge.

Ibrahim and Ismail's Story: The Quarrel

Ibrahim and Ismail had quarreled for years over a piece of land that Ismail had inherited, but no one in El Mina thought this would lead to bloodshed. Both men were hot-tempered, but not foolish. Neither of them wanted to provoke a feud that might leave their sons and nephews dead. On a hot July day though the men parted after unusually bitter words. Driving off in his truck, shouting at Ismail, Ibrahim accidentally struck his rival's 11-year-old niece. The girl lapsed into a deep coma and died. Tension soared as everyone feared that Ismail and his brothers would strike at Ibrahim's family.

When the girl died, Ibrahim and his brothers left El Mina for their mother's village. There, his grandfather urged Ibrahim to find a way to end the dispute. Everyone talked about a feud 30 years earlier that had taken many lives.

Three days later, Ismail was approached by a man respected for his role in ending disputes. He asked Ismail's family to accept a traditional court which would set conditions for a peaceful resolution. Ismail and his kin agreed and all concerned met at the home of a man who was on good terms with both families. After long discussion, all agreed that while the girl's death had been an accident, her family should receive some compensation. They also agreed to resolve the dishonorable squabble that indirectly caused the accident. Ibrahim's family agreed to pay the substantial sum of 500 dollars to the girl's family and to give up their claims to the disputed land. In return Ismail's family agreed not to seek blood vengeance. Tension gradually eased and Ibrahim was relieved that he and his family could go about their lives without fear of sudden and deadly assault.

Given the importance of defending family honor, it is fortunate that Egyptian tradition provides peaceful ways of resolving affronts to honor. Tradition gives a victim's family only three days for violent revenge, and it permits the wrongdoer and his relatives to protect themselves by fleeing to their mother's kin. The institution of the traditional court allows older, often more powerful relatives to mediate a settlement (Fakhouri, pp. 109–114; Ghosh, pp. 69–70, 135–137). It is a testament to the effectiveness of these customs that while norms call for men to defend their honor, the murder rate in Egypt is in fact very low.

Social Groups and Social Controls in the City

Egyptians have been city dwellers for thousands of years, so urban life is very much a part of Egyptian culture. In the past century, Egypt's urban population has expanded rapidly. Migrants from the countryside have poured into Cairo, Alexandria, and other cities, so that today nearly half of all Egyptians live in urban areas. Cairo is an exceptionally crowded city, it packs in almost 100,000 people per square mile. (See Table 4.1.) Though migrants keep up ties with their villages for many decades, city-dwellers develop a rich social life of their own. Many former peasants who came to Cairo in past decades live in densely settled and colorful old downtown districts like Bulaq, which are well known in Egyptian literature and folklore.

TABLE 4.1 Urban Concentration 2005

One out of every four Egyptians lives in Cairo, the country's largest city, but only one German in 20 lives in Berlin, the largest city in Germany. One of every two Egyptians who lives in a city, lives in Cairo.

	Largest City in the Country	Population of Largest City	Percent of Urban Population Living in Largest City	Percent of Total Population Living in Largest City
Egypt	Cairo	15,250,000	48	23
Japan	Tokyo	34,000,000	40	27
Mexico	Mexico City	22,350,000	28	22
Namibia	Windhoek	190,000	28	9
United States	New York	21,800,000	9	7
Germany	Berlin	4,200,000	6	5

Sources: Thomas Brinkhoff, "The Principal Agglomerations of the World," http://www.citypopulation.de/World .html

WORLD BANK, World Development Indicators, 2004, http://devdata.worldbank.org/data-query/

FOOD AND AGRICULTURE ORGANIZATION OF THE UNITED NATIONS, "FAO Statistical Databases," 2004, http://apps.fao.org/faostat/

There, in crowded poor neighborhoods old four- and five-story apartment buildings face each other across unpaved, rutted alleys, many no more than six feet wide. Lines of laundry hang criss-cross overhead, and in front of shops racks of merchandise encroach on the street. Coffeehouses place benches and tables out in front of the café. Peddlers sell clothing, sweets, vegetables, and prepared foods like beans in various sauces. Storefront workshops produce furniture, shoes, jewelry, and even industrial machinery, spilling some of their operations out into the alleys. Cars can pass through these crowded streets only with great difficulty; goats, sheep, and buffalos stand in muddy corners chewing grain, and donkey carts clog the intersections.

Recent migrants to the city often cannot afford to live in the old city neighborhoods. They live in squatter settlements, like Cairo's Imbaba and Zawya on the outskirts of the city, in tiny houses constructed of packing crates, tin sheets, pallets, or, at best, concrete blocks. Many have settled in Cairo's large graveyards, making their homes in tombs and memorial buildings. Squatter neighborhoods lack running water, electricity or sewers, mail delivery, police patrols, fire stations, and public schools. In some neighborhoods, people work together to install sewer pipes, which run to cesspools in the street.

In Cairo, as in Egypt's villages, people want to have close ties with their extended families, to live with them in the same buildings or at least in the same neighborhood. But the housing shortage makes this difficult. As adult children marry, they may be unable to find apartments near their parents, and so the extended family may be scattered, with married siblings living in different neighborhoods, perhaps far from their parents. Especially in poor neighborhoods though, people act like their neighborhood is a village and their neighbors are relatives. Residents emphasize their closeness, even to strangers, by addressing each other by kin terms. A younger woman calls an older, unrelated man, "uncle." Women the same age call each other

As millions of Egyptians pour into already crowded cities, much of life is lived in the street rather than in the home. A crowded street in Luxor is typical of poorer neighborhoods in many Egyptian cities. Shopping for food, a daily activity for poor Egyptians is often done by men. Although some women are present, men dominate this streetscape. We see that public space in Egypt is typically male space.

"sister." Egypt is a "touch" society (but only in same-gender interaction). Men greet their friends and relatives by kissing first on one cheek, then the other. Men may hold hands as they walk, and women walk down the streets together arm in arm. Egyptians of the same gender are comfortable standing quite close to each other when they talk, and they smile a lot and look intensely into each other's eyes.

In the city, the clan is no longer the center of men's social life. Instead, men look to social groups called *shilla*. These are small groups bound by friendship or family ties—friends from the village or from school, a group of brothers and their friends, and some of their friends' brothers. Often the members of a *shilla* have a regular table in the coffeehouse or a regular weekly get-together, and they are also mutual-aid networks. A group member who has prospered and moved high in the government bureaucracy will expect to help his friends and relatives.

A Cairo neighborhood is full of people: Shopkeepers stand in their doorways; men sit in coffee shops and at tables in the street. Women look out of their windows and stand on the rooftops to talk to friends in adjoining buildings. Many people live in small apartments or houses at street level. You can look in the windows and watch their televisions and they can watch the street. Egyptians don't hesitate to intervene with neighbors or even strangers if there is a problem. An argument on the street between a vendor and a customer or between two young men brings all the merchants out of their stores and gathers a crowd of passersby. Those nearby willingly jump in and take sides or calm down the antagonists. In a way, the propensity of Egyptians to get involved permits people to dramatize disagreements. Antagonists shout, pound on tables, make threatening gestures, and wave their arms. People rely on others, even strangers, to stop their conflict before it escalates too far (Wilson, pp. 108–109).

In the narrow, crowded streets of Cairo it is not unusual for a car to hit a pedestrian. Then the driver of the car will leap out and begin bewailing the accident and beseeching God's help. He will probably load the victim into the car to drive off to the hospital. The driver may act out of genuine contrition; we'll never know; because as soon as they hear a thump, the crowd gathers and buzzes with anger at the careless driver. The watching crowd also doesn't hesitate to chase down a thief, or even a murderer, and they will hold the suspect for the police. A man who is angry at a woman will sometimes write her name and telephone number on a banknote (like a dollar bill). Strangers who handle the bill will phone her and call her names (Al Kammar, *Middle East Times*).

Islam and Social Controls

Egypt today is in a ferment of moral discussion. Egyptians have always understood their values and norms in terms of Islam, but now, with a religious revival in full swing, talk about Islam is ubiquitous. Many norms of behavior are being redefined, and there is a continual debate about what the appropriate Islamic norms are in a given situation. People struggle to become better Muslims, and this struggle plays a very powerful role in social control.

Geneive Abdo describes visiting a barbershop where a local, unofficial *sheik* (one who has no special religious education, but who is respected for his piety) is explaining to the customers why women should be veiled. She visits the *dars,* or religious lesson of a sheik who answers questions from a crowd of several hundred, "ranging from whether using facial cream was against Islam to whether children were allowed to take revenge against a father who killed their mother." When one young man confesses that he yelled at his wife until she cried, the sheik berates him: "This is an example of how men can be jerks" (Abdo, pp. 31–32).

People go to hear fashionable or famous preachers, or watch them on TV. They buy casette tapes of sermons. Women meet in Quran study groups and search out passages about women and men. In an atmosphere of intensified piety, people are actively trying to decide what their religion requires of them and to live by it. Abdo reports taking many taxis in Cairo and discovering a real difference between taxi drivers who play pop music tapes and drivers who play Quran recitations: "Those who played Egyptian pop music, attached photographs of bikini-clad women to their dashboards, contorted their necks to stare at my legs in the back seat . . . (but) the men of religion were interested only in their driving." Also, the religious drivers asked a "reasonable fare" and didn't haggle over money (Abdo, p. 4).

SOCIAL INEQUALITY IN EGYPT

It is really remarkable that there is so little deviance in Egyptian society, because there is no shortage of frustration and strain. It has to be a tribute to the effectiveness both of government repression and of informal social controls in small groups.

Egyptians live in a society deeply divided by economic inequalities, with shrinking opportunities and increasing competition. Many people feel worn out with struggle.

Class Inequality

Sociologists use the term **class inequality** in discussing several related matters. They use it to talk about inequalities in the distribution of economic resources like income and wealth and to ask how broadly or narrowly these resources are spread through the society. They also use it to discuss **social classes,** groups of people whose economic resources and lifestyles are similar, and which may form real, self-identified social groups. Finally, sociologists use the term *class inequality* in discussing **social mobility,** the extent to which people in different social classes have a chance to move up or down in the social stratification system.

The class stratification system in Egypt is quite distinctive. It bears the imprint of Egypt's history as a socialist society, when the government took control of land and capital and strove to distribute resources more equally. It also shows the effects of Egypt's recent "opening" to capitalism and global business. Today, most Egyptians are quite poor. Egypt's yearly Gross National Product averages only U.S. $1,354 per person, which is equivalent in purchasing power to $3,810 per person in the United States. About one-fifth of all Egyptians live on less than what $2.00 a day per person could buy in the United States (United Nations, *Human Development Report,* 2004; El-laithy et al., pp. 21–22). At the very top of the stratification hierarchy there is a very small class of very wealthy Egyptians—probably no more than 1 percent of the population. A good way to understand Egyptian class inequality is to say that the top and the bottom of the Egyptian hierarchy are very far apart, but most people cluster near the bottom. As a result, if you examine distribution of income by quintiles (see Table 1.5, p. 51), you will find that Egypt has a relatively equal distribution of incomes—much more equal than Mexico, for example. In 1999, the most recent year for which income distribution data is available, the richest 20 percent of all Egyptians received 5 times as much total income as the poorest 20 percent. (The poorest 20 percent of Egyptians received 8.6 percent of all income and the richest 20 percent received 43.6 percent.) Data on earnings by occupation reveal a similar level of inequality: Skilled workers earn 6 times as much as unskilled workers, and supervisory and professional employees earn 12 times more than laborers (World Bank, *World Development Indicators,* 2004).

Economic Resources and Social Class

For any society, knowing about income and wealth distribution gives us only half the picture of class inequality. We also want to know who these people are: Who are the Egyptians in the top income fifth? Who are the poorest Egyptians? Where do they live and what is the source of their earnings? Egypt is making a transition out of its socialist experiment. That means it is official government policy to encourage private enterprise, but, so far, only one-third of Egyptian workers are employed in the private sector—in industry or manufacturing, retail sales or services. People with connections to the private sector operate in a different world than do people in public sector jobs. They earn much more money. This discrepancy in pay is one of many sources of frustration and anger for Egyptians (Wickham, pp. 61–62).

One-third of all workers are government employees, working either in the government bureaucracy, the army, in the civil service (as postal clerks, teachers, bus drivers, mail carriers, etc.), or in government-owned companies like the Helwan Steelworks, the state-owned oil industry, or the Suez Canal Company. (*The Economist,* March 20, 1998, p. 4; The American University in Cairo, Social Research Center, 2001). A very large number of Egyptians can get no regular employment at all. They make their way as best they can in the **informal sector** or else they migrate abroad to find work. Because relatively few people own or work for private businesses, "ownership of the means of production," in Karl Marx's sense, isn't the most important source of income or class position in Egyptian society. Much more important is a person's **power** or access to government-controlled resources. In Egypt, unequal access to government power results in unequal rewards. People who can get jobs as government employees (as skilled factory workers, clerical workers, or professionals) enjoy an enviable job security, even though their pay is usually low. They are likely to treat their jobs as economic resources—a way to get medical insurance, or a way to find jobs, or contracts or connections, for relatives and friends. They may supplement their wages by accepting bribes for ordinary services or by skimming government funds that come through their hands. They don't hesitate to skip work when their family needs them, and they may even leave work early every day to go to a better-paid, but less secure second job.

Even for those who are not government employees, access to government resources is critical to prosperity. Owners of private businesses operate in an economy which is largely government owned. Banks are government owned, as is transportation, and many industrial supplies must be purchased from government factories. Import and export licenses must be granted by the government and paperwork must find its way through the vast government bureaucracy. Business owners can't use their property profitably without government permission.

The same is true in agriculture. Ninety-five percent of Egyptian farms are tiny—below five acres. Many of these landowners have the government to thank for their holdings, having received them in the post-1952 land redistribution. But new landowners didn't receive outright ownership of their land. They were required to join farm cooperatives which decide what crops should be grown, and supply seeds and fertilizer, storage, transportation, and marketing. Farmers are given credit by government banks and sell their crops to the government at prices the government sets. Egyptians look upon their government officials very differently than do the Japanese. In their eyes the bureaucracy certainly is not a rational, dispassionate agency committed to the public good. Ministries and bureaucrats operate in their own self-interest and they are open to influence and bribery. To get ahead, Egyptians need good connections, through family or *shilla* networks.

Social Classes in Rural Egypt

Many Egyptians are desperately poor, without enough resources to buy sufficient food for their families. According to the World Bank, 17 percent of Egyptians lived in poverty this severe in 2000. They had incomes equivalent to less than what $2.00

a day could buy in the United States. Poverty rates are especially high for the twenty-five million Egyptians who depend on agriculture for their livelihood. In southern Egypt, traditionally Egypt's poorest region, poverty rates even rose during the prosperous years between 1995 and 2000, from 29 to 34 percent. The poorest rural people are landless agricultural workers who must find work on other people's farms, seasonally or by the day (Food and Agriculture Organization of the United Nations, FAO Statistical Databases; El-laithy et al., pp. 11, 21–22). About one million Egyptians (occupying 62 percent of all farms) are sharecroppers, farming land for which they must pay rent in the form of a percentage of their crop. A smaller number of tenant farmers pay their rent in cash. The rest of the farmers own their own land, but almost all of them (95 percent) have very small farms—under five acres (Kurian, 1992, p. 568). They are better off than the landless, but are still poor and, as we have seen, dependent on the support and goodwill of the government. (See Table 2.4, p. 118.)

Mina's Story: Life on the Land

Mina is in her early forties. All her life she has lived in Bisat, a rural community at the edge of Egypt's western desert. Her family and her husband's family have farmed the land here as long as anyone can remember. At 15 she married her cousin Yussef, her father's brother's son. They farm less than a feddan *(an acre) of land. To make ends meet, Yussef has had to find employment for part of the year at a factory in a nearby town. Mina works in the fields at planting and harvest times, along with her sisters and sisters-in-law, her cousins and her aunts. The rest of the year they do their household chores in each other's company, baking bread, cooking, raising children, and going to the local market where Mina sometimes sells her cheese. Life is not so placid for Mina and Yussef's son Hassan, who is 23. There is no land in Bisat for him to farm, so last year he went to Cairo, hoping his cousin there could help him find work. "Here I am," he says, "sharing a miserable room and looking for work every day. Sometimes a builder hires me and I get 7 to 10 pounds (about $3) for a day's work. Some days I get nothing. Often I live on* fuul *(boiled beans) and nothing else for days. How will I ever be able to marry and raise a family?"*

Since such an overwhelming percentage of rural Egyptians are poor, it is easy to miss the rural elite. As a result of the land redistributions, there are relatively few large farms. Only 5 percent of farms are larger than five acres—but these farmers own 49 percent of the land! Egyptian soil is so fertile that five to twenty acres is a good size for a commercial farm and the owner will be quite prosperous. Such farmers usually live locally and farm their land with hired labor. They are part of a rural upper class, together with village professionals like the town lawyer and doctor and perhaps a successful storekeeper. They live in comfortable houses, with gardens and shaded courtyards, and employ servants. Villagers look up to them, and they are able to send their children to university in the city.

But while these landowners are the elite of village society, in national terms they are not part of the upper class. This distinction belongs only to the largest landowners—one-tenth of 1 percent of farmers who own more than 50 acres of land. These farmers don't live locally; they let their land out to tenant farmers, hire a manager, and live in the city. Many of them are actually foreign corporations from Saudi Arabia, Europe, or the United States that buy Egyptian land and employ landless laborers to produce crops like cotton and sugar for export.

Social Classes in Urban Egypt

Class differences are highly visible in Egyptian cities too, and city residents are aware of the hierarchy of classes and where they stand in it (MacLeod, p. 34). In Cairo people of different classes live in distinctively different neighborhoods. The poorest live on the dusty fringes of the city in squatter settlements. Those who are luckier or slightly better off live in old crowded downtown slums like Bulaq or in the concrete high-rise towers of government-built "satellite cities" on the outskirts of town. More prosperous people live in spacious neighborhoods with solid apartment houses and paved streets. The wealthy elite are found in downtown luxury apartment towers or in gracious, tree-lined enclaves of private homes. Different social classes spend their leisure in different places too: the poor in the coffeehouses and on the rooftops of their quarter; the middle class in their homes and in the downtown coffeehouses, restaurants, and movie theaters; the rich in country clubs and modern western hotels. Only the rich own cars; everyone else must ride the slow, sputtering buses, jammed with people, or else walk. People of different classes dress differently too. Lower-class men are likely to wear the traditional *gallibiyya,* a long, loose cotton shirt, and lower-class women wear a loose black cotton overgown with a black head scarf when they are out in public. Middle-class Egyptian men generally wear western-style clothing and middle-class women wear some form of western dress, often chosen for its conservatism and modesty. The upper classes are easily identified by their fashionable clothes, imported from Europe (MacLeod, p. 34).

The Lower Class. Many Egyptians who live in large cities saw their economic fortunes improve in the late 1990s. By 2000, only 9.2 percent of urban Egyptians were counted as poor (by Egypt's very low standard). More city dwellers found work in a construction boom, and more men were able to migrate and send money home to their families. But the economic boom of the late 90s benefited the rich more than the poor, and the gap between privilege and poverty grew. Today, the global economy has cooled and Egypt's finances have suffered. The construction boom has come to an end. A team of World Bank economists, led by Heba El-laithy of the University of Cairo, was pessimistic in 2003, suggesting that there is a strong possibility that many Egyptians who escaped poverty between 1995 and 2000 have slipped back into poverty again in this decade. In 2004, the Egyptian government resumed its earlier practice of distributing food vouchers to the poorest of the poor, a sign that poverty is worsening again (El-laithy et al., pp. 11, 17, 21; Mitchell, May 5, 2004).

Those most likely to be poor are people who live in households headed by someone who is illiterate. You should probably picture an illiterate family from a rural part of Upper Egypt, that moves to a city, perhaps Cairo, and then has a very hard time making a life for themselves. They probably live in a squatter settlement, on the desert outskirts of the city. Six million Cairo residents now live in these illegal communities, self-built quarters of shacks and tents without electricity, piped water, schools, or health clinics. Sewage runs in open ditches in the street. There is no safe drinking water and health problems are rampant. Some of these squatter settlements are built in the city's cemeteries, where poor people have moved into the stone tombs

TABLE 4.2 Illiterate Men and Women

Despite substantial reductions in illiteracy, almost half of Egyptians are illiterate and women are far more likely to be illiterate than men.

	Illiterate Women		Illiterate Men	
	1970	2002	1970	2002
Egypt	83	56	54	33
Namibia	49	17	36	16
Mexico	30	11	20	7

United Nations Human Development Report, 2004 http://hdr.undp.org/statistics/

in which rich Egyptians inter family members' remains (*The Economist,* March 20, 1998, p. 10; Bayat, pp. 1, 5; Rodenbeck, p. 84; Abu-Lughod, J., p. 218). (See Table 2.3, p. 117 and Table 4.2 above.)

Imagine that our poor urban family doesn't have many connections in the city. Without *wasta,* and without the ability to read and write, family members haven't a prayer of getting a secure government job. It is much more likely that they will work in the **informal sector,** which employs an estimated 26 percent of all Egyptian workers. Informal sector is often a polite way of saying that people scrounge for work. They work off-the-books, often as temporary laborers, or they work as unlicensed street vendors, outside the regular markets, outside the tax system, sometimes selling "pirate" goods—illegal copies of cassette tapes or foreign designer clothes. More than 200,000 street vendors flood Cairo's downtown. Thousands of people work the garbage dumps of big cities, picking through the trash for recyclable materials to sell. Others buy and sell old clothes from door to door, collect and sell used cigarette butts, shine shoes, hawk used newspapers on the street. Organized groups illegally control the streets of a quarter, where they park and protect cars for a fee. Some informal sector workers are not poor. They are educated, recent graduates unable to find work, or government workers who need second jobs. They make use of their literacy and bureaucratic know-how, by writing letters for illiterate Egyptians or taking sidewalk passport photos. Hundreds work as "facilitators," freelance guides to the bureaucracy, who for a fee will help people find their way through the bewildering corridors of Mugamma, Cairo's huge government building (Rodenbeck, p. 80; Hedges, June 7, 1994, p. A4; Bayat, p. 4).

Rasha's Story: Life in Mottakam

Rasha worked nimbly at the rug. Her family's rising income depended more and more on her ability to turn recycled rags into colorful rugs. For years, times had been very good for her father, Isak. Twenty years ago he left the desperately hard life of a tenant farmer near Asyut, in the south, to join his brothers in Mottakam, Cairo's Garbage City. Coptic Christians, like Isak and his family, cluster together in Mottakam. When Isak arrived in Mottakam, his brothers were making a meager living for themselves by raising pigs and goats on the garbage they collected from Cairo's wealthier neighborhoods. Then the Zabeleen, *as these Coptic communities are called, discovered that there was really money to be made in recycling. They took over the garbage dumps and garbage collection, selling plastic, aluminum and rags as scrap or for recycling. With seed money from international agencies the* Zabeleen *turned garbage into money. Rasha's family did well enough that their children were able to go to school through 6th grade. Rasha can read and write.*

Rasha's brother, Wali, is an accomplished businessman at 13 years of age. "Even when I was a child," he says, "I helped sort garbage. I made a few pounds by putting aside the shampoo bottles and reselling them to dealers. Now Proctor and Gamble pays us to shred their bottles into scrap so no one can reuse them. Then I thought, why should I spend all my time looking for these bottles when my friends can help me? I promised to buy any bottles my friends could find. Then I resell them to the Proctor and Gamble people. Now I am learning to read so that I can be sure I am not cheated when I sign a contract."

"Everything would be wonderful," Wali and Rasha say, "if it were not for our governor and his afrangi *(foreign) friends. They'll leave nothing for us." In an effort to clean up Cairo's legendary dirty streets, Cairo's governor has signed contracts with waste disposal companies from Italy. Block by block they are taking over the collection of the garbage that the* Zabeleen *depend on. "The government doesn't really care about us," complained Isak. "If we starve so that tourists can take pretty pictures, that's fine with them. I think they were surprised when we took to the streets to protest, but we won't give up our livelihoods without a struggle."*

The Middle Class. When thinking about Egyptian social class, you must remember the sociological concept of **relative poverty.** Many Egyptians consider themselves middle class, even though their incomes are barely above poverty line, because their family has two rooms to live in rather than one, or owns a radio. In the same situation, you would consider yourself desperately poor. About half of all Egyptians (and about three quarters of urban Egyptians) identify with the middle class, but actually their circumstances vary greatly. Saad Edin Ibrahim divides the Cairo middle class into three **strata** (or layers); the lower middle stratum (including 26.5 percent of Cairenes), the middle stratum (36.1 percent), and the upper middle stratum (15.3 percent) (cited in MacLeod, pp. 34–35). The lower middle class includes manual workers who, in many other societies, would consider themselves "working class."

Egypt's industrial workforce is small, only about 10 percent of the whole labor force, mostly in government-owned enterprises. Relatively skilled industrial workers, who are literate and secure in their jobs, tend to think of themselves as middle class, dress like middle-class people, and have middle-class aspirations for their children. They see themselves as socially equal to other government employees, like clerks or lower civil service workers, whose wages are indeed similar. In fact, their wives and daughters very well may be clerical workers. The bottom of the lower middle class lives barely above the poverty line and they live in the same neighborhoods as the poor.

Those who are better off may have a larger apartment, with perhaps as many as four rooms, a TV, refrigerator, and maybe a few other appliances. In cases in which the husband has a skilled job in a private company the family will be better off, since pay is much higher in private companies than in the public sector, though jobs are less secure. Many lower-middle-class families would be poor were it not for income earned by the wife, who works in a regular job in the formal economy (MacLeod, p. 36). Women are steadily entering the labor force, with about 35 percent of women aged 15 and above in paid work (United Nations, *Human Development Report,* 2004).

The middle stratum of the middle class has a more secure hold on its class position. They are university educated and many are young professionals or senior clerical workers in the government bureaucracy. They are self-employed workers in the skilled trades, like plumbers and electricians, or they are shopkeepers or small merchants. Many live in the modest neighborhoods where their businesses are located, but they are actually quite prosperous (Barakat, pp. 89–90; Rodenbeck, p. 82). Middle-middle-class people live in much better apartments, usually of three or four rooms, and they have more elaborate home furnishings and appliances. They expect their children to go to a university.

The upper middle class shades off into the upper class. These people are much more secure than the rest of the middle class. They are established professionals, government bureaucrats, army officers, the prosperous owners of private businesses. Upper-middle-class Egyptians live in air-conditioned modern apartment houses, or in large apartments in old-fashioned middle-class districts. Their homes may be lavishly furnished with inherited antiques or modern European furniture. They can afford servants and even perhaps to send their children to a university abroad.

The Upper Class. The Egyptian upper class is very small, but it is growing. Ibrahim estimates the upper class in Cairo, the national center of business and government, as not more than 1 percent of the population. According to Hooglund, in 1990, only 2,000 families in all of Egypt had incomes above $14,000 per year, so you can imagine how small the upper class is (Ibrahim, cited in MacLeod, p. 35; Hooglund, p. 114). The upper class includes the elites of the government bureaucracy and the top managers of government-owned industries. It includes the most successful owners of private capital—entrepreneurs, big wholesale merchants who engage in international trade, and the owners of big construction firms favored by government contracts. The most successful professionals who work for the public and private elites are members of this class too. The occupations of upper class individuals and the sources of their wealth are varied, but they are linked together by business ties, social relationships, and kinship. Upper-class people are dependent on each other to maintain their wealth. After all, exporters need government licenses and permissions; lawyers need clients, and bureaucrats, no matter how powerful, earn relatively low wages; they use their official positions and their contacts in the private sector in order to earn upper-class incomes, often through private commissions. For example, in recent years President Mubarak's sons have become very wealthy acting as business agents in the airline industry. They earned commissions from foreign airplane manufacturers when they negotiated contracts to supply planes to Egypt's government-owned airline.

Old and New Wealth. In Egypt today there is an old upper class and a new upper class. The old upper class was formed in colonial era Egypt, though many of its members were able to preserve their wealth and connections in socialist Egypt. This elite formed a small, self-conscious group in Cairo and Alexandria. They lived amid family antiques in a few exclusive, guarded villa neighborhoods, spoke French, and supported Egyptian literature and theater. Their children attended exclusive private schools together and they socialized together at English-style country clubs. This elite still prospers in Egypt, but since it always sought to live privately and conceal its wealth, the old elite is overshadowed today by the newly rich.

Egypt's new millionaires have made their money since Sadat's *infitah,* the opening to global capitalism. Some are the sons of old elite families, but others are enterprising operators, some of really modest background, who parlayed a nest egg earned abroad or a gift for speculation into tremendous wealth. Some of the newly rich have made their money in industrial production—steel, appliances, aircraft, but others have profited from currency speculation or from skimming business loans from international banks. Ex-officials and their sons grew rich from bribes paid by western multinational corporations eager to break into Egypt's markets for arms, aircraft, communications systems, and so on. Others made their fortunes investing in the oil-rich Gulf states and have brought back both their new wealth and Islamist styles of dress, architecture, and piety. As new money flows into Egypt, a whole secondary layer of business people has grown wealthy selling consumer goods to the newly rich. They are architects and developers, interior decorators, advertising consultants, dealers in cars, jacuzzis, and cell phones. Entertainers, lawyers, and doctors who serve the rich have also prospered (*The Economist,* March 20, 1998, p. 6).

The newly rich have not hesitated to show off their wealth, making the contrast between rich and poor more obvious to everyone. A huge new apartment tower in the suburb of Giza boasts "villas" of 17,000 square feet each, selling for up to $15 million. A new golf course, constructed in the desert on the road to Suez, has carefully watered and manicured green fairways and 300 villas, advertised as "a lifestyle for the privileged few." It sits right next to a bleak, rundown group of concrete public housing blocks, surrounded by eroded sand and blowing trash, home to 20,000 (Ibrahim, Y., Aug. 17, 1995, p. A4; Ajami, pp. 235–237).

Ahmad's Story: The Developer

Ahmad Moustafa looked out over the Nile from the balcony of his Zemalek apartment. At 54 he wished his country had done as well as he had in these turbulent times. He marvelled at his own capacity to find a way to profit in every circumstance. A Mercedes, a luxury apartment in Cairo's most fashionable quarter, hand-tailored suits made in Italy, a glamorous wife, and a son to follow in his footsteps—not bad!

When the monarchy ended in 1952 and the estates of large landowners were broken up, Ahmad's father took the family to live quietly at one of their country properties. But Ahmad went to university, did his army service, and finished his degree in engineering. A classmate helped him get a job in the Ministry of Construction and then he married the daughter of his commanding officer.

In the 1980s, Ahmad saw the opportunities in luxury construction. He went into partnership with his old classmate and they pooled their resources. His father-in-law helped him get a bank loan and with 10 million pounds in hand they were able to buy an old colonial mansion in Garden City from the squabbling heirs who had just inherited it. The house cleared away, they planned 16 apartments, sold for 2,400,000 pounds each, and a well-timed "gift" to a crucial colleague in the ministry and others at the city council made it possible to build two extra floors, another four apartments. In the end, accounting for construction costs and bribes, net profits amounted to 24,000,000 pounds. Ahmad never looked back: three more apartment complexes, a golf course, and now the condo development in the resort at Sharm el Sheikh. Ahmad's son manages land acquisition and is soon to marry the daughter of one of the top bureaucrats of a major bank. They may well fly all the guests to Sharm for the wedding.

Social Mobility in Egypt

For ordinary Egyptians today opportunities for upward mobility are shrinking. Population growth outpaces job growth and young people face high rates of unemployment. This situation is particularly upsetting to Egyptians because their expectations were formed during several decades of rapid economic growth after the 1952 revolution, when living standards rose and opportunities for upward mobility expanded rapidly.

Closed and Open Systems. Sociologists make a theoretical distinction between two kinds of societies: **closed stratification systems** and **open stratification systems.** In closed systems, people must remain in the social class into which they were born and no amount of talent or effort can have any effect. In contrast, in open systems, parents are unable to pass any advantage on to their children. All children have an equal chance to prosper or fail, based only on their ability and hard work. In real life, no stratification system is completely closed or completely open, but it is useful to think about the two theoretical extremes in order to understand the situation in Egypt today. Before Nasser and the revolution of 1952, Egypt's stratification system was based primarily on inherited land and wealth. It was very difficult for people who didn't have these to acquire any. After 1952, Egypt changed from a rather closed system to a more open one, and opportunities for social mobility increased.

The Revolution and Social Mobility. Nasser created vastly more opportunities for Egyptians in two ways. First, he expelled the existing upper class, by ending colonialism and nationalizing almost all Egyptian businesses. European managers, Greek, Christian, and Jewish merchants, and even wealthy Muslim business owners fled the country. Their departure deprived Egypt of their skills, but created many new openings for those loyal to the revolution (Kurian, 1992, p. 550). A new class of Egyptian managers grew. Second, Nasser quickly moved to create a modern economy under state ownership. Economic expansion laid the foundation for a new middle class, and Nasser deliberately poured the nation's resources into training Egyptians for modern industrial jobs. He opened schools and universities and made education available to ordinary Egyptians. He created a modern health care system as well. Suddenly teachers, doctors, nurses, engineers, architects, accountants, managers, and industrial workers were required in great numbers. To encourage young people to go to school, Nasser promised each college graduate a job in the bureaucracy or in government-owned industry. In Nasser's time, the sons of postal workers became doctors, and the sons of peasants became skilled workers (MacLeod, pp. 31–34; Fakhouri, pp. 40–45; Vatikiotis, pp. 390–396, 457–458).

Aspirations and Realities. Although the percentage of Egyptians who fall into the class of the very poor has become smaller, that doesn't reassure most people. Education has raised their aspirations. At the same time, they fear that the possibilities for upward mobility are shrinking. Every year 1.2 million people enter the labor force for the first time and half of them cannot find jobs. The official unemployment rate stands at 10 percent (unofficially it is 20 percent) and that isn't counting the 3 million workers (one-quarter of the total labor force) who cannot find regular jobs but work in the informal sector (*The Economist,* Jan. 5, 2001, p. 36; July 7, 2004, p. 48; U.S. Department of Labor, pp. 1–4). Recently the government increased the number of poorly paid government jobs, but this satisfies no one. The pay is too low to support a family and the work is often humiliating. Trained engineers are hired to file papers that don't need to be filed. Egyptians call such government jobs "eating dust." Yet they are better than nothing, and when the government recently tried to limit the number of those who could apply, rioting broke out. The cost of providing these jobs is also a substantial drain on Egypt's resources (Fekry, July 13, 2001).

However, Egyptians still look to education as the route out of poverty, and even quite modest jobs as clerks or semiskilled workers require a high school degree. Many educated young people find their expectations disappointed. Nearly one quarter of those unemployed in Cairo today hold university degrees (Rodenbeck, p. 82). Intensified competition and unsatisfied aspirations fuel social unrest.

Migration. The most common response to shrinking opportunities is migration. About 1.9 million Egyptian men—out of a labor force of 22 million—work outside Egypt today. Men don't take their families abroad with them and women never become migrant workers. Migrant work pays well; that is its great attraction. Those working abroad send home an average of $1,600 apiece yearly.

In total, the money migrants send home, called **remittances,** amounted to almost three billion dollars in 2003–2004. About half of Egyptian migrants go to Saudi Arabia and most of the rest to Libya, Jordan, and Kuwait. Smaller numbers go to the United States, Germany, and the United Arab Emirates, but they send the most money home, probably because they are the most educated and skilled. But in the post–September 11 world, it is becoming more difficult for Egyptians to use migration as a route out of poverty. The number of Egyptians migrating reached its peak in 1997, and since then migration is down 12 percent (*Middle East and North African Business Report,* Oct. 31, 2004; El-laithy et al., p. 232; International Labor Organization—Labor Migration Database). (See Table 4.3, p. 241.)

Don't think of migrant work as something done only by the poor and unskilled. Men of every class work abroad, especially the insecure children of the rural and urban middle classes—the sons of small landowners, shopkeepers, and government bureaucrats. They often work as engineers, teachers, and doctors. Egyptian universities graduate a great many students with degrees in education—more than 17,000 per year—but 80 percent of them go abroad to teach (Kurian, 1992, p. 569).

Idris' Story: The Teacher

Idris had always thought of himself as a man with a bright future. His parents had been born in the countryside, but in the flush times of the early sixties they came to Cairo. Idris was a bright child and did well in school, and his parents believed his intelligence and hard work would bring success. But this was not to be. By the time Idris left teachers' college in the early 1980s, there were no jobs for teachers in Egypt. For two miserable years he searched desperately for any job, but only found work tutoring neighborhood children to pass their exams.

TABLE 4.3 Money Sent Home by Those Working Abroad

Mexicans and Egyptians working abroad send home billions of dollars each year. Money sent home by Mexicans has increased steadily since 1980 to more than 13 billion dollars, but money sent home by Egyptians peaked in 1992 at 6 billion dollars and has steadily declined to less than 3 billion. The disruption of Iraq's economy in the 1991 Gulf War and the decline of Saudi Arabia's economy have left fewer jobs in the region for Egyptians.

	Value of Money Sent Home by Those Working Abroad in U.S. Dollars		
	1980	1992	2003
Mexico	$ 698,000,000	$3,070,000,000	$13,266,000,000
Egypt	$2,696,000,000	$6,104,000,000	$ 2,961,000,000
Namibia	No Data	$ 8,000,000	$ 4,800,000

Sources: Balance of Payments Statistics Yearbook, 2004, International Monetary Fund (Washington, DC, 2005)

University of California, Davis, Migration Dialogue: Remittances http://migration.ucdavis.edu/mn/data/remittances/remittances.html

Idris was rescued by the offer of a job as a teacher's assistant in a private school in Kuwait. A college friend was teaching there and had some small influence. Idris was delighted, even though working in Kuwait meant leaving his family. He arrived in Kuwait penniless; the bribe he paid for his exit visa took the last of his cash.

But then Idris hated Kuwait. Even though he was an educated man, an Arab, and a Muslim, he was treated with contempt. And he thought Kuwait was a wasteland—no culture, no night life, no nothing. Idris lived with other Egyptians, rarely going out and sending most of his money home to his family. They needed it too. His father's wages as a factory worker failed to keep pace with rising prices.

On one of his infrequent visits home, Idris married Aisha, whom he had known since childhood, and in the middle of the Kuwaiti school year he became the father of twins. He couldn't even return home for their birth; it was either a hospital room for Aisha or an airline ticket for him. What, thought Idris, had become of his life? What hope could there be for the future? Even in eight or ten years, when his name finally came up on the waiting list for a teaching job in Egypt, the salary would never be enough to support his wife and family and also help his parents.

Compared to the tremendous class and gender inequalities in Egyptian society, other status inequalities seem minor. There are racial and religious inequalities in Egypt, but they are of lesser importance.

Racial Inequality

Egypt is a racially mixed society. Its people come from Africa, the Middle East, Central Asia, and Europe, but they have been mixing and intermarrying for thousands of years. As a result, Egyptians vary in their skin colors and facial features. There is no doubt that light skin is a source of prestige. Before the 1952 revolution, many families in the landowning elite were aristocrats descended from Egypt's earlier rulers (including Greeks, Turks, and Macedonians). They were conscious of their lighter skin and sought similar spouses for their children (Hooglund, p. 119). Today light skin is still associated with elite status, with wealth and power. Movie stars and women in advertisements tend to have light skin. On the other hand, skin color is only one of many sources of prestige in Egypt, including gender, education, occupation, family background, and city origins. Furthermore, while Egyptians are aware of skin color, they are not race conscious. That is, they do not classify people by race: "she is black," or "he is white." They might note that among a family of siblings, some have lighter skin and others darker skin, but they would not feel a need to decide if the family was "white" or "black." Another way of putting this is to say that race is not a **master status** in Egypt. Skin tone does not determine a person's access to jobs, education, or choice of spouse in any major way.

Religious Inequality

Now that Egyptians are so conscious of being Muslims, living in an Islamic society, we need to ask: What does this mean about their attitudes towards people who are not Muslims? The evidence is not particularly reassuring. Probably the most conspicuous case of hostility to non-Muslims is the treatment of Jews in Egypt. Once there was a diverse and flourishing community of more than 80,000 Egyptian Jews. Some had lived in Egypt since ancient times and others had come to Egypt as refugees from persecution in Europe all through the medieval and modern periods. Jews were always second-class citizens in Egypt, whose rights were not the same as the rights of Muslims, but they were tolerated, and in a sense welcomed for their contributions to business and government. But over the course of the second half of the twentieth century almost all Egyptian Jews left Egypt in response to escalating anti-Semitism.

Modern anti-Semitism first emerged in Egypt in the 1930s, through the activities of Egypt's largest and oldest Islamist group, the Muslim Brotherhood. The Brotherhood attacked Egyptian Jews in the response to the growing conflict between Arabs and Jews in Palestine, then a British colony where Jews were settling and pressing for the creation of a Jewish state. The Brotherhood did not distinguish between Egyptian Jews who supported the idea of a Jewish state and those who opposed it or were indifferent to it. This pattern persisted through the rest of the twentieth century and remains today: Anti-Semitism in Egypt grows out of hostility to Israel. It is not restricted to Islamists; secular Egyptians are also anti-Semitic (Benin, pp. 241–267).

The government began enacting anti-Semitic legislation in the late 1940s. It first struck at the citizenship and property of those considered Zionists (supporters of the recently independent State of Israel) and later targeted all Jews, without qualification. Some Jews had been very active in Egyptian politics, identifying themselves as Egyptians first and only secondarily as anti-Zionist Jews. They found that only conversion to Islam would permit them to continue to play a public role in Egyptian life (*Cairo Times*, March 28, 2001). Today, with intensified conflict between Israel and the Palestinians, and with the U.S. invasion of Iraq, anti-Semitism has grown stronger in Egypt. Many Egyptians attribute their country's misfortunes to Jewish conspiracies. Anti-Semitic scenes and plot twists turn up often in popular films, and even *Al-Ahram,* the moderate, semi-official Cairo newspaper often carries anti-Semitic articles and cartoons. In 2002, anti-Semitic ideas turned up in the most-watched television drama. Every year during Ramadan Egyptian television stations feature serialized dramas, shown in the evening when families gather for the *iftar,* the dinner that breaks the day's fast. That year, the most popular serial, picked up by stations all over the Arab world, was "Horseman without a Horse," forty-one episodes that dramatized the history of the Middle East, incorporating ideas from The Protocols of the Elders of Zion, the famous anti-Semitic forgery so widely publicized during the Nazi era (*The Economist,* Jan. 22, 2000; Wakin, no date; MacFarquhar, Nov. 2, 2002).

The Coptic Christians

Prejudice is greatest against Jews in Egypt, but they are an absent minority. What about Coptic Christians, Egypt's largest minority? Their treatment is more contradictory. Copts make up somewhere between 5 percent and 20 percent of the population. The true total is a matter is dispute, since the government does not enumerate Copts. Some people say the government is afraid to know how large the Coptic minority has grown. Sociologically speaking, Copts are a **religious minority group,** not just in numbers, but in terms of their lack of power. Arabic-speaking Muslims are the social **majority** in Egypt, and were so even when their numbers were small, because they controlled the military, the government, and the laws. At many points in Egyptian history, the Muslim majority permitted Copts to maintain their own communities and religious institutions, as long as they accepted their subordination to Muslim authority. At other times, Coptic institutions and property were attacked by the Muslim majority, despite their official protection under Islamic law (Nisan, pp. 115–121; Ibrahim, Y., March 15, 1993, pp. A1, A8).

The Life of a Religious Minority

Egypt's Coptic community has traditionally been divided between those living in Cairo and Alexandria and those living in rural areas in Upper Egypt. Before the twentieth century, urban Copts often served as clerks and administrators for Egypt's Muslim rulers. Boutros Boutros-Ghali, former secretary general of the United Nations, is descended from a prominent Coptic family with a long tradition of government service. When Copts were forced out of government positions by the British colonial administration, they turned to the professions and many became doctors and pharmacists (Nisan, pp. 122–127). Affluent, urban Copts have little informal social contact with their Muslim neighbors, except to some extent when they attend a university. But the situation is far different for poor Copts in the countryside and the cities.

Poor Coptic Christians and Muslims are often neighbors and they come into close social contact as part of the same neighborhood social networks. Coptic and Muslim women shop for one another, watch each other's children, and lend each other money. Christian and Muslim neighbors attend each other's weddings and funerals and participate in the more social aspects of each other's religious celebrations. For example, it would not be unusual for Christian men to attend their town's annual festival at the Muslim shrine, nor would it be strange for a Muslim woman to go to Easter services with her Christian neighbor (Early, p. 73).

In some ways, Copts can be considered a highly **assimilated** minority, one which has taken on the culture of the dominant group. Copts cannot easily be distinguished from their Muslim neighbors. Centuries ago, Copts adopted Arabic as their daily language; the ancient Coptic language is rarely used. Copts wear the same clothing as other Egyptians and eat the same foods too. In daily life, only a visible cross or a Christian name (such as Butros) distinguishes Copt from Muslim (Hooglund, pp. 141–142). Although they are underrepresented in government jobs, Copts do hold two of thirty-one positions in Mubarak's cabinet, and there are many important Coptic businessmen (*The Economist,* Jan. 8, 2000, p. 41).

Militant Islam and the Copts

In the early 1990s, when the militant Islamic groups Gama'a and Islamic Jihad were at the peak of their strength, there was a significant increase in anti-Christians actions. Militants attacked and killed as many as 200 Copts and vandalized and burned churches. Coptic children were shunned by their public school classmates, and women with the traditional tattooed cross were taunted and attacked in public. The government's response was contradictory. For several years, before it succeeded in destroying the Islamic groups, the government stationed police guards outside churches. In 2003, President Mubarak surprised Egyptians by declaring the Coptic Christmas (January 7) a national holiday, like the Prophet Muhammad's birthday. And photos of the president's son Gamal, attending midnight Mass, were shown on television news. But at the same time, in their efforts to co-opt Islamist sentiment, government officials sometimes make statements that reflect deep hostility towards the Coptic minority. In the past decade, many Copts who can afford it have been emigrating, mostly to the United States (Nisan, pp. 127–133; Ajami, pp. 206–209; Jehl, March 15, 1997, p. A3; Friedman, Jan. 8, 2003; Nabeel and Shryock, pp. 30, 229).

SOCIAL CHANGE AND THE FUTURE

Egypt today is in an unstable situation. The society is simmering with problems and pressures for change, but so far, as of 2005, the government has managed to keep the lid on. Everyone wants to know: How long can this go on? Power is concentrated in the hands of President Mubarak, and he is getting old. Economic change is raising expectations that go unsatisfied for many people. Population growth is outpacing the ability of the economy to create jobs. In response to religious revival and economic need, gender roles are being reshaped. Political change is obviously the most powerful force of all, and we haven't been able to get this far in describing Egypt without referring to the politics of Islamism again and again.

Economic Change

Egypt's economy today is in a very contradictory state: Gas tanks are full, but dinner plates are empty. Rich Egyptians now buy so many Mercedes-Benz cars that the company started an assembly plant in Egypt to serve local demand. At the same time, most Egyptians can afford to eat meat only a handful of times a year. In the

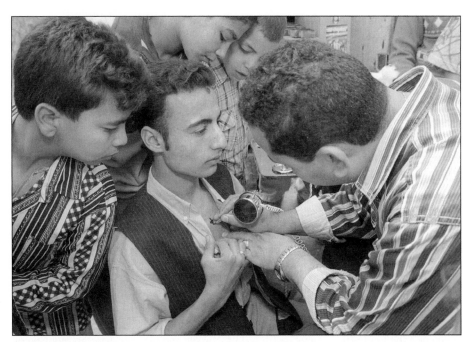

In their language and dress Egypt's Coptic Christians are often indistinguishable from their Muslim neighbors. Tattooed crosses are one way that Copts can express their distinctive identity. Although this tattooed crucifix is being applied on a man's chest, tattoos of the cross are often placed on the wrist as a more visible symbol.

1990s, under pressure from the International Monetary Fund, and with the help of U.S. foreign aid and debt relief, the government began to privatize the economy. There are now privately owned steel companies, appliance manufacturers, telecommunications companies, aircraft manufacturers, and lots of construction businesses. But in 2000 and 2001, and especially after September 11, 2001, Egypt was badly hurt by the global economic downturn. The pace of privatization slowed. Share prices, property values, and currency values fell, while unemployment rose. And the recession badly hurt Egypt's income from oil and tourism (*The Economist,* March 20, 1998, pp. 1–5, Jan. 5, 2002, p. 36, July 21, 2001, p. 38).

In 2003, the government officially devalued the currency, making Egyptian goods cheaper for people in other countries. That boosted exports and tourism, but made imported goods more expensive for Egyptians. The price of basic foods went up between 33 and 109 percent. Overall, GDP grew at a relatively slow 3.1 percent, while consumer prices rose 5.5 percent (*The Economist,* July 17, 2004, pp. 47–48; July 24, 2004, p. 92; Fisher, May 4, 2002).

Even at the height of the boom, most of the new businesses were owned by the sons of the old upper class who are well connected to the governing elite. Outside of that upper crust, most new businesses are tiny; they are the shoestring operations, the local grocery and candy stores, the market stalls that serve a growing population. And job growth has not kept pace with population growth. There is a growing split between older, middle-class Egyptians who have jobs, houses, and schools for their children, and younger Egyptians, even middle-class people, who can't find jobs, can't marry, and can't afford housing. Poverty continues to intensify, and unemployment would be even worse if the bureaucracy stopped hiring (Fisher, May 4, 2004).

Even though Egypt is privatizing, the economy is still strangled by its traditional bureaucracy. Nasser began to overstaff the bureaucracy decades ago in order to provide jobs for all educated Egyptians. Now bureaucrats start work at nine and leave at two and spend much of the time in between on tea breaks and conversation. They are poorly paid, so many use their positions merely as opportunities to collect bribes or help relatives advance their fortunes. Registering new property—a house or business you have bought—still requires seventy-seven different bureaucratic procedures in thirty-one different offices! (Vatikiotis, pp. 406–411, *The Economist*, March 20, 1998, p. 4).

Privatizing the Land

The Mubarak government is deeply committed to modernizing and privatizing Egyptian agriculture. This means phasing out **subsistence agriculture,** in which peasant families grow food for their own consumption, usually on tiny plots of land, using lots of labor but little machinery. To do this, the government has substantially weakened the land reform laws instituted by Nasser and allowed foreign businesses to buy up huge tracts of fertile land (Mitchell, T., pp. 22–23). In 1997 Egypt's government ended a freeze on land rents and changed the laws so landlords are now allowed to revoke leases. The new law, No. 96, affects 6 million peasants, nearly 10 percent of the population, most of whom cannot afford the new market rents and risk dispossession. Some landowners have hired armed guards to force tenants off their land, and some peasants have been killed resisting (Bush, 2000; Jehl, Dec. 27, 1997; Hirst, Oct. 1, 1997, p. A16).

The government hopes that pushing peasant farmers off the land will make it easier to move Egypt towards mechanized cultivation of commercial crops, like fruit, cotton, and rice for export. Hosni Mubarak has staked his prestige and Egypt's scarce funds to divert part of the Nile to Toshka, a region of fertile but dry desert land 40 miles from Lake Aswan (the lake formed by the huge Aswan Dam on the Nile). There, Sun World International, a highly successful agribusiness in California's Mojave Desert, has been retained to create a 100,000-acre commercial farm, employing as many as 60,000 people (Ireton, 2000; Khalil, 2000; Fulmer, 2000).

The Food Gap and Inequality

Today, Egypt suffers from a **food gap:** Despite rising agricultural production, the country must import food to feed its people. Money that might be spent on schools, housing, and health care is used for foreign wheat. Egypt's food gap is puzzling, because production of grain has kept up with and even exceeded population growth. The explanation lies in the use to which the grain is put. Increasingly, wheat and corn grown in Egypt are used as animal feeds to raise cattle for beef sold to those affluent Egyptians who can afford a diet rich in meat. Then the government must import wheat for subsidized sale to the poor. Half of all wheat is now imported. Also, for-

TABLE 4.4 Dependence on Food Imports
Despite substantial agricultural production, Mexico and Egypt import very large amounts of basic grains to feed their populations.

	Egypt		Mexico	
	1970	2002	1970	1999
Tons of Grain Imports	1,260,000	10,348,000	835,000	17,945,000
Percent of Daily Calories from Grain Imports	18.5%	39.7%	9%	69%

Source: Food Balance Sheets for 1970 and 2002, Food and Agriculture Organization, Online FAOSTAT DATABASE, http://apps.fao.org/.

eign companies grow thousands of acres of cotton and sugar for export. Obviously, this also reduces domestic food production in Egypt (Metz, p. 358; Mitchell, T., p. 21). (See Table 4.4, above.)

Population Change

Because Egypt's economy has grown little, it has proved difficult for the society to absorb its growing population—neither job growth nor housing construction have kept pace. In 1947 there were 19 million Egyptians, by 1976 there were nearly 37 million, and by 2000 there were 68 million. Although Egypt's population is not expected to increase as rapidly in the future, substantial growth is still expected. By some estimates, Egypt will have nearly 105 million people by 2025 (Omran and Roudi, p. 4).

The Demographic Transition

Egypt, like many other developing countries, is in the midst of very important changes in population patterns. **Demographers** (the scientists who study population) call these changes a **demographic transition.** Before 1950, Egypt had a high birthrate, but there was a high death rate too. Many babies failed to survive to adulthood and consequently population growth was slow. Then, after 1950, there was a big change. Death rates fell rapidly: In 1950 24 people out of every 1,000 Egyptians died every year; by 1990 only 8 out of every 1,000 died yearly. This striking drop in death rates started when the Nasser government embarked on a huge campaign to make free or low-cost health care available to all Egyptians. Between 1952 and 1976 government expenditure on public health increased 500 percent. At the same time, however, birthrates stayed high, so in consequence, population soared. Recently Egypt has entered another stage in the **demographic** transition: Birthrates are falling, while death rates remain low. As a result, the rate at which its population is growing has slowed. In 1950 the birthrate in Egypt was 48 births yearly for every 1,000 Egyptians, but by 1990 the birthrate had fallen to 33 per 1,000 yearly. Birthrates continue to fall, but so far the rates are still high enough to keep population expanding (Hooglund, pp. 124, 148–152; Omran and Roudi, p. 4).

Urbanization and Population Growth

Better health care brought down death rates. What changes made birthrates fall? One critical change has been the migration of people from the countryside to the cities and their involvement in an urban economy. In 1950 only one Egyptian in three lived in an urban area, but by 1990 half of all Egyptians lived in cities. In 1992 rural women had an average of five children each, but urban women had only three. In the cities, women in the paid labor force are likely to have fewer children. Also, city families see that educated children earn more than those who are barely literate. If a family thinks it likely that they will be able to send their children to school, then it pays to have fewer children so they will be able to afford to educate them. Conversely, a very poor family that knows education is out of the question will find it more rational to have many children, all of whom can work and bring in some income to help the family.

Population Policy

Since 1966 Egypt's government has encouraged family planning and the use of contraceptives to limit population increase. The government has created a national network of family planning clinics, conducted an extensive media campaign in favor of small families, and made contraceptives widely available. These efforts have not been as successful as the government hoped: Egyptians tend to distrust anything that their government promotes. Nevertheless, it is clear that programs to reduce family size have met with some success. In 1992 almost half of all married Egyptian women reported that they used a modern contraceptive method such as the diaphragm or the intrauterine device. The same survey also reported that 67 percent of married women wanted no more children (Omran and Roudi, p. 13). But despite these very real successes, the number of Egyptians continues to rise, due in part to the **momentum factor.** Each family is having fewer children, but there are so many more families that population growth continues at a rapid rate. (See Table 4.5, p. 249.)

Changes in Gender Roles

When it comes to deciding how they should play their roles, women and men in Egypt today are beset by conflicting expectations. In an increasingly pious society, there is pressure on women to put their religious duties first, but at the same time, economic need and increasing education push women to greater independence and a more conspicuous public role. Men also want to fulfill religious expectations, but more and more they find economic barriers in their way.

Women's Roles

Students from western societies often bring to the study of Muslim women some cultural assumptions about women that they don't even know they have. In the West, feminism has fought the assumption that women are "the weaker sex," passive, inferior, submissive. Students often assume that women in Islamic societies must fight these same stereotypes. But Islamic culture has never imagined women like this. Islamic culture sees women as active and powerful, both sexually and personally. If

TABLE 4.5 Population Momentum:
Births—and the total population—rise despite a fall in the number of births per woman. The rising number of births reflects the growing number of women in the childbearing years.

	Women in the Childbearing Years 15–49	Births	Average Number of Births to a Woman in Her Childbearing Years*	Population
Egypt				
1960	6,200,000	1,200,000	6.6	27,000,000
1980	9,800,000	1,700,000	5.5	43,000,000
2000	15,800,000	1,800,000	3.2	68,000,000
Mexico				
1960	13,900,000	1,800,000	6.7	56,000,000
1980	16,000,000	2,400,000	4.7	69.000,000
2000	20,800,000	2,500,000	3.5	85,000,000

Source: International Data Base, United States Census, http://www.census.gov/ipc/www/idbsprd.html.

Note:* Total Fertility Rate

anything, women are seen as so dangerously powerful that men must impose limits on them to keep order in society (Mernissi, 2001; Abdo, p. 57). Traditional Egyptian culture views women as dangerously distracting and tempting to men, who cannot be trusted to control themselves. This way of thinking dates far back in Egyptian history, to the Greek and early Christian eras. If women are dangerously tempting to men, then they should act in such a way as to avoid attracting male desire, and men should protect their female relatives from unrelated men. In Egypt people think that women require *hudud,* "boundaries," in Arabic, like the walls of a house that form a protected space. In Arabic both a house without secure outside walls, and a woman without a *hijab,* a covering veil, are described as *awra,* or naked (Mernissi, pp. 6–8).

Modest Dress. Women should dress modestly, in a way that conceals their sexual attractiveness. The Quran, in a passage often cited as the source of modesty norms for women, required the wives of the prophet to cover themselves:

> And say to the believing women that they should lower their gaze and guard their modesty; that they should not display their beauty and charms except what (normally) appears of them; that they should draw their veils over their bosoms and display their beauty only to their husbands. (quoted in Esposito, 1991a, p. 99)

This passage from the Quran is rather vague, and the requirements of modest dress have varied widely in different periods in Egyptian history. As we will see, all over Egypt, women are now caught up in intense debate over what constitutes modest dress.

Chastity. Women are also expected to be chaste. Chastity has a broader meaning in Egypt than it generally does in western societies. Of course it means, first of all, that women should be virgins when they marry and after marriage should have sex with no one but their husbands. Virginity is a special treasure, which a girl and her family carefully preserve and guard until marriage. Egyptian journalist Abeer Allam remembers that his high school biology teacher sketched the female reproductive system, pointed to the entry to the vagina and declared, "This is where the family honor lies" (Jehl, June 20, 1999, p. A1).

Lost virginity is a disaster for a young woman, for whom marriage will likely become impossible, and for her shamed family. Consider this incident: A 10-year-old daughter of an affluent family crashed her bicycle into a wall and tore her hymen. Her family rushed her to the doctor, who wrote an affidavit describing the injury. This document preserved the girl's marriageability.

But chastity goes beyond merely avoiding sex. Women shouldn't start conversations with strange men, or smile at them, or make direct eye contact with them. Such behavior seems flirtatious and endangers a woman's reputation. A wife, alone in the house, or with other women only, would not open the door to her husband's friend, nor would he wish to enter because it might appear improper (Wilson, p. 91).

Purity.   There is a traditional custom in Egypt, practiced today by both Muslim and Christian Egyptians, which is linked to norms about virginity and chastity. Its proponents call the custom **female circumcision,** but Egyptian feminists who have campaigned against it call the custom **female genital cutting.** In female circumcision, the clitoris is wholly or partially removed. It is an ancient North African custom that has nothing to do with Islam.[1] The mutilation, usually performed on pre-adolescent girls is painful and risky, since it may result in hemorrhage, infections, incontinence, or later difficulty in childbirth. At least 85 percent of Egyptian women have been circumcised and most plan to have their daughters circumcised as well. Folk beliefs hold that an uncircumcised girl will be dangerously masculine and will be wild and chase after men. Most women believe that it will be harder for their daughters to find husbands if they are uncircumcised. Egyptian feminists and human rights groups have been fighting female genital cutting since the 1970s, when the famous writer Nawal al-Saadawi (who was also a medical doctor and the Minister of Public Health) was first imprisoned for her opposition to it. Egypt's highest court ruled female genital cutting illegal in 1997. Some Islamic authorities argue that since the practice is not mentioned in the Quran, it is not required. Other, more conservative religious leaders argue that since the Quran does not forbid female circumcision it should be allowed (Fakhouri, pp. 86–87; Atiya, pp. 11–13; Crossette, Dec. 29, 1997, p. A3; WIN News, Summer, 1997, pp. 31–32; *The New York Times,* Dec. 16, 1997, p. A3; July 12, 1997, p. 3).

Female genital cutting is often the place where westerners draw the line on **cultural relativism,** where their tolerance for cultural diversity runs out and **ethnocentrism** begins. It is a good place to start thinking carefully about ethnocentrism.

---

[1]Unicef (the United Nations Children's Fund) estimates that 130 million women, most of them in Africa, have undergone genital cutting. Seven nations account for 75 percent of the cases of female genital cutting in Africa: Egypt, Ethiopia, Kenya, Nigeria, Somalia, and Sudan. The mutilation is banned in eight countries: Burkina Faso, the Central African Republic, Djibouti, Egypt, Ghana, Guinea, Senegal, and Togo (Crossette, Jan. 18, 1999, p. A10).

Is it ethnocentric to condemn female genital cutting? Can you condemn it without being ethnocentric? Must sociologists accept uncritically every aspect of each culture? Women's organizations in Africa make it very clear that they welcome your support for their efforts to end the practice, but western criticism that depicts their societies as backward or barbaric is unwelcome and makes their struggle harder. (See Fernea, 1998, pp. 269–272.)

Gender Segregation.   Separate social spaces for women and men also protect women from the attentions of men and protect men from sexual impulses. Men and women tend to gather separately. We call this **gender segregation.** After dinner at a family party, men and women gravitate into separate rooms. The public realm clearly belongs to men. Even in the daytime, there are more men than women in the streets and men gather in mosques and coffeehouses. After dark almost everyone outside is male. Traditionally, if a woman must venture out into this male territory, it is proper for a male relative to accompany her. Men stroll with friends, sit in restaurants, and go to the movies. In the daytime, women walk outside together, linked arm in arm. They may go with their children to the movies, and they gather in each other's homes. In poor neighborhoods, women move freely through the alleyways near their houses, fetching water or food from the market, or calling children in for meals, but not venturing far afield. In Cairo, there are separate, female-only sections on trains and buses, and many women prefer them. Swimming pools at private clubs have separate swim hours for men and women.

Changing Roles for Women

Egyptian women find themselves caught between two potentially conflicting trends. Many women are becoming more pious and more influenced by new Islamist preachers. They want to be good Muslims and follow religious norms for modesty, chastity, and gender segregation. But at the same time, as Egypt's economy modernizes, women are drawn more and more into public roles, and they find new opportunities for self-expression. Egyptian women are debating how they can reconcile piety with public life, and they are creating very interesting new norms and customs.

The changes began with education for women. When Nasser urged families to send their daughters to school, and then permitted women to attend high school and university, he set in motion a series of changes that are still being played out today. Girls who go to school become accustomed to going out in public, and they form friendships outside the family. Don't assume this has a westernizing or secularizing effect. Girls may shop for make-up together, but they may equally well listen to tapes of the latest preacher and experiment with how to wear the veil.

Girls who go to high school typically work for at least a couple of years before marriage and perhaps afterwards as well. If they are lucky or well connected they may get a job in a government office as a clerical worker or secretary. These jobs are not particularly challenging or well paid (they file papers and run copy machines and keep simple accounts). Government offices are very much overstaffed and everyone spends a lot of time drinking tea and chatting. Nevertheless, women employees greatly enjoy office life, with its bustle of visitors and links to a larger world. (See Table 4.6, p. 252.)

TABLE 4.6   Percentage of Egyptians 16–20 Years Old Attending School in 1992 and 2000

Women in the countryside are much less likely to go to high school and university than women in cities. Rural women are also less likely to go to school than rural men. Overall, fewer than half of young Egyptians continue their education beyond age 15.

	Rural			Urban	
	Male	Female		Male	Female
1992	44	23		58	53
2000	46	28		59	55

Source: Demographic and Health Surveys, Macro International, http://www.measuredhs.com, March 8, 2005.

TABLE 4.7   Women in Politics and the Economy

Egyptian and Japanese women play a substantial role in the economy, but are largely excluded from political roles. Less than one in every ten political leaders in Egypt and Japan are women.

	Female Legislators (% of total)	Women in Government at Cabinet Level (% of total)	Female Professional and Technical Workers (% of total)
Egypt	2	6	30
Japan	5	6	46
United States	12	32	55
Mexico	18	11	40
Namibia	19	16	55
Germany	29	36	49

Sources: Interparliamentary Union, "Women in National Parliaments," http://www.ipu.org/english/home.htm United Nations, Human Development Report, 2004 http://hdr.undp.org/statistics/

College-educated women can become teachers, doctors, lawyers, and engineers, but jobs are scarce and they often find themselves working in employment far below their level of training. Uneducated women sometimes work in factories; they sell produce or cooked food in the streets or even own and manage coffeehouses. Overall, about 35 percent of Egyptian women work for wages outside their homes—in offices, factories, stores, and on farms. Almost 40 percent of them work on farms, and 54 percent work in professional or service jobs. Egypt's industrial economy is rather small, and only 7 percent of working women are employed in factories (United Nations, *Human Development Report,* 2004). It is mostly younger women who work; their mothers' generation was much less likely to venture away from home. That means working women can often rely on their mothers-in-law or other female relatives for help with child care. (See Table 4.7, above.)

Women who attend school and work have much more opportunity to spend time away from their male relatives and the supervision of their families. An educated, employed young woman in Cairo is likely to be reluctant to marry her country cousin. They are too far apart culturally to make an easy match, and the young woman will probably reject the idea of a village life spent under her mother-in-law's eyes. Urban Egyptians, especially those who have completed high school or college, are far more likely to find their marriage partners in school, at work, or elsewhere outside the family circle. In universities, women and men who are not relatives get a chance to meet and talk together in classes, on campus paths, and in the cafeteria. Still, Egyptians do not date before marriage, not even in the city.

Many forces encourage Egyptian women to seek education and jobs. Parents want their daughters to go to high school, if they can possibly afford it. An educated girl is more likely to find an educated husband, perhaps with a good job, from a better-off family. Once girls have graduated from high school, they like the idea of working and getting out of the house. But poor, uneducated women sometimes work also when their husbands are unemployed or earn too little. Women whose husbands have left Egypt to find work abroad also find themselves, at least temporarily, the heads of their families. The government supports working women by giving maternity leave to those who are government employees and by making free birth control available at government clinics. Women who now serve in the parliament (the National Assembly) as well as in neighborhood and village councils set active role models for young women (Ibrahim, B., pp. 294–295). The percentage of professors in universities or colleges who are women was higher in Egypt in the 1990s than in France or Canada; the percentage of engineering students who are women was higher in Egypt than in Canada or Spain (*1996 Unesco Statistical Yearbook,* cited in Mernissi, 2001, pp. 27–28).

New Roles and Role Conflict

When Egyptian women attend school or work outside their homes, they experience both new satisfactions and new anxieties. Venturing into the public world is fraught with conflicts and complications.

First of all, the idea of a woman being "just" a housewife is foreign to Egyptian culture. *Housewife* is a respected, honored status in Egypt. Especially among poor Egyptians, a woman who is a good housekeeper, who can always stretch the budget to feed the family, arrange good marriages for her children, and solve their medical problems, is admired by all her neighbors and relatives. People recognize her wisdom and hard work and go to her for advice. Many poor women who must work outside their homes—in factories, as servants, as peddlers, or market women—would prefer not to. Such jobs put women under a cloud of moral suspicion. They are out in public and often under the authority of men, who, it is understood, might try to take advantage of them. And the work is menial, heavy, and poorly paid, so the role, as well as the status, is unrewarding. Many lower-middle class girls aspire to go to university and get higher status professional jobs. But public education may not prepare them well enough to pass the entrance exams. If their families cannot afford private tutoring, they may not be admitted. Or, they may actually graduate university and then fail to find jobs. Many of these girls reorient their hopes and choose other statuses that confer prestige. They decide that being a good Muslim is their primary goal in life and being a wife and mother their most important duty. They are willing to work if the family needs their income, at any job they consider honorable, but work is not their focus (Wickham, pp. 166–167).

Such women are dealing with one of the many **role conflicts** Egyptian women must navigate. In role conflicts people must deal with the incompatible role expectations that go with different statuses. More than ever, women want to have rewarding careers, be good Muslims and be good wives. But how can they follow norms of modesty and still go out into a world of strangers? For example, when women must travel to and from work or school, this creates problems because there are no clear norms specifying how men should treat unrelated women, particularly strangers, in public places. There is a traditional assumption that any woman away from the protection of her family, especially at night, is sexually available, a prostitute. Even when it is clear that respectable women are on their way to work, they are often harassed. Every Egyptian woman must find some way to deal with role conflicts (MacLeod, pp. 63, 107–115; Fernea, 1998, pp. 240–288).

Role Conflicts and Modest Dress. Think about your society for a moment. Does the way people dress have symbolic meaning? Do people use their clothes to tell the world who they are and what they believe? A business suit or jeans, loose pants or fitted ones, expensive watches, nose rings, briefcases and backpacks, all convey social messages. The same thing is true in Egypt. On the street in Cairo, about three quarters of the women who pass by are wearing some version of "modest dress" or "Islamic dress." This always includes the *hijab. Hijab* translates literally as "veil," but actually it is a scarf, pinned or tied under the chin to completely conceal the neck and pulled forward at the forehead to cover the hair.

If you ask young women in Cairo why they wear the *hijab,* they will all tell you that they wear it because Islam requires it. It is a serious statement. Wearing the *hijab* shows that piety matters to you. More, it says that you value Islam; that you are proud of your culture and Muslim heritage. Westerners tend to see the *hijab* as a sign of the oppression of women, the suppression of their identity. But for Egyptian women, wearing the *hijab* is an assertion of identity. Sometimes putting on *hijab* is even an act of rebellion, when girls are more religious than their parents.

The *hijab* asserts religious identity, but it expresses other identities too. There are many different styles of "modest dress" and the style you adopt says more about who you are (Menezes, *Cairo Times*). Many educated working women—teachers, engineers, bureaucrats—adopt a professional style of modest dress, wearing the *hijab* over a long skirt with a blazer and turtleneck or a full tunic with long sleeves. Affluent teenagers, pushing the boundaries, wear their *hijab* with tight jeans and a long, loose tunic. Away from home, the tunic comes off to reveal a skimpy shirt. Women who have made a deep commitment to religiosity sometimes adopt the *niqab,* a long unfitted gown in a solid color, often black, with waist-length *hijab,* face-veil, and even gloves, concealing all but their eyes. Remember that for all women, the *hijab* is a garment worn in public, or in the presence of men who are not relatives. In their homes, women remove their scarves and put on lighter, less enveloping dresses.

The *hijab* has been around long enough now that it is a fashion accessory as well as a statement of identity. There is an active, lively debate among women, and men

Karimat El Sayed is a Physical Chemistry Professor of Solid State Physics at Ain Shams University in Cairo. Professor El Sayed received the 2003 L'Oreal-Unesco Award For Women in Science. Accompanied by her students she takes a pleasant break from her research. Professor El Sayed is older and, like many professional women in her generation, wears a hat, while her younger students cover their hair with the hijab or headscarf. Their hijabs tell the world they are good Muslim women at the same time they are modern physics graduate students. In your society, do many women become physicists?

too, about the *hijab*. Are men fooled into thinking that every woman who wears the *hijab* is a decent woman? Do men prefer veiled women when they choose a wife? Are women who wear *niqab* extremists who go too far? Is it alright to wear a *hijab* made of patterned cloth? How about fringe? Is it acceptable to let the *hijab* slide back and reveal a little hair? Egyptian women are pleased to have a fashion that is completely Muslim and not a creation of western style. More and more now, young women modify the classic black or white *hijab,* wearing patterned and bright-colored scarves, tying them in unusual ways. You could say that wearing the *hijab* says you value Islam, but modifying the *hijab* says individual expression is also important to you (Menezes, El-Rashidi, Al Ahram).

It is important to understand, though, that women in every variety of dress are out in public. Even women in *niqab* go to university; they go to mosque services; they work in clinics established by Islamist groups, and at Islamist newspapers and Web site offices. Becoming religious doesn't necessarily push women back into their homes; it gives them new places to go!

Solving Role Conflicts. Egyptian women don't talk about it this way, but as sociologists, we'd like to suggest that wearing the *hijab* helps solve role conflicts.

Modest dress declares that a woman respects Islam even though she works. It gives her respectability and thus allows her to move about more freely in public (Wickham, p. 170). Modest dress declares that a woman is a professional, not a sex object. It reassures her father, or brother, or husband. It is likely that modest dress also reduces sexual harassment in public places. Men who annoy a woman wearing western dress break only a poorly defined secular norm, but men who harass a woman in Islamic dress profane Islam.

Several sociologists have even argued that women in Islamic dress find it easier to interact with men, since their dress defines the situation as nonsexual, as this university student explained:

> Before I wore the veil, I always worried what people might think when they saw me speak to a man in the cafeteria or outside the class. I even wondered what the man himself thought of me. Since I wore the veil, I don't worry anymore. No one is going to accuse me of immorality. (Quoted in Mule and Barthel, p. 330. See also Ahmed, p. 224; Fernea, p. 244)

Zaynab's Story: A Good Wife

Zaynab met her future husband, Kamal, an engineer, at the government office where she still works. Zaynab's father Mamduh, a mechanic for Egyptair, the national airline, was delighted. He had begun to despair that Zaynab, already 24, would ever marry, but now she would—and an engineer at that. What a catch for an uneducated man's daughter! Mamduh hoped Zaynab would leave her job and stay home where a wife and mother should be. When Mamduh was a boy in a tiny village in Upper Egypt, no woman left her home. But after the birth of her children, Zaynab returned to her office. "It's my life," she said, "my friends are there. Besides, no family can live on one income; Kamal, the children, and I would starve!"

Mamduh was not entirely surprised. Zaynab had turned down a previous offer of marriage from a young man who had demanded that she leave her work. But Zaynab astonished her entire family in 1997 by announcing that from then on she would wear "Islamic dress," the hijab over a loose dress. Zaynab, her parents, and her husband were not especially religious. Kamal thought it was ridiculous that the wife of an educated man should "cover herself," but Zaynab persisted. "Men do not respect a woman on Cairo's streets," she argued, "only a 'covered woman' will be left alone. Besides, even women at the university are 'covered' " (MacLeod, pp. 110–124; Ahmed, pp. 222–225; Mule and Barthel, pp. 328–331).

Women's Rights. While westerners (and secular Egyptians) tend to see Islam as an obstacle to women's rights, it doesn't look that way to most Egyptian women. They reject western feminism, which they see as fomenting unnecessary hostility between women and men. Instead, they look to the Quran for a genuinely Islamic legitimation of changing women's roles. Young women find the Islamic norms embodied in *Sharia* an important protection against the difficulties of life in a poor and male-dominated society. *Sharia,* for example, provides that a woman retains the right to the property she owns at the time of marriage. She also has sole ownership of any new property she acquires in the course of her marriage; her wages or her inheritance are hers, not her husband's (Hoodfar, pp. 5–7, 12–14). It was well into the nineteenth century before even a few European societies gave women such rights. People don't always fully comply with Islamic law, but a claim made under it is not easily denied. In Egypt *Sharia* is taken far more seriously than western principles of human or women's rights. Some educated women go to Quranic study groups that reinterpret the Quran, stressing passages that address men and women as spiritual equals (El Gawhary, pp. 26–27; Fernea, pp. 241–245). Some women even dispute the interpretation of the Quran with male clerics.

Changing Roles for Men

For Egyptian men, the changing economy has led to tremendous frustration and strain, as they try to satisfy role expectations. In the past, in rural Egypt, most men could achieve respect in their communities. Land was the foundation of life and men controlled the land. Groups of men, tied together by common interests, cemented by kinship, worked together to cultivate, irrigate, and harvest the land. This unity of work and family gave men tremendous power. They took pride in the masculine tone of their world. And they could afford to marry young and carry out their Islamic duties as husbands and fathers. But today, in the countryside, many men are marginalized. They are losing their land as the result of new land laws, or because their parents' landholding are simply too small to support all the children and their families.

In the city, government bureaucracies cannot grow fast enough to keep up with the rising number of high school and college graduates. Factory workforces are slashed as enterprises pass from the state into private hands. Migration abroad has become more difficult. Men feel they cannot control their futures and cannot even control their families! Clans and networks of male kin have less power in the city. Women increasingly go to school or work outside their homes. Worst of all, in Egypt today, men face barriers in carrying out their obligation to marry as soon as possible and to remain chaste until marriage. In 38 percent of the marriages that took place in 1999, the groom was over the age of 30 (*United Nations Demographic Yearbook*). (See also Table 4.8, below.)

Young people in western societies don't mind waiting to marry, so you may not immediately understand the significance of this problem. For Egyptian men, marrying is a real religious obligation, and it is also something their families and others

TABLE 4.8 Marriages

Marriage rates for every country have declined since 1971. Egypt's marriage rates have declined by nearly 20%.

	Number of Marriages for Each 10,000 Persons 1971	Number of Marriages for Each 10,000 Persons 2002
Egypt	103	84*
Japan	104	59
Mexico	72	55
Germany	70	48
United States	105	78

Sources: 1990 Demographic Yearbook, United Nations, 1992

2002 Demographic Yearbook, United Nations Statistics Division, Demographic Yearbook System
http://unstats.un.org/unsd/demographic/products/dyb/dyb2.htm

*Data for 1999

expect of them. Young men face constant pressure: Everyone asks, "So when are you getting married?" "Why aren't you engaged yet?" I know a woman who would be a perfect wife for you." And chastity is a reality for unmarried Egyptian men. If they are lucky enough to spend any time at all with a young woman, it is likely to be in public, or surrounded by relatives at a wedding or family party. Marriage is really the only way of having any kind of sex life.

While they wait for marriage, men must behave properly so potential in-laws will not reject them. Drinking, chasing women, swearing, getting into trouble with the police all dishonor a man and his family and make marriage problematical. Expectations like these are not so burdensome when men marry young, but if a man must wait years or decades to marry, he may readily run into trouble.

Obstacles to Marriage. When it comes to marriage, Egyptian men are caught between rising expectations and falling resources. Egyptian norms require that in order to marry a man must be able to pay for certain customary expenses. He must purchase the engagement gift (usually a gold ring and several gold bracelets), though his parents and even the bride and her family may help with this. He must pay for the wedding celebration and pay the "key money" for a rented apartment or pay for the purchase of an apartment. And he must furnish the whole apartment. People in Cairo estimate the whole sum needed for a lower-middle class college graduate at between 6,000 and 15,000 Egyptian pounds. With an entry-level government job paying about 60 to 80 pounds a month, you can imagine how hard it is for a young man to accumulate such a sum. The money might be earned by working abroad, but as we have seen, it has become more difficult to migrate.

At the same time, as Egypt modernizes, Egyptians' social ambitions are rising higher. University graduates don't want to do manual work. They want white collar salaried jobs, preferably in management and in government. Sales jobs are looked down upon as rather humiliating or shady, and service-sector jobs, where you would actually be serving someone, are seen as demeaning. So parents want a salaried government employee as a husband for their daughter. But when they find out he makes only 80 pounds a month, that's not good enough either. Young men find they need a government job in the daytime, supplemented by a private-sector job, waiting tables or driving a taxi, at night. At the same time, a young man can see an ad in the newspaper placed by foreigners who advertise jobs for maids or nannies at $500 to $800 a month! Imagine the blow to a young man's self-esteem.

Role Conflicts and Islam

All of these conflicting expectations cause problems for Egyptian men and women, especially the growing number with university education. The help they find in solving their dilemmas comes mostly from within Islam. First of all, conventional Islamic authorities, the *ulamas* appointed by the government, have looked to Islamic law, *Sharia,* for solutions to the marriage problem. For example, some jurists at Al Azhar, Egypt's leading Islamic university, have ruled that with the agreement of the bride's family, a man may pay a smaller dowry and accept help from the bride's family in buying a home (Shoreth).

Islamic jurists have tried in another way to adapt the law to help men purchase apartments. In most western countries today, the use of mortgages, long-term loans to buy houses, is common. But Islamic law forbids lending money at interest and this would seem to place mortgage loans beyond the reach of Muslims. There is hardly a consensus on this issue, but some prominent Muslim authorities have reluctantly approved mortgages for certain purposes. The Grand Sheik of Al Azhar, Mohammed Sayyed Tantawi, commented that in general no one should take a loan, except for life's necessities. Necessities, the sheik indicated, could include buying an apartment, car, or air conditioner (El Fiqi, Nov. 11–17, 1999).

As many Egyptian families face declining incomes and rising costs, the nature of marriages has become, in some instances, radically redefined, but still there is an effort to keep the marriage bond within the scope of Islamic practice. Young couples who cannot afford apartments arrange *Urf* marriages. *Urf* marriages or *Gawaz Urfi* are created by a contract signed by the bride and groom and by two witnesses. These marriages are not officially registered. They are legal, but leave women without the security of a dowry, or the possibility of alimony and child support (Allam, Feb. 18, 2000; Albahey).

Legal solutions can go only so far in solving men's role conflicts. More and more men are now looking to Islamic activist groups for help in understanding the causes of their problems and in recovering their dignity. Through involvement in neighborhood mosques and Islamic networks, men find a sense of belonging and purpose. Carrie Wickham, reporting on her study of lower- middle-class university graduates, puts it very clearly: Participation in Islamic activist movements transformed "poorly skilled graduates with bleak economic prospects into fellow soldiers in the noble task of Islamic reform" (p. 153). Islamist movements speak to the bitterness of graduates who believe they should be part of society's elite, but instead find no work or only demeaning work. The Islamist movement tells discontented young men that they can join in working for a true Islamic society in which "merit— both moral/spiritual and practical/professional would be justly acknowledged and rewarded" (Wickham, p. 160).

On a more practical level, the Islamist movements offer young men alternative paths to social esteem and alternative roles. They tell men they can be the protectors and supports of their community, the community of believers, or *umma*. Men can engage in charitable work, support Islamist candidates for office, campaign at their university for separate classes for men and women, contribute money to help the Palestinians, or even, for the most radical, enlist in jihad abroad. Political action provides a source of male pride and dignity. Also, many men who feel spurned by their society find themselves welcomed with enthusiasm by Islamist groups. They are treated with respect and praised when they come to pray in the mosque or when they attend study groups. Religious leaders may treat teenage boys to after-school meals or pay them to run errands. They tell the boys they are the chosen ones, destined for great things. Such messages sink deeply into thirsty ground.

Finally, Islamist groups offer men an honorable way to readjust their expectations downward and achieve marriage without the highly paid, prestigious jobs they had hoped for. Men and women learn that university degrees and white-collar jobs are unimportant; that what matters in life is studying Islam and any honest work is acceptable to support a life in Islam. Wickham emphasizes that for the activist men she studied "as their expectations regarding higher education, career advancement, and material wealth diminished, so too did the graduates' feelings of disappointment and frustration." Islam also offers help to men who can in no way afford to marry: Fasting and prayer could take the mind off sex and "decrease the longing" (Wickham, pp. 166–168, 170). Wickham's study gives us an unusually rich understanding of the appeal of Islam in Egypt. You can see that it speaks to many different needs of young people.

Abdel's Story: A Life in Islam

"I was dead," Abdel told his cousin. "When Fatima's family announced her engagement to the banker, I died. 'You are a good man, Abdel,' her brother told me, 'but Fatima is 27 and she cannot wait forever. You're a government clerk. On your salary you can never marry Fatima.' When I heard that, it destroyed me. I wandered the streets and all the hopes I had in college died. I wasn't an engineer; the only job I could find was filing papers. I wasn't a husband. I wasn't a father. I wasn't a man.

One day I stopped to rest at the mosque. I had no religious feeling, but I had no money for a coffee shop either. The sheik saw me and gave me a cup of tea and something to read. I began to tell him all my troubles and he was kind. He gave me books to read and answered my questions about Islam. Although I didn't know it then, I had entered jihad. I struggled with my ignorance and doubt. By now, thanks be to God, I've found my way. When the sheik offered me a job as a tutor, I took it. By helping the children I was building my life and building the community of Islam.

The sheik has a niece, Nadia. She's from his village in the delta. We'll marry after Ramadan. Nadia doesn't need a car or cable television. A room in the sheik's house is enough. I was dead, but now I have found life and faith in Islam."

Political Change

You may think of the Egyptian government, like many other Middle Eastern governments, as the still eye of the storm. A great variety of political currents perturb the political air over Egypt, but so far President Hosni Mubarak has managed to crush any real opposition and keep his authoritarian regime frozen in place. The opposition he has tied up could be very powerful though, if unleashed. First of all, there is a pro-democratic movement, including younger, educated, "technocratic" men, even within Mubarak's own party, the National Democratic Party (NDP) and within his own family. Then, there is the whole range of the Islamist movement, from the most apolitical pietists, to jihadi terrorists. Democracy advocates hope the government will change enough to forestall popular discontent. Islamists know that they will win either way: If the government democratizes, a modern Islamist government will be freely elected. And if the government does not democratize, young people will become more and more frustrated and radicalized and a radical Islamist movement may be able to seize power.

Political Reform

In 2005, Hosni Mubarak was nearing the end of his fourth six-year term as president. He and the NDP party have governed Egypt for almost twenty-five years. Mubarak was Anwar Sadat's vice president and became president when Sadat was assassinated in 1981. He has ruled the whole time under emergency decrees that suspend the constitution and allow the government to ban opposition parties, restrict freedom of the press and freedom of speech, and try political prisoners before harsh emergency security courts. Complex election rules make vote-rigging easy, and in any case, Mubarak is elected by a peculiar procedure in which parliament selects just one candidate (Mubarak) for a referendum vote.

But demands for democracy in Egypt are growing, not least because the government seems to function so badly, with banking, school, health care, and legal systems all in a state of neglect. For years now, such opposition parties as are permitted to exist have been demanding direct presidential elections. And there have been scandals that reach very high up in the government, with close associates of the ministers of agriculture, information, and parliamentary affairs accused of accepting bribes. Recently, the government has made some gestures in the direction of reform, but most Egyptians believe that Mubarak is not willing to permit real democracy, only just enough reform to keep the government in power (MacFarquhar, Aug. 11, 2004, p. A4).

The Problem of Succession

Although Mubarak stepped up to the presidency from the vice president position, he has never appointed a vice president of his own. He is 76 years old and there have been a couple of scares about his health. It appears that Mubarak is trying to renew his aging party and government, without actually permitting any challenges to it. Speculation centers on Gamal Mubarak, the president's son, an urbane 41-year-old who previously worked in England as an investment banker. Egyptians wonder whether Mubarak plans to somehow bequeath the presidency to his son. In 2000, Gamal was appointed to the NDP's twenty-five member secretariat, and he heads a party policy committee that has come out with a number of reform proposals, none yet put into effect (*The Economist,* Dec. 6, 2003, p. 42; MacFarquhar, Dec. 21, 2003).

In the meantime, there have been small changes, none of which add up to democracy. Three aged government ministers were dismissed and replaced by younger, more dynamic men, as were half of the twenty-six regional governors. In a well-publicized gesture, the 2003 party congress ended with the release of 900 Islamist political prisoners (but between 10,000 and 20,000 remain jailed). The government abolished one state security court, but left power with the other two. At the same time, parliament renewed the emergency laws. In 2005, Mubarak proposed changes in the Constitution to allow multiple candidates to run for president. But candidates will still have to be approved by parliament, the same parliament that obediently nominates Mubarak election after election. Egyptians are skeptical of the likelihood they will see democracy. One official laughed at an assertion by American Condoleeza Rice that after Sadam Hussein's fall there would be a "march of democracy" in the Arab world. "Cinderella. How nice of her," he scoffed, "Is she dreaming?" (Perlez, Oct. 3, 2002, p. A12; *The Economist,* July 17, 2004, p. 47; Oct. 4, 2003, pp. 44–45, MacFarquhar, Feb. 27, 2005, pp. 1, 4).

The Islamist Movement

All the maneuvering in Egypt towards and away from democracy takes place in the shadow of the Islamist movement. The Islamist movement is a good example of a **social movement,** a creation of large numbers of people who organize to change the world or some aspect of it. We have certainly discussed Islamism quite a bit already in this chapter. But now we can clearly depict the various layers of the movement. We can distinguish among three different strands of the movement. The first is **cultural Islam,** the very widespread growth of piety in Egyptian society and of identification with Islam. Many people who participate in cultural Islam belong to no organized political group. Then there is **political Islam,** which includes all the Islamist political organizations that want to bring about an Islamist state, a government that will be in some sense Islamic. Finally, one part of political Islam is **jihadi Islam,** those organizations willing to use terrorism and revolution to achieve an Islamic state. Obviously, jihadi Islam gets the most attention in the west, but it is important to realize that it is a small part of the Islamist movement.

Cultural Islam. Cultural Islam is a response to an identity crisis in Egypt. Globalization has made many Muslims feel that their society is being overrun by western culture. Satellite television, movies, and cassette tapes have brought sexually suggestive material into everyone's view. Even just walking down the street in Cairo, you can see posters advertising American films or French underwear that flaunt scantily clad models. Western fashions and American toys are everywhere. Along with western media, western standards of beauty have invaded Egypt. Traditionally, a full-figured woman was regarded as desirable in Egypt, but now there is pressure on women to be thin. Government broadcasters recently made it known that anchorwomen and other female TV personalities must be slim and wear western dress and makeup. Diet clinics have appeared in Egyptian cities; some are even attached to clinics sponsored by mosques (Marcus)! Once Cairo's skyline was dominated by the minarets of mosques, but now new office and apartment towers make it look like any western city. In many parts of Cairo, the golden arches of McDonald's are as visible as the mosques. It is worth noting that Mohammed Atta, one of the leaders of the September 11 attacks, was a city planner. He was furious at what he regarded as the destruction of Cairo's architectural heritage to make room for tourists.

It is important to realize that this whole pattern of American cultural influence and anti-American reaction is by no means limited to Egypt, or even to non-western societies. You can look at France or Canada and find movements aimed at preserving their national culture and resisting American influence. But in Egypt, preservation of Islamic culture, of Egypt's heritage, has become identified with the Islamists.

In response to the "cultural invasion" from the West, as Caryle Murphy puts it, Egyptians "are asserting their existential cultural guidepost, Islam. They are returning to their Islamic 'roots' because they see Islam as a protective armor against a humiliating loss of identity" (p. 8). The one theme that all branches of the Islamist movement have in common is anti-Americanism and hatred of Israel. A decade ago, Islamism focused much more on perceived moral problems within Egypt, but Mubarak's government has blocked any attempt at Islamist reform within Egypt. During the same period, the peace process in Israel fell apart, and conflict between Israelis and Palestinians reached a new intensity. Now the fate of the Palestinians has become a major concern in Egypt. Arab television news stations now bring into every apartment and coffee shop nightly images of bloody Israeli raids and women and children wailing in front of their crushed houses (Golden). Anti-Americanism has intensified greatly since the American invasion of Iraq in 2003. Egyptians are convinced that the United States is actively hostile to Islam and is seeking to conquer and dominate the Arab world. This is an idea upon which the Islamists and the Mubarak government can agree.

But cultural Islam is a broad movement; it encompasses a wide range of responses. It includes the privileged young woman who adopts a fashionable *hijab* and watches the sermons of Amr Khaled, the most popular televangelist in Egypt and beyond. Khaled sells more cassette tapes than Egypt's top pop singers (*The Economist,* June 29, 2002, pp. 44–46). Mr. Khaled, a former accountant, preaches a moderate, personal form of Islam. He has no beard and wears a suit. According to sociologist Asef Bayat, Khaled "articulates a marriage of faith and fun." He is compassionate and colloquial, not grim and moralizing like traditional preachers, and he talks about the ethics of everyday life: wearing *hijab,* dressing neatly, not smoking, improving relationships. When he preaches, his audience cries and laughs and feels an emotional release (Bayat, May 2003).

At the other extreme from Khaled is a part of Islamic culture that could be called ultra-orthodox. It is, Caryl Murphy says, "puritanical, xenophobic and intolerant." Fundamentalist Islam wants to purify the Muslim world of corrupt western influences and return Islam to an imagined past golden age of the Prophet and the early caliphs, when homogeneous peoples unified around heroic figures in a pure, rural idyll. Ian Buruma and Avishai Margalit write that this is an "anti-liberal" impulse, distinct from anti-Americanism. It is a reaction against modern society, against individualism, science, diverse populations, the freedoms associated with cities, artistic and sexual freedom. Typically, Buruma and Margalit contend, this fundamentalist reaction focuses on Jews, homosexuals, and feminists as the symbols and sources of western decadence. So the Taliban, in Afghanistan, for example, were determined to put women in seclusion, cover them up, and keep them out of public life. Al Qaeda saw the twin towers in New York as the towers of Babylon, symbol of ungodliness and decadence. However, warn Bururma and Margalit, "there is no clash of civilizations." Anti-modernism is not restricted to Islamic societies. These same ideas inspired Nazism and Japanese militarism, and they are echoed today by Christian fundamentalists in the United States, and by Jewish and Hindu fundamentalists as well (Buruma and Margalit, p. 7).

Political Islam. This term simply refers to Islamic activists and organizations that aim to replace secular governments with Islamic governments that will support an Islamic society. But there is a huge variety of Islamist groups and tendencies and a ferment of ideas and debates. The groups agree on nothing except a general goal: a more Islamic society (and on who their enemies are—Israel and the United States). What an Islamic state or society would be remains relatively undefined, beyond the idea that it would be based on *Sharia* and would be a just society. The attention of the West is pinned on Bin Laden's Al Qaeda, but most political Islamist groups reject violence.

Under Islamic rule, the Islamists promise, there will be an end to corruption, a more equal society, and a society that will prosper because it is god fearing and moral. Islamic rule also promises to moderate the harsh inequalities of capitalism, by forbidding speculation and loan sharking, enforcing charity, and requiring the wealthy to invest their money productively, creating jobs for others and services for the community. Many Muslims see in Islamic fundamentalism the hope of "something uniquely Islamic between capitalism and socialism that will marry private enterprise with social justice and a sense of family and community" (Smith, P., pp. 85–88).

It is important to understand that the appeal of political Islam is not solely ideological. Islamist ideas are communicated in a very rewarding social context. Particularly in the newly settled neighborhoods on the outskirts of Cairo, Islamist groups have established a network of social groups that anchors residents' lives and institutions that give people concrete help. Political Islamists see Islamic reform proceeding from the bottom up: the individual, then the family, the neighborhood, and finally the whole society, rather than through a direct attack on the government. One of Wickham's informants told her that the problem with jihadis "is that they are in a rush. They have their eyes on the end, but they don't attempt to find the proper means. While they are prepared to use force, we stress the means of upbringing and persuasion" (Wickham, pp. 127, 129–130).

The mosque is an important center of Islamist life. There are daily prayers and sermons, seminars and weekly religious classes for men and women. These offer some of the few opportunities for young men and women to interact outside the home. Mosques have lending libraries for books and cassette tapes of sermons, and there are also independent Islamic publishing houses and bookstores that sell Islamic journals, magazines, newspapers, books, and pamphlets (Wickham, pp. 133–135, 152).

A very important benefit of Islamist life is that people help each other through networks formed in the mosque. If you need to find an apartment, find a job, get a visa, or find a spouse, mosque contacts are a wonderful resource. Also, the mosque provides access to Islamic institutions that parallel government institutions. There are jobs in Islamist publishing houses and Islamist-run health clinics. The mosque has charitable funds to distribute to the needy and provides subsidized day care and health care services. When a woman decides to adopt modest dress, the local Islamic circle provides the veil and dresses as a gift (Wickham, pp. 125, 153, 155).

Islamist groups run health clinics, schools, day care centers, and furniture factories to provide jobs to the unemployed. They sell meat at discount prices to the poor and give free books and tutoring to poor children. They help young professionals like doctors, dentists, and lawyers by giving them loans to set up clinics and offices and by underwriting health and life insurance policies. Islamic militants seem earnest and dedicated, and above all, honest, especially in contrast to Egypt's corrupt government (Weaver, 1993, p. 82, 1995, p. 61; Hasan, pp. 60–63).

Nabeel's Story: The Sympathizer

Ever since he was a small boy, Nabeel had loved cars, trucks, tanks, planes—things that moved. His parents despaired when he failed the high school entrance examination, but he thrived in the local technical and vocational school, learning to be a mechanic. On graduation, Nabeel looked for a job in Asyut, the city in Upper Egypt where he was raised,

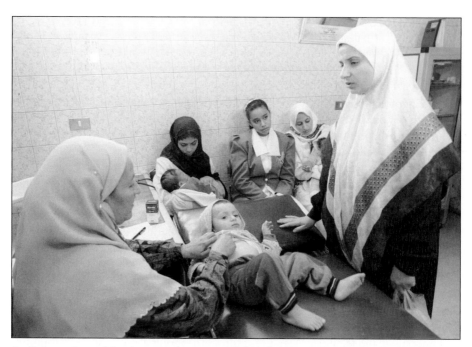

A clinic run by an Islamist group in a poor neighborhood in Cairo. These clinics generate support for the Islamists among the poor who have no other means of obtaining modern medical care. Private care is too expensive, and government clinics too few. The clinics also create support for Islamists among medical professionals like this young woman doctor who might otherwise find few professional opportunities in Egypt. Many Egyptian professionals have had to emigrate to find work. How do the poor in your society obtain medical care?

but there was little work to be found, only unskilled and poorly paid labor. Unhappy, but resigned to the need, Nabeel left to join one of his uncles in Cairo who promised to help him find work. Nabeel's uncle found a job for him repairing postal vans, but the pay was low and he had to make a large payment to the garage manager "for his help." After three years, Nabeel, now 22, owned only his clothes and a few books. His wages fed him, but let him save little. When his mother was ill, Nabeel sent most of his small savings to pay for doctors and medicines.

Cairo was not the bright promise it had once seemed. He was poor, had no future, and every day rich men and women drove past him in expensive cars and foreign clothes. Nabeel was shocked by the women in Cairo; they walked the street uncovered and immodest. Bared bosoms were displayed on every movie poster! It was all part of the influence of the afrangi—the westernized Egyptians who thought and acted as foreigners, not Egyptians, and not Muslims.

Later that year, Nabeel's mother came to visit him in Cairo and he took her to a free health clinic run by the Muslim Brotherhood. There were dedicated young doctors there who took their work seriously. The doctor really listened to Nabeel's mother and she was able to diagnose her breathing problems and get the asthma under control. Nabeel was overjoyed,

but he was also furious at the government clinics that had made his mother wait and wait,
then hadn't helped her. Nabeel listened to sermons by imams who sympathized with al
Jihad. They called for an Islamic Egypt where the government would care about ordinary
Egyptians and there would be jobs and decent wages for all. "Perhaps," thought Nabeel,
"this is the path we need to follow."

In Egypt, the largest and most influential moderate Islamist group is the Muslim Brotherhood, first organized in 1928 by Hassan al-Banna, a schoolteacher who dreamed of bringing back the golden age of the caliphate. The early Brotherhood had a secret paramilitary wing that tried unsuccessfully to assassinate President Nasser. Nasser executed the Brotherhood leadership, jailed thousands of members, and banned the organization in 1954. In prison, Sayyid Qutb wrote what has become the most influential anti-modernist text and argued that an unjust government could be declared infidel and overthrown. In the 1970s, Sadat released many Brotherhood leaders and allowed the organization to operate and recruit. As we will see, Qtub's ideas became influential at this time and inspired radical students who broke with the Brotherhood to join jihadi groups.

The Brotherhood found many recruits among university students and young professionals in the 1980s. It organized within professional associations and universities, taking over many groups in internal elections. Islamists gained important positions in mass media, education, and community social services. As Saad Edin Ibrahim puts it, the Islamists "steadily infiltrate(d) Egypt's public space" (Ibrahim, p. 71). Now the Muslim Brotherhood insists it has renounced violence and will work for an Islamic state by peaceful, legal means in Egypt, though it approves violence against Israel in Palestine. The leadership includes many very respectable men who don't espouse anti-modernist ideas. One leader, Abdul Fotouh is a doctor and university professor. "In general," he says, "I don't find the western way of life at odds with Islam. At the end of the day, we have a common set of humanist values: justice, freedom, human rights and democracy." Another doctor, Gamal Hishmet, is one of seventeen Muslim Brotherhood members of parliament, though they were all elected as independents, since the Brotherhood remains a banned party. Clean-shaven, in a suit and tie, he visits his district, the town of Damanhur, weekly to hear his constituents' problems. They say he is the only politician they ever see, except on election day (*The Economist,* Sept. 13, 2003, p. 7; MacFarquhar, Jan. 20, 2002, p. 3).

Jihadi Islam.   From the 1970s to the 1990s, a period when the government gave free rein to Islamists, radical activists were able to organize on college campuses. Most students were uninterested in politics, but they were gradually drawn in to charitable and professional activities. Islamists came to dominate student government and clubs. Gradually, students were drawn deeper into the Islamist world. Some came under the influence of Sayyid Qtub's ideas and were attracted to two radical offshoots of the Muslim Brotherhood, Gama'a al-Islamiyya and Islamic Jihad. In the 1990s, these groups also attracted followers in the poor squatter settlements of Cairo and in rural towns. Jihad and Gama'a were anti-modern in philosophy and jihadist in strategy. They were willing to use violence and terrorism to challenge the government and redefine the norms of Egyptian society (Ibrahim, p. 69).

In the 1990s, Gama'a and Jihad began to assert their power, using violence to redefine the norms of Egyptian society. In poor neighborhoods dominated by Gama'a, groups of young male militants armed with knives and guns went about enforcing *Sharia* (Islamic law), as their religious leaders, their *sheikhs* defined it. They burned video shops selling tapes they considered immoral—tapes which showed men and women touching or which seemed insulting to Islam. They burned the office of the biggest billboard manufacturing company, which puts up revealing pictures of popular Egyptian actresses (Dawoud, p. 1).

They also mounted a powerful attack on Egypt's secular intellectuals, accusing certain writers of heresy and apostasy, crimes punishable by death under *Sharia*. It began in 1992 with the assassination of Farag Foda, a well-known author who wrote as a Muslim, but criticized the fundamentalists and rebutted their claim to know the only true Islam. In 1994 militants stabbed Naguib Mafouz, one of Egypt's most venerated novelists. Mafouz is a Nobel Prize winner, who has criticized both the Islamists and the Mubarak government. Next came the famous case of Nasr Hamed Abu Zeid, a professor of Arabic literature, whose work is a scholarly and erudite analysis of early Islamic texts. Abu Zeid was targeted as a secularist for daring to discuss the Quran as a text subject to interpretation. He was declared apostate and then Islamist lawyers went to court to dissolve his marriage on the ground that an apostate could not be married to a Muslim woman. Abu Zeid and his wife eventually fled Egypt. Then in 1997 came the infamous massacre of tourists visiting the temples at Luxor (Miller, pp. B7, B9; Ajami, pp. 205–221).

Starting in 1992, the Mubarak government began its attacks on jihadi militants (and on the more moderate Muslim Brotherhood as well). The repression was bloody and thorough, as we have described on pages 220–221. By the end of the 90s, revolutionary Islam had been militarily defeated in Egypt. Egyptian terrorists decided that they could only conduct their warfare abroad, where some individuals helped organize Al Qaeda.

Islamism and Egypt's Future

By the end of the 1990s, many experts agreed that jihadi Islam had passed its peak and was on the way to defeat. In his book, *The Failure of Political Islam,* Olivier Roy argued that everywhere that radical, fundamentalist Islamists had come to the point of putting their ideas into practice they had failed. They failed in Algeria, where the military kept them from power, in Egypt where the government hunted them down, and in Iran, where a new generation rebelled against the strictures of the 1979 Islamist revolution. He predicted that the future held a more moderate, pragmatic political Islam (*The Economist,* Sept. 13, 2003, p. 8).

Since 2001, however, jihadi Islam has gained new life. United States' support for Israel's actions in the occupied territories and the U.S. invasion of Iraq have inspired an outpouring of anti-Americanism and the conviction that the United States is anti-Muslim. While most Egyptians condemn jihadi violence, and believe it is the wrong strategy for achieving an Islamic society, there is some thrill in seeing the terrorists take the initiative and put the West on the defensive.

What will happen to Egypt in the near future? Most people are increasingly pious, but against terrorism. However, they find life harder and harder and their personal situations more precarious. The government is controlled by an aging group of autocratic bureaucrats, and tensions in the Middle East continue to rise. Egypt will be fortunate to end up with a moderate, democratic, Islamist government, but less appealing scenarios are easy to envision.

Thinking Sociologically

1. How do Islamic norms shape daily life in Egypt?
2. What are the norms for "modest dress" in your society?
3. How has modernization in the Egyptian education system and economy changed the roles women play? How has the religious revival changed Egyptian women's roles?
4. Is it ethnocentric to condemn female genital cutting?
5. What role conflicts do men in your society experience? What strategies do men pursue to resolve them?
6. Compare the power of women and men in Egyptian families. What power and influence do women have? How about in your own society?
7. Discuss the importance of work in the informal sector and work abroad for Egyptians and Mexicans. Is there an informal sector in your society? Who works in it?
8. Is the social stratification system in Egypt becoming more open or more closed? How about the stratification system in your society?
9. Based on what you have read in this chapter, do you think the Islamist movement in Egypt will become stronger or weaker in the next few years?
10. In what ways has the experience of colonization shaped the cultures of Egypt and Mexico? How has it affected attitudes towards the West?

For Further Reading

ABDO, GENEIVE, *No God but God: Egypt and the Triumph of Islam.* New York: Oxford University Press, 2000.

AHMED, LILA, *Women and Gender in Islam.* New Haven, CT: Yale University Press, 1992.

ARMSTRONG, KAREN, *Islam: A Short History.* New York: Modern Library, 2000.

FERNEA, ELIZABETH WARNOCK, *In Search of Islamic Feminism.* New York: Doubleday, 1998.

FERNEA, ELIZABETH WARNOCK, AND ROBERT A. FERNEA, *The Arab World, Forty Years of Change.* Anchor, 1997.

FLUEHR-LOBBAN, CAROLYN, *Islamic Society in Practice.* Gainesville: University Press of Florida, 1994.

HADDAD, YVONNE YAZBECK, AND JOHN ESPOSITO, eds., *Islam, Gender and Social Change.* New York: Oxford University Press, 1998.

IBRAHIM, SAAD EDDIN, *Egypt, Islam and Democracy: Critical Essays.* Cairo: The American University in Cairo Press, 2002.

LIPPMAN, THOMAS, *Understanding Islam: An Introduction to the Muslim World.* New York: Penguin, 1990.

MURPHY, CARYLE, *Passion for Islam: The Egyptian Experience.* New York: Scribner, 2002.

SINGERMAN, DIANE, AND HOMA HOODFAR, eds., *Development, Change, and Gender in Cairo: A View from the Household.* Bloomington: Indiana University Press, 1996.

WICKHAM, CARRIE ROSEFSKY, *Mobilizing Islam: Religion, Activism and Political Change in Egypt.* New York: Columbia University Press, 2002.

Bibliography

ABDO, GENEIVE, *No God but God: Egypt and the Triumph of Islam.* New York: Oxford University Press, 2000.

ABU-LUGHOD, JANET L., *Changing Cities.* New York: HarperCollins, 1991.

AHMED, LILA, *Women and Gender in Islam.* New Haven, CT: Yale University Press, 1992.

AJAMI, FOUAD, *The Dream Palace of the Arabs: A Generation's Odyssey.* New York: Pantheon Books, 1998.

———, "Nowhere Man," *The New York Times Magazine,* Oct. 7, 2001, pp. 19–20.

ALBAHEY, YASMINE, "Down with Urfi Marriages," *Middle East Times,* July 4, 2003, http://metimes.com/2K3/issue2003-27/opin/down_with_urfi.htm.

AL KAMMAR, SAID, "The Silent Opposition in Egyptian Politics," *Middle East Times,* Sept. 29, 2000, www.metimes.com/2K/issue2000-39/commu/silent_opposition_in.htm.

ALLAM, ABEER, "Urfi Delivers the Goods, at Half the Price," *Middle East Times,* Feb. 18, 2000, http://metimes.com/2k/issue2000-7/eg/urfi_delivers_the.htm.

———, "Egypt: Number of Executions Jumps," *The New York Times,* June 14, 2002, p. A8.

———, "Egypt: Police Arrest Suspected Militants," *The New York Times,* Sept. 25, 2002, p. A10.

———, "Egypt: Members of Muslim Group Arrested," *The New York Times,* Jan. 3, 2003, p. A6.

———, "Egypt: Police Arrest 13 in Outlawed Islamic Group," *The New York Times,* Dec. 12, 2003, p. A21.

———, "Egypt: Torture Charged," *The New York Times,* March 2, 2004, p. A6.

———, "Egypt: 26 Jailed in Antigovernment Plot," *The New York Times,* March 26, 2004, p. A6.

———, "Egypt: New Crackdown on Brotherhood," *The New York Times,* May 18, 2004, p. A9.

THE AMERICAN UNIVERSITY IN CAIRO SOCIAL RESEARCH CENTER, "Economic Participation of Women in Egypt," 2001, http://www.aucegypt.edu/src/wsite1/index.htm.

ATIYA, NAYARA, *Khul-Khaal: Five Egyptian Women Tell Their Stories.* Syracuse, NY: Syracuse University Press, 1982.

BARAKAT, HALIM, *The Arab World: Society: Culture and State.* Berkeley: University of California Press, 1993.

BASSIOUNI, M. CHERIF, *An Introduction to Islam.* Chicago: Rand McNally, 1989.

BAYAT, ASEF, "Cairo's Poor: Dilemmas of Survival and Solidarity," *Middle East Research and Information Project,* June 1997, http://www.merip.org.

———, "Faith and Fun: Can One Have It All?" *Al-Ahram Weekly On-Line,* May 22–28, 2003, http://weekly.ahram.org.eg/2003/639/fel.htm.

BENIN, JOEL, *The Dispersion of Egyptian Jewry: Culture, Politics and the Formation of the Modern Diaspora.* Berkeley: University of California Press, 1998.

BROWN, NATHAN J., *The Rule of Law in the Arab World: Courts in Egypt and the Gulf.* Cambridge: Cambridge University Press, 1996.

BURUMA, IAN, AND A VISHAI MARGALIT, "Occidentalism," *The New York Review of Books,* Jan. 17. 2002, pp. 4–7.

BUSH, RAY, "An Agricultural Strategy without Farmers: Egypt's Countryside in the New Millennium," *Review of African Political Economy,* Vol. 27, no. 84 (June 2000), pp. 235–249.

CAMPO, JUAN EDUARDO, *The Other Side of Paradise: Explorations into the Religious Meanings of Domestic Space in Islam.* Columbia: University of South Carolina Press, 1991.

CROSSETTE, BARBARA, "Court Backs Egypt's Ban on Mutilation," *The New York Times,* Dec. 29, 1997, p. A3.

———, "Senegal Bans Genital Cutting of Girls," *The New York Times,* Jan. 18, 1999, p. A10.

DANISZEWSKI, JOHN, "Disabling Acid Attacks on Women Are on the Rise in Egypt, *Los Angeles Times,* June 1, 1997, p. A09.

DAWOUD, KHALED, "Militant Video Burners Get 5 to 15," *Al-Ahram Weekly On-line,* March 11–17, 1999, issue no. 420, http://www.ahram.org.eg/weekly/1999/420/eg11.htm.

DONNER, FRED M., "Muhammed and the Caliphate," in John L. Esposito, ed., *The Oxford History of Islam.* New York: Oxford University Press, 1999, pp. 1–62.

EARLY, EVELYN, *Baladi Women of Cairo: Playing with an Egg and a Stone.* Boulder, CO: Lynne Rienner, 1993.

THE ECONOMIST, "A Survey of Egypt: New and Old," March 20, 1998, pp. 1–18.

———, "Egypt's Vulnerable Copts," Jan. 8, 2000, p. 41.

———, "Israelis Whom Egyptians Love to Hate," Jan. 22, 2000, p. 48.

———, "Egypt's Economy: Lonely as a Pyramid, without Tourists," Jan. 5, 2001, pp. 36–37.

———, "Egyptian Unemployment: Summer of Fury," July 21, 2001, p. 38.

———, "Egypt's Islamists: Kinder, Gentler Islam," June 29, 2002, pp. 44, 46.

———, "In the Name of Islam," special survey, Sept. 13, 2003, pp. 3–16.

———, "Egyptian Politics: Surgery on Hardened Arteries," Oct. 4, 2003, pp. 44–45.

———, "Egypt's Presidency: After Mubarak, Who's Next?" Dec. 6, 2003, p. 42.

———, "Egypt: New Surgeon, Same Old Scalpels," July 17, 2004, pp. 47–48.

———, "Emerging Market Indicators," July 24, 2004, p. 92.

DEL FRATE, ANNA ALVAZZI, "Victims of Crimes in Developing Countries." Rome: United Nations Interregional Crime and Justice Research Institute, Publication No. 57, 1998, http://www.unicri.it/cvs/publications/index_pub.htm.

EL-FIQI, MONA, "Borrowing in the Balance," *Al-Ahram Weekly Online,* Nov. 11–17, 1999, issue no. 455, http://web1.ahram.org.eg/weekly/1999/455/ec3.htm.

EL-LAITHY, HEBA, MICHAEL LOKSHIN, AND ARUP BANERJI, "Poverty and Economic Growth in Egypt, 1995–2000," World Bank Policy Research Working Paper 3068, June 2003.

EL-RASHIDI, YASMINE, "Young and Hip, Veil Optional," *Al-Ahram Weekly On-Line,* Oct. 3–9, 2002, http://www.ahram.org.eg/weekly/2002/606/li2htm.

EL-GAWHARY, KARIM, "An Interview with Heba Ra'uf Ezzat," *Middle East Report,* Vol. 24, no. 6 (Nov.–Dec. 1994), pp. 26–27.

ESPOSITO, JOHN, *Islam: The Straight Path.* New York: Oxford University Press, 1991a.

FAKHOURI, HANI, *Kafr El-Elow: An Egyptian Village in Transition.* New York: Holt, 1972.

FEKRY, AHMED, "Egyptians Demonstrate over Rising Unemployment, *Middle East Times Online,* July 13, 2001, http://metimes/com/2K1/issue2001-29/bus.

FERNEA, ELIZABETH WARNOCK, *A View of the Nile.* Garden City, NY: Doubleday & Co., 1970.

———, *In Search of Islamic Feminism.* New York: Doubleday, 1998.

FERNEA, ELIZABETH WARNOCK, AND ROBERT A. FERNEA, *The Arab World: Forty Years of Change.* New York: Doubleday Anchor, 1997.

FISHER, WILLIAM, "Egypt Suffering Labor Pains," *Middle East Times,* May 4, 2004, http://metimes.com/2K4/issue2004-20/eg/egypt_suffering_labor.htm.

FLUEHR-LOBBAN, CAROLYN, *Islamic Society in Practice.* Gainsville: University Press of Florida, 1994.

FOOD AND AGRICULTURE ORGANIZATION, *Food Balance Sheets, 1970 and 2002.* Online FAOSTAT Database, http://www.apps.fao.org/.

FOOD AND AGRICULTURE ORGANIZATION OF THE UNITED NATIONS, "FAO Statistical Databases," 2004.

FRIEDMAN, THOMAS, "After the Storm," *The New York Times,* Jan. 8, 2003, p. A23.

FULMER, MELINDA, "Desert Farmer Taps into Global Markets," *Los Angeles Times,* Oct. 8, 2000, p. C1.

GERGES, FAWAZ A., "The End of the Islamist Insurgency in Egypt?" *Middle East Journal,* Vol. 54, no. 4 (Oct. 1, 2000), pp. 592–612.

GHOSH, AMITAV, *In an Antique Land.* New York: Knopf, 1993.

GOLDBERG, JEFFREY, "Behind Mubarak," *The New Yorker,* Oct. 8, 2001, pp. 48–55.

GOLDEN, TIM, "Crisis Deepens Impact of Arab TV News," *The New York Times,* April 16, 2002, p. A16.

GLAIN, STEPHEN, J., *Mullahs, Merchants, and Militants: The Economic Collapse of the Arab World.* New York: St. Martin's Press, 2004.

HADDAD, YVONNE YAZBECK, AND JOHN ESPOSITO, eds., *Islam, Gender and Social Change.* New York: Oxford University Press, 1998.

HASAN, SANA, "My Lost Egypt," *The New York Times Magazine,* Oct. 25, 1995, pp. 60–63.

HEDGES, CHRIS, "As Egypt Votes on Mubarak, He Faces Rising Peril," *The New York Times,* Oct. 4, 1993, p. A8.

———, "In Bureaucrats' Castle, Everyone Else Is a Beggar," *The New York Times,* June 7, 1994, p. A4.

HIRST, DAVID, "Reaping Worry along the Nile," *Newsday,* Oct. 1, 1997, p. A16.

HOODFAR, HOMA, "The Impact of Male Migration on Domestic Budgeting: Egyptian Women Striving for an Islamic Budgeting Pattern," *Journal of Comparative Family Studies,* Vol. 28, no. 2 (Summer 1997), pp. 73–99.

HOOGLUND, ERIC, "The Society and Its Environment," in Helen Chapin Metz, ed., *Egypt: A Country Study,* 5th ed. Washington, DC: Federal Research Division, Library of Congress, 1991.

IBRAHIM, SAAD EDDIN, *Egypt, Islam and Democracy: Critical Essays.* Cairo: The American University in Cairo Press, 2002.

IBRAHIM, YOUSSEF, "Muslims' Fury Falls on Egypt's Christians," *The New York Times,* March 15, 1993, pp. A1, A8.

INTERNATIONAL LABOR ORGANIZATION, "Economically Active Population Estimates and Projections: 1950–2010," http://laborsta.ilo.org/.

INTERNATIONAL MONETARY FUND, *Balance of Payments Statistics Yearbook, 2004.* Washington, DC: International Monetary Fund, 2005.

INTERPARLIAMENTARY UNION, "Women in National Parliaments," http://www.ipu.org/english/home.htm.

———, "The ILO International Labor Migration Database," http://www.ilo.org/public/english/protection/migrant/ilmdb/index.htm, last updated Aug. 31, 2004.

IRETON, FRANCOIS, "The Evolution of Agrarian Structures in Egypt," in Nicholas Hopkins and Kirsten Westergrad, eds., *Social Change in Rural Egypt.* Cairo: American University in Cairo Press, 2001, pp. 41–65.

JEHL, DOUGLAS, "Above the City's Din, Always the Voice of Allah," *The New York Times,* March 6, 1996, p. A4.

———, "Killings Erode Cairo's Claim to 'Control' Militants," *The New York Times,* March 15, 1997, p. A3.

———, "Egyptian Farmers Resist End of Freeze on Rents," *The New York Times,* Dec. 27, 1997, p. A6.

———, "Arab Honor's Price: A Woman's Blood," *The New York Times,* June 20, 1999, pp. 1, 8.

KAMEL, YOMNA, AND SARA MASHHOUR, "Jumping on the Bandwagon More and More Stars Take the Veil," *Cairo Times,* Nov. 14–20, 2002.

KERSHAW, SARAH, "Cairo, Once 'the Scene,' Cracks Down on Gays," *The New York Times,* April 3, 2003, p. A3.

KHALIL, ASHRAF, "Egypt Bulls Ahead on 'Megaprojects,' " *Chicago Tribune,* Dec. 26, 2000, section 1, p. 3.

KISHOR, SUNITA, "Women's Empowerment and Contraceptive Use," in Maher Mahran, Fatma H. El-Zanaty, and Ann A. Way, eds., *Perspectives on the Population and Health Situation in Egypt.* Cairo, Egypt: National Population Council and Calverton: Maryland: Macro International, Inc., 1998.

KURIAN, GEORGE, ed., *Encyclopedia of the Third World,* Vol. 1. New York: Facts on File, 1992.

LEWIS, BERNARD, "What Went Wrong?" *The Atlantic Monthly,* Vol. 289, issue 1 (Jan. 2002), pp. 43–48.

LIPPMAN, THOMAS, *Egypt after Nasser.* New York: Paragon House, 1989.

———, *Understanding Islam: An Introduction to the Muslim World.* New York: Penguin, 1990.

MACFARQUHAR, NEIL, "Egypt Sentences Sociologist to 7 Years in Quick Verdict," *The New York Times,* May 22, 2001, p. A6.

———, "Egyptian Group Patiently Pursues Dream of Islamic State," *The New York Times,* Jan. 20, 2002, p. 3.

———, "Saddam's 'Weapons' Costly, 'Bush-Sharon' Cheap," *The New York Times,* Nov. 7, 2002, p. A4.

———, "Mubarak Pushes Egypt to Allow Freer Elections," *The New York Times,* Feb. 27, 2005, pp. 1, 4.

MACLEOD, ARLENE, *Accommodating Protest: Working Women, The New Veiling and Change in Cairo.* New York: Columbia University Press, 1993.

MACRO INTERNATIONAL, "Demographic and Health Surveys," http://www.measuredhs.com.

———, "Egyptians Wonder If Mubarak's Son Will Stir Things Up," *The New York Times,* Dec. 21, 2003, p. 10.

———, "Looking for Political Reform? See the Grim Reaper," *The New York Times,* Aug. 11, 2004, p. A4.

MARCUS, AMY DOCKER, "It's Not Easy Being Lean in Cairo Today," *The Wall Street Journal,* March 4, 1998, p. A1.

MENEZES, GABRIELLE, "Religious Chic between Beauty and Modesty, Fashion for Higabs Multiplies," *Cairo Times,* Sept. 25–Oct. 1, 2003, http://cairotimes.com/.

MERNISSI, FATIMA, *Islam and Democracy.* Reading, MA: Addison-Wesley, 1992.

———, *Scheherazade Goes West: Different Cultures, Different Harems.* New York: Pocket Books, 2001.

METZ, HELEN CHAPIN, *Egypt: A Country Study,* 5th ed. Washington, DC: Federal Research Division, Library of Congress, 1991.

MIDDLE EAST AND NORTH AFRICAN BUSINESS REPORT, "Egyptian Expatriates' Remittances Amount to Almost $3 Billion," *MENA Report Newsletter,* Oct. 31. 2004, http://www .menareport.com/story/TheNews.php3?sid=288013&lang=e&dir=mena.

MILLER, JUDITH, "With Freedom, Cairo Intellectuals Find New Stress," *The New York Times,* Jan. 31, 1998, pp. B7, B9.

MITCHELL, PAUL, "Egypt Reintroduces Food Vouchers as Poverty Worsens," May 5, 2004, http://www.wsws.org/articles/2004/may2004/egyp-mo5_prn.shtml.

MITCHELL, RICHARD P., *The Society of the Muslim Brothers.* London: Oxford University Press, 1969.

MITCHELL, TIMOTHY, "America's Egypt: Discourse of the Development Industry," *Middle East Report* (Mar.–Apr. 1991), pp. 18–34.

MULE, PAT, AND DIANE BARTHEL, "The Return to the Veil: Individual Autonomy versus Social Esteem," *Sociological Forum,* Vol. 7, no. 2 (1992), pp. 323–332.

MURPHY, CARYLE, *Passion for Islam: The Egyptian Experience.* New York: Scribner, 2002.

NABEEL, ABRAHAM, AND ANDREW SHRYOCK, eds., *Arab Detroit: From Margin to Mainstream.* Detroit: Wayne State University Press, 2000.

NAJJAR, FAUZI M., "The Debate on Islam and Secularism in Egypt," *Arab Studies Quarterly,* vol. 18, no. 2 (Spring, 1996).

THE NEW YORK TIMES, "Egypt to Appeal Ruling on Genital Cutting," July 12, 1997, p. 3.

————, "Jail Term in Egypt for Mutilation Death," Dec. 16, 1997, p. A3.

NISAN, MORDECHAI, *Minorities in the Middle East.* London: McFarland, 1991.

OBERMEYER, CARLA MAKHLOUF, ed., *Family, Gender and Population in the Middle East: Policies in Context.* Cairo: The American University Press in Cairo, 1995.

O'CONNOR, DAVID, *A Short History of Ancient Egypt.* Pittsburgh: Carnegie Museum of Natural History, 1990.

OMRAN, ABDEL R., AND FARZANNEH ROUDI, "The Middle East Population Puzzle," *Population Bulletin,* Vol. 48, no. 1 (July 1993), pp. 1–39.

PERLEZ, JANE, "Egyptians See U.S. as Meddling in Their Politics," *The New York Times,* Oct. 3, 2002, p. A12.

REMNICK, DAVID, "Going Nowhere," *The New Yorker,* July 12 and 19, 2004, pp. 74–83.

RODENBECK, MAX, "Religion," in John Rodenbeck, ed., *Cairo.* Singapore: APA Publications, 1992.

ROY, OLIVIER, *Globalized Islam: The Search for a New Umma.* New York: Columbia University Press, 2004.

RUGH, ANDREA, *Family in Contemporary Egypt.* Syracuse, NY: Syracuse University Press, 1984.

RYAN, CURTIS R., "Political Strategies and Regime Survival in Egypt," *Journal of Third World Studies,* Vol. 18, no. 2 (Oct. 1, 2001), pp. 25–46.

SACHS, SUSAN, "Egypt's Women Win Equal Rights to Divorce," *The New York Times,* March 1, 2000, p. A1, A5.

————, "Muslim Televangelist Delivers a Winning Message," *The New York Times,* Dec. 24, 2001, p. A4.

SADAT, JEHAN, *A Woman of Egypt.* New York: Simon & Schuster, 1987.

SHERIF, YOUSSEF, "Gays under Attack in Egypt," *Middle East Times,* March 12, 2004, http://metimes.com/2K4/issue2004-11/eg/gays_under_attack.htm.

SINGERMAN, DIANE, *Avenues of Participation: Family, Politics and Networks in Urban Quarters of Cairo.* Princeton, NJ: Princeton University Press, 1995.

SINGERMAN, DIANE, AND HOMA HOODFAR, eds., *Development, Change, and Gender in Cairo: A View from the Household.* Bloomington: Indiana University Press, 1996.

SMITH, JANE, "Islam and Christendom," in John L. Esposito, ed., *The Oxford History of Islam.* New York: Oxford University Press, 1999.

SMITH, PAMELA ANN, "Where Capitalism Is Shaped by Islam," *Utne Reader* (Mar.–Apr. 1994), pp. 85–88.

SPRINGBORG, ROBERT, *Mubarak's Egypt: Fragmentation of the Political Order.* Boulder, CO: Westview Press, 1989.

STARRETT, GREGORY, *Putting Islam to Work: Education, Politics, and Religious Transformation.* Berkeley: University of California Press, 1997.

STATCOMPILER, *Demographic and Health Survey of Egypt, 1995,* http://www.measuredhs.com/date/indicators.

TEKCE, BELGIN, LINDA OLDHAM, AND FREDERIC SHORTER, *A Place to Live: Families and Child Care in a Cairo Neighborhood.* Cairo: The American University in Cairo Press, 1994.

UNITED NATIONS, *1990 Demographic Yearbook,* New York: 1992.

———, 2002, Demographic Yearbook, http://unstats.un.org/unsd/demographic/ products/ dyb/dyb2.htm

———, 2002 *Demographic Yearbook,* http://unstats.un.org/ unsd/demographic.

———, "United Nations Surveys on Crime Trends and the Operations of Criminal Justice Systems," Fourth Survey, 1994, http://www.unodc.org/unodc/en/crime_cicp_ surveys.html.

———, Human Development Report, 2004, http://hdr.undp.org/statistics/data/.

———, *Human Development Report, 2004.* http://hdr.undp.org/statistics/

UNITED STATES BUREAU OF THE CENSUS, *International Data Base 2000.* http://www.census.gov/ipc/www/idbsprd.html.

VATIKIOTIS, PETER J., *The History of Egypt,* 3d ed. Baltimore: Johns Hopkins University Press, 1991.

WAKIN, DANIEL, "Anti-Semitic 'Elders of Zion' Gets New Life on Egypt TV," *The New York Times,* Oct. 26, 2002, pp. A1, A6.

WEAVER, MARY ANNE, "The Trail of the Sheikh," *The New Yorker,* Apr. 12, 1993, pp. 71–88.

———, "The Novelist and the Sheikh," *The New Yorker,* Jan. 30, 1995, pp. 52–69.

WICKHAM, CARRIE ROSEFSKY, *Mobilizing Islam: Religion, Activism and Political Change in Egypt.* New York: Columbia University Press, 2002.

WILSON, SUSAN, *Culture Shock: Egypt.* Portland, OR: Graphic Arts Center Publishing Co., 1998.

WIN NEWS, "Egypt: New Research Shows Many More Women Mutilated," Vol. 23, no. 3 (Summer 1997), pp. 31–33.

WORLD BANK, World Development Indicators, 2004.

Five hours east of Montreal and New York by air, less than an hour from London and Paris lies Berlin, the capital of a reunited Germany, one of the most prosperous countries on earth and the birthplace of Albert Einstein, Ludwig van Beethoven, and other figures who shaped western civilization.

LOCATION: In the center of Europe. France, Belgium, and the Netherlands border Germany to the west; Denmark and the North Sea to the north; Poland and the Czech Republic to the east; and Austria and Switzerland to the south.

AREA: 135,000 square miles or 391,500 square kilometers; the size of California or Japan.

LAND: Lowlands in the north, highlands in the center, and a mountainous region in the south bordering the Alps.

CLIMATE: Temperate similar to the northeastern United States, Canada, or Japan.

POPULATION: 82 million in 2005, expected to decline to 79 million in 2050.

Germany's population is aging: 17 percent are 65 or over.

INCOME: Germany is a wealthy industrial nation. GNP per person averaged $24,051 in 2004.

EDUCATION: The average adult (25+) has completed almost 12 years of school.

RELIGION: 42 percent Protestant; 35 percent Catholic.

MINORITIES: Germany has a large immigrant population. In 1998 there were 7.3 million foreign residents in Germany— almost 10 percent of the population. 2.1 million were Turks and more than 1 million are from the Balkans. Jewish population has grown to 100,000.

CHAPTER FIVE

Germany: Social Institutions and Social Change in a Modern Western Society

INTRODUCTION

"The sociological imagination," said American sociologist C. Wright Mills, "enables us to grasp history and biography and the relations between the two." It tells us that "neither the life of an individual nor the history of a society can be understood without understanding both." Mills argued that people often see their problems as "personal troubles" having to do only with themselves. They fail to see that their lives are shaped by "public issues," problems or transformations in society that impact them and many other individuals (Mills, 1959). If Mills is right, then Germans, of all peoples, must surely have sociological imagination. In the century just past, Germans lived through many devastating social crises and transformations, episodes of change that make clear the intersections between individual lives and societal history.

Giesele's Story: An Eventful German Life

You would have liked my father. He was a big tough guy from Stettin. His family were dockworkers, but somehow he ended up in Berlin on the police force. When I was young he used to carry me on his shoulders to go shopping. My mother would say he carried me so often, they'd have to hire someone to teach me how to walk! My father would always say that it was a brighter world before Germany went to war in 1914. But I was born later, in 1921, after the First World War. My father carried us all on his shoulders in difficult times.

In high school Frieda was my best friend, even though I was a policeman's daughter and she was a professor's daughter. We both wanted to be language teachers. In 1936, Frieda told me her family was leaving Berlin. Germany had become too dangerous for Jews. Until that day I had paid no attention to politics. My father had often said that he didn't care for Hitler, but I had no idea why. One day, not long after that, my father came home at noon, took off his police uniform and never put it on again. He had been forced to resign. A group of Hitler thugs had set fire to a Jewish store and wouldn't let the fire brigades put it out. My father, a lieutenant by that time, had his men force the Nazis back at gun point so that the fire brigades could do their work. I didn't become a policeman to let a bunch of thugs burn down Berlin, he said.

My boyfriend Rolf wouldn't listen to a word said against Hitler. The Führer was a strong man and would make Germany great again, he said. We argued all the time. I never thought we would marry, but when Rolf was called into the army after Germany invaded Poland in 1939, I realized I might never see him again. After our wedding Rolf said the Russians held no terrors for him. He'd rather face a thousand Russians than face my father again.

Rolf came back from Russia in 1943 an old and broken man. His lungs had been damaged by pneumonia and he'd lost three fingers to frostbite. He was bitter and depressed. He didn't say so, but I knew we would lose the war. Allied bombing destroyed our house, so we moved to a shack that my father had built on his garden plot in an eastern suburb. The cold and hunger bothered Rolf less than the thought that the Russians would overrun Berlin. They'll pay us back for Leningrad and the Ukraine, he said. We left piles of dead women and children and marched the men off to build bridges for our tanks. When the bridges were done, we shot them.

Rolf's lungs gave out before the Nazis finally were beaten, but though things were very bad, we had some hope. The Russians found our names, my father's and mine, on a list of enemies the Nazis planned to send to the camps. The Russians thought we could be trusted as loyal anti-Nazis and I was offered a teaching job in East Berlin.

Some of the German anti-fascists whom the Russians brought to power were people of courage, but for them, freedom was following the communist party line. It became harder and harder for me to follow the party, especially since my second husband, Johann, was an active Christian. My supervisors told me that if I didn't leave the church, I would lose my job. I was as stubborn as my father and lost my job.

By 1985, Johann and I were old enough to travel to West Berlin. If you were 65 and had some money, the DDR would let you come and go. Johann had a small pension and my son Heinz, an engineer, helped us. We carried the news of our continuing resistance to party dictatorship to the West and we brought back church newspapers published in the West that printed our stories. Churches all over East Germany made copies of these articles for their parishioners. It's hard to believe that church bulletins had the liveliest journalism in East Germany, but they did. When the Wall came down, it was a triumph, but the good times didn't last. East Germany's economy was on the brink in the 1980s, and reunification pushed it over. Our products were a joke in the West. They called the East German car, the Trabi, the world's largest paperweight. Today, the capitalists at Volkswagen and Daimler build their cars in Moldavia or Mexico, not in the former East Germany. Our son is out of work; he is picketing an industrialist's conference in Dusseldorf next week. We're going to march with him. You should join us.

The twentieth century was hard on Germans. They experienced humiliating defeat and devastation in two world wars and they lived under the greatest variety of political systems: a monarchy, a republic, a fascist state, an authoritarian Soviet satellite state, and a democracy. After World War II, East Germans and West Germans experienced two different economic systems: socialism and capitalism. Finally, east Germans today are finding their lives transformed as their society is absorbed into a reunified Germany.

It will be helpful for you to learn about German society for several reasons. First of all, you will become acquainted with all the varieties of political and economic institutions that are found in modern western societies. For example, Germans practice their own national variety of capitalism. If you live in a capitalist society, you will see that German capitalism is different from your nation's capitalism. Also, by studying Germany you will learn how changing social institutions shape people's lives. Sociologists, because they deal with real-life societies, cannot conduct experiments in the same way that physicists or even biologists can. But in the past 45 years, Germany has been a kind of natural experiment in the consequences of adopting two different sets of political and economic institutions. You can see how different institutions in East and West Germany shaped contrasting values and norms and interpersonal relationships.

Finally, it is important to study German society because so many important sociologists were German. They used their experiences with dictatorship and democracy, with bureaucracy and social inequality, in creating some of sociology's most important concepts and theories. To really understand Karl Marx's theories or Max Weber's works, you need to know about German society.

Social Change Today: Reunification

One of the most fascinating things about Germany is that dramatic social change is going on today. Reunification is an experiment in deliberately remaking social institutions that is happening before our eyes. Germany was originally divided into two separate states in the wake of its defeat in World War II. The eastern part of Germany, occupied by the Soviet Union, became East Germany (the German Democratic Republic, or GDR), a Soviet satellite state with a socialist economy, an authoritarian government, and sealed borders—symbolized by the famous Berlin Wall. The western part of Germany, occupied by Britain, France, and the United States, became West Germany (the Federal Republic of Germany, the FRG, or the Federal Republic, as Germans called it); a close ally of its former enemies in their fight against communism. West Germany became a western-style parliamentary democracy and one of the world's richest, most powerful capitalist economies. It was twice the size of East Germany and had a population four times larger (62.6 million, versus 16.4 million in the GDR in 1990) (Heilig, Buttner, and Lutz, p. 4).

Until Gorbachev came to power in the Soviet Union and loosened the Soviet hold on eastern Europe, no society had ever before abandoned socialism and adopted capitalism. Now, since 1988, East Germany, like Poland, Hungary, the Czech Republic, and many other former Soviet-bloc nations, has been engaged in adopting some form of democratic political institutions and capitalist economic institutions. In East Germany, the transformation has taken the particular form of re-unification with West Germany, or, in reality, absorption into West Germany. West German institutions have remained essentially unchanged, while the former GDR (East Germany) has changed its government and economy, values and norms, and social group life. Acknowledging that the process of unification is not yet really complete, Germans refer to "the western Länder" (the states that composed the former West Germany) and "the eastern Länder" (the states that were East Germany). Recently they have taken to calling the unified Germany "the Berlin Republic" to distinguish it from the FRG and the GDR.

Inge's Story: In The New Germany

Since the Wende (literally, the "turning," as in "a turning of the road," the term Germans use for the fall of the East German regime and reunification), life in Leipzig (in the former GDR) has changed more than Inge Reuter ever imagined. New Year's Eve, for example, Inge and her husband went out to a restaurant—alone. In the old days there were no restaurants worth going to, and no one had any money anyhow. They spent all their New Year's eves (and most other weekend nights as well) gathered around someone's kitchen table, eating bread and cheese, and drinking beer, laughing and singing and enjoying the company of family and friends. That was all they had: friends and plenty of time to enjoy them. No one worked very hard, because working hard didn't get you more pay, and even if it did, there was nothing to buy.

Now Inge finds herself a successful businesswoman, and nostalgic for the old days. When the western companies began to build all the new shopping malls outside Leipzig, she started a cleaning company. She is busy all the time, hiring and training employees, supervising, getting new contracts, and doing her accounts far into the night. There are no more kitchen-table parties. It's not just time either: The old crowd has split up. Some, like Inge, have prospered, but others are still unemployed. They are no longer all in the same boat, and tensions have sprung up among them. Everyone is out for themselves now; working hard to earn money and busy spending it. It seems like things have become more important than friendship.

Life has changed too in western Germany, though not as drastically as in the east. As Germany struggles to absorb the east, there are new economic burdens and people in the west have seen their standard of living decline.

Joachim's Story: In the New Germany

Joachim Hasselblad has just completed his technical training in advertising, at the age of 26. He is very disappointed that the company with which he apprenticed has not hired him and he has only been able to find contract work. If he can keep the contracts coming without pause (not very likely, he assumes), he can make as much as $40,000. Not bad for the first year out of training, you might say. Joachim bitterly denies it. "I'm going to lose 40–50 percent to taxes! That's to pay for rebuilding the east, and to pay for all those pensioners in the east who never paid in with real German money, but will collect anyhow. And all they do is complain—after all we've done for them! Oh, I know," says Joachim, "its not just the east. It's the pressure of global competition. Employers can't afford high wages and pensions and long vacations and all the other benefits anymore. They are moving factories east to Poland and Slovakia. But why should it be my generation that has to pay the price?"

Inge and Joachim come from two different societies: East Germany and West Germany, but they are both Germans, and as Germans they do still have much in common. Forty-five years of division into two societies did not erase all their common heritage. Their societies have a history that was shared up until 1946, and it has left preoccupations and scars common to both societies. Also division did not entirely alter the German culture common to both East and West. Let us begin by examining the two Germanys' common history and culture.

GERMAN HISTORY: CENTRAL THEMES

First of all, Germany's national history is briefer than that of Egypt or Japan. Germany didn't even exist as a separate nation until modern times. Nevertheless, Germany's history has been very eventful. It is studded with wars, treaties, monarchs, changes of borders, and successive governments and policies. We cannot begin to tell you the whole involved story in a sociology text. Instead we will describe a few key issues that Germans have repeatedly fought over. The first is: Should Germany have a single government with centralized power or should it be a collection of small states with most power held on the local level? Over the centuries Germans have fought about this and they have also fought about whether Germany should be an authoritarian nation, with unrestricted power in the hands of its rulers, or whether it should be a democracy, with a constitution, a bill of rights, and a parliamentary system to give its citizens political say and protection from rulers' power. Finally, Germans have struggled about what protection the government owes its citizens against the impersonal destructiveness of market forces in an industrial society. In this battle, a system of social welfare protections has been the alternative to government control of the economy.

Centralized Power versus Local Power

Germany was not fully united as a nation-state until 1871. Before that, Germany experienced many centuries when periods of national unification alternated with fragmentation into small kingdoms. In the first and second centuries B.C., Germanic tribes settled the area that is now modern Germany, battling the Romans, and after the collapse of the Roman Empire they spread over northern Italy, Britain, and France. In early medieval times (A.D. 800) Charlemagne unified these peoples in an empire known in Germany as the First *Reich* (or empire) and elsewhere as the Holy Roman Empire. After Charlemagne's death, his empire broke up into hundreds of small kingdoms. Through the centuries they sometimes formed local unions, then broke up again. In modern times, centralization gained. Prussia was first united after the Thirty Years' War ended in 1648. In 1815, after Napoleon's defeat, the Congress of Vienna established a German Confederation of 39 monarchies, headed by Austria under Prince Metternich as chancellor. After the Franco-Prussian War, in 1871, German states voluntarily joined Prussia in a Second Reich, a new imperial Germany, led by the Prussian King Wilhelm I and his prime minister, Otto von Bismarck. This time the Reich took the form of a federal union, with all the small monarchies represented in a Federal Council.

Imperial ambitions for military might and global political power led Germany into World War I, a war the nation expected to win within months. When, after four grueling years of trench warfare, Germany finally conceded defeat, it lost some territory and was forced to disarm, but it remained one state through the Weimar Republic and Hitler's Third Reich. Only after World War II did Germany once again suffer division—into two separate states. But as we shall see, West Germany, the FRG, mindful of the harm done by Germany's past imperial ambitions, established itself as a federation of states, carefully balancing centralized power with the rights of separate state governments.

Authoritarianism versus Democracy

Germany has a long tradition of authoritarian rule and a much newer commitment to democracy. Monarchs with absolute power ruled Germany at least from the time of Charlemagne, and the most successful joined absolutism with empire, a strong military, and especially in the modern period, an efficient bureaucracy, which the monarch tried to keep subordinate. But in the nineteenth century, absolutism came under attack in Germany, from liberals influenced first by the French Revolution and later by German socialism.

During the time of the German Confederation some aristocrats, influenced by liberal thought, joined with officials of the bureaucracy to press Metternich for reforms like a constitution, parliamentary government, guarantees of civil liberties, and market freedoms. The French Revolution of 1830 inspired further efforts, and liberals, allied with artisans and peasants, actually seized power briefly in the German Revolution of 1848. They succeeded in establishing a constitutional monarchy in the form of a federation of states. But the alliance among middle-class liberals and artisans and peasants soon broke down, because the latter two groups wanted more radical reform. Then conservatives seized their chance to restore monarchical absolutism.

It was Bismarck who healed the split between liberals and monarchists by dividing power between the king and parliament in such a way as finally to favor the king. His strategy of attracting the support of liberals through a policy of militarism and imperialism was to prove surprisingly durable, from the 1870s, straight up to World War I, and then, of course, in Hitler's Germany as well. Germans were continually attracted to the idea of military strength used to conquer an empire under the leadership of a heroic, absolute ruler.

One interlude in German history built democratic institutions. Germany's military defeat in World War I was accompanied by workers' revolts all over the country, which deposed monarchies and replaced them with revolutionary councils. In Berlin, the Social Democratic Party proclaimed a federal republic, instituted a parliament, drafted a constitution with universal suffrage, and elected a president. The new republic was the Weimar Republic, named in reference to the birthplace of Germany's beloved poet Goethe, who symbolized German humanism, in contrast to Prussian despotism and militarism. But despite its democratic values, the Weimar Republic left the door open to authoritarianism. Bowing to German tradition, the republic created a strong president, elected for seven years with extensive powers. When Communists put down an antidemocratic coup, Social Democrats allied themselves with the military to suppress the Communists. This opened the way to extremism on both right and left and prepared the way for Hitler's rise in the desperate times of the depression of 1929–1933.

Once in power, Hitler established an extreme authoritarian dictatorship, arresting liberal, socialist, and communist critics, and putting all independent institutions under Nazi control. The secret police, special courts, and concentration camps were used to crush all opposition. State governments were replaced by appointed governors, trade unions were abolished, and other political parties were disbanded. Hitler appointed himself *Führer* of the Third Reich. Nazi propaganda glorified the authoritarian state, the heroic leader, and military power. Military might was used for conquest, adding *Lebensraum* (living space) to the new German empire, and for a racist genocide against the Jews, at least six million of whom were slaughtered in the Nazi holocaust.

After the Nazi defeat, the federal Republic was founded as a democracy, consciously building on the legacy of Weimar democracy. East Germany, while formally adopting democratic institutions, actually became another authoritarian regime.

Welfare Capitalism versus Socialism

Germany experienced a late and rapid industrialization during the final quarter of the nineteenth century. Primarily agricultural in 1875, by 1900 Germany employed more people in industry and mining than in farming. It became the biggest industrial power in Europe. Germans flocked to industrial cities and towns and population grew by 50 percent. Germany specialized in heavy industry: coal mining, iron production, and manufacture of chemicals and electrical equipment. Laboring under the oppressive conditions of early capitalism, industrial workers were attracted to Germany's tradition of Marxist socialism.

Marx wrote *The Communist Manifesto* in time for the Revolution of 1848. Characteristically, for Germany, it fused a demand for popular democracy with the call for socialism. In authoritarian Germany, these two goals were joined: Working people wanted the right to form trade unions, the right to political representation, and the power to control industry themselves. When the 1848 revolution was crushed, more than a million German republicans left their country for the United States. Others remained to form many democratic and socialist opposition parties, including the forerunner of today's Social Democratic Party.

Fear of socialism motivated every German government of the late nineteenth and early twentieth centuries. Bismarck, always the clever politician, succeeded both in repressing socialism and in co-opting it: He outlawed all Social Democratic organizations and trade unions, while at the same time attracting Social Democratic support by instituting comprehensive social insurance to protect workers against the cost of illness, accident, old age, and disability.

Later governments were more obvious in their opposition to socialism. After Bismarck, the German monarchy pursued militaristic nationalism and overseas colonies to distract the public from social reform. Even the Weimar government, though founded with the help of revolutionaries and Social Democrats, became so fearful of socialists and communists that its president Hindenburg appointed Hitler chancellor rather than seek Social Democratic support. After World War II, Germany faced the future with a strong socialist tradition, an equally enduring history of opposition to socialism, and a culture that, since Bismarck, had assumed social welfare to be the government's business.

East and West Germans are united by their common history. They all understand Germany's historic conflicts over centralism, authoritarianism, and socialism. Germans are also united by a common culture inherited from their shared past.

GERMAN CULTURE: CONTINUITY AND CHANGE

Because Germany was for so long divided into separate monarchies, there are still regional variations in customs and identity. The cultures of Prussia (in the north) and Bavaria (in the south) are distinct. Nevertheless, we can easily single out certain enduring values and norms in German culture. Germans have long been known for their love of order, their respect for authority, their seriousness, hard work, and social responsibility. These values still animate Germans today in both the former GDR and the FRG.

Order

Germans prefer order in all aspects of their lives. Norms require promptness, tidiness and cleanliness, careful conformity to the law, and a proper formality in relating to others. If you have a business appointment with a German executive you must get right down to business, because when your time is up, the manager will become impatient and soon send you on your way (Hall and Hall, pp. 35, 53, 83–84). Social small talk will not be appreciated. If you are late to a job interview, there is no way you can get the job, and if you are late to dinner, your hosts will be insulted and annoyed. Stores must close by 8 P.M. on Saturdays and are closed all day on Sundays. Sunday is supposed to be a day of rest. If you mow the lawn or use power tools or hang out laundry to dry, you will scandalize your neighbors (*The Economist,* Sept. 2, 2000, p. 44).

Germans also carefully order the space around them. Spending the day at the beach, West German families pile up sand as high as 4 feet in a wall around their blankets, defining their own private territories (Gannon, p. 75). In a business, the offices of different departments are separated by closed doors and the department chief carefully closes the door of his private office. It would be very rude to pick up or move a chair in someone's home or office in order to make yourself more comfortable (Hall and Hall, pp. 40–41). In a German hotel, the maid arranges a foreigner's jumbled shoes in a neat row and lines up the toothbrushes.

Obedience

Germans have long seen it as their duty to obey the law and to submit to the authorities—government officials, bureaucrats, police officers, and judges who make and enforce the laws. Ordinary Germans believe it is their duty to correct anyone they see disobeying the law. They don't hesitate to reproach strangers. Neighborhoods have informal rules about when and where you can wash your car or put out the trash and when children are allowed to play noisily outdoors. People will reproach a neighbor whose windows are unwashed or whose lawn grows too high. Germany has complex recyling laws, which people patiently follow. They must sort their trash into four different color-coded bins, take wine bottles down to a special dumpster on the corner, and return jars and bottles to the supermarket (Hall and Hall, p. 47; Landler, Jan. 1, 2003, p. A4).

Germans cross only when the light is green and let their dogs off the leash only in specially marked areas. Dogs, like people, are expected to obey and obedience schools for dogs are very popular. They teach dogs and their owners how to behave in public places like trains, shops, and restaurants. Dogs that complete the course successfully are given a diploma, the *Hundefuhrerschein I* (Cohen, June 20, 2000, p. A4).

While many other cultures rely on informal understandings, Germans like to make all the rules explicit. It is typically German to make thousands of detailed laws and regulations that people carefully obey to the letter. In each German state detailed laws specify how schools should operate: from the marking system to the types of punishments permitted. Businesses must conform with endless and growing legal regulations: health and safety laws, laws regulating competition, and laws specifying the structure of corporate boards and their membership.

Ulrich and Helga's Story: The Marriage Contract

Ulrich and Helga, after living together for a year, have decided to marry. Tonight they are sitting over glasses of wine with their friend Otto, a lawyer, to draw up a prenuptial agreement. "We agree to share domestic tasks equally," the document reads. "We will take turns in cooking, cleaning, and dishwashing, laundry, grocery shopping, and bill paying. We each agree to contribute 10 percent of our salaries monthly toward a fund for buying a house, to retain 10 percent for private use, and to place the rest in a joint bank account. We agree that each of us shall have the right to go out alone with male or female friends, but we pledge ourselves to sexual fidelity. We agree that if we have a child, Helga will stay at home for six years and, during that time, Ulrich will support her and the child." Ulrich, Helga, and Otto see nothing unusual about this document. All their married friends have done something similar and they believe it is good to discuss all these matters explicitly and reach a formal agreement.

Seriousness

Germans take life seriously. They are very concerned with ideas and principles and they insist on things being done right. Many observers have characterized German culture as "intellectual." West German TV features many earnest discussion programs in which people sit at round tables and solemnly debate current issues. The TV audience sits before them at smaller tables, sipping drinks and listening attentively (Buruma, p. 23). Germans are idealistic. They want to find the right principles and follow them, no matter what.

In the nineteenth century, Germany was a breeding ground for trade unionism and socialism, developing a tradition of working-class organization and an analysis of class conflict expressed most influentially by Karl Marx. German dedication to improving the condition of working people influenced societies all over the world, and particularly in the United States, where many German immigrants became involved in the antislavery movement and the trade union and socialist movements. As immigrants in America, they fought successfully for higher wages, shorter hours, limits on child labor, safer working conditions, and recognition of contracts with labor unions.

Dedication to principle has had some admirable results, but some ghastly ones too. German fascination with absolute principles facilitated Nazism. People were willing to accept a simple principle—"Aryan supremacy"—that explained everything in life and told them what to do, and they closed their eyes to its immoral consequences. But you mustn't forget that German conscientiousness also underlay resistance to Hitler by some German aristocrats, Catholics, and Communists.

Hermann's Story: The Police Officer

Hermann Schnabel is a 17-year veteran of the Hamburg police force, recently promoted to detective. He has been assigned to track down foreigners who have overstayed their visas and are now in Germany illegally. One day Hermann is called by an angry landlord to a shabby walk-up apartment building on the industrial outskirts of the city. "That woman up there never pays her rent on time, and she looks so foreign and her apartment smells funny; I want you to investigate," the landlord demands. Climbing up to the top floor, Hermann finds a terrified woman who falls weeping at his feet. "Please don't arrest me," she pleads, "it's not for me, but for my daughter. If you send us home my relatives will circumcise her. Do you know what that means? I can't let her be mutilated like that." Hermann does know what it means. He has heard this story before. And this is on top of yesterday's encounter with an Algerian journalist who wrote an exposé of a fundamentalist militia. If he is sent home, the militia will hunt him down and kill him. Mumbling with embarrassment, Hermann takes a 20-mark bill out of his wallet and gives it to the woman, then flees.

Trudging back to the station house, Hermann feels anguished and torn. "It's my assignment," says one side of his mind; "it's my duty." "I can't do this," says another side. "I can hear my history teacher telling us, 'Germans must never simply acquiesce in persecution again.'" "How can I send foreigners home to be killed or mutilated?" Back at the station house, Hermann drags himself into his captain's office. "I can't do this," he says. "I want to resign from the illegal alien detail. Please, can you transfer me to another duty?" "Well Hermann, I'm not surprised," says the captain. "You're the third officer in the last four months to ask for transfer off this duty. Maybe I'll ask for a transfer too."

Careful Work

Dedication to work is another aspect of German seriousness. Germans are renowned for their hard work and efficiency and their "insistence on precision." Germany has long excelled in industries that produce quality goods to exacting standards, like machine tools, cars, cameras, arms, and small appliances. Cars like Mercedes Benz are built to be driven for hours on the German *Autobahnnen* (highways) at speeds over 100 miles an hour. In 2004, a proposal that goods produced in Germany be labeled "Made in E.U." (European Union) set off a roar of protest. The "Made in Germany" label had become "a pillar of postwar German identity," associated as it was with quality, fine craftsmanship, and precision engineering. Germans were embarrassed by a recent survey that ranked Mercedes behind Lexus and Infiniti in dependability—it was an assault on their national reputation (Landler, May 9, 2004, WK14). German business managers are slow to reach decisions, because they require a great deal of very detailed technical information. Slide presentations, reams of data, long histories of background events, are all carefully attended to and digested (Lewis, p. 375; Hamilton, p. 58).

The Burden of History

Not only do Germans take their principles and their work seriously, they take their history very seriously too. They worry about Germany's past susceptibility to authoritarian government, to racist ideologies, and to demagogues like Hitler. Do you come from a society with an ugly past? Is there racial oppression or genocide in your country's history? If so, you will understand some of the painful dilemmas Germans face. Young Germans long to put the Nazi horror behind them; to be part of a "normal nation." "How long do we have to keep apologizing?" they ask. But if they try to close the books on Nazism, doesn't that show insensitivity to Hitler's victims? For example, there is the issue of Germans criticizing Israel. Have they any right to do so? "Whenever Israel is discussed in Germany," said Foreign Minister Joschka Fischer, the fundamental debate about German identity is never far behind." Recent books and a television documentary about the devastation of Dresden and other German cities by British and American firebombing in World War II broke a half-century taboo on discussing German suffering in the war. Germans ask, is it morally acceptable to portray ourselves as victims during the Nazi era? (*The Economist,* May 25, 2002, p. 48; Schneider, Jan. 18, 2003, p. B7; Bernstein, March 15, 2003, p. A3; Buruma, Oct. 21, 2004, pp. 8–12).

Taking Responsibility. In the aftermath of World War II, Germans hastened to forget the horrors of Nazism. But in the late 1960s, a new generation of young West Germans insisted on confronting the public with the truth about Nazi crimes. Germans began a serious national self-examination of their guilt, a process of *Trauerarbeit,* as they call it (the work of mourning) that continues to this day (Buruma, p. 21). West German schools made study of the Holocaust a required part of the curriculum.

Government policy reflects Germans' fear of repeating the past. The constitution grants draftees the right to refuse to fight on grounds of conscience (Buruma, pp. 24–25). Germany has also made it state policy to welcome refugees from political persecution, despite Germans' discomfort with foreigners. And Germany has maintained a careful tolerance of free speech, despite distaste for nonconformists. The government has moved very carefully in its efforts to root out Islamic terrorist cells in German cities because of the reluctance of politicians, spies, and policemen "to be accused of Gestapo tactics or Stasi tactics" (The Stasi was the East German secret police) (Kramer, Feb. 11, 2002, pp. 36–37; Bernstein, Sept. 26, 2004, p. 14).

Questioning Authority. Since World War II, Germans have worried about the dangers in their traditional respect for authority. In Hitler's time, people treated Nazi groups with respect, as they paraded and drilled in their smart uniforms. After World War II, many Germans said that they had been "just obeying orders" when they massacred civilians and sent Jews off to concentration camps. If that was the result of obedience, West Germans reasoned, they were going to have to educate their children to resist authority and make their own moral choices. Nowadays, German school exams ask questions like "Discuss the problem of how an individual is to behave in a state based on false norms" (Buruma, pp. 183–184).

Divergent Values in East and West

Though East and West Germany had much in common, during the forty-five years of their separation their cultures diverged. After all, the two societies were completely isolated from each other, divided by an armed border. East Germans were not allowed to cross the border, and West Germans could do so only with difficulty. For several decades even phone calls across the border were blocked. In the West, German culture was shaped by consumer capitalism and in the East it was changed by socialism.

West German Consumerism

West Germany became one of the world's most affluent societies. Yearly per person income was $23,030 in 1992, putting the West Germans behind only Japan, Sweden, and the United States in international income comparisons. In West Germany smooth, carefully engineered highways were filled with Mercedes Benzes, BMWs, Audis, and Porsches, zooming along at 100 miles per hour. Modern high-speed trains connected cities filled with upscale shopping districts and malls, sleek apartment towers, and new housing estates. Landmark buildings destroyed in World War II were perfectly rebuilt or restored. Few neighborhoods in West German cities were old or crumbling, dirty or neglected. You could not help but notice that this was a rich society. (See Table 5.1.)

The Value of Possessions. In West Germany, people were busy making money and spending it. They had many labor-saving devices but were always in a hurry. Meetings with friends were carefully scheduled on busy calendars. In many regions, the simplest single-family house cost $300,000 and people spent heavily on luxury furnishings: leather couches, oriental rugs, and original paintings. Designer clothes and upscale cars and trendy sports equipment were the means to declare one's status and express an individual identity (Rademaekers, pp. 9–10). West Germans

TABLE 5.1 Measures of Affluence
Americans, Germans, and Japanese have far more extensive connections to global communications, entertainment, and information than Egyptians and Mexicans do.

	Television Sets Per 1,000 Persons	Cell Phones Per 1,000 Persons	Internet Users Per 1,000 Persons	Personal Computers Per 1,000 Persons
United States	835	488	552	659
Japan	731	637	449	382
Germany	586	727	411	431
Mexico	283	255	99	82
Namibia	38	80	27	71
Egypt	217	67	28	17

Sources: United Nations, Human Development Report 2004, http://hdr.undp.org/statistics/data/advanced.cfm

World Bank, World Development Indicators 2004, http://www.worldbank.org/data/dataquery.html

invested a great deal of money and time in their homes and they enjoyed their possessions in privacy.

The Value of Leisure. In recent decades, West Germans moved away from the traditional German dedication to work. They devoted themselves less to duty and more to pleasure. West Germans achieved the highest wages, the shortest workweek, and the most holidays of any industrialized nation. They worked an average of 37 hours per week, compared to 41 in the United States, and over 60 in Japan. Plus, they got six weeks of paid vacation, with an extra month's pay at vacation time, a Christmas bonus, and noncash benefits equal in value to 80 percent of their take-home pay (Glouchevitch, pp. 112–113). On their long vacations, West Germans were dedicated travelers, filling the beaches of the Greek islands, Miami, and Cuba during the winter months and seeking the latest tropical resorts on remote Asian islands. Travel agents did a booming business in tour packages.

The Value of Individualism. West Germany was an **individualistic** society: People saw themselves as individuals, autonomous actors, free to join groups or remain separate. They valued their privacy and their right to speak as individuals. Businesses and politicians addressed citizens through advertising and the mass media, but people were expected to make individual decisions and act on the basis of their own needs and judgments. When Wal-Mart opened stores in Germany with their usual greeter at the door, shoppers were offended. The friendly salespeople were too intrusive, people complained, and they didn't want cashiers touching their things either, by packing their purchases for them (Rubin, Dec. 27, 2001, p. 1). In West Germany it was not unusual or deviant behavior to belong to no group beyond the family, friendship circles, and a rather formal work group membership. Few West Germans did volunteer work with the elderly or any other needy group.

John Ardagh vividly described West Germans' sense of their separateness as individuals and their distance from the rest of society. For example, at a West German health club an elderly person needing help or a mother who needed someone to watch her child for a moment would not turn to other club members. If asked, their response would be "That's not my business—the officials (staff) are paid for that." The West German welfare state provided generous support for people who were disabled, addicted, or ex-prisoners. This is perhaps fortunate, since individual West Germans tried to avoid such people and felt no obligation to help them. No one described West German individualism more clearly than an old East Berlin couple, interviewed by *The New York Times* after reunification: "In the old East Germany people were closer. . . . We helped each other," they said, "In the west, people say this is my space, it is separate from you, and do not disturb my space" (Ardagh, pp. 526, 527–528; Cohen, March 8, 1993, p. D3).

East German Socialism

In the East consumer goods were drab and sometimes in short supply. Housing was cheaply built and often in disrepair. People had to take their vacation in East Germany or in nearby Soviet-bloc nations. Life moved slowly; people spent hours waiting in line in stores and for buses, but everyone seemed to have lots of time; time to go visiting, take coffee breaks, chat with a neighbor, or cheer up people at the old-age home (Darnton, pp. 297–309).

When Peter Marcuse visited the two Germanys in 1989, just before the Wall came down, he saw "the society of the elbows" and "the society of the coffee breaks." In West Germany he thought that people were always elbowing each other out of the way in their hurry to get to the cashier or on the plane. In East Germany he was amazed to find that all work at his office stopped every day at 10 A.M. sharp. The secretaries cleared off a table, laid a cloth and dishes, and put up the kettle, and everyone in the office came in and had coffee and cake and chatted together. No one answered the phones and appointments waited (Marcuse, p. 43). East German customs reflected distinctive values, different from those in the West.

The Value of Labor. Socialist theory holds that workers are the most important part of any economy, because their labor produces the goods on which wealth is based. Capitalists are really parasites who feed on workers, because they take their profits out of what workers produce. In East Germany there were no capitalists—no businesspeople, no entrepreneurs. To make a profit or charge interest was seen as profoundly immoral. Socialist East Germany taught respect for labor. Each elementary school class was paired with a factory unit where they visited and helped out and got to know individual workers. Classes planted gardens and learned to use machinery. The East German government tried to give heroic workers as much publicity as entrepreneurs like Donald Trump received in the United States. The only problem was that people were aware that workers in East Germany didn't live as well as workers in capitalist West Germany.

Because they valued labor so highly, East Germans believed that people's jobs should be productive and satisfying, not mindless or debasing the way labor so often was in capitalist societies. This ideal came from the writing of Karl Marx. But East Germans frequently complained about their society for its failure to provide satisfying work. Shortages of supplies, or mixups in deliveries often shut down production, and because materials were of poor quality the goods produced were often shoddy. Everyone was employed, but there really wasn't enough work for everyone, so many people were working way below their capacities. These problems bothered people, because they really believed in the value of work.

The Value of Equality. Egalitarianism was a very strong value in East Germany. If ordinary working people are the real source of wealth, then it makes sense for everyone to be paid what workers are paid; no one deserves any more. East German society was strongly committed to providing necessities for all. Everyone had a job; there was no unemployment. Housing was very cheap, though its quality was poor. There was no homelessness. Basic foods like bread and cheese and beer were cheap. Health care was free, education was free, old people received pensions, and preschool day care was available to all. But luxuries were distrusted. The only car for sale was the sputtering, smelly Trabant; clothing was all cheap and styleless. **Conspicuous consumption,** acquiring possessions as signs of wealth and status, was condemned. In fact, a key event in undermining the East German regime after the fall of the Soviet Union was a series of revelations about the privileges of the ruling Communist Party elite. When East Germans learned that the party chief's wife traveled to Paris every month to get her hair cut, and that the party leadership lived in luxury homes in guarded compounds and drove Mercedes Benz cars, they were furious.

The Value of Collectivism. An important part of socialist culture in East Germany was belief in the virtues of group participation and distrust of individualism. People were expected to involve themselves in **collectives** (organized groups): to join youth organizations, women's organizations, the Communist Party; to attend meetings at their office or factory. Individualism was suppressed. If you avoided joining group life, and insisted on setting yourself apart, that was seen as "antisocial" and it was actually a legal offense.

East German **collectivism** was at one and the same time resented and absorbed. The coffee break Peter Marcuse observed was a benign aspect of East German collectivism. People did really become very involved with their co-workers socially and emotionally. They depended on friends and workmates for mutual aid, much more so than in the West. Friends helped each other find scarce goods and cope with bureaucracy. Typical friendship groups of perhaps two dozen people often linked individuals with very varied occupations, from doctors to auto mechanics, who all had contacts or skills to share with the group. But oddly enough, these warm, close-knit groups which exemplified the value of collectivism were in their own way a form of retreat from the demands of official socialism. East Germans called it "niche society" (*Nischengesellschaft*), and it was seen as a passive protest against the regime. Friendship groups were a substitute for official party organizations like the youth and women's groups that the government insisted people join. These groups were disliked and they disappeared immediately after reunification.

SOCIAL INSTITUTIONS OF THE TWO GERMANYS

In some ways the two Germanys were very similar: both were modern industrial societies with specialized social institutions. If you were a Bushman visiting Germany, you would probably notice little difference between the East and the West; the contrast with your own small-scale hunting and gathering society would be overwhelming. In both Germanys large-scale formal organizations—businesses, collective farms, parliaments, political parties, trade unions, management boards, planning boards, universities, armies, government ministries, and so forth—were critical to the functioning of society.

Bureaucracy

Max Weber, the most famous German sociologist of the early twentieth century, saw **bureaucracy** as the defining feature of modern industrial societies. As a person living in a modern society, you certainly have a feeling for what bureaucracy is. Weber saw **rationalization** as the essence of bureaucracy: Formal rules and procedures for attaining specific goals are substituted for traditional or spontaneous forms of social relations.

In addition to formal rules, Weber saw some other special features in bureaucracies: People perform specialized jobs, and they are ranked in a hierarchy, so they take orders from superiors. Employees can make a career of work in a bureaucracy, climbing the levels of the hierarchy. Bureaucracies are also impersonal. They treat people as cases, not individuals, and they place great emphasis on careful record keeping. Weber argued that though it has definite drawbacks, bureaucracy is the most effective way to organize large numbers of people to serve practical, well-defined goals. He expected that whatever its political and economic system, any modern society would require bureaucracy (Gerth and Mills, pp. 196–216). Like Weber, we can certainly see bureaucracy well illustrated in Germany. It is clear that German culture, with its stress on obeying authority and following the rules, is quite supportive of bureaucratic organizations. German bureaucrats take their jobs seriously and people trust them not to be capricious or corrupt.

Katerina's Story: The Proper Bureaucrat

Katerina Wolf is a certified social worker in the office of Immigration Services in Berlin. Her department handles the cases of Aussiedler *(ethnic German "resettlers") from lands that were once German, but were taken by the Soviet Union after Germany's defeat in World War II. Germany has a policy of accepting as a citizen anyone who is of German ancestry. Since the fall of the Soviet Union, three-quarters of a million Soviet Germans have applied.*

Today, Stefan Z., an ethnic German who comes from East Prussia, has come to consult about his case. Katerina is looking down, studying his file while he sits down. When she looks up, she is stunned. He is the most handsome young man she has ever seen. Despite his accent, he has a beautiful voice and a winning smile; she can hardly focus on what he is saying. When she finally concentrates she understands two things: He is asking her out to coffee and he is asking her to speed up the process of getting state aid for an apartment. "But you're not even close to the top of the list," she exclaims in surprise; "there are many people before you." "Please, it's not for me," he begs, "my parents—they are old, sick—we have only a tiny room; it's not well-heated—they suffered for many years." "Just look at their papers," he pleads, unfolding a worn packet of letters from dissidents in the Soviet Union, Lutheran ministers, and even a TV personality. Folded between the pages is a 100-mark note. Katerina gasps. Forcing herself to respond, she shoves the papers toward Stefan and in a voice choked with anger she says, "You cannot do this—others are in need also. You are a German now; you must follow the rules—everyone does. This is not the East; not Russia!" Astonished at his rebuff, Stefan rises in awkward silence and moves toward the door. Katerina's eyes follow him; then she stares dumbly at the door until her supervisor approaches with a questioning look.

The Capitalist Economy in West Germany

In 1945 Germany lay in ruins after its surrender. The people were starving, the cities were smoldering rubbish heaps, about half the factories were destroyed, and roads and railroads were torn up by the bombing. Inflation made the German currency worthless, so people who had food or anything else of value refused to sell it. Germans call this time *die Stunde Null,* zero hour, the lowest point, which had to be a new beginning. But in capitalist West Germany, once rebuilding began, production grew with astonishing rapidity. They called it "the German economic miracle." People once again had enough food and clothing and shoes. Millions of houses were built and cities were reconstructed. By the 1950s, West Germany had achieved full employment, and it exported more goods than any other country except the United States (Turner, pp. 59–62). By the 1980s, West Germany had become one of the world's richest countries, in the same league with the United States and Japan. You can learn about the basic features of capitalism—private property, competition for profits, and market forces—by studying West Germany.

Private Ownership

In Germany businesses are almost all privately owned, and they compete in their efforts to make profits. This makes the economy very dynamic. You may be surprised to learn that Karl Marx was one of the first to recognize the productivity of capitalism. In his 1848 *The Communist Manifesto* Marx wrote: "The bourgeoisie (that is, the class of capitalists) during its rule of scarce one hundred years, has created more massive and more colossal productive forces than have all preceding generations together" (Marx, pp. 13–14).

Many German businesses are corporations. They have no single owner; rather, shareholders have the right to vote on company decisions, and the company is legally headed by boards of directors and run by managers appointed by the boards. German manufacturing companies are famous all over the world, and some of their names may be familiar to you. Cars are produced by BMW, Volkswagen, and Porsche. There are major chemical companies like Bayer and electrical manufacturing companies like Siemens. Big banks like Deutsche Bank are also privately owned.

West Germany also has an unusually large number of middle-sized businesses (called the *Mittelstand*) which often are owned and managed by single individuals or families. These companies account for half of all west German production, employ two-thirds of all workers, and produce two-thirds of all exports. Many produce precision parts, like machine tools, parts for cars, and laser cutters. Farms are also privately owned. Most are very small (averaging about 35 acres) and they are owned by the families that work them. Less than 1 percent of the farms are larger than 120 acres (Glouchevitch, pp. 57, 63; Nyrop, pp. 182–184).

The Profit Motive and Competition

Like other capitalists, the owners and managers of west German firms are in business to make money. They try their best to maximize the profits of their enterprises in order to increase their own wealth and prestige. In search of profits, they try to produce and sell more, to produce more cheaply, to develop new products that customers will want to buy, and to find new customers for their products. In an economy based on the **profit motive,** businesses find themselves in **competition** with each other, for customers, and for the best workers and suppliers.

For example, in the 1960s, Volkswagen did fabulously well selling budget-model VW "Beetles" to buyers all over Europe and America. But as buyers became more affluent they abandoned the Beetle for more luxurious cars, made by other German and non-German manufacturers. VW profits fell and the company might even have gone out of business had it not designed several new, fancier cars and vans. Today buyers seem to want their cars to be big and powerful and luxurious, and German companies are successful in international competition because they can meet this demand.

German firms also compete for capable workers, and workers compete for the best jobs. The most profitable companies are able to provide very fine apprenticeship programs that lead to well-paid jobs and opportunities for promotion. Many German high school students choose apprenticeship rather than university, and the programs run by big companies are considered very desirable. Students must compete for admission and companies have their pick of students with the best grades and recommendations, and the best presentation at interviews.

Market Forces

Capitalist economies are sometimes called **free-market systems** because, in theory at least, the interaction of supply and demand determines how much is produced, and by whom, and at what price it is sold. Adam Smith, the first theoretician of capitalist economies said that the market acts like an "invisible hand," directing workers to this firm, or capital investments to that firm. Smith was amazed at how smoothly the market worked, weeding out the inefficient and the overpriced, encouraging innovation, and giving the buyers what they demanded.

German-Style Capitalism

West Germany built one of the world's most successful capitalist economies, but it built in characteristically German style. German capitalism is different from Japanese capitalism and different from American capitalism. The particular nature of German capitalism is consistent with German culture and values.

When West Germany was established in 1949, the British and American forces wanted it to become like Adam Smith's ideal capitalist society: an economy of many small producers, all competing feverishly, and all subject to the operation of market forces, without government interference. Today this ideal is often called **laissez-faire capitalism.** But as soon as the West Germans began running their own government they set about controlling and limiting the operation of free-market forces. For laissez-faire competition they substituted government regulation, **oligopoly,** and labor-management cooperation. Germans call their economy a "social market economy."

Valuing order and social responsibility, Germans find the workings of free-market forces unacceptably cruel and disorderly. In unregulated competition, some companies become so successful that they drive out all others, becoming monopolies and destroying competition itself. Also, unregulated market economies often exhibit strong **business cycles,** periods of boom when profits rise, businesses grow, and more workers are hired, followed by terrible depressions when companies go bankrupt and many workers are unemployed. Workers may be forced to accept very low wages and bad working conditions, just to have a job. Even business owners in Germany want the government to step in to control free-market competition. For example, the head of the 100,000-member German Retail Trade Association recently explained why business owners are pleased with government restriction of business hours: "Germans need rules and regulations, and want a well-ordered, harmonious society, not the law of the jungle" (Whitney, Jan. 16, 1995, p. A6).

Government Regulation

Germans agree that it is right for the government to set the rules for business and use its power to make sure the economy works well. Complex laws regulate business practices, the use and disposal of toxic materials, the kinds of advertisements permitted, work conditions in factories and offices, how businesses should bargain with unions, and how corporate management should be structured. For example, by law stores are permitted to have sales only twice a year, in January and July. When Wal-Mart cut prices on food staples, provoking a price war with other stores, the government intervened. Cutting prices below cost is illegal in Germany because it puts small stores at a disadvantage (Rubin, Dec. 27, 2001, p. 1). While Germans sometimes complain about the difficulty of complying with so many regulations, they think that their society is better off because of the role government plays in the economy.

The German government also uses its resources to steer the economy. The government makes plans for economic development (sometimes in coordination with industrial associations), and it gets business to do what it wants by using incentives. Tax breaks spur capital investment and are used to target investment in vital industries. Subsidies and tariffs protect small farmers against competition from large commercial farms (Nyrop, pp. 218–220). The most important way the German government intervenes in the economy is by providing benefits to workers to guarantee their security (see pp. 310–312, "The Welfare State").

Oligopoly

West Germany allowed a good deal of **oligopoly** (situations in which a few very large firms dominate an industry), again for the purpose of making its capitalist economy more orderly and controlled. The firms in oligopolies can get together to control market forces instead of being at their mercy.

Today, Germany's biggest businesses and banks have **interlocking directorates.** They hold shares of each other's stock, and bank representatives and directors of large companies sit on each other's supervisory boards. Through these connections they are able to cooperate with each other instead of competing. German companies also form industrial associations, in which the biggest companies lead others in planning investment and research for a whole industry.

Labor-Management Cooperation

German capitalism is distinctive in the emphasis it places on workers' security. In Germany, businesses must be profitable, but maintaining "the social peace" by recognizing the rights of labor is an equally important value. This is apparent in the organization of firms and in management goals.

Approximately one-third of German workers are union members and almost all of their unions belong to a powerful central federation, the German Trade Union Federation (DBG). Employers and unions run big businesses together in a unique system known as **codetermination.** By law, all big companies have two boards of directors, a management board and a supervisory board. Union representatives must make up half the members on the supervisory boards. Workers councils, elected by employees in medium- and large-size firms, can actually veto some management decisions, including decisions on hiring and firing and job elimination. The idea that workers should have a say in running the businesses where they are employed goes all the way back to nineteenth-century Marxism. German workers first demanded it in the revolution of 1848, and workers' councils were enacted into law for the first time in 1920 (Glouchevitch, pp. 134–142; Nyrop, pp. 232, 234; Andrews, Feb. 14, 2001, p. W1). You can see that Marx's ideas had a big influence on West German society as well as on East German society.

Competition versus Cooperation

Codetermination has become controversial in Germany, as economic growth has sagged. Some people argue that codetermination holds the economy back. All those rules make the economy rigid, and labor regulations make it hard for companies to cut costs and compete in a globalized economy. As a result over the last few years, codetermination has become somewhat hollowed out. Unions are losing membership, especially in the east, and employers' associations are losing members even faster. Unions have allowed an important loophole in codetermination to widen: They have allowed "workers' councils" in individual firms to negotiate "Alliances for Employment" that diverge from industrywide agreements. German companies are also getting around codetermination by hiring more temporary workers, by contracting work out to smaller companies, and by moving manufacturing operations out of Germany, mostly to the low-wage countries of eastern Europe (*The Economist,* Sept. 6, 2003, p. 45; Feb. 21, 2004, p. 49).

The Socialist Economy in East Germany

Socialism existed as an ideal before any society actually adopted a socialist economy. It was meant to be a new form of modern industrial society that would correct the defects and abuses of industrial capitalism. Now that you know something about capitalism, the logic of socialism will be easier to understand.

In the nineteenth century, Karl Marx was the social thinker most influential in describing and criticizing capitalism and calling for a socialist alternative. Marx was German, but he fled Germany and lived in France and finally England. The capitalism he saw in Europe was a harsh system. Factory workers toiled long hours in unsafe conditions for very low pay. Even young children were employed in factories. Every decade or so there was a financial crisis and a huge economic depression, and millions of workers found themselves without any means of support. The market economy, Marx said, far from being a miraculous system that automatically works for the public good, as Adam Smith claimed, is actually an irrational, ruinous system, in which successful business owners (**capitalists**) get richer and richer by **exploiting** their workers (that is, paying them less than the value of the products of their work). Marx also condemned the **irrationality** of capitalism, which he said produces what is profitable, not what the public needs. Marx expected that once workers knew about socialism, they would revolt against the capitalist system, seize control of their governments, and create worker-states, where working people would run the economy to benefit the public. Marx considered collective ownership, planning, and cooperation the essence of socialism.

The first socialist economy was created in the Soviet Union after the 1917 Bolshevik Revolution. Following World War II, variations of Soviet-style socialism were established in all the Soviet-bloc countries of eastern Europe: East Germany, Poland, Czechoslovakia, Hungary, Yugoslavia, Bulgaria, Romania, and Albania, and in other socialist countries like Cuba and Mozambique. In Asia, China adopted its own socialist system after Mao Zedong's revolutionary forces triumphed in 1949.

Collectivization

East Germany's postwar administration established socialism while the country was still occupied by the Soviet army. The first step was **collectivization,** when privately owned farms and businesses were turned into public property. In East Germany, collectivization began with the estates of great landowners (who owned approximately half the farmland). About two-thirds of this land was distributed to small farmers and the rest was organized into large collective farms. The businesses of active Nazis were seized and also certain types of enterprises considered essential, like banks and power utilities. These became "peoples' plants" operated at first by the administration of the Soviet Zone and later by the GDR. Later, many more firms were harassed out of business by taxation and difficulties with government supplies or price controls. By 1952 over three quarters of industrial workers were employed in state-owned enterprises. Small farmers were also pressured to join collectives (Turner, p. 109). Collectivization continued until, by 1985, 95 percent of agricultural land was farmed by collectives and 98 percent of the labor force was employed in collectivized enterprises, which earned 96 percent of total national income (Burant, pp. 121–122; Ardagh, p. 373).

A Planned Economy

The East German economy was a **planned economy.** Economic decisions were not left to market forces; rather, various planning boards set economic goals and decided what would be produced, and by whom, and how resources would be used and at what prices products would be sold. The government not only planned the economy, it also commanded: It told the various economic institutions and actors what to do. For this reason, some sociologists call socialist economies **command economies.** Ideally, a planned economy would extend political democracy to the economy, because important economic decisions would be made by the people or their representatives, not by the tiny class of capitalists. A planned economy would work for the public good by producing what people really need and deliberately distributing it equally, so everyone would have at least the minimum to live in health and dignity. Congresses of the ruling Communist Party (called the SED) passed successive two-year and then five-year economic plans that decided what the society should invest in, where resources should go, and what trade should be permitted (Turner, pp. 111, 112).

Cooperation, Not Profit Seeking

Socialists in East Germany expected that once collective ownership and a planned economy were created, new relationships among people would develop too. Socialist society would be humane: Competition would be replaced by cooperation; individual greed by a spirit of comradeship. People would no longer try to make profits by selling things or by exploiting others; instead they would do work that benefited everyone.

In fact, over the forty years of socialism in East Germany, people did stop thinking in terms of profit. They thought of providing basic goods for everyone, and the idea of persuading people that they needed more and more so that you could sell more and make more money became foreign to them. When Peter Marcuse visited East Germany in 1989–1990, he talked with a hotel manager about the new private bicycle store down the road. The manager was puzzled: "When everyone has a bike, they won't be able to sell any more," he explained. The capitalist idea of inventing racing bikes, then mountain bikes, then dual-use bikes, and convincing people they needed them was totally beyond him (Marcuse, pp. 263–264).

German-Style Socialism

East German socialism had a lot in common with the socialist systems of other eastern European Soviet satellite states. In large measure this was so because Soviet domination set limits to what institutional variation was allowed. The socialist economy in East Germany was distinctive in that it was heavily industrial, it was run by a huge bureaucracy which was not corrupt, and it was quite productive. Serious, skilled East German workers turned out relatively high-quality goods in great demand throughout the socialist world. The GDR economy was also quite effective in raising the living standards of the poorest East Germans and making all citizens more equal.

Productivity

The East German system never aspired to produce luxuries for anyone. Its goals were to achieve material comfort and security for everyone, equally shared, and to build an economy collectively and democratically run by the people. An idealistic East German socialist told John Ardagh that "this society may be far from perfect, but at least we have eliminated real poverty, and that's more than you have done in the West." In terms of output, East Germany's socialist economy made great progress in the early postwar years, rapidly restoring production to prewar levels. This was quite a feat, considering that the East received no aid from the United States and instead had to pay reparations to the Soviet Union. The U.S.S.R. dismantled and took away factories producing 40 percent of East Germany's industrial goods; this was twice the damage done by the war. Also, the Soviets took 25 percent of East Germany's output, without compensation (Ardagh, pp. 371, 373; Turner, pp. 110–111).

Between 1963 and 1973, GDR national income grew at an annual rate of 5 percent, and East Germany became the strongest Soviet-bloc economy. Consumer goods like cars, refrigerators, washing machines, and TVs became widely available. Much more housing was built. According to the World Bank, in 1974, per capita income was higher in the GDR than in Britain. But this was the high point of East German production. Thereafter, the oil crisis of the 1970s made it difficult for the GDR to sustain capital investment and production of consumer goods at the same time. Growth and improvement in living standards slowed (Turner, p. 139; Ardagh, p. 372; Steele, p. 7).

Collective Ownership

In East Germany, people took the idea of collective ownership very seriously. But large numbers of people rejected it. Their problems with collective ownership revolved around a central issue: When enterprises are "collectively" owned, who really owns and controls them? The people who work in them? All the people? The government? In East Germany, "collective ownership" was really **state ownership** and control. In effect the state owned the means of production in the name of the people and it acted, so it said, in their interests. The East German government really tried to make people feel like members of collectives. In every workplace there were dozens of committees and hundreds of meetings about the "plan," and employees made thousands of suggestions; but in actuality, the "plan" was made at the top levels of the party and orders came down from the top through all the levels of the party, down to each factory department, and everyone knew it.

East Germans themselves had never demanded collective ownership; they never made a socialist revolution. Collectivization was imposed by the Soviet Union, and many people didn't want it. The most common form of opposition was flight to the West by small farmers, small businesspeople, and workers too. By 1961, when the Berlin Wall was built, 2.5 million East Germans (from a total of 19 million in 1948) had fled their country. Many people defied collective ownership in a smaller, less risky way—they worked privately in addition to their regular jobs, doing house building, baby-sitting, car repair, dressmaking, and so on. This hidden private economy was probably quite large (Ardagh, pp. 390–391). Some east Germans believe their experience demonstrates that socialism is a hopeless failure, impossible to achieve. Others believe a truly democratic socialism might be possible, but that the Soviet Union never permitted East Germany to try it.

Planning and Bureaucracy

East Germany's experience is very interesting, because it shows something about the strengths and weaknesses of bureaucracy. A huge state-planning bureaucracy developed in East Germany. There were factory committees, regional and state planning boards, *Kombinaten,* the huge combines of factories, with their production quotas, joint prices, and distribution outlets. German-style, bureaucrats took their jobs relatively seriously. They were not open to bribery and they didn't use their power to favor their relatives. They behaved like good bureaucrats, systematically and rationally advancing the goals of their organization.

Nevertheless, Marx would have been greatly disappointed in the East German government bureaucracy. Marx had predicted that under socialism the state would need to rule for the proletariat at first; but eventually, as collective institutions developed, the state would "wither away" and the people would run their economy and society directly. This ideal future state would be **communism.** Neither East Germany nor any other socialist society has even come close. In all socialist societies, collective ownership has meant increased centralization of power in the hands of a ruling party and a swollen government bureaucracy.

Max Weber always said that Marx was wrong on this score. He believed no industrial society—capitalist or socialist—could do without bureaucracy. While aware of the advantages of bureaucracy for rationally coordinating large organizations, Weber would not have been surprised to hear about its limitations.

Planning in East Germany turned out to be clumsy and inefficient. You could say that it was like having the Department of Motor Vehicles run the whole economy. Once a plan had been made, it was very difficult to change it, even if it didn't seem to be working. Information from the factory moved very slowly up the layers of party bureaucracy. For example, if a condom factory had been sent too little latex, it would take a long time for word to get back to the planning boards and a long time for them to respond. Perhaps a bathing suit factory had received too much latex, but they just hid it away to compensate for future shortages. Factories often came to a stop when some vital material was lacking, or else everything waited while the factory manager made an informal arrangement trading some parts he had stockpiled for the missing material stockpiled in some other factory.

> A lion in a GDR zoo complains to the zookeeper that he's being discriminated against. "All I ever get to eat is bananas and every now and then an apple, but the lion in the next cage gets meat all the time."
>
> "But there's a good reason for that," says the warden. "The lion next to you is in a cage planned for a lion, but you're in a cage planned for a monkey." (Marcuse, p. 127)

Recently economists have argued that defects in planning are an intrinsic, fateful flaw of socialism. Robert Heilbroner contends that it is impossible, in principle, for a large modern economy to be run by central planning. No one could ever build a computer with sufficient capacity to keep track of all the supplies, products, prices, and exchanges. Blind as it is, market allocation of production avoids this colossal bookkeeping task.

It seems clear that while the East German government was committed to raising standards of living, reliance on centralized planning caused many unforeseen problems. For example, it took the East German government until the 1970s to decide that building housing had to be a priority, and then the plan poured resources into housing. Investment was diverted away from factories, which kept on producing with old, outdated machinery. As a result, the quality of East German products declined, and it became harder to export them to countries outside the Soviet bloc. Also, aging factories and power plants spewed more and more pollution into the air and water and land. But since the plan called for increasing production of housing and consumer goods, this problem was ignored. This is one of the saddest defects of socialism: It proved to be no better, and perhaps worse, than capitalism at controlling environmental pollution (DeBardeleben, pp. 144–164).

Because planning was so clumsy and imprecise, it could deal best with highly standardized goods. Newly built housing endlessly repeated the same modular concrete apartment blocks; clothing was offered in only a couple of basic designs; even cars came in only one model. State-owned stores were identified only by number: "Women's Clothing Store #32," "Butcher Shop #1658." Such standardization, combined with the poor quality of much consumer goods, made East Germany a kind of "gray society," lacking color and variety, in sharp contrast to the bright lights, vivid advertising, and glittering shopping districts found in the West.

Inequality in East and West

Despite the differences in their economic systems, the societies of East and West Germany shared a common commitment to reducing economic inequality. Both societies were relatively successful in limiting inequalities of income, and the welfare state further equalized families' resources. West Germany showed a moderate degree of income inequality. In the mid-1980s, the poorest quintile of West Germans received 7.0 percent of total income, while the richest fifth received 40.3 percent or 5.8 times as much (World Bank, 1993).[1]

Data on East German income distribution show that income was more equally distributed in the East than the West. In 1980 the poorest fifth of East German households received 12.2 percent of total income, and the richest fifth received 29.8 percent, approximately 2.5 times as much (United Nations, p. 7). In the East, in the 1980s, the average factory manager was paid only about twice as much as the average factory worker. In West Germany in 1990, pay for a managing director averaged about 4.5 times that of an average factory worker (Ardagh, pp. 174, 374).

Ethnic, Religious, and Racial Minorities

While Germany has relatively mild income inequalities, racial, ethnic, and religious inequalities are more significant. West Germany first welcomed immigrants in the 1950s and 60s, when rapid economic growth led to labor shortages. The Federal Republic negotiated agreements with poorer countries to supply temporary laborers. These *Gastarbeiter* ("guest workers") first came from Italy, Spain, and Greece, and later from Turkey, Morocco, Tunisia, and Yugoslavia. They worked at unskilled jobs in mines and factories and construction. In the beginning, single men immigrated to Germany, intending to earn money and return home. In fact, during the 1960s and early 70s, 14 million immigrants came to Germany and 11 million returned to their native countries.

Germany stopped recruiting temporary workers in 1973, but allowed remaining foreign workers to bring their families to join them in Germany. Over the past five years, net immigration into Germany has averaged about 200,000 per year. By 2002 there were 7.3 million foreign residents in Germany, making up about 9 percent of the population; 2.5 million are Turks and more than 1 million come from the Balkans (the former Yugoslavia and nearby countries). An additional 3 million ethnic Germans came to Germany from the former Soviet Union, Poland, and Romania. Some of these ethnic Germans are Jewish. They have swelled the Jewish population of Germany from 29,000 at the beginning of the 1990s to an estimated 100,000 in 2002. Germany now has the largest immigrant population of any country in Europe. One in five babies born in Germany today is not ethnically German. Many of Germany's immigrants are Muslims from Turkey, Yugoslavia, and North Africa. Immigrants are clustered in western German industrial cities; in Frankfurt 30 percent of the population is foreign, including 80,000 Muslims, mostly Turks. There are

[1]In comparison, the richest quintile of Mexicans received 19 times as much income as the poorest fifth. And in the United States, the richest fifth received 8 and a half times as much income as the poorest. (See Table 1.5, p. 51.)

Three and a half million Muslims live in Germany and on November 21, 2004 some 20,000 demonstrators filled the streets of Cologne's city center to protest the use of violence in the name of Islam. One young Muslim demonstrator has a poster reading, "Islam is for the people;" another's poster proclaims, "Islam is Peace."

twenty-seven mosques. In Stuttgart and Munich about a quarter of the population is foreign (Cohen, Dec. 30, 2000, pp. A1, A6; Friedrichs, p. 1754; Federal Statistical Office, Germany, Dec. 31, 2003; Sept. 19, 2003; *The Economist,* May 1, 2004, p. 50; Butler, Nov. 15, 2002, p. A5).

Many countries have ethnic minorities and minority religious groups. In many cases minorities face prejudice, perhaps racial discrimination, perhaps obstacles to practicing their religion. But in Germany the problems of immigrants evoke extraordinary anguish. Any shadow of unfair treatment of ethnic or religious minorities reminds Germans of the racial policies of Nazi Germany and stimulates tremendous guilt and shame. Germans are particularly sensitive about immigrants who apply for political asylum. Throughout the 1990s, Germany was the destination of choice in Europe for those fleeing war and persecution—in Bosnia, Kosovo, Somalia, Iran, and other disaster-ridden nations. Germany accepted close to two million such refugees (*The Economist,* May 6, 2000, pp. 25–27).

While conscience tells Germans to welcome immigrants, they really don't want foreigners, especially those who are darker-skinned and Muslim. German citizens will readily tell a visitor, "Germany is not an immigration country." It is the common view that having German blood makes you German, and long residence, or even birth in Germany, does not if you are of foreign stock (Turner, p. 163; Ardagh, p. 276; Schlaes, pp. 19–20, 36). In polls, a third of east Germans and a quarter of west Germans say they think Germany is "overrun" with foreigners. The party platform of the Christian Democrats in 2001 proclaimed "Our Christian culture, marked by Christianity, ancient philosophy, humanism, Roman Law, and the Enlightenment, must be accepted." It explained "that does not mean the abandonment of particular religions and cultural practices, but acceptance of our values and organization for living together" (*The Economist,* July 1, 2000, p. 48; Cohen, May 13, 2001, p. 11).

As unemployment has increased in Germany, outspoken prejudice against foreigners, particularly Turks, has increased also, especially in eastern Germany and especially among the less educated. In 1992 and 1993 there was a shocking series of violent assaults on Turkish families and on immigrants seeking asylum. These attacks continued through the decade, mostly in eastern Germany, prompting unhappy debate about German intolerance. In 2000 an African immigrant was killed by a group of neo-Nazis in Dessau and other Africans were attacked in Eisenach. A bomb in Düsseldorf wounded nine immigrants, six of them Jews. Foreign minister Joschka Fischer chastised Germans, reminding them that a majority that keeps silent may abet a crime. This allusion to the Nazi era was lost on no one (Cohen, Aug. 1, 2000, p. A7).

Immigrants, especially Turks, tend to live in run-down inner-city neighborhoods, somewhat separated from other Germans. Germans don't invite Turks into their homes, although German children do learn to tolerate their foreign classmates. In a society as much given to legal regulation as Germany, it is significant that there are no laws against racial discrimination, other than in pay. Ads for jobs or apartments often say "only Germans," or "only Europeans," and bars often prohibit entry to Turks. By law, a German worker has preference over a foreigner for a job (Ardagh, pp. 287, 288, 297). It was only in 2000 that Germany changed its 1913 citizenship law, which declared that anyone of German "blood"—whether born in Germany or elsewhere—was German and could always claim citizenship. Those not of German blood—even if they had been born in Germany—could never become citizens. This law always evoked Nazi racial theories and claims of racial superiority. The new law will give automatic citizenship to German-born children of foreigners, if they have one parent who has been in Germany for at least eight years (Cohen, May 22, 1999, p. A3).

Ali's Story: The Immigrant

Ali Mustafa came to Germany with his parents from Turkey when he was 10 years old. In some ways he is completely German. His speech is perfect, his dress European and sophisticated. He went to university and law school in Frankfurt, where he lives today. His law firm deals with international business law and his work takes him around Europe and sometimes to Asia. German companies like to employ his firm when they do business in the Middle East. Ali is unusual: His wife is German. While marriages between Germans and other Europeans are now common in Frankfurt, German–Turkish marriages are rare.

At a family dinner celebrating the end of Ramadan, fifteen people sit down together for a Turkish feast. Ali's 70 year-old mother wears a head scarf and speaks German poorly. His brother's wife wears no scarf, but her German isn't very good either. The children, the next generation, are fluent German-speakers. When they visit Turkey, people call them little Germans.

"Germans in Frankfurt can't quite make up their minds about Turks," Ali says. "They need us—to sell them vegetables and run their coffee shops, to clean their hospitals and old people's homes. But they are terrified of Islamic terrorists. How can I convince them that Islam means peace and tolerance? I'm willing to reach out and talk to Germans, to learn their culture and teach them about mine. But if they want me to convert to Christianity, to forget that I am Turkish, then I say forget it!" (This vignette draws on interviews reported by Cohen, Dec. 30, 2000, pp. A1, A6.)

Representative Democracy in West Germany

There is no characteristically "German" form of government. In the past century, Germans have lived under the most varied political orders—from the small, independent kingdoms of the early nineteenth century, to the great monarchy which Prussia dominated at the end of the nineteenth century, and then on to the Weimar parliamentary democracy which fell to Nazi dictatorship. When the governments of the two Germanys were created after World War II, there were precedents for almost any modern form of government. West Germany embraced **democratic** political institutions and East Germany was given an **authoritarian** government.

The West German government, which today governs all Germans in the reunified Germany, was created under the influence of the occupying forces of the United States and Britain, who were determined to establish a democracy—that is, a political system in which the citizens choose their leaders and participate in making government decisions and the government functions according to rules set down in a constitution, which also guarantees basic human rights. But West Germans themselves, horrified by Nazi carnage, reached back in their history to identify with a German democratic tradition. It was no accident that they chose for their flag the red, gold, and black bands first carried by the republican revolutionaries of 1848, which was also the flag of the Weimar Republic. West Germany, like all modern societies, was much too big to be a **direct democracy** in which all the citizens actually meet together and directly make the decisions which affect their lives. Instead, it established an **indirect democracy,** a **representative democracy** in which people express their preferences by voting for the candidates of competing political parties.

A Federation of States

The particular type of representative democracy adopted in West Germany is characteristically German. It reflects both Germany's tragic history and its present-day values. With typical German thoroughness and attention to detail, the West German political system was designed to make it difficult for a dictator like Hitler ever to seize power again. First of all, West Germany chose to avoid a centralized government like that of Nazi Germany. Instead, West Germany adopted a **federal system** (like that of the United States and Canada). It consisted of ten states, to which five additional states were added when Germany was reunified. Many of the states were based on old German principalities, which had united in past German confederations. In this federal system, the rights of the states limit the power of the central government. In Germany the states control education, radio and TV, police, environmental regulation, cultural affairs, and local government and planning (Turner, p. 39; Ardagh, p. 86).

Every state elects its own parliament and its own prime minister and has an office, a kind of embassy, in the federal capital. All personal income taxes and corporate taxes are shared 50–50 between the states and the federal government, although federal law ensures that tax rates are the same in all states.

Parliamentary Government

West Germany also chose a parliamentary system of representative democracy, similar to the governments of other western European democracies. In a parliamentary system, the head of the government (in Germany, the chancellor) is elected by the upper house of parliament, not directly by the citizens. The vote takes place along party lines, so when a particular party or coalition of parties wins a majority of seats, its leader almost automatically becomes chancellor.

The upper house of the parliament (or *Bundestag*) is the nation's most powerful political institution. The lower house (the *Bundesrat*) is composed of delegates of the states. Representatives are elected to the *Bundestag* following an intricate system of **proportional representation** designed to frustrate the seating of small extremist parties, like the Nazi Party. Every German casts two votes for representatives: one for a district candidate, elected as an individual, and one for a party list of candidates. Half the seats go to district candidates and half to party list candidates, in proportion to their party's share of the vote. Any party that fails to win either three election districts or 5 percent of the party lists is denied representation (Dalton, pp. 281–285; Turner, pp. 40–41). In Germany today, power is carefully divided between the federal government and the states, between the upper and lower houses of parliament, and among the parties.

Political Parties

Finally, as specified in the constitution of the Federal Republic, the West German political system is fundamentally a **party system.** Political parties, distinguished by their differing political perspectives, compete for votes. In parliament they follow party discipline; that is, their members almost always vote as blocs. Political parties make the system orderly. When they vote for a party or its candidates, voters know what they are getting. The party system keeps the government responsible to voters; legislators know that if they do not act as they promised, voters can always turn to another party and vote them out of office (Dalton, pp. 249–250).

In West Germany after World War II there were two major parties, the Christian Democratic Union and the Social Democratic Party; and two lasting minor parties, the Christian Social Union (which usually acted in coalition with the CDU) and the Free Democratic Party (which allied itself with either of the two major parties). The CDU was the party of the moderate right, advocating anticommunism and a commitment to capitalist economies. The SDP, the oldest German party, was traditionally committed to socialism and democracy, but since World War II, it has been a moderate left party, clearly anticommunist and oriented to a market economy, but with a strong belief in the welfare state (Dalton, pp. 251–276; Nyrop, pp. 264–273).

West Germans were also free to create other political organizations to make their opinions heard and to compete for political power. **Interest groups** speak for people who share common needs and problems. They lobby the government for desired legislation and policies. In the Federal Republic the "big four" interest groups were business, labor, the churches, and farmers, represented by organizations like the Federation of German Industries, the German Federation of Trade Unions, the Catholic Church and the Evangelical Church in Germany (an association of Protestant churches), and the German Farmers Association (Dalton, pp. 210–227).

Starting in the 1960s, new groups of political organizations developed which often challenged the traditional interest groups. These new groups, known collectively as the New Politics movement, included environmentalist organizations, the women's movement, and the peace movement. In 1980 people involved in these groups created a new party—the Green Party, which became an influential minor party and in 1998 became the minor partner in a coalition government with the SPD. The Greens express younger Germans' serious concerns about pollution, nuclear weapons and nuclear power, militarism, gender inequality, and alienating work (Dalton, pp. 227–228, 266–269).

Constitutional Rights

The 1949 Basic Law (or constitution) which established the political system in West Germany, also granted citizens certain basic rights: freedom of speech and assembly, freedom of the press, equality before the law, religious freedom, and freedom from discrimination based on race, sex, religious or political beliefs, and the right to relief from military service on grounds of conscientious objection. All these rights had been lost under the Nazi regime, so restoring them was a very important step toward democracy. But ironically, the Nazi experience led the new German government to qualify some of these rights in order to protect the democracy. Thus, it is constitutional to ban parties that advocate the overthrow of democracy and this provision has been used against both Nazi and Communist parties. Similarly, the right of free speech cannot be used to attack democracy or to advocate Nazism. For example, in 2004, in a major police raid on private homes, police arrested more than 300 people suspected of putting neo-Nazi music files on the Internet for others to download. The songs, by skinhead bands, had lyrics that incited hatred against Jews and immigrants, a punishable offense (*The New York Times,* March 15, 2004, p. A6).

Authoritarian Government in East Germany

You must understand that East Germans did not choose their form of government. East Germany's government was created during the Soviet occupation after World War II and sustained until 1989 when Soviet domination ended. The GDR was what was called a "Soviet satellite state"—a country kept in the orbit of the Soviet Union's power by that country's threat of military force. East Germany tried once to escape Soviet domination in the uprising of 1953, which the Soviet army brutally put down. Afterwards, East Germans put up with their Soviet-installed regime as best they could. They learned to put aside the traditional value of obedience in favor of "working the system" in order to get by. For example, if you ordered parts to fix your car in the proper way, you could wait years for them, but West German money earned illegally and spent on the black market could get you what you needed right away. To get a good professional or technical job, or to qualify for it, you had to pretend to be an enthusiastic supporter of the regime. East Germans were schooled in petty disobedience and in contempt for authority.

When they were first created, East Germany's political institutions paralleled those of West Germany. There were five federated states, upper and lower houses of parliament, and a minister-president elected by a majority of the upper house (or People's Chamber). The Constitution of 1949 resembled West Germany's Basic Law and guaranteed fundamental rights like freedom of assembly and speech, freedom of the press, religious freedom, the right to strike, and the right to emigrate.

But as early as 1947, these institutions of representative democracy became an empty shell, within which a second set of centralized and authoritarian political institutions developed. Real power became highly centralized in one party, the Social Unity Party or SED, and within the Party, in the hands of the top SED leaders, the *Politbüro.* Early on, the states ceased to have any separate powers, and they were replaced by administrative districts in 1952 (Turner, p. 101). Although basic civil rights were formally guaranteed, in actuality those rights were denied in a repressive **police state** that permitted no opposition to SED rule.

A Sham Democracy

Officially, the East German state was a parliamentary democracy with a total of five competing parties. In fact, four of the parties were really puppets of the SED, run by leaders acceptable to the ruling party and never permitted to challenge SED power. This was how it worked: East Germans did not get to choose between candidates or party slates when they voted. An organization called the National Front put together a single slate of candidates, representing all five parties and also the "mass organizations" like trade unions, farmers' cooperatives, women's and youth organizations. East Germans could vote only for or against this "unity slate," and the vote was always reported as overwhelmingly in favor of it.

In any case, the power of the People's Chamber was very limited. It met only about six times a year, for a day at a time and unanimously passed only about a dozen bills a year, all submitted to it on direction from the Central Committee of the SED. Even Jonathan Steele, a sympathetic observer, commented, "there is no chance of voters exerting any influence against SED policy" (Steele, p. 145). Western critics of Soviet-style socialism argued that the SED had no intention of allowing democracy, since they knew that if East Germans had a choice they would vote out the SED and get rid of the socialist regime. This is probably true: When East Germans were given a choice in 1989–1990 after the collapse of the Soviet Union and the fall of the Berlin Wall, they voted to join West Germany and adopt its political and economic systems.

The One-Party State

Real power in East Germany was exercised by the political institutions of the SED. At the top was the *Politbüro,* the supreme party organization, composed of about twenty-five senior officials, ministers, and army officers, and headed by the general secretary. Below was the Central Committee, then the Party Congress, then the regional congresses, and at the bottom the local party organizations. In theory, the *Politbüro* was elected by the Central Committee, which was elected by the Party

Congress and so on, but in reality, the top levels were self-selecting and party members had no influence on their choice. **Centralism** was the official principle of government in the GDR. Decisions were to be made at the top, and lower-level organizations were expected to act on orders without question.

In East Germany, the leaders of the SED lived in a separate guarded suburb outside Berlin. They selected the individuals who would get special training at party schools to become party officials. The party membership lacked access to the means for making their voices heard. For example, when the Party Congress issued a new Five-Year Plan, it was sent out to every branch of the party and state for discussion. Union locals met to discuss how the Plan would affect their work and to make suggestions. But union members were all full-time workers who met after work. They had no researchers or libraries or statisticians, and they were given only two weeks to discuss a proposed plan (Steele, p. 135). You can see that it would be very difficult for them to challenge a plan or even document any well-founded doubts. Party officials had an enormous advantage over them in resources, time, and power.

Democratic Centralism

Despite its centralization of power, SED leaders claimed that the GDR was, in fact, a democracy. It was not a parliamentary democracy like West Germany, but rather a new socialist kind of democracy they called **"democratic centralism."** The SED's leaders believed that a single party could integrate within itself all the different social groups so democracy would take place in debate within the party, not in competition among parties. SED leaders prided themselves on the high degree of political involvement among East Germans. They said political participation made East Germany more democratic than the western democracies, where citizens took little part in ongoing politics, most not even bothering to vote in elections every couple of years.

In East Germany, the government urged people to belong to the SED and other political parties, join mass organizations, run for office and join committees, and attend meetings—and large numbers of people did so. Approximately one in six East Germans over 18 (or about 2.3 million people) were SED members, and they belonged to over 84,000 local organizations. Nearly 100 percent of adults were trade union members. Hundreds of thousands more people were members of state legislatures or legislative committees, National Front committees, production councils, and PTAs. Millions joined youth and women's organizations (Burant, pp. 182, 187, 201; Dalton, p. 43).

GDR leaders proudly emphasized that people from all different classes participated in the SED and could rise to positions of power. The SED monitored the class background and current status of party members and described its membership as 56 percent working class (Steele, p. 142). They argued that the SED was democratic because all different classes were represented in it. In the West, people believed their society was democratic because many different views were represented in parliament, even though almost all representatives were middle class or upper class. In the East, it was relatively easy to join the party hierarchy, and in fact it was a major channel of upward mobility. But to rise to leadership, you had to be ideologically loyal. Thus, people from many classes were represented, but only one viewpoint—that of the SED—was allowed.

Gunter's Story: Criticizing the West

Gunter, a 53-year-old east German factory worker lived all his life under "democratic centralism." Since reunification, he has been introduced to western-style democracy, and he is critical of it. "In the GDR, a man like me or my son could hope to have a place in the life of the nation. In today's Germany, no one has a minute for you unless you drive a big car! Is this democracy? A democracy of the Mercedes? Everyone is free to have their say as long as they have money! Even the Socialists are Doktoren! *When was the last time you saw a man with callused hands in the Bundestag? Honecker [past general secretary of the SED] was a fool, but he knew that in a democracy, everyone has a part."*

A Police State

The East German government demanded political mobilization and ideological loyalty from its citizens, but just to make sure there was no opposition, the government suppressed all dissent. A large secret police force, a network of informers, a guarded border, and an army prevented the expression of opposition to the SED or to socialism, and prevented the penetration of seditious ideas from outside East German borders. Any group larger than seven people needed official permission to meet (Ferree, p. 96).

Censorship. In East Germany, the newspapers, radio, and television were all state-owned and state-run. News reporting was considered part of the campaign to build socialism, so events within the GDR and outside that might cast the regime in a bad light were simply not reported. For example, when the worker movement Solidarity challenged the Communist Party in Poland in 1980, it was never mentioned in the GDR news media. Newspapers and radio gave lots of news about sports and the arts, but there was no reporting on crime or consumer shortages. Party congresses were reported in predictable boring detail, economic reports were always positive, and headlines like "Delegates Unanimously Praise Workers' Collectives" were so obviously canned that they defeated their own purposes. TV programs were similarly relentlessly upbeat. Since most East Germans could tune in to West German TV, they learned about censored news anyhow, and it fed their cynicism about the GDR (Ardagh, pp. 391–392).

Prohibition of Travel. One of the things that angered East Germans most about their repressive regime was the ban on travel to the West. To leave East Germany or its Soviet-bloc neighbors you needed special government permission, seldom granted. Married couples were never permitted to exit at the same time and individuals, like athletes or musicians, permitted to tour the West were carefully watched by spies. Only old people were allowed to visit relatives in West Germany.

In 1961 construction of the Berlin Wall completed the sealing of the border between East and West. The entire border was fenced and guarded by 50,000 GDR border police, who patroled a mined no-man's-land and were trained to shoot anyone attempting to cross.

The Threat of Force. Ultimately, the SED kept its power in East Germany through the threat and use of force against its citizens. There were police, secret police, border guards, a regular military, and volunteer militia units. East Germany's military was not large, but it was conspicuous. People were also aware of the threat of the Soviet army, which had been brutally used to put down rebellions in East Germany in 1953 and in Hungary in 1956.

Most sinister was the *Stasi,* the secret police, which in the very repressive days of the 1950s and 1960s imprisoned and tortured dissidents without trial. By the 1980s the *Stasi* was simply in the business of spying on people, looking for dissent. The secret police force was huge: It had a regular staff of 85,000, as many as half a million paid informers—ordinary people who spied on their co-workers, neighbors, friends, or even spouses—and secret files on a third of all GDR citizens. Until the *Wende,* no one knew how big the *Stasi* was. People just had the feeling that it was important to watch what you said all the time. When the true size of the *Stasi* operations was revealed after 1989, people were horrified and furious.

The Welfare State

When you read about the political and economic institutions of East Germany and West Germany, you see how very different the two societies were. But in one very important respect, both Germanys were similar. They were both **welfare states,** and welfare institutions worked effectively and met with popular approval in both societies. In both East and West, the welfare state meant the same thing: It meant that the government accepted responsibility for its citizens' social welfare. Germans today will tell you that welfare benefits support "the social peace" and relieve class tensions. Though their taxes are high, they believe the benefits are worth it. In the West, the welfare state meant that the government pledged to guarantee citizens the right to certain benefits and services, like health care and housing, even if they couldn't afford to buy them on the free market. The East German welfare state was more extensive than the West's but it was based on a similar belief that the government has an obligation to provide for the well-being of its citizens. Both societies also took responsibility for making certain that all young people were able to get an education that prepared them for a job.

The institutions of the welfare state date back long before the division of Germany. The welfare state began in the 1880s, under the rule of Kaiser Wilhelm I and his prime minister, Otto von Bismarck, as a conservative response to the trade union and socialist movements of the time. They instituted three historic components of a universal welfare system: national health insurance, accident insurance, and old-age/disability insurance. Unemployment insurance was added in 1927.

During the twentieth century other European countries followed Germany's example, establishing similar welfare programs. In the United States, where the obligation of the state to ensure the social welfare of its citizens is not fully accepted, only two of the usual welfare programs—old-age pensions and unemployment insurance— have been enacted.

The West German Welfare State

West Germany added to this basic welfare package. The government gives all parents a yearly family allowance for each child, regardless of income or marital status.

TABLE 5.2 Health Spending and Life Expectancy

Germany and Japan spend only half as much per person on health care as the United States, but average life expectancy is a few years longer.

	Spending on Health Care Per Person Yearly	The Number of Years You Can Expect to Live
United States	4,887	77
Germany	2,820	78
Japan	2,131	82
Namibia	342	42
Mexico	544	74
Egypt	153	69

Source: United Nations Human Development Report 2004 http://hdr.undp.org/statistics/data/advanced.cfm

There is also a program of rent allowances for low-income families, to make sure they can afford market rents and prevent homelessness. Finally, there is a small "welfare" component: allowances for people who for some reason cannot work (Nyrop, pp. 97–98).

West Germany's social insurance and welfare programs are expensive. Approximately one-third of the country's GNP is spent on health and welfare. Social programs are paid for by high income taxes, payroll taxes, and mandatory employer contributions. Health insurance, for example, is paid for by required contributions from employees and employers equal to about 6 percent of salary (Nyrop, p. 94; Glouchevitch, p. 111). (See Table 5.2 above.)

The East German Welfare State

In East Germany, the welfare state went even further. As Jonathan Steele reported, in East Germany the state "takes responsibility for providing almost everything from stable consumer prices to a job for every school leaver. People expect the state's promises to be kept. They make higher claims on it than most people do in the West" (Steele, p. 13). Although the overall standard of living in the East was much lower than in the West, no East German was excluded from education or health care for lack of money. No one was homeless or jobless; no elderly people or single mothers were left without social and financial support.

East Germany provided the standard European universal welfare institutions: health insurance, accident and disability insurance, old-age pensions, unemployment insurance, and family allowances. Health care was readily available, without charge, from state-employed medical professionals, so patients neither laid out money in advance nor filed paperwork. The quality of health care was high and the atmosphere caring.

Family benefits were generous: Women received six months' maternity leave at full pay for their first child and a full year at reduced pay for subsequent children. Years spent caring for children were credited in figuring pensions. Families received allowances for their children until they reached age 18. Newly married young couples were given free "starter loans," with repayment waived incrementally as children were born. Day care was inexpensive and readily available (Edwards, p. 46).

Children and teachers from an East Berlin day-care center are out for an afternoon walk. Cars were scarce in East Germany, but high-quality, inexpensive day care was easily obtained by working mothers.

Many additional benefits were provided through the workplace and administered by the unions, including holidays in union hotels, factory hospitals and clinics, day-care centers, sports facilities, adult classes, libraries, discount shops, and housing (Steele, p. 131; Burant, p. 98).

Finally, an important element in the East German welfare state was management of wages and prices through the Plan, which made basic goods available to everyone at subsidized prices, at the cost of making luxuries scarce and expensive. Prices of basic foods like bread and milk and sausage, rents, gas and electric, and commuter fares were frozen. Even the prices of theater and concert tickets and restaurants were subsidized. Rents were especially low: about 4 to 5 percent of average family income. (To imagine what this means, figure that a family earning $500 a week would pay only $25 a week in rent.) Forty percent of government spending went to these subsidies (Burant, pp. 88–89).

Educational Institutions

You can learn a lot about a society from its system of education. Both East Germany and West Germany had educational institutions that not only reflected the natures of the two societies, but also socialized students to take their places in those societies. West Germany's system was designed to carefully sort children based on their intelligence, talent, and effort, preparing each child for his or her position in the class system. West German schools were set up in a way that limited the power of the German government over education. East German schools tried to treat all children the same and teach them all the value of manual work. When it came to selecting an elite for higher education, East German schools sorted by political, ideological criteria. Schools were tightly controlled by the government.

Schooling in West Germany

Control over education in West Germany was located at the state and local level, not the national level. Curriculum and teacher's pay were set by the state, but school buildings and equipment were supplied by the locality and varied greatly in quality. The basic system, however, was standard throughout West Germany. States tried hard to assure all students an equal start in primary school. There was no **tracking** (ability grouping) at the primary level: All the children were taught the same lessons in heterogeneous classes. Schools, however, were seen as narrowly academic. Their influence in children's lives was deliberately restricted. The schools taught academic subjects only, and the school day was compressed, starting at 8:00 A.M. and ending at 1:30 or 2:00 P.M. Children went home for lunch. West Germans didn't see character building, team sports, or leadership development as the responsibility of the schools. They thought parents, churches, and voluntary groups, like the Boy Scouts, should be in charge of all sports and nonacademic activities. Similarly, while schools taught about democracy and the constitution and how the German government worked, there were no student government organizations or even any debating teams. There were no school plays, assemblies or gyms, or even school libraries (Ardagh, pp. 241–243).

At the end of the fourth grade (in some states sixth grade) West German children faced a crucial life transition. Based on their grades, their teachers' assessments, and their parents' wishes, they transferred to one of three types of secondary schools. From there on, German schools were seriously tracked and the kind of secondary school one attended had lasting life consequences (Hamilton, pp. 73–74, 77–78).

Three High School Tracks. Students considered to have the strongest academic ability went to academic high school (or *Gymnasium*), which they attended until age 19. It was roughly equivalent to American high school plus one or two years of college. In 1990 31 percent of German students attended *Gymnasium.* Most of them were from middle-class families. Students whose grades were satisfactory and who passed a rigorous entrance exam were admitted to university, and about 75 percent of those qualified went right on to further study. Those who were admitted to university paid no tuition and were given allowances for living expenses, so they didn't need to work while they were in school ("A Profile of the German Education System," p. 21; Hamilton, p. 85; Ardagh, p. 249).

Twenty-eight percent of German students moved from primary school to technical institutes (or *Realschule*). These were vocational schools that specialized in commercial or technical fields and also provided some academic education. Technical institutes went through tenth grade and when students graduated at 16 they went on either to apprenticeship or to a technical college (*Fachhochschule*), which trained for careers like nursing or accountancy. Those who didn't go on to technical colleges got jobs as lab technicians, precision mechanics, secretaries, or personnel managers, and so forth (after completing apprenticeships in these jobs). *Realschule* educated a true cross-section of the German population.

The largest and least academically qualified group of students (33 percent) attend vocational high school (*Hauptschule*) until age 15.[2] These schools prepared students for apprenticeship or work in manual, clerical, and semiskilled service jobs. They became construction workers, auto mechanics, file clerks, and salespeople in retail stores. The *Hauptschule* was usually a neighborhood school, often in the same building as the primary school, and its prestige was low. Students at *Hauptschule* were usually from working-class families. Even students in vocational school were required to show their grades to employers when they sought jobs, so it was important to work hard in school (Hamilton, pp. 80, 85).

Second Chances. Students who started out doing poorly, but later decided they wanted a university education had some chance of catching up. Technical school students were allowed to switch over to the academic high school after graduation, though they often lost a year or two in making the switch. In some states as few as 2 percent did so, but in others up to 16 percent made the move up. Also, there were adult-education courses that prepared people for college entrance later in life (Hamilton, pp. 78–79; "A Profile of the German Education System," p. 21).

Apprenticeship. The most impressive characteristic of West German education was that in every track education culminated in marketable skills that qualified students for good, full-time jobs immediately upon graduation. For most students this was accomplished through a system of apprenticeship. They spent four days a week in the workplace and one day a week in vocational school. Apprenticeships were provided by German companies, which paid for the training (Gittler and Scheuer, pp. 18–19).

Young people in West Germany apprenticed as auto mechanics and personnel managers, postal workers, computer programmers, graphic designers, copywriters, plumbers, railway conductors, shoe sales workers—for white-collar and blue-collar jobs in over 350 occupations. You might even think that German apprenticeships overtrained young people. Even relatively unskilled jobs were treated with the greatest seriousness. For example, shoe sales workers served a full apprenticeship and learned about sales, sizing, cash-register operation, the process of shoe manufacture, and bookkeeping. Ordinary workers were very competent as a result, which added to their status, and they were also qualified to advance to the next step of promotion. Every shoe salesperson had the knowledge necessary to be manager. More than half of all apprentices went to work for the company that trained them, but others moved into jobs with companies not offering apprenticeships or into related occupations that didn't have apprenticeships (Hamilton, pp. 35, 143–144).

---

[2]Another 8 percent of German students attended comprehensive high schools, which are uncommon in Germany ("A Profile of the German Education System," p. 21).

Georg's Story: The Apprentice

At 18, Georg Messer is in his final year of apprenticeship with the famous Konigsdorfer Shoe Company in Hamburg, training to be an Industriekaufmann, *an office worker in an industrial firm. Georg felt lucky to get this apprenticeship; it was highly competitive. One thousand graduates applied for 25 places. Konigsdorfer chose young men and women who were socially skilled and presentable and whose records attested to their ability to work hard and carefully. Having served in 12 different departments at Konigsdorfer, Georg is finishing his apprenticeship in the Cost Accounting Department, working closely with his mentor and applying new computer models to develop prices for the spring shoe line. He uses his knowledge of international exchange rates, import-export tariffs, and the costs of materials and labor, learned in the one-day-a-week formal instruction* (Berufsschule), *which is part of his apprenticeship.*

We asked Georg if he is ever sorry he didn't go to Gymnasium (academic high school) and on to university. "No, not at all. Why should I be," he answered. "I was really getting tired of school by the time I was 15. This apprenticeship has let me out in the real world, and the one-day-a-week formal school makes sense, because I use what I learn in Berufsschule *here at the factory. Did I tell you I've been offered a job, in the Cost Accounting Department? I can begin as soon as I take my qualifying exams. My bosses seem certain I'll pass. You know I'll have a responsible job with a real adult salary and plenty of room for advancement by the time I'm 18."*

Schooling in East Germany

In East Germany, education was highly centralized and politicized. The purpose of schooling was clear: Schools were to create the "new socialist human being," or as an official statement explained, to teach children that "the task of every young citizen is to work, to learn and to live in a socialist way, selflessly and with determination for the benefit of the Socialist Fatherland of the DPR" (Rodden, pp. 15, 16). For this purpose, the education ministry was tightly controlled by the party, and education was intensely ideological. Teachers were specially selected for their ideological orthodoxy and loyalty to the party. The teacher of German history, for example, had to prove he or she had the proper "class perspective." The children's work was evaluated by political criteria. "How does this drawing, this essay, contribute to the struggle," the teacher was to ask. Liberal arts, creative thinking, and independent critique were all deplored. Exam questions included the following: "Why was it fortunate for the world, for Europe, and for the German *Volk* that the DPR was founded? The school day was long, there were Saturday classes, and most children under age 10 went to after-school care, where they sang "Tractor Thomas" or wrote "friendship letters" to the "Lenin Pioneers" of the USSR (Rodden, pp. 13–17, notes p. 424).

Education was designed to symbolize, and indeed to create, equality, as well as ideological conformity. Almost all children received the same basic education: a ten-year program of schooling called the POS (Polytechnische Oberschule). These schools were not tracked; all the children received the same education, which emphasized technical knowledge. The only children who didn't attend the POS were athletes, musicians, or dancers who were specially trained for international competitions. The schools were very successful in teaching technical material to the vast majority and preparing children for jobs. The graduation rate was almost 100 percent and children came away skilled and trained in the German virtues of "order, cleanliness and punctuality" (Rodden, pp. 13–15). Only about 13 percent of children continued their education after tenth grade. They went on to eleventh and twelfth grade, and from their ranks were chosen those admitted to university. This group, though, was chosen primarily for ideological conformity, rather than for intellectual excellence (Rodden, p. 177).

DEVIANCE AND SOCIAL CONTROL

In every society, people sometimes engage in **deviant behavior:** They disregard or defy the norms of society and act in ways that other people condemn. To maintain order and limit deviance, every society needs ways of imposing **social controls,** systems of **social sanctions** and social pressures that spur individuals to conform. East Germany and West Germany had distinctively different systems of social controls.

In East Germany, because of collectivism, centralization, and police power, the state had tremendous power over individuals. The government was able to monitor what individuals did and said and use sanctions to ensure that people conformed. The government responded most severely to deviance it considered a political challenge to the SED or to socialism. A great deal of behavior seen elsewhere as private was defined as political in the GDR. For example, listening to rock music was considered a political act. In the West, in contrast, an emphasis on individualism, compartmentalization, and civil liberties shielded individuals from state power and left them freer of official social controls. West Germany had to rely much more on action by individuals and on individual conscience to limit deviance. Faced with political deviance, the West German government found it difficult to act.

Totalitarian Social Controls

East Germany was often characterized by western critics as a **totalitarian state,** that is, a society in which the government intrudes into all aspects of public and private life, so that the individual is nowhere sheltered from state power. In a totalitarian state the government imposes its ideology through control of the media and education. It controls the police, the economy, and the ruling party. Through these institutions, the state exercises supreme power over individuals. In a totalitarian state there is no "independent public space" free of government control (Philipsen, p. 79).

Collectivism, Centralization, and Social Sanctions

It is important to understand that all formal East German social groups were in some way government controlled. Some, like the party, the unions, the youth groups, and the Women's Federation were more tightly controlled, and others, like the work collectives and social clubs were more independent, but in every group there were party members pushing the party line and *Stasi* agents noting what people said and did. People were induced to participate in official organizations by means of powerful positive and negative social sanctions controlled by the SED.

Centralization meant that anything you did in one group could have consequences in every aspect of your life. People could not expect to be promoted at work unless they took leadership roles in basic organizations like the Youth Federation or Women's Federation (Scharf, pp. 141–142). Those who joined the party, enthusiastically gave their time to other voluntary groups, and voiced their belief in socialist ideology were more likely to be admitted to university, given responsible jobs and promotions, good apartments, even perhaps permission to travel to the West. You could lose these desirable rewards too. If your child defected to the West, you might lose your responsible job and get work only as a janitor; if you joined a church, your child might be turned down for the university; if you opposed the party line at work, you might never get a better apartment.

Adult Organizations. Adults were expected to join many official organizations—unions, of course, professional associations, sports leagues, the Women's Federation, volunteer social service groups, and possibly the SED or another party. Adult workers were also expected to participate in collectives in their place of work, and about half did so. Collectives were social groups: They kept scrapbooks with pictures of members' families, records of members' health, and minutes of meetings. They went on picnics and trips and did weekend volunteer work maintaining the factory's summer camp and staging plays, concerts, or educational events (Steele, p. 136). Though East Germans felt coerced by this system, they also found personal satisfaction in it. People felt the work collectives, clubs, and volunteer groups were humane; they belonged and others cared about them.

Petra's Story: The Party Member

Petra is a hospital radiologist in Potsdam. In the old days, before 1990, she was a union member, a member of the Democratic Women's Federation and the Society for German–Soviet Friendship. Further, as an SED member, she played a role in the party organization in her hospital. She had been a swimmer since primary school and retained her membership in the sports league. Petra was busy, managing her household and children in addition to attending meetings after work, but she enjoyed meeting people and valued the respect with which her friends and co-workers viewed her accomplishments. She felt like she was a participant in making her society run.

Dieter's Story: The Drop-Out

For Petra's younger brother Dieter, reunification came just in time. Dieter, a musician, had not joined the Association of Composers and Musicians, and he had stopped going to meetings of the Free German Youth. He pierced his nose and hung out in the bars downtown with other "punk" youth. Dieter had completed an apprenticeship as a primary school music teacher, but somehow the government never placed him in a job. Now Dieter has moved to Berlin and found a job in a private nursery school. It doesn't pay very much and Dieter can't afford his own apartment, so he is still sleeping on the couch in the apartment where the other members of his band live. Dieter says he can live with that.

Youth Organizations. Children and teenagers spent a great deal of their time in organizations controlled by the government. First of all, all children attended the same kind of government-controlled schools (there were no private schools). Ninety-nine percent of them joined the Young Pioneers, the official children's organization, and 75 percent went on to join the Free German Youth, the official youth group from which the SED recruited new members. Children spent a lot of time after school and on weekends in Pioneer activities like cleaning up public areas, collecting paper for recycling, or helping old people to shop, carry coal, or shovel snow. Thousands attended Pioneer camp each summer as well (Steele, p. 175).

Teenagers were attracted to youth clubs, which offered discos and hobby groups, and cheap vacations, all under the watchful eyes of party cadre. Once they finished school or apprenticeship, young people were pressed to join youth commissions or youth teams on their first job. Youth teams in the workplace had their own "plan" to fulfill (Edwards, pp. 124, 129, 130, 135, 141, 144). In its mobilization and indoctrination of children, the GDR resembled the Nazi state.

Women and Group Life. Throughout its 50-year history the government of the GDR worked to bring women into the labor force, both for ideological and for political reasons. In ideological terms, Marxism teaches that "socially useful work" is an essential human activity and that no one can fully develop as a person without it. Paid work was politically desirable too, as a means of integrating women into East German society, making them part of the collectives, unions, and volunteer groups that were the fundamental social units. As early as 1950, the GDR began working to counter the Nazi belief that women belonged at home. By the 1980s, 88 percent of women aged 15 to 60 were either employed or in school, the highest percentage in any country in the world (Edwards, pp. 50, 78, 82). And East German women typically remained in the workforce throughout their childbearing years, supported by low-cost day-care centers, shorter hours, and time off for childbirth. Early in its history, East Germany was short of labor, so it helped to have women work. But by the 1980s, the GDR had trouble finding enough jobs for all its people. Still, women were urged to work—in response to political, not market priorities.

The Elderly. East Germany also tried to prevent isolation of elderly people. Old people were encouraged to continue at work, or maintain contact with their old collectives and unions, and to join old people's clubs or other clubs. Factories and primary schools were "twinned" with old people's homes or clubs. They visited the elderly, did repairs for them, and ran trips and parties for them. Union committees also kept in touch with retired members. In turn, elderly people frequently visited schools or youth groups to give talks about the past, the Nazi era, and the building of socialism. A separate adult volunteer society ran old people's clubs, delivered meals on wheels, and provided home aides (Edwards, pp. 170–172, 193–196).

The Effectiveness of Social Controls

Social control in East Germany was focused on preventing political opposition to the SED and its style of socialism. The government was less concerned with deviance it defined as nonpolitical, except insofar as it saw all crime as political because it reflected poorly upon the merits of socialist society. Ordinary crime was handled in a style that was unmistakably both socialist and German. There was great emphasis on responding to deviance within worker- or neighborhood-based collectives. For example, factory managers were required to report to the policy any workers "who show serious signs of developing a work-shy outlook, who try to obtain a livelihood in an unworthy way, who break work discipline through constant abuse of alcohol or who show by their social behavior that they need extra instruction" (quoted in Steele, p. 158).

Some deviance was handled within the factory itself. Workers elected conflict commissions of eight to ten members which acted as courts for disciplining fellow workers in cases of quarrels, insults, petty theft, or damage to factory property. These panels were taken seriously and were quite effective. They might require convicted individuals to apologize to another person or to the collective, to repair or pay for damage, be publicly reprimanded, or pay a fine. The party newspaper published conflict commission cases weekly. Local disputes commissions played the same role in residential neighborhoods, adjudicating cases involving quarrels, noise, drunk driving, or even child abuse. Offenders convicted by the regular courts were expected to return to their old jobs after imprisonment and be looked after and helped to go straight by their fellow workers (Steele, pp. 139, 140, 157).

East Germany kept an unusually large uniformed police force, and they maintained files on all citizens, regardless of whether or not they committed any crimes. But except in cases of "political crimes," the police operated in typically German legalistic fashion, processing crimes and complaints strictly by the book (Ardagh, p. 316).

Defining Political Deviance. East German statistics cannot be relied on for accuracy, but it seems likely that there were in fact relatively low crime rates. Political deviance was another matter entirely. East Germany's leaders understood that many people did not support the regime; they were, in one way or another, **dissidents.** Open dissidence was treated harshly. Dissidents and their families were blocked from universities, jobs, and apartments. They were watched and followed by the secret police, so others avoided them. In extreme cases they were jailed, or even expelled from the country. Even people who were not explicitly "political" but simply tried to "drop out" of conventional life were defined as antisocialist. Hippies, folk musicians, punk rockers, and unconventional artists were all viewed with suspicion. When rock music came to East Germany in the 1970s, the SED considered it harmful and threatening. Much rock was individualistic: It explored private, subjective feelings, and other rock was critical of government and society. As early as 1976 the SED decided that only carefully controlled rock music could be played in official discos by "disco moderators," who received special training in Marxism-Leninism and could be trusted. All other rock music performances were banned (Ramet, pp. 91–92).

But despite its tremendous power to sanction deviance, the East German government was caught in a dilemma. Leaders wanted both to suppress dissent and to give the appearance that there was no dissent, that East Germans enthusiastically supported the SED. In particular, SED leaders wanted to play down the amount of violence required to keep their regime in power. As much as possible, they wanted to avoid the open use of force. Above all, they wanted to avoid a recurrence of open revolt like the June 1953 rebellion, put down in such an ugly way by Soviet troops. On the other hand, they weren't willing to let dissidents leave East Germany, because they were afraid that millions of people would do so, revealing the pervasiveness of discontent.

The government hoped that by involving all citizens, from early childhood, in government-controlled organizations, they could build willing support for the regime. Government and people engaged in a sort of silent struggle, with the government trying to control all aspects of its citizens' lives and the people trying to create private space shielded from state power. By trying to control so much of people's lives, the government turned every aspect of life into an arena of political struggle. Many people who were otherwise apolitical found themselves defined as dissidents and in opposition to the government. Many people retreated from the public realm to country cottages and gardens and the kitchen-table society of friends and family. Informal friendship circles were particularly important to young people. Among friends they listened to music, talked politics, defined individual identities, and participated in a youth culture which was outside of government control (Lemke, pp. 68–71).

In the mid-1970s, the SED, under the leadership of Erich Honecker, decided that it would be better to allow people selected safety valves for their discontent, rather than increase the level of repression. The SED selected two seemingly harmless outlets: television and the church. They decriminalized the watching of western TV, figuring that since so many of West Germany's serious-minded TV programs were devoted to social problems like poverty and drug abuse, watching western TV would decrease the attractiveness of the West. The SED also permitted the Protestant Church, harassed since the 1950s, to increase its level of activity. The church became the only institution independent of the state and it took on an enormously important role in opposing the East German regime (Ardagh, p. 384).

The Church and Dissent

East Germany is a traditionally Lutheran part of Germany and the Catholic Church is rather small and inactive there, so Honecker sought his rapprochement with the Lutheran Church, promising some degree of church independence in exchange for a pledge that the church would stay out of politics. Honecker hoped the church would attract discontented people and direct their energies into religion, not political opposition. As a result, the church came to offer "the only organized public alternative to the official value-system, and thus attracted many people not otherwise very religious" (Ardagh, p. 385). All kinds of deviants—homosexuals, punks, rebellious youth, rock musicians, peace activists, and would-be emigrants—were attracted to the church (Goeckel, pp. 211, 216–217).

The church hierarchy, pastors, and congregations constantly argued over the role of the church: How far should it go along with the state? How much should the church allow its premises to be used for dissent? This very discussion, which called into question the legitimacy of the government, was profoundly seditious, even when church authorities decided in the end to suppress political activity. The very existence of the church as an institution outside the hierarchies of the SED made the state nervous. Even in the 1980s, when the SED permitted the building of new churches, permitted religious programs on state radio, and permitted departments of theology to train ministers, the state still discriminated against church members and especially pastors. Their children were usually excluded from higher education. They were officially put in a special category, the *Sonderlinge*—literally "the peculiar"—with a very small admissions quota and active Christians were not permitted to become schoolteachers or government officials (Ardagh, p. 387; Darnton, p. 226).

In the late 1980s, as the domination of the SED weakened, the churches, somewhat reluctantly, became the natural focus of dissident activity. In many cities peace groups, environmentalist groups, and human rights groups began meeting in churches and they pressured church officials to allow and protect greater freedom of speech within the church. Concerts and church services arranged by these groups drew more and more people and became weekly events that spilled over into candlelight marches, demonstrations, and vigils. In the fall of 1989, as the regime crumbled, church services in small towns attracted crowds, and while praying for divine intervention, people began to speak out against the government. Following the pattern established in Leipzig and Berlin, village churches held weekly prayer meetings and candlelight marches, and the authorities, as they felt their power undermined, began to back off from confronting the demonstrators (Philipsen, pp. 141–150; Darnton, pp. 222–226). In this way, the churches, the only independent institutions, became the nurseries of dissident organization.

Deviance and Social Control in the Federal Republic

You can see a clear contrast: East Germany was a **collectivist** society that treated individuals as members of groups, but West Germany was an **individualistic** society that saw individuals as autonomous actors, free to join groups or remain private. West Germans belonged to fewer groups than East Germans, and the groups they did belong to were under no centralized control. The West German pattern of deviance and social control continues today in the reunified Germany.

Social Groups in an Individualistic Society

As Hall and Hall put it, in West Germany social institutions were compartmentalized. Politically, the nation was divided into states, and the federal government shared power with them. In business, work was divided among departments, which jealously guarded their territory. Information was seldom shared freely among work groups (Hall and Hall, pp. 44–45). People kept their friends and their work separate, their school life and social life separate, and their friends and neighbors separate. How they behaved in one social group likely had little bearing on their treatment in another. As we have seen, for children school life and after-school friendships and activities were quite separate.

Women and Group Life. Short school days had a major effect on women's lives in West Germany. Children didn't start school until age 6 or 7, there were few day-care centers or even kindergartens, and those that existed were privately run and relatively expensive. School, once begun, was only a half-day affair, and there was little after-school care available either. Then, of course, the shops closed at 6:30, so someone had to be home to take care of children and shop in the afternoons (Marsh, p. 311). West German society assumed that it was the responsibility of individual families, not the society or government, to work out this problem. As a result, West German women were much less likely to work than East German women, and actually less likely to work than women in England or France or the United States.

Under 40 percent of West German women worked in the 1980s, and only a third of these women had children. They brought home only 18 percent of family income. It was the pattern in West Germany for women to work for several years before marriage and childbearing, at which time they left the labor force, reentering it only when their children were grown. As a result, there were few women in professional careers: Only 5 percent of lawyers and 3.4 percent of senior civil servants were women, although 20 percent of doctors were female. In banking, business, and industry, only about 2 percent of all top positions were held by women. Mostly, women found less skilled jobs, primarily in traditionally female occupations like office work and sales, and they earned only about half as much as men. Even women in salaried jobs earned only two-thirds of men's pay. The unemployment rate was about twice as high for women as for men (Ferree, p. 93; Ardagh, pp. 192–194; Nyrop, pp. 123–124).

Responses to Deviance

West Germans responded to deviance in ways that are both characteristic of parliamentary democracies and characteristically German. Because of the burden of their Nazi past, West Germans were fearful of any government intervention that smacked of totalitarianism. They didn't want the government spying on people or controlling private organizations or limiting freedom of speech. But as Germans they valued an orderly society and they expected people to conform closely to the law. As we have seen, West Germans took it upon themselves to correct other people's behavior—in the streets, in the neighborhoods, at work. Also, West Germans were notoriously litigious—that is, they readily litigated, or brought lawsuits against each other. Neighborhood residents would sue a restaurant that stayed open too late, or a homeowner who didn't follow the rules for mowing the grass. At work, employees used grievance procedures to contest mandatory overtime they considered unjustified or a missed promotion.

> ### Johanna's Story: The Lawsuit
> Johanna Silberschnitt still blushes with embarrassment and anger when she talks about the lawsuit her neighbors brought against her family for excessive noise. They tried, she protests, to observe all the rules about quiet hours and laundry hours and hallway neatness in their apartment house. "But when you have four boys under the age of 10, you have to expect some noise," she remarks. In the end, the courts upheld the Silberschnitts, but "though we won the battle, we lost the war," Johanna says. It was hard to face angry neighbors day after day, and teachers began to look at the older boys as troublemakers. Finally, her in-laws helped them with the down payment and they bought a house in a new development outside town. It's further from the shops and school, Johanna says, but it's worth it. "There is no one living beneath us hearing footsteps and there are a lot more young families in the neighborhood, so people understand."

Political Deviance in the Berlin Republic

Following reunification of the two Germanys, East Germany's entire system of social control was dismantled: the Stasi, the SED, the Women's Federation, the youth organizations, the factory Conflict Commissions, the ideological school curriculum: All disappeared. All of Germany was to run on the western model.

The result has been an unanticipated upsurge in political deviance, especially in the former East Germany and predictable difficulty on the part of the reunified German government in responding to it. More young men were seen in the streets with shaved heads and paramilitary gear, wearing Nazi symbols. Violent underground computer games like "Aryan Test" and "Total Auschwitz" drilled antiforeigner youths in running a concentration camp or gassing Turks. "Skinzines" (underground right-wing magazines) included *Macht und Ehre* (Power and Honor) and *Schlachtruf* (Battle Cry) and brought news of neo-Nazi groups worldwide. "Hate rock" (a neo-Nazi blend of punk and heavy metal) was the most powerful part of the movement. There were at least fifty *Faschobands,* including *Volkszorn* (The People's Anger) and *Zyklon B* (the name of the poison gas used in Nazi death chambers) (Rodden, p. 199). Neo-Nazis staged many attacks on foreigners and also firebombed synagogues and vandalized Jewish cemeteries. According to government figures, far-right groups committed 746 acts of racial violence in 1999 (about six times the level of the early 1980s, but down by a third since the early 1990s *The Economist,* Aug. 12, 2000, p. 18).

Many skinhead youth support the ultraconservative parties (like the German People's Union and the National Democratic Party). The ultraright parties are all antiforeigner. Campaign posters for the German People's Union in 1998 called for "German Money for German Jobs." Supporters termed foreigners "parasites" who feed on the "*Aryan Volk,*" and "*Zecke Verrecke*" (death to the ticks) is one of the slogans of the movement. It may seem strange that antiforeigner sentiment is so strong in a part of Germany where there are in fact very few foreigners. Immigrants are only one-half of one percent of the population in the east, compared to 10 percent in the western states. Foreigners are really **scapegoats** for young east Germans' problems (Rodder, p. 198).

Young people in the east have been less hesitant to embrace neo-Nazism because they were never taught about the horrors of the Nazi era and they were never expected to take responsibility for it. The socialists and communists who came to power in the east after the division of Germany had been steadfast opponents of Nazism. They tried and jailed and executed many former Nazis and then declared that the guilty had been punished and East Germans no longer had to bear the burden of guilt for the past. Taboos about Nazi rhetoric, dress, and symbols that are very strong in the west have little force in the east (Buruma, pp. 156, 157, 181).

Erich's Story: The Skinhead

Erich Kessel (age 17) is a high school student in Bitterfeld in the eastern state of Saxony. Like his friends, Erich cuts school a lot. He lives in a cracked, water-stained apartment tower complex near the abandoned chemical plants. He wears black leather, shaves his head, and sports T-shirts with neo-Nazi slogans. Late last Saturday night, Erich's high school principal spotted him and his best friend spray-painting swastikas on the gravestones in the old Jewish cemetery. The principal was furious. "You give all Ossis a bad name," he railed. "Why don't you come to school and learn a trade? Make something of yourself so your parents could be proud of you." "What's the point," said Erich. "With the plants closed down, half this town is out of work. My father has been sitting around drinking beer for 12 years now. And they keep bringing in more and more Jews, and give them good apartments and welfare. Hitler was right: There's a tide pouring out of the East, Jews and

Poles and Russians, taking all the good jobs and stealing our women, breeding a new race of Untermenschen *(inferior people). You'll see, soon you'll all thank me and my friends for trying to save Germany."*

Responding to Anti-Semitism

How much should Germany do to suppress neo-Nazis? What does Germany owe to Jews fifty years after the Nazi era? Germans have conflicted responses to these very troubling questions. Almost all Germans deeply deplore anti-Semitism. They are genuinely horrified by anything smacking of Nazism. But they are just as repelled by anything that reminds them of totalitarianism. They don't want their government to restrict free speech, or the rights of political dissidents, or the rights of religious minorities. They don't want government agencies like the *Stasi* spying on people. As a result, their responses to neo-Nazis are often contradictory. In some cases Germans take individual action, helping a disabled man attacked by skinheads, or throwing a known neo-Nazi out of a bar (Ardagh, pp. 504–505). In several cities, after neo-Nazi attacks, thousands of Germans turned out in demonstrations to show their opposition to intolerance and anti-Semitism. In November 2000, 200,000 people marched through Berlin to remember the victims of *Kristallnacht,* the 1938 attack on Jews that many see as the beginning of the Holocaust. Banners and balloons proclaimed "No to Neo-Nazis" (*The New York Times,* Nov. 10, 2000, p. A12). For

Meet Roy Brandt, better known to his friends as "Bomber." Roy is teaching his three-year-old son to give the Nazi salute. Some Germans react to the rapid changes brought by reunification and European union by reviving symbols of the Nazi past. Although neo-Nazis are a tiny minority in Germany, rising unemployment and substantial immigration have resulted in a sense of unease among many Germans.

the first time, in 2001 the government tried to ban a neo-Nazi party, the National Democratic Party, on the ground that it seeks to overthrow the republic and the constitution. Support for the measure was quite mixed, with many people hesitant to suppress any free speech, however ugly, unless it is an explicit call to violence. And in the end, the ban failed (Landler, Sept. 21, 2004, p. A16; *The Economist,* Oct. 28, 2000, p. 50).

Some German actions are aimed at making reparations to Jews and others who suffered in Nazi Germany. In 2000 the German government and some major German companies signed an agreement to create a $5 billion fund to compensate Nazi-era slave workers and forced laborers. There were 640,000 such victims at the end of World War II, although only 61,000 are still alive (Andrews, July 18, 2000, p. A3). In 2001 an ambitious Jewish Museum opened in Berlin to great fanfare. And Jews occupy a privileged position in German immigration policy. Five thousand Jewish families a year have their visas approved and receive work permits and full benefits packages rivaling those of ethnic German immigrants. The Berlin official in charge of immigration in Berlin explains, "This should be seen as a form of reparation. Jews were murdered and we feel better if we do this" (Erlanger, Sept. 10, 2001, p. A8).

Responding to Terrorism

Now Germans have recognized a new form of political deviance—Islamic terrorist cells. After the September 11 attacks in New York, it became clear that many of the terrorists had lived in Germany while planning and coordinating their attacks. Mohammed Atta, apparently the pilot of one of the planes that struck the World Trade Center, was the leader of an *al-Qaeda* cell in Hamburg. His group held meetings by pretending to be an Islamic prayer group. Two other leading hijackers lived in Hamburg too. The terrorists chose Germany for two reasons. They could easily blend in and go unnoticed, especially in cities like Hamburg with large Muslim populations. Also, Germans have been so eager not to be like Nazis and not to be like *Stasi* that they have been hesitant to use the power of the state against political deviants.

The September 11 attacks mobilized Germans to tighten things up. The parliament repealed a provision of the constitution that gave special protection to religious groups. Now even religious groups can be banned if they advocate terrorism or proselytize hate. In December 2001 Germany banned an Islamic group called The Caliphate and carried out more than 200 raids on members. Also, the government tightened security laws, scrapping privacy protections that had made it difficult to get access to bank account and income information, computer records, even addresses and telephone numbers. Now the government is even considering adding fingerprints to passports and identity cards. And there is talk as well about tightening immigration laws (Erlanger, Oct. 1, 2001, p. B1; Oct. 5, 2001, p. B6; Dec. 13, 2001, p. B5).

SOCIAL CHANGE AND THE FUTURE

The story of the *Wende* (German reunification) is a wonderful example of how historic social change actually takes place. Years of quiet organizing by dissident groups suddenly blossomed into exhilarating collective action in the demonstrations

Celebrating the fall of the Berlin Wall in 1989, these young German men are intoxicated with the excitement of making history. Emboldened by participating in mass demonstrations, they have actually climbed the Wall. Only days before, they would have been shot by East German police if they had dared to cross the no-man's land which bordered the Wall.

that led to the fall of the Berlin Wall. But the pace of change slowed after that, and the discouraging process of institutionalizing a revolution began.

The *Wende* really began with Gorbachev, because he loosened the hold of the Soviet Union upon all its eastern European satellites. When Hungary moved toward democracy and opened its border with Austria, early in 1989, East Germans began fleeing through Hungary to the West. In the first nine months of 1989 alone, 130,000 East Germans defied their government by leaving the country.[3] Because it was unable to stop this flood of emigration, the government's authority was fatally undermined. Gorbachev himself made it clear that Soviet troops would no longer be available to prop up the SED. That emboldened more people to flee, and it made the SED seem more vulnerable. In October 1989, SED chief Erich Honecker stepped down and new leaders began to reorganize the party.

In November 1989, millions of people demonstrated in East Berlin and Leipzig. They carried banners reading "No More Fear," "Socialism: Who Destroyed Its Meaning?" "Stop Privileges," and "Those Who Don't Move Don't Feel Their Chains." One said only "1789–1989." The crowds roared, "We are the people." After that, events moved quickly. First, the whole ministry resigned, then troops and

[3]Almost 345,000 people left East Germany by the end of 1989, 2 percent of the country's remaining population. Those who left were mostly young, educated, and skilled, making their loss the more painful (Craig, 1994, p. 36). Many hospitals lost so many staff their operation was crippled.

tanks rolled into the streets of East Berlin, only to be withdrawn; then the whole *Politbüro* resigned. Finally, on November 9, an SED spokesman was holding a news conference and someone handed him a handwritten note. He read it off casually, perhaps inaccurately, and reporters announced that the Wall was officially opened! Then Berliners took matters into their own hands. Hundreds of thousands of people from both sides of Berlin converged on the Wall. They argued with the guards, who looked frightened, but didn't shoot, and then suddenly one guard opened a gate. The crowd surged through and suddenly there were thousands of people through the Wall, and then on top of it—dancing, hugging, drinking wine, exchanging flowers, hammering at the Wall, and destroying it with pickaxes. The crowd chanted, "We are ONE people."

Collective Behavior and Social Movements

The fall of the Berlin Wall was one of the great revolutionary moments of the twentieth century, a moment when events move so fast that a crowd, and even individuals in that crowd, hold history in their hands. Just imagine: Those young, frightened border guards could as easily have started shooting as opened the gate. They made history!

Sociologists who study spontaneous history making like this call the phenomenon **collective behavior.** Events on this scale don't happen often, because they require an unusual combination of conditions. First of all, they occur in response to preexisting grievances. People are likely to engage in collective behavior when they are convinced that the authorities won't listen to them any other way. Collective behavior happens most readily in an already existing crisis, when there are structural strains in the society and social controls have weakened. People have a feeling that the possible gains from collective action outweigh the risks that authorities will punish them. Even then, collective action may not occur unless two other prior conditions are present. People need some way to communicate with each other so they know other people share their grievances and will act with them. Then, there is usually some precipitating incident that focuses long-standing complaints.

In Berlin in 1989, demonstrations grew out of years of organizing activity by dissident groups. Dissidents, working mostly through the Protestant churches, organized the growing demonstrations and helped people voice beliefs about the need for change. Then the collapse of the SED precipitated action and many more people spontaneously joined in. In the crowd at the Wall people improvised norms and individual actors played a major role in the actual events.

When the Berlin Wall was opened on November 9, events began to move very quickly. Until then, the dissident movement had focused on demands for democracy—in a separate, socialist East Germany. But the masses of November 9 suddenly looked through the Wall and saw the prosperous West—a society that worked. "We are ONE people," they declared, and the rush to reunification was born. The dissidents who led the movement were horrified. But Helmut Kohl, the chancellor of West Germany, saw a unique opportunity. Hastily, he announced a plan for rapid reunification, figuring that it could take place only while Gorbachev was still in power. In March 1990, East Germans democratically elected a new parliament; by July, the economic union of the two countries was a reality; and on October 3, the two nations were officially joined as one again.

Reunification and Institutional Change

Germans were euphoric: no one had ever expected Germany to be whole once more, nor had anyone anticipated the end of Soviet domination in the East. But euphoria was short lived. It soon became clear that in 40 years, West and East had become two very different societies, with contrasting values, different ways of thinking and interacting, as well as two incompatible economic systems. People realized that reunification would be difficult and very expensive. The East required new political institutions: new political parties, a new legal system, and new local governments at every level. It needed newly privatized economic institutions to replace the old state-owned structures. Schools, hospitals, and social welfare institutions had to be reorganized along western lines. And the terrible legacy of environmental damage had to be cleaned up. As institutions changed, East Germans had to reorient themselves to new roles and norms.

Reorganizing the Economy

The course of economic change was set by decisions taken early in the process of reunification. The governments of East and West Germany chose to merge the East into the Federal Republic as rapidly as possible, in part in an effort to stem the tide of emigration which was disruptive to West German society and damaging to the East as well.

The first step toward economic merger was the 1:1 currency union which took effect on July 1, 1990. Once East Germans had *deutschmarks* to spend, they bought western goods which were cheaper and of better quality. A Trabant had cost 10,000 marks, but a far superior used BMW from the West cost 4,000 marks (Ardagh, p. 431). Without buyers for their goods, without the state subsidies that had kept them afloat, and without guaranteed markets in other Soviet satellite nations (now opening their own borders to western goods), East German factories were driven out of business. Within a year unemployment in the east reached 30 percent.

Privatization. Simultaneously with the currency union, the German government began a process of complete privatization of the East German economy. East German companies would immediately either be sold to private investors or shut down. The government created a new agency, the Public Trust (or *Treuhandanstalt*) to carry out privatization. The Public Trust's job was daunting. As one East German industrialist explained, "No one knew how to transform an economy from socialist central planning to a free market. There was no road map" (Siegfried Schlottig, quoted in Protzman, p. D1).

The *Treuhand* took over more than 13,000 formerly state-owned companies. The agency's work went slowly at first. But by 1995 privatization was almost complete. Perhaps a third of east German companies proved unsaleable and were shut down; others were sold after reorganization by the *Treuhand*. There were 4.1 million people who worked in the companies taken over by the *Treuhand*, but at the end of privatization, only 1.5 million of their jobs still existed (Protzman, pp. D1, D2).

Government Aid. Simultaneously with privatization, the German government began pouring money into eastern Germany, at a rate of about $140 billion per year. At first it went mostly for industrial restructuring and for retraining, unemployment benefits, and subsidized work. Then huge subsidies went into rebuilding the roads, railroads, sewers and power lines, phone systems, and power plants. Money was spent restoring historic churches and public buildings. This enormous investment was paid for by income tax surcharges (*The Economist,* May 27, 2000, p. 51).

Adopting Western Political Institutions

Superficially, political incorporation of eastern Germany into the Federal Republic proceeded more smoothly than economic reunification. All the old political institutions of the GDR disbanded upon reunification and the East adopted the legal system, constitution, and political institutions of the Federal Republic. The traditional five states of eastern Germany, which had been abolished in the centralizing GDR, were reestablished. The old puppet political parties of the GDR, with two important exceptions, disappeared, and the major West German parties established themselves in the East. One exception was the CDU, then the governing party, which had already existed as an eastern party, and therefore inherited a membership and some organization. The other party that continued in existence was the SED, which purged itself of its top leadership and then continued under a new name, the Party of Democratic Socialism (PDS). So it did not take long to create all the standard West German political bodies in the former GDR.

On a deeper level, however, the establishment of democratic institutions in eastern Germany has remained problematical because easterners had no experience in active political participation. Once it became clear that the two Germanys would reunify, the West German parties moved their operations into the East. They played a dominating role in all the 1990 elections. Eastern Germans were overwhelmed by the TV ads, the posters, the rallies with huge sound systems, the election parties with beer and traditional costumes.

REUNIFICATION AND CULTURAL CHANGE

> There is a new joke now in east Germany: " 'We are one people,' says the easterner. 'So are we, says the westerner.' " (Whitney, Jan. 24, 1995, p. A3)

Institutional changes in the economy and government were quickly accomplished in the former GDR. But cultural reunification has been much more difficult to achieve. A decade after reunification Germans worried about "the walls in our heads and hearts (that) have been growing in both parts of Germany." "We have divided more than we have come together," said one east German local official (Cohen, Oct. 25, 1998, p. 6). Eastern Germans feel resentful of westerners, who have been so quick to condemn and discard everything eastern. "What do you expect to achieve by constantly telling 15 million people that everything they did was wrong?" demanded one easterner (Cowell, July 7, 1998, p. A8). It is helpful to contrast east Germany with other former communist countries like the Czech Republic and

Poland. People have struggled to adopt market economies in those countries, but they are doing it for themselves and they feel proud of their efforts, while in east Germany, "each new day reminds eastern Germans that they lost the cold war and must defer to the victors" (*The New York Times,* Sept. 1, 1996, p. E8). Many eastern Germans are suddenly nostalgic for their old society. There is even a word now for this feeling: *Ostalgie.* "Not everything in the GDR (East Germany) was bad," said one easterner. "Maybe we couldn't buy luxury goods, but food was cheap and no one went hungry. At least everyone had a job. And human relations were better. I needed my neighbors and they needed me. We all helped one another. Now people are more isolated. We don't even say hello to each other anymore" (Cohen, Oct. 25, 1999, p. A1; *The Economist,* Nov. 13, 1999, p. 55).

Anomie in the Former East Germany

To fully understand the problems of cultural integration after reunification in Germany, we need to turn to the work of a famous French sociologist, the great Emile Durkheim. At the end of the nineteenth century, Durkheim wrote about the harmful consequences of rapid change in modern societies. He said that in a period of profound change, such as a time of rapid economic modernization, an economic collapse, or a revolution, old standards of behavior, values, and beliefs become irrelevant and a state of **anomie** (or normlessness) prevails. Old social controls on individual behavior become ineffective; new ones don't yet exist and people feel directionless and lost. They may expect too much from the changed society, and they often become depressed or aggressive. Rates of deviant behavior like suicide, violent crime, and drug and alcohol abuse climb rapidly.

Life in eastern Germany after reunification presents a classic example of anomie. At first, when the Wall came down, there was euphoria. People thought that with Germany reunified, all their problems would be solved. But then everything changed. Timothy Garton Ash explained

> Nowhere in post-Communist Europe has the change in every aspect of life been so sudden and total as in east Germany. Not just the political, economic and legal system but the street signs, the banks, the post offices, the health insurance, the cars, the products in the shops, why even the bread has changed. (Ash, p. 22)

Socialism, a set of ideals that many people respected, even if they thought it had not been achieved, seemed to have been decisively defeated. People were asked to adopt a whole new way of life previously considered reprehensible. They were asked to act as individuals, to put consumer desires first, and to value private enterprise and profit making. Some people rapidly adapted, but for many others it was as if the world had turned upside down.

Frau Metz's Story: The Teacher

"There couldn't be a worse time to be a teacher," declares Charlotte Metz, a seventh-grade history teacher in the mining town of Cottbus. "I truly don't know what to teach my students. You know, I really believed in socialism. I taught my students Marxism–Leninism and I thought we were building the workers' state. I cried when the Wall came down. But then I saw pictures of the West. I even visited my relatives in Berlin, and it wasn't all poverty and crime and drug addiction as we had been told. But now look

what reunification has done here: the mines are closed and almost all the men are out of work. That would never have happened in the GDR."

"Teach your students both sides," Charlotte's husband interjects. "Let them make up their own minds." "I do. . . . I try to," Charlotte replies, "but I can't teach any of it with conviction. I don't know what's true anymore or what's the right way to run our country. And there's something worse. My students don't want to know. Yesterday, when I started my lesson on the division of Germany, they put on their earphones. Yes, they actually pulled out their Walkmans and put on their earphones!"

Many eastern Germans described their state of anomie quite clearly. In 1994, the Reverend Christian Führer, who was a leader of the dissident movement in Leipzig, explains, "People here feel a real schizophrenia. No one wants to go back to the days of dictatorship, but at the same time we're not really happy with the new system. It's full of challenges for which we are totally unprepared." . . . Brutal competition and the lust for money are destroying our sense of community. Almost everyone feels a level of fear or depression or insecurity" (Kinzer, Oct. 14, 1994, p. A14).

Birthrates and Death Rates. Anomie in eastern Germany had chillingly concrete social consequences. Birthrates had been falling gradually in both East and West Germany, but after the fall of the Berlin Wall birthrates in the East fell precipitously. By 1993, there were 60 percent fewer births than there had been in 1989. Rates fell most for married women in the prime childbearing years. Such a sharp decline is almost unprecedented in twentieth-century history, though something similar did happen in Berlin in the last years of World War II. Marriage rates fell to the lowest level in the world today. "Many eastern couples are reluctant to have children, because they are unsure whether they will be able to survive in the newly competitive society," concluded *The New York Times* in 1994 ("Living, and Dying, in a Barren Land," p. 54; Kinzer, Jan. 25, 1994, p. A3). By 2003 the total number of births per year in the east had increased by a third, but it was still only half what it had been in the 1980s (Federal Statistical Office). (See Table 5.3, p. 333.)

Even more disturbing was the sharp rise in death rates in the former GDR. For women between the ages of 25 and 45, the death rate rose by nearly 20 percent between 1989 and 1991, and for men of the same age it rose 30 percent. Most astonishingly, for girls 10 to 14 the death rate rose 70 percent. Eastern German men in 1990 were 156 percent more likely to die of injuries or suicide than men in western Germany (*The Economist,* April 23, 1994, p. 54). Durkheim would not be surprised to learn that with time, the crisis in eastern death rates has subsided. Life expectancy is now about the same for women in all parts of Germany, though life spans are still slightly shorter for men in the east than in the west (*This Week in Germany,* Oct. 8, 2004).

Cultural Values in East and West

It is now more than 15 years since the fall of the Berlin Wall. Can anomie and cultural divides last this long? The evidence is conflicting. A 2004 survey shows that values remain quite different in the west and the east. Western Germans ranked freedom as their most important value: 49 percent said so, and only 35 percent said equality was more important. Eastern Germans saw it the opposite way: 36 percent to 51 percent. Some say eastern Germans still feel like "second class citizens" (*The Economist,* Sept. 18, 2004, p. 58).

But in an odd way, western German attitudes towards the east are changing. The old DDR is becoming an object of *Ostalgie* to westerners, even young people who never experienced the old East Germany. A 2003 film about East Germany, *Goodbye Lenin,* became one of Germany's biggest successes at the box office. In the film, a young man in east Germany tries to create the illusion that the Wall has never fallen in order to protect his sick mother from the shock of reunification. There are also television shows inspired by life in the DDR, T-shirts with pictures of the *Trabi* (the East German car) and Web sites selling vanished East German products. Crowds came to the New National Gallery in Berlin for a show of postwar East German art, including a great deal of "socialist realist" art. And hip young Berliners are seeking out apartments in the sprawling, ugly old apartment towers in the east, which are suddenly cool (*The Economist,* Sept. 13, 2003, p. 57; Fitzgerald, Oct. 1, 2003, p. E1; Roth, Jan. 24, 2002, pp. F1, F8).

Women in the New Germany

Though it had many faults, East German society had one virtue appreciated by its citizens: There were many benefits to help parents, and especially mothers, raise their children while working outside the home. As we have seen, affordable day care was widely available, most children stayed in school for a full day and ate lunch at school, there was generous maternity leave (a year at 80 percent of full pay), and the state enforced and guaranteed child support by absent fathers. Abortions were legal and available through the national health insurance system (Duggan and Folbre, p. 23; Ferree, p. 94). Women were accustomed to marrying young, having children early, and working throughout their childbearing years.

By 1989, 91 percent of East German women of working age were employed, and working women contributed 40 percent of average household income. They held an unusually large percentage of skilled factory jobs and professional jobs. Women were certainly not completely equal to men: They were concentrated in typically "feminine" occupations like education, nursing, and textile production, and they did most of the housework and child care, even when they worked full-time (Dolling, pp. 34–37; Nickel, pp. 50–51: Ferree, pp. 91, 93).

After reunification, eastern German women suddenly found themselves living on the western plan. The cost of day care doubled relative to income, and maternity leave pay fell to only 25 percent of full pay. The state no longer fully guarantees child support. School lets out before lunch and women are expected to be at home waiting for their children. Now two-thirds of unemployed eastern Germans are women. Finally, abortion is now illegal in eastern Germany, as in western Germany, except in very limited circumstances (Nyrop, p. 123; Ferree, p. 93; Duggan and Folbre, p. 23). (See Table 5.3, p. 333.)

By 2003, only 70.5 percent of women in east Germany were employed. More women worked part-time and fewer worked full-time. Nevertheless, east German women remained more likely to work than west German women, and more likely to work full-time (Federal Statistical Office, 2005). (See Table 5.4, p. 333.) It remained considerably easier to get child care in eastern Germany than in the western states,

TABLE 5.3 Births, Deaths and Marriages in Germany, 2003

Even fifteen years after reunification, marriage and birth rates are still lower in the former East Germany than in the former West Germany and the death rate remains higher in the former East Germany.

	Marriages Per 10,000 Persons	Birth Per 10,000 Persons	Deaths Per 10,000 Persons
Former East Germany*	37	72	112
Former West Germany*	49	89	102
Germany	46	86	103

*Excluding the city of Berlin

Source: Statistical Office of the Lander and the Federal Statistical Office, http://www.statistik-portal.de/ Statistik-Portal/en/en_jb01_jahrtab3.asp

TABLE 5.4 Working Mothers of Young Children in Germany

Women of children under 6 in the former East Germany remain more likely to work and to work full time than their sisters in the former West Germany. This may reflect the emphasis that the socialist culture of East Germany placed on the value of work and the opportunities it created for mothers of young children to work.

	Mothers of Children Under 6			
	1996		2003	
	Full Time	Part Time	Full Time	Part Time
Former East Germany	37%	14%	32%	21%
Former West Germany	12%	23%	11%	30%

Federal Statistical Office Germany, "Women with Preschool Children," March 7, 2005, http://www.destatis.de/ presse/englisch/pm2005/p1020024.htm.

and all-day day care was much more available in the east than the west. There are also indications that eastern women are more successfully adjusting to the new, re-unified Germany than are east German men. Huge numbers of young men and women are leaving east Germany for the cities of the west, but the women are more likely to find jobs in the west in service industries such as health care. Many men can't find jobs in the west and end up returning home to the east. As a result, sex ratios in the east are now unbalanced: there are 20 percent more men than women aged 15–50 (Harris, March 10, 2004).

Women and Population Change. You could say that as women leave eastern Germany, the number of "potential" mothers is falling. There are fewer women to have the future children of eastern Germany, adding to the decline in population. Even in Dresden, the prosperous capital of the eastern state of Saxony, forty-three schools closed in 2004 because of a lack of children. But it's true that population is falling in western Germany also, just not as rapidly. Overall, German women don't have enough babies to reproduce the population. On average, they have only 1.4 babies each. Reiner Klingholz, director of the Berlin Institute for Population and Development, calculated that without immigration, Germany's population will fall from the current 82 million to 24 million at the end of the twenty-first century. Even including immigration, at current rates, Germany's population will shrink by 700,000 by 2020. And a bigger proportion of Germany's population will be old: By 2050, Klingholz predicts, one-third of Germans will be over 65, twice the current proportion. That will put an enormous strain on Germany's public health care system and on the public pension system. Germans worry that there will be too many schools, too many hospitals, too many roads, and a deserted, depopulated countryside (Landler, Nov. 18, 2004, p. A3).

Why are German women having so few children? Some women say that German culture doesn't really value children. Neighbors complain when babies cry or noisy children play outside. "They want their houses, they want their cars, they want their cars, they want their peace," one mother explained. Families would rather buy a fancy car than have another child. Immigrants have larger families than native-born Germans, but the children of immigrants quickly adopt German lifestyles and have fewer children. Also, women find it difficult to combine work and motherhood. They opt for smaller families in order to keep their career options open. Recognizing the problem, the government plans to spend 1.5 billion euros a year after 2005 on child care and to invest 4 billion euros a year on all-day schools (Landler, Nov. 18, 2004, p. A3; *The Economist,* Dec. 6, 2003, p. 47).

Germany Today: Life in the Berlin Republic

We want the story to have a happy ending: Germany reunified, grateful east Germans enjoying democracy and capitalist affluence; virtuous west Germans proud of the help they gave their eastern brothers and sisters. Unfortunately, more than a decade after reunification the happy ending has not arrived. Perhaps it will, given sufficient time, but right now, Germany is faced with unanticipated difficulties and conflicts.

The Status of Economic Reunification

The situation in east Germany is a wonderful example of the power of **expectations.** At the start, Germans had faced economic unification with great optimism. Then-Chancellor Helmut Kohl promised easterners they would see "blooming landscapes" fill the east's gray and polluted land within five years. Germans were so optimistic in 1989 that they were bound to be disappointed in the years that followed.

Actually, in many ways eastern Germans are much better off than they were before 1989. Their wages are much higher. Legislation at the time of reunification aimed at equalizing wages, and easterners now earn about 80 percent of what westerners earn. They are able to buy consumer goods undreamed of before 1989. Housing has improved greatly. People are abandoning the grim cement housing projects of Communist East Germany and building new suburbs of modern single family homes. More than 750,000 new houses have been built since 1993. The greatest accomplishment of the years since reunification has been in ridding the east of pollution. With the old factories closed down and modern sewage-treatment plants constructed, severely polluted rivers have been cleaned up. The air is much cleaner, thanks to new modern cars and $50 billion spent on clean-burning new power plants (*The Economist,* Sept. 30, 2000, p. 26).

But many east Germans feel worse off. They worry terribly about unemployment, which they have never experienced before. They are shocked at the new inequalities present in their society and unprepared for the risk and uncertainty that goes with life in a capitalist economy. Even the new material abundance seems to them somewhat heartless.

Unemployment is the real root of all the trouble. In government statistics, unemployment in the east is running approximately double unemployment in the west—16–20 percent, compared to 8–10 percent. In the obsolete industrial cities along the border with Poland, unemployment runs as high as 35 percent. There is a lot of disguised unemployment too. Many people over 50 have been encouraged to retire early. Everyone admits there is a whole generation of middle-aged people who will never work again. Especially in depressed industrial areas, east Germans feel like they are a welfare colony, maintained on the charity of the west, and it angers them very much, because in the past they took pride in their workmanship, their productivity, and their role as the leading socialist economy (Andrews, Sept. 10, 1998, p. A12; Landler, July 21, 2004, p. A4).

Also, easterners have not failed to notice that with reunification the leaders and managers of East German society were thrown out and they were replaced by westerners. In business, banking, law, communications, government, and the universities, the top jobs are still occupied by imported *Wessis* (*The Economist,* Sept. 30, 2000, p. 26).

The New Economy of the East. In some parts of the east, economic redevelopment has been successful. Dresden, the capital of the eastern state of Saxony, has been beautifully reconstructed, its baroque historic center restored. It is now, as in the past, a popular tourist destination. Many hi-tech start-ups have come to the Dresden area, bringing jobs in data-processing, biotechnology, optical precision instrument manufacture, electrical and medical engineering. The Dresden area now calls itself "Silicon Saxony" (Landler, Nov. 21, 2003, pp. C1, C2; *The Economist,* Sept. 18, 2004, p. 58).

But many more towns are like Hoyerswerda, in Brandenburg, which is Germany's fastest-shrinking city. Hoyerswerda has lost 39 percent of its residents, and its unemployment rate is still 23.5 percent. Ironically, Hoyerswerda's problems actually result from modernization of its factories. The city's biggest employer, Schwarze Pumpe, employed 18,000 people before reunification, but after privatization and modernization, it employs only 1,000 (O'Brien, May 28, 2004, pp. W1, W7). We see the same pattern in eastern Germany's old chemical industry. In Bitterfeld, a dangerously polluted old industrial town, Bayer invested 630 million euros (including a government subsidy of 100 million euros) to build a new complex. The factory, which in the past required hundreds of workers, is now run by eight chemists, who monitor the computers in the control room (O'Brien, Sept. 8, 2004, pp. W1, W7). As industries close down or modernize, people leave eastern towns.

About one in seven eastern Germans has moved to western Germany or abroad since 1990, and population in the eastern states has dropped 10 percent. There are fewer working-age people and fewer children and elderly people make up a larger and larger percent of the eastern population (Zielbauer, Dec. 25, 2002, p. A3).

Germany in the Global Economy

Although eastern Germany is in much worse shape economically than western Germany, in important ways all of Germany suffers from the same problem: lack of competitiveness in the global economy. Germans talk about a sense of malaise, or even despair. They believe that the future looks black, because in order to compete with poorer, lower-wage countries—eastern European countries like Poland or the Czech Republic, or even China and Vietnam—Germans will be forced to give up the good life they have long enjoyed.

In a very real sense, Germany has never accepted the system of **laissez-faire capitalism,** an individualistic, free-market system, that seems so natural to Britons and Americans. This was, of course, true of socialist East Germany, but it was true as well of capitalist West Germany. Germans in the east and west both believed in a social welfare system, a **welfare state,** in which people look upon the government as a protector. It goes back to Bismarck: People expect the government to shield them from the ups and downs of the economy, to provide unemployment insurance, health insurance, and old-age pensions, and also to legislate short work hours, long vacations, and job security for employees. Germans get six weeks of vacation per year, plus another nine to twelve days of holiday. There is a thirty-five hour work-week. Germans work fewer hours per year than employees anywhere else in the industrialized world. They can retire at 65 with a pension equal to about half of their average earnings. Unemployment benefits are generous and can continue indefinitely. Some east Germans have been collecting unemployment since 1989. Journalist Richard Bernstein says Germans remember the economic collapse of Weimar Germany that paved the way for Nazism, and as a result, they have a "cultural preference for what is called social peace versus the brutalities . . . of American-style capitalism." If social welfare laws and the complex process of codetermination create economic rigidities, that has been a price Germans have been willing to pay in exchange for stability (Bernstein, March 19, 2003, p. A4; July 2, 2003, p. A4; Andrews, Feb. 28, 2002, pp. C1, C5; *The Economist,* Aug. 30, 2003, p. 35; July 31, 2004, p. 13).

Making Germany Competitive. Everyone sees the problem: All the benefits that have made life good for working Germans in the past fifty years now make Germany less competitive in the global economy. But Germans really aren't ready to accept the solution: They must have lower wages, less job security, and fewer benefits. Chancellor Gerhard Schröder has staked his future and the future of the Social Democratic Party on economic reform. His Agenda 2010 package included legislation to restrict unemployment benefits to just one year, shift some pension costs to employees, reform labor laws so employers can fire workers more easily, and cut taxes. Schröder hopes that economic reform will revive the economy so that overall, Germans will be better off, even in a more free-market world. So far, the pain of the reforms is more evident to Germans than any gains (Bernstein, Oct. 18, 2003, p. A5; July 6, 2004, p. A3; Norris, Jan. 9, 2004, pp. W1, W7).

At the same time, businesses aren't waiting for government action, and German workers are resisting change. In 2004, car maker Opel, a German brand owned by General Motors, demanded major job cuts—a third of its workforce or 10,000 jobs. Workers responded with a wildcat strike (a strike not authorized by their union), which is highly unusual in Germany. Mercedes Benz tried to eliminate customary hourly breaks and institute a forty-hour workweek, and workers walked out of the company's plants all over Germany. In the end, Mercedes-Benz workers agreed to a longer workweek and lower pay in the future in exchange for promises of job security until 2012. Siemens threatened to move 2,000 jobs assembling telephones to Hungary and won an extension of the workweek to forty hours, without any extra pay. And in eastern Germany, the weekly protest marches that built up to the collapse of East German communism resumed in Magdeburg, Leipzig, and other cities, with old slogans revived to protests cuts in unemployment benefits (*The Economist*, Aug. 14, 2004, p. 45; July 31, 2004, p. 51; Oct. 23, 2004, p. 61; Landler, July 16, 2004, pp. W1, W7; Oct. 19, 2004, pp. W1, W7).

The Economy and Education

An unfortunate consequence of economic woes is the undermining of the German system of education, inherited from West Germany and now in use throughout the country. First of all, Germans were shocked by an international study that ranked 15-year-olds in thirty-one countries in reading, math, and science. German high school students ranked a miserable twentieth. Now German politicians, parents, and educators are in the midst of an unhappy self-examination. What has gone wrong with German schooling, once famous for its excellence? Some people point to the high pupil-teacher ratios, others to the aging staff of teachers. Some blame the short school day and others the large population of children from immigrant families (*The Economist*, Dec. 15, 2001, p. 43).

Other worries focus on Germany's system of vocational high schools and apprenticeships. Germans have been so proud of this system, which in the past educated young people to a high level of competence and placed them into secure, career-track jobs. The problem now is that as the economy slowed after 2000, there were fewer jobs available for young graduates, and businesses offered fewer paid apprenticeships. As many as 100,000 young people between the ages of 17 and 25 have neither jobs nor apprenticeships. Some remaining apprenticeships train people for jobs that no longer exist. The principal of one vocational high school in Berlin reported that 90 percent of her students could find no apprenticeship (O'Brien, July 31, 2004, pp. W1, W7).

There are also new problems with university education. Since 1972, Germany has promised a free university education to every graduate of an academic high school. Now that system is becoming strained. Enrollment has increased, partly because of high unemployment, but since economic problems are squeezing government budgets, spending on universities has been cut. Classes are overcrowded, library acquisition budgets are cut, science research labs ill-equipped. State governments are trying to introduce rather minimal tuition fees of about $600 a semester,

The continuing pressure by German industry and government to cut back pay and benefits has led to a wave of strikes and considerable unrest among Germany's workers. Here thousands of workers protest outside the Bremen factory of the German-American firm DaimlerChrysler. The overalls of the workers and their red banners place them in the century long socialist tradition of German workers. Their banner reads "Hands Off Our Pay!"

especially for students who take more than six and a half years to graduate. Students have protested furiously, both against cuts in university budgets and against the idea of charging tuition. If universities charged, student allege, Germany would become a much more unequal society (*The Economist,* May 10, 2003, p. 44; Jan. 10, 2004, p. 45; Bernstein, May 9, 2004, p. 8).

Political Change

Unresolved economic problems have led to political uncertainty in Germany. Chancellor Gerhard Schröder has taken a big gamble with his program for economic reform. So far, Germans have seen only losses: fewer jobs, longer hours, lower pay, fewer benefits. Young people have been particularly hard-hit. If economic reform began to lift the economy, and bring down the unemployment rate, Schröder's liberal Social Democratic Party would get the credit. But so far, they are only getting the blame. By 2004, polls showed support for the SPD down to 20 percent, though it rose back up to 31 percent later in the year. But this is a very poor showing for a major party in power facing an election in 2006, if not before. The surprise is that the conservative CDU, the Christian Democratic Union, the SPD's major opponent, is doing badly also. In 2004, in state elections in Brandenburg and Saxony, two big eastern states, the Social Democrats did badly and the Christian Democrats did even worse. The Christian Democrats distinguish themselves from the Social

Democrats by their even more active enthusiasm for labor market reforms. In effect, the SPD is saying: Vote for us—we will reform the economy. And the CDU is saying: We will take economic reforms even further. At the same time, voters are rejecting economic reform (*This Week in Germany,* Oct. 15, 2004; *The Economist,* Sept. 25, 2004, pp. 15–16).

A Multiparty System

How is it possible for both the SPD and the CDU to get smaller shares of votes? If you live in a two-party, winner-take-all system like the United States, you may be puzzled. It is very unlikely that we will ever see the Democrats and Republicans together receive less than half the total votes. But Germany has a **multiparty system,** with a system of **proportional representation.** Parties can send representatives to parliament without winning elections outright. When candidates of a party receive, for example, 12 percent of the votes, they get 12 percent of the seats.

The Minor Parties

"People are very skeptical about the two major parties and their competence," said Professor Peter Lösche of Göttingen University. One result is that overall voter turnout is dropping, from over 70 percent in western Germany to about 50 percent today. And support for the major parties is shrinking (Bernstein, Oct. 10, 2004, p. 3; *The Economist,* Sept. 11, 2004, p. 47). More people vote for the minor parties instead, either as a protest or in an attempt to find a party that will represent their interests. But even while Germans vote for minor parties, they worry about the growth of minor party strength. "The number of people who do not believe in any of the big parties is growing rapidly," said Wolfgang Bosbach, the vice chairman of the CDU's parlimentary group. "And you know, this is how it developed in the Third Reich, when people didn't believe in democracy any more and the extremes on both sides grew stronger" (quoted in Bernstein, Oct. 10, 2004, p. 3). Bosbach exhibits a common German fear of a return to fascism; it seems unlikely things will get so bad. Probably by 2006, more voters will come back to the major parties. Nevertheless, in the meantime, the minor parties are increasing their strength. People don't feel they are wasting their votes when they vote for minor parties. When neither of the major parties elects a majority of the parliament, the leading party has to find a minor party partner and govern in a **coalition government.** For example, starting in 1998, the Social Democrats governed in coalition with the Green Party. German voters' political preferences are altering the balance among Germany's minor parties and in so doing they may be making history.

Parties of the Extreme Right. The parties that worry Germans the most are of those of the extreme right: the German People's Union and the National Democratic Party. People were shocked in 2004 when the neo-Nazi NDP took 9.2 percent of the votes in state elections in Saxony and secured twelve seats in the state parliament. Most shockingly, that was nearly as large a percentage of the votes as the SPD received. This was the first time in thirty-six years that the ultraright party had been able to elect any representatives to parliament. In the neighboring state of Brandenburg, the German People's Union received 6.1 percent of the vote. And in the western State of Saarland, the NDP got an unprecedented 4 percent of the vote. The ultraright parties have built regular party organizations, which are particularly strong in rural areas, and are planning to run joint candidates in the federal parliamentary elections in 2006.

The extreme right parties have been particularly successful in attracting unemployed young men who are not high school graduates. In the recent state elections in Saxony, 21 percent of 18- to 29-year-olds voted for the NPD. These men respond to party demands that Germany close its borders and send foreign workers home. Their language is antiforeigner and anti-Semitic. Such appeals are particularly successful in the east, where nearly one in five people is out of work (*The Economist,* Sept. 25, 2004, pp. 63–64; Landler, Sept. 20, 2004, p. A3; Dempsey, Sept. 6, 2004, p. A5).

The PDS. The PDS (Party of Democratic Socialism), the successor to the SED, is enjoying a resurgence of support in the eastern Länder (echoing a similar revival of Communist parties in all the former Soviet-bloc nations). In 1990 the PDS captured 11 percent of the eastern vote. Then in 1994 it was up to 19.8 percent, and in 1998, 21 percent. Despite a poor showing in the west, the large eastern vote in 1998 gave the PDS more than 5 percent of the total national vote, qualifying the party for full status as a minority party in parliament. In 1999 it sent delegates for the first time to the European Parliament, after winning almost 6 percent of German votes. Though it remains overwhelmingly an eastern party, the PDS is beginning to attract some support in the west, especially in industrial cities and among trade union members. The ex-Communists have made Gerhard Schröder's reform program the focus of their attacks, calling it "poverty by law" (*The Economist,* Oct. 9, 1999, p. 59; Aug. 14, 2004, p. 45; Ash, p. 22; Cowell, July 7, 1998, p. A8; Andrews, Sept. 28, 1998, p. A10).

The Green Party. The Green Party has enjoyed tremendous influence as the junior partner in the Schröder government. In 1998 it replaced the FDP (the Free Democratic Party) as the "kingmaker" in German politics: the small party needed by either the SPD or the CDU to form a ruling coalition. As a governing party, the Greens were able to achieve many of the legislative reforms they had advocated, including liberalized citizenship laws, new controls on the export of weapons, an environmentally friendly energy tax, recognition for same-sex marriage, new consumer-protection laws, and a decision to phase out nuclear power in Germany. What a list of accomplishments! (Hockenos, pp. 20–22; *The Economist,* "Survey of Germany," Feb. 6, 1999, pp. 14–15; Andrews, July 7, 1999, p. A5).

Green Party ministers in Schröder's cabinet have been notably capable and popular. However, since 1998, the Greens have pulled back from many of their more radically left-wing positions. They supported sending German soldiers to Kosovo and Afghanistan (though, like most Germans, they opposed the war in Iraq). The Green Party has become an advocate for fiscal conservatism—for avoiding deficits by keeping spending and taxes in balance. At the same time, however, discontent on the left-wing of the SPD hints at a possible new, rival left-wing minor party. Trade unionists opposed to Schröder's free-market reforms, and led by Oskar Lafontaine, a former SPD chairman, are threatening to form a new left-wing party. Such a party could take the place of the PDS in the west and perhaps attract some Green Party radicals (*The Economist,* Sept. 11, 2004, pp. 47–48).

Does this sound confusing to you? If you are accustomed to an American-style two-party system, parliamentary coalition politics can be a challenging puzzle. Looking toward the 2006 election, the challenge for Chancellor Schröder, the SPD, and the Greens will be to keep voters' loyalty while pushing through a free-market reform program that undermines trade union power and state protections that Germans have long taken for granted. If the economy continues to sag, voters may punish the parties now in power. But where they will take their loyalty is currently unclear.

Thinking Sociologically

1. Describe the values and institutions that made East Germany a socialist society.
2. Germany and Japan are both capitalist societies, but in some ways they are quite different. What differences do you see in their attitudes toward consumerism, leisure, and individualism? How do their economic institutions differ?
3. Do you live in a capitalist society? If so, is its style of capitalism similar or different in any way from Germany's or Japan's?
4. Germany, Japan, and the United States are the world's three biggest capitalist economies. Refer to Table 1.4 and compare how equally or unequally these three societies distribute income to their citizens.
5. In institutional structure, Germany, Japan, and Mexico all are representative democracies. What are some of the differences in the ways their political institutions work?
6. Compare the system of higher education in Germany with the system in your society. What advantages or disadvantages do you see in each?
7. Explain why many people in eastern Germany have experienced anomie since reunification. Can you think of some examples of people experiencing anomie in your own society?
8. How is Germany responding to the prospect of a declining total population and an aging population?
9. Compare attitudes to immigrants in Germany and in Japan. How does your society react to immigrants?

For Further Reading

ARDAGH, JOHN, *Germany and the Germans.* New York: Penguin, 1991.

BAER, HANS, *Crumbling Walls and Tarnished Ideals: An Ethnography of East Germany before and after Unification.* New York: University Press of America, 1998.

DARNTON, ROBERT, *Berlin Journal, 1989–1990.* New York: Norton, 1991.

EINHORN, BARBARA, *Cinderella Goes to Market: Citizenship, Gender and Women's Movements in East Central Europe.* London: Verso Press, 1993.

FULBROOK, MARY, *Anatomy of a Dictatorship: Inside the GDR 1949–1989.* New York: Oxford University Press, 1995.

GLAESER, ANDREAS, *Divided in Unity: Identity, Germany and the Berlin Police.* Chicago: Chicago University Press, 1999.

MARCUSE, PETER, *Missing Marx: A Personal and Political Journal of a Year in East Germany, 1989–1990.* New York: Monthly Review Press, 1991.

MARKOVITS, INGA, *Imperfect Justice: An East-West German Diary.* New York: Oxford University Press, 1995.

RODDEN, JOHN, *Repainting the Little Red Schoolhouse: A History of Eastern German Education 1945–1995.* New York: Oxford University Press, 2000.

RUESCHMEYER, MARILYN, AND CHRISTIANE LEMKE, eds., *The Quality of Life in the German Democratic Republic.* Armonk, NY: Sharp, 1989.

Bibliography

ANDREWS, EDMUND L., "Gift from Kohl in an Election Year: Temporary Work for East's Jobless," *The New York Times,* Sept. 10, 1998, p. A12.

———, "Former Stronghold Turns Frustrations against Kohl in Voting Booth," *The New York Times,* Sept. 28, 1998, p. A10.

———, "Old Greens in Germany Challenged by Upstarts," *The New York Times,* July 7, 1999, p. A5.

———, "Germans Sign Agreement to Pay Forced Laborers of Nazi Era," *The New York Times,* July 18, 2000, p. A3.

———, "Germany Weighs Overhaul of 'Consensus' Capitalism," *The New York Times,* Feb. 14, 2001, pp. W1, W7.

———, "With Germany in Recession, Many Ask Why," *The New York Times,* Feb. 28, 2002, pp. C1, C5.

ARDAGH, JOHN, *Germany and the Germans.* New York: Penguin, 1991.

ASH, TIMOTHY GARTON, "Kohl's Germany: The Beginning of the End?" *The New York Review,* Dec. 1, 1994, pp. 20–26.

BAER, HANS, *Crumbling Walls and Tarnished Ideals: An Ethnography of East Germany before and after Unification.* New York: University Press of America, 1998.

BERNSTEIN, RICHARD, "Germans Revisit War's Agony, Ending a Taboo," *The New York Times,* March 15, 2003, p. A3.

———, "Germans Balk at the Price of Economic Change," *The New York Times,* March 19, 2003, p. A4.

———, "Modern German Duty: The Obligation to Play," *The New York Times,* July 2, 2003, p. A4.

———, "German Parliament Votes to Cut Welfare Benefits and Taxes," *The New York Times,* Oct. 18, 2003, p. A5.

———, "Halls of Ivy May Receive Miracle-Gro in Germany," *The New York Times,* May 9, 2004, p. 8.

———, "Voters in Much of Europe Seem to Want the Ins Out," *The New York Times,* July 6, 2004, p. A3.

———, "Germany Struggles to Assess True Aims of Islamic Group," *The New York Times,* Sept. 26, 2004, p. 14.

———, "A Small City in Germany Mirrors a National Malaise," *The New York Times,* Oct. 10, 2004, p. 3.

BURANT, STEPHEN R., ed., *East Germany: A Country Study,* 3d ed., Area Handbook Series. Washington, DC: U.S. Government Printing Office, 1988.

BURUMA, IAN, *The Wages of Guilt: Memories of War in Germany and Japan.* New York: Farrar, Straus & Giroux, 1994.

———, "The Destruction of Germany," *The New York Review of Books,* Oct. 21, 2004, pp. 8–12.

BUTLER, DESMOND, "Germany Plans to Raise Status of Nation's Jews," *The New York Times,* Nov. 15, 2002, p. A5.

CHILDS, DAVID, *The GDR: Moscow's German Ally.* London: Allen & Unwin, 1983.

COHEN, ROGER, "The Growing Burden of Germany's Unification," *The New York Times,* March 8, 1993, pp. D1, D3.

———, "Germany's New Face: Age 22, at Threshold of Change," *The New York Times,* Oct. 25, 1998, p. 6.

———, "Germany Makes Citizenship Easier for Foreigners to Get," *The New York Times,* May 22, 1999, p. A3.

———, "Germany's East and West: Still Hostile States of Mind," *The New York Times,* Oct. 25, 1999, pp. A1, A16.

———, "A Dog's Best Friend, It Seems, May Be a German," *The New York Times,* June 20, 2000, p. A4.

———, "German Faults 'Silence' about Attacks on Immigrants," *The New York Times,* Aug. 1, 2000, p. A7 YNE.

———, "Germany's Financial Heart Is Open but Wary," *The New York Times,* Dec. 30, 2000, pp. A1, A6.

———, "How Open to Immigrants Should Germany Be? An Uneasy Country's Debate Deepens," *The New York Times,* May 13, 2001, p. 11.

COWELL, ALAN, "Gloom in German East May End Kohl's Streak," *The New York Times,* July 7, 1998, pp. A1, A8.

CRAIG, GORDON A., *The Germans.* New York: Putnam, 1982.

———, "United We Fall," *New York Review of Books,* Jan. 13, 1994, pp. 36–40.

DAHRENDORF, RALF, *Society and Democracy in Germany.* New York: Doubleday Anchor, 1969.

DALTON, RUSSELL J., *Politics in West Germany.* Boston: Scott, Foresman, 1989.

DARNTON, ROBERT, *Berlin Journal, 1989–1990.* New York: Norton, 1991.

DEBARDELEBEN, JOAN, "The Future Has Already Begun," in Marilyn Rueschmeyer and Christiane Lemke, eds., *The Quality of Life in the German Democratic Republic.* Armonk, NY: Sharp, 1989, pp. 144–164.

DEMPSEY, JUDY, "Schröder's Party, Under Fire for Cuts, Is Routed in State Election," *The New York Times,* Sept. 6, 2004, p. A5.

DOLLING, IRENE, "Culture and Gender," in Marilyn Rueschmeyer and Christiane Lemke, eds., *The Quality of Life in the German Democratic Republic.* Armonk, NY: Sharp, 1989, pp. 22–47.

DUGGAN, LYNN, AND NANCY FOLBRE, "Women and Children Last," *The New York Times,* Jan. 8, 1994, p. 23.

THE ECONOMIST, "Living and Dying in a Barren Land," April 23, 1994, p. 54.

———, "Germany Survey," Feb. 6, 1999, pp. 1–18.

———, "Germany's Ex-Communists: Creeping Up," Oct. 9, 1999, p. 59.

———, "Germany: Coming Together, Ten Years On," Nov. 13, 1999, pp. 52–55.

———, "Germany: The First Test," May 6, 2000, p. 52.

———, "Eastern Germany's Slow Revival," May 27, 2000, p. 51.

———, "Germany: The Trouble with Foreigners," July 1, 2000, pp. 48–49.

———, "Germany's Neo-Nazis," Aug. 12, 2000, pp. 18–19.

———, "Germany: The Church Victorious," Sept. 2, 2000, pp. 44–45.

———, "German Unification: Togetherness: A Balance Sheet," Sept. 30, 2000, pp. 25–28.

———, "Germany: Banning Nazis," Oct. 28, 2000, p. 50.

———, "German Education: Dummkopf!" Dec. 15, 2001, p. 43.

————, "Taboos in Germany: They're Being Broken," May 25, 2002, pp. 48–49.

————, "German Universities: Pay Up, Young 'Uns," May 10, 2003, p. 44.

————, "German Reform and Democracy: The Exhausting Grind of Consensus," Aug. 30, 2003, p. 35.

————, "Germany's Trade Unions: Ever Weaker," Sept. 6, 2003, p. 45.

————, "East German Products: Ostalgie," Sept. 13, 2003, p. 57.

————, "Germany's Declining Population: Kinder, Gentler," Dec. 6, 2003, p. 47.

————, "German Universities: Lower Education," Jan. 10, 2004, p. 45.

————, "German Industrial Relations: Slowly Losing Their Chains," Feb. 21, 2004, p. 49.

————, "German Immigration: Brains Not Welcome Here," May 1, 2004, p. 50.

————, "German Politics: Children of the Bourgeoisie, Unite!" June 12, 2004, p. 49.

————, "Business in Germany and France: Europe's Workplace Revolution," July 31, 2004, p. 51.

————, "European Labor Reform: Keep Up the Momentum," July 31, 2004, p. 13.

————, "Germany: It's Those People, All Over Again," Aug. 14, 2004, pp. 45–46.

————, "German Politics: Teutonic Shift," Sept. 11, 2004, pp. 47–48.

————, "Eastern Germany: Getting Back Together Is So Hard," Sept. 18, 2004, p. 58.

————, "German Elections: A Plague on Both Your Parties," Sept. 25, 2004, pp. 15–16.

————, "German Politics: Angela, Gerhard and the Neo-Nazis," Sept. 25, 2004, pp. 63–64.

————, "German Labour: The Day the Factories Stopped," Oct. 23, 2004, pp. 61–62.

EDWARDS, E. E., *GDR Society and Social Institutions.* New York: St. Martin's Press, 1985.

EINHORN, BARBARA, *Cinderella Goes to Market: Citizenship, Gender and Women's Movements in East Central Europe.* London: Verso Press, 1993.

ERLANGER, STEVEN, "A Memory-Strewn Celebration of Germany's Jews," *The New York Times,* Sept. 10, 2001, p. A8.

————, "Shocked Germany Weakens Cherished Protections," *The New York Times,* Oct. 1, 2001, p. B1.

————, "In Germany, Terrorists Made Use of a Passion: An Open Democracy," *The New York Times,* Oct. 5, 2001, p. B6.

————, "Germany, under New Antiterrorist Law, Bans a Radical Muslim Group," *The New York Times,* Dec. 13, 2001, p. B5.

FEDERAL STATISTICAL OFFICE GERMANY, "Ever More Children Born in Germany Have Foreign Parents," Sept. 19, 2003, www.destatis.de/presseveranstaltungen.

————, "Fewer Births in 1999 but more than in past years," July 4, 2000, http://www.destatis.de/presse/dentsch/pm2000/p2400023.htm.

————, "Births in the New Länder and Berlin-East after 1989–90," http://www.statistikbind.de/presse/englisch/pm/p7291023.htm.

————, "Child Care in Western and Eastern Germany," March 16, 2004, www.destatis.de/presse/presseveranstaltungen.

————, "Micro Censuses 2003: Gainful Employment of Mothers Rises," April 28, 2004, http://www.destatis.de/presse/deutsch/pm2004/p1910026.htm.

————, "Women with preschool children," March 7, 2005, http://www.destatis.de/presse/englisch/pm2005/p1020024.htm.

FERREE, MYRA MARX, "The Rise and Fall of 'Mommy Politics': Feminism and Unification in (East) Germany," *Feminist Studies,* Vol. 19, no. 1 (Spring 1993), pp. 89–115.

FITZGERALD, NORA, "Artifacts of Überkitsch Evoke Old East Germany," *The New York Times,* Oct. 1, 2003, pp. E1, E9.

FRIEDRICHS, JURGEN, "Ethnic Segregation in Cologne, Germany 1984–94," *Urban Studies,* Vol. 35, no. 10 (Oct. 1998), pp. 1745–1762.

GANNON, MARTIN J., *Understanding Global Cultures*. London: Sage, 1994.

GAZDAR, KAEVAN, *Germany's Balanced Development: The Real Wealth of a Nation*. Westport, CT: Quorum Books, 1998.

GERTH, H. H., AND C. WRIGHT MILLS, *From Max Weber: Essays in Sociology*. New York: Oxford University Press, 1958.

GITTER, ROBERT J., AND MARKUS SCHEUER, "US and German Youths: Unemployment and the Transition from School to Work," *Monthly Labor Review* (March 1997), pp. 16–20.

GLAESER, ANDREAS, *Divided in Unity: Identity, Germany and the Berlin Police*. Chicago: Chicago University Press, 1999.

GLAESSNER, GERT-JOACHIM, "Technology Policy and Educational Transformations," in Marilyn Rueschmeyer and Christiane Lemke, eds., *The Quality of Life in the German Democratic Republic*. Armonk, NY: Sharp, 1989, pp. 77–94.

GLOUCHEVITCH, PHILIP, *Juggernaut: The German Way of Business*. New York: Simon & Schuster, 1992.

GOECKEL, ROBERT R., "Church and Society in the GDR," in Marilyn Rueschmeyer and Christiane Lemke, eds., *The Quality of Life in the German Democratic Republic*. Armonk, NY: Sharp, 1989, pp. 210–227.

HALL, EDWARD T., AND MILDRED REED HALL, *Understanding Cultural Differences*. Yarmouth, ME: Intercultural Press, 1990.

HAMILTON, STEPHEN F., *Apprenticeship for Adulthood*. New York: Free Press, 1990.

HARRIS, EMILY, "Former East Germany Suffering a Shortage of Women," *National Public Radio, Morning Edition,* March 10, 2004.

HEILIG, GERHARD, THOMAS BUTTNER, AND WOLFGANG LUTZ, "Germany's Population: Turbulent Past, Uncertain Future," *Population Bulletin,* Vol. 45, no. 4 (Dec. 1990), pp. 1–46.

HOCKENOS, PAUL, "Letter from Berlin: Greens and PDS," *The Nation,* Vol. 273, no. 13 (Oct. 29, 2001), pp. 20–22.

KINZER, STEPHEN, "650 a Baby: Germany to Pay to Stem Decline in Births," *The New York Times,* Jan. 25, 1994, p. A3.

———, "A Wall of Resentment Now Divides Germany," *The New York Times,* Oct. 14, 1994, pp. A1, A14.

KIRCH, HENRY, *The German Democratic Republic*. Westview Profile/Nations of Contemporary Europe. Boulder, CO: Westview Press, 1985.

KOLINSKY, EVA, "Everyday Life Transformed: A Case Study of Leipzig since German Unification," *World Affairs,* Vol. 156, no. 4 (Spring 1994), pp. 159–174.

KRAMER, JANE, "Letter from West Germany," *The New Yorker,* Dec. 19, 1983, pp. 102–121.

———, "Private Lives: Germany's Troubled War on Terrorism," *The New Yorker,* Feb. 11, 2002, pp. 36–51.

LANDLER, MARK, "New Deposit on Aluminum Cans Tests German Sense of Order," *The New York Times,* Jan. 1, 2003, p. A4.

———, "Eastern Germany Is Able to Prevent Industrial Flight to Third World," *The New York Times,* Nov. 21, 2003, pp. W1, W2.

———, "Germans Have a Breakdown over Quality," *The New York Times,* May 9, 2004, p. WK 14.

———, "Dispute Disrupts Daimler in Germany," *The New York Times,* July 16, 2004, p. W1.

———, "East Germany Swallows Billions and Still Stagnates," *The New York Times,* July 21, 2004, p. A11.

———, "Rightists Make Strong Strides in Eastern German State Elections," *The New York Times,* Sept. 20, 2004, p. A3.

———, "Far-Right Gains in Germany Not Seen as Specter of Weimar," *The New York Times*, Sept. 21, 2004, p. A16.

———, "G.M. Workers in Germany Protest Job Cuts a 3rd Day," *The New York Times*, Oct. 19, 2004, pp. W1, W7.

———, "Empty Maternity Wards Imperil a Dwindling Germany," *The New York Times*, Nov. 18, 2004, p. A3.

LANDUA, DETLEF, "Germany after Unification: Still a Twofold Society," *International Journal of Comparative Sociology*, Vol. 34, no. 1–2 (Jan./Apr. 1993), pp. 75–86.

LEMKE, CHRISTIANE, "Political Socialization in the 'Micromilieu,'" in Marilyn Rueschmeyer and Christiane Lemke, eds., *The Quality of Life in the German Democratic Republic*. Armonk, NY: Sharp, 1989, pp. 59–73.

LEWIS, FLORA, *Europe: A Tapestry of Nations*. New York: Simon & Schuster, 1987.

LONG, ROBERT EMMET, ed., *The Reunification of Germany*, The Reference Shelf. New York: Wilson, 1992.

MARCUSE, PETER, *Missing Marx: A Personal and Political Journal of a Year in East Germany, 1989–1990*. New York: Monthly Review Press, 1991.

MARKOVITS, ANDREI S., AND PHILIP S. GORSKI, *The German Left: Red, Green and Beyond*. New York: Oxford University Press, 1993.

MARX, KARL, AND FRIEDRICH ENGELS, *Manifesto of the Communist Party*. New York: International Publishers, 1948, 1966.

MAYER, MARGIT, AND JOHN ELY, *The German Greens: Paradox between Movement and Party*. Philadelphia: Temple University Press, 1998.

MERTES, MICHAEL, STEVEN MULLER, AND HEINRICH AUGUST WINKLER, eds., *In Search of Germany*. New Brunswick: Transaction Publishers, 1996.

MILLS, C. WRIGHT, *The Sociological Imagination*. New York: Oxford University Press, 1959.

THE NEW YORK TIMES, "The Progress of German Unification," Sept. 1, 1996, p. E8.

———, "Germany: Police Take Aim at Neo-Nazi Music," March 25, 2004, p. A6.

NICKEL, HILDEGARD M., "Sex-Role Socialization in Relationships as a Function of the Division of Labor," in Marilyn Rueschmeyer and Christiane Lemke, eds., *The Quality of Life in the German Democratic Republic*. Armonk, NY: Sharp, 1989, pp. 48–58.

NORRIS, FLOYD, "In Germany, Shifting the Cost of the Pension to the Worker," *The New York Times*, Jan. 9, 2004, pp. W1, W7.

NYROP, RICHARD F., ed., *Federal Republic of Germany: A Country Study*, 2d ed., Area Handbook Series. Washington, DC: U.S. Government Printing Office, 1982.

O'BRIEN, KEVIN J., "Last Out, Please Turn Off the Lights," *The New York Times*, May 28, 2004, pp. W1, W7.

———, "Lessons in Reality for Apprentices," *The New York Times*, July 13, 2004, pp. W1, W7.

———, "Eastern German Chemical Industry Stages a Comeback," *The New York Times*, Sept. 8, 2004, pp. W1, W7.

PHILIPSEN, DIRK, *We Were the People: Voices from East Germany's Revolutionary Autumn of 1989*. Durham, NC: Duke University Press, 1993.

"A Profile of the German Education System," *American Educator*, Vol. 18, no. 1 (Spring 1994), pp. 21–22.

PROTZMAN, FERDINAND, "East Nearly Privatized, Germans Argue the Cost," *The New York Times*, Aug. 12, 1994, pp. D1, D2.

RADEMAEKERS, WILLIAM, "The Oh So Good Life," in Robert Emmet Long, ed., *The Reunification of Germany*. New York: Wilson, 1992, pp. 8–12.

RAMET, PEDRO, "Disaffection and Dissent in East Germany," *World Politics*, Vol. 37, no. 1 (Oct. 1984), pp. 85–111.

RODDEN, JOHN G., *Repainting the Little Red Schoolhouse: A History of Eastern German Education 1945–1995*. New York: Oxford University Press, 2000.

ROTH, ALISA, "In Chic New Berlin, Ugly Is Way Cool," *The New York Times,* Jan. 24, 2002, pp. F1, F8.

RUBIN, DANIEL, "German Grumps Hobble Wal-Mart," *The Houston Chronicle,* Dec. 27, 2001, p. 1.

SA'ADAH, ANNE, *Germany's Second Chance: Trust, Justice and Democratization.* Cambridge: Harvard University Press, 1998.

SCHARF, C. BRADLEY, *Politics and Change in East Germany.* Boulder, CO: Westview Press, 1984.

SCHNEIDER, PETER, "The Germans Are Breaking an Old Taboo," *The New York Times,* Jan. 18, 2003, pp. B7, B9.

SHLAES, AMITY, *Germany: The Empire Within.* New York: Farrar, Straus & Giroux, 1991.

STATISTICAL OFFICE OF THE LANDER AND THE FEDERAL STATISTICAL OFFICE, http://www. statistik-portal.de/statistik-Portal/en/en_jbol_jahrtab3.asp.

STEELE, JONATHAN, *Inside East Germany: The State That Came In from the Cold.* New York: Urizen Books, 1977.

STERN, FRITZ, *Dreams and Delusions: The Drama of German History.* New York: Knopf, 1987.

TURNER, HENRY ASHBY, JR., *The Two Germanies since 1945.* New Haven, CT: Yale University Press, 1987.

UNITED NATIONS, DEPARTMENT OF INTERNATIONAL AFFAIRS, "National Accounts Statistics: Compendium of Income Distribution Statistics," *Statistical Papers,* Series M, No. 79, 1985.

THE WEEK IN GERMANY, "Life Expectancy Up for East Germans," Oct. 8, 2004, www. germany.info/gic.

UNITED NATIONS, *Human Development Report 2004,* http://hdr.undp.org/statistics/data/ advanced.cfm.

———, "Poll Turnaround for Schröder's SPD," Oct. 15, 2004, http://www.germany-info.org/relaunch/info/publications/week/2004/041015/politics4.html.

WHITNEY, CRAIG R., "Comfortable Germans, Slow to Change (Especially if It Means More Work)," *The New York Times,* Jan. 16, 1995, p. A6.

WORLD BANK, World Development Indicators 2004, http://www.worldbank.org/data/ dataquery.html.

ZIELBAUER, PAUL, "As Eastern Germany Rusts, Young Workers Leave," *The New York Times,* Dec. 25, 2002, p. A3.

Index